A History of

CHRISTIAN THOUGHT

•

Volume I

A History

of

CHRISTIAN
THOUGHT

by

Otto W. Heick

VOLUME I

FORTRESS PRESS   PHILADELPHIA

FOREWORD

The present volume is a revision of the first volume of *A History of Christian Thought*, a co-operative venture of the late Dr. J. L. Neve and myself, first published in 1943.

In the past two decades this work has received a wide circulation among students of theology in both the United States and Canada. The section on American Theology in Volume II has also been published in Germany. The book has been written with an eye to the needs of the undergraduate student. Most non-English expressions have been translated and the original sources have, in most cases, been referred to or quoted from an English edition. Some inconsistencies, I am afraid, have remained.

The work has been prepared principally for Protestant readers. In addition to the large section on the Reformation in the present volume, the doctrinal development in the ancient Church is presented in great detail, for both Luther and Calvin regarded the decisions of the first ecumenical councils concerning the Trinity and the incarnation as a correct exhibition of the New Testament message, while the Antitrinitarians of the Reformation age looked askance at the Nicene and Chalcedonian creeds. The brief section on the Middle Ages is meant to give the Protestant student a basic understanding of the Catholic theology against which the Reformers revolted.

I am deeply indebted to the Reverend Eric R. W. Schultz, M.Th., B.L.S., librarian of Waterloo Lutheran University, Waterloo, Ontario, for his careful reading of the manuscript and his many useful suggestions.

Since 1948 it has been my privilege to teach History of Christian Thought to an appreciative student body at Waterloo Lutheran Seminary. Hence, at the close of my teaching career, I would like to dedicate these pages to the younger generation of pastors of the Eastern Canada Synod of the Lutheran Church in America. Theology is never irrelevant. Next to Scripture, the teachers of the Church are useful guides to an effective ministry even in the age of nuclear power.

Soli Deo gloria.

OTTO W. HEICK

Waterloo, Ontario
August, 1964

TABLE OF CONTENTS

Book One

THE ANCIENT CHURCH

Book Two

THE MIDDLE AGES

Book Three

THE REFORMATION

ABBREVIATIONS

ANF   *Ante-Nicene Fathers, Translations of the Writings of the Fathers Down to A.D. 325.* Grand Rapids, Mich., 1951-1953.

CR   *Corpus Reformatorum.* Edited by G. C. Bretschneider and H. E. Bindseil. Halle, 1834-1860.

EA   *D. Martin Luthers sämmtliche Werke.* Frankfurt and Erlangen, 1826-1857.

LCC   *The Library of Christian Classics.* Edited by John Baillie, John T. McNeill, Henry P. VanDusen. 26 vols. Philadelphia: The Westminster Press, 1953—.

LW   *American Edition of Luther's Works.* Philadelphia: Muhlenberg Press and St. Louis: Concordia Publishing House, 1955—.

MSG   *Patrologiae Cursus Completus, seu bibliotheca universalis, integra uniformis, commoda, oeconomica omnium ss. patrum, doctorum scriptorumque ecclesiasticorum.* Edited by J. P. Migne. *Series Graeca. Paris,* 1844-1904.

MSL   *Patrologiae Cursus etc. Series Latina.* 221 vols. Paris, 1844-1904.

NPNF   *A Select Library of Nicene and Post-Nicene Fathers of the Christian Church.* 2nd series; New York, 1890—.

PE   *Works of Martin Luther.* Philadelphia: A. J. Holman Co. and Muhlenberg Press, 1915-1943.

PRE   *Realencyklopädie für protestantische Theologie und Kirche.* Edited by Albert Hauck. Leipzig, 1896—.

RGG   *Die Religion in Geschichte und Gegenwart.* 3rd ed.; Tubingen, 1957—.

ST.L.   *D. Martin Luthers Werke.* Kritische Gesamtausgabe. Georg Walch. Edited and published in modern German. 23 vols. St. Louis, 1880-1910.

WA   *D. Martin Luthers sämmtliche Schriften.* Weimar, 1883—.

Book One

THE ANCIENT CHURCH

CHAPTER I

INTRODUCTION

I. Subject Matter and Method

This work is a history of Christian doctrine, not just a history of the development of the official dogma of the Church. This is evident in the history of the ancient Church and of the Reformation, for a large part of the discussion of the ancient Church has only an indirect bearing upon the development of dogma. The section on the Middle Ages also includes material which is only distantly related to the dogma of the Church. The same holds true for the second volume, which is pre-eminently a history of Protestant theology and theological developments which attempt doctrinal reconstruction.

In distinguishing between dogma and general Christian thought, the following may be said: In dogma, that is, in the confessions of the Church, we have the tangible results of fundamental Christian thought on matters of divine revelation. The name dogma is applied to the crystallized statements which were received by the Church. The Church Fathers designated their reliable and authoritative doctrines of faith as dogmas as contrasted with the mere opinions of philosophers and heretics. Gradually the Nicene Creed came to be regarded as dogma in the strictest sense. Modern man is inclined to turn away from authorized doctrines, from a *kanōn tes aletheias* or *regula fidei*— that is, from doctrines claiming to be rules of faith. Originally, the message of salvation through Christ was brought to a world in which all the influences of pagan philosophy and religious heresies were at work to oppose and to counteract that message. The young Church was in need of confessional guides and of "rules of faith." These, as expressions of the Church's experience, came to be recognized as

3

public confessions, and through the centuries they have guided the peoples of many races in their religious life. When we accept the confessions, we do not equate the Apostles' Creed, the Nicene Creed, the Augsburg Confession, the Thirty-nine Articles, and the Westminster Confession with "general Christian thought."

The title of this work has been chosen chiefly for the larger freedom it gives us to include matters of general theological interest. This freedom is needed particularly in the study of the Middle Ages, and even more in the second volume, in which we deal with the development of theological positions under the influence of modern philosophy.

Adolph von Harnack, Friederich Loofs, Reinhold Seeberg, and their predecessors have made "history of dogma" (*Dogmengeschichte*) the standing title for the branch of theology dealt with here. This special interest in the "dogma" of the Church, even on the part of liberalism, is easily explained. Rationalism overtook the Church of Germany in the eighteenth century and discredited the historic dogmas expressed in the so-called ecumenical creeds of Christendom. In the ensuing struggle between the conflicting theological tendencies—radicals, conservatives, and middle-of-the-road supernaturalists—Wilhelm Muenscher, the "father of German history of dogma," set himself the task of tracing, with historical criticism, the genesis of the confessional writings which claimed authority in the Church. He was supported by a number of like-minded historians who followed him. There has since been considerable reaction in Germany against limiting the subject matter of the history of dogma to the confessions.[1]

Will the title *History of Christian Thought* obligate us to deal not only with the history of doctrine, but also with the history of Christian ethics? In other words, though pre-eminence must be given to

---

[1] For a detailed discussion of the situation see Friederich Loofs, "Dogmengeschichte," in *Realencyklopädie für protestantische Theologie und Kirche* (hereinafter referred to as *PRE*), IV, 752 ff., especially 760 ff. Cf. G. Krueger, *Was heisst und zu welchem Ende studiert man Dogmengeschichte?*, 1895; Carl Stange, *Das Dogma und seine Beurteilung in der neueren Dogmengeschichte*, 1898; and O. Ritschl, *Dogmengeschichte des Protestantismus*, 1908-1927. Stange criticizes Harnack, Loofs, and Kaftan for their traditional conclusion of the history of dogma with the confessions of the sixteenth century. Three American writers, W. G. T. Shedd, H. C. Sheldon, and G. P. Fisher, substituted the title "history of doctrine" for "history of dogma" in order to include the movements following the Reformation.

the doctrine of the Church in parts of this work which are devoted to the history of dogma, must we not include the corresponding ideas of Christian ethics? In the *Didache* we read of the "two ways," the way of life and the way of death. The Montanists, the Novatians, and the Donatists, the writer of the *Shepherd of Hermas*, Tertullian, Cyprian, Callistus, and Augustine, were stimulated by an intense interest in the ethical purity of the Church. The problem of repentance became such a major concern in the Middle Ages that Luther found in it the starting point for the Reformation. Throughout history, the subjects of dogmatics and ethics are intimately related. Thus there can be no serious objection to the choice of title on this ground.

Having in some measure justified the use of our title, we must turn to the question: How can we limit ourselves in the review of the seemingly limitless material that lies before us? Our title commits us to deal with the history of Christian thought. We must be on our guard against losing ourselves in dogmatics and polemics. The task is always a historical one. While the aim of the historian does not relieve him of the duty of criticism, there is a difference between polemics and objective historical criticism.

Further, it must be our aim to confine our critical-historical views to historic Christianity. Certain radical forms of religion have abandoned the foundations of the Christian Church. Our discussion keeps in view the doctrinal interests of historic Christianity. We are not studying the history of philosophy, even though we must frequently review developments in the field of philosophy. Our aim is to trace the history of Christian thought and to derive our conclusions from that study.

II. Brief Review of the Study of the History of Dogma

The Middle Ages saw no object in a study of the history of dogma, because the teaching of the Church was held in the words of Vincent of Lérins (d. 434), to have been believed "everywhere, always and by all" (*quod ubique, quod semper, quod ab omnibus creditum est*). In other words, dogma has existed since the beginning of the Church. The assimilation of dogma has been gradual, however, and of this alone has there been a history. We must not overlook the intense historical and human development in the gradual working out of the principles and issues in the final formulation of Christian truth. The mistake of the Church in the Middle Ages lay in its conception of tradition as a quantity that was handed down from age to age free from the purifying process of criticism.

The Reformation opened the way for history of dogma as a subject for critical investigation. Luther established the principle that dogmas have no authority as decrees of councils and popes unless they accord with the Scriptures.[2] His view did away with the principle that creedal statements made by councils must be adopted without investigation. As first the Lutheran Reformers had unbounded confidence in the doctrinal developments of the first five centuries. Nevertheless, Luther expressed a criticism of the *homoousios* in the Nicene Creed.[3] Melanchthon drew attention to certain Platonic influences in the early Christian doctrines.[4] He found a strong adulteration of Christian dogma in the ages following Leo the Great. Flacius, in his pioneer work on Church history, characterized these centuries as a continuous process of beclouding specifically evangelical doctrines, with an occasional witness to the truth incapable of arresting the fatal development.[5] Although such views stimulated inquiry and historical investigation, the conservatism of the latter part of the sixteenth century and of the seventeenth did not encourage any critical attitude toward the "ecumenical creeds."

Arnold, a theologian of the Pietist group, questioned dogmas in his *Unparteiische Kirchen—und Ketzerhistorie* (1699-1700), a work in which he made it his object to show that orthodoxy is fallible, and that the truer expressions of piety have come from the heretics and the sects. The men of the Enlightenment declared the creedal statements of the past to be historical problems which must be investigated with regard to their origin, development, and validity for succeeding generations. It was his interest in such investigation that made Wilhelm Muenscher, a theologian of the rationalist school, the father of the modern history of dogma. The problem that concerned him in his presentation was: How and by what agencies has Christian dogma

[2] *Works of Martin Luther* (Philadelphia: A. J. Holman Co. and Muhlenberg Press, 1915-43; hereinafter referred to as *PE*), II, 43 and elsewhere.

[3] Weimar edition of Luther's works (hereinafter referred to as *WA*), VIII, 117.

[4] *The Loci Communes of Philip Melanchthon,* ed. H. C. Hill (Boston: Meador Publishing Co., 1944), p. 70.

[5] Cf. pp. 454 ff.

gradually received the character and form in which we have it today?[6] In the main it must be said that these men, in observing the changes in the development, failed to see and evaluate the abiding elements of truth in the dogmas.

Schleiermacher's influence upon the history of dogma has also been felt. He was interested in the element of continuity in the new life of Christianity. The same emphasis can be observed in Johann August Wilhelm Neander (d. 1857) and Karl Rudolf Hagenbach (d. 1840). Ludwig Friedrich Otto Baumgarten-Crusius (d. 1832) and Johann Georg Veit Engelhardt (d. 1839) also belong to this class.

A contribution from Hegel's conception of history came through Ferdinand Christian Baur's *Lehrbuch der Christlichen Dogmengeschichte,* published in 1847. In Hegelian fashion, Baur conceived of Christianity as the unfolding of the divine Idea in space and time. Peter, as the thesis, represents the Jewish phase of development, Paul as the antithesis, the Hellenistic phase. The Church of the second century represents the synthesis.

It is of interest to observe that this Hegelian principle of development was a workable basis for some confessional Lutherans. Theodor Kliefoth, in his *Einleitung in die Dogmengeschichte* (1893), saw in the history of dogma the organic unfolding of Christian truth in the life of the Church. In this conception the influence of Schleiermacher is also evident. Gottfried Thomasius wrote the two-volume *Die Christliche Dogmengeschichte als Entwicklungsgeschichte des kirchlichen Lehrbegriffs* (1874 ff.), which was supplemented and modified in a second edition by Gottlieb Nathanael Bonwetsch and Reinhold Seeberg (1886 ff.). Thomasius aimed to describe dogma as a development starting from the revelation in Scripture and resulting in the Lutheran Reformation of the sixteenth century. His description continually distinguished between theological opinion and crystallized dogma. Later histories of dogma have profited much from this remarkably rich work. Among other writers on the history of dogma who were influenced by the Hegelian conception of history, we mention Philipp Marheineke, Heinrich Schmid, and Karl Friedrich August Kahnis, who

[6] His writings on the subject were *Handbuch der Christlichen Dogmengeschichte,* 4 vols. (1797 ff.), covering the first six centuries, and *Lehrbuch der Christlichen Dogmengeschichte* (1811).

combined influences from Schleiermacher, Hegel, and Carl Immanuel Nitzsch.

Adolph von Harnack wrote a history of dogma in three large volumes. This work is in a class by itself and has become famous. It appeared between 1886 and 1890 under the title *Lehrbuch der Dogmengeschichte*. It was translated into English in seven volumes by Neil Buchanan (1894) from the third edition (1894). Harnack also prepared a *Grundriss* ("outline") of his work which reached a sixth edition in 1922. Like the rationalists in the eighteenth century, Harnack maintained that the New Testament contains a twofold gospel, the gospel *of* Jesus and the gospel *about* Jesus. According to the former, the Son was not a part of the message which he proclaimed. The original kerygma dealt only with the fatherhood of God and the brotherhood of man. The disciples, above all Paul, superimposed the gospel *about* Jesus upon the simple gospel *of* Jesus. Thus the founder of the Christian faith became the God and Savior in whom the Christian believes. Harnack made the gospel of Jesus the criterion of dogma and considered the liberation of the Church from a dogmatic Christianity to be the real aim of the history of dogma.[7]

By dogma, Harnack meant particularly the dogma of the ancient Church, the christological dogma as it had found expression in the decrees of the ancient councils and in the Apostles' Creed, the Nicene Creed, and the Athanasian Creed. Harnack insisted that this dogma had become antiquated, attempting to prove it by referring to three distinct divisions within Christianity. First, he claimed that in the Eastern Orthodox church, after a period of development that closed with John of Damascus, dogma had become petrified. The life of that church now lay in its cultus. Second, in the Roman Catholic church, according to Harnack, the Greek dogma had undergone a modification through the Augustinian system, preserving its specifically Hellenistic character, however, in the Decrees of Trent. The later Vatican dogma of the infallibility of the pope had practically shelved these decrees and made obedience to the hierarchy the controlling

Dogmatic Christianity equals petrified Christianity

---

[7] Upon the publication of his *Dogmengeschichte*, his father, Theodosius Harnack, remarked, "Just to mention the most important thing, whoever takes an attitude toward the resurrection as you do, is in my eyes no longer a Christian theologian." Quoted from F. W. Kantzenbach, *Evangelium und Dogma* (1959), p. 184.

principle. Third, the Protestant Reformers had adopted the Greek dogma, thereby contradicting their own principles regarding doctrinal authority in the Church, since Protestants hold that dogmas are always subject to revision. The Lutheran church in particular, Harnack maintained, was inconsistent with its own principle when it adhered to a dogmatic Christianity.

Upon the basis of his conception that the history of dogma issues in its own dissolution, Harnack naturally had no interest in following the history of confessional development in the age of the Reformation. He stopped his special investigation with the Council of Trent and with a brief report on Protestantism in its first stage of doctrinal development. The doctrinal "inconsistencies" of the Reformers and their internal differences he left to be treated in a special department of Church history. It is of great interest to note that in thus radically limiting the history of dogma to the rise and dissolution of dogma in the ancient Church, Harnack had no successors, not even in the confessionally independent Loofs, who dedicated his own work to Harnack.

The popularity of Harnack's work has its explanation. It was published in an age of opposition to dogma and to creeds. Harnack did not really deny the inner impulse of Christianity to express its faith and convictions in public statements, but he looked upon the attempt to give binding significance to such statements as something that never had functioned and was incapable of functioning in the Church. In his indifference to this study and with his immense store of learning, he became the historian of an anti-creedal attitude in the field of history of dogma. Quite naturally he became a leader to many outside the Lutheran church who took a liberal attitude toward the confessions of faith. His work appeared at a time when the Ritschlian points of emphasis were an attraction to many theologians in Germany and abroad. Harnack offered an entirely new method in dealing with the history of dogma as a branch of theology. The traditional categories for organization of the material were dismissed. The details of his outlines were dictated by the genetical development. A conspicuous feature lies in his repeated attempts to view many individual events as an expression of conditions in the Church as a whole, often

9

leaving the critical reader with the feeling that the author has risked too much by conjecture.

The next three authors to be discussed, Loofs, Seeberg, and Wiegand, did not follow Harnack in limiting the history of dogma to the special "Hellenistic" dogma of the ancient Church and its supposed dissolution in the opening stages of the Protestant Reformation. Instead, they continued and improved the historico-genetic method begun with Muenscher and further developed by Gieseler and Engelhardt, who were the first to liberate themselves from the Hegelian influence introduced by Baur.

In 1889, Friederich Loofs published his famous *Leitfaden zum Studium der Dogmengeschichte*. Although he was a student and friend of Harnack, Loofs declined to follow Harnack in making the so-called synoptic Jesus the criterion of the dogma of the Church. He took the apostolic kerygma as the starting point of his investigation. However, he too regarded the Alexandrian-Athanasian version of the Trinity as foreign to the New Testament.

Reinhold Seeberg published the two volumes of his *Lehrbuch der Dogmengeschichte* in 1895 and 1898. He later revised it and expanded it into four volumes. Seeberg had studied under Thomasius at Erlangen, the Lutheran university where he began his own academic career. Differing from both Harnack and Loofs, Seeberg maintained the unity of the New Testament and the essential agreement of dogma with the kerygma of the Scriptures. Seeberg defined dogma as a formal expression of the truth believed and confessed by the Church. In dogma, the Church gives its faith a fixed and normative form. It must of course be acknowledged, said Seeberg, that the christological dogma had attained its form through the use of the intellectual categories dominant at the time this dogma was formulated. Therefore, faith must not be equated with dogma. Instead, we must always distinguish between faith, or the substance of dogma, and the form in which the framers of the ancient dogma sought to express the truth. Guided by this principle, we may acknowledge the biblical character of the creeds of Nicea and Chalcedon while remaining critical of the terminology employed at these councils.

Friedrich Wiegand's *Dogmengeschichte*, in two volumes published in 1912 and 1919, shares the characteristics of Loofs and Seeberg in many ways. He has many references to Harnack, but he covers the whole of the history of dogma. The readable way in which Wiegand reviews the well organized material constitutes the pedagogical value of his work. His remarkable gift of popularizing and still covering the essential issues is seen in his three volumes on *Dogmengeschichte* (1928-29).

A follower of Albert Schweitzer, Martin Werner, has more recently tried to explain the history of dogma as the Hellenization of the gospel. The origin of dogma, he holds, is a symptom of the delay of the second coming. Dogmatic Christianity is a de-eschatologized version of the kerygma of Jesus.[8]

The four American writers to be mentioned next treated not just dogma, but doctrinal interests in general.

In the preface to his *History of Christian Doctrine*, W. G. T. Shedd confessed his indebtedness not only to the historians of Germany, but also to such great lights of the English Church as Hooker and Bull, Pearson and Waterland. He mentioned Baumgarten-Crusius and Hagenbach as having "to some extent furnished material itself." [9] On the Reformation, Shedd wrote as a strict Calvinist. Charles Porterfield Krauth directed a searching critique against Shedd's treatment of Lutheranism.[10] Shedd followed the topological method, which is now generally abandoned. After a general introduction, he discussed the history of each topic through the centuries. He included Latitudinarianism and Unitarianism, and closed with a history of the confessions in the manner of an introduction to comparative symbolics.

H. C. Sheldon also used the topological method.[11] He discussed the topics in a review of five periods: the years 90 to 320; 320 to 726; 726 to 1517; 1517 to 1720; 1720 to 1895. The categories for this topical treatment were always the same: (1) The Godhead; (2) Creation and Creatures; (3) Redeemer and Redemption; (4) Church and Sacraments; (5) Eschatology. In discussing the last period, Sheldon spoke of Leibnitz, Wolff, Kant, Fichte, Schelling, Lotze,

[8] Cf. Martin Werner, *The Formation of Christian Dogma*, trans. S. G. F. Brandon (New York: Harper & Bros., 1957).

[9] Shedd, *History of Christian Doctrine* (3rd ed.; New York: Charles Scribner's Sons, 1866), I, 8.

[10] Krauth, *Conservative Reformation* (Philadelphia: J. B. Lippincott and Co., 1875), pp. 329-54.

[11] Sheldon, *History of Christian Doctrine* (New York: Harper & Bros., 1886), Vols. I-II. The latest edition, the fourth, was published in 1906.

Hegel, Schleiermacher, Schopenhauer, von Hartmann, and Herbart in Germany; Comte, James Mill, John Stuart Mill, and Herbert Spencer in France and England; also of the Moravians, Methodists, Arminians, Baptists, Swedenborgians, Unitarians, Universalists, of the theological schools on the Continent and in England, and of the denominations in America, etc. That is, the author took the liberty of departing from the history of doctrine and made his work a history of Christian thought, even approaching a history of philosophy of religion.

George Park Fisher abandoned the topological method.[12] He also abandoned the traditional arrangement of the material under the headings "general" and "special" doctrinal history. His German precursor in this was Engelhardt, to whom Fisher expressed obligation. He also mentioned Neander, Schaff, Moeller, Harnack, Loofs, Baur, and the Ritschlian writers. Seeberg's great work was not available when Fisher wrote, nor had the work of Loofs appeared in its fourth modified and amplified edition. Fisher treated the material in distinct units as natural history. He appreciated Ritschl's criticism of the "anatomical" procedure of the old topological method, and followed his demand for a "physiological" procedure, by which was meant a chronological treatment of the matter. In dealing with all the modern schools of theology, Fisher made his work a history of Christian thought, although his title is *History of Christian Doctrine*. A lecturer must support Fisher's work with much additional information and an intuition for historical observation in order that the contents may be made sufficiently impressive for pedagogical purposes. Yet the painstaking fairness and moderation of Fisher in every respect has attracted many readers.

Arthur Cushman McGiffert, a professor in Union Theological Seminary, New York, was the first American student of Harnack, whose position he maintained in his book *The Apostles' Creed* (1902).[13] He was an independent, moderately liberal theologian of the Ritschlian type. His two short books *Protestant Thought before Kant* (1911)[14] and *The Rise of Modern Religious Ideas* (1922)[15] are written with

---

[12] Fisher, *History of Christian Doctrine* (New York: Charles Scribner's Sons, 1886).
[13] New York: Charles Scribner's Sons.
[14] *Ibid.*
[15] New York: The Macmillan Company.

the judgment of a matured scholarship. Toward the end of his life he published a *History of Christian Thought* in two volumes.[16] In the first volume (1932) he dealt with the New Testament origins of Christian thought and with the Fathers of the Eastern Church; in the second (1933), with the developments in the West beginning with Tertullian and closing with Erasmus. He had intended to add a third volume on the history of modern thought, enlarging upon the contents of his two shorter books mentioned above, but died in 1934 before this volume could be finished. It should be added that McGiffert was also the author of a life of Luther which has been widely appreciated.[17]

The English theologians have written very ably on the same materials treated by the Germans, but in a different way. J. F. Bethune-Baker wrote *An Introduction to Early History of Christian Doctrine to the Time of the Council of Chalcedon* (1903), a monograph.[18] Most of the English writings in this field are monographs, a number of which are referred to in this first volume. As a rule they deal with such doctrinal problems as the Trinity, Christology, the Holy Spirit, the sacraments, predestination, and especially the many questions in controversy between Conformists and Nonconformists.

English historians have centered their interest upon outstanding personages of the ancient Church. Thus we have such works as *The Theology of Justin Martyr* by R. E. Goodenough; [19] *The Theology of Tertullian* by R. E. Roberts; [20] *The Meaning of Homoousios*[21] and *Nestorius and His Teachings*,[22] both by J. F. Bethune-Baker; *Apollinarianism* by C. E. Raven;[23] and the two-volume work of Alexander Souter, *Pelagius' Expositions of Thirteen Epistles of St. Paul*.[24] The scholarship in these monographic productions is not second to that of the Germans. The inclination to conduct the investigations in the form of monograph and biography may have its

[16] New York: Charles Scribner's Sons.
[17] *Martin Luther, the Man and His Work* (New York: The Century Co., 1911).
[18] London: Methuen & Co., Ltd., 1938.
[19] New York: G. E. Stechert & Co., 1923.
[20] London: Epworth Press, 1925.
[21] Cambridge: The University Press, 1901.
[22] *Ibid.,* 1908.
[23] New York: The Macmillan Company, 1924.
[24] *Ibid.,* 1922, 1926.

explanation in the aim of the Anglo-Saxon mind to present the varied matters in tangible units.[25]

It would be misleading, however, to think that the British writers have no aptitude for larger contributions to the history of Christian thought. Their monographs often present great syntheses. They have not created histories of dogma such as those of Thomasius, Harnack, Loofs, and Seeberg, but they have shown a peculiar aptitude for presenting critical investigations which deal constructively with the materials of the whole field. The influence of Harnack is observable in most of them. We mention the two works by Percy Gardner, *Growth of Christianity*[26] and *Evolution in Christian Doctrine*,[27] and also *Christianity in History, a Study of Religious Development*, 1917, by J. V. Bartlet and A. J. Carlyle.[28]

Earlier than these was the very stimulating but much criticized book, written in America, by A. V. G. Allen, *Continuity of Christian Thought: a Study of Modern Theology in the Light of its History*.[29] This book grew out of an attempt to take refuge from the Augustinian and Western tradition by going back to Clement of Alexandria, Origen, and Athanasius.[30] In influential quarters of England there is, according to Vollrath,[31] a deep appreciation of religion and theology expressed by the Greek mind. We are told that "Origen is the greatest representative of a type of Christian thought which has not yet done its full work in the West." Here is determined opposition to the tenets of Augustine.

For a recent contribution reference must be made to *Early Christian Doctrines* by J. N. D. Kelly.[32] In this volume a leading patristic scholar of Great Britain presents a history of the first great creative period of the Church. The discussion extends from the close of the Apostolic Age to the Council of Chalcedon, A.D. 451. The author treats

---

[25] This is the suggestion of W. Vollrath, *Theologie der Gegenwart in Grossbritannien* (1932), pp. 142 ff.

[26] New York: The Macmillan Company, 1907.

[27] London: Williams and Norgate, 1918.

[28] Out of print.

[29] Boston: Houghton-Mifflin Co., 1884.

[30] See Charles Lewis Slattery, *Alexander Viets Griswold Allen* (New York: Longmans, Green & Co., 1911).

[31] *Op. cit.*, p. 143.

[32] New York: Harper & Bros., 1958.

extensively the doctrines of the Trinity and Christology, the authority of Scripture and tradition, sin, grace, and the sacraments.

In conclusion, a reference to the Lundensian school of thought will be in order. The Lundensians insist that the history of Christian thought must have a unified theme. In this respect, Aulén says, Adolph von Harnack's great work was better than the more encyclopedic work of Reinhold Seeberg. However, Aulén is not in agreement with the liberalism and humanism of Harnack who attempted to show that the christological dogma of the ancient Church and of the Reformation had met its defeat. The Lundensians (with certain exceptions peculiar to their system) are decidedly on the conservative side. Their outstanding merit lies in their critical discussion of theological liberalism. They also criticize Seeberg's method, and would prefer to see at the basis of his work a Christian *Grundmotiv* with a "dynamic of love." The Lundensians thus attempt to point to the motif underlying the development of the dogma of the Church.

The main Lundensian contributors to this field are Gustaf Aulén and Anders Nygren. From Aulén we have *Die Dogmengeschichte im Lichte der Lutherforschung* (1932); *Christus Victor* (1931),[33] which is a historical study of the three main types of the idea of the atonement, and *Den kristna gudsbilden* (1927), which was translated into German in 1930 under the title *Das christliche Gottesbild in Vergangenheit und Gegenwart*. In this volume the author traces the "picture" of God through the course of history, beginning with the biblical period, through the ancient Church, the Middle Ages and the Reformation, down to the recent theology in Sweden, Germany, and England.

The principal work in this field is Nygren's *Agape and Eros*.[34] Both

---

[33] Translated into English by A. G. Hebert (New York: The Macmillan Company, 1937).

[34] This work was originally published as three separate volumes in Stockholm. The first volume, *Den kristna kaerlekstanken,* appeared in 1930, a German version being issued at the same time. The English translation was made by A. G. Hebert, who added a valuable "translator's preface" (1932). The succeeding two volumes were translated into English by Philip S. Watson, who also wrote a very helpful preface (1938-39). The work was re-edited in one volume under the title *Agape and Eros* (Philadelphia: Westminster Press, 1953). Apart from the quotations given in this review, all citations refer to the 1953 edition.

words mean love in Greek, but, as Hebert emphasizes, they express two completely different concepts. They indicate "the Christian and the Greek attitude to life." Agape is "primarily God's own love, manifested in the life of the Son of man who came to seek and save that which was lost, above all in his death on the cross." It includes the love which God through his Spirit enkindles in the Christian heart in response to his love. Agape is "the downward movement of the self-giving divine love"; but Eros, of pagan or Platonic origin, is "the upward movement of the human soul to seek the divine." In his discussion of Eros, Nygren's interest is in neither the biological nor the psychological aspect of the "sensual desire" so prominent in Greek art. His interest is in Plato's "heavenly Eros," in "the endeavor of the soul to escape from the fetters of sense and seek the satisfaction of its highest spiritual needs in the eternal and true." In speaking of Agape and Eros, the author wants to discuss grace and nature as the two ways of salvation, observing them as contrasts or rather antitheses: Agape is the work of God's grace to transform nature into his image. In the words of the Translator's Preface to Volume I: "The history of Christian thought is the tangled story of the integration of the biblical and Christian tradition with the Greek tradition, of Agape and Eros." Again in the words of the translator: "It is fundamental to Christianity that God is both Creator and Redeemer. The God who created the world is the God of Agape. As creator He is the author of the natural world and of human life with its upward movement, which Aristotle describes in terms of Eros, and in this natural world and in the natural goodness of human life, God is present, and His glory is manifested. But it is only in Redemption, that is, by Agape, that He is personally revealed, both in the incomplete revelation of Agape in the Old Testament, and in the perfect manifestation by Christ." [35]

The student of this area of Swedish thought must remember that a Lundensian theology, while dealing with many topics of the history of doctrine or dogma, is primarily a history (or philosophy) of religion. Instead of confining itself to the content of Christian doctrine, Lundensianism seeks to define the relation of that doctrine (Agape) to the subjective or natural religious consciousness (Eros) of man.

[35] 1932 edition, p. xii.

16

III. The Historical Dogma

Does Dogma Represent a Development?

Dogma—and by this we mean all the abiding truths of the various dogmas—is in the Scriptures. But the Scriptures do not offer this truth in formulated statements. Some matters are clearly expressed; others are only indicated. There is a need for a proper interpretation of Scripture which is guided by the "analogy of faith" (cf. Rom. 12:7). In this regard all of the Christian churches have reached the same conclusion. There are cases of willful heresy (Titus 3:10). But can all failure to find the truth be characterized in this way? Occasionally there may be diversity of opinion with regard to the law of reasoning in arriving at a certain truth from the Scriptures. Objectively, the truth of the dogma is in the Scriptures; but there is a subjective and a group element which is an important factor in expressing this truth.

The statement of Vincent of Lérins has been quoted, namely, that the teaching of the Catholic Church has been believed "everywhere, always, and by all." His reference was to what the Church of his time expressed in the Niceno-Constantinopolitan Creed and in the Roman Symbol. The Roman church today speaks of dogma as the progressive unfolding of the truth by divine, supplementary revelation through the Church, that is, through the councils and through the pope.

If we look at the ecumenical and the particular confessions that are accepted by the Lutheran church, and if we consider the confessional history of the Reformed churches, there can be no reasonable objection to saying that the content of these confessions represents a development. Later ages, in their confessional experience, have stood upon the shoulders of preceding ages. It is interesting to observe a few of the prominent features which show the development of dogma.[36]

There has been a logic in the succession in which topics of the history of doctrine have come up for special consideration. First arose the problem of the relation of the Son to the Father. Gradually the question of the relation of the Holy Spirit was added. Thus the problems relating to the Trinity and the pre-existence of Christ won

---

[36] The evolution that we shall admit must not be confounded with an evolution of the naturalistic type which fails to see the supernatural elements in the beginnings and history of Christianity.

the attention of the early Church. Of course the truth on this subject is in the Scriptures. But these discussions began in the pre-Catholic age when the Scriptures did not exist in the form of a recognized canon, at a time when the knowledge of scriptural truth was sporadic and when heresy (Ebionitism, Gnosticism) was at work to pervert the apostolic tradition. The bishops, as guardians of the Church's tradition, were of great importance in this process of clarification. Then there followed the endeavors to define the relation of the divine and human natures of Christ in his historical existence. We are reminded of the conflict between the Antiochean and the Alexandrian schools. An interest in soteriological problems followed, issuing in the conflict between Augustine and Pelagius. Finally, doctrines were held in connection with repentance: the agelong discussion of the admissibility of a "second repentance"; discussions of the atonement, and of the Eucharist. On these and other subjects we see developments and misconceptions all through the centuries. Yet the logic of history in the succession of these topics is always noticeable.

The Greek, the Roman, the German, and the Anglo-Saxon mind each has made its special contribution. Each has worked with the heritage from the Apostolic Age. There is a unity of interest also in the fact that one age and one race usually takes over the heritage from its predecessor. At times the heritage is translated into the individuality of the new race, but with certain eliminations and modifications that impoverish Christianity. At other times the new race offers conditions favorable to greater religious depth. This matter can be described more profitably later when the purity of dogma is considered.

Philosophical influences have also shared in the development of Christian doctrines on their way toward crystallization into dogmas. Mention should be made of Neo-Platonism and Stoicism in the ancient Church, and nominalism and realism both in the Middle Ages and in the time of the Reformers.

The bent of mind and the individuality of certain leaders in the development of Christian thought must not be overlooked. We mention Irenaeus, Tertullian, Origen, Athanasius and the great Cappadocians, Theodore of Mopsuestia and Cyril of Alexandria, Leo the Great, Augustine, Gregory the Great, Thomas Aquinas, Luther, Melanchthon, Zwingli, Calvin. There is room for a psychological study of the in-

dividuals and of the races. Origen shows the Hellenistic type of mind; Tertullian, Cyprian, and Augustine the Latin type; Luther the German; and Calvin the French.

Other very decisive elements which have entered into the making of dogma are the weight of scriptural testimony and the providentially directed constellation of historical situations in critical moments of world events. Why was it that Athanasianism—in spite of all the political intrigues at the Byzantine court in favor of Arianism; in spite of the fact that Arianism was embraced at the time of the migration of peoples, by all the tribes destined to constitute future civilization except the Franks—why was it that Athanasianism, almost crushed, its standard-bearer constantly persecuted, nevertheless kept the field and had the future? Was there no providence in that event at Toledo in 589? [37] Considerations of this nature are taboo to the purely "scientific" historian. The Christian theologian cannot help but give them some thought.

The Purity of the Church's Doctrine: Its Criterion

The criterion of religious truth must be seen in the redemptive work of Christ as it was taught by the Apostles and expressed in the Holy Scriptures. Hence it belongs to the task of the history of Christian doctrine to ask whether the purity of the dogmas has not been lost in the development. During this development there has been a constant danger of assimilating foreign elements such as extra-Christian mysticism, legalism, etc.

It is interesting to watch the process of the nationalization of certain doctrines. Let us emphasize that this very process may mean, and in many cases has meant, the surrender of a very important contribution. Luther and Melanchthon, in their fine appreciation of the teachings and practices of the past, recognized this. There are special heritages and endowments that must be watched, respected, and treated with an open, though critical mind. In the ancient Church the Greek mind made its special contribution through Irenaeus, Origen, the Cappadocians, and Cyril of Alexandria. In the transition to the Middle Ages, through Augustine, Ambrose, Leo the Great, and Gregory the Great, the Roman mind was functioning and shaping

---

[37] See our remarks at the close of Chapter IX.

dogma. In the Reformation we have in Luther and in the influences behind him and about him the specifically German type of thought. In the interpretation of Calvin by John Knox and the English Reformers, we have the Anglo-Saxon type of thinking. The history of doctrine is interested in the question whether dogmas have been Hellenized or Romanized, Germanized or Anglicized, and whether they have lost their purity in the process. In themselves, Seeberg remarks, such processes of nationalization do not necessarily mean a corrupting of the dogma; they only indicate that "the thoughts of the Christian religion, at certain great epochs, were thoroughly digested" and entered into the very civilization of certain nations. "But," he continues, "the danger of these processes consists in this, that the respective peoples or ages do not merely translate Christianity into their own peculiar understanding, but they alter its contents and change it into a lower form of religion." [38] Here the history of Christian thought must proceed with criticism. Where there has been actual adulteration of dogma, there is a legitimate call for reformation. In such a reformation, however, there is the possibility of new errors that may call for even further reformation.

The Place of the Dogma in the Life of the Church

Here, differently from above, we must take "dogma" to mean an accepted creed or confession. We think here of the confessional standards in the historical churches.

But are there not anti-creedal churches? To this question Philip Schaff replies:

> Experience teaches that those sects which reject all creeds are as much under the authority of a traditional system of a few favorite writers, and as much exposed to controversy, division, and change, as churches with formal creeds.[39]

Are creeds or confessional denominational standards infallible? What is the difference between Rome and Protestantism on this matter?

To Rome, the creeds are only a part of the Church's tradition. Dogma, as part of this tradition, is infallible. Conservative Protestantism denies

[38] Reinhold Seeberg, *Lehrbuch der Dogmengeschichte* (hereinafter referred to as *Lehrbuch*), I (1920), 667 ff.

[39] Philip Schaff, *Creeds of Christendom* (New York: Harper & Bros., 1919), I, 9.

an infallible Church, and therefore can admit the truth of a dogma only in so far as its teachings are proved scriptural in the experience of the investigating members of the Church. These churches will say that their confessions are scriptural in their essentials.

What is included in a confessional subscription to the Church's doctrine? The statement is frequently made that the theological form must not be included as obligatory because it changes with the times. There is a great deal of truth in this qualification. But this qualification is one that can leave out of consideration certain elements that should be seen. What do we mean by the theological form? Here we may distinguish between terms that are employed and the frame of a given article in which the terms occur. Two things are essential in confessional subscription: (1) the rejection of a given heretical doctrine; (2) the affirmation of the truth which stands opposed to this heretical position. But we must keep in mind that not all confessions are alike; within the confessions, the different articles may offer special cases. There are instances where the "frame" of the discussion and the "terms" employed should not be made binding on the subscriber. Again there are examples in which the theological form is inseparable from the very substance of the confessional idea. This very form coins the thought in a very peculiar way; it expresses the thought once and for all. The form limits the confessional thought and determines its direction. It keeps this confessional idea from assimilating heterogeneous elements. In this respect it may be remarked that certain terms in the Nicene Creed such as "essence," "person," and the *homoousios*, which our age has begun to discredit because of their Hellenistic origin and asociation, do have their confessional significance. They convey to us the fundamental idea to be professed. Luther once said that he hated the *homoousios*, but was holding to the fact (*res*). We have no new forms and terms that would convey this idea. Those that are offered as substitutes fail to satisfy. In spite of modern criticism, especially on the part of Ritschlian theologians, this ancient terminology has preserved the truth of the gospel for the Church.

The Denominational Situation

The conservative Reformation (Lutheran and Reformed) took over the dogma of the ancient Church with regard to Christology and the trinitarian relation, as well as the Augustinian heritage with regard to sin and grace. The Socinian and Anabaptist movements were opposed to binding creeds and were interested respectively in the rationalization and spiritualization of the leading features of the objective faith. Deism in England, naturalism in France, rationalism in Germany, as results of the new philosophy in a new age, prepared the way for the abandonment of dogma.

What position are we to take on the question of truth, when there are extreme differences among the Protestant bodies? <u>Protestants started with a common acceptance of the ancient symbols, but separated into two camps, the Lutheran and the Reformed.</u> On the surface, their differences seem to be based on a disagreement concerning the means of grace. There are similar differences with regard to the relationship of the divine and human natures of Christ. Neither are the Lutheran and Reformed positions alike in the adoption of Augustinianism. These differences have been expressed in the confessions they have produced. We may say that <u>the Lutheran and Reformed confessions reveal a different comprehension of the gospel, and the result has produced a different piety and a different church life.</u> The viewpoints and controlling principles are not the same. <u>Luther is guided for the most part by the question: "What must I do to be saved?" Calvin's leading interest is the glorification of God in the congregation of believers.</u> Each of the two systems has a historically developed way of salvation with points of agreement, if individual tenets are taken by themselves, but persistent differences permeate each system as a whole. We will deal with these differences in our study of the founders of these two churches. The truth, as well as the misapprehension of the truth, must not be dealt with polemically, but in a way that objectively presents the historical facts.

BIBLIOGRAPHY

1. *Minutes of the Councils*
   BOYD, W. K. *The Ecclesiastical Edicts of the Theodosian Code.* New York: Columbia University Press, 1905.
   BRIGHT, W. *Notes on the Canons of the First Four General Councils.* New York: Oxford University Press, 1892.
   FULTON, J. *Index Canonum.* New York: Whittaker Co., 1892.

HARDOUIN, J. *Collectio Maxima Conciliorium Generalium et Provincialium.* Paris, 1715.

MANSI, J. DOM. *Collectio Sacrorum Conciliorum.* Florence and Venice, 1759-1798; new print, 1903.

MITCHELL, E. K. *Canons of the First Four General Councils.* Philadelphia, 1898.

O'LEARY, L. E. *The Apostolic Constitution and Cognate Documents.* New York, 1905.

SCHWARTZ, E. *Gesammelte Schriften,* Vol. III. Munich, 1959.

2. *Histories of the Councils*

DU BOSE, W. P. *The Ecumenical Councils.* 4th ed. New York: Charles Scribner's Sons, 1910.

HAMMOND, W. A. *The Six Ecumenical Councils.* Oxford: J. H. Parker Co., 1843.

HEFELE, VON K. J. *Konziliengeschichte.* 9 vols., 1855—. 2nd ed., Vols. 1-3, 1873—. French ed., 8 vols., Paris: 1907—.

3. *Writings of the Church Fathers*

The American Library of "The Ante-Nicene" and of "The Nicene and Post-Nicene Fathers." Edited by A. ROBERTS *et al.* Grand Rapids, Mich.: W. B. Eerdmans Co., 1951-53.

Corpus Scriptorum Ecclesiasticorum Latinorum. Vienna, 1866—.

GEBHARDT, O. VON AND HARNACK, ADOLPH VON. *Texte und Untersuchungen.* Leipzig, 1882—.

Die grieschischen Schriftsteller der ersten drei Jahrhunderte. Berlin Academy, 1897—.

The Library of Christian Classics. Edited by JOHN BAILLIE and HENRY P. VAN DUSEN. 26 vols. Philadelphia: Westminster Press, 1953—.

LIETZMANN, H. *Kleine Texte.* 1902—.

Maxima Bibliotheca Patrum. 27 vols. 1677—.

MIGNE, J. P. *Patroligiae cursus completus . . . quie ab Aevo Apostolico ad Tempora Innocentii III (anno 1216) pro Latinis et ad Concilii Florentini Tempora (anno 1439). Series Scriptoresque Ecclesiae Graecae,* 161 vols., pro Graecia Floruerunt, Paris: 1857-1904. *Series Latina,* 221 vols., Paris: 1844-1904.

The Oxford Library. Edited by EDWARD PUSEY, JOHN KEBLE, and JOHN HENRY NEWMAN. 48 vols. 1837—.

Patristic Texts. Cambridge, 1897—.

Texts and Studies. Following the *Texte und Untersuchungen.* Edited by J. A. ROBINSON. 1891—.

CHAPTER II

PRECURSORY THOUGHT

Before beginning a survey of Christian thought, the reader will find it helpful if he knows something of the intellectual and spiritual environment over against which earliest Christian thought appeared. This chapter is devoted to a brief look at some of the pertinent features of this background. Three main topics must be examined: Graeco-Roman philosophy, conditions in Judaism, and the foundations of the New Testament.

I. GRAECO-ROMAN PHILOSOPHY

Passing over the pre-Socratic philosophy, it is to be said that several of the ancient philosophical systems have left their marks upon the history of Christian dogma. Epicureanism, of course, with its sensualism, materialism, and eudaemonism,[1] declined under the attacks of Christian polemic. Aristotelianism had no influence upon the ancient Church. The time for the influence of this philosophy came in the Middle Ages. This leaves for our review, besides the philosophy of Socrates, only Platonism, Stoicism, and Neo-Platonism as philosophical presuppositions of Christian thought in the ancient Church. It will be found that some of these systems influenced Christian thinkers in two ways: Either they suggested the form in which to express the truth of the Christian faith or, under their impact, biblical concepts underwent a veritable transformation. The former, in our opinion, occurred in the controversies over the divine nature of the man Jesus. The latter transpired when the dualistic psychology of Hellenism rent asunder the psychosomatic unity of man as set forth in Scripture.

Socrates connected absolute knowing with the absolute good. Clear

---

[1] A system of ethics which is defined and enforced in terms of personal happiness or well-being.

knowledge, he taught, was bound to produce good actions; evil actions follow from ignorance. Virtues are teachable; they are innate in man; they need only to be brought into being. God, though invisible, is the author of virtue in man. As he governs nature, so he also leads man in his conditions. Man's soul shares in the divine only insofar as he participates in God's wisdom. Freed from the physical body, his soul is immortal.

We can understand why Justin Martyr would speak of Socrates as having been practically a Christian.[2] The early Christians referred to Socrates as a moral example. Here we are reminded of the moralistic trait in the Christianity of many of the Fathers of the first centuries, to which there must be frequent reference. The Socratic identification of knowledge with goodness reminds us of positions taken later by the Gnostics and by Clement of Alexandria, as well as of the stress that was laid upon knowledge as the essential of Christianity by the Greek Church Fathers.

Among the ideas of Plato the following are of interest in the history of Christian doctrine. There is a dual world: the world of ideas or forms and the world of phenomena or things. The only real world is that of ideas. The world of phenomena, which is constantly changing, is fundamentally nonexistent; it receives real character only insofar as it partakes of the ideas. For Plato this metaphysical differentiation between the two worlds is also ethical. Only the world of ideas is the world of good. The summit of the world of ideas and of the good is God.

Plato's idea of God is that he is "good" and therefore the source of all good and beneficial things. He cannot be the cause of evil. We must seek some other cause for our troubles. God is also "unchangeable." He is not a "sorcerer" who "appears designedly at different times in different shapes, deceiving us and making us conceive false opinions of him." Since God is the perfection of goodness, beauty, and excellence, any change in him would mean a change for the worse. In the *Timaeus*, God is called a "creator," "father," and "artificer," who formed the universe after "an eternal pattern." Such ideas would naturally find favor with Christian thinkers, and would influence them in the fashioning of their own theology.

[2] *Apology*, I, 6.

25

The human soul is assumed to be pre-existent. In Platonic thought, the soul has committed transgression in the world of ideas. For purposes of expiation and purification, the soul has been sent into the world of phenomena and united with a body. It is the task of the soul to slough off this bodily prison and "house of correction" and to return to the world of pure spirit. The principal ways of accomplishing self-redemption are through the theocentric contemplation of the world of ideas and the practice of mystical asceticism. The soul remembers the ideas which it once viewed in its pre-existent state, and it is seized with a deep yearning for them. An enthusiastic, erotic homesickness uplifts the soul and prepares it for its return to the world of ideas. This intellectual and mystical ascent of the soul is accomplished by a curbing and repression of the body. Through asceticism the desires of the body are subordinated to the reasoning powers of the soul. This subordination is accomplished either by harmonious union of body and soul, or by a complete repression of the body. From the process of harmonization arise the four cardinal virtues of wisdom, courage, temperance, and justice, the "natural virtues" of medieval theology. Asceticism can also have for its aim the complete destruction of all sensual phenomena and world relations. One of Plato's fundamental maxims was this: "By fleeing the world one becomes like God, so far as this is possible." Here we have that asceticism which was hinted at in the New Testament and which reappeared in monasticism.

The pre-existent human soul belongs properly to the world of ideas and is therefore immortal. Plato was especially interested in the immortality of the soul. He provided an array of proofs such as immateriality, simplicity, vitality, and the ability to grasp eternal ideas, which were used later by Christian theologians. In the *Phaedo* we read that "the soul is in the very likeness of the divine, and immortal and intelligible and uniform and indissoluble and unchangeable." Again: "If the soul be truly affirmed to be self-moving, then must she also be without beginning and immortal." Plato reports Socrates as saying shortly before his death: "I am confident in the belief that there truly is such a thing as living again, and that the souls of the dead are in existence, and that the good souls have a better portion than the evil.

26

. . . You may bury me if you can catch me; . . . and be of good cheer, and say that you are burying my body only."

The soul's self-redemption, when successfully worked out, will result in the final attainment of the "beatific vision" of eternal beauty and goodness. For the bad there will be future punishments. These punishments, after having continued for ages, will finally come to an end. This idea is the source of Origen's teaching concerning the restoration of all things and of the later Roman Catholic doctrine of purgatory. Some men, however, who have become steeped in sin and wickedness, will be beyond pardon. These will be "hurled into Tartarus, which is their suitable destiny, and they will never come out."

Stoicism, founded by Zeno of Citium (d. 264 B.C.), was the noblest example of ancient pagan ethics. In many respects it made a close approach to Christianity, even influencing the nascent religion. Upon the ruins of pagan polytheism, stoicism built a system of practical ethics that was not without its points of worth, merit, and excellence. It was represented by such men as Brutus, Cato, Cicero, Seneca, Epictetus, and Marcus Aurelius.

In Stoicism we find features of peculiar materialism. Like Aristotle, Zeno taught that the world, composed of spirit and matter, is the consequence of two principles. The spirit, as the active principle, is the mover; matter, as the passive principle, is the moved. These two principles are but different aspects of one ultimate reality. This reality is material and physical. Pure spirit does not exist. In matter there are coarser and finer forms. Mind is a finer form of matter; the body, a coarser form. Abstract qualities are also corporeal. Even God is thought of in the same terms: The world is actually his body. Here we have some of the thought underlying Tertullian's theology.

Stoicism was naturally pantheistic. What the soul is to the body, God is to the world. He is the great world-soul, the mover of matter, the fire which warms and animates it, the intelligence which guides it, the law which governs it, the Logos or reason of which man's reason is a part. Since all the seeds of life and development are present within the Logos, it is called the "spermatic Logos."

This identification of God with the living universe is pantheism. God becomes the absolute mechanical necessity, the destiny, the fate which determines everything.

27

But Stoicism was also theistic. As Weber states, the Stoics maintained "a kind of compromise between pantheism and theism." [3] God is viewed as the benevolent providence which guides everything teleologically. He is the "good king and true father" of all things. He is perfect, kind, good, benevolent, a lover of mankind, who has rewards for the virtuous and punishments for the evil.

The *summum bonum* of Stoicism was virtue, and its chief ethical maxim was: "Practice virtue for virtue's sake." Happiness is not the chief end of life but only an incidental by-product. However, the holy man will be the happy man. Hence the great law of life should be: "Live according to nature or live according to reason." The holy man is able to accept with resignation and indifference anything and everything which may come to him.

The root of evil, or sin, is seen to lie in ignorance and in the absence of reason, as with Socrates. He who really knows the good will love it, and is bound to love it. Sensuality is man's worst enemy, and suppression of it is his first duty. Stoicism was not blind to sin as a general condition of mankind, and it aimed at conversion.

There was a cosmopolitanism about Stoicism that helped to prepare the soil for Christianity. Since there is one divine reason, the Logos, which pervades the entire universe and of which all men are partakers, it follows that the human race is a solidarity. By the same token there can be only one law of nature and one rule of moral conduct. This applies to every man, whether slave or emperor, and every man is morally free. The idea of the universal fatherhood of God stands out clearly. We are all children of the same Father. Aratus said: "We are all His family"; and Cleanthes: "We, too, are His offspring." [4] The inevitable consequence is the universal brotherhood of man. In his *Letter on Slavery*, Seneca maintains that all men spring from the same root and are included in one large family. If it be true that all men are brothers, then we ought to aid and forgive our foes. All men must work together for the highest good and for the welfare of the whole body. Still, as an exclusive philosophy of the upper classes, Stoicism fostered a haughty aloofness and self-sufficiency of spirit

[3] Alfred Weber, *History of Philosophy,* trans. Frank Thilly (New York: Charles Scribner's Sons, 1907), p. 143.

[4] For references to Aratus and Cleanthes in connection with Acts 17:28, see Theodor Zahn, *Kommentar zum Neuen Testament,* V (1927), 618 ff.

which were surely inimical to and incompatible with Christian humility.

A most significant philosophical phenomenon for Christian theology and the last one we shall mention is Neo-Platonism. It terminated both Greek philosophy and ancient religion as it appeared in the mysteries. Neo-Platonism was a cosmopolitan philosophy which included the fundamental tendencies of Platonism: the religious morality of later Stoicism, the ideals of Philo, and some general oriental influences. In time Christianity also influenced Neo-Platonism; it in turn affected the early teachers of Christianity.

With Neo-Platonism we enter the third century of the Christian era. The characteristic defender of Neo-Platonism was Plotinus, who lived between the years A.D. 204 and A.D. 269. His system is epitomized in the *Enneads*. The central concept of this system is an "emanistic pantheism." The world is considered an emanation of "the One" or God. The final goal of all things is returning to and being reabsorbed into "the One," thus restoring the original unity of all things.

God is a simple, perfect, absolute existence. He is One, and in Him there is no plurality or diversity. Furthermore, he transcends all being and knowledge. His transcendence precludes any positive statement we may make concerning him. If we attempt to say anything about him by way of definition, we simply limit him. We cannot even say that he thinks or feels or wills; we can only say what he is not. We must, then, be content with negative statements. So far as human knowledge, whether theological or philosophical, is concerned, Plotinus insisted very strongly upon God's unapproachableness and his apartness from the world.

Although God is the source of all things, he nevertheless did not create the world. For one thing, he does not need the world; and for another thing, he did not will to create the world. The world is only an emanation or "overflow" from God. In this process of emanation or overflow, there are three stages: (1) the *Nous* or "Pure Mind"; (2) the *Psyche* or "Soul"; and (3) Matter. The world of phenomena issues out of the union of the soul with matter, through which the soul becomes bound up with mortality and evil. The entrance of the soul into the human body constitutes a genuine fall. This fall is caused by the soul's fixing its gaze upon the earth rather than upon God. While the body is fundamentally evil, the soul may be benefited by its period of tabernacling within the body. It will gain cognizance of evil, learn to utilize its own powers, and thus start on its return to God.

In speaking about return or absorption, the process is reversed, and development proceeds from the lower to the higher. It is the task of the soul to return to God by severing its connections with the crass materiality of the body and by rising higher and higher in gradual stages. Failure to do this will send the soul after death into another body, either human, animal or vegetable, according to the nature and depth of its sin. The pure souls are colonized in the stars; only the very purest may return to God. The means by which this ascending development takes place are mystical ecstasy and ascetic ethics. In the state of mystical ecstasy the soul transcends itself and rises to the world of ideas, where it not only recognizes that it is God but actually becomes God.

What is the effect of Neo-Platonism on Christianity? Traces of Neo-Platonism are to be found not only in the heretical excrescences of Christianity, but even in the teachings of the Church Fathers. The Neo-Platonic conception of the transcendence, unknowableness, spirituality, and timelessness of God had its effect not only on Dionysius the Areopagite, but also on Augustine. More significant in their aftereffects on Christian doctrine were the combination of monism with dualism, and the idea of a development from God to the world and from the world to God.

II. JUDAISM

In the message of the Old Testament prophets, the law of God as given to the people of Israel had occupied an important place. It was an exceedingly spiritual quantity. In the giving of the law God revealed himself to his chosen people as the living God of history. More and more the prophets had been showing that the goal of the Old Testament, with its law written on stone, was a new covenant in which the divine law would be written in the hearts of men (Jer. 31:31 ff.). The time came when the living word of prophecy ceased in Israel. After the exile there was a restoration of the law. Gradually this religion developed into the "Judaism" of Jesus' day. To the

30

Gospel writers it was very different from the religion of the Old Testament, which was characterized by that personal relation of gratitude and confidence of the soul in God reflected in the Psalms. The religion of post-exilic Judaism was one of legalism. To the interest in fulfillment of the law was added a system of sacred legislation which included the oral tradition handed down by the elders. Inward piety and moral veracity were lost, and Judaism became a religion of externalism. The Pharisees especially considered themselves the custodians of this religion. It is this situation that explains many of the utterances of Jesus against the Pharisees. The teaching of work-righteousness, as in the Book of Tobit (12:8, 14:9) and the Apocalypse of Baruch (45:2), helps to explain many Pauline statements. These views vitiated the conception of the mission of the Messiah. He was expected to bring reward for the righteous and freedom from alien oppression. A highly developed eschatology was taught.

The Jewish diaspora was especially significant for the Christian Church. The Jews guarded their identity by holding to their monotheism and maintaining synagogues for teaching the law. The fact that the Old Testament could be read in Greek translation brought Jewish and Greek modes of thought into closer contact. As a result, especially in Egypt, the Jews of the diaspora became interested in Greek philosophy. The first traces of a union between Greek speculation and the belief of the Jews in revelation are found in the writings of Aristobulus and in the Wisdom of Solomon, both of which were quoted by Christian theologians of the first century.

This Greek-Jewish philosophy reached its culmination in Philo of Alexandria, who was a contemporary of Jesus. Philo had an abstract conception of God. This created for him the problem of God and world, of spirit and matter. He bridged the chasm by mediating potencies reminiscent of the Platonic ideas, the Jewish angels, the Pythagorean numbers, and the mythological demons. The Logos or "divine reason" was the highest of these potencies. This middle being was called the son of God, the first-begotten of God, the second God. This language recurs in the attempts of the Church Fathers to describe the relation of Christ to God. The Logos was the organ for the world's creation, according to Philo. Man's soul is from God, but it has fallen and become imprisoned in the body and involved in sin and evil. Man's

31

task is the conquering of his sensuality and the suppression of his inclinations. For this, man needs the assistance of God. The highest piety manifests itself in an ecstatic relation of the soul to God. Philo's influence has been felt in the development of Christian dogma.

III. The Fundamental Testimony of the Scriptures

In the preceding sections we have been reviewing the ideas of noble thinkers standing outside the Christian revelation whose writings created a large part of the literary atmosphere in the days of the early Church Fathers. Not only did they influence the Fathers, but there are passages in both Testaments with direct or indirect reference to extra-biblical thought. But the Scriptures have a significance for Christian dogma which cannot be claimed for the literature that has just been reviewed.

What is the relation of the Scriptures to the history of dogma? The teachings of Jesus and the Apostles constituted the special object of thought for the early Christian Fathers. This teaching was at first a living Word, not confined to the New Testament writings. The latter were but partially known and only gradually came into the possession of the whole Church. There were special impulses for the creation of a recognized canon. The Gnostics aimed to prove the legitimacy of their peculiar speculations by a number of apocryphal writings which they regarded as Christian and apostolic, for example, the Gospel of Mary, the Gospel of Thomas, the Acts of Peter, and others. How far to extend the canon became a burning issue for the ancient Catholic Church. The Church Fathers had to interpret the Church's writings in a way that harmonized with the tradition of the Church (*regula fidei*). Irenaeus is a typical representative of the Church's interest in this matter. To him, the criterion of a truly Christian doctrine was its biblical character.

To Christianity the New Testament, as the fulfillment of the Old, is the normative criterion of Christian truth. This does not mean that individual passages of Scripture should be used to prove or disprove Christian truth irrespective of their historical connection. The Holy Scriptures, both Old and New Testament, represent a historical organism. This must be remembered when we speak of them as normative and use them as criteria of truth. To say this is not to ignore the fact that there was a "gospel before the Gospels," the spoken word proclaimed by the Apostles.

In this last part of this chapter on thought precursory to the dogma of the Church, we must speak very briefly of a few ideas and facts of Scripture which soon became issues for Christian thought in the history of doctrine.

Who Was Jesus?

The early Church Fathers were forced to express themselves on this question against the Gnostics, Ebionites, Samosatenes, and Arians. In the positive endeavor to formulate the conception of Christ's relation to the Father and then later to the Holy Spirit, the arguments centered around this question. The teachings of the New Testament furnished the foundations.

Matthew speaks of Jesus as the revealer of God (11:27). He has the authority to interpret God's law (5:22, 28, 34, 39). He is commissioned with the right to forgive sins (9:6). Before His death He established a new covenant (26:28).

These statements of Matthew are corroborated by Mark and Luke. According to their testimony, Jesus of Nazareth was a true prophet of God, mighty in deed and word. Mark emphasizes the messianic power of Jesus by which he forgives sins (2:5), exercises authority above the Mosiac law (2:28), and bestows upon his followers the saving power of his ministry. Luke adds to this conception the picture of Jesus as the Friend of sinners, who has come to restore the lost in Israel (4:16 ff.; 5:8 ff.; 7:37 ff.; 19:1 ff.; 23:39 ff.).

The teachings of the Fourth Gospel are in full harmony with this picture from the Synoptics. Jesus is He of whom Moses and all the Scriptures testify (John 5:39, 46), and whose day Abraham rejoiced to see (8:58). Jesus calls both the Pharisees (3:1 ff.) and the sinners (4:1 ff.; 5:14) to repentance and faith. He manifests his power amid a diversity of human want and misery (2:1 ff.; 5:1 ff.; 6:1 ff.; 9:1 ff.; 11:1 ff.). He is also, in the conception of John, Lord of the Sabbath (5:9; 9:14) and of the sacerdotal precepts of the Pentateuch (2:19 ff.; 4:23). As the Servant of the Lord (Isaiah 53), he is the Lamb of God who bears the sins of the world (John 1:29).

The deeds and words of the earthly Jesus are also the foundation of Paul's faith (I Cor. 2:2). Paul did not subtract or add any essential incidents. He faithfully delivered to his congregations what he received through the tradition of the first Christian community (15:3). According to the Gospel of Paul, Jesus, though being in the form of God, was made in the likeness of men (Phil. 2:6 ff.), born of a woman under the law (Gal. 4:4). John the Baptist's preaching of a baptism of repentance to all Israel bore witness to Jesus as the coming Savior (Acts 13:23 ff.). The fact that Paul believed in the miracles of Jesus is shown by his belief in his own miraculous power and that of the other Apostles in their service of Jesus (Acts 14:3, 15:12; Rom. 15:19; II Cor. 12:12). The transitory though divine character of the law which Paul emphasized so emphatically in his letters to the Romans and Galatians, he learned from Jesus himself. Jesus, according to the message of Paul, in the night preceding his death established a new covenant by virtue of his blood or death, giving the disciples his body to eat and his blood to drink (I Cor. 11:23 ff.). Paul is in full harmony with the other Apostles concerning the crucifixion, death, burial, and resurrection of Jesus.

According to the unanimous witness of the New Testament, the resurrection from the dead is the proof of Jesus' claim. This great fact made Jesus the *Kyrios*, which means "the Lord of glory" (Acts 4:33, 10:36; I Cor. 2:8; I Pet. 1:21; James 2:1).[5] This is also the basis for the promise of Christ's continued presence with his believers and of his final return for judgment (Matt. 28:20; John 16:22).

Special attention must be given to the two terms "Son of man" and "Son of God." The real foundation for speaking of Jesus as the Son of God is in his incarnation as taught in the prologue to John's Gospel. It is said that the Synoptics, which stress the human side of Christ, offer the earlier testimony, and that John's Gospel is of a later date. Note, however, that John says nothing on this point that disagrees

---

[5] In the Orient and in Egypt, gods and rulers were frequently addressed as *Kyrioi*. In the Septuagint *Kyrios* corresponds, apart from its use in ordinary conversation, almost regularly to the divine names of Yahweh or Elohim and related forms. By saying that God has made Jesus of Nazareth *Kyrios* (Acts 2:36), the New Testament declares Jesus to be God, before whom every knee should bow (Phil. 2:10). Cf. "Lord" in *Bible Key Words* (New York: Harper & Bros., 1958), Vol. VIII, trans. from Gerhard Kittel's *Wörterbuch zum Neuen Testament*, III, 1038 ff.

with the Synoptics, two of which have the story of the virgin birth.[6] The later date of John's testimony has the additional advantage of a larger perspective. Christ himself did not begin by announcing himself as the Son of God, but aimed to lead men to a gradual conviction by experience.

The uniqueness of Jesus is further expressed in the Pauline Letters and the General Letters. Paul speaks of Christ as "the second Adam," the new federal head of humanity (Rom. 5:12; I Corinthians 15:45-49), "the firstborn of all creation" (Col. 1:15), "the firstborn from the dead" (Rom. 8:29), "the image of the invisible God" (Col. 1:15), and on an "equality with God" (Phil. 2:6). Paul clearly sets forth the pre-existence of Christ. In I Peter, Christ is represented as "a lamb without blemish and without spot" (1:19), "the shepherd and bishop of your souls" (2:25), "a chief corner stone" (2:6), and "the just" who died for the "unjust" (3:18). The writer of Hebrews designates Him "a priest for ever after the order of Melchizedek" (5:5, 6) and "the new and living way" (7:19; 10:20). These designations provided the early Christians with the basis for the christological development of the Church.[7]

What Was the Mission of Jesus?

Closely associated with the doctrine of the person of Christ is that of his work in the world. This question includes the ideas of atonement, justification, and the establishment of the Church, about which numerous controversies centered.

The atonement is set forth in the peculiar patterns of the different New Testament writings. In Mark 10:42-45, Jesus speaks of giving

[6] There are critical scholars who decline to accept the New Testament testimony as to the earthly beginnings of our Lord. They contend that the story of the virgin birth recorded by Matthew and Luke is the product of the imaginative mind of the primitive Christian community. It was these early Christians, they say, who raised Jesus of Nazareth to the proportion of a heavenly, supra-mundane being, born of a virgin and coming again upon the clouds of heaven. But in the New Testament testimony itself there is no real foundation for such a conjecture. The critical attitude of these men seems to be rooted in the naturalistic bent of their own minds. Cf., for instance, Rudolf Bultmann, *Theology of the New Testament* (New York: Charles Scribner's Sons, 1952), I, 131. See also in Vol. II of the present work the discussion of the men of the historico-religious school and of modernism in both Great Britain and America.

[7] Cf. E. Brunner, *The Mediator,* trans. Olive Wyon (Philadelphia: Westminster Press, 1934), pp. 316 ff.

his life as "a ransom for many." Exegetes have differed widely as to the significance of this statement, yet it is to be associated with redemption. The words of institution of the Lord's Supper embrace the idea of forgiveness: "this is my blood of the New Testament, which is shed for many for the remission of sins" (Matt. 26:28). In foretelling his own death, Jesus stated that it was voluntary and vicarious (16:21). The apostolic tradition clearly associated the death of Jesus with the forgiveness of sins and salvation. Paul claims that he received from the early Apostles the teaching that "Christ died for our sins according to the scriptures" (I Cor. 15:3).

The problem which confronted the early Church was how to reconcile the ignominious death of Christ on the cross with the exalted mission of the promised Messiah. The Jews argued that such a death proved that Jesus was not the Messiah. Jesus' death on the cross was interpreted as a great crime on the part of the Jews who rejected him, yet as a power and a blessing to those who accepted him. The "stumbling block of the cross" (I Cor. 1:23) was the culmination of Christ's saving work and the crown of his messianic mission. The early Christians found the Old Testament in harmony with this idea.

The theme of Paul's preaching was "Jesus Christ and him crucified" (I Cor. 2:2). In Galatians 3:13, the Apostle presents Christ's death as vicarious, "being made a curse for us." The atonement was effected logically and in harmony with the divine justice and mercy. Christ suffered voluntarily as a sinless Savior on behalf of men who could never pay the penalty of sin, and thus reconciled man and God (II Cor. 5:21; I Thess. 5:10; Gal. 1:4; Rom. 4:25, 8:32; Col. 1:13; II Cor. 5:18). In becoming a curse for us, Christ suffered the curse of the law. He became our substitute, revealing and vindicating the divine righteousness. This is far more than retributive justice, and it exalts the righteousness of God (Rom. 3:24 ff.).

In I Peter, the death of Christ is also set forth as redemptive (3:18), but is presented in relation to moral cleansing rather than to legal acquittal from guilt. This Letter does not enter into the involved arguments of the Pauline theology, but sets forth the vicarious character of Christ's suffering as the ground for sinners' comfort and hope (1:18, 3:18).

The writer of Hebrews sets forth the atonement under the figure

of the priesthood. The imperfection of the old Levitical priesthood
(7:11) called for a new priesthood of perfect and perpetual significance. This change was effected in Christ, who abolished the old order
and opened up the new and living way unto God. His sacrifice atoned
for sin once for all (9:28), and offered to men a testament of his
benefits (9:20).

In the Apocalypse the death of Christ is redemptive. It is in "the
blood of the Lamb" that saints receive purification from sin (1:15;
7:14; 22:14). The symbol of the Lamb is one of vicarious suffering,
mercy, and love (5:12).

According to the First Letter of John, Christ, the Righteous One,
fulfills a twofold function: He not only delivers us from sin, but he
is also our advocate with the Father (2:1). His blood "cleanses us
from all sin" (1:7). The atonement from sin unto righteousness is
clearly expressed in the designation "propitiation" (2:2; 4:10). Salvation is a present blessing as well as a future reality (3:2).

We see, therefore, that the New Testament presents and develops
the idea of the atonement as a distinct part of the messianic mission
of Jesus in terms of his death, blood, suffering, resurrection, and
propitiation.[8]

Justification is a doctrine which received special development and
emphasis in the writings of the Apostle Paul. The roots of the forensic
conception of righteousness lie in the Old Testament (Hab. 2:4), but
in Judaism the law was conceived of as making man good. Righteousness came by the law. For Paul, the purpose of the law is to make
man conscious of his guilt. It can never take away man's sin (Rom.
7:7; I Cor. 15:56). Since the whole race is under the condemnation
of sin, the righteousness of God is required to take away sin. How is
this brought about? God freely pronounces the unrighteous man
righteous through faith in Christ. Justification is a forensic act. The
idea stands in contrast with the teaching of the Pharisees who posited
righteousness by works. It is by faith alone that man apprehends the
righteousness achieved by Christ (Gal. 2:20; 3:3). It is not that God
recognizes faith as meritorious. "Of faith" means "according to grace"
(Rom. 4:16). This "righteousness of God by faith" is not imputed
apart from Christ. It is for Christ's sake that believers are declared

[8] Brunner, *op. cit.*, pp. 475 ff.

righteous. Justification grows out of the atonement. Christ's death is therefore called a propitiation. "He was delivered for our transgressions and raised again for our justification." From justification flows peace, sanctification, and the new life (Rom. 5:1; Eph. 5:25; Titus 2:14).

While this idea of justification is Pauline, other New Testament writers are in accord with it. According to the writer of Hebrews, God produces good works in us (13:21; 11:7), though not in the sense of meritorious works. Peter recognizes moral integrity as a divine requirement (I Peter 2:24; 3:14), and warns his readers not to abuse the freedom which they have in Christ (2:16). James emphasizes works, not basing the edict of justification exclusively upon faith. Yet the works of which he speaks are the works which follow faith. While he seems to differ from Paul, he nevertheless avoids the legalism of Judaism (James 2:20 ff.).

The doctrine of justification is not thoroughly systematized either in the Pauline Epistles or in the other writings of the New Testament. It remained for the teachers of the Church to formulate and develop the scattered conceptions into consistent representations in which the one frequently supplements the other.

The establishment and organization of the Church constituted a distinct part of Christ's mission. The implications expressed in the founding of the Church, particularly with respect to polity, occasioned unlimited controversies in the history of dogma.

The Synoptic Gospels teem with statements concerning the "kingdom of God" or the "kingdom of heaven." This theme was uppermost in Jesus' thought. In analyzing what Christ meant, we dare not overemphasize the kingdom's eternal significance. To Pilate he said: "My kingdom is not of this world" (John 18:36). The true program for the coming of the kingdom is to work for regeneration in the hearts of men by the power of the Holy Spirit through the means of grace. The kingdom is a process comparable to the leaven in the meal (Matt. 13:33). The character of the kingdom depends upon a condition in the hearts of men. According to Jesus' teachings, the kingdom lies in the experience of the forgiveness of sin and in the reign of divine love in the hearts and lives of those who receive his grace and offer their devoted service (4:17 ff.; 13:44-45). Jesus established the kingdom as a growing process with the design of universality. The parables reflect this idea (Mark 4:26 ff.). The principles of the kingdom are to permeate all social relationships of life. On this subject theology presents the many works on Christian ethics, Christian sociology, and the practical life of the churches. This is not the place for details except to say that it is possible to overlook the claims of Christian sociology as the fruit that must follow faith. In the teachings of Jesus the kingdom transcends every temporal, mundane achievement. In the last analysis it is an eschatological entity, the "wholly other." [9]

While Jesus appointed disciples and promised the establishment of the church, it remained for history to develop the external organization. The word church (ecclesia) appears only twice in the Synoptic Gospels (Matt. 16:18; 18:17).

The need for an organized Church is seen in the Book of Acts. At first the early Christians met in homes (4:31-37). The growth of the Christian movement called for the appointment of deacons to assist in daily ministrations (6:5).

Paul spoke more frequently of the Church than of the kingdom of God not because he was primarily interested in external organization, but because he felt responsible for the organization of the various communities of believers. He thought of the kingdom as "righteousness and peace and joy in the Holy Spirit" (Rom. 14:17). He conceived of the Church as local communities of believers and followers of Christ (I Cor. 1:2; 12:28; 15:9). The early Epistles of Paul do not refer to ecclesiastical officers (cf. Galatians and I Corinthians). In all probability the party factions in Corinth grew up because of the fluidity of organization. It is in his first Letter to the Corinthians that the Apostle speaks so extensively of the *charismata* or "gifts of grace." The later Epistles show that there had been a development in the organized life of the Church, for official leaders appear as deacons, presbyters, and bishops. It is generally conceded that the offices of bishop and presbyter were the same in New Testament times. The Pastoral Epistles especially portray a highly developed organization.

[9] Cf. C. H. Dodd *et al., The Kingdom of God in History* (Chicago: Willett, Clark and Co., 1938) and E. F. Scott, *The Kingdom of God in the New Testament* (New York: The Macmillan Company, 1931). The eschatological aspect of the kingdom has received consistent emphasis in the works of the historico-religious school and more recently in the writings of the dialectical theologians.

While the Apocalypse speaks of the seven churches of Asia and refers to the general community of the elect from all tribes and nations, it does not add anything essential to the Pauline teaching concerning the organization of the early Christian communities. It has remained for history to deal with the problems of Church polity.

The sacraments were also part of the controversies waged in the development of Christian doctrine. According to the testimony of the New Testament, Jesus established the two sacraments of baptism and the Lord's Supper.

Baptism as a rite was practiced by the Jews and by the devotees of the mystery religions, as well as by the early Christians. John the Baptist introduced new connotations in the rite he employed. Christian baptism, as instituted by Christ, differs from the purification of the Jews and the rite of John the Baptist. In the narratives of Acts, this baptism was practiced "in the name of Jesus." In Matt. 28:19-20 there appears a triadic formula, supported also by many other references.[10]

Apparently there was a definite tradition or course of instruction connected with baptism in the early Church. Its confessional character called for the formulation of the belief and practice. Accordingly, a baptismal confession was crystallized (Rom. 6:3; Acts 19:2; Heb. 10:22; Eph. 4:5). This baptismal formula and tradition served as a basis for the Rule of Faith and later the Apostles' Creed. Anglican scholars call attention to the fact that baptism in the early Church was preceded by penitence and was often followed by the practice of laying on of hands, "confirmation" (Acts 8:14-15; Heb. 6:2). They see a legitimate basis for speaking of these other rites as sacraments.[11]

In addition to the baptismal formula, there was also a tradition concerning the Lord's Supper (I Cor. 11:23 ff. and in the Synoptic Gospels) which was associated with Christian instruction and confession. The New Testament gives little insight into the Communion feast other than the repeated references and words of institution. The only exception is the *agape* feast which was related to the Lord's Supper.

Eschatology occupied a unique place in the thought of early Chris-

[10] I Cor. 6:11, 12:4; II Cor. 13:13; Rom. 15:16, 30; Eph. 2:19-22; II Thess. 2:13.

[11] E. G. Selwyn (ed.), *Essays, Catholic and Critical* (New York: The Macmillan Company, 1926), p. 376.

tianity. This may account for the comparatively late composition of the canonical Gospels. On the one hand, early Christians, mindful of the promise of Christ's early return and eagerly awaiting this event, were satisfied with the oral gospel and the dominance of the Spirit. These Christians felt no need for a written New Testament. On the other hand, when His coming seemed unduly delayed, confusion arose. It became necessary for the Apostle Paul to write admonishingly concerning this doctrine (cf. I and II Thessalonians).

Jesus himself inaugurated those eschatological hopes upon which the disciples meditated after his death. In Acts, these hopes appear very vivid (1:11). Paul endeavored to co-ordinate this tradition with his program of world-wide missions (II Thess. 3:5). The writer of the Apocalypse elaborated upon this doctrine in terms of Jewish apocalyptic symbolism and in the light of the Roman imperial powers. The symbolic character of this book gave rise to many conflicting opinions in the development of Christian doctrine. Later, Augustine clarified Christian thinking on this point to a very large extent.

In addition to the doctrine which grew up on New Testament soil there are other traditions. For example, in the house-tables of the Pauline Epistles we note the development of definite traditions of an ethical character, particularly with respect to virtues and vices (cf. Rom. 12; Eph. 6; Col. 5:18 ff.). Likewise we note numerous admonitions concerning offices, regulations of worship, and the like (I Tim. 3:1; Titus 1:7; I Cor. 14; Heb. 6:1-2). Some of these traditions were crystallized in the *Didache*.

The early Christians became conscious of various doctrinal and practical problems which called for solution. In the Pauline Epistles particularly, we see the efforts of the inspired Apostle to establish standards of conduct and teaching. In I Corinthians, for example, Paul deals with marriage, the sacraments, the doctrine of the resurrection, and other questions troubling the local community of believers. A growth and development of Christian tradition can be seen which is sometimes very fluid, at other times more or less definite. These developments constitute the starting point for the development of Christian doctrine. However, the New Testament does not offer formulated and systematized doctrines for the Church. Rather, it states the principles and sets the standards for working out the doctrines needed for the guidance of the Church.

BIBLIOGRAPHY

1. Graeco-Roman Philosophy

ANGUS, S. *The Religious Quests of the Graeco-Roman World.* London: J. Murray, 1929.

ARMSTRONG, A. H. *An Introduction to Ancient Philosophy.* London: Methuen Press, 1947.

————. *The Architecture of the Intelligible Universe in the Philosophy of Plotinus.* Cambridge: Cambridge University Press, 1940.

ARNOLD, E. V. *Roman Stoicism.* Cambridge: Cambridge University Press, 1911.

CORNFORD, F. M. *Plato's Theory of Knowledge.* London: Routledge and Paul, 1935.

GLOVER, T. R. *The Conflict of Religions in the Early Roman Empire.* London: Methuen and Co., 1909.

LIETZMANN, H. *A History of the Early Church.* Cleveland: Meridian Books, 1961.

WENDLAND, P. *Die Hellenistisch-Römische Kultur.* 1912.

2. Judaism

BOUSSET, W. *Die Religion des Judentums im neutestamentlichen Zeitalter.* 1903.

CHARLES, R. H. *The Apocrypha and Pseudepigrapha of the Old Testament.* 2 vols. Oxford: Oxford University Press, 1913.

DAUBE, DAVID. *The New Testament and Rabbinic Judaism.* London: University of London (Athlone Press), 1956.

DAVIES, W. D. *Paul and Rabbinic Judaism.* London: SPCK, 1948.

DEISSMANN, ADOLPH. *Light from the Ancient East.* Translated by LIONEL R. M. STRACHEN. 1927.

FOAKES-JACKSON, F. J. and KIRSOPP LAKE. *The Beginnings of Christianity.* 4 vols. London: Macmillan Co., 1920-33.

GRANT, FREDERICK C. *Ancient Judaism and the New Testament.* New York: Macmillan Co., 1959.

MONTEFIORE, C. *Judaism and St. Paul.* London: M. Goschen Ltd., 1914.

MOORE, G. F. *Judaism in the First Three Centuries of the Christian Era.* 2 vols. Cambridge, Mass.: Harvard University Press, 1927.

SCHUERER, EMIL. *History of the Jewish People in the Time of Jesus Christ.* Translated by SOPHIA TAYLOR and PETER CHRISTIE. 5 vols. New York: Charles Scribner's Sons, 1891.

STRACK, HERMANN and PAUL BILLERBECK. *Kommentar zum Neuen Testament aus Talmud und Midrasch.* 4 vols. 1922-26.

3. The Fundamental Testimony of the Scriptures

BULTMANN, RUDOLF. *Theology of the New Testament.* 2 vols. New York: Charles Scribner's Sons, 1952—.

CULLMAN, OSCAR. *Christ and Time*. Philadelphia: Westminster Press, 1962.

_____. *The Christology of the New Testament*. Philadelphia: Westminster Press, 1959.

_____. *Earliest Christian Confessions*. London: Lutterworth Press, 1949.

FOAKES-JACKSON, F. J. and KIRSOPP LAKE. *The Beginnings of Christianity*. London: Macmillan Co., 1920–.

HOSKINS, EDWYN, and DAVEY, NOEL. *The Riddle of the New Testament*. London: Faber and Faber, 1947.

MANSON, THOMAS W., MAJOR, H. D. A., and WRIGHT, C. J. *The Mission and Message of Jesus*. New York: E. P. Dutton and Co., Inc., 1951.

PORTER, F. C. *The Mind of Christ in Paul*. New York and London: Charles Scribner's Sons, 1930.

RICHARDSON, ALAN. *An Introduction to the Theology of the New Testament*. New York: Harper & Bros., 1959.

SCHLATTER, A. *Die Geschichte des Christus*. 1923.

STAUFFER, ETHELBERT. *New Testament Theology*. London: SCM Press, 1955.

ZAHN, THEODOR. *Grundriss der Neutestamentlichen Theologie*. 1932.

CHAPTER III

THE POST-APOSTOLIC FATHERS

I. The Earliest Fathers and Their Writings

The so-called Apostolic or Post-Apostolic Fathers were those early Christian writers who immediately succeeded the Apostles, and whose period of activity extended over the years A.D. 90 to A.D. 140. The expression Apostolic Fathers originated in the belief that these men had been pupils of the Apostles. Since some of the Fathers were not contemporaries of the Apostles, the designation is not strictly accurate. The significance of these men lies in the fact that they formed the connecting link between the time of the Apostles and the Old Catholic Age. They furnish the starting point for the history of doctrine.

Some may feel that these Fathers exhibit only individual opinions, and thus are of no value for the history of doctrine. The scanty writings which have come down to us are the specimens of a much larger literature which was influential in its day. What Grote says of the classical literature of Greece is applicable to the literature of the early Church: "We possess only what has drifted ashore from the wreck of a stranded vessel." [1] Their writings were so significant in their day that some were almost admitted into the New Testament canon. There is no doubt that they provide us with a cross section of the mode of religious thought in the Gentile-Christian congregations of the time.

The writings which are available for a study of this period are the following:

The so-called *First Letter of Clement;* written in A.D. 96 or 97 by Clement of Rome and addressed to the church at Corinth. It contains

[1] Cf. G. P. Fisher, *History of Christian Doctrine* (New York: Charles Scribner's Sons, 1911). p. 41.

44

general moral and doctrinal instructions and particular admonitions with regard to a quarrel which had arisen between the presbyters and certain rebellious laymen of that church.[2] Although Clement accepted the doctrines of Paul, he failed to fathom them and lost himself in legalism.[3]

The *Shepherd of Hermas* was written by a member of the Roman church. This is an exhortation to repentance, and is composed of five visions, twelve mandates and ten similitudes. In this document, the Church appears as an ancient lady, while the "Angel of Repentance" is represented by a shepherd. The ancient Church regarded the *Shepherd of Hermas* as a canonical book until the warning was issued not to "count it among the prophets nor the writings of the Apostles." The objection was that it had been written "in our times" (middle of the second century) by a certain Hermas whose brother was Pius, Bishop of Rome (139-154). The book was supposedly written around 140; but because of Vision II, 4, it has been dated as early as the year 97.[4]

The *Seven Letters of Bishop Ignatius* of Antioch are addressed to the congregations in Ephesus, Magnesia, Tralles, Rome, Philadelphia, Smyrna, and to the Bishop of Smyrna. The date of composition is placed between 110 and 115. In these letters there are extremely interesting thoughts on Christ's pre-existence, on the reality of his incarnation, on the Christian as a "Godbearer" (*theopheros*), and on the Church and the bishop as the representative of the Church's unity.

The *Letter of Bishop Polycarp of Smyrna*. This was written to the congregation at Philippi close to the date of the seven letters of Ignatius, probably in 155.

The so-called *Letter of Barnabas* was written by an unknown author, not by St. Paul's companion. There is no agreement as to the date of composition. Some place it as early as A.D. 70, while others date it as late as 117 and 138. This writing, which is characterized by a strong opposition to Judaism, interprets the Jewish ceremonial law as an allusion to Christ and his redemption.

The so-called *Second Letter of Clement* was written about 150 by

[2] For the situation as it existed in Corinth, see p. 97.
[3] Cf. Wilhelm Wrede, *Untersuchungen zum ersten Klemensbrief* (1899).
[4] Cf. Theodor Zahn, *Der Hirte des Hermas* (1886).

an unknown author and is the most ancient homily that has been preserved. It is strongly legalistic in tone.

The Exposition of the Oracles of the Lord, consisting of five books, was written about 125 by Bishop Papias of Hierapolis. Only a few fragments of this work have been preserved. These are especially significant because of their chiliastic descriptions which were drawn from Jewish apocalyptic books.

The *Didache, or Teaching of the Twelve Apostles*, is a church manual for catechists and congregations. The first part, which is catechetical, presents moral precepts in the form of the two ways—the way of life and the way of death. The second part contains instructions for church worship and rules for congregational life. The document closes with eschatological statements.[5] Harnack dates it between 120 and 160.[6]

The *Preaching of Peter* (*Praedicatio Petri*) is a so-called missionary sermon of Peter. It is really a pseudonymous work which originated between 110 and 130. Only fragments of this writing remain.[7]

II. DOCTRINAL CONCEPTS PRESENTED BY THE FATHERS

The Concept of God

It is difficult to speak of the common theology of the Fathers. In a sense, they had no common theology. They lacked the needed distance and perspective. Furthermore, no need was felt for formulated doctrines. These early Christians were still deeply impressed with Christ's life and sufferings, in the face of which there were no impulses for the creation of doctrinal statements. The chief interest of these Christians was in the demands of the new Christian life. They formulated decisive principles on the "two ways" (cf. the *Didache* and *Barnabas*). Their doctrinal expression was sporadic and accidental.

In contradistinction to the polytheistic faith of heathenism, the Post-Apostolic Fathers adhered tenaciously to monotheism in the Old Testament sense. Hermas begins his book with the command: "Above

[5] The first edition of this very important document was made by Philothelos Bryennios in 1883.

[6] Cf. *PRE*, I, 722. Cf. *The Library of Christian Classics* (Philadelphia: Westminster Press, 1953—), hereinafter referred to as *LCC*, I, 162.

[7] See G. Ficker in E. Hennecke, *Neutestamentliche Apokryphen* (1924).

all things believe that there is One God, who created and ordered all things, who brought everything to existence from nothingness, and who comprehends all things, although He Himself is incomprehensible." To all of them God is the almighty Lord, the creator, upholder, and ruler of the world. Although He created the world, he himself is not a part of it. He is invisible, incomprehensible, uncreated, everlasting, and in need of nothing. At the same time he is the merciful Father who manifests himself by love to men, especially to sinners. He created the world for men and the Church. These thoughts are mainly of Old Testament and Jewish origin, and exhibit little Hellenic influence.

A kind of trinitarian relationship in the Godhead was recognized by some of these Fathers as indicated by remarks such as the following: The *First Letter of Clement* speaks of God and the Lord Jesus Christ and the Holy Spirit.[8] In *Similitudes*, VI, Hermas has an approach to a trinitarian relation when he speaks of the Father as Lord of the farm, of the Son as servant, and of the flesh as bearing the Holy Spirit.[9] A passage from Ignatius is very interesting. He speaks of Christians as being stones of the temple of the Father, made ready for the building of God our Father, carried up to the heights by the engine of Jesus Christ, that is the cross, using the Holy Spirit for a rope.[10] It appears that the Post-Apostolic Fathers were familiar with the baptismal formula and its crystallization in the trinitarian relationship. The Trinity, however, was not made a subject of speculation. This was particularly the case with regard to the Holy Spirit. There was the natural difficulty of conceiving of the Spirit hypostatically or personally. In view of the fact that the Church still had its charismatics (gifts of the Spirit) as the media through which the productive and creative activity of the Spirit was transmitted, there was little occasion for discussing the Holy Spirit.

The Person of Christ

The divinity of Christ was an accepted fact among these Fathers. To Ignatius, Christ was "my God" and "our God." The *First Letter of Clement* speaks of Christ as "the sceptre of the majesty of God,"

[8] 58, 2; 56, 6.
[9] Cf. *Similitudes,* V, VII.
[10] *Ephesians,* IX, 1.

and the *Homily of Clement* declares: "We ought so to think of Jesus Christ as of God, as of the Judge of the quick and the dead." [11] Governor Pliny reported in his letter to the Emperor Trajan that the Christians "are accustomed to sing a hymn to Christ as God" (*Christo quasi Deo carmen dicere soliti sunt*).

The humanity of Jesus was also clearly recognized. The *Didache* characterizes Jesus not only as the chosen and beloved of God, but also as the "servant of God." Ignatius speaks of him as "conceived by Mary" and as being "of the seed of David." [12] The *Homily of Clement* says: "Christ the Lord who saved us, though he was originally Spirit, became flesh and thus called us." [13] The Apostolic Fathers did not speculate concerning the relation between Christ's divinity and humanity, or the relation of his divinity to that of the Father.

The pre-existence of Christ was also asserted clearly and positively. Before time and space began, Christ was God, exalted above the angels; and yet he was differentiated from the Father. He assisted at creation and later appeared in the flesh to open the kingdom of God to the ransomed.[14] Hermas says: "The Son of God is older than his creation so that he was the counsellor of his creation to the Father." [15] Hermas also designates the pre-existent Christ as the Spirit, and calls his incarnation a tabernacling in the flesh. The impression has arisen that Hermas identified the Son of God with the Holy Spirit, and so espoused a Binitarianism instead of a Trinitarianism. More exact investigations lead to another result. Zahn declares: "It is certain that Hermas assigns a pre-historic, i.e., an eternal, existence to the Son of God as personally differentiated from the Holy Spirit." [16]

The Way of Salvation

In the conception of the Fathers there is less clarity concerning the saving work of Christ than there is concerning the person of Christ. It is true that such statements as the following are found concerning

[11] I, 1.
[12] *Ephesians*, XVIII, 2; *Trallians*, IX.
[13] IX, 5.
[14] Cf. Ignatius, *Magnesians*, VI, 1; Hermas, *Similitudes*, V, 6.
[15] *Similitudes*, IX, 12, 2.
[16] Theodor Zahn, *Ignatius von Antiochien* (1873), p. 261.

the atonement. "Let us fix our gaze upon the blood of Christ and let us know that it is precious to his Father, because it was poured out for our salvation, and brought the grace of repentance to all the world." [17] "It was for this reason that the Lord endured to deliver up his flesh to death that we should be sanctified by the remission of sin, that is, by his sprinkled blood." [18] "Christ gave his blood by the will of God for us, and his flesh for our flesh, and his soul for our souls." [19] In the *Epistle to Diognetus* there is a beautiful testimony to the vicarious significance of the death of Jesus for man:

> He himself gave up his own Son as a ransom for us—the holy one for the unjust, the innocent for the guilty, the righteous one for the unrighteous, the incorruptible for the corruptible, the immortal for the mortal. For what else could cover our sins except his righteousness? In whom could we, lawless and impious as we were, be made righteous except in the Son of God alone? O sweetest exchange. O unfathomable work of God! O blessings beyond all expectation! The sinfulness of many is hidden in the Righteous One, while the righteousness of the One justifies the many that are sinners.[20]

Polycarp, Justin Martyr, Irenaeus and all the Fathers speak of the vicarious suffering of Christ. There is no reflection upon the question why and how Christ's work has redeeming power. The Fathers liked to speak of the gifts which God had brought to mankind. Among these is the forgiveness of sins, as understood by the Greek mind. The pre-eminent gifts are the "knowledge of the truth" and "eternal life." The *Homily of Clement* calls Christ the Redeemer and the Captain of Immortality, "through whom God revealed the truth and the heavenly life to us." [21] It is clear that the Apostolic Fathers made prominent only those elements of the Christian revelation which were of special value to them and their times. The result was this one-sidedness and this meagerness of conception which impress the reader of today. While there are no errors in these views, a unified and systematic teaching is lacking.

A positive error occurred when the gift of Christ came to be viewed principally as the revelation of a new law (*nova lex*). Christ was

[17] *I Clement*, VII, 4.
[18] *Barnabas*, V, I.
[19] *I Clement*, 49, 5.
[20] *LCC*, I, 220 -21. This document is an apology for the faith written about A. D. 130. See also the introduction to this epistle, *ibid.*, pp. 205 ff.
[21] XX, 5.

taken to be the new lawgiver. In the *Shepherd of Hermas* there are many statements expressing this sentiment. As a result, there is scarcely any trace of the Pauline doctrine of justification in the writings of the Fathers. They viewed man's relation to God as being regulated, not by faith, but by works. It is true that the *First Letter of Clement* has a passage which is strongly reminiscent of Paul:

> All these, therefore, were highly honoured, and made great, not for their own sake, or for their own works, or for the righteousness which they wrought, but through the operation of his will. And we too, being called by his will in Christ Jesus, are not justified by ourselves, nor by our own wisdom, or understanding, or godliness, or works which we have wrought in holiness of heart; but by that faith through which, from the beginning, Almighty God has justified all men; to whom be glory for ever and ever.[22]

This passage is without parallel in the rest of the Apostolic Fathers, and even Clement himself says in other places: "Blessed are we, beloved, if we perform the commandments of God in the concord of love, that through love our sins may be forgiven." [23]

It is obvious that the emphasis has begun to fall upon works and their merit. A far-reaching road was being prepared for a subsequent development. This is evidenced by statements like the following: "Work with thy hands for the ransom of thy sins." [24] "If ye turn to the Lord with your whole heart and work righteousness the remaining days of your life, and serve Him strictly according to His will, He will heal your former sins." [25] "Almsgiving is therefore excellent as a repentance for sins; fasting is better than prayer; but almsgiving is better than either, . . . for almsgiving becomes lightening of the burden of sins." [26] Due to Jewish and heathen impulses, the idea arose that it is possible to perform an excess of good works, which is made the foundation of a higher morality. The *Didache* declares: "If you will wear the entire yoke of Christ, you will be perfect; if not, then do what you can." [27] Hermas says: "If you can do more than what God commands, you will earn more glory for yourself and you will have more honor before God." [28]

[22] *I Clement,* 32.　[23] *Ibid.,* 50, 5.　[24] *Barnabas,* XIX, 10.
[25] Hermas, *Mandates,* XII, 6, 2.
[26] *Homily of Clement,* XVI, 4.
[27] *Didache,* VI, 2.
[28] *Similitudes,* V, 3, 3.

The errors connected with moralism have already begun to insinuate themselves. Grace, faith, and forgiveness have yielded ground to the new law and good works. The righteousness revealed in the gospel (Rom. 1:17) is no longer understood as the righteousness of Christ imputed to the believer. Instead, these men (and all writers of the Catholic tradition) conceive of righteousness as the actual newness of the Christian life: the righteousness which a Christian does rather than that which he believes (cf. I John 3:7). Faith has lost its central position. It now is simply one of the many virtues evident in the life of believers.

The Church

To Clement of Rome the Church is the company of saints, the flock of Christ, and God's own possession. Even pre-existence is attributed to it. The *Homily of Clement* declares that the first Church, the spiritual Church, was created before the sun and moon.[29] Hermas says that it was created first and before all things. The Church is the real goal of creation. Its connection with Christ is as intimate as that of the body with the soul. According to its being, the Church can only be "one" and "holy." Such was the case in the beginning, and such will be the case at the end. We belong to the Church if we do the will of our heavenly Father. The Church is also historical and empirical. As such it contains within itself objectionable elements. Hermas expresses this idea in the following simile: "As the trees are all alike in winter, when they have cast their leaves, and it is not evident which ones are dead and which ones are full of vital energy, so in this world neither the righteous nor the unrighteous are recognized, but all appear alike."[30] Hermas anticipates that it will not always be so: "After these [*i.e.,* the wicked] are cast out, the Church of God shall become one body, one understanding, one mind, one faith, one love. And then the Son of God shall be exceedingly glad . . . because He has received his people pure."[31]

Ignatius compares the personal union between Christ and the believer to the relationship of the congregation to the bishop. He makes an easy transition from soteriology to ecclesiology. The bishop is the

[29] XIV, 1.
[30] *Similitudes,* III, 2, 3.
[31] *Ibid.,* IX, 9, 4.

centripetal point of the congregation. Just as wherever Christ is, there is the Church Catholic, so "wherever the bishop appears, there let the people be." [32] The bishop is the best weapon and protection against heresy. With this in mind, Ignatius says: "Shun divisions as the beginning of evils. Do ye all follow your bishop as Jesus Christ followed the Father, and the presbytery as the apostles, and to the deacons pay respect." [33] Although Ignatius never wearied of reminding the congregations to adhere to the bishop in view of the threatening dangers of heresy, he did not intend his statements to be understood in a hierarchical sense. The episcopate was still congregational, and not diocesan. Nevertheless his statements were soon used in the interest of a hierarchy.

It is important to note that Ignatius thought of the Church not only as a local congregation, but also as a universal institution, extending throughout the whole world. He was apparently the first to use the word "catholic" to express the Church's universality.

The Church appears on the one hand as an ideal, eternal magnitude belonging to the sphere of God. On the other hand it is viewed as an empirical product which not only exists in the world, but which is also rendered peccant by the influences of the world.

The Holy Scriptures

The Apostolic Fathers regarded the Word of God as a unique possession of the Church. They depended upon the Old Testament in its entirety and recognized it as an absolute authority. Wherever "the Scriptures" are mentioned or quotations are introduced with "it is written," we may be sure the Fathers were thinking of the Old Testament. It was regarded as "the revelation of the past, present, and future." [34] There were some who believed that Christianity had become the true Israel and the custodian of the Old Testament after the rejection of the Jews. Others, like Barnabas, believed that God never made any revelation to the Jews. All agreed that the

---

[32] *Smyrnaeans,* VIII, 2.

[33] *Ibid.,* VII, 2; VIII, 1.

[34] *Barnabas,* I. Cf. Justin, *Dialogue with Trypho,* XXI. The tense relation that existed at this time between the Jews and the Roman state undoubtedly expedited the emancipation of the Church from Judaism. Cf. S. G. F. Brandon, *The Fall of Jerusalem and the Christian Church* (London: SPCK, 1951).

Old Testament belongs to the Christians and not to the Jews. The Old Testament was interpreted entirely in terms of the Christian faith. Gradually Old Testament institutions—especially the priesthood and the sacrificial idea—came to be looked upon as emblematic of the Christian congregation. Such a conception and interpretation of the Old Testament destroyed any historical insight into it. With few exceptions this concept and its application continued to prevail until the Reformation.

The words of Jesus occupied a high position of authority with the Fathers. It is comparatively seldom, however, that an exact quotation of them is given. Next to the words of Jesus stood those of the Apostles. The *First Letter of Clement* frequently cites the Old Testament as religious authority, but also alludes to or quotes from the writings of the New Testament.[35] Clement expressly admonishes the Corinthian congregation to re-read the letter "which the blessed Apostle Paul" wrote to them, and to permit themselves to be instructed by it.[36] Careful investigations have proved that the thirteen Pauline Epistles and the four Gospels were known to the Apostolic Fathers. But they did not use these writings in the form of a closed collection or canon. It should be noted that the formation of the New Testament was not precipitated primarily by heretical antitheses such as Gnosticism. It was due to normal impulses which proceeded from motives lying within Christianity itself. The Church's struggle with heresy simply strengthened the incipient New Testament canon and brought it to a formal conclusion sooner than would otherwise have been the case. The subject will be discussed at greater length in Chapter VI.

The Sacraments

At first baptism was administered in the name of Jesus, but gradually in the name of the Triune God: Father, Son and Holy Spirit. It was considered the real instrument for imparting the gift of Chris-

---

[35] The letter cites Matt. 5:7—13, 2; 13:3—24, 5; 26:24—46, 8; Luke 1:75—48, 3; 6:31—13, 2; 17:1—46, 8. Further references are to Acts (20:35—2, 1), Rom. (33, 1; 35, 5), I Cor. (13, 1; 34, 8; 37, 2), II Cor. (13, 1) Gal. (5, 2), Eph. (59, 3), I Tim. (61, 2), Tit. (2, 7), Heb. (17, 1; 27, 2).

[36] *I Clement,* 47, 1.

tianity.[37] Barnabas says: "We go down into the water laden with sins and filth, and rise from it, bearing fruit in the heart, having reverence and hope in Jesus in our spirits." [38] Hermas declares: "There is no other repentance than this, that we go down into the water and receive the forgiveness of past sins." [39] Baptism confers the forgiveness of sins. It is also the "seal" that we have received the Holy Spirit and, with him, the assurance of a new life of faith and hope in Christ. With the forgiveness of sins man receives a new heart and also the obligation to live according to Christ's commandments. On the meaning of baptism as a seal for the gift of the Holy Spirit, Hermas and especially Second Clement followed the language of Paul (II Cor. 1:22; Eph. 1:13, 4:30).

Baptism secures the forgiveness of past sins. But what about those of the future? It was concern over this question which started a development that led to the sacrament of repentance. The early Christians had a deep recognition of sin, but a marked distinction arose between the unavoidable sins of daily occurrence and some special sins of a graver nature that must be absent in the life of a true Christian. Here was the beginning of the later theory of "venial" and "mortal" sins. The prevailing idea was that repentance for sins was an inner experience that lasted for the Christian's lifetime. It had been the teaching of Judaism that in the messianic last times there would be no further opportunity for repentance because the Lord would function as judge.[40] What hope was there for Christians who sinned after baptism? It was this concern that drove many Christians into extraordinary despair and pangs of conscience. Passages such as I John 5:16-17 and Heb. 6:4-6, 10:26-27, and 12:17 could be misused to limit repentance as a means of grace . How should troubled souls find relief? Hermas devoted himself to this problem. He announced that in an exceptional way God is willing to permit a second repentance. Hermas exhorted the fallen to earnest repentance as the condition of participation in the present and in the final revelation of God's grace.[41] The chief defection from the biblical standard lies in the

---

[37] *Didache*, VII, 1-3.
[38] *Barnabas*, XI, 11.
[39] *Mandates*, IV, 3, 1.
[40] *Apocalypse of Baruch*, 85, 12; IV Esdras, VII, 112-115.
[41] *Mandates*, IV, 3.

failure of these writers to understand grace as the forgiveness of sins which extends continually throughout the whole of life.[42]

In the Lord's Supper the coming and presence of Christ are prayed for and experienced. The growing realistic conception of this sacrament is indicated by the following statement of Ignatius: "The Eucharist is the flesh of our Saviour Jesus Christ, which suffered for our sins, which the Father in his goodness raised from the dead." He speaks of the "breaking of the one bread, which is the medicine of immortality, an antidote that we might not die, but live in Jesus Christ forever."[43] The Eucharist still meant a "thankoffering." The sacrificial conception had not yet appeared. The celebration of the Supper was charged with a strong eschatological significance, as is indicated by the famous eucharistic prayers with their petition: "Let grace come, and let the world pass away."[44] Among the Apostolic Fathers there was no speculation on the meaning of the words of the institution. While they considered the Lord's Supper a mystery of greatest importance, they had no mature thoughts on the subject.[45]

Eschatology

The Fathers had the consciousness that they were living in the last times. The immediate return of Jesus was anticipated. It was this expectation which held the congregations together. The Church considered it imperative to keep an eye for the approaching end and to work for moral betterment, so as not to be surprised by its appearance. In looking for the consummation, Christians learned to observe the signs of the times and to watch for definite indications which would precede Christ's coming. The precedent signs were to include false prophets and seducers, an increase of wickedness and persecutions, the Anti-Christ, and the resurrection of the dead. Papias defended chiliasm in a very gross and materialistic form. He spoke of a thousandfold fruitfulness of vines and crops. According to Barnabas, the return of Christ would be followed by his temporal reign for a thousand years. Although the historical Church comprised both good and bad, the final judgment would bring about a separation of the

---

[42] Cf. Seeberg, *Lehrbuch*, I, 157 ff. [43] *Ephesians*, XX, 2. [44] *Didache*, X, 6.
[45] For a more comprehensive view of the doctrine of sacraments in the ancient Church, see pp. 215 ff.

righteous from the unrighteous. The resurrection was defined in a decidedly Jewish and anti-Hellenic sense, as the resurrection of the flesh. The final judgment of the world remained the chief event together with the certainty that the holy would go to heaven to God, and the unholy to the place of eternal punishment.[46]

BIBLIOGRAPHY

American Library of "The Ante-Nicene Fathers," Vol. I. Edited by A. ROBERTS et al., reprint Grand Rapids, Mich.: W. B. Eerdmans Co., 1951.

BIHLMEYER, K. *Die Apostolischen Väter,* 2nd ed. by W. SCHNEEMELCHER, 1957.

CORWIN, VIRGINIA. *St. Ignatius and Christianity at Antioch.* New Haven: Yale University Press, 1960.

DIBELIUS, MARTIN. *Der Hirte des Hermas.* 1920.

GOLTZ, E. VON DER. *Ignatius von Antiochien als Christ und Theologe.* 1894.

GOODSPEED, EDGAR J. *The Apostolic Fathers.* New York: Harper & Bros., 1950.

————. *Index Patristicus sive Clavis Patrum Apostolicorum Operum.* Naperville: Alec R. Allenson, Inc., 1960.

HARRISON, P. M. *Polycarp's Two Epistles to the Philippians.* Cambridge: Cambridge University Press, 1936.

IGNATIUS. *The Epistles of St. Ignatius.* Translated by J. H. SRAWLEY. London: SPCK, 1919.

JAMES, M. R. *The Apocryphal Books of the New Testament.* Oxford: Oxford University Press, 1955.

KNOPF, RUDOLF, *et al.* "Die Apostolischen Väter" in HANS LIETZMANN (ed.), *Handbuch zum Neuen Testament.* 1923 ff.

LAKE, KIRSOPP. *The Apostolic Fathers.* 2 vols. 1917 ff. Greek-English edition in the Loeb Classical Library, 1930. Cambridge, Mass.: Harvard University Press, 1959.

Library of Christian Classics. Edited by JOHN BAILLIE and HENRY P. VAN DUSEN, Vol. I. Philadelphia: Westminster Press, 1953.

LIGHTFOOT, J. B. *The Apostolic Fathers.* Grand Rapids, Mich.: Baker Book House, 1956.

ROBINSON, J. A. *Barnabas, Hermas and the Didache.* London and New York: SPCK, 1920.

STARK, R. A. *The Christology of the Apostolic Fathers.* Chicago: Chicago University Press, 1912.

TORRANCE, T. F. *The Doctrine of Grace in the Apostolic Fathers.* Grand Rapids, Mich.: W. B. Eerdmans Co., 1959.

WUSTMANN, G. *Die Heilsbedeutung Christi bei den Apostolischen Vätern.* 1905.

ZAHN, THEODOR. *Ignatius von Antiochien,* 1873.

[46] Cf. Irenaeus, *Against Heresies,* V, 33, 3f. and Eusebius, *Church History,* III, 39, 12.

CHAPTER IV

THE GREEK APOLOGISTS

I. ORIENTATION

The second century was an age of severe conflicts for Christianity. It was exposed to attacks from Judaism and Gnosticism. Heathendom as a whole, backed by the Roman Empire, turned against Christians, who were looked upon as a menace to the state. Both the morals and the faith of Christians were impugned. Consequently, Christianity had to prove its right to exist. Defenders equipped with the necessary scholarship were needed to meet this foe. A group of writers arose who are both interesting and important for our study because it is in these Apologists that the first system of Christian theology is attempted.

Two tasks occupied the attention of the Apologists. First, they aimed to defend Christianity against the gross calumnies and misrepresentations of the heathen writers and against the rumors current among the people. Heathenism had made a significant attack on Christianity through the medium of the philosopher Celsus and his work *The True Word*, which appeared in A.D. 178. Only fragments of this work remain. Celsus, the most typical spokesman of heathenism, declared the entire Christian teaching to be utter folly and pure myth. He claimed that numerous discrepancies and fabrications were to be found in the Christian Scriptures. The idea of the incarnation of God was especially repugnant to him. These objections were answered by the Christian Apologists, who sought to formulate a science of Christian truth. On the one hand, heathenism, viewed from the standpoint of ethics and history, was sharply criticized as a religion of demons. On the other hand, the Apologists recognized copious elements of truth in the heathen religions and especially in Greek philosophy. The Apologists found these elements of truth to be derived historically from the Old Testament, or metaphysically from the "seminal Logos" (*logos spermatikos*) which appeared in Christ as the "entire Logos" (*ho pas logos*) or psychologically from the soul, which is by nature Christian, or ethically from the sense of morality which is inborn in every man. By the application of the contemporary philosophical conception of the Logos, Christianity was set forth as the true philosophy. The Apologists offered a positive doctrine—especially in reference to the Logos—in the form of a Christian philosophy. Where it was possible and suitable to their purpose, they justified the Christian doctrine by drawing certain analogies between Christianity and heathenism. Some of the Apologists turned from apologetics to polemics and pointed out the folly, immoral character, and intolerance of heathenism.

Alongside the religion of heathenism, and quite inseparable from it, stood the menace of the Empire. Here lay the second task of the Apologists. The growing intolerance of Rome and the increasing taste of the emperors for Christian blood were matters which called loudly for a public Christian voice.

Our present discussion is limited to the Greek Apologists. The most important of these and likewise the most frequently quoted are the following: Aristides, Justin Martyr, Tatian, Athenagoras, and Theophilus of Antioch. Of these, Justin is an especially outstanding figure. The time of the Apologists' activity was from about A.D. 130 to A.D. 180. Of course, Irenaeus, Origen, Minucius Felix, Tertullian, and Cyprian were Apologists too. For the history of doctrine they must be reserved for later consideration.

II. A Review of Their Writings

Marcianus Aristides addressed an *Apology* to the emperor Antoninus Pius, A.D. 150.

In the same year Justin Martyr also wrote an *Apology* with a supplement known as the *Second Apology* to this emperor. He furthermore wrote a *Dialogue with Trypho, the Jew* and a treatise *On the Resurrection.* Justin is the most important of all these writers.[1]

[1] Cf. Moritz von Engelhardt, *Das Christentum Justins des Märtyrers* (1878); A. Staehlin, *Justin der Märtyrer und sein neuester Beurteiler* (1880); E. R. Goodenough, *The Theology of Justin Martyr* (New York: G. E. Stechert & Co., 1923); E. Seeberg, *Die Geschichtstheologie Justins des Märtyrers* (1939).

Tatian of Syria wrote an *Address to the Greeks* (A.D. 150), which contains a severe criticism of paganism.

Athenagoras wrote (*ca.* 177) a *Petition for the Christians*, which was addressed to the emperors Marcus Aurelius and Commodus. This Apologist also wrote a treatise *On the Resurrection*.

Theophilus, Bishop of Antioch, wrote three books *To Autolycus*, addressed to a heathen friend.

With the exception of a few fragments the following writings have been lost: Quadratus, *To the Emperor Hadrian;* Claudius Apollinarius of Hierapolis, *To Marcus Aurelius, To the Greeks,* and *Of the Truth;* Miltiades, *To the Greeks, To the Jews,* and *To the Secular Prince concerning the Christian Philosophy;* Melito of Sardis, *To Marcus Aurelius;* Ariston of Pella, an anti-Jewish *Dialogue between Jason and Papiscus.*

III. Some Basic Thoughts of the Greek Apologists

Concept of God

The Apologists emphasized that God is one. He has created the world out of nothing and he preserves it. In their description of the Divine Being the Apologists spoke in negative terms: He is "invisible," "unbegotten," "incomprehensible," etc.[2] They hesitated to express what is best in God for fear that the Divinity might be dragged down into the sphere of the creature as in the mythologies of the heathen world.

The Apologists taught that it was through the Logos that God created the world. God, being spaceless and infinite, was in need of the Logos as a middle being to bridge the gap and chasm between him and the world. What did the Apologists say about this Logos, a much-discussed topic of their age?

The Logos

The prior question is: Why did the Apologists speak of Christ in terms of Logos? The answer of Seeberg is worthy of quotation: "This was a favorite term of the cultured classes. Whenever it was mentioned

[2] Aristides, *Apology,* I. Justin, *Apology,* I, 10, 13, 25, 49, 53; II, 6 and *Dialogue,* 127. Tatian, *Address to the Greeks.* Athenagoras, *Petition for the Christians,* 10, 13, 16, 44, 21. Theophilus, *Autolycus,* I, 4, 3; II, 3, 22.

the interest of all was at once secured. The choice of this term proves
how completely the thought of the Church was centered in the exalted
Christ. If it had thought chiefly of the man Jesus, it might easily have
characterized Him as a second Socrates. It thought of Him as God,
in God and with God, and therefore selected a term such as Logos in
order to make the matter plain to the heathen." [3]

According to the Apologists, the Logos existed before he became
incarnate. He existed as the divine reason (*nous*) in God, just as a
thought exists in man before it issues forth in verbal utterance. To
this pre-existent Logos, Theophilus applied the word *endiathetos*,
which was used by the Stoic philosophers and also by Philo.[4] The
Logos was conceived of as the divine immanent reason.

The Logos was operative in the creation of the world and later
in the prophets and wise men.[5] According to Justin, the Logos has a
most intimate relationship with the reason of man, and man's perception of truth is derived from the Logos. All men partake of the seminal
Logos. From this source heathen philosophers received all the truth
which was contained in their systems. It was the Logos who spoke
through the prophets of the Old Testament.[6] In the fullness of time
the Logos was born of the Virgin Mary, became man, and took unto
Himself flesh, blood, and a human soul. He still remained God. The
purpose of the incarnation of the Logos was to teach mankind the
higher philosophy which embraces the one God, the "New Law"
requiring a righteous life, and immortality, bringing with it rewards
and punishments.[7]

From all eternity the Father was Logos-natured. For the purpose
of creation the Logos was projected as an independent personal being.
By an exercise of God's will, the Logos sprang forth as the thought
is uttered in speech (*logos prophorikos*). This involved no separation
or loss in the Godhead, but was like a fire which is not diminished by
kindling another from it.[8] To express the idea of how the Logos

[3] Reinhold Seeberg, *Textbook of the History of Doctrines,* trans. Charles E.
Hay (Philadelphia: Lutheran Pub. Soc., 1904), hereinafter referred to as *Textbook,* I, 113.
[4] *To Autolycus,* II, 10.
[5] Justin, *Apology,* I, 44.
[6] *Ibid.,* II, 8, 13 f.
[7] *Ibid.,* I, 12-19.
[8] Justin, *Dialogue with Trypho,* 61, *passim;* Theophilus, *op. cit.,* II, 10, 22.

became differentiated the word *gennethēnan* was used, and the word *ktizesthai* avoided. The Logos was called "the first production of the Father," "the first-born work of the Father." [9] The Logos appeared as the angel of the covenant in the Old Testament, and in the fullness of time he took upon himself our nature. This personal differentiation of the Logos from God was something new, and it was Christian when considered in the light of the Stoic philosophy. It should be noted, however, that according to the Apologists there was no personal differentiation of the Logos before the creation. Although Christ and the Logos were identified, the historical Christ was pushed into the background, and the Son of God was understood to be the pre-existent Logos.

The Apologists taught the subordination of the Son to the Father. According to Justin, the Father alone is the real God; the Logos is only a Divine Being of second rank. With respect to the Father the Logos is something else (*heteron ti*) and another (*allos tis*). He is the Father's organ and servant, and is dependent on him. While the Father is eternal, infinite, incomprehensible, unchangeable, and transcendent, the Son is not.[10] Loofs remarks that the other Apologists were not so strong in their insistence upon subordination.[11] However, subordination was a tenet which continued to trouble the developing Christian Church.

The Trinity

The Apologists were familiar with the triadic baptismal formula. Theophilus was the first to use the term *trias*.[12] The Apologists considered the Godhead a triad rather than a trinity. This is seen in the fact that while the Spirit was distinguished from the Logos and the Father, he was subordinated to both. Since the Logos inspired the prophets and was at work everywhere, there was little room for the activity of the Holy Spirit. Fortunately the Apologists had no occasion to speak to the heathen about the Holy Spirit, as they themselves had not clarified their ideas on the subject.

[9] Tatian, *op. cit.*, 5.

[10] *Dialogue with Trypho*, 56, 62, 128-29.

[11] Loofs, *Leitfaden zum Studium der Dogmengeschichte* (hereinafter referred to as *Leitfaden*), p. 122.

[12] Theophilus, *op. cit.*, II, 15.

61

Anthropology

The Apologists rejected Stoic fatalism. They taught that God has given man freedom of the will. This freedom enables man to make decisions in favor of goodness and truth. Man learns the correct use of his freedom through Jesus' teaching and is able to be victorious in his struggle with carnal weakness and demonic temptations. Man finally arrives at union with God.[13] With these conceptions the Apologists failed to perceive man's natural depravity.

Church and Sacraments

The Church of Christ is the true Israel, the People of God, a new generation, a generation of the pious, etc. When the Christians were blamed for not serving in the army, the Apologists replied that the Christians do a much better thing—they pray that the emperor may be successful and victorious. Instead of being dangerous to the empire, the Christians are really the ones who hold it and the world together.[14]

Baptism in the name of the Holy Trinity was considered a washing of forgiveness and a regeneration. It brings pardon and the new life, and is therefore necessary to salvation.[15]

The Eucharist was conceived of by Justin in these terms: "We have been taught that the food blessed by the word of prayer employed by Him, from which our bodies and blood are by its transformation nourished (*kata metabolēn*), is also the Body and Blood of the same Jesus who was made flesh." [16] Because of this statement, Justin has been cited as teaching transubstantiation. These words are not to be taken in this sense. Yet the idea is that "the divine Logos is mysteriously present in the bread and wine, as in the Incarnate Christ." [17] Two conceptions of the Eucharist can be observed throughout church history: (1) the realistic conception, which sometimes culminates in the metabolic view; and (2) the spiritualistic or symbolic conception. Justin belongs to the line of realists, whereas Augustine, later, is found on the symbolic side.

[13] Justin, *Apology*, II, 6; *Dialogue with Trypho*, 30.
[14] Theophilus, *op. cit.*, II, 14.
[15] *Dialogue with Trypho*, 30.
[16] *Apology*, I, 66.
[17] Fisher, *History of Christian Doctrine*, p. 68.

Eschatology

The Apologists maintained the thoughts of primitive Christianity concerning eschatology in opposition to Hellenism and Gnosticism. Rejecting the Greek notion of immortality, they emphasized that God created man with body and soul, and that through death and resurrection he wills to complete his work of creation.[18] The emphasis with which they championed this point was occasioned by the opposition they met at the hands of the Gnostics. The Apologists also taught the parousia of Christ[19] and the millennial kingdom.[20] When Christ appears both good and bad will stand before him to receive the reward of their deeds.

Christianity as a Philosophy

To the Apologists, Christianity appeared as a true philosophy—in fact, *the* true philosophy. Some declared Christianity to be the absolute truth, of which heathenism was the direct antithesis. Others thought of heathenism as being only the imperfect bud, while Christianity was the full-blown and perfect flower. At any rate, all of them pointed to Christianity as a higher and more reliable philosophy. In heathenism and Christianity the aim is identical, namely, to arrive at a trustworthy knowledge of the true God, virtue, and immortality. But Christianity is a better and absolutely reliable philosophy because it rests not upon its own speculation but upon perfect revelation.

The channels through which this perfect revelation has come are twofold. The first is the Scriptures of the Old Testament. Since they are inspired by God and the Logos, they are inerrant. The philosophers, the Apologists held, derived many of their ideas from this source. A lively interest in the Old Testament was stimulated in the churches. The second channel of this perfect revelation is the Logos. Before his incarnation, the Logos spoke through the prophets and wise men. When he became man, he continued his work in person. Starting with the teachings of Christ, the Apologists proved them from the Old Testament, and then compared them with the corresponding thoughts of heathen philosophy.

[18] Cf. Athenagoras, *On the Resurrection;* also Theophilus, *op. cit.,* II, 13-14, *passim.*
[19] Justin, *Apology,* I, 20, 52, *passim.*
[20] *Dialogue with Trypho,* 81-82.

IV. Evaluation

It seems to be a *fait accompli* in the histories of doctrine that <u>ration-alism and moralism are the distinctive marks of the Christianity of the Apologists</u>. Moritz von Engelhardt wrote: "Justin wishes to be, and according to his faith is, a Christian. But he is a Christian who shows in everything his dependence upon the world-view as held by heathen-ism." [21] And again: "Justin is at once a Christian and a heathen." [22] In the opinion of Harnack, the Apologists made Christianity a "deisti-cal religion." In content their theology hardly differs from the ideal-istic philosophy of their contemporaries. Their religion, Harnack held, is a rationalistic religion with emphasis on one God, virtue, and immortality.[23] Over against this severe criticism, Anders Nygren makes an act of reparation to the Apologists, and especially to Justin. Against the background of the Lundensian motif research, Nygren refuses to be led astray in his judgment by the apparently philosophical language of the Apologists. When the Apologists speak of Christianity as a "New Philosophy" and "New Law," Nygren maintains, they do not surrender the essence of the "Agape-type" of religion. He points out that in later antiquity philosophy was occupied "not with ponder-ing theoretical, rational problems, but with the cure of souls, to bring help to a troubled and suffering generation." It is not a theoretical, but a practical, religious interest which drives Justin to philosophy, and for him its task is to give instruction about God and set man in relationship with Him. For Christianity to be the true philosophy means that it is "the true religion, the right way of salvation, the only one that can lead to real fellowship with God." This way is possible for man "solely as God in Agape comes down to man and meets him through revelation." [24]

Nygren holds that Justin's definition of Christianity as a "New Law" has no legal meaning. The New Law, according to Justin, is the New Covenant; it is not a sum of new commandments, but Christ Himself, whose Agape is manifest in the Cross which, as Nygren insists, holds a central part in Justin's thought. Prior to his discussion

[21] *Op. cit.,* p. 210.
[22] *Ibid.,* p. 485.
[23] Adolph von Harnack, *History of Dogma,* trans. Neil Buchanan (New York: Russell & Russell, 1958), II, 224.
[24] *Agape and Eros,* pp. 267 ff.

of Justin, Nygren admits: "Nevertheless, their [the Apologists'] general view is that of the Apostolic Fathers. In both cases the point of departure is not the love God gives so much as the love He requires of men." [25]

In passing critical judgment upon the Apologists, it must be remembered that every practical apologetic proof forced them to accommodate themselves to the language of their opponents. In contrast to Harnack, the theology of the Apologists is philosophical in form, but there is a great wealth of genuine New Testament piety back of their philosophical terminology. The method, however, becomes dangerous. In the course of time, language will inevitably affect the content of its message. In this respect the Apologists set a bad example for succeeding generations.

BIBLIOGRAPHY

American Library of "The Ante-Nicene Fathers." Edited by A. ROBERTS et al. Vol. I. Grand Rapids, Mich.: W. B. Eerdmans Co., 1951.

CARRINGTON, P. *The Christian Apologetics of the Second Century.* New York: Macmillan Co., 1921.

Corpus Apologetarum Christianorum. Edited by J. C. OTTO. 9 vols. 1842–. 3rd ed., 1876–.

Library of Christian Classics. Edited by JOHN BAILLIE and HENRY P. VAN DUSEN. Vol. I. Philadelphia: Westminster Press, 1953.

PUECH, A. *Les Apologists grecs du II siècle de notre ère.* 1912.

REVIERE, J. *St. Justin et les apologists du second siècle.* 1907.

[25] *Ibid.,* p. 265.

CHAPTER V

PERVERSIONS OF CHRISTIANITY

This chapter presents some of the earliest sectarian aberrations from the catholic or universal Church. Most of these "sects" no longer exist under their former names, but many of their principles still live as historical tendencies in present-day religious thought.

The heretical perversions of Christianity in the ancient Church took their rise from two chief sources. The first source, which was at once Jewish and Gentile in character, lay outside Christianity. The second was found within Christianity itself. The chief representatives of these various perversions may be classified as follows: (1) Judaizing Christianity, which was essentially Jewish in its origin; (2) Gnosticism, which was of heathen parentage; (3) the heresy of Marcion, whose ideas were derived partly from heathenism and partly from Christianity; and (4) Montanism, which was rooted mainly in Christianity.

I. Ebionitism

It is necessary to discuss only the principles of Judaizing Christianity that were incompatible with Christianity. Complete salvation, the Judaizers maintained, could be secured only through the medium of Judaism (cf. Paul's Letter to the Galatians). The Judaizers repudiated the gospel of Paul and regarded him as an apostate from the law. Justin was acquainted with such Christians. However, he distinguished between those who considered the law binding only on Christians who were Jews by birth and those who imposed the law on Gentile Christians as well. It is probably correct to call the stricter of these two groups "Ebionite." Jerome refers to them as "Nazarenes" who believed in Christ as the Son of God, born of the Virgin Mary. Yet, in his opinion, "while they want to be Jews as well as Christians, they are actually neither Jews nor Christians." [1] To this description Eusebius[2] adds the information that this group, although retaining the virgin birth, as did Arius, denied the pre-existence of Christ. He limits the term "Ebionite" to the most radical faction which denied the virgin birth as well as the pre-existence of the Logos. To the Ebionites proper, Jesus was merely a man on whom the Holy Spirit had descended for the first time at his baptism. Christ's work was that of a prophet and teacher who enlarged the law by precepts of greater strictness.

This Jewish Christianity received an influx of Gentile ideas, and resulted in a kind of Jewish-Christian Gnosticism. This was emphasized in a book written by Elkasai in the reign of Emperor Trajan. Angelic powers played a great role. The virgin birth was rejected. Christ Himself was thought of as the Primal Man who was continually becoming incarnate. The law was retained, but the sacrificial system was abrogated. Its place was taken by all kinds of lustrations and by an ascetic mode of life. The Gnostic views of Jewish-Christianity influenced ancient Church literature and produced the so-called Pseudo-Clement's writings.[3] Under the name of Peter and his alleged pupil, Clement of Rome, the principles of Judaizing Christianity were set forth in a strongly polemical fashion.

By the fifth century Ebionitism had practically disappeared as a disturbing factor within Christianity. Nevertheless, the religious syncretism evident in this movement was of great historical significance in that it contributed to the origin and rise of Mohammedanism as the third great monotheistic religion of the world.

II. Gnosticism

Our knowledge of Gnosticism is derived from the Church Fathers, such as Justin, Irenaeus, Tertullian, Origen, Hippolytus, and Epiphan-

[1] Jerome, *Letters*, 112, 113; cf. *Commentary on Isaiah*, s.v. Isa. 9:1. Both terms evidently signify the members of this sect as "poor saints" (Rom. 15:26). "Ebionite" derives from the Hebrew word for poor, though Tertullian, for example, connected the name with one Ebion, the alleged founder of the sect (*Prescription against Heretics, 33*).

[2] *Church History*, III, 27.

[3] See the text in *The Ante-Nicene Fathers: Translations of the Writings of the Fathers down to* A.D. 325, ed. Alexander Roberts and James Donaldson (Grand Rapids, Mich.: W. B. Eerdmans Co., 1951-53), hereinafter referred to as *ANF*, VIII, 69 ff.

ius. These, however, do not always agree. In addition, we have few original documents such as, *The Letter of Ptolomaeus to Flora, The Pistis Sophia,* and a number of fragments. For orientation see the bibliography of this chapter. There has been a resurgence of studies of Gnosticism since the discovery of the Dead Sea Scrolls. In this brief review the ancient sources are quoted only occasionally.

The investigations of Bousset have made it clear that Gnosticism began as a movement within paganism. It was a result of the process of religious fusion which had begun before the advent of Christianity. Following the religious syncretism of the time, Gnosticism approached Christianity with the intention of adding it to the long list of contributing religions.

As it appears in the light of history, a number of interesting reasons explain the whole Gnostic movement. First, the ancient world had exhausted its resources and was now dying of a terrible hunger—a hunger for salvation. Only a powerful stimulant could ward off its imminent death. Second, although many of the ancients rejoiced over the salutary and rejuvenating influences which Christianity had introduced, some of them were not at all satisfied with a religion which proclaimed the deity of Christ and the foolishness of the Cross. Third, the intellectual and cultivated minds of the day felt that the Church did not make as much of philosophical thought and principles as it should. Fourth, to those who were acquainted with the elaborate and mysterious ceremonies of heathenism, the worship of the Church seemed dry and barren.

Led by these considerations, Gnosticism proposed to remedy the situation by forming an alliance between the religions of paganism and that of the Church. The endeavor to rejuvenate the ancient world, favored by the syncretistic drift of the age, resulted in the boldest and grandest syncretism the world has ever seen. All the previously isolated and heterogeneous elements of religion, philosophy, and culture were to be blended into one. Revelation was to be combined with the "wisdom of the world," and Christianity was to be made a truly "modern" religion. This gigantic undertaking was decidedly favored by the all-prevailing drift of the age in the direction of syncretism, the disposition to amalgamate mythology with philosophy, to explain and assimilate, as far as might be, Oriental religions, systems, and cults. Gnosticism was the first attempt in the history of the Church to bring the world into subjection to the Church by interpreting Christianity in harmony with the world.

Gnosticism was an eclectic movement in which were represented cosmological myths, the philosophical thoughts of the Greek and Oriental paganism, and the truths of Christianity. The religons of Babylonia, Syria, Asia Minor, Persia, and India, the Judaism of Philo, and the message of Jesus and the Apostles all were fused in the Gnostic crucible. Gnosticism possessed certain features in common with Christianity, such as the divine plan of salvation, the Christian tradition, and the centrality of Christ in human history. But these features were badly distorted. As a rule heathen features predominated. The emphasis was placed on the idea of evolution, the cosmogonic theories, and the pagan mystery-worship.

In the Christian system, faith is held to be the faculty through which salvation is acquired. For the Gnostics, however, *gnosis* or higher knowledge was the channel of salvation. *Gnosis* did not mean intellectual knowledge acquired by mental processes, but was rather a supernatural knowledge which came from divine revelation and enlightenment. Like the Greek philosophers who asserted the existence of a race of intellectual patricians, the Gnostics claimed to possess a deeper knowledge of divine things than did the ordinary believer. Hence the name *gnostikoi* ("the men who know") was used in certain Gnostic circles. This esoteric system of Gnosticism appeared more profound than did current Christianity with its popular creed. In spite of its much vaunted claim to a higher knowledge, Gnosticism never attained to a higher goal than the precincts of its ancient mythology.

Although the Gnostics were deeply interested in the fabrication of speculative religious philosophies, this was not their chief concern. In fact, philosophical considerations were really secondary with them. The underlying idea of Gnosticism was the avowed purpose to present a way of salvation to a sick world. All mystic speculations were subordinate to the idea of redemption. Being fundamentally redemptive in purpose, Gnosticism sought to establish not merely *a* religion, but *the* universal religion. In addition to its speculative and mythological aspects, Gnosticism claimed to have a divine revelation from God. Divine revelation, mystical experience, symbolical forms of enchantment, and the practice of asceticism were the means by which the higher life was to be achieved. The heathen mysteries were imitated and employed to impart saving knowledge. Religious organizations with elaborate rituals were established.

Let us now proceed to point out a few of the characteristic features of Gnosticism:[4]

The Dualistic Theory

It is important that we understand this dualistic conception, because it is here that we find the origin of the Gnostic conception of world and man, of sin and woe, and the resultant necessity of redemption.

Gnosticism derived its dualism from the Syrian systems which had been shaped under Parsee or Zoroastrian influences. Persian dualism was physical and consisted of two antagonistic principles—light and darkness. In Gnosticism this physical dualism of light and darkness became a metaphysical dualism of spirit and matter. In this system the world of matter (*hyle*), which is under the governance of the evil principle, is from all eternity in violent conflict with the world of spirit (*pneuma*) which is ruled by the good God. In this conflict some of the spiritual elements became imprisoned in the world of matter. This was the beginning of the world and man, and likewise of sin and misery.

The more Hellenistic systems (Basilides and Valentinus of Alexandria) were inclined to Platonic ideas. Here the dualistic opposition was not hostile, but "non-essential and non-substantial." This dualism, which was pre-eminent in the realm of ideas, was modified by the emanation theory; but it remained dualism nevertheless.

The Emanation Theory

This theory, which was held especially by the Alexandrians and was extensively developed by them, served to explain how the world and man came into existence. The system of Valentinus in particular had a highly fantastic and speculative process of cosmogony and theogony. From the hidden God there emanated a long series of divine

[4] Cf. Nygren, *Agape and Eros*, pp. 293 ff.

essences (*aeons*) whose inherent divine power diminished as the distance from the original divine source increased. This process of depotentialization continued until a point was reached where the spiritual element came into contact with matter and was imprisoned in a material body. Thus man and the world were created.

The Creator

The last link in the theogonic chain was the Creator or Demiurge. He occupied a middle position between the world of spirit and the world of matter, and was usually identified with the Jehovah-God of the Old Testament. Although not absolutely hostile and evil, the Demiurge was an inferior and antagonistic being—a blind intelligence, who was ignorant of the Good God and who unwittingly had brought the world and man into existence. Arguing from the characteristics of the Jewish law as described by Jesus, the Valentinian Ptolomaeus maintained that they could not have originated from the devil, but must have come from the Demiurge—"the Middle God" or "Just God." This God was regarded as an angelic being, not free from malice, who governed with a loveless external justice.

The Problem of Redemption

The chief problem of Gnosticism was: How can man be liberated from the world of matter and be made a partaker of the world of light? Man deserves to be emancipated because something of the spiritual world still remains within him. How then is redemption effected? The origin of redemption is to be looked for in the world of spirit. The Demiurge had brought about the creation of the world and man, with concomitant sin and woe, and necessitated a redemption of the spiritual elements in man. But the Demiurge would not and could not carry out the plan of redemption. Therefore, the Highest Aeon came as a redeemer to secure perfect emancipation.

Jesus Christ, the Redeemer

Gnostics held the person of Christ in high regard and his appearance was praised as a great turning point in history. It was this note in Gnostic teaching which deceived so many Christians. An atonement for sin through the death of Christ was not considered necessary. All that Gnosticism needed was a teacher "to dispel ignorance and to abrogate death." [5] The attention of men was directed away from Christ's specifically soteriological work and fixed upon his teaching. Christ's teaching, said Gnosticism, is intended to help us overcome the material world, either by the practice of asceticism or by fleshly libertinism. His teaching gives man an insight into the world-relations, and familiarizes him with the mysterious formulas of enchantment by which he may transcend the planetary spheres, mount up to God, and obtain entrance into the realm of light.

Docetism

Christianity knows of no doctrine of atonement save through the incarnate Son of God. Gnosticism rejected the doctrine of the incarnation. It declared that Christ could not possibly have a body: (1) because the absolute cannot enter into a real union with the finite; and (2) because matter is evil, and the spiritual world is ever in conflict with it. It was thought that the Christ had joined himself for the time being with the body of a profoundly spiritual man called Jesus. As Fisher puts it, the divine was merely "in temporary juxtaposition with humanity." [6] This union was effected either at the birth or at the baptism of Jesus, and it was dissolved shortly before the crucifixion. It followed, therefore, that the Christ was not really crucified. The crucifixion of Christ was an optical illusion in which the man Jesus was the real sufferer. Thus Gnosticism, with its docetic conception, denuded the Redeemer of any real humanity, and destroyed the historic person of Christ. Gnosticism clearly derived its ideas of the Redeemer from pagan mythology. Hence it was never able to effect any genuine union between the Christ and Jesus of Nazareth. [7]

The Classification of Men

Earlier Gnosticism divided men into two classes, but later Gnosticism added a third. According to the proportion of spirit in their natural constitution, men were said to be either spiritual, psychical, or

---

[5] Irenaeus, *Against Heresies*, I, 15, 2.

[6] Fisher, *op. cit.*, p. 54.

[7] In this connection, read the fine observation by H. L. Martensen, *Christian Dogmatics*, trans. William Urwick (Edinburgh: Hamilton, 1866), Sec. 128.

carnal. The first class was represented by the true Christians or Gnostics, of whom there were few. The second class was composed of Jews and Christians, who had faith but not *gnosis*. The last was identified with heathenism. Inclusion in the first class was considered to be the chief object of redemption. It was taught that "these are not only by practice, but also by nature pneumatic [spiritual], and will necessarily be saved." The psychics, or ordinary Christians, might be saved through faith and good works; but the carnal or hylics, to whom the majority of men belonged, would be lost.[8] Regeneration was defined as the separation of the spiritual from the sensual. This separation was thought of as a chemical rather than an ethical process. This was one of the glaring points of difference between Christianity and its Gnostic perversion. The Gnostic system was never interested in ethics and morality. All ethical and moral considerations were pushed aside in the interest of the one all-absorbing idea—the emancipation of the spirit from the thralldom of matter. In the ethical realm the practice of the Gnostics was never uniform. Some demanded strict abstinence from sexual pleasures, while others went to the opposite extreme and lived according to the principle that the flesh can be mortified only by excessive gratification. Vegetarianism was also a feature of the system.

Eschatology

The Gnostic system had no place for a bodily resurrection because of its belief in the inherent evil of matter. Neither was there to be any final judgment. Gnosticism taught that the emancipated soul would simply ascend to the place of its origin—the kingdom of light—where it would present itself, repeat the mysteries, and finally be reabsorbed into the fullness of the Godhead. Gnosticism held out no hope for a personal immortality. Souls which had not received the mysteries would be thrown back into bodies. The worst sinners would be cast into the outer darkness of complete annihilation.

The Mysteries

These were symbolic rites, mystic ceremonies, and magical formulas which were used to popularize the cosmic theory and to give assur-

[8] Irenaeus, *op. cit.*, I, 6, 2.

ance of salvation. Originating in the heathen mysteries of the time, they served to place a heathen construction on the Christian idea of redemption. These esoteric features were part of the scheme to make Christianity the universal religion of the enlightened.

Attitude Toward Scriptures

The Old Testament was either totally rejected or interpreted allegorically to suit Gnostic thought. The Gnostics became the first exegetes. The documents commented upon were altered to conform to the predilections of the commentators. A great deal was made of the unwritten apostolic traditions and teachings. In addition, a voluminous literature of apocryphal and pseudonymous books was published for the dissemination of Gnostic doctrines.

Effects of Gnosticism on the Church

The intimate acquaintance of the Church with Gnosticism produced several distinct results: The claim of Gnosticism to be the universal religion led the Church to assert the catholicity of her own position. Since Gnosticism had concerned itself so greatly with the Old Testament and the apostolic writings, it became the imperative duty of the Church to settle forever the question of the inspiration of the Old Testament and to determine the contents of the New Testament canon. Gnosticism contended that Christianity was fundamentally a doctrine, and the Church replied by stating what that doctrine really was. In order to standardize the doctrine of the Church, appeal was made to the Rule of Faith (*regula fidei*). From this rule, which varied somewhat in the different localities, sprang the ancient creeds of Christendom. When Gnosticism began to assume alarming proportions, the Church was obliged to call for able defenders. The bishops came forward and fought the heresy throughout the entire realm. In this way the prominence of the bishops was secured, and added impetus was given to the development of episcopal polity. Although defeated in the end, Gnosticism succeeded in imparting some of its own mysticism to the Church. Finally, Gnostic asceticism prepared the way, at least in part, for the monasticism of the Church.

The Significance of Gnosticism

It will be of interest to consider three estimates of Gnosticism. First, in a gross overestimate of the Gnostics, Harnack says: "They were simply the theologians of the first century. They were those Christians who sought to make a rapid conquest of Christianity for the Hellenic culture, and vice-versa." [9] He refers especially to the Basilians and Valentinians who refused to separate themselves from Christianity. These schools were *de facto* not Christian, and their representatives were not Christian theologians. It was in these circles where the pioneer work was done in the creation of the New Testament writings, dogmatics, and ethics. It was theology, but in no respect a Christian theology. Bousset, on the other hand, sees in Gnosticism a movement which was essentially retrogressive and extra-Christian—"the reaction of the ancient syncretism against the rising universal religion." [10]

In contradistinction to Harnack, Nygren holds that Gnosticism is one of the foulest perversions of Christianity. "Here the Eros motif overwhelms Christianity as a flood." [11] Although the Gnostics frequently used the term Agape, "the Eros motif holds sway completely." Agape lost its original meaning and was transformed not into "the heavenly Eros" of Plato, but rather into "vulgar Eros," and that in its lowest form. Agape is equated with downright sensual passion. In the Gnostic system, Agape is God's own fall. The gross calumnies of incest charged by pagan writers had some basis in this type of heretical Christianity. [12] The eclipse of the fundamental dogmas of creation, incarnation and resurrection is complete. The highest God has nothing to do with the world of sense. The incarnation is denied as "the foul mystery" of Christ's birth. Finally, the rejection of belief in the resurrection is absolute. Thus the "Hellenization of the gospel" reached its climax in the teaching of Gnosticism. [13]

---

[9] Harnack, *History of Dogma*, I, 227.

[10] W. Bousset, *Die Hauptprobleme der Gnosis* (1907), p. 7.

[11] Nygren, *op. cit.*, p. 289.

[12] Cf. the example quoted by Epiphanius, *Panarion*, XXVI, 4, referred to by Nygren, *op. cit.*, p. 309. For the further references, see the remarks in Seeberg, *Textbook*, I, 99.

[13] Nygren, *op. cit.*, pp. 303 ff.

III. MARCION'S ATTEMPTED REFORMATION

How is Marcion to be classified? The Church Fathers looked upon him as a Gnostic. Certain features of his system justified this view, especially his dualism of the just God and the good God and his rejection of the real incarnation of Christ. Furthermore, it is known that Marcion was more or less influenced by the Syrian Gnostic Cerdo, who taught that "the God, proclaimed by the law and the prophets, was not the Father of our Lord Jesus Christ. For the former was known, but the latter was unknown; while the one also was righteous, but the other was benevolent." [14]

The investigations of Zahn and Harnack have made it clear that Marcion should be placed in a class by himself. As proof of this we cite the following reasons: Marcion was guided exclusively by a soteriological and not a metaphysical interest; according to him the way of salvation was through faith instead of through gnosis. He did not acknowledge the emanation theory and the Gnostic explanation of the origin of sin. A much abbreviated New Testament canon was regarded the source of truth. He did not aim to form mystic associations holding speculative tenets within the Church. Instead, he sought to reform the Church by establishing rival congregations in opposition to the Catholic parishes.

Nygren also considers Marcion as distinct from the Gnostics. Marcion was the champion of the Agape motif of the New Testament, and therefore reacted violently against the incipient nomism of the primitive Church. He wanted to be a reformer, but accepted the basis laid by Gnosticism. [15]

To Marcion, the gospel was an absolute paradox. While in biblical thought the God of redemption is identical with the God of creation, Christ is not the Creator's Son, according to Marcion, nor is man the Redeemer's creature. "If Christ were the Creator's Son it was with justice that He loved His own (creature), if He comes from another God His love was excessive, since He redeemed a being that belonged to another." [16] In Gnosticism, God is the Unknown, but man is akin to him. In Marcion, on the other hand, God is a stranger to man and man is a stranger to God.

---

[14] Irenaeus, *op. cit.*, I, 27, 1.
[15] Cf. Nygren, *op. cit.*, pp. 317 ff.
[16] Tertullian, *On the Flesh of Christ*, 4.

As may be seen, Marcion assumes that there are two gods, the Creator God (the Demiurge) and the Redeemer God. The God of the Old Testament is the creator of the world. He is also the Just God who cared only for Israel, although he ruled that nation with rigorous justice and maltreated it with his law. The Old and New Testament are absolute opposites. The Old Testament is the book of Nomos (law), the New the message of Agape (love). Yet it is not difficult to see, as Nygren observes, that in denying that creation is the work of God himself, Marcion robs Agape of its real significance. If the Redeemer God has no obligation toward man, man has no obligation toward God either.[17] Man is no longer a sinner, but merely unknown by God.

Marcion also failed to clarify Christ's relation to the Good God. "Christ is distinguished from the Father in name only, for in Christ God was revealed through Himself (*in Christo Deus per semetipsum revelatus est*). The Father and the Son represent just such an equation as do the Son and the Gospel. "Marcion was a Modalist as were other ancient Christian teachers; but he was probably a more conscious one than they." [18] As a rule, Christ was identified with the Good God. He abrogated the law, and by way of retaliation the Just God secured his crucifixion at the hands of the Jews. But Christ, who had a docetic body, did not really die. He merely went into Hades, where he liberated the Gentiles. The pious of the Old Testament were passed by.

Man is saved, Marcion taught, not by an effect resulting from the death of Christ, but simply by believing what Paul teaches about the Good God. This kind of faith enkindles a love which in turn leads man to a life of asceticism. Marcion, for example, rejected marriage, as was the case with some of the Gnostics, as an abomination. To abstain from marriage brings deliverance from the lustful flesh. But he also forbade marriage as a means of defying the Demiurge lest his realm be enlarged.[19]

Marcion repudiated all of the Old Testament. So far as the New

---

[17] Nygren, *op. cit.,* p. 326.

[18] Harnack, *Marcion: Das Evangelium vom fremden Gott,* p. 162.

[19] *Ibid.,* pp. 148-49. (Quoted in Nygren, *op. cit.,* p. 331). As to references cf. Tertullian, *Against Marcion,* I, 29; IV, 17, 29, 34, 38, *passim.*

Testament was concerned, he admitted only a mutilated Gospel of Luke and ten corrected letters of Paul. The Pastoral Letters and the Letter to the Hebrews were excluded. Marcion's early attempt (*ca.* A.D. 160) to set up a recognized canon of apostolic writings stimulated the Church to clarify its own views on the subject. His rejection of the allegorical interpretation of Scripture had a beneficial effect on the Church.

The Marcionite controversy led the Church to the clearer understanding of the fact that the Creator and the Redeemer are indeed one God, and that in God justice and mercy are combined.

IV. MONTANISM

Montanism marked the transition from the extra-Christian heresies to the reactionary and reformatory movements within Christianity. About the year 156, Montanus, a recently converted pagan priest, appeared upon the scene. He claimed that he was possessed of the spirit of prophecy which still operated actively in the Church, as was acknowledged by the Church Fathers. Later he was joined by two women, Maximilla and Priscilla, who had deserted their husbands with Montanus' sanction. Montanus professed to represent a special form of prophecy. He declared himself to be the manifestation of the Paraclete promised in John 14. The period of revelation was closing, said Montanus, and with its conclusion would come the end of the world. Indeed, one of the prophetesses maintained: "After me there will be no further prophecy; then shall the end be." [20] Montanus charged his followers to gather at the town of Pepuza in Phrygia where the descent of the New Jerusalem was to occur.[21] Montanism thoroughly recognized the previous stages of revelation in the Old and New Testaments and the ecclesiastical doctrine which had developed therefrom. Up to this point it was entirely orthodox and removed from every type of heresy.

The new feature which the Paraclete had to reveal was concerned with the sphere of ethics and ecclesiology. In the sphere of morals and discipline Montanism represented the sternest rigor, surpassing that of the New Testament. This program was carried out in detail

[20] Epiphanius, *Haereses,* 82, 2.
[21] *Ibid.,* 49, 1.

by Tertullian after he had become a Montanist. He prohibited second marriages, and in the main even marriage itself. He ordered the strictest fasting, unreserved preparation for martyrdom, and separation from the world. Only those Christians who met the demands of the Paraclete were "pneumatic" (spiritual). These constitute the true Christians, the communion of saints. This Church alone, and not the externally organized Church, possesses the full power of absolution. In consequence of this, Tertullian wrote: "Therefore the Church will indeed forgive sins; but only the Church of the Spirit can do this through the Spirit-filled people, and not the Church which consists of a number of bishops." [22] Thus Montanism manifested an ecclesiastical reaction as well as an attempt at spiritual reform.

Montanism was the first movement of any distinction that endeavored to call the Church back to "the first love," whose decline the Exalted Lord deplored in Rev. 2:4. It was a powerful protest against the incipient secularization of the Church and of the tendencies to institutionalize its life and work. On the other hand, it was extreme in its harsh and radical demands.

Montanism paved the way for a series of movements which have continued down through the history of Christianity, such as those of the Novatians, the Donatists, the Waldensians, the radicals of the Reformation period (Mennonites and others), and the modern Pentecostal and Holiness churches. Like these movements, Montanism was a reaction, and an attempt to preserve the eschatological mood of early Christianity which was rapidly disappearing at the end of the second century. By rejecting Montanism, the Church repudiated its earlier sectarian character. As Loofs states the matter: "The elimination of Montanism reacted mightily upon the Church. It strengthened the prestige of the Canon. It sanctioned the spirit of conniving at moral laxity, and as a result the differentiation between a higher and lower morality. It raised the position of the bishops, and promoted the development which changed the Church from a communion possessing the assurance of salvation to an institution which must guarantee salvation." [23]

[22] *On Modesty*, 21.
[23] Loofs, *op. cit.*, p. 175.

BIBLIOGRAPHY

1. General Reference
BRADEN, CHARLES S. *These Also Believe.* New York: Macmillan Co., 1949.
CLARK, E. T. *The Small Sects in America.* Nashville: Cokesbury Press, 1937.
DAVIES, HORTON. *Christian Deviations.* London: SCM Press, 1961.
NEVE, J. L. *Churches and Sects of Christendom.* Blair, Neb.: Lutheran Publishing House, 1952.
SCHMID, H. *Handbuch der Symbolik.* 1890 ff.

2. Ebionitism
BRANDON, S. G. F. *The Fall of Jerusalem and the Christian Church.* London: SPCK, 1957.
BRANDT, W. *Elchasai.* 1912.
EPIPHANIUS. *Haereses,* 29-30.
EUSEBIUS. *Church History,* III, 27.
HIPPOLYTUS. *Philosophumena,* VII, 34; IX, 13-16.
HOENNECKE. *Das Judentum im 1. und 2. Jahrhundert.*
IRENAEUS. *Against Heresies,* I, 26, 2.
JEROME. *Letters,* 112, 113.
JUSTIN. *Dialogue with Trypho the Jew,* ch., 47 ff.
ORIGEN. *Against Celsus,* II, 1, 3; V, 6, 65.
————. *Homilies,* VIII.
SCHOEPS, H. J. *Theologie und Geschichte des Judentums.* 1949.

3. Gnosticism
BAUER, W. *Rechtgläubigkeit und Ketzerei im ältesten Christentum.* 1934.
BOUSSET, W. *Die Hauptprobleme der Gnosis.* 1907.
DORESSE, JEAN. *The Secret Books of the Egyptian Gnostics.* Translated by PHILIP MAIRET. London: Hollis and Carter, 1960.
FAYE, E. DE. *Gnostiques et Gnosticisme, étude critique des documents des gnosticisme chrétien aux II et III siècles.* 1925.
Gnosticism: a sourcebook of heretical writings from the early Christian period. Edited by ROBERT M. GRANT. New York: Harper & Bros., 1961.
HILGENFELD, A. *Die Ketzergeschichte des Urchristentums.* 1884.
Letter of Ptolomaeus to Flora.
Pistis Sophia.
REITZENSTEIN, R. *Die hellenistischen Mysterienreligionen.* 1927.
SCHULTZ, W. *Documente der Gnosis.* 1910.

4. Marcion's Attempted Reformation
BLACKMAN, E. C. *Marcion and His Influence.* London: SPCK, 1948.
HARNACK, A. Marcion: *Das Evangelium vom fremden Gott.* 1924.
HIPPOLYTUS. *Refutations,* VII, 29-31.
IRENAEUS. *Against Heresies.*
JUSTIN. *Apology, I,* ch., 26, 58.

Origen. *Against Celsus*, VI, 74, 53.

Tertullian. *Against Marcion.*

5. *Montanism*

Bonwetsch, N. *Texte zur Geschichte des Montanismus.* 1914.

―――. *Geschichte des Montanismus.* 1881.

Epiphanius. *Haereses*, 48-49.

Eusebius. *Church History*, V, 16.

Labriolle, P. de. *Les sources de l'histoire du Montanisme.* 1913.

Rolffs, E. *Urkunden aus dem antimontanistischen Kampfe des Abendlandes.* 1895.

Soyres, J. de. *Montanism and the Primitive Church.* London: Bell and Co., 1878.

Tertullian. *On the Veiling of Virgins.*

―――. *The Chaplet.*

―――. *On Flight in Persecution.*

―――. *An Exhortation to Chastity.*

―――. *On Monogamy.*

―――. *On Modesty.*

―――. *On Fasting.*

Weinel, H. *Die Wirkungen des Geistes und der Geister im nachapostolischen Zeitalter bis auf Irenaeus.* 1889.

CHAPTER VI

THE FOUNDATION OF DOGMA

In this chapter we seek to answer the following questions: What was the source and norm of truth for the early Church? Upon what foundation was the dogmatic system of the Church erected? By way of introduction, these questions may be answered briefly in the following manner.

As early as the first part of the second century the Church recognized the authority of the Old Testament, the words of Christ and the Apostles, and the Sacred Scriptures soon to be gathered into a recognized canon.

The fundamentals of the Christian religion which were used in the parochial and missionary work were being crystallized into creedal statements.

In that day of incessant struggle with heresy, the episcopate came to be looked upon as the powerful guardian and the reliable interpreter of the Scriptures and the Rule of Faith.

All three of these factors require a more detailed exposition. The first two, the canon and the rule of faith, will be dealt with in this chapter. The third—the development of the episcopate—is so closely related to the conception of the Church that it must be treated in connection with this more general subject in Chapter VII.

I. The Canon of the Holy Scripture

Unclarified views hindered the formation of a canon of Scripture. On the one hand, some of the post-apostolic writings such as the *Shepherd of Hermas*, the *Epistles of Barnabas and Clement*, the *Apocalypse of Peter*, and the *Acts of Paul*, had come to be regarded as having equal value with the writings of the Apostles. On the other hand, the

Letter to the Hebrews, the Letter of James, and Second Peter were not in the Bibles of the Occident until about the middle of the fourth century. From then on the word canon, which in the second century had been applied to the Rule of Faith, was used to designate the accepted body of Holy Scripture.

There were several influences at work which forced the Church to determine what books should constitute the canon. The following influences are worthy of mention: Marcion created for his followers a canon of sacred writings which omitted those books that did not support his conception of the gospel. The *Muratorian Fragment* (*ca.* 170-80) represented another attempt to formulate a canon of Scripture. The *Peshitta* appeared at the end of the second century as the canon of the Syrian church. The pneumatics with their unbounded enthusiasm led the Church to scrutinize all alleged revelation in the light of the words of Christ and the Apostles. This group of the early Church, which had the sanction of Paul (I Cor. 14:1 ff.; cf. I Thess. 5:19-20) occasionally went to great excesses in individual cases. Gradually the Church found itself engaged in a real struggle with pneumatics of all kinds, with men and women who claimed to be organs of the Holy Spirit. The Letter of Clement to the congregation at Corinth was directed at this evil. The wild enthusiasm of the Montanists showed what would happen to the Church if free rein were given to the pneumatics. The speculations of the Gnostics and their efforts to prove their views from the apostolic writings constituted a powerful inducement to the Church to establish an authoritative and actually recognized canon of the New Testament. Finally, an apocryphal literature, such as the *Acts of the Apostles,* and numerous apocalyptic writings (*Sibyllines*), were shooting up like weeds in a garden. In these the greatness of the past was magnified by the report of wonderful miracles. The Apostles were portrayed as being workers of miracles who, without exception, raised the dead, made dogs and donkeys speak, healed broken statues, put life into smoked fishes, and killed demons.

When a book was being considered either for admission into or for exclusion from the canon, a twofold test was applied. First was the historical test. The age had a deep consciousness of the fact that it was the Apostles to whom Christ had committed the preaching of the gospel, and that the same Spirit who had been operative in the writers of the Old Testament had been at work in the Apostles also. The writings considered for admission into the canon were tested by whether the authors had been Apostles. If these authors had not been Apostles, it was asked whether their relation to the Apostles was such as would warrant the placing of these writings on a level with the apostolic books. Second, the internal test asked if a given book possessed the character of spiritual elevation which made it worthy to be ranked with apostolic writings. Thus, certain books of the Post-Apostolic Age were finally dropped from the number of those which were considered for incorporation in the canon.

The canon of the second century was comprised of the Four Gospels, the thirteen letters of Paul, the First Epistle of Peter, the First Epistle of John, and perhaps also Jude and the Book of Revelation. Thus the collection which came into being did not differ essentially from the writings which had been preferred and used by the earlier period.

Just as it was believed that the Old Testament was inspired, so inspiration was claimed for the New Testament writings. At first inspiration was thought of as a state of ecstasy in which the sacred authors wrote as purely passive agents. In a statement ascribed by some scholars to Athenagoras,[1] the soul of the prophet while engaged in prophesying is compared to a flute. In a spurious writing of Justin Martyr, *Cohortatio ad Graecos*,[2] the author compares the prophet to a lyre which is played by the Holy Spirit. The Montanists held to ecstatic inspiration, and Tertullian made the ecstatic condition an essential of inspiration.[3] It was against them that Miltiades directed the statement, "The prophet does not need to speak in ecstasy."[4] Irenaeus rejected the view that the writers of Scripture remained purely passive in the act of inspiration. Although he believed in verbal inspiration, Irenaeus observed that Paul frequently transposed the word order in his sentences, "due to the rapidity of his discourses and the

---

[1] G. Thomasius, *Die christliche Dogmengeschichte als Entwicklungsgeschichte des kirchlichen Lehrbegriffs* (1874—), I, 128; Cremer's article on inspiration in *PRE*, IX, 187.

[2] VIII, 10.

[3] *Against Marcion*, IV, 22: ". . . we maintain in the case of the new prophesy that to grace ecstasy or rapture [*amentia*] is incident." Cf. *On the Soul*, 21.

[4] Eusebius, *Church History*, V, 17.

impetus of the spirit which is in him." [5] Clement of Alexandria included ecstasy among the marks of the false prophets. [6] Origen ascribed the peculiar style of the New Testament writers to their personal individuality. As to content these authors are always right, but their style, Origen says, is at times marred by solecisms. [7] Origen also admitted that the measure of inspiration varied. This variation is reflected in Paul's distinction between a "word of the Lord" and his own opinion (I Cor. 7:2). [8] Origen explained some of the statements and expressions in Scripture which seemed illogical or even absurd by use of the allegorical method. [9] These authors agreed, however, that it is principally the Lord who speaks in the Bible.

II. The Rule of Faith

What was the Rule of Faith? In our discussion of the Post-Apostolic Age we made mention of a rule for faith and life, to which the *Didache* makes especial reference, but which can be traced back even to the later books of the New Testament literature. What the Church Fathers meant by the Rule of Faith has been a much debated question among such specialists on this subject as Zahn, Harnack, Kattenbusch, McGiffert, and Kunze (*kanōn tes aletheias, regula veritatis, kanōn tes pisteōs, regula fidei*). According to Zahn, it was merely the profession made at baptism. Kattenbusch, seconded by Harnack, Loofs, and others, takes it to be the Church's interpretation of the baptismal formula. Kunze emphasizes that it was an anti-heretical profession supplemented and interpreted by Scripture. We may conclude from this that the Rule of Faith was a brief expression in creedal form of the fundamentals of the Church's entire teaching. It is important to refer at this point to a work of Irenaeus (*Epideixis*) which shows the large range of these fundamentals in a vivid way, and even transcends the doctrinal sphere by touching upon numerous matters of an ethical, devotional nature.

Next we come to the baptismal formula—that brief epitome of the faith upon which the Church was establishing itself. The baptismal

[5] *Against Heresies,* III, 7, 2.
[6] *Stromateis,* V, 311.
[7] *Commentary on John,* IV, 1 ff.
[8] *Ibid,* I, 5.
[9] *De Principiis,* IV, 1, 16, ff.

formula may be traced back to a fixed doctrinal tradition found in the New Testament epistles which Seeberg[10] illustrates as follows: profession (I Tim. 6:12; Heb. 10:23; 4:14); things that have been committed (I Tim. 6:20; II Tim. 1:12, 14); faith (Jude 3:20; Titus 1:13; Col. 1:1); word of truth (I Peter 1:22; cf. Col. 1:5); form of doctrine (Rom. 6:17, 16:17; II John 9 ff.; Heb. 6:2); the gospel (Rom. 2:16, 16:25; Gal. 2:2; I Cor. 15:1); sound teaching (II Tim. 1:13); words of faith (I Tim. 4:6).

We may have to distinguish between a wider and a narrower conception. Expressions such as "gospel" and "faith" seem to comprise the whole Christian teaching, namely: Christ's descent from David, his divinity, his suffering, resurrection, and ascent into heaven, his being seated at the right hand of the Father, the work of the Spirit, baptism and the Eucharist. There seems to have been a difference between the foregoing catechetical material and the profession (*homologia*) which was made at baptism. What Paul writes in I Cor. 15:3-4 sounds like an echo of the baptismal formula: "For I have delivered unto you first of all that which I also received," (and now follows "that," *hoti*, which is identical with our quotation marks), "how that Christ died for our sins according to the Scriptures, and that He was buried, and that He rose again the third day according to the Scriptures; and after that He was seen by Cephas, then of the twelve." I Tim. 6:20 may refer to a similar form.[11]

Paul Feine reconstructs the following formula from the New Testament writings as an existing rule of faith:

> I confess one God, the Father, the Creator of the World (or: of Whom the world is, or: by Whom and through Whom and to Whom the world is, or: Who has made heaven and earth, or: One God and One Father of the world, Who is over all and in all). And (I confess) Jesus Christ, the Lord (or: our Lord), the Son of God (the only begotten), born of the seed of David . . . Who suffered under Pontius Pilate (or: Who was crucified under Pontius Pilate), died for our sins, was buried, preached the Gospel to the dead (or: Who descended to the dead), was resurrected the third day, sitting at the right hand of God after having entered heaven, to Whom are subject the angels and the powers, Who shall judge the living and the dead (or: Who shall come to judge the living and the dead, or: Who is ordained by God as Judge of the living and the dead)

[10] *Lehrbuch, passim.*

[11] Special investigations along this line have been made by A. Seeberg, *Katechismus der Urchristenheit*, 1903.

through Whom we receive forgiveness of sins and the gifts of the Holy Ghost and the hope of resurrection of the dead (or: the resurrection of the dead and the eternal life, or: and the hope of eternal life.)[12]

While this perfectly trinitarian faith may be taken as the matrix from which a recognized formula for baptism and the so-called Apostles' Creed eventually issued, it does not mean that baptism was being administered in the name of the triune God at that time. At first baptism was in the name of Christ.[13] The emphasis was always placed upon faith in Christ "from the seed of David, born of the Virgin, suffered under Pilate, raised from the dead by the Father, sitting at the right hand of God whence He shall come for judgment." This is easily explained. Since the earliest Christians were Jews who already believed in the one God, it was not necessary for them to reaffirm that faith. The essential thing for them was to confess their faith in Jesus the Christ, hence the use of the older christological form. But gradually we find the Post-Apostolic Fathers mentioning the fact that baptism was administered in the name of the triune God.[14] In view of the contemporaneous testimony of Irenaeus and Tertullian, we come to the conclusion that during the period from about 130 to 140, the baptismal formula had become trinitarian for the whole Church. By reconstructing the baptismal formulas which were used in certain localities, for instance, in Egypt Feine shows that the trinitarian formula of Matthew was employed about the year 100. This change from the christological to the trinitarian form was to be expected when Gentiles were coming into the Church. It was necessary for them to confess their faith, not only in Christ as their Redeemer, but also in the one God and the Holy Spirit. Therefore it was natural to follow the command of Christ related in Matthew. In connection with this trinitarian form, Eastern creeds varied in their expressions, but resembled more or less the so-called Apostles' Creed. Kunze reconstructs the Creed of Antioch, and Zahn another creed from the *Didascalia*. The question may be asked why these creeds or rules of faith were not freely recorded. The answer is that in the Old

---

[12] Paul Feine, *Gestalt des Apostolischen Glaubensbekenntnisses in der Zeit des Neuen Testaments* (1925). Similar constructions by Reinhold Seeberg and Lietzmann should be compared with Feine's. See *Sitzungsberichte der Akademie der Wissenschaften in Berlin* (1919).

[13] Cf. Acts 2:38, 10:48, etc.

[14] *Didache*, VII, 1; Justin, *Apology*, I, 61.

Catholic Age, Christians were pledged to silence regarding the mysteries of the Christian faith (*disciplina arcani*). The Creed, it was held, ought not be recorded with ink on paper; instead, it should be written on the "tablets of the heart." Hence we have only periphrastic references in the writings of the Fathers.

The Old Roman Symbol was quoted as a whole for the first time by Marcellus of Ancyra (348) and then by Rufinus (400).[15] All agree that this symbol is much older than the others. Kattenbusch undertakes to trace it back to about 100. Reinhold Seeberg admits that it goes back at least to the beginning of the third century. McGiffert traces it back to the latter part of the second century.

The following is the text of the Old Roman Symbol as translated into English:

> I believe in God the Father Almighty.
> And in Jesus Christ, His only Son, our Lord;
> Who was born by the Holy Ghost of the Virgin Mary;
> Was crucified under Pontius Pilate and was buried;
> The third day He rose from the dead;
> He ascended into heaven; and sitteth on the right hand of the Father;
> From thence He shall come to judge the quick and the dead;
> And in the Holy Ghost;
> The forgiveness of sins;
> The resurrection of the body (flesh).[16]

The relation of the Old Roman Symbol to the creeds of Asia and the East in general presents a perplexing problem. The question is, whether the Eastern creeds came into existence independently of the Old Roman Symbol, or whether this Roman creed was the source of all the ancient forms, even of those in the East. On this question there is an unsettled controversy. Scholars are sharply divided into two camps. Kattenbusch, Harnack, and McGiffert insist that the Roman Symbol is the parent of all other forms, including those of Asia Minor. On the other hand, Zahn, Burn, Sanday, Kunze, and Reinhold Seeberg (following Caspari) defend the independence of the Eastern creeds. Interesting as it is, the argument cannot be incorporated in this text.

---

[15] Marcellus's quotation of this symbol is preserved by Epiphanius, *Panarion,* 72. For Rufinus' reference to it see *A Select Library of Nicene and Post-Nicene Fathers of the Christian Church* (2nd series; New York: Christian Lit. Co., 1890), hereinafter referred to as *NPNF,* III, 541 ff.

[16] See the Greek and Latin texts as given by A. C. McGiffert, *The Apostles' Creed* (New York: Charles Scribner's Sons, 1902), pp. 42 ff.

Nothing definite is known as to the origin of the Old Roman Symbol; everything is conjectural. Neither is anything reliable known about the common source of the creeds of Asia Minor.

Our present Apostles' Creed is not identical with the Old Roman Symbol. Additional phrases have been inserted in the Apostles' Creed. Knowing that up to the fifth century Rome had maintained a jealous watchfulness over the integrity of its creed, we are forced to ask how a change could have taken place.

It must be remembered that it was only up to the fifth century that the Roman church used the Apostles' Creed as the baptismal confession. Then a remarkable change took place. The Ostrogoths, under Odoacer, brought their Arianism into dangerous contact with Rome. The Roman church immediately decided to use the Nicene Creed in place of the Old Symbol because of its clear antithesis to Arianism.[17] Three centuries later the Roman church returned to the use of the Apostles' Creed in baptism and in the services of the sanctuary.[18] In the meantime the present form of the Creed developed in Western Gaul. This development was due to the habit of the extra-Roman churches of adding some phrases of particular significance. This altered form of the Creed was then accepted by Rome because the additions had a historic right; in fact, most of them had been used since the earliest times by the churches of various localities.[19] The form which now came into use was soon accepted in the whole West, and in this form it was later taken into the Catechism of Luther and the Heidelberg Catechism.

In the Apostles' Creed a few particulars which have been matters of interest in the history of dogma should be enumerated:

Article I in the Old Roman Symbol read: "I believe in God the Father Almighty." The Creed of Aquileia added, "invisible and impassible" against Sabellianism and Patripassianism. At a time when heathenism was the chief opposition, the Eastern creeds inserted "one" before "God." The present text has the additional phrase "Creator of heaven

[17] A hundred years earlier, the Nicene Creed had replaced the Apostles' Creed in the East.

[18] See the reasons given by Harnack in *PRE*, I, 754.

[19] It may be mentioned here that the Apostles' Creed did not come back into use at the same time in the East. This explains why the Nicene Creed is used exclusively in Eastern Christianity today.

and earth." The same, or a similar phrase, was contained in the Rule of Faith in the Ante-Nicene Creed as a confession against the Gnostics, who made a distinction between the true God and the Demiurge who was considered the maker of the world.

In Article II, the phrase "conceived of the Holy Ghost" was not used in the earlier Symbol of the East, neither was it in the Old Roman Symbol. This phrase appeared as a creedal statement for the first time in 359 in a confession of orthodox bishops. Because this statement was taught in Luke 1:31, 35, it was taken into the received text.

"Of" (*ek*) the Virgin Mary came to be preferred to *dia,* because it brought out more clearly the reality of Christ's incarnation and life in opposition to the docetic heresies. Some forms had "truly born."

"Suffered" and "dead" are additions to the received text, but we meet these expressions even in the Eastern symbols. There was no doctrinal tendency in these amplifications; the aim was merely at greater completeness.

The same can be said of the phrase, "He descended into hell," which was not in the Old Roman Symbol, but was found in the Aquileian Creed. The meaning is that Christ descended into the abode of the dead before his resurrection. This was believed in the first century on the basis of the Scripture.

In Article III, the word "Catholic" in the sentence "I believe in the Holy Catholic Church" is an addition to the received text. It is first found in the Creed about 450 in Southern Gaul, but it had already been used by Irenaeus. The meaning is this: The Church is co-extensive with the dissemination of Christians. This was the meaning of the term "catholic" as used by Ignatius and the early Christians. "Catholic" concurs also with the meaning of the term "church" (*ecclesia*) in the New Testament, which Luther always translated as "congregation" (*Gemeinde*).

Though the phrase "the resurrection of the flesh" is identical in the Roman form and in the received text, it cannot be dismissed without a few explanatory remarks because it has been a subject of discussion throughout the centuries. In both forms we have "resurrection of the flesh" (Latin: *carnis;* Greek: *sarkos*). The terminology of Paul in I Cor. 1:15 favors the use of the term "body." But the early Church, in its struggle with Marcion and the Gnostics, insisted upon employing the word "flesh." [20] McGiffert offers the following remark: "This insistence upon a fleshly resurrection over against the denial of it was due not only to the feeling on the part of many Christians that the future life was impossible without a resurrection of the material body, but also to the fear that the loss of the belief in the resurrection of the present flesh for judgment would lead to immorality and impurity." [21]

The Old Nicene Creed, like the Apostles' Creed, represents a development of the rule of faith. These creeds arose in different localities of the East and, while differing from each other, were both shaped by the Eastern mind. The Creed of Caesarea was used as a basis for the Creed which was formulated at Nicea in 325 against Arianism.[22] Like the Roman Symbol, the Nicene was intended to be a confession of faith on the part of the catechumens. These Eastern creeds differed from those of the Western Church. The Western creeds were brief, practical, and static. The Eastern creeds were, as Schaff rightly describes them, "more metaphysical, polemical, flexible, and adapting themselves to the exigencies of the church in the maintenance of her faith in conflict with heretics." [23] These characteristics were accentuated in the creed which was formulated at Nicea. This creed was not intended, nor was it suitable, for baptism because of its theological and unliturgical nature. It was created chiefly for the purpose of representing a christological rule of faith. The biblical expressions of the Caesarean Creed were not sufficiently definite and exclusive with regard to heresy. It was necessary to substitute theological terms and phrases not contained in the Scriptures. This had to be done in order to meet the subterfuges of Arianism. While the phrases and terms (such as the *homoousios*) were not derived from the Scriptures, nevertheless their content and meaning were fundamentally scriptural. Under the circumstances, the theological and polemical form was necessary. Such a form affected the practical use of the symbol in the services of the

---

[20] Tertullian, *On the Flesh of Christ,* Chap. I, *On the Resurrection,* and *Against Marcion,* IV, 37; V, 7, 9-10. Irenaeus, *Against Heresies,* II, 29; V, I, 18; 2; II; 31.

[21] McGiffert, *op. cit.,* p. 167.

[22] Compare the review of the gradual construction and history of the Nicene Creed in J. L. Neve, *Introduction to the Symbolical Books* (Columbus, Ohio: Wartburg Press, 1956), pp. 61 ff.

[23] Philip Schaff, *Creeds of Christendom,* I, 25.

Church. The feeling existed that the Nicene Creed should be confessed at the solemn act of baptism and also in the liturgical worship of the Church. It was this consideration which gave us the present text, the so-called Niceno-Constantinopolitan form of the Creed.

We have traced the source of the baptismal formula as it gradually evolved into the Apostles' and the Nicene Creed. The contents of these creeds show that there were now two great problems before the Church: (1) Father and Son, and yet one God; and (2) Jesus the Son of God, and yet the Son of Mary. The solution of these problems marks a large part of the history of dogma in the ancient Church.

BIBLIOGRAPHY

1. *The Canon of the Holy Scripture*
   BLACKMAN, E. C. *Marcion and His Influence.* London: SPCK, 1948.
   KENYON, F. K. *Our Bible and the Ancient Manuscripts.* New York: Harper & Bros., 1958.
   KNOX, J. *Marcion and the New Testament.* Chicago: Chicago University Press, 1942.
   MOFFATT, J. *Introduction to the Literature of the New Testament.* New York: Charles Scribner's Sons, 1921.
   SOUTER, A. *The Text and Canon of the New Testament.* London: Duckworth Press, 1956.
   ZAHN, T. *Introduction to the New Testament.* 3 vols. Grand Rapids, Mich.: Kregel Publications. 1953.

2. *The Rule of Faith*
   FEINE, P. *Die Gestalt des Apostolischen Glaubensbekenntisses in der Zeit des Neuen Testaments.* 1925.
   FLESSEMAN, E. VAN LEER. *Tradition and Scripture in the Early Church.* Assen, Van Gorcum, 1954.
   KATTENBUSCH, F. *Das Apostolische Symbol.* 2 vols. 1894.
   KUNZE, J. *Glaubensregel, Heilige Schrift und Taufbekenntnis.* 1889.
   McGIFFERT, A. C. *The Apostles' Creed.* New York: Charles Scribner's Sons, 1902.
   SWETE, H. B. *The Apostles' Creed.* London, 1908.

CHAPTER VII

THE EPISCOPATE AND EARLY IDEAS OF THE CHURCH

Introductory Discussion

Before Cyprian and Augustine very little was done to formulate a doctrine of the Church. Serious reflection on the nature of the Church is necessary for the creation of a dogma of the Church. Such reflection is confined chiefly to those times when there is occasion to discuss the relation of the *Una Sancta Ecclesia* ("One Holy Church") to the historical appearances of the Church, as was the case at the time of the Reformation. Although this question was involved in the conflict with Novatianism and Donatism, the Church of the first centuries was inclined to identify the essential Church with its external existence as established on the Rule of Faith and the authority of its leaders. The distinction we have in mind when we hear of the visible and the invisible Church, or the Church in a wider and narrower sense, was almost nonexistent. It is true that the earlier centuries were not entirely devoid of motives for making certain small contributions to the dogma of the Church, as the following discussion will show. But errors, such as the extravagances of the pneumatics (Montanists, Novatians, and even the Donatists), were not sufficiently important to inaugurate the formulation of an exhaustive doctrine of the Church. There were other considerations as well. For one thing, the Church had not had enough actual experience to warrant a conclusive treatment of so practical a topic. For another thing the theologians of the Catholic period were too much occupied with such subjects as the Trinity, Christology, and Anthropology to find time for fundamental discussions of the Church. Finally, Christians of the first centuries were so

93

aware of the reality of the Church that there was little cause for doctrinal reflection about it.

Ignatius, Bishop of Antioch (*ca.* 115), was the first to use the term "catholic."[1] This was a new expression of the unity of the Church as taught by Paul: "There is one body and one Spirit . . . one Lord, one Faith, one Baptism" (Eph. 4:4-5). The Apostolic Fathers had emphasized this teaching.[2] Ignatius saw the unity of the Church in the Eucharist.[3] To this may be added: (1) baptism in the name of the triune God, as enjoined in the *Didache* (*ca.* 7) and reported as a general practice by Justin Martyr;[4] (2) the *Disciplina*, in accordance with the ethical requirements of the Lord; (3) the observance of fasting and prayer, especially the regular use of the Lord's Prayer; and (4) the Rule of Faith, with its crystallization in the baptismal formula. Those who adhered to these things were regarded as being in the unity of the catholic faith. The catholicity of the Church's character was asserted again and again by the Fathers of the Catholic Age, especially by Irenaeus, Tertullian, Origen, and their successors. Irenaeus wrote: "No matter how different the language of the world, the contents of tradition are the same everywhere, and neither the churches founded in Germany have another faith or another tradition, nor those in Spain, Iberia, Gaul, nor those in the East, Egypt, and so forth; but as God's sun is one and the same for the whole world, so the preaching of the truth enlightens all men who are willing to see the truth."[5]

In the development of the dogma of the Church there were two interests which served as guiding factors: (1) The purity or apostolicity of the Church's teaching. This interest led to a recognition of the bishop for the purpose of safeguarding the truth expressed in the Scriptures, in the Rule of Faith, and in the baptismal formula. From this interest issued a recognition of the bishop-presbyters over against the pneumatics. This extended to a recognition of one bishop in each congregation; then a special recognition of the bishops located in places where the Apostles had labored. Ultimately this led to the rec-

[1] *Smyrnaeans,* VIII; cf. *Martyrdom of Polycarp,* VIII, 1.
[2] *I Clement,* XLVI, 7; XXVII, 1. Ignatius, *Ephesians,* V.; *Philadelphians,* IX.
[3] *Philadelphians,* IV.
[4] *Apology,* I, 61.
[5] *Against Heresies,* I, 9, 5.

ognition of a college of bishops and of a monarchical episcopate at Rome. (2) The holiness of the Church, or the purity of the Church's life, or the interest in repentance as an institution of the Church. Purity of teaching and purity of life were the two outstanding motives for developing the Church and its institutions. It is interesting to observe that generally speaking the East had a special bent for formulating dogma for the catholic Church, whereas the Western part of the Church preferred to devote itself to the establishment of institutions which would cultivate and safeguard the Christian life of its members. These two motives constantly parallel and frequently overlap each other. The distinction between East and West is not always exclusive; yet, in the main, the two motives can be clearly traced.[6] Below we examine these two motives in greater detail.

APOSTOLICITY OF TEACHING

Originally the preaching and spiritual leadership of the Christian congregations were in the hands of a class of men who were recognized as being in a special sense the organs of the Spirit. We refer to the Apostles, prophets, evangelists, pastors, and teachers (Eph. 4:11; I Cor., chaps. 12 and 14). From the *Didache* we learn that the Apostles and evangelists traveled from place to place, while the prophets, pastors, and teachers were permitted to settle in one congregation. The prophets differed from the teachers in that they had the *charisma* of prophecy. According to Paul and John, their messages were subject to trial by the Church (I Thess. 5:21; I Cor. 12:10, 14:29; I John 4:1). The *Didache* says that if the prophets' lives are Christlike, their messages are not to be tried. To try their messages would constitute a sin against the Spirit.[7] The unknown author of the letter attributed to Barnabas regarded himself a pneumatic teacher and claimed authority on that account. At the time of Paul, and also in the earlier decades of the Post-Apostolic Age, these prophets and teachers were the real leaders in spiritual matters.[8] The prophets offered free prayer at the Eucharist.[9]

---

[6] See the interesting observation of Seeberg, *Textbook*, I, 174 ff.

[7] *Didache,* 11-12.

[8] Cf. the *hēgoumenoi* in Heb. 13:7, 17, 24, or the *proēgoumenoi* in *I Clement,* 6.

[9] *Didache,* 10, 6.

As yet the office of the bishops or presbyters was far from being what it later became. At this time bishop and presbyter meant one and the same thing. In each local congregation there were a number of men, appointed or elected, who were called either bishops or presbyters (cf. Titus 1:5, 7; I Tim. 3:1; 4:14; 5:17, 19). In Phil. 1:1, Paul addresses himself not to one, but to a number of bishops. According to Acts 20:17, 28, all presbyters of the Ephesian church were appointed bishops. Clement of Rome knew of no distinction between bishops and presbyters, and the *Didache* speaks of only two classes of officers elected by the congregation—bishops and deacons.[10]

What was the work of these bishop-presbyters in the early Church? It was that of "oversight" (*episkopein*). Such work naturally fell to men of experience—the *presbyteroi* or elders. The men appointed or elected to this office were responsible for good order in the conduct of the congregational services as demanded in I Corinthians 14:40. It must have been their duty to see to it that services were held in which the prophets and teachers would edify the congregation. Originally the bishop-presbyters were not the regular preachers and teachers of the early Church, but simply directors and overseers. Their position, which was much like that of the rulers of the synagogue (see Acts 13:15 and Luke 4:17, 20), demanded good judgment and executive ability in matters of church government.

It was natural for the bishop-presbyters gradually to add the work of the pneumatics to their own duties. This was a change which Paul himself had favored. It was the task of the bishops to preserve not only good order, but also sound doctrine (Acts 20:28-31). This gave them the right, and even made it their imperative duty, to "try the spirits" by applying the test of orthodoxy to the messages of the prophets (I Cor. 14:29). Furthermore, in the absence of a prophet, one of the presbyters or bishops would be obliged to take his place (I Tim. 5:17; Titus 1:9; cf. *Didache* 13, 4; 15, 1-2). Therefore the bishop himself had to be sound in doctrine and "apt to teach" (I Tim. 3:2). Only gradually did it come about that one of the group of bishop-presbyters took the exclusive title of bishop.

Clement, one of the bishop-presbyters, in his letter to the Corinthian church, gives us interesting information on this subject. We

[10] *Ibid.*, 15, 1.

learn that at Rome, around the year 96, the pneumatics did their work under the authority of the bishops, and that they preached, taught, and even offered prayer at the Eucharist. At that time the Corinthian church was involved in a troublesome dispute due to the fact that two prophets there demanded the entire leadership of the church. Such a situation was, to use Clement's words, an "unholy revolution." In his letter Clement appealed to the Old Testament, declared the bishops were the successors of the Apostles, and insisted upon the superiority of the bishops over the prophets *jure divino* ("by divine authority").[11] It must be understood, of course, that the assumption of sacerdotal functions by the bishop-presbyters cannot be dated from any particular time for all parts of the Church. It was a gradual development.

The Monarchical Episcopate

Bishop Ignatius of Antioch, who died about 115, was not only the first man to employ the term "catholic," but also the first to speak of one bishop at the head of the presbyters and deacons in each congregation.[12] He urged the monarchical episcopate as a necessity for the Church.

As yet there was no thought of one bishop for the whole Church. Ignatius urged the congregation to be loyal to its bishop and to the presbyters under him. He compared the bishops to Christ and the presbyters to the Apostles. The burden of his exhortation was that as the Church Universal has its center in Christ, so the individual congregation should find its center in the bishop. What the Apostles are to the Church at large, the presbytery is to the individual congregation. The individual congregation, subject to the bishop and the presbytery, is a copy of the Church Universal which is led by Christ and the Apostles. Christ and the preaching of the Apostles, therefore —not the episcopacy—condition the unity of the Church Universal.[13]

How did this arrangement for one bishop at the head of a local church originate? The most natural answer to this question is that it came from the church at Jerusalem. From Acts 15 we learn that James, the brother of our Lord, presided over the council of Apostles

[11] *I Clement*, 41 ff.
[12] *Smyrnaeans*, VIII.
[13] *Trallians*, II, III; *Magnesians*, II; *Smyrnaeans*, VIII; *Ephesians*, VI.

and presbyters in Jerusalem; or at least he spoke for them. According to a report from Hegesippus,[14] James was succeeded by Simeon, who was also a relative of Our Lord. So a kind of episcopacy had become a tradition in Jerusalem. From there the episcopacy was easily carried to Antioch. The origin of this episcopate should not be sought in Rome. Clement of Rome indicates in his letter to the Corinthians that he was only one of the bishop-presbyters. *The Shepherd of Hermas*, which was written in Rome about 150, likewise knows of no monarchical episcopate. We know that Marcion held a conference at Rome about 140, not with a bishop, but with a college of presbyters.[15] The monarchical episcopate, which by the time of Irenaeus and Tertullian was recognized throughout the entire Church, was introduced by gradual steps.

The reason for supporting the bishops was found in the necessity of presenting a fixed authority against the Gnostic tendencies spreading through Asia Minor. The unity of the Church in one faith had to be preserved. This was always the chief motive in urging the monarchical episcopate, as can be seen from the writings of the Anti-Gnostic Fathers.[16] The bishops of the individual churches co-operated with each other in the task of keeping all the Christian churches in the unity of the faith. Bishop Polycarp of Smyrna traveled to Rome to confer with Bishop Anicetus (150). At the same time Hegesippus visited Rome and Corinth. About the year 170 the Corinthian Bishop Dionysius sent a number of catholic letters to the congregations in Athens, Nicomedia, Crete, Pontus, and Rome.[17] The bishops also wrote credentials and letters of recommendation, with certain marks, for itinerant Christians.

THE BISHOPS OF "MOTHER-CHURCHES"

The Church, in its struggle with heresy, depended absolutely on the teaching of the Apostles. The endeavor was to receive, preserve, and transmit the apostolic tradition in its purity and integrity. The

---

[14] Eusebius, *Church History*, II, 23, 4; IV, 22, 4.

[15] Epiphanius, *Panarion*, 42, 1.

[16] Irenaeus, *Against Heresies*, I, 10; IV, 26; V, 20. Tertullian, *On the Veiling of Virgins*, II. Clement of Alexandria, *Stromateis*, V, 6; VII, 17. Origen, *Homily on Genesis*, II, 3.

[17] Eusebius, *op. cit.*, IV, 23.

heretics, who were the first exegetes of the New Testament writings, claimed to have received secret commissions to interpret the Scriptures from the Apostles. How was the Church to defend its conception of the apostolic teaching as expressed in the Rule of Faith and in the baptismal formula? The Church looked to the bishops of the "mother-churches" where the Apostles themselves had labored— Smyrna, Ephesus, Jerusalem, Corinth, Philippi, Thessalonica, and especially Rome. It was claimed that there were such churches all over the world, wherever the martyred Apostles or their co-laborers had taught.[18] The argument was that in these "mother-churches" the purity of the apostolic tradition had been guarded with extraordinary care.[19] Tertullian spoke of the heretics in the following fashion:

> Let them therefore produce the origins of their churches; let them display the order of their bishops, running through succession from the beginning in such a way that the first bishop had as his teacher and predecessor some one of the Apostles or of the Apostolic men who were closely associated with the Apostles.[20]

The center of interest was in the unbroken chain of episcopal succession. Hegesippus devoted himself to the succession of bishops in Rome and other places.[21]

In attributing a special *charisma* of truth to the bishops, Irenaeus went beyond Ignatius. According to Irenaeus, the bishops in the succession had received "a sure gift of truth" (*charisma veritatis certum*); and they were regarded as the possessors of a trustworthy tradition.[22] But more than this, it was believed that they possessed a special gift which guaranteed a correct interpretation of the apostolic tradition. Their office was that of mediating to the Church the correct interpretation of the final revelations contained in the New Testament. There was no claim to special revelations as was the case with the Montanists.[23] It should be observed that in the view of Irenaeus the gift functions through the tradition as handed down by those in the succession.[24] After he had become a Montanist, Tertullian desired to

---

[18] Irenaeus, *op. cit.*, III, 2-3; III, 12, 5.
[19] *Ibid.*, III, 33, 8.
[20] *Prescription against Heretics*, 32; cf. 21, 36, 37.
[21] Eusebius, *op. cit.*, IV, 11, 22.
[22] Irenaeus, *op. cit.*, IV, 26, 2.
[23] *Ibid.*, IV, 26, 5; cf. Tertullian in the pre-Montanist period of his life, *Against Praxeas*, 2.
[24] Irenaeus, *op. cit.*, IV, 26, 2.

recognize as bishops only those who could be counted among the *spirituales*.[25] Cyprian, slightly modifying the view of his teacher, held that all bishops are *spirituales;* if they are not, they have no real right to be bishops.[26] He actually taught that the bishops are guided in their decisions and writings by inspirations and visions. This has reference to special illuminations granted for special duties.[27] The Church once more had its pneumatics, only now it was claimed that the bishops were the possessors of the gifts formerly held by the prophets.[28]

We have seen that there was a bishop at the head of each church and that there was no thought as yet, of one bishop for the Church at large. Every bishop had a significance for the Church Universal because each was engaged in the task of preserving the apostolic doctrine in its integrity for the Church of all places and of all ages. George Park Fisher says: "The bishop is no longer the mere head of a local church; he has a relation to the Church Universal. He has a part in the episcopate which is one and single." [29] As centers of the Church, the bishops constituted an organism, and as such they represented the whole Church.

Among the mother-churches Rome was regarded as pre-eminent. It was here, tradition had it, that the great Apostles Peter and Paul had taught and died. The apostolic tradition, as it was preserved by the Roman bishops, was considered especially trustworthy. Men did not believe it possible that reliable traditions in any of the mother-churches could disagree with what was preserved in Rome.[30] The Roman church was also in possession of a confession of faith, the Roman Symbol, which was accepted by the other churches in the West. In Rome, heretics were kept out of the Christian communion with better success than was the case in Alexandria and Constantinople. Thus it came about that Rome was looked upon as a guardian of the Church's unity. The Roman bishops were conscious of the position they occupied. Bishop Callixtus (217-22) claimed such titles for him-

---

[25] *On Modesty,* 21.
[26] Cf. Seeberg, *Textbook,* p. 181.
[27] *Letters,* 11, 3, 4; 57, 5; 68, 5; 66, 10, 63, 1; 73, 26.
[28] Cf. p. 96.
[29] *History of Christian Doctrine,* p. 79; cf. Cyprian, *On the Unity of the Church,* 5.
[30] Cf. Irenaeus, *Against Heresies,* III, 1, 2.

self as *Pontifex Maximus* ("highest pontiff") and *Episcopus episco-porum* ("bishop of bishops").[31] Censuring the Roman bishop, Tertul-lian insisted on the equality of the various churches: "If you are near Achaia, you have Corinth. If you are not far from Macedonia, you have Phillipi. . . . If you can turn to Asia, you have Ephesus. If you are bordering on Italy, you have Rome where also we have a conven-ient authority."[32] Cyprian referred to Rome as the *matrix et radix* ("womb and root") of the Church[33] and said that, according to Matt. 16:18-19, Christ had built the Church on one man. However, he maintained that after the resurrection Christ had assigned the like power to all the Apostles.[34]

Cyprian shared in the general belief that the Roman church was the church of which Peter had been bishop. Rome represents (*monstretur*), so to speak, the unity of the Church Universal, as Peter represented that unity among the Apostles. The church of Rome is the representation of the great idea of the Church's unity. Cyprian therefore directed the Church of his day to the See of Rome "where priestly unity had taken its beginning."[35] In spite of the emphasis upon the idea that Rome was the outward symbol of unity, Cyprian refused to recognize any special authority of the Roman bishop over the other bishops. He quoted the words of Christ: "He who hears you hears me"[36] and he even drew the attention of those who were so interested in Matthew 16 to the error of Peter recorded in Gala-tians 2. This shows that Cyprian did not grant any unique significance to the Roman church as did the bishops Callixtus and Stephen.[37] Cyprian's peculiar conception, however, was too speculative and too idealistic to maintain itself in the *praxis* of Church life. The tendency of the age was in the direction of a powerful authority concentrated in a hierarchy.

PURITY OF LIFE

The problem of repentance gave occasion for advancing episcopal authority. The interest in the apostolicity and purity of the Church's

[31] See Tertullian's sarcastic reply in *On Modesty*, 1; cf. 15, 21.
[32] *Prescription against Heretics*, 36.
[33] See Cyprian, *Letters*, 48, 3.
[34] *On the Unity of the Church*, 4.
[35] Cf. *Letters*, 48, 3; 74; 59, 2, 14; 67, 3.
[36] *Ibid.*, 66, 4.
[37] Cf. also Eusebius, *op. cit.*, V, 24.

teaching led to the recognition of the episcopate. The conflict which was waged over the problem of maintaining the holiness of the Catholic Church led to an advance in the conception of the Church.

Early Christians had held that grave sins committed after baptism could not be forgiven.[38] The *Shepherd of Hermas* had already made the distinction between mortal and venial sins. Hermas claimed to have received a special revelation that the chance for a "second repentance" would be offered in view of the imminent consummation of the world.[39] However, the Montanists were unyielding in their rigorous church-discipline. Before joining the Montanist ranks, Tertullian reluctantly accepted the theory: "I am afraid of the second chance; I should rather say, the last hope."[40] The reference of the stricter party, which later came to be known as the "Novatians," was to sins of a "serious and destructive" nature, such as the following: homicide, idolatry, fraud, denial of the faith in times of persecution, blasphemy, adultery, and fornication. Sins of this kind were regarded as "irremediable," requiring excommunication from the congregation of saints.[41] Novatian wanted to build up a congregation of the pure[42] in opposition to Cornelius and the less rigorous practice which had come into vogue since Callixtus' special ordinance. Since he was surrounded by churches of a differing practice, Novatian insisted upon the rebaptism of those who joined him. Novatian also insisted upon the appointment of opposition-bishops in other places. Thus he maintained a schism in the church which had already been in evidence under Bishop Hippolytus.

Callixtus, Bishop of Rome (217-222), publicly sanctioned and established the new order. The conflict between the two parties as to which sins could not be forgiven by the Church was narrowed down to two offenses: "in times of peace, especially fornication; in times of persecution, denial of the faith and apostasy." Callixtus published a new penitential order in which he allowed a second repentance in case of fornication. He defended his step against Hippolytus with biblical arguments which could be accepted without

[38] See p. 54.
[39] *Mandates*, IV, 1, 8; cf. IV, 3, 6.
[40] *On Repentance*, 7.
[41] Cf. Tertullian, *On Modesty*, 19.
[42] Cf. Eusebius, *op. cit.*, VI, 4, 1.

hesitation.[43] But the chief point of interest in the present investigation is this: Callixtus settled the problem as a "conscious hierarch."

The Church thus far had been regarded as being made up of the holy people of God who held in common the faith of the Apostles, that is, the faith of the bishops. Callixtus took the position that the Church is an institution which is subject to the control of the bishop who pardons or retains sins by divine authority and by his own sovereign judgment. The bishop, he taught, is lord over the faith and the life of the people by virtue of an absolute supremacy divinely bestowed upon him. In this way Callixtus became the author of the Roman conception of the Church. The manner in which Callixtus defended his penitential order is significant: He insisted that the regulation of repentance belonged to the council of bishops. He appealed to the power of the keys (*potestas clavium*) given to Peter as representing the bishops of the Church. Since it was already believed that Peter had been the first Bishop of Rome, the obvious conclusion was the monarchical episcopate with its visible culmination in the Roman See. For this step the way was fully prepared.

It was Cyprian, Bishop of Carthage (248-258), who laid the doctrinal foundation for the conception of the Church in the Post-Nicene Age and for the development of the Church into the Roman hierarchy. He did so both in his book *On the Unity of the Church*, and in the letters he wrote. His thinking was stimulated by the contemporary conflict over the regulation of repentance. Tertullian, his great teacher, who had joined the Montanists, was bitterly opposed to the penitential order of Callixtus, against which he published his most radical writing, *On Modesty*. The practice introduced by Callixtus had become universal by about 250. It was then that the violent persecution broke out under Emperor Decius. Many Christians denied the faith either by making offerings to idols, buying certificates to show that they had done so, or by making false statements regarding their relation to Christianity. The Church was now forced to decide whether such deniers of the faith should be readmitted or not. Apostasy from the faith was added to the sins of the flesh with which the order of Callixtus had dealt. Cyprian decided that the lapsed should be readmitted into the Church provided they

[43] Cf. Seeberg, *Textbook*, I, 176.

showed signs of genuine repentance and made public confession. A peculiar situation developed which stimulated Cyprian to his fundamental utterances on the position of the bishops. Certain presbyters took the matter into their own hands and admitted the backsliders. Cyprian at once took the position that such presbyters should be excluded from the Church. He worked in harmony with Bishop Cornelius in Rome, directing his efforts against Novatian. In 252, an assembly of bishops was held in Carthage to settle this matter. The bishops alone were called upon to make the decision.

Cyprian took the position that the Church, as an institution for the salvation of mankind, comprised the good and the evil alike. Admitting that in individual cases God might judge differently, Cyprian insisted that the Church alone could guarantee salvation. Orthodoxy constituted no guarantee when the individual was outside the Church. "*Extra ecclesiam nulla salus.*" [44] "*Si quis ecclesiam non habet matrem, Deum non habet patrem.*"[45] The Church was established upon the bishops. They could be judged by no one except God. To criticize the bishop was rebellion. Cyprian did not stress apostolic succession as a test of the validity of the episcopal office, but he did emphasize the idea that the bishop was the successor of the Apostles and the legitimate interpreter of the apostolic tradition. He further emphasized the college of bishops (the episcopate) as the authority of the Church, and he willingly recognized the pre-eminence of Rome. Yet Cyprian had no intention of favoring the papal system. His theory of safeguarding the unity of the Church was nonetheless soon overtaken by the actual development which established the Bishop of Rome as the visible head of the Church.

BIBLIOGRAPHY

1. Writings of the Post-Apostolic Fathers
AUGUSTINE. Anti-Donatistic writings.
CYPRIAN. *On the Unity of the Church.*
————. *Letters.*
HIPPOLYTUS. *Philosophoumena*, IX.
IRENAEUS. *Against Heresies.*
TERTULLIAN. *On Repentance.*
————. *On Modesty.*

[44] "There is no salvation outside the church," *Letters,* 73, 21.
[45] "If someone has not the church for his mother, he has not God for his father," *On the Unity of the Church,* 6.

2. *The Episcopate before the Reformation*
   BENSON, E. W. *Cyprian, His Life, His Times, His Work*. New York: D. Appleton Co., 1897.
   HATCH, E. *Organization of the Early Christian Churches*. London: Rivington Co., 1886.
   REVILLE, J. *Les Origines de l'episcopat*. 1895.
   ROLFFS, E. *Das Indulgenzedikt des Bischofs Kallist*. 1893.

3. *Post-Reformation and Present-Day Developments*
   CLARKE, H. W. *History of English Nonconformity*. London: Chapman and Hall, 1911 ff.
   EHRHARDT, ARNOLD. *The Apostolic Ministry*. Edinburgh: Oliver and Boyd Co., 1958.
   FAIRWEATHER, E. R. and HETTLINGER, R. F. *Episcopacy and Reunion*. London: Mowbray and Co., 1952.
   HERGENROETHER, P. *Lehrbuch des Katholischen Kirchenrechts*. 1905.
   HOOKER, R. *Ecclesiastical Polity, 1594-1662*. Edited by J. KEBLE. 3 vols. 3rd ed.; London: Parker, 1845.
   KIRK, K. E. (ed.). *The Apostolic Ministry*. New York: Morehouse-Gorham, 1947.
   LADD, G. T. *Principles of Church Polity*. New York: Charles Scribner's Sons, 1882.
   MANSON, T. W. *The Church's Ministry*. Philadelphia: Westminster Press, 1948.
   NIEBUHR, H. RICHARD, and WILLIAMS, DANIEL D. (eds.). *The Ministry in Historical Perspective*. New York: Harper & Bros., 1957.
   SOHM, R. *Kirchenrecht*. 1892.

CHAPTER VIII

TEACHERS AND TEACHINGS IN THE OLD CATHOLIC AGE

The Old Catholic Age (170-325) established a theology against Ebionitism; against the religious philosophy of the Gnostics; against Marcion; against the views of the Monarchians, i.e., the Samosatenes (dynamistic) and the Sabellians (modalistic). Other characteristics of this age were as follows: the development of the Rule of Faith; the establishment of the canon of the Holy Scriptures; first steps toward an episcopal organization; the rejection of Montanism; and the persecution of the Church.

The principal schools and teachers of the Old Catholic Age were:

The School of Asia Minor, with Irenaeus (d. *ca.* 200) and his pupil, Hippolytus, as leading teachers;

The School of Alexandria, represented by Clement (d. before 216) and Origen (d. 254);

The School of North Africa, led by Tertullian (d. *ca.* 225) and Cyprian (d. 258).

These schools represent the three main ideas of Christian love, and are exemplified by the three outstanding Ante-Nicene theologians: Irenaeus, Origen, and Tertullian. They represent respectively the Agape, Eros, and Nomos types. "This does not mean, however," as Nygren remarks, "that any one of the three types succeeded in displacing the others." [1] Rather, they existed side by side in the Church. Because of Gnosticism, Eros had been recognized as heretical, while Agape had been compromised by Marcion. This explains the limitations of the idea of Agape in the theologies of both Irenaeus and Tertullian. The Nomos type had not been under suspicion and therefore

[1] Nygren, *Agape and Eros,* pp. 355 ff.

the basically Nomos theology of the Apostolic Fathers and Apologists could assert itself unhindered.

As to the interrelation of these schools, Irenaeus represented an earlier stage; Origen and Tertullian represented two extremes. Origen, with his use of the Alexandrian Logos-speculation as the principle of Christian gnosis, barely escaped degrading Christianity to the level of a philosophy, and lost himself in the maze of spiritualism. On the other hand, Tertullian, who fastened his whole attention upon nature, aimed at substantializing God and the soul. He settled upon a one-sided realism. Irenaeus avoided the dangers of both by his thorough biblicism, by his sound attitude toward tradition, and by his christo-centric theology.

I. Irenaeus: Founder of a Biblical Theology

Irenaeus, who was bishop at Lyons in Southern Gaul at the time of his death (*ca.* 200), had lived in Asia, where he knew Polycarp personally. In theology, Irenaeus was typical of the School of Asia Minor. This School was "the outcome of John's ministry, and was distinguished by a firm grasp of Scripture, solid faith, conciliatory treatment of those within, and energetic polemics against heretics." [2] Although the Johannine origin of Irenaeus' theology is worthy of emphasis, it must not be forgotten that Irenaeus was filled with the spirit and thoughts of Paul more than was the case with any other of the leading theologians of his age.

Like Tertullian, Irenaeus was opposed to philosophical speculation in matters of religion. Gnosticism shows, he said, where we shall arrive if we follow philosophy. Being of an intensely practical turn of mind, Irenaeus was averse to every kind of *a priori* speculation, for God is known to us not through speculation, but through revelation. Hence we should not concern ourselves with such idle questions as what God did before creation. Christ is understood to be the revelation of God. As such he is pre-existent and co-eternal (*semper co-existens*). The Father and the Son belong together from all eternity. Just as Christ is the revelation of God, so God has always been revealing the Son; and the relation between the two includes the personal

[2] J. H. Kurtz, *Church History,* trans. John Macpherson (London: Nodder & Stoughton, 1888-90), Vol. I, Par. 31, 1.

differentiation.[3] The manner in which the Father generated the Son is altogether incomprehensible.[4] We should therefore abide by the language of Scripture and not depart from the Rule of Faith. Irenaeus began with the historic Christ whom he regarded as the revelation of God the Father. He thus transcended the viewpoint of the Greek Apologists. His thinking was christocentric, not Logos-centered. In other words, his interest was centered in Christ the God-Man as the mediator of our salvation,[5] not in the Logos as the mediator between God and the world. However, Irenaeus made but a small contribution to a scientifically articulated dogma of the Trinity. This was chiefly due to his refusal to deal with speculative questions.

Soteriology was the material principle of Irenaeus' entire theology. Against Gnosticism, Irenaeus raised the fundamental thought that the God of creation is the same as the God of redemption.[6] Christ the God-Man, who is the personification of the eternal self-revelation of God, is the mediator of man's salvation. The first Adam misused his free will and disobeyed God, in consequence of which he fell, and with him, all mankind. Through the fall man lost the divine image and became the victim of death. The divine plan of gradually leading man to actual Godlike-ness was interrupted. Physical death constituted a certain negative remedy. But God immediately inaugurated a positive plan for the salvation of man and for leading him to the intended goal—actual Godlike-ness. God entered into a fourfold federation with man. The first federation covered the time from Adam to the flood; the second, the time after the flood under Noah; the third, the giving of the law under Moses; and the fourth is the period in which man is to be renewed and all things brought to completion and perfection through the gospel.

Under this fourth federation God became man in Christ, who, as the Second Adam, entered into solidarity with our sinful race. Christ proved his holiness in the hours of temptation, overcame the common enemy, and thus regained the possibility of Godlike-ness for man. In this way Christ restored the interrupted development and led it to a

---

[3] Irenaeus, *Against Heresies*, II, 30, 9; III, 18, 1; II, 25; 28, 2.
[4] *Ibid.*, II, 28, 4, 5.
[5] *Ibid.* II, 13, 8; 28, 5.
[6] *Ibid.*, IV, 20, 2; 6, 2.

conclusion in himself. This is the so-called *anakephalaiōsis*[7] or recapitu-lation-thought of Irenaeus. <u>Christ appeared as the Second Adam</u>. As the first Adam, who fell, had produced a generation of sinful men, so <u>Christ, the Second Adam, produced a new generation of righteous men in whom the divine image is restored</u>. In Christ the new man becomes immortal. *Quando incarnatus et homo factus, longam homi-num expositionem in se ipso recapitulavit. In compendio nobis salutem praestans, ut quod perdideramus in Adam, id est, secundum et simili-tudinem esse Dei, hoc in Christo reciperemus.*[8] Through his obedience Christ did what Adam had failed to do. Christ destroyed sin and Satan. All stages of human life, from infancy onward, are sanctified by the life of the Second Adam. This thought of Christ's works and suffer-ings for us is carried out even to his descent into Hades, into which his followers shall likewise descend and from which they shall come forth at the resurrection as Christ did.[9] After all has been completed and the mission of Christ is accomplished, Christ's special position in the economy of the Trinity will cease. The hosts of redeemed man-kind will then occupy the place of Christ, and God will be all in all.[10] <u>Christ, the God-Man, occupied the center of Irenaeus' thinking, and not Christ the Teacher, as was the case with the Apologists</u>. Irenaeus raised the question: *Cur Deus homo?* ("Why did God become man?") and then answered it thus: "In order that we might become gods, that is, Godlike." [11]

The Epoch-Making Significance of Irenaeus' Theology

Zahn says: "<u>Irenaeus is the first writer of the Post-Apostolic Age who deserves the name of a theologian</u>." [12] Loofs calls Irenaeus' theology "the Catholic form of an older theological tradition" which

---

[7] *Ibid.,* II, 2, 8. The same term is used in Ephes. 1:10.

[8] *Ibid.,* III, 18, 1. Elsewhere, this remarkable passage is translated as follows: "But when He became incarnate and was made man, He summoned up in Him-self the long line of human beings, and furnished us, in a brief, comprehensive manner, with salvation; so that what we had lost in Adam—namely, to be accord-ing to the image and likeness of God—that we may recover in Jesus Christ." *ANF,* I, 446.

[9] Irenaeus, *Against Heresies,* III, 19, 3; 20, 4; *passim.*

[10] *Ibid.,* IV, 38, 4.

[11] *Ibid.,* II, 14, 7; cf. IV, 38.

[12] *PRE,* IX, 410.

had its home in Asia Minor.[13] Harnack expresses a certain dislike at connecting Irenaeus (through Polycarp) with the ministry of the Apostle John. The objection is that in this way "Irenaeus is given authority which he cannot claim by virtue of the character of his theology." Yet Harnack admits that the conception of Christianity as expressed in Irenaeus' theology has become "a decisive factor in the history of dogma." [14] There are leading elements in the doctrinal system of Irenaeus which the Church could not avoid adopting and using as the basis for the further development of a system of Christian truth. Thomasius passes a correct judgment when he cites Irenaeus as "the most conspicuous representative of the Church's consciousness," and characterizes his theology as "sound to the core" (*grundgesund*).[15] His soundness is seen particularly in these three things: his theology is biblical; it sustains a deep reverence of the apostolic tradition; it is christocentric.

Concerning the biblicism of his theology, it may be said that there is in Irenaeus, for the first time, a consideration and understanding of the Scriptures as a whole. The relation of the Old Testament to the New is indicated and the teaching of Paul is understood. From the trying conflict with fundamental heresies there has come a classification of views with regard to many of the fundamentals of Christianity. There is a scriptural and evangelical ring in the system of Irenaeus. Thus a truly catholic theology appeared, a theology which the Reformation of the sixteenth century recognized as catholic over against the Roman Catholic innovation of later times.

A closer study of Irenaeus' writings shows that his teaching was not without erroneous elements, especially in the field of soteriology. Like the Anti-Gnostic Fathers, he emphasized the freedom of man's will, and therefore could not free himself from that ethical apprehension of the Gospel which we have noticed in the Apologists. The evangelical ring mentioned above was absent in his discussion of sins committed after baptism and in his understanding of faith as a doing of God's will. Likewise, the teaching of the deification of man as a result of the incarnation of God reveals a serious limitation in his theology.[16]

[13] Loofs, *op. cit.*, p. 139.
[14] Harnack, *History of Dogma*, II, 236.
[15] Thomasius, *op. cit.*, I, 145.
[16] Cf. Nygren, *op. cit.*, pp. 409 ff.

II. CLEMENT OF ALEXANDRIA AND ORIGEN

The School of Alexandria was represented by Clement and particularly by Origen. In this school it was the speculative tendency which was dominant. Theology was viewed as a science and was expressed in terms of philosophical thought. Beyond creating the background for this type of theology, Clement's contribution was small. The theology of Origen, while often negative, nevertheless abounded in helpful suggestions which contributed toward the solution of the trinitarian and christological problems. Origen became a great stimulus to theology.

The city of Alexandria in northern Egypt had been founded in 332 B.C. by Alexander the Great, from whom it took its name. Originally intended to be a commercial center, it succeeded in becoming an intellectual center also. It seems that when men come together to trade their material possessions, it frequently happens that they trade their intellectual property as well. Alexandria became the common meeting-ground for Greek philosophy, ancient Egyptian thought, the Oriental cults, and Judaism. It would have been strange if Christianity had not entered the intellectual and scholastic life of the city. By about A.D. 185 there existed in Alexandria a famous school to prepare catechumens for Christian baptism. The pronounced scholastic character of the school may have been due to either a conscious imitation of, or a direct opposition to, the various systems of thought found in that place. As far as is known the rather obscure figure Pantaenus was the first teacher of this school. He had formerly been a Stoic philosopher.

Clement (d. before 216), of whom we know more, had been a learned pagan philosopher. In his search for knowledge he came to Alexandria and placed himself under the influence of Pantaenus, later succeeding him as teacher. As compared to Origen, Seeberg notes, Clement was a "talented dilettante with the virtues and vices which belong to such character." [17] A study of Clement's writings substantiates this.

Some of these writings have been lost, among them, his interpretation of the Scriptures in eight volumes. A large work composed of three parts has been preserved. In the first part of this work, *A Word*

[17] Seeberg, *Textbook,* I, 141.

of *Admonition to the Greeks*, which is both apologetic and polemic, Clement exposes the foolishness and vanity of heathenism. The second part, entitled the *Instructor*, in three books, offers a guide for the Christian life of those who are destined to be *gnostikoi*. This may well be called the Church's first comprehensive work on Christian ethics. To it, Clement added a monograph on the question *Which Rich Man May Be Saved?* The third part, which comprises eight books, is entitled *Stromateis*, meaning patchwork or miscellanies. It takes its name from its aphoristic style and the variety of its contents, and aims at presenting an introduction to the perfect Christian knowledge (*gnosis*). It discusses the relation of Christian truth to philosophy and of faith to knowledge, and thus delineates the ideal of the Christian Gnostic. This part lacks unity of thought. It is indicative of the fact that Clement was not a systematic thinker.

Clement was a thoroughgoing eclectic. He praised Plato, but followed the ethics of the Stoa. He contributed more than any other to the creation of that attitude of mind which formed the background and foundation of the systematic theology of the Greek Fathers.[18]

Origen (d. 254), who was the pupil of Clement, was the greatest among the representatives of the Alexandrian School. So universal was his mind that he has been "celebrated as a philosopher, philologist, critic, exegete, dogmatician, apologist, polemicist . . ." whom "posterity has with equal right honored as the actual founder of an ecclesiastical and scientific theology, and reproached as the originator of heretical opinions." [19] In 203 he became teacher at the School of Alexandria. After his excommunication, which was probably due to the jealousy of Bishop Dimetrius, he taught at Caesarea.

A large part of Origen's work was in the field of biblical criticism. In this field he produced his *Hexapla* comprising fifty volumes—a work in which he placed in parallel columns all the then known texts and translations of the Old Testament, indicating their agreements and variations, in many cases adding his own critical remarks. This work, on which he labored continuously for twenty-seven years, disappeared when Caesarea was destroyed by the Arabians.[20] It should be men-

---

[18] Cf. Nygren, *op. cit.*, pp. 349 ff.

[19] Kurtz, *op. cit.*, par. 31, 5; cf. par. 51 f.; par. 52, 6.

[20] Fragments of it have been collected and these represent Vols. 15 and 16 of J. P. Migne, *Patrologiae Cursus Completus, seu bibliotheca universalis, integra*

tioned that much of Origen's work was devoted to an exegetical investigation in the sphere of interpretation and application.[21] Worthy of special mention is Origen's dogmatic work which has been preserved in a Latin translation entitled *De Principiis* ("About First Principles"). This was the first attempt to present a comprehensive system of Christian doctrine based upon the Scriptures and the Apostolic Tradition and the philosophical knowledge of the age. The creative character of this work has exerted a great influence upon Christian dogma both positively and negatively.[22] The eight books, *Contra Celsum*, also contain important material for an exposition of Origen's system of theology.

The Philosophical Character of Alexandrian Theology

The theology of Clement and Origen differed greatly from that of Irenaeus and Tertullian. Pre-Catholic conditions maintained themselves longer in Alexandria than in Asia Minor and Carthage. The situation in which Clement found himself explains the Hellenic form of much of his theology. By Origen's time the Catholic tradition had also become established in Alexandria; but it did not do away with the peculiar type and tendency of theology in the School. Clement regarded philosophy as having the same pedagogical significance for the Greek world as law had for the Hebrew world. Philosophy is the light of reason which the Logos has imparted to mankind. It is the preparation for the higher light which shines in the gospel. Through Greek philosophy the soul is prepared for the reception of faith on which truth erects the edifice of knowledge.[23] Philosophy is the means by which the real nature of Christianity is disclosed to the thinking man. Even today philosophy will do this service for man. Such were the thoughts of Clement, and they lay also at the foundation of the system of Origen. Origen looked upon Chrisianity as a higher philosophy. Christ towers above Zeno and Plato because he

uniformis, commoda, oeconomica, ominum ss. patrum, doctorum, scriptorumque ecclesiasticorum (Series Graeca), hereinafter referred to as *MSG* for the Greek Series, *MSL* for the Latin Series.

[21] The *Semeioseis* or *Scholia* are interpretations of difficult passages of Scripture; the *Timpi* are commentaries on books of the Scripture, especially Matthew and John; and the *Homilies* are expository addresses.

[22] See the English translation in *ANF*, IV, 239 ff.

[23] Cf. Nygren, *op. cit.*, pp. 387 ff.

overcomes polytheism, and his religion is for the common man as well as for the thinker. The Alexandrian School was a continuation of the principles which were expressed by Philo and by the Greek Apologists. This school marked the first consistent synthesis between biblical revelation and philosophical speculation.

Is philosophy a legitimate factor in the work of theology? This age-old question which men continue to ask was suggested by the peculiar type of Alexandrian theology. It cannot be denied that what Clement and Origen were aiming at was an inner necessity for Christian theology. Christianity is universal in character. This means that it is the religion which is destined to exercise the controlling influence over the world's thought. Kurtz says: "When once the substantial truth of divine salvation had cast off the Judaistic husk in which the kernel had ripened, those elements of culture, which had come to maturity in the Roman-Greek world, were appropriated as the means for giving to Christian ideas a fuller and clearer expression. The task now to be undertaken was the development of Christianity on the lines of Graeco-Roman culture." [24] The Apologists began the work along this line. Tertullian did a great deal of it without intending to do so.

The Alexandrians dealt with philosophy in such a way that it appeared to be an integral part of the whole system. The Gnostics had also done this, but without any consideration for the apostolic tradition or the Rule of Faith. When Origen substituted "Christian gnosis" for a "pseudonymous gnosis," he did so with the intention of being guided by the Scriptures, although he frequently failed in this because of his allegorical exegesis and his philosophical trend of mind. No matter how impossible his system was as a whole, no matter how much we may reject his many errors and his synthesis of religion and philosophy in its practical details, nevertheless, Christianity does possess the inner impulse to establish itself as a system, and to pour its contents into the mental forms which have been developed by the work of philosophy. In this sense Origen was a pioneer in the quest for theological method. Irenaeus' refusal to recognize philosophy prevented him from making any contribution to the solution of the trinitarian problem, but the contribution of Origen and his successors was great.

[24] Kurtz, *op. cit.*, Par. 19; cf. Par. 7, 25-26.

Pistis and Gnosis

The peculiar theology of both Clement and Origen pivoted on the relation of faith to a deeper knowledge of the content of faith. Clement said, "To know is more than to believe." [25] Faith is the outward acceptance of God and of the doctrine of Christ in the literal sense; but the Christian Gnostic possesses an initiated vision which apprehends salvation inwardly and comprehends it.[26] This attitude or experience gives the Gnostic a higher motive for his ethical functioning. He does not do the Christian's work for reward, but for its own sake and out of love to God.[27] In faith there is already an element of that knowledge (*gnōsis*), and therefore faith is sufficient for salvation. The simple believer has already received the needed perfection and the assurance of salvation in his baptism. The believer is one who is taught by God, and as such he is a pneumatic. These thoughts separated Clement from the views of the Gnostics, who said that from their birth men are either hylics or pneumatics, and that only the latter can be saved. The simple faith, however, is to be lifted to something higher—to a vision of the divine mysteries. It is here that philosophy can aid, but even here Clement was opposed to an unlimited speculation.

A true Gnostic, Clement said, is one who bases his thinking on the faith of the Church.[28] In these thoughts Origen agreed entirely with Clement. The cultured man, who sees the Logos in Christ, is the perfect Christian. He sees divine truth in all things. Every fact is merely a symbol to him of abstract teachings which express higher truth. Seeberg notes that from this theology

> there resulted two forms of Christianity. In contrast with the barely believing and uncultivated beginner, inclined to externalities, stands the Christian who beholds the mysteries of God and who with heart and understanding receives God to abiding fellowship. The Stoic discrimination between the wise and the advancing is here transferred to Christianity. . . . The "Gnostic" of Clement stands higher than his "believer." [29]

Origen on the Interpretation of Scripture

Allegorical interpretation was common to the Church Fathers of this and the following periods. It was Origen who systematically

---

[25] *Stromateis*, VI, 14.
[26] *Ibid.*, VI, 11-12; V, 1; VII, 12; VI, 10.
[27] *Ibid.*, IV, 18.
[28] Cf. *ibid.*, VII, 7.
[29] Seeberg, *Textbook*, I, 142.

developed this method of interpretation in Book IV of his *De Principiis. Against Celsus* is also full of references to this way of interpreting
Scripture. It has been fittingly remarked that it was "this method
which enabled him to conceal the foolishness of the gospel and to
glorify it as wisdom." [30] Origen needed this allegorical method in
order to establish the system of his peculiar doctrines. According to
him, the Cosmos—God's first revelation—is threefold; spiritual, psychic,
and material. In the same way the Scriptures, which constitute God's
second revelation, are threefold. First, the Scriptures have a somatic
or literal sense upon which the simpler souls of the multitude depend.
Exegesis is to find that sense, but its intent is to conceal the true sense.
Second, the Scriptures have a psychical or moral sense which refers to
the individual in his ethical relations.[31] Third, the Scriptures have a
pneumatic or speculative sense. This is the real spiritual content of
Scripture—the profounder meaning which is sealed to all save the
mature believer.[32] There are cases where the literal sense must be
rejected altogether, as, for instance, in Genesis 19:20 ff.; 25:1 ff.;
29:27-28; 30:3, 9. The literal sense is intended to conceal the spiritual
sense in order that pearls may not be cast before swine. The mature
believer will press beyond the literal sense and discover the esoteric
tenets of the Divine Word.[33]

Origen on the Trinitarian Relation in God

In Neo-Platonic fashion Origen saw reality only in the spiritual as
opposed to things material and visible. This led him to an abstract,
Platonic conception of God. As the Father, God is one and is opposed
to the many things. These things have their cause in him. He alone is
real being. Anthropomorphic expressions are to be carefully avoided.
God is goodness and omnipotence, and for this reason he presses
toward a revelation which takes place through the Logos. God cannot
be thought of without revelation. Creative activity belongs to his very
being. His being appears in the many things which He is creating.

---

[30] For example, see VI, 7; V, 60. Cf. the estimate of Porphyry in Eusebius,
Church History, VI, 19, and also Origen, *Against Celsus*, IV, 38.

[31] Cf. the elaborate discussion in Origen, *De Principiis*, IV, 1.

[32] *Ibid.*, I, 1-2.

[33] See R. P. C. Hanson, *Allegory and Event* (Richmond: John Knox Press,
1959), pp. 131 ff.

But revelation includes limitation. In creating man a free agent, God limited himself.

The Son reveals the Father to us. Origen followed Neo-Platonism, which taught that the *nous* (intellect) proceeds from the Divine Being. The Son proceeds from the Father as the will proceeds from a human being.[34] This procession is expressed in the conception of a generation (*genesis*) of the Son from the Father. By speaking of an eternal generation, Origen made a large contribution to the dogma of the Trinity. The Father is always begetting the Son.[35] Origen was thus a strong opponent of Monarchianism, which had its supporters in Rome. He looked upon the Logos as a person, and taught that the Son, begotten of the Father from all eternity, was a hypostasis from all eternity.[36] Origen's teaching differed from all previous conceptions of a hypostatic Logos. This was especially true with reference to the Apologists, who took the position that the hypostasizing of the Logos occurred in time for the purpose of creation and incarnation. According to Origen, the generation of the Son took place not simply as the condition of creation, but as a necessity in itself, for where there is light there must be shedding forth of rays. Because the life of God is not bound by time, his life in the Son must also lie outside of time. It is not, therefore, an act of God accomplished once and forever, but continuing exercise of his eternal, living power.[37]

This was the first advance toward stating the Son's co-eternity with the Father as expressed in the ancient creed of Nicea. This thought opened the way to another equally important term of the creed, *homoousios*.[38] It should be remembered that Origen did not succeed wholly in overcoming his subordinationism.[39] He even maintained that prayer should be addressed to the Father alone.[40] But Origen's subordination was restricted within the narrowest possible limits. In opposition to Gnostic theories of emanation, he rejected the expression that the Son came "from the essence of the Father." In opposition to the *homoousios* as used in the Patripassian sense, he maintained that

[34] *De Principiis,* I, 2, 6.
[35] *Ibid.,* I, 2, 4.
[36] *Ibid.* I, 2, 9 f.; IV, 28; *Against Celsus,* V, 37.
[37] *Ouk estin hote ouk en.*
[38] *De Principiis,* I, 2, 12; *Against Celsus,* VIII, 12.
[39] *Against Celsus,* V, 39; VI, 60; II, 9.
[40] *Ibid.,* VIII, 13; cf. VIII, 26.

the Son is different in his being from the Father. He taught the generation of the Son from the will of God because he saw in him the objectified divine will. He called Christ a creature (*ktisma*), but only insofar as He is generated from God and does not have a life independent of God. What Origen taught was a subordination, not of essence or nature, but of existence or origin.

Origen felt obliged to express himself on the Holy Spirit, to whom the Rule of Faith assigned third place in the Trinity. In describing the relation of the Son to the Father, Origen made use of analogies suggested by the philosophers.[41] He proceeded differently with regard to the Spirit. Here he relied entirely on revelation.[42] Although the Spirit is a production of the Son, nevertheless he is a hypostasis and is divine in character. He is active, not like the Logos in all intelligent things, but in the souls of the saints. The Spirit's sphere of activity is the smallest, but also the most important. The Father governs in the sphere of being, the Son in that of reason, and the Spirit in the souls of Christians.

According to Origen, the Trinity can be represented graphically by three concentric circles of which the Father is the largest, and the Spirit the smallest. The Trinity is at once economic and ontological. God reveals himself, and he cannot be thought of without constantly revealing himself in that way.

Origen on Cosmology and Anthropology

There was a history before history.[43] Since God has been revealing himself through all eternity, the world also is eternal—that is, the world of spirits, not this visible world.[44] The mediator in God's creative activity is the Son. The spirits, who were originally alike, were created free agents and their destiny was to be fixed by their own determination. The spirits were intended to arrive at a condition of constancy and were then to make room for new creations. But the world of spirits became the scene of a fall into sin. Some of the spirits did not participate in the fall (such as the soul of Jesus and

[41] The Neo-Platonian Plotinus spoke of the *nous* proceeding from God, as Origen spoke of the *Logos.*

[42] *De Principiis,* I, 3, 1-4.

[43] *Ibid.,* II, 8, 3; 9, 2.

[44] *Ibid.,* 1, 2, 10; II, 9, 6.

others), while others did to a greater or lesser degree. Their condition in the world of creation was fixed by their abstinence from, or by their participation in, the fall.

The creation which is recorded in Genesis was for the purpose of punishment and purification. In the creation the spirits received bodies which corresponded to their merits. Their attitude toward good and evil showed itself in their external appearance. On the one hand, there were those who attained to the heights of goodness; these appear as divinities, as thrones, or as stars which are looked upon as living beings. On the other hand, there were the creatures, namely, Satan and the devils, who fell first and deeper than the others; these appear now in dark and coarse forms. Between these two classes are the spirits or souls of men in their own form of corporeal being; it was for these that the world was created.[45] Man is to be purified in and through a terrestrial life. For this man is endowed with the freedom through which he may attain to the position of the angels.

The souls of men, then, are fallen spirits. In the pre-existent world from which he came, man received his *nous*, or intellect, from the Logos. By reason of the fall that *nous* lost its participation in the divine fire and cooled down into a soul.[46] The freedom of the soul in its material body is emphasized. In spite of this, the soul comes into this world polluted with sin and is surrounded by temptations from the demons.[47] Man is therefore in need of redemption. Origen taught that the actions of the souls in their pre-existent state also determined the situations of men in the world of history, even with regard to such things as parental origin, place of birth, and the region and environment in which this earthly life is to be spent.[48]

Origen on Soteriology

Having developed the pre-historic part of his system which may be called "the prelude in heaven," Origen proceeds to biblical history. The revelation contained in the Scriptures is for man's redemption. To the natural law there is added the Mosaic law. Next comes the gospel—first the literal Gospels, and then the eternal gospel which

[45] *Ibid.*, III, 4, 5; II, 1-4.
[46] *Ibid.*, II, 8, 3.
[47] *Against Celsus*, III, 62.
[48] *De Principiis*, II, 9, 8.

needs no covers or illustrations. From what we have learned of Origen's distinction between *pistis* and *gnosis,* and between the external and internal sense of Scripture, we know what he meant by these stages in his historic revelation.

The significance of Christ is twofold. On the one hand, there are the uncultivated beginners who cannot believe without externalities and who must therefore be impressed. To these Christ brought redemption by paying a ransom for the deliverance of man from the devil. On the other hand, there are the real Gnostics, the real Christians who behold the mysteries of God. To these Christ appeared as a priest to open the depths of knowledge and to make them participants of His divine life, so that they might become gods themselves.

There was a difference between the Christian *gnosis* of Origen and the *pseudo-gnosis* of the Gnostics. The Gnostics denied the historicity and reality of the facts of redemption, while Origen believed and taught them. However, these facts are needed only by the uncultivated beginner (*nepios*). The real or Christian Gnostic requires neither Christology nor soteriology, i.e. a doctrine in which the historic facts of redemption are accounted for. The Christian Gnostic has Christ in an immediate way. Divinity and humanity present no problem to him. The historic facts of revelation represent real truth, but they are not the truth. This reminds us again of Origen's distinction between faith and theology.

In dealing with the work of Christ, Origen proceeded with his characteristic distinction between two classes of Christians, the Christians of simple faith and the Christians of advanced knowledge. To the first class Christ presented himself as the God-Man and the Physician. To the second class he was the Teacher and the Divine Principle. The latter, whom we may call the Christian Gnostics, no longer require the Physician, for Christ has taught them the deeper mysteries. "Blessed are they who have arrived at the point where they do not need the Son of God as the Physician who heals the sick, nor as the Shepherd, nor as the Redeemer, but who have Him as Wisdom and Reason." [49] The highest work of Christ consisted in his doctrine of the divine mysteries. In this work the Logos used the man Jesus as his organ.

[49] *Against Celsus,* III, 61, 62.

Origen accepted what the Scriptures teach concerning the redemptive significance of the passion and death of Christ. But it is only the Christians of simple faith who need this. The object of Christ's passion and death is to liberate men from the dominion of the demons. The Christians of simple faith are to be helped by objectifying this redemption in the doctrine of the death of God's Son in which an atonement was made and a ransom paid.

What are the elements of Origen's doctrine of atonement? Through sin the souls of men had come under the sovereignty of the devil. Jesus offered his soul unto death as an exchange (*antallagma*) or ransom (*lytron*) in order that they might be redeemed from the devil. The devil was not aware that he was unable to endure the presence of a sinless soul. He was deceived into accepting the ransom because he did not possess the touchstone whereby the ransom might be retained.[50] Origen expressed himself as follows:

> But to whom did He give His soul as a ransom for many? Surely not to God! Perhaps the Evil One. For he reigned over us until the soul of Jesus had been given to him as a ransom—to him who deceived himself, thinking that he could be master over it, not realizing that it did not suffer the agony which he applied to hold it down.[51]

Thus the souls of men became free from the power of the devil and his demons.[52] Origen was the first to interpret Christ's death as a deception of the devil. Nevertheless, it is of interest to note that the necessity of a propitiation before God was recognized. Christ bore in our stead the penalty which rightfully belonged to us. God was reconciled to us and we to God. To these biblical thoughts Origen added his own peculiar ideas that the work of reconciliation extends beyond the world of men to the realm of angels, and that Christ continues his redeeming work through the ages.

The Person of Christ

It was for the sake of the simple and imperfect Christian, the Christian who is not capable of deeper knowledge, that Christ had to become the God-Man. To satisfy his religious need the doctrine of

[50] *Commentary on Matthew*, s.v. Matt. 16:8.
[51] *Loc. cit.*
[52] *Against Celsus*, II, 47; VIII, 54, 64, *passim*.

Christ had to be put in a form which excludes the errors of Docetism and Ebionitism.

Christ had a human soul which formed the connection between the Logos and the body of Jesus.[53] This soul was a pure spirit which had not participated in the pre-historic fall. It was this soul, together with the human body, which suffered, and not the Logos, who is incapable of suffering. Origen was careful to leave the natural properties to each of the two natures of Christ. The man Jesus was really mortal. He really suffered and died. Against Celsus' accusation that the Christians considered the dying Jesus to be God, Origen insisted that the Logos is incapable of change, and therefore cannot die. When it is said that the God-Man really died, such an expression must not be understood to mean what it seems to say. Here we have an anticipation of Zwingli's denial of the communication of Christ's attributes and of his treatment of *alloiosis,* treating such an expression as a *phrasis loquendi* ("manner of speaking").

Origen felt obliged to insist upon a real union of the two natures of Christ. What kind of union was it? It is not merely a communion (*koinōnia*) between the two natures, but a real union (*henōsis*). Positively speaking, it is a spiritual or mystical union, much like that which exists between Christ and the believer. The Logos—the all-permeating reason or *nous*—has a controlling influence over the man Jesus. The influence of the Logos deifies the humanity of Christ more and more. Origen went so far as to say that because of its virgin birth the body of Christ was from the act of incarnation even more divine than our bodies. Origen arrived at a union of the divine and the human in Christ by teaching a moral influence of the Logos over the man Jesus which led to a gradual deification of His body. The union between the Logos and the soul and body of Christ became so close that Scripture applies the predicates of divinity interchangeably. The Logos gradually absorbed the body of Jesus until finally he was transformed into spirit and admitted into union with the Godhead.

Harnack says of Origen's Christology: "All imaginable heresies have been touched upon, though limited by precautions. . . . The only exception is modalism."[54] The last reference is to Origen's fundamental opposition to modalistic Monarchianism.

[53] *De Principiis,* II, 6, 3, 4; *Against Celsus,* I, 66; II, 9, 4, *passim.*
[54] *Grundriss,* p. 152.

The Sacraments

Baptism is for the forgiveness of sins. The act of baptism is a symbolic exhibition of the soul's purification through Christ, just as Christ's healing miracles were symbolical of man's continual liberation from the demons through the Logos. The actual benefit which the individual derives from baptism comes from the prayers connected with the act.[55]

Baptism is the sacrament through which sins are forgiven. For sins committed after baptism a forgiveness is available through repentance. In a truly evangelical way Origen holds that repentance consists primarily in the confession of one's sins to God, but also to the "spiritual man" (I Cor. 2:15) who "forgives whatever God 'forgives' and 'retains' such sins as are incurable," for example, idolatry, adultery, and fornication.[56]

Eschatology

The goal to be reached is the union of man with the Logos and the deification of human nature. Complete redemption comes with death and the things which follow. In eschatology Origen broke with the tradition of the Church. His spiritualizing method permitted him to put forward a different interpretation of these things. Those who are saved receive a pneumatic body and enter paradise. The place for the rejected is hell. There they experience the fire of judgment which Origen understood to be the individual's conscience tortured by the sense of its sinfulness. But this is a purifying fire, and even the wicked, including the devil, will after infinite ages, finally reach the intended goal.[57]

III. TERTULLIAN: FOUNDER OF WESTERN THEOLOGY

The Man and His Work

Tertullian was born about 150 and died about 225. He never was

---

[55] *Commentary on John*, VI, 33.

[56] *On Prayer*, XXVII, 8 ff. In another passage however, Origen concedes that there is room for *one* repentance for the graver sins of life. *Homilies on Leviticus*, XV, 2; cf. also *ibid.*, XI, 2; XII, 3 and *Against Celsus*, III, 51.—On Origen's view of the Eucharist, see pp. 223-24.

[57] *Apokatastasis tōn hapantōn* (Acts 3:21); *Against Celsus* V, 15. *De Principiis*, II, 10, 4; I, 6, 3; cf. *ibid.*, II, 3, 7; 10, 3 f; 11, 11 2 ff; III, 6, 4-9 and *Against Celsus*, V, 17, 23; VI, 72; *passim.*

more than a presbyter. Like Cyprian, who revered him as his teacher,[58] he belonged to the School of North Africa. His writings indicate the various influences to which he had been subjected. There was his own training in Stoicism, his reading in the early apologetic literature of the Church, and the strong influence of the tradition of Asia Minor transmitted through Irenaeus.[59] Tertullian was very outspoken in his emphasis upon tradition as the authority for the Church. In his writing, *Prescription against Heretics,* he advised the Christians not to argue with the heretics on the basis of Scripture, but rather to deny them the right of appeal to that source. The reason which he advanced was that the heretics had lost all legitimate connection with the Church. He pointed to the churches of the Apostles as the depositories of apostolic teaching, and to the succession of bishops as the custodians of a reliable tradition.[60] It is one of the remarkable instances of historical irony that this same man became a schismatic himself in the latter part of his life and joined the Montanists. It should be remembered, however, that Montanism was an aberration in matters of practice only, and did not depart from the Rule of Faith.

Was Tertullian a jurist before his conversion? Theology has an interest in this question because of the nomistic views expressed in his writings. Eusebius refers to him as "a man versed in Roman law." [61] But the passage may only serve to show how much the cultured people of the West were saturated with the juridical spirit.[62]

In his theologizing Tertullian was moved by practical motives. He had no interest in theological or philosophical knowledge for its own sake. His thinking moved in paradoxes. No one of the Church Fathers was so extreme in emphasizing the Church's positivism. "To know nothing of the things that may be in conflict with the Rule of Faith," he exclaimed, "is to know everything" (*adversus regulam* [i.e., *fidei*] *nihil scire omina scire est*).[63] Faith is consent in a state of absolute obedience. The more unreasonable the articles of faith are,

---

[58] Jerome relates that no day passed in which Cyprian did not say to his servant, *Da mihi magistrum* ("Hand me the teacher"); *Catalogue of Illustrious Men,* 53.

[59] Cf. Loofs, *op. cit.,* pp. 152 ff.

[60] *Prescription against Heretics,* 32; 36.

[61] Eusebius, *Church History,* II, 2.

[62] Cf. Seeberg, *Lehrbuch* (1920), p. 435.

[63] *Prescription Against Heretics,* 14.

the more opportunity there is for faith to develop its strength. The more impossible the object of faith is, the more certain it is.[64] On the basis of such an expression Tertullian has been epitomized in the sentence: *Credo quia absurdum est* ("I believe because it is absurd"). This expression was not of his own creation. On the other hand, Tertullian, who built everything upon authority and paradox faith, declared in his apologetic writings that the proof of the truth of Christianity lies in its reasonableness, and he proceeded to use rational-psychological methods in offering his proof. This shows the dualism of faith and knowledge which was present in medieval scholasticism and which has always been a problem in Protestant theology.

Tertullian belonged to the North African School, which was opposed to the speculations of Origen and Clement. The North Africans stressed the apostolicity of the Church's teaching as expressed in the Rule of Faith and in holiness of life. Both Tertullian and his successor Cyprian were leaders in these matters. The practical aspect of Tertullian's religion, evident in his writings, later led him to join the Montanists. Tertullian looked upon philosophy as a guide leading to error. In order to prove the truth of Christianity he did not marshal the heathen philosophers as did the Greek Apologists. Rather, he invoked the untutored, unsophisticated soul to give its witness to the existence of God. The untutored soul's unpremeditated expressions, such as "Which may God grant" and "If God will," spring out of the depth of the heart and are the best attestation to the truth.[65] In his eyes the philosophers, above all Plato, were "caterers to all heresies." [66] He referred to the serenity of Socrates in the presence of death as a forced and affected composure.[67] He exclaimed: "What indeed has Athens to do with Jerusalem? What concord is there between the Academy and the Church? What between heretics and Christians? Our instruction comes from the 'porch of Solomon'. . . . Away with all attempts to produce a mottled Christianity of Stoic, Platonic, and dialectic composition!" [68]

[64] *Prorsus credibile est quia ineptum est . . . certum est quia impossibile est;* On the Flesh of Christ, 5.
[65] *On the Soul,* 2.
[66] *Ibid.,* 23.
[67] *Ibid.,* 1.
[68] *Prescription against Heretics,* 7; cf. *Apology,* 46.

Tertullian was not independent of philosophical thought. The influence of Stoicism, in particular, is quite apparent in some of his theological conceptions. According to his view, all that exists is corporeal, even God and the soul. Much of his theology rests upon the principle that there is nothing spiritual without corporeity. *Omne quod est, corpus est sui generis.*[69] *Quis negabit Deum corpus esse, etsi Deus spiritus est?*[70] *Corpus est anima.*[71] It can easily be seen why a theologian devoted to this principle should have been a teacher of traducianism.[72] Tertullian's position tended to be fundamentally opposed to the Alexandrians as well as to the Gnostics. Realism was his fundamental principle. The reality of nature and the visible world, the reliability of the senses, the significance of the corporeity and the substantiality of the spirit—these things constituted the basis of his thoughts. With a keen sense he detected the divine in the creation, the divine reason shining through the orders of creation. He delighted in the study of nature, to trace the Creator and the inscriptions of truth in the cosmos, and to analyze the soul for the purpose of discovering in it the witnesses to God's existence. This realism was the basis of Tertullian's theology, his weapon in the struggle with Gnosticism, and a one-sided spiritualism. It was from this starting-point that he argued for the substantiality of God, for the unity of the race and its history, for the origin of sin in the soul of man, for the historicity of revelation, for the truth of the divine-human person of Christ, and for the facts of redemption and the resurrection of the body. In arguing for the existence of God he placed great stress upon the cosmological and physico-teleological proofs.[73]

As a systematic theologian, Tertullian did not succeed in presenting a unified theology on the basis of one great leading thought, as did Irenaeus. He was in essential agreement with Irenaeus in emphasizing the significance of the incarnation, in adopting the Old Testament as well as the New as a source of truth, and in recognizing the rule of faith. Irenaeus' entire theology was organized around the christo-

[69] *On the Flesh of Christ,* 11: "Everything that exists is a bodily existence."

[70] *Against Praxeas,* 7: "Will he who denies that God is a body also deny that he is Spirit?"

[71] *On the Soul,* 5: "The soul is corporeal."

[72] *Ibid.,* 27.

[73] *Against Hermogenes,* 35; *Against Praxeas,* 7; cf. *On the Soul,* 11.

centric principle, while in Tertullian's theology certain things have the appearance of being added elements. It was more in the isolated discussion of individual topics that Tertullian showed his creative force.

Tertullian's "economic conception of the Trinity" [74] is of interest, and we shall deal with it fully in a separate chapter (IX). Nevertheless, the thought in which we are interested at this point is one in which Tertullian moved on ground occupied by Irenaeus. Like Irenaeus, Tertullian taught that there is a Trinity for the purpose of revelation only. After all has been accomplished, the distinction between the persons will cease. [75] This reminds us of Irenaeus' recapitulation theory. But Tertullian differed from Irenaeus in going back to the thoughts expressed by the Greek Apologists: The disposition of God, in which He unfolds Himself, is for the purpose of bringing the world into existence. The existence of the Son as a separate person in the Trinity became necessary because of the creation of the world. With Tertullian, as with the Apologists, this conditioned a subordination of the Son to the Father.

Tertullian as the Founder of Occidental Theology

The terms which Tertullian employed were soon found to be helpful when the dogmas of the Trinity and Christology were crystallized into their final form.

It was Tertullian who first used the word "Trinity" and introduced the terms *substantia* and *persona* to describe the interrelation of the three persons in the Trinity. [76] With Origen, and later Athanasius, he was a pioneer in paving the way for the Church's conceptions of the Trinity, even though he did not succeed in avoiding subordinationism.

It was Tertullian who, in struggling with the Docetism of Marcion and the Gnostics, coined terms to describe the two natures of Christ and their relation to each other. These terms sound like an anticipation of the formulas employed in the Chalcedonian and Athanasian Creeds: Each nature contains its own attributes; there is no confusion,

[74] Cf. Paul's use of the term *oikonomia* (Eph. 1:10, 3:2, 9; Col. 1:25; I Tim. 1:14).

[75] *Against Praxeas*, 4; with reference to I Cor. 15:24-25.

[76] *Ibid.*, 2 ff.; *Apology*, 21.

but a conjunction of the human and the divine.[77] Against Docetism he emphasized that Christ was really man, possessed of a rational human soul and spirit. Christ's suffering was in the "human substance" of his person. Because of the union of the human and the divine, Tertullian spoke of the "sufferings of God," and said that God was "truly crucified." [78] Tertullian, then, had the same significance for the Christology of the West that Origen had for the East.

On sin and grace (in connection with repentance and baptism) Tertullian was the pioneer theologian along lines which became more or less normative for the Western Church (largely through Cyprian). The reference is not to his theory of traducianism, which was not really adopted by the Western Church, but to his doctrine of original sin.[79] In this he was generally followed by the Fathers of Augustine's time. The reason for his emphasis on the freedom of the will, which seems out of harmony with his teaching on original sin, is to be found in his conflict with Gnosticism and Manichaeism. In stressing the freedom of the will he taught that even after the fall man was able to choose between the opposites of good and evil.[80] This teaching led him to views concerning the way of salvation which were in entire accord with the teachings of the later Roman Catholic Church. It is true that he completely recognized the importance of Christ's death, making it the foundation of man's salvation.[81] He even knew of grace as a creative principle which changes man's heart, but his description of grace did not fit into the system which was developed by Augustine. Tertullian viewed the entire religious and moral life of the Christian from the angle of obligation. He chose expressions which pictured man as God's debtor, and which spoke of meriting, and of rendering satisfaction. Christ is pre-eminently the bringer and interpreter of the new law, the *nova lex*.[82] The relation between God and man is that of two private persons in which the one has offended the other and therefore owes a satisfaction such as was required by the Roman law. Tertullian wrote: "You have offended Him, but there is

[77] *Ibid.*, 27 ff.
[78] *On the Flesh of Christ*, 5.
[79] *On the Soul*, 39.
[80] *Ibid.*, 21; *Against Marcion*, II, 5 ff.
[81] *On the Veiling of Virgins*, 16.
[82] *Against the Jews*, 3, 6-7; *On Monogamy*, 8; 14; *On Prayer*, 11, 22; *On Repentance*, 3.

a way of reconciliation. You have one to whom you can render satisfaction and who will be glad to accept it." [83]

Guilt and punishment are removed by baptism, but man earns his salvation in baptism by repentance. Baptism imparts the power of sanctifying grace. The sanctifying power is attached to the water. Through it the Holy Spirit is obtained, whom Tertullian, true to his realism, conceived to be something material. Satisfaction is to be rendered for sins after baptism. This is done by repentance, which consists of a deep sorrow; of confession, in which the sinner humbles himself; and of sighing, weeping, and fasting. Thus man atones for his transgression, offers satisfaction to God, and earns forgiveness for himself. By such punishment man liberates himself from the eternal punishments.[84] The most valuable satisfaction a man may offer to God is martyrdom.

Not only are the divine commandments to be observed with scrupulous care; the "evangelical counsels" must also be carried out. Tertullian praised abstinence from marriage.[85]

Tertullian taught that men are justified through faith. By faith he meant not only acknowledgement of Christ as Savior, but also fulfillment of the divine commandments. Tertullian was a remarkable forerunner of Roman Catholic theology. In fact, Nygren is right when he passes the judgment on Tertullian that his "outlook united Old Testament nomism and Roman moralism and jurisprudence. The result is a theology of merit whose influence on the later history of Christianity was calamitous. . . . In Tertullian, Nomos has taken form as nowhere in the history of Christianity." [86] The irrational element in God's Agape was highly offensive to him.[87]

We shall dispense with a special treatment of Cyprian here, because we have discussed in extenso his leading interest and significance in another connection (Chapter VII). It should be admitted, as Kurtz remarks, that "in originality, profundity, force, and fullness of thought, as well as in speculative and dialectic gifts, the practical-minded bishop stands far below the somewhat eccentric presbyter." [88]

[83] On Repentance, 7.
[84] Ibid., 9.
[85] See the treatise To His Wife.
[86] Nygren, op. cit., pp. 347-48.
[87] Ibid., pp. 344-45.
[88] Kurtz, op. cit., Par. 31, 11.

IV. Augustine and the Ecumenical Catholic Age

The Ecumenical Catholic Age was the time between the first and the last of the ecumenical councils (325-787). During this time the following took place: (1) settlement of the trinitarian, christological, and soteriological problems; (2) completion of the episcopal-hierarchical organization; and (3) maturing of the Western and Eastern types of Catholicism. For fuller discussion of these characteristics, see also Chapter XIII.

The schools and teachers of this period were:

The Antiochean School, represented by Theodore of Mopsuestia (d. 429); Theodoret (d. 457); Ephraem, the Syrian (d. 387); John Chrysostom (d. 407); and Nestorius (banished in 432).

The Neo-Alexandrian School: Athanasius (d. ̄373); the Great Cappadocians: Basil of Caesarea (d. 379); Gregory Nazianzus (d. 390); Gregory of Nyssa (d. 394); Cyril of Alexandria (d. 444); Eutyches (deposed in 448).

The Occidental School: Ambrose (d. 397); Jerome (d. 420); Augustine (d. 430); Leo the Great (d. 461).

The Fathers mentioned were the leading theologians in the trinitarian and christological controversies. Theodore of Mopsuestia and Nestorius, Athanasius, and the three great Cappadocians, together with Cyril of Alexandria and Leo the Great, contributed negatively or positively to the formulas expressed in the Creeds of Nicea and Chalcedon.

Augustine in Special Phases of His Development

At the source of the remarkable doctrinal development which has controlled Christian belief in the Trinity and Christology stands a man who had a far greater and lasting influence than all his predecessors. This man, Aurelius Augustine, in addition to his intense interest in the doctrine of the Trinity, became the leading genius in a temporary solution of the anthropological and soteriological problems, raising questions which constituted the central interest of the Reformation in the sixteenth century. Augustine, Bishop at Hippo Rhegius, is so significant that this chapter on the oustanding theologians of the Ecumenical Catholic period must offer a connected description of Augustine in special phases of his development.

This review cannot cover all of the features of the theological interest of this religious genius. To complete the picture, see also the discussion of Augustine's conception of the Trinity at the close of Chapter IX; especially Chapter XI, which reviews his conflict with Pelagianism; and the discussion of his expression on the sacraments in Chapter XII.

Augustine's Significance

Tertullian and Cyprian were the first to give positive direction and distinctive characteristics to Western theology, but it was the influence of Augustine's writings which determined decisively the special character of Occidental (Roman) theology. His influence upon Western theology is comparable to that of Origen upon the theology of the East, but far greater. Indeed, Augustine was the father of Occidental Christianity. Many features of Roman Catholicism must be traced back to ideas, principles, and suggestions in his theology. In the Donatist controversy, he gave the formula of Cyprian the meaning *unitas ecclesiae* which Protestantism cannot accept. In his later years Augustine defended the principle of coercion and persecution of heretics and schismatics by false exegesis of the text, "Compel them to come in." [89] There is hardly a dogma of the Roman Catholic church that does not bear the marks of Augustine's influence. The best in the theology of Scholasticism was stimulated by his thoughts. Even in method the Scholastics learned from Augustine. The mysticism of the Middle Ages, in its conservative as well as in its radical forms, functioned under influences from Augustine. The dogma of the Trinity was completed by Augustine for the West with all the specific features that contributed to the later schism between East and West. Augustine's theology along this line was accepted by the Reformation. Furthermore, his doctrine of sin and grace, with its determined aim at emphasizing the *sola gratia*, in which he was not in entire harmony with the fundamentals of Rome, made him a teacher not only of the Reformers of the sixteenth century, but also of their conservative followers in succeeding generations.

It is possible to make too much of the moral defects in the life of Augustine before his conversion. His *Confessions*, written in 397, are the true mirror of a saint's sincerity. Concerning his relation first with

---

[80] *Epistles,* 173, 10.

one woman in Carthage for fifteen years, and shortly before his conversion in Milan with another (in both cases with faithfulness to the woman), it must be remembered that outside of the Church such relations were without ethical reproach among the pagans of that day. Augustine was still not a Christian. The relationship was a monogamous concubinage which was distinguishable from a legitimate marriage, first, in that the wife was not of equal position; second, in that the relationship could be dissolved; and third, in that the "natural" children of such a union were not legitimate heirs to the property left by the father. Augustine visited with his "wife" and child in Thagaste, and was received by his mother Monica. Later, Augustine condemned this relationship in the strongest terms, as we would expect of a sincere Christian. In the severity of his repentance he was prompted by his growing appreciation of the monastic life, which to the Church Fathers in that day was the bridge from the impurity of heathenism to the ethical standards of Christianity. Even before his conversion, Augustine's character was not so questionable as some historians have painted it.

In his search for truth, salvation, and satisfaction, Augustine became a Manichaean for nine years (373-384). Christianity had not appealed to his speculative mind. Rather, he was attracted by the speculative dualism of Manichaeism, which stressed the conflict between light and darkness, and redemption through liberation of the elements of light from the embrace of darkness. The Manichaean process of redemption involved ascetic abstinence from all that was connected with darkness, and a continence which corresponded to the degree of saintliness attained as one passed from the ranks of the auditors to those of the elect. Augustine always remained in the class of the former. About the year 382, he began to turn away from the fantastic cosmological systems of the Manichaeans. Ultimately he separated himself from them in a series of writings that mark an important stage in his inner development.[90]

It was at this time that Augustine came under the influence of Neo-Platonism. In place of God and evil as dualistically conceived among the Manichaeans, he learned to think of God as the eternal real substance and of evil as voluntarily turning away from the good which

---

[90] See the anti-Manichaean writings in *NPNF*, Vol. IV, Part I.

alone is being. This attitude of mind, and his renunciation of everything that could not claim to have divine authority or reality, he later called his "conversion." In 386 he came under the influence of Bishop Ambrose of Milan. In a well-known occurrence in a garden of Milan, while he was in a most receptive frame of mind, his attention was called to Rom. 13:13-14. This was the moment of his life when God first enabled him to turn his will against the powers of sensuality which had been depriving him of the spiritual freedom for which he was longing. His new and intense interest in Neo-Platonism gave a highly philosophical character to his thought and meditation at this time.[91] It was on philosophical subjects that he wrote in the country near Milan, where he had retired with his son Adeodatus and friends to prepare for baptism.

Augustine, while preparing himself for Christian baptism, tells of impressions from reading the Psalms.[92] He knew the contents of the baptismal formula in the form of the Apostles' Creed, and all through his life the liturgy and hymns of the Christian services in the Church at Milan resounded in his soul.[93] In addition, Augustine recognized the authority of the Church in the great messages of Ambrose which were based on the generally accepted Rule of Faith. Therefore, his deep interest in the problems of a philosophy which seemed to have so much in common with Christianity should not be used to minimize the specifically Christian ideas in the heart of this candidate for Christian baptism. Seeberg, concerned with harmonizing the purely philosophical and the genuinely Christian elements in Augustine at this period, comments: "The authority of the Church has furnished Augustine the soul-contents of his faith, but philosophy gave him the form." [94] Augustine took the position that authority must precede the operation of reason: *Crede ut intelligas* ("Believe that you may know"). Knowledge is necessary for the perfecting of faith.[95] The results of this first stage under the special influence of Neo-Platonism

[91] Neo-Platonism, Nygren remarks, is a school which Augustine did not leave. As a matter of fact, "all his life he remained a Neo-Platonic Christian or, if you will, a Christian Platonist," *op. cit.,* p. 458.

[92] *Confessions,* IX, 4, 8.

[93] *Ibid.,* IX, 6, 14.

[94] *Lehrbuch,* II (1923), 409.

[95] *On the Morals of the Catholic Church,* I, 47. *On the Profit of Believing,* 13, 29. *Epistles,* 89; 120, 8. *Sermons,* 43, 4; 118, i. *De Magistro,* II, 37.

are seen in his writings.[96] Augustine recognizes the historical Christ, but it is the Teacher with his example who attracts Augustine's attention. There is not yet the evangelical appreciation of his death and resurrection.[97]

In 391 Augustine became presbyter of the church in Hippo Rhegius, and in 395 he became bishop. This relation to the Church as teacher and leader offered impulses for his development as a churchman. He felt keenly his lack of maturity in doctrinal matters. This feeling drove him to a diligent study of the Scriptures, an interest which soon began to color his language. From now on he spoke less of reason and almost exclusively of faith, following the authority of the Church. Tracing the development in some detail, we call attention to the following points: (1) To the Neo-Platonic conception of God as an absolute Being distinguished from the conditioned multiplicity and variableness of the world,[98] Augustine now adds an emphasis upon God as the world's personal Creator and Governor.[99] (2) Influenced by Neo-Platonism, Augustine devoted a great deal of thought to the construction of an analysis and definition of evil which distinguished between reasoning and non-reasoning creatures.[100] Later he came to regard sin as the voluntary yielding of man to the temptations from the devil.[101] It is the will of man that governs all faculties of the soul, puts them into motion, and forces them to operate.[102] Faith, in the last analysis, is an act of the will.[103] (3) Extricating himself more and more from Neo-Platonism, Augustine moved away from the aesthetic enjoyment of God to find enjoyment in living a life of obedience. This was in line with his estimation of the will as the governing faculty of the mind. (4) The Augustinian teaching of redemption has always been a matter of great interest. Two great scholars, O. S. Scheel and J. G. Gottschick, and have written searching studies on this subject and have

[96] Cf. *On the True Religion.*

[97] Cf. O. Scheel, *Die Anshauung Augustins von Christi Person und Werk,* pp. 59 ff.

[98] *City of God,* XI, 10, 1.

[99] *Ibid.,* XII, 25; V, 9, 4. It also appears in his thoughts on the Trinity. See Loofs' article in *PRE,* II, 270-71, and his *Leitfaden,* pp. 365 ff.

[100] For a lucid description, refer to the article in *PRE* just cited.

[101] "On the Freedom of the Will," *NPNF,* V, 443 ff.

[102] *On the Trinity,* X, 11, 17.

[103] *On the Spirit and the Letter,* 57.

arrived at opposing conclusions.[104] Scheel sees in the Augustinian theory of redemption the influence of Christ upon the sinner. He says that Augustine's peculiar philosophical conception of Christ's divinity had kept him from an ethical-soteriological estimate of the death of Christ. Gottschick, on the other hand, starting from Augustine's strong emphasis on the forgiveness of sins, undertakes to show that Augustine meant redemption as a reconciliation of God in the sense of Anselm: placating or satisfying God.[105] It will have to be admitted that when Augustine spoke of Christ's death as a satisfaction offered to God,[106] he did not mean satisfaction in the Anselmic sense. Augustine shared the prevalent view of his day and regarded Christ's death as the price paid for man's release from the rightful claims of the devil.

It will not be possible to reduce all of Augustine's statements on the subject of redemption to a consistent theory. The following points are most prominent: Augustine's piety never lost the deep sense of guilt.[107] This conviction of guilt led him to a grateful appreciation of the remission of sins in baptism. In this state of mind he placed a high estimate on the cross of Christ. While stressing the significance of Christ as our King, Augustine never tired of praising him as the Savior of sinners.[108]

Augustine's View on the Church

Augustine's part in the Donatistic controversy became the occasion for developing further the popular ideas about the Church which we have traced historically in Chapter VII.

The Donatists were opposed to the election of Archdeacon Caecilian as bishop in Carthage because he was the candidate of the party favoring readmission into the Church of those who had lapsed during the Diocletian persecution. The party of a stricter discipline elected

[104] Otto Scheel, *op. cit.* Johannes Gottschick, "Augustins Anschauung von den Erlöserwirkungen Christi," *Zeitschrift für Theologie und Kirche* (1901), pp. 97-213, with reply by Scheel, "Zu Augustins Anschauung von der Erlösung durch Christus," *Studien und Kritiken* (1904), pp. 401-433, 491-554.

[105] Cf. Seeberg, *Lehrbuch*, II, 428.

[106] *Sermons,* 152, 11.

[107] Cf. Loofs, *Leitfaden,* pp. 396-97, which refers to Gottschick and to many places in Augustine's writings.

[108] Cf. Seeberg, *op. cit.,* II, 425, with many references. The continuation of these thoughts must be followed in our study of the conflict between Augustine and Pelagius in Chapter XI.

Majorinus, and it was under his successor Donatus (d. 355) that the whole conflict became an issue for the Church. The Church dealt with the difficulty at the Synod of Arles, 314. The Donatists took the position that the Church must be a communion of real saints. The bishops, like the Apostles, must be holy men. An element of the old pneumatics was reviving itself in the Donatists. The Novatians had demanded the holiness of the members, and the Montanists had established themselves on the principle that the Church, as the communion of saints, must not defile itself with the readmission of the excommunicated who had fallen into grave sins. In similar fashion, the Donatists insisted that the Church, as the bride of Christ, must be holy. For this reason the Church must not have bishops who betrayed the truth in times of persecution. A Church of such bishops loses the validity of the sacraments—of ordination and even of baptism, which must be repeated. Not all of the Donatists were so radical; Tyconius, for example, was an exception.

After 370, Optatus of Mileve wrote on *The Schism of the Donatists* from the standpoint of the Catholic Church. It was chiefly Augustine, after he had become bishop, who used his whole influence to reconcile the contending parties, which were of about equal strength. The conflict, which was confined to the African church, covers the period between 393 and 420.

The Catholics acknowledged the orthodoxy of the Donatists, and at the Synod of Arles (314), they also recognized the Donatist sacraments. The Catholics established the position that the validity of the sacraments does not depend upon the moral condition of the one who administers them.[109] Augustine, however, would not admit that the Donatists were a real representation of the Church. He called them a quasi-church because they were occupying a sectarian position and building a partisan wall which was not resting upon the cornerstone. To Augustine the Donatists were outside of catholicity.[110] Augustine admitted the validity of the Donatist sacraments, although he did so against the general tradition of the North African church. Thus, Donatists who returned to the Church did not have to be rebaptized. Nevertheless, Augustine insisted strenuously that outside of the Catho-

---

[109] *Against the Letters of Petilian,* III, 68.
[110] Here Augustine accepted the position taken by Optatus in *The Schism of the Donatists,* III, 7, 10.

lic Church the sacrament of baptism is "of no avail for the forgiveness of sins." [111] The Donatists' charge of "unholiness" against the Catholic Church, because of a few bishops at the time of the Diocletian persecution had not been faithful, was a matter of indifference to Augustine in this controversy.[112] Absolute holiness of the Church cannot be expected in this life. The passages of Scripture referring to such holiness speak of the future and the state of perfection.[113]

Augustine's conception of the Church combined several considerations. First, he strongly emphasized the duty to recognize the Church Catholic; it is a visible appearance. This Church alone, possessing the Faith of the Apostles, the sacraments, and the ministry, is in a condition to expand over the entire world and to save and to sanctify its members. Outside of this Catholic Church, which is the body of Christ, there is no truth, no salvation.[114] Separation from the Church is sacrilege.[115]

Second, from the Church as an outward organization, Augustine distinguishes the Church as a communion of the saints (*communio sanctorum, congregatio sanctorum, societas credentium, Christiana societas, bonorum societas*). In this "invisible union" we have those who love God and one another, and who pray for the Church.[116] He distinguishes between those who are outwardly in the Church and those who really belong to it.[117]

Third, Augustine distinguishes between the predestinated and non-predestinated. Only the man who is predestinated can maintain himself as a true member of the Church through the gift of perseverance.[118] Among these there may be some who do not even belong to the Catholic Church.

Augustine's views on the Church are incomplete without adding a

[111] *On Baptism,* I, 12-18; V, 8-9; VI, 5-7.
[112] Augustine, *Breviculus Collationis cum Donatistis,* III, 19 ff.
[113] *Ibid.,* III, 9; Optatus, *op. cit.,* II, 20.
[114] *Epistles,* 141, 5.
[115] It is interesting, however, that Augustine, though he acknowledges the primacy of the apostolic chair (*ibid.,* 43, 7) and sees in it a "representation of the unity of the church," knows nothing of a special authority invested in Peter or his successors.
[116] See references in Seeberg, *op. cit.,* II, 465 ff.
[117] *On Baptism,* I, 26; III, 26; IV, 4; VII, 100. *Against the Letters of Petilian,* II, 247. *On the Unity of the Church,* 74.
[118] *On Rebuke and Grace,* 9, 22; *On the Gift of Perseverance,* 2.

brief review of the ideas expressed in his great work, *The City of God*, which covered thirteen years of intensive thought (413-426).

As a first philosophy of history, this work of twenty-two books has often been compared with Hegel's *Philosophy of History*. It is erected upon the conception of two states, the people of God and the people of this world, differing fundamentally in their principles, but continually touching each other. These two states are described as having their prototypes in the separation of the evil angels from the good. The historical development appears in the descendants of Cain and Abel, continuing in the contrast between the followers of Christ and those of Anti-Christ: *civitas Dei, et civitas terrena huius mundi* ("the city, or state, of God and the city of this world").[119]

The occasion for this work was the charge of the pagans that Christianity had brought about the fall of Rome through the barbarians in the year 410. Augustine wanted to show that the cause of this fall was the deterioration of righteousness in Rome. Thus he secured the foundation for describing the genius of the state as contrasted with that of the true Church of Christ.

In Augustine's thought, the city of the world, as the counterpart of the city of God, is equivalent to the political state. Although rooted in the fall, the state is willed by God to maintain order, welfare, and peace.[120] Augustine was decidedly conservative along these lines. To hold property, in his eyes, was not wrong.[121] Even wars, though evil in themselves, might be "waged by the good," for the protection of the life and liberty of people in distress.[122] Unfortunately, the earthly kingdoms are nothing but "great robberies" (*magnae latrociniae*).[123]

Augustine recognizes the necessity of the state, but because of man's sinfulness, and because the state is erected upon the foundation of pride, love of self, and the flesh, the ideal of righteousness cannot be realized.[124]

In comparison with the city of the world, the city of God is the family of the redeemed. While its members are not of the world,

[119] *The City of God*, XV, 1 ff.
[120] *Ibid.*, II, 32, 2; IV, 33; V, 1 ff.; XIX, 17, *passim*.
[121] *Commentary on John*, 6:25-26.
[122] *City of God*, I, 21; *Epistles*, 138, 13.
[123] *City of God*, IV, 4.
[124] *Ibid.*, XIV, 28.

they are living in the world. For this reason they "make no scruple to obey the laws of the earthly city, whereby the things necessary for the maintenance of this mortal life are administered." [125] If the state is to prosper, it will observe the precepts of the Christian religion, and happy are we, Augustine says, for Rome now has a Christian emperor. If the emperor is wise, he will make his power the handmaid of God's majesty, "for the greatest possible extension of His worship." [126] Supported by the power of the Christian state, the Church may put into practice the word of its Lord "to compel man to come in to the feast of everlasting salvation." [127] For Augustine the Church as the kingdom in space and time is the fulfillment of the millennial hope of Revelation 20! Christ now rules through those men by whom the Church is ruled, that is, the bishops! [128]

Augustine gave a theological justification to the state-church arrangement of Constantine and his successors. An element of realized eschatology may be seen in Augustine's view of Church and state. The contradiction in this concept is very evident, though. On the one hand, the Church as the kingdom of God in space and time is a spiritual entity in which Christ rules through the saints; on the other, it is the number of the baptized governed by the bishops. Because of his glorified view of the empirical Church, Augustine remained unaware of the disparity of these ideas. Consequently, in the Middle Ages both the Roman hierarchy and the critics who regarded the papacy as the very incarnation of the Anti-Christ could appeal to Augustine.

BIBLIOGRAPHY

1. Irenaeus

IRENAEUS. *Adversus Haereses.* Edited by W. W. HARVEY. 2 vol., 1857; also *ANF*, Vol. I.
_____. *Epideixis.* See *Texte und Untersuchungen*, Vol. XXXI, Pt. 1, 1907; also *Patrologia Orientalis*, Vol. XII, 1919.

BONWETSCH, N. *Die abendlandische Theologie um 200 nach Christo.* Part I: *Irenaeus.* 1925.
BOUSSET, W. *Kyrios Christos, Geschichte des Christusglaubens von den Anfängen des Christentums bis Irenaeus.* 2nd ed., 1926.

[125] *Ibid,* XIV, 17.
[126] *Ibid.,* XXVI, 24.
[127] *Epistles,* 173, 10; cf. 93; 185. *Commentary on John, s.v.* John 11:14.
[128] *City of God,* XX, 9.

Dufourcq, A. *Saint Irèné*. 1926.

Harnack, Adolph von. *Geschichte der altchristlichen Literatur*. 1891.

Hitchock, F. R. M. *Irenaeus of Lugdunum, a Study of His Teaching*. Cambridge: Cambridge University Press, 1914.

Kunze, J. *Die Gotteslehre des Irenaeus*. 1891.

Lawson, John. *The Biblical Theology of Saint Irenaeus*. London: Epworth Press 1948.

Robinson, J. A. *St. Irenaeus and the Apostolic Preaching*. London: Macmillan Co., 1920.

Werner, J. *Der Paulinismus des Irenaeus*. 1889.

Wingren, G. *Man and the Incarnation*. Translated by Ross McKenzie. Philadelphia: Muhlenberg Press, 1959.

Zahn, T. *Forschungen zur Geschichte des neutestamentlichen Kanons*. 1891.

2. *Clement*
Clement. *Works*. Edited by J. Potter. 2 vols. Oxford, 1715. Reproduced in *MSG*, VIII-IX.

ANF, Vol. II.

Bigg, C. *The Christian Platonists of Alexandria*. Oxford: Clarendon Press, 1913.

Hort, F. J. A. *Six Lectures on the Ante-Nicene Fathers*. London: Macmillan Co., 1896.

Merk, C. *Clemens Alexandrinus, in seiner Abhängigkeit von der griechischen Philosophie*. 1897.

Patrick, I. *Clement of Alexandria*. Edinburgh and London: Blackwood and Sons, 1914.

Scherer, W. *Clemens Alexandrinus, und seine Erkenntnissprinzipien*. 1907.

Tollington, R. B. *Clement of Alexandria, A Study of Christian Liberalism*. London: Williams and Norgate, 1914.

3. *Origen*
Origen. *Works*. *MSG*, Vols. 11-17.

_____. *Against Celsus* and *De Principiis*. English translation in *ANF*, Vol. IV. Compare also *LCC*, Vol. II.

Bigg, C. *The Christian Platonists in Alexandria*. Oxford: Clarendon Press, 1913.

Butterworth, G. W. *Origen on First Principles*. London: SPCK, 1936.

Faye, E. de. *Origène, sa Vie, son Oeuvre, sa Pensée*. 3 vols. 1923—.

Hanson, R. P. C. *Allegory and Event*. Richmond: John Knox Press, 1959.

Klein, C. *Die Freiheitslehre des Origenes*. 1894.

Koch, H. *Pronoia und Paideusis, Studien über Origenes und sein Verhältnis zum Platonismus*. 1932.

Nygren, Anders. *Agape and Eros*. Philadelphia: Westminster Press, 1953.

Voelker, W. *Das Vollkommenheits Ideal des Origenes*. 1931.

ZOELLIG, A. *Die Inspirationslehre des Origenes.* 1902.

4. *Tertullian*

TERTULLIAN. *Works in CSEL,* Vols. I-II. 1954. English translation in *ANF,* Vols. III-IV, and *LCC,* Vol. V.

BRANDT, T. *Tertullian's Ethik.* 1928.

ESSER, G. *Die Seelenlehre Tertullians.* 1893.

EVANS, E. *Tertullian's Treatise against Praxeas.* London: SPCK, 1948.

HAUCK, A. *Tertullians Leben und Schriften.* 1887.

HOLL, K. "Tertullian als Schriftsteller," *Preussische Jahrbücher,* 1897. Compare also *Gesammelte Aufsätze zur Kirchengeschichte,* Vol. III, 1928.

LORTZ, J. *Tertullian als Apologet.* 2 vols. 1927—.

NYGREN, ANDERS. *Agape and Eros.* Philadelphia: Westminster Press, 1953.

ROBERTS, R. E. *The Theology of Tertullian.* London: Epworth Press, 1924.

STIER, J. *Die Gottes—und Logoslehre Tertullians.* 1899.

WIRTH, K. H. *Der Verdienstbegriff bei Tertullian.* 1892.

5. *Augustine*

AUGUSTINE. *Works. MSL,* Vols. 32 ff.; also, *CSEL,* Vols. 23 ff.

————. *Selected Works.* English translation, *NPNF,* First Series, 8 vols. Also *LCC,* Vols. 6-8.

BECKER, H. *Augustin, Studien zu seiner geistigen Entwicklung.* 1908.

————. *Augustin, ein Lebens and Characterbild auf Grund seiner Briefe.* 1910.

BINDEMANN, C. *Der heilige Augustinus.* 3 parts. 1844-1869.

BOEHRINGER, F. *Aurelius Augustinus; Bischof von Hippo.* 1878.

BOURKE, U. J. C. *Life and Labours of St. Augustine.* London: Simpkin, Marshall, Hamilton, Kent and Co., 1880.

BUSCH, R. W. *St. Augustine, His Life and Times.* London: Religious Tract Society, 1883.

COLLETTE, H. C. *St. Augustine, His Life and His Writings as Affecting His Controversy with Rome.* London: W .H. Allen, 1883.

A Companion to the Study of St. Augustine. Edited by ROY W. BATTENHOUSE. New York: Oxford University Press, 1955.

CUNNINGHAM, W. *Augustine and His Place in the History of Christian Thought.* London: C. J. Clay and Sons, 1886.

DOERRIES, H. "Fünfzehn Jahre Augustin-Forschung," *Theologische Rundschau.* 1929 Heft 3.

HOLL, K. *Augustins innere Entwicklung.* 1923.

HOERREGARD, M. I. *Augustins Bekehrung.* 1923.

HUDSON, J. *St. Augustine, Bishop of Hippo.* London: Macmillan Co., 1899.

McCABE, J. *St. Augustine and His Age.* London and New York: G. P. Putnam's Sons, 1907.

MONTGOMERY, W. *Saint Augustine, Aspects of His Life and Thought*. London and New York: Hodder and Stoughton, 1914.

NYGREN, ANDERS. *Agape and Eros*. Philadelphia: Westminster Press, 1953.

POSIDUS. *Vita Augustini*.

THIMME, W. *Augustins geistige Entwicklung in den ersten Jahren nach seiner Bekehrung*. 1908.

TROELTSCH, E. *Augustin, die kirchliche Antike und das Mittelalter*. 1916.

WEINAND, H. *Die Gottesidee: der Grundzug der Weltanschauung des heiligen Augustinus*. 1910.

6. *Augustine's View of the Church*
AUGUSTINE. *Against the Donatists*. PNF, Vol. IV.

————. *Against the Letter of Parmenian*. PNF, Vol. IV.

————. *Against the Letters of Petilian*. PNF, Vol. IV.

————. *Breviculus collationes cum Donatistis*.

————. *On Baptism*. PNF, Vol. IV.

————. *On the Correction of the Donatists*. (Letter 185). PNF, Vol. IV.

————. *On the Schism of the Donatists*. MSL, Vol. 11. Also CSEL, Vol. 26.

FREND, W. H. C. *The Donatist Church: a movement of protest in Roman North Africa*. Oxford: Clarendon Press, 1952.

CHAPTER IX

THE DOCTRINE OF THE TRINITY

The term "Trinity" does not appear in the Scriptures. This does not mean that the doctrine expressed by that term is not scriptural or Christian. The fact is that the trinitarian conception of God is the underlying and governing thought of the biblical history of redemption. In addition, the trinitarian faith expresses a doctrinal experience of the Church, the necessity of which has been tested by the practical needs of piety through many centuries. The problem presented itself unconsciously in the baptismal formula of earliest Christianity. It was soon felt as a burning problem in all parts of the Church. The interest was not just metaphysical, it was religious. At times—for example, in the Apologists and in Origen—the philosophical interest blended with the religious. But Athanasius was not a philosopher; he was a churchman. Even Augustine, a real philosopher and a dialectician, in discussing the trinitarian "relations," was prompted not by speculative but by religious interest.[1] The problem of the Trinity was a matter of practical interest to the Church as the congregation of believers. It began with the overwhelming conviction, confirmed by Scripture, that the presence of Christ in the Church is like that of God the Father himself. The early Christians prayed to Christ as they prayed to God. Naturally they thought about the relation of Christ to the One God. The trinitarian formula for baptism, in Matt. 28-19, included the Holy Spirit. If in that age of intense monotheism Christ had not been deeply experienced as the reality of God himself, the trinitarian formula would have died a natural death, as did other purely philosophical doctrines. The problem persisted and grew in intensity toward the close of the ancient period of the Church. John of Damascus and Augustine undertook to say a final word for the

[1] Cf. Augustine, *On the Trinity.*

143

East and the West respectively on this matter. The problem was settled only temporarily. The Trinity is a mystery and as such it is open to discussion in all ages of the Church. It will never do to dismiss the historic significance of the work of the ancient Church on the trinitarian problem by treating it as useless speculation of the Greek mind. The Latin mind, which functioned as the regulative factor in this process, was intensely practical and frequently counterbalanced the speculation of the Greeks. However, the statements of John of Damascus are not beyond criticism.

I. First Stages in the Trinitarian Development

The early writers of the primitive Christian Church were not given to doctrinal speculations about the baptismal formula. They used the trinitarian formula; but this formula did not provoke them to a discussion of the relation among the Three. Concerning Christ's relation to the Father, the early writers regarded Christ as the Son of God and ascribed to him those attributes which can be predicated of God alone. With Father and Son, the Holy Spirit is mentioned in many cases.[2] Baur and Harnack maintained that the first Christians, particularly Hermas, held Ebionitic or adoptionistic views. Even so independent an investigator as Loofs, who dedicated his work to Harnack, admits that this position is not convincing.[3] It must be admitted that the language of the Post-Apostolic Fathers was frequently binitarian. The Spirit was taken as the Spirit of Christ, as in II Cor. 3:17. This did not mean an actual identification of the Spirit with the Son. It was simply an abbreviation in expression. There was the natural difficulty of speaking of the Holy Spirit in hypostatic terms.

The early Apologists, in their aim at creating a Christian theology, discussed the relationship between Father and Son. About 180, Theophilus wrote concerning the Godhead: "In like manner also the three days, which were before the luminaries, are types of the Triad (*trias*) of God and His Word and His Wisdom."[4] Although the meaning of this passage is rather vague, Seeberg assures us that "the

[2] We refer especially to H. B. Swete, *The Holy Spirit in the Ancient Church* (London: Macmillan Co., 1912), pp. 11 ff.

[3] *Leitfaden*, p. 182, n. 4.

[4] *To Autolycus*, 11, 15.

Trinity is certainly an article of the common faith. . . . Although the Apologists find little occasion to speak of this mystery, the apprehension of it constitutes for them the profoundest problem and supreme desire of their hearts." [5] Seeberg quotes from Athenagoras, who characterizes the Apologists as being "carried away with this desire only, to see God and the Logos with Him. What is the unity of the Son with the Father? What the fellowship of the Father with the Son? What the Spirit? What the union and difference of those who are thus united—the Spirit, the Son, the Father?" [6]

In discussing the relation of the Son to the Father, the Apologists introduced the term "Logos" from John's Gospel. This was attended, however, with the danger of identifying John's Logos with that of Philo. The Apologists did not altogether escape this danger, as is evidenced by the fact that they failed to recognize a personal differentiation of the Logos from the Father before the creation of the world. This led them to subordinate the Son to the Father. They did not yet think in terms of a co-equality between Father and Son. Adopting Philo's distinction of *logos endiathetos* (immanent *logos*) and *logos prophorikos* (uttered *logos*), they for the most part regarded the hypostasizing as conditioned by the cosmic drama of creation and revelation. The *Logos* was the Father's agent in creating and ordering the world and in revealing truth to men.[7]

Irenaeus, in his conflict with Gnosticism, taught without speculation and simply on the basis of the Rule of Faith that Son and Spirit participate in the divine substance.

Tertullian defined God as Father, Son, and Holy Spirit, and to express his thought he used the word *trinitas*. He championed hypostasianism against the monarchianism of Praxeas. The following citations illustrate his thought:

Everywhere I hold one substance in three cohering.[8]

All are of one, by unity of substance; while the mystery of the dispensation is still guarded, which distributes the Unity into a Trinity, placing in their order the three, the Father, the Son, and the Holy Spirit; three however . . . not in substance but in form, not in power but in

[5] *Textbook,* I, p. 114.
[6] Athenagoras, *Petition,* 12.
[7] Cf. Justin, *Apology,* I, 59; 64, 5; II, 6, 3.
[8] *Against Praxeas,* 12.

appearance; for they are of one substance and one essence and one power, inasmuch as He is one God from Whom these degrees and forms and aspects are reckoned under the name of the Father and of the Son and of the Holy Spirit.[9]

To make his meaning clearer he drew analogies from nature: Father, Son, and Holy Ghost are to each other as the root, shrub, and tree; and as the fountain, stream, and river.[10] This language shows that subordinationism was still in the mind of Tertullian. The Father is the whole substance, while the Son is only a derivation who participates in the divine substance to a lesser degree than the Father. As with the Greek Apologists, the hypostasizing of the Son as the Logos did not take place until the time of creation.

The immediate problem which the Church had to solve was stated in two questions: (1) How could the Church escape from subordinationism, i.e. from viewing Christ as a kind of "second God" (*heteros theos*)? (2) How could the Trinity of special persons (hypostasianism) be maintained without sacrificing Christian monotheism? Thus far subordinationism had been the safeguard of monotheism.

It was the many-sided genius of Origen that helped to solve the problem. Like Tertullian, Origen was strongly opposed to Monarchianism with its emphasis on monotheism to the exclusion of hypostasianism and tri-personality. Abandoning the view of the Apologists and of Tertullian that the Logos was a person only from the time of creation, Origen declared that the Logos was a person from all eternity. "His generation is as eternal and everlasting as the brilliancy produced by the sun." [11] He also states that: "The Father did not beget the Son and set Him free after He was begotten, but He is always begetting Him." [12] This suggestion of an eternal generation was a needed contribution. Unconsciously it was a step in the direction of the co-eternity and co-equality of the Son with the Father, as expressed in the Church's doctrine of the Trinity. Origen arrived at the same terminology as Irenaeus: Origen by philosophical speculation; Irenaeus by following the Scriptures and the Apostolic Tradition.

[9] *Ibid.*, 2.
[10] *Ibid.*, 8.
[11] *De Principiis*, I, 2, 4.
[12] *Commentary on Jeremiah*, IX, 4. Cf. *De Principiis*, I, 2, 4.

II. The Elimination of Monarchianism

The word "Monarchian" was first used by Tertullian[13] to designate those defending the monarchy or sole government of God. The aim of Monarchianism was to be commended. Monarchianism sought to save the Unity of God (that is, monotheism) by rejecting hypostasianism and tritheism. "Monarchianism," says Seeberg, "made an effort to reconcile monotheism, the most precious treasure of Christianity, as contrasted with the heathen world, with the divinity of Christ without resorting to the expedience of the 'second God.' In this consists its historical significance."[14] The Monarchians were also opposed to a philosophical Christianity and Logos Christology.

There were two types of Monarchians—the dynamistic and the modalistic. The first type is called adoptionistic by Harnack, humanitarian by Fisher. The dynamistic Monarchians regarded the divinity in Christ as a mere power of influence (*dynamis*). Their starting point was the human person of Jesus who was eventually deified. The second type, on the other hand, thought of Christ as a mode or manifestation of God the Father. Both rejected the Logos-Christology as being Gnostic: the first in the interest of the historic or synoptic Christ; the second in the interest of the monarchy and divinity of Christ. Thomasius calls these two types Ebionitism and Docetism in a higher form. He also points out their differences:

> The one maintains the personality of the historic Christ and sacrifices His essential divinity; the other maintains His essential unity with the Father and sacrifices the personal differentiation. The one starts from below with the historic-human person of Christ and degrades Him to a mere man; the other begins with the celestial Christ who has complete divinity dwelling within Him and so endangers His true humanity.[15]

Both types of Monarchianism seem to have originated in Asia Minor. Since Rome was the great centripetal force in those days, these views were soon in evidence there. For a time it seemed as if a modified form of Modalism would prevail in Rome. In Carthage, Tertullian fought the battle against the Modalism of Praxeas.

[13] *Against Praxeas*, 3.
[14] *Textbook*, I, 163.
[15] G. Thomasius, *Die Christliche Dogmengeschichte*, I, 168-69. Cf. J. C. Ayer, *Source Book of Ancient Church History* (New York: Charles Scribner's Sons, 1948), pp. 221 ff.

Dynamistic Monarchianism

Although a historic connection with Ebionitism cannot be proved, Dynamism resembled the Ebionite conception which contended that Christ was a mere man who was chosen, inspired, and exalted by God. The emphasis was placed upon the excellence of His character. He was the Son of God solely by adoption.

Before referring to the chief representative of this group, two others should be mentioned: (1) The Alogoi, who centered their interest in the human, synoptic Christ, born of the Virgin, divinely adopted when the Spirit descended upon him at baptism, and exalted at the resurrection; and (2) the Theodotians and the Artemonites, who held similar views.

Paul of Samosata, Metropolitan of Antioch in Syria, was the most conspicuous of the dynamistic Monarchians. He has been described as unspiritual, worldly, imperious, vain, pompous, insidious, sophistic, covetous, and even immoral.[16] Briefly summarized, his teaching was as follows: God must be thought of as one person. It is permissible to speak of a Logos or Son, and a Wisdom or Spirit in God; but these are nothing more than attributes of God. God has been projecting this divine reason or Logos from all eternity. It is merely an impersonal influence (*dynamis*). Jesus, who was born of the Virgin, was a man (*katōthen*) upon whom God exercised his Logos-influence. The indwelling of this divine wisdom from above (*anōthen*) made the man Jesus the Son of God. A parallel to this is seen in the indwelling of wisdom in the prophets, except that this indwelling occurred in a unique way in Christ as the temple of God. Jesus exhibits merely a moral union between God and man. "Through immovable steadfastness in this relationship He united Himself intimately with God by the influence of the spirit and unity of will, thus securing the power to perform miracles and fitness to become the Redeemer, and in addition attaining a permanent oneness with God." [17]

In spreading his views, Paul of Samosata went so far as to remove the hymns of praise addressed to Christ as Lord. This was especially offensive to sensitive Christians. The condemnation of Paul's doctrine was not secured until three synods had been held between 264 and

[16] Eusebius, *Church History*, VII, 27 ff.; Epiphanius, *Panarion*, 65.
[17] Harnack, *History of Dogma*, III, 34 ff.

269. The first two were without result because he knew how to conceal the heterodox character of his views. It was only at the third synod that the presbyter Malchion, a practiced dialectician and formerly a rhetorician, succeeded in unmasking him at a public disputation. The word *homoousios* was here rejected because Paul had used it to designate God and the Logos as one person.

Paul of Samosata exemplified Dynamism at its height and the rejection of his doctrine marked a turning-point in the history of Christology in the Church. Harnack observes: "With the deposition of Paul of Samosata, it was no longer possible to gain a hearing for a Christology which denied the personal, independent pre-existence of the Redeemer." [18]

Modalistic Monarchianism

Dynamistic Monarchianism was a tendency in only a few of the Church's leaders. The very opposite was true of Modalism, which affected the vast body of the Church's membership. Modalism appealed very strongly to the ordinary believer who saw in it a veritable safeguard of monotheism. Tertullian saw the situation in its true proportions, when he wrote:

> The simple, indeed (I will not call them unwise and unlearned), who always constitute the majority of believers, are startled at the dispensation (of the Three in One), on the very ground that their very Rule of Faith withdraws them from the world's plurality of gods to the one only true God; not understanding that, although He is the one only God, He must yet be believed in with His own economy. The numerical order and distribution of the Trinity, they assume to be a division of the Unity.[19]

It turned out that Modalism became very widespread and influential in the West. It was not Adoptionism, but rather the doctrine that God *in toto* was incarnate in Jesus, that was the dangerous opponent of the Logos-Christology between A.D. 180 and A.D. 300.

The chief interest of Modalism was to maintain Christian monotheism without sacrificing the divinity of Christ. The Modalist sought to solve the problem by identifying Christ with the Father and by regarding him as one of the successive forms in which the Father manifested himself. This led, on the one hand, to Patripassianism.

[18] *Grundriss, p.* 48.
[19] *Against Praxeas,* 3.

149

which taught that it was really the Father who suffered and died; and on the other hand, to Docetism, although in a higher form than the docetism of the Gnostics.

One of the first representatives of the modalistic Monarchians was Noetus of Smyrna. These statements by him characterize Modalism:

> When the Father had not yet been born, He was rightly called the Father; but when it had pleased Him to submit to birth, having been born, He became the Son, He of Himself and not of another.[20]
>
> Christ is Himself the Father, and . . . the Father Himself was born, He suffered and died.[21]
>
> For Christ was God and suffered for us, being the Father Himself, in order that He might be able also to save us.[22]

About 190, Praxeas, an adherent of Noetus, came to Rome, bringing with him the doctrines of his teacher. While Praxeas agreed in the main with Noetus, he made more of a distinction between the Father and the Son: "The Son indeed suffers, but the Father suffers with Him."[23] Praxeas represented a certain blending of the modalist with the dynamistic type of Monarchianism. Praxeas' teaching even recruited followers in Carthage, which caused Tertullian to write his great work *Against Praxeas* (*Adversus Praxeam*).

The most significant of all the Modalists, however, was Sabellius.[24] In 215, he taught his doctrines in Rome. He differed from Noetus and Praxeas in that he gave the Holy Spirit a place with the Father and the Son.[25]

His system may be outlined as follows: God is a Unity (*Monas*). There are no distinctions in the divine Being, but God the divine Unity reveals himself successively in three different modes or forms (*onomata, prosōpa*). In the Father, God reveals himself as creator; in the Son, as redeemer; and in the Spirit, as sanctifier. These are not three hypostases; they are rather three roles or parts played by the one person. In other words, all three are one and the same person. The thought may be illustrated by a figure from the stage. One *per-*

---

[20] Hippolytus, *Refutations*, IX, 10.

[21] Hippolytus, *Against Noetus*, 1.

[22] *Ibid.*, 2.

[23] Tertullian, *Against Praxeas*, 29.

[24] As sources we mention: Hippolytus, *Refutations*, IX, 11-12. Epiphanius, *Panarion*, 62; cf. 69, 7. Athanasius, *Orations Against the Arians*, III, 4, 36; also IV (probably not by Athanasius) 2, 3, 9, 13, 17, 25.

[25] Epiphanius, *op. cit.*, 32, 1.

sona dramatis will impersonate three different characters or roles before the audience, and yet there is in reality only one person. To use a Sabellian analogy: Man has three names, body, soul, and spirit; but there is only one person. The one sun possesses light, heat, and roundness; but there is only one sun. So God has three names: Father, Son, and Holy Spirit; but there is only one person. The Father, Son, and Holy Spirit are identical, and it was this supposed identity which lay at the bottom of the entire system. The God of Sabellianism was therefore a Unity, a monad, a single Person viewed under three different forms. After the *prosōpon* of the Father accomplished its work in the giving of the law, it fell back into its original condition. Advancing again through the incarnation as Son, it returned by the ascension into the absolute being of the Monad. It revealed itself finally as the Holy Spirit, to return again, after securing the perfect sanctification of the Church, into the Monad that knows no distinctions, there to abide through all eternity. Sabellius characterized this process as an expansion and contraction.

Although Sabellius was ultimately excommunicated and his teaching rejected, nevertheless he unconsciously prepared the way for the *homoousios* in the orthodox Christology of a later time. While his absolute identification of the three persons in the Trinity was a positive error, he hinted at a more positive truth, namely the co-essence, co-equality, and co-eternity of the three persons.

The modified Monarchianism of the Roman bishops from Victor to Callixtus should also be noted. The situation in Rome was both confusing and detrimental to the Church. On the one hand was Hippolytus, the champion of hypostasianism and subordination; on the other hand, Sabellius, advocate of modalistic Monarchianism. Bishop Callixtus regarded it as his task to discover some formula of compromise by which Hippolytus and Sabellius might be excluded and the strife ended. To this end he taught that the Father, Son, and Holy Spirit are the names of the one indivisible Spirit and that they are one and the same thing. The divinity of Christ is identical with the Father; yet the flesh of Jesus should be called the Son, since it is inhabited by the God-Spirit who deified the man Jesus.[26] Hippolytus correctly called this doctrine a combination of the teaching of Sabellius and

---

[26] Hippolytus, *Refutations*, IX, 6.

and Theodotus.[27] It should be observed that Callixtus really labored to avoid Patripassianism by teaching that the Father did not suffer except in and with the Son. Kurtz remarks fittingly: "Decidedly Monarchian as this formula of compromise undoubtedly is, it seems to have afforded the bridge upon which official Roman theology crossed over to *homoousian* hypostasianism." [28] While his deification of the man Jesus seems to smack of Dynamism, Callixtus created a kind of Godlike hypostasis for the Son which proved helpful in subsequent Nicene theology.

III. FURTHER STRUGGLE FOR CLARIFICATION OF VIEWS

Of the two types of Monarchianism, Modalism achieved the greater success. But even Modalism gave way gradually to the Logos-doctrine. In the Orient it bowed to the form represented by Origen; in the West, to that of Tertullian. The old problem was still before the Church: How was subordinationism to be overcome? It will be remembered that Origen had suggested the idea of the eternal generation of the Son from the Father, and the Church's teachers had not lost sight of his thought. It is interesting to note how the various views were clarified in the struggle for the elimination of Monarchianism.

Novatian

Novatian was the learned presbyter who, after Cornelius had been elected Bishop of Rome (251), headed the revolt in favor of applying the strictest discipline to the lapse. His treatise, *On the Trinity*, written sometime between 240 and 250, shows how completely Tertullian's views replaced the modified Modalism which had reigned in Rome from Victor to Callixtus. The writing is as decided against the Monarchians as it is in favor of the Trinity. Novatian declared that the Son was "always in the Father, else the Father would not always be the Father." [29] He was extremely careful to avoid the charge of ditheism as made by the Monarchians. The best way to do this, he thought, was to admit that the Son had a beginning, and that in a

[27] *Ibid.,* IX, 23.
[28] Kurtz, *op. cit.,* Par. 33, 5.
[29] *On the Trinity,* 31.

certain sense the Father precedes the Son. The Father alone is eternal and unborn, while the Son is a personal derivation from him. Thus subordinationism was still present. Novatian is interesting to us because (1) he based himself squarely on hypostasianism, and (2) in his system the Holy Spirit appeared as the third person of the Trinity.

The Controversy Between the Two Bishops Dionysius

Bishop Dionysius of Alexandria was a pupil of Origen and, like his teacher, was the head of the Alexandrian catechetical school for some time. He adhered to the Logos-doctrine and believed in the personal differentiation of the Son from the Father. The errors of subordination, which usually attended hypostasianism, did not trouble him greatly.

As a hypostasianist, Dionysius rejected the modalistic doctrine of Sabellius, which had gained many recruits in Libyan Pentapolis. In writing against Sabellius his zeal carried him too far in the opposite direction, and Dionysius was charged with declaring that "the Son of God is a creature . . . in essence alien from the Father, just as the husbandman is from the vine, or the shipbuilder from the boat; for that, being a creature, He was not before He came to be." [30] Athanasius admits that, although the charge was correct, yet it was based on but a fragment of Dionysius' teaching which could not properly be construed as the foundation of a true judgment. This teaching gave offense to intelligent Christians in Alexandria in whose consciousness the eternal existence or generation of the Son was firmly lodged. They accordingly brought complaint against their bishop before Dionysius of Rome (ca. 260).

In his reply, the Roman Dionysius did not condemn the erring colleague, but he did oppose any attempt to destroy the monarchy of the divine Being. The Son and the Spirit must be held in close connection with the Father. "It must needs be that with the God of the universe the Divine Word is united, and the Holy Ghost must repose and habitate in God." [31] The divided Trinity is to be brought together and summed up in one God, the almighty ruler of all things. The Son is not to be regarded as a creature. It must not be taught that

[30] Athanasius, Defense of Dionysius, 4. NPNF, IV, 177.
[31] Cf. the fragments preserved by Athanasius in "Defense of the Nicene Definition," NPNF, IV, 165 ff.

He had a temporal beginning. The Church must defend the *homoousios* and believe simply in "God the Father Almighty, and in Jesus Christ His Son, and in the Holy Ghost."

In a voluminous work designed to clear himself of heresy, the Alexandrian Dionysius replied that he had not been entirely understood. He agreed with his opponents, he declared, and had no intention of denying *homoousios*, although the expression is not biblical. In stating his own views of the Trinity, he said: "We expand the monad undivided into the Trinity, and again combine the Trinity undiminished into the monad." [32] Such an explanation was apparently satisfactory, and the controversy was not revived. The agreement between the two parties was an auspicious omen. All parts of the Church were gradually coming together on the subject.

IV. ARIANISM VERSUS ATHANASIANISM

The two men who fought the great battle over Arianism were both from the church at Alexandria. They were the archdeacon Athanasius, who earned the title "Father of Orthodoxy," and his opponent, the presbyter Arius. The systems they taught were diametrically opposed to each other, and their fundamental ideas could not be compromised. The Church was obliged to decide between them.

The Genesis of Arianism

It is interesting to note the relation of Arius to certain teachers of the past. On the one hand, he was vastly indebted to Paul of Samosata, with whom his teacher, Lucian of Antioch, had acquainted him. Says Harnack: "This school (Antioch) is the nursery of the Arian doctrine and Lucian, its head, is the Arius before Arius." [33] Like Paul of Samosata, Arius was opposed to modalistic monarchianism and strongly in favor of hypostasianism of the subordinationist type. Athanasius was correct in accusing the Arians of teaching the Samosatene doctrine without having the courage to admit it. On the other hand, Arius drew some of his ideas from certain uncautious remarks of Origen; as for instance, the latter's reply to Celsus, in which he

---

[32] Athanasius, "On the Opinion of Dionysius," *ibid.*, pp. 182-83.
[33] *History of Dogma*, IV, 3.

said that the Logos is "intermediate between the nature of the un-created and that of all created things." [34]

Arius labored with a twofold purpose in view. Together with the Church he wished to preserve the Logos-Christ as an independent being. With the Monarchians he desired to save the monotheistic principle of Christianity. In combining these two interests he was compelled to emphasize subordinationism to such an extent that the eyes of the Church were opened wide to a fact that had long remained concealed, namely that the idea of a decided subordination of the Son to the Father constituted a danger to the full conception of the divinity of Christ. Arianism was only subordinationism heretically developed.

Arius was evidently a skillful practical psychologist. In spreading his doctrines he wisely put them in verses (*thaleia*) which the people might sing at their work and so be indoctrinated the more easily.

In this endeavor to explain Christ, Arius introduced a mythological figure—a *tertium quid*, half-God and half-man—something like the Demiurge of the Gnostics. This Christ was not a mere man. He was a demigod: divine, but not co-equal with the Father. This had been taught by the subordinationists of the past, such as the Apologists, and in a way even by Tertullian. Arius argued that there is a real differ-ence in essence between the Father and the Son. The Father alone is a real divine Being, while the Son is only a creature (*ktisma*). The idea of co-eternity was rejected. "There was a time when the Son was not." [35] To the Son belong all the predicates that belong to the creature. After Arius had established the difference in essence (*ousia*) between the Father and the Son, he proceeded to point out the differ-ences between the Son and other creatures, and to explain the Son's mission in the world. The Son was created before time and space in order that he might mediate in the creation of the world and that he might also reveal God to the world. For this purpose he was endowed in advance with a special divine glory — a glory which he deserved in view of the virtuous life he was going to lead. The Son, to Arius, was not God, but divine.

Arius, with Paul of Samosata, taught that it was the man Jesus who became divine. Arius held that the Son or Logos was a finite

---

[34] *Against Celsus,* III, 34.
[35] Arius, *Thalia.* See the context of this statement in Ayer, *op. cit.,* pp. 302-304.

being who was made divine because God foresaw his future ethical achievements. Behind this teaching was an abstract conception of God, according to which God is an absolute monadic unity without differentiation in himself, and hence unable to create the world without the mediation of the highest created Being. Thus, a mythological element was introduced into Christianity and the Christian faith was transformed into the worship of a demigod.

The First Ecumenical Council

Alexander, Bishop of Alexandria, was irrevocably opposed to the views of Arius, and at a large synod held in 321 at Alexandria he had Arius deposed and excommunicated. However, Arius was not without sympathizers. Many, like the influential Eusebius of Nicomedia, openly favored him. Others, like Eusebius of Caesarea, were for tolerating Arius, although they did not agree with him. Emperor Constantine, who had heard of the situation, was disposed to treat the matter as an inconsequential church quarrel in which nothing essential was involved. His trusted advisor, Bishop Hosius of Cordova, was of a different mind. It is likely that it was Hosius who persuaded the emperor of the seriousness of the controversy. Constantine called the first General Council of the Church in 325 at Nicea. In attendance were about three hundred bishops and many others of lower rank. Alexander, prepared for a verbal battle, attended along with his archdeacon, Athanasius, who was to become the mighty champion and bulwark of orthodoxy in the Arian controversy.

Three parties were represented: (1) The Homoousians, weak in numbers, but strong in their conviction, led by Alexander and Athanasius; (2) the Arians, headed by Eusebius of Nicomedia; and (3) a large group embracing those who did not understand the situation and whose main interest was peace—Eusebius of Caesarea belonged to this group.

Alexander upheld firmly the eternal generation of the Son (Origen). The birth of the Savior from the Father is without beginning. To deny this would be to deny the eternity of the Father's light. The Sonship of Christ, being eternal, is therefore different in kind from that of human beings. The Son is truly a necessary part of the Father's being.

Eusebius of Nicomedia presented an Arian creed which was promptly voted down. Then Eusebius of Caesarea offered his creed in which Christ was called the "Logos of God." This creed would have satisfied the Arians, and indeed most of the assembled bishops, but Athanasius and Alexander could not subscribe to it. Hosius of Cordova suggested that the word *homoousios* be used in speaking of Christ. This term was finally agreed upon. It was out of the Creed of Caesarea that the new confession of faith was formed. The characteristic phrases of the new creed were these: "Out of the essence of the Father, generated, not made, of like essence with the Father." To the whole creed was appended the following damnatory clause: "But the holy and apostolic church anathematizes those who say that there was a time when He was not, and that He was made from things not existing, or from another person or being, saying that the Son of God is mutable or changeable." [36]

Athanasius and His Theology

Athanasius (d. 373) was not a man of great originality in opening up new springs of religion as was Augustine. He saw the practical essentials in religion and theology and organized the fundamental interest of the Church about the religion of redemption. He brushed aside the purely philosophical interests of the followers of Origen and established the Church upon Christ as the Redeemer. It was from this specifically religious position that he secured the rejection of Arianism at the Council of Nicea.

In addition to this theological position, the decisive factor in the victory of homoousianism was the unfaltering determination of Athanasius during a long life of persecution and oppression. The life of Athanasius reads like a page from fiction. He was exiled five times, and yet he proved victorious in the end. At Nicea his eloquence was so convincing that the small minority of the Homoousians prevailed over the large and influential majority of Arians and Semi-Arians. He was equally strong in the literary conflict that followed the action of Nicea.

The leading thoughts of Athanasius: Arianism leads to practical polytheism. If Christ is not co-eternal and of one essence with the

[36] For documents relating to the controversy, see *NPNF,* XIV, 3 ff., and *LCC,* III, 329 ff.

Father and at the same time not just a man, as was admitted by Arius, then he is a middle being or demigod, comparable to the Demiurge of the Gnostics. This would result in the worship of a creature. Why should there be any need for such a middle being? Is God the Creator too proud to come into direct contact with his creatures? Furthermore, if it was impossible for him to create the world without a middle being then it was also impossible for Him to create the Son without a middle being.[37] This was directed not only against Arius, but also against the Logos-speculations of the Apologists. The Logos-doctrine in the old philosophical form began to disappear and the word Logos, which was contained in the Symbol of Eusebius, was omitted from the Nicene Creed.

The full divinity of Christ must be admitted. Athanasius insisted that if Christ is in any sense divine, as Arus taught, then he belongs to the unseparated and undivided monad of the Deity. The Son existed personally from all eternity. The three hypostases, however, are not to be separated from one another. "The relation between the Father and Son is like that between a fountain and a stream that gushes from it. Just as a river springing from a fountain is not separated from it, although there are two forms and two names, so neither is the Son from the Father, nor the Father from the Son." [38] Thus the co-eternity and the co-equality of the Son with the Father must follow. Such a Son is different in origin and nature from created beings. He is "other-natured" (*heteroousios*) with regard to created beings, but is "same-natured" (*homoousios*) with the Father. This is the co-essence of the Son with the Father. If then the Son, who is "same-natured" with the Father, differs from the Father in person, then the Son cannot have been created; He must have been generated. If the Father has always been the Father—which is obviously necessary since there can be no change in the Godhead—then the Son must have been generated from all eternity. In other words, the Son must have been eternally the Son.[39]

It was upon these thoughts that Athanasius based his insistence upon the full divinity of Christ and upon a real Trinity expressive of a

[37] *Against the Arians*, II, 25, 29-30.
[38] *Exposition of the Faith*, 2; *Against the Arians*, III, 4.
[39] *Against the Arians*, I, 14; cf. III, 66; I, 27.

carefully guarded monotheism. Only thus could he base prayer to Christ, the administration of baptism, and above all, the redemptive character of the Christian religion with the forgiveness of sin and the hope of resurrection.

Athanasius saw in the Scriptures and in the Rule of Faith the authority for the teaching of the Nicene faith. Against the objection of the Arians that the terms of the Nicene Creed are not in the Scriptures, he replied that they do express the substance of Scripture teaching.[40] He interpreted the Bible in the light of its teaching on Christ and on redemption. He even appealed to Christian experience on this subject. He saw an expression of all these essentials in the apostolic teaching of the Church.[41]

The Temporary Defeat of Homoousianism

Although the Nicene victory seemed complete, it was nevertheless far from permanent. The majority of those who voted for the homoousian creed had but a meager conception of its real meaning. Consequently the sixty years which followed the Nicene Council were not peaceful. Athanasius had been appointed Bishop of Alexandria in 328. and for a time all went well. But in 335 at the Synod of Tyre, Eusebius of Nicomedia preferred charges against him with the emperor, and Athanasius was deposed, Time and time again the bishop was forced into exile and then permitted to return. When Athanasius died in 373, it seemed that the great things for which he had fought had been completely defeated. These sixty years were dark ones for Homoousianism, and it appeared that Arianism would gain the ultimate victory.

The Final Victory of Homoousianism

From the very beginning Arianism had within it the seeds of defeat. The statement of faith, which had been formulated at Nicea in the "Old Nicene Creed," had been opposed by two parties. The first was the small group of Arians. The other, however, was a large group, more conservative in principle. This conservative group regarded the word *homoousios* as an echo of Sabellianism. It preferred to use the

[40] *De Decretis* ("Defense of the Nicene Definition"), 21; cf. 18.
[41] *Against the Arians,* I, 48; II, 34; III, 28, *passim.*

word *homoiousios*.[42] The two parties were agreed in two things: (1) in their aversion to the word *homoousios*, and (2) in their hostility to each other. This state of affairs in the ranks of the opposition worked out well for the cause of Athanasius. The Arians gradually became more radical, while the Homoiousians became more conservative. The result was that under Emperor Valens, an outspoken Arian, the Homoousians and the Homoiousians were driven together and gradually constituted an alliance for Athanasianism.[43]

In addition to the effect produced by the fusion of the Homoousians and the Homoiousians, still another factor directed the Church's attention to the truth of Athanasianism. This factor was the powerful influence of the three great Cappadocians in the East—Basil of Caesarea, Gregory of Nazianzus, and Gregory of Nyssa[44]—and of Ambrose in the West. Seeberg remarks:

> The modification which has been made in the ancient Nicene doctrine is very evident. Athanasius (and Marcellus) taught that there is the one God, leading a threefold personal life, who reveals Himself as such. The Cappadocians thought of three divine hypostases which, as they manifest the same dignity, are recognized as possessing one nature and the same dignity.[45]

Athanasius started with the one divine nature (*ousia*, or *hypostasis*) indicating the threefold personal life. The Cappadocians began with the three divine hypostases (or *prosōpa*) and they labored to bring these under the one divine *ousia*. Each hypostasis has its peculiarity, property (*idiotes*), or attribute. The Father is unbegotten, the Son generated, the Spirit proceeding. All have the same divinity, energy, and power, the same divine substance and nature, and therefore the same dignity and glory. The mystery for Athanasius lay in the Trinity; for the Cappadocians, in the Unity.

> It was with labor and difficulty that the latter guarded themselves against polytheism. But it was only in this way that the Nicene doctrines were, for the Orientals, freed from the taint of Sabellianism, and that the personality of the Logos appeared to be sufficiently assured. The Cappa-

---

[42] *Homoiousios* should not be translated "similar" in comparison with *homoousios* meaning "equal." In using the term *homoiousios*, the conservative group wanted to safeguard the real hypostasis of the Son against the tendency of Modalism.

[43] For details of this period see Seeberg, *Lehrbuch*, II, 87 ff.

[44] For a selection of their writings see *NPNF*, Vols. V, VIII and *LCC*, Vol. III.

[45] Seeberg, *Textbook*, I, p. 232.

docians interpreted the doctrine of Athanasius in accordance with the conceptions and underlying principles of the Logos-Christology of Origen. They paid a high price for their achievement, the magnitude of which they did not realize—the idea of the personal God. Three personalities and an abstract, impersonal essence resulted. In this form the *ousia* and *physis* are a heavy weight upon the doctrine concerning God, for they are in conflict with the personality of God. It was a partial corrective of this that they after all—inconsistently—identified the Deity with the Father, which was again a relic of the earlier Subordinationism. . . . Thus, in place of the conception of the one-natured, threefold God, had come the doctrine of the like-natured, triune God.[46]

Clarification of Views on the Holy Spirit

Arius and his followers, in connection with their conception of the Son as the highest of all creatures, regarded the Holy Spirit as the first creature brought forth through the Son. The Nicene Creed of 325 said simply: "We believe in the Holy Spirit." The Spirit was recognized because of the trinitarian expression in the early baptismal creed (Matt. 28:19) and the early doxologies and hymns which glorified the Spirit with the Father and the Son.[47]

Gregory of Nazianzus relates that there was a great diversity of opinion among the theologians concerning the Spirit, who was variously regarded as an energy or influence, a creature, or an angelic being. Some deemed it best not to make any definite statements concerning the Spirit.

Athanasius, in a later period of his life, helped to solve this problem. He had become convinced that, if we are to hold to the baptismal formula, the Spirit cannot be a creature. If the Spirit is a creature, something of a different nature is introduced into the Godhead and we have a diad instead of a trinity. The Spirit, like the Son, must be *homoousios* (co-essential, consubstantial, same-natured). He undertook to prove this on the basis of the Spirit's work of sanctification. Athanasius wrote on this subject in four letters to Bishop Serapion. Bishop Macedonius of Constantinople opposed this position and declared that the Holy Spirit is a creature subordinate to the Son. The Synod at Alexandria (362), presided over by Athanasius, estab-

---

[46] *Ibid.*, pp. 232-33. Here Seeberg reviews the religious motive underlying this theology in a most interesting way. The reference is to expressions such as those from Basil, *Letters*, 38, 3-4; 52, 2 and Gregory of Nazianzus, *Orations*, 31, 1; 28, 31.
[47] Cf. Swete, *op. cit.*, pp. 231 ff.

lished the *homoousia* of the Holy Spirit and declared Him to be a
person like the Father and the Son. The disciples of Macedonius were
styled Pneumatomachians and later were called Macedonians. The
leading theologians, such as the three Cappadocians and Didymus the
Blind, followed in the footsteps of Athanasius. The baptismal formula,
taken directly from the Scriptures, was the decisive factor. Cyril of
Jerusalem had taught the divinity of the Spirit as a person.[48] The
Cappadocians aided with detailed argumentation.[49]

After the death of Athanasius (373) the expressions on the Holy
Spirit, as we have them in the present form of the Nicene Creed, were
sanctioned at the so-called Second Ecumenical Council at Constantinople (381). At a synod held in Rome (380), the Occident decided against
all expressions of doubt with regard to the deity of the Spirit. The
Spirit was understood to be a hypostasis, like the Father and the Son.
The Spirit's work was interpreted as the completion and application
of Christ's redemptive work. As to the difference between the Son
and the Spirit it was stated that the Son is generated and sent forth,
while the Spirit proceeds.[50]

Voices from the West

The Latin theologians stood on the side of Athanasius. The modified monarchianism of the Roman bishops from Victor to Callixtus
shows that Western theology recognized the element of truth contained in Modalism. Latin theologians emphasized the unity in the
Godhead. With this unity they combined the Alexandrian distinction
between the persons of the Godhead without resorting to a Logos-
speculation that would militate against the co-eternity and the co-
equality of the Son.

Hilary (d. 367), in *On the Trinity*, defended with biblical terms
the independency of the persons and the unity of their being. In
On the Councils he aided the union between East and West by
admitting the *homoiousios* with the *homoousios*. Hilary pointed to
the distinction between the persons by referring to John 5:25: the
Father gives; the Son receives. As to person, the Son is different

---

[48] Cf. Cyril of Jerusalem, *Catechism*, 17, 5; 13, 33-34.
[49] Basil the Great, *On the Holy Spirit*, 29, 72; cf. Gregory of Nazianzus, *Orations*, 31.
[50] For a detailed discussion, see Swete *loc. cit.*

from the Father. The Father begets the Son, while the Son is begotten by the Father. Hilary, like Origen, referred to the generation as an eternal act. Because of generation the nature common to the two spells the unity of being.[51]

Ambrose (d. 397) followed the Cappadocians. He thought of three persons being one in one substance, divinity, will, and operation.[52]

The development of the dogma of the Trinity has now been traced up to the time when the present Nicene Creed replaced the original form of 325.

As it was the imperial power which had bestowed victory upon the Nicene Faith and then upon Arianism, so now it was the imperial influence which acted decisively in favor of the Neo-Nicene faith. In 380 Emperor Theodosius issued an edict establishing the new orthodoxy. In 381 he convened the Second Ecumenical Council in Constantinople at which the Nicene Creed was confirmed and adopted and Arianism suppressed.

As has already been indicated, the original creed, adopted at Nicea in 325, is not identical with that which we use today. Nor was the present form of the Nicene Creed, the so-called Niceno-Constantinopolitan Creed, created at the Council of Constantinople in 381. That this old view is erroneous has been fully demonstrated by the investigations of Caspari, Hort, Harnack, Kattenbusch, and others. According to Hort and Harnack, what has been called the Niceno-Constantinopolitan Creed is a modification of the baptismal formula which was used in Jerusalem. Into this formula were incorporated the most significant phrases of the Nicene Creed, together with an additional statement regarding the Holy Spirit. How this came to be regarded as the creed made at Constantinople cannot be explained with certainty. All we know is that from about 500 this form came to be used in place of the original Nicene Creed. The Niceno-Constantinopolitan form does not have the highly significant words "out of the essence of the Father." The damnatory clauses are also omitted. The *filioque* is a later addition.

---

[51] See the writings of Hilary, "On the Trinity" and "On the Councils," in *NPNF*, Vol. IX. Cf. A. Beck, *Die Trinitatslehre des heiligen Hilarius* (1903).

[52] See Ambrose, "Exposition of the Christian Faith," in *NPNF*, X, 201 ff.

V. THE COMPLETED DOCTRINE IN THE ATHANASIAN CREED

The doctrine of the Trinity was practically completed by the Council of Constantinople (381). There were two later theologians, however, who gave the final expression to this doctrine as it was held in the East and the West respectively. John of Damascus (d. *ca.* 754) represented the Eastern Church; Augustine (d. 430), the Western.

John of Damascus was not a productive genius like Augustine. His significance lay in that he summarized the dogma of the Trinity as it was held in the East. In the third part of his standard work, *De fide orthodoxa,* he presented God as one substance and three hypostases—Father, Son and Spirit.[53] The three hypostases, however, are not related to each other after the manner of three men. "They are one in all respects . . . except those of non-generation, generation, and possession" and their relation is that of a mutual permeation (*perichōresis* or *permeatio*) or interpenetration without any commingling. Although John rejected subordinationism, he spoke of the Father as the source of the Godhead and of the Spirit as proceeding from the Father through the Logos. He exhibited thereby a remnant of the old Greek subordinationism. He found his justification in two words of the Nicene Creed—"One God"—words which are indeed subject to misunderstanding. This prepared the way for the later controversy over the *filioque.*

Augustine, representative of Western theology, restated the Latin view of the Trinity in his great work *On the Trinity.*[54]

With Augustine the emphasis lay upon the unity of God. The Trinity is the one God. In substance, nature, energy, and will God is one. This was carried out with great consistency. For instance, the Son is represented as taking part in his own sending and incarnation.[55] The persons of the Trinity are not different from one another; with respect to the entire divine substance they are identical

---

[53] For an English translation of this work, see *NPNF,* Vol. IX.

[54] The English text is found in *NPNF,* III, 17 ff. Cf. T. Gangauf, *Augustinus spekulative Lehre von Gott* (1865); O. Scheel, *Die Anschaung Augustins ueber Christi Person und Werk* (1901); W. S. Bishop, *The Development of the Trinitarian Doctrine in the Nicene and Athanasian Creeds* (London: Longmans, Green and Co., 1910); M. Schmaus, *Die psychologische Trinitätslehre des heiligen Augustin* (1927).

[55] *On the Trinity,* II, 5, 9.

with each other.[56] In this sense Augustine used the word *homoousios*. The Son and the Spirit are not sent because they are in any sense inferior or subordinate to the Father, but because they proceed from him.[57] Each of the three persons is equal to the entire Trinity, and the entire Trinity is not more than one of the persons. Augustine spoke as though the essence of Being is a Person after all. Yet Augustine, in agreement with the Church's tradition, insisted on the three persons in the Trinity. How, then, was he able to do this after his previous statements on the unity? Simply by introducing the logical category of relationship.[58] In the one God there are three forms of existence, and the one cannot be without the other. The three persons are not related to God as the species to the genus nor as properties to the substance.[59] Quantitative and qualitative distinctions are carefully excluded. There is the relation of mutual dependency among the persons. Father, Son, and Spirit behold in themselves the entire undivided unity which belongs to each of them under a different point of view, as generating, generated, or existing through spiration.[60]

Augustine's analogies, taken from the human soul, are as interesting as they are familiar: (1) sight—the thing seen, vision, and the intention of the will uniting the two; (2) thought—the thing in memory, the inner vision, and the will uniting the two; (3) spirit—memory, intelligence, and will; and (4) love—the lover, the beloved, and the love itself. These analogies express the idea of a harmonious spiritual entity impelled and controlled from a threefold center, and also the thought that three are equivalent to one.[61]

Augustine made it impossible to think of the God of redemption without thinking of him as Father, Son, and Spirit. This thought called for emphasis on the unity and demanded the reduction of the hypostases to relative trinitarian distinctions within the divine monad. Augustine was aware of the inadequacy of human language as a medium of expressing absolute truth. "Nevertheless, when it was

[56] *Ibid.,* VII, 6, 11; VIII, 1; VI, 7, 9.
[57] *Ibid.,* VI, 20, 27.
[58] *Ibid.,* V, 11, 12.
[59] *Ibid.,* V, 5, 6; VII, 3, 6; VIII, 1.
[60] *Ibid.,* XV, 14, 23.
[61] *Ibid.,* XI, 2; cf. XV, 3, 5 and IX, 22.

asked, What are the three? human speech at once toils with great insufficiency. Yet we say three persons, not in order to express it, but in order not to be silent." [62]

The closing words of Augustine's great work are beautiful and worthy of remembrance. "Lord our God, we believe in Thee, the Father, the Son, and the Spirit. For truth would not have said, Go baptize, . . . [Matt. 28:19], unless Thou be a Trinity. . . . I would remember Thee, I would love Thee. . . . Lord, Thou One God, Divine Trinity, whatsoever I have written in these books by suggestion of Thee the One, mayest Thou the Three accept; if anything of myself, mayest Thou the One and Thou the Three overlook it." [63]

The fundamental features of Augustine's doctrine of the Trinity were crystallized in the *Symbolum Quicunque*, popularly known as the Athanasian Creed. This creed has been recognized only by the Western Church.

VI. SUMMARIZING OBSERVATIONS

There are those who insist upon seeing the origin and rise of the trinitarian idea in the early Christians' exalted estimate of the man Jesus. They say he was looked upon as a hero, as a semi-divine being or demigod. Gradually his admirers exaggerated this idea so that Christ stood before them as God. This forced upon them the question as to his relation to the Father-God. If this were a correct estimate of Jesus, then the trinitarian conception would simply have to be recorded as an aberration. To those that hold this, the admission of the Trinity would constitute an element incompatible with pure monotheism.

The conservatives, even the progressives among them,[64] look upon the doctrine of the Trinity as the very foundation of the biblical history of redemption. It is in the mission of Christ that they begin with an explanation of the Trinity, not with God as the absolute. To them the Trinity is not a matter of speculation, but of religion. Even the untutored Christian in his prayer-life moves unconsciously in the truth of the trinitarian relation of the Godhead. It is a con-

[62] *Ibid.*, V, 9-10.
[63] *Ibid.*, XI, 21, 51.
[64] Consider, for example, the dogmatics of Barth, Brunner, and Tillich.

viction also which is in harmony with the self-consciousness of Christ (cf. Luke 4:18; Matt. 11:27; 16:27; 19:28; 28:19; John 5:15 ff.; 8:29; 10:17, 29-30, 33, 38; 14:9 ff.; 17).

The religious character of the position of Athanasius in his rejection of Arianism has been emphasized. The permanent truth in his argumentation lies in two things: (1) Christ is God because he is the Redeemer. (2) At the same time, the being (essence) of God is one. In no sense can Christianity admit a second and a third subordinate being in the Godhead. When speaking of God, it must always be the one God who at the same time is Father, Son, and Spirit, not successively, as the Sabellians stated it, but *de facto*, as the Athanasian Creed expresses it.

There is an abiding truth in the Greek emphasis upon the hypostases in the Trinity expressed by the three Cappadocians and John of Damascus. The abiding truth lies in the relation of the one trinitarian God to mankind in an actual history of revelation, redemption, and communication.

Augustine started with the Western emphasis upon the unity in the Trinity. The Roman bishops leaned to a modified Monarchianism in the Sabellian direction. The three persons are not to be denied, but Augustine saw them only in "relationships." With Athanasius he was on his guard against making Christ a "second God." In describing the relations of the One to the Three, he rejected qualitative distinctions such as those employed by Hilary, and reluctantly employed the term "person." [65] Augustine's attempt to harmonize the persons with the unity resulted in a speculative system which was in constant danger of losing the reality of the divine revelation through history.[66] Still there was a great historic significance in the really fundamental features of the Augustinian statements as expressed in the Athanasian Creed. They served as a safeguard against the degeneration of the Trinity into tritheism.

In closing, we call attention to two historic moments when Athanasianism was at the point of losing to Arianism, but emerged victorious. The first of these moments was the period after 350. Athanasianism seemed to be crushed following its condemnation in the West

[65] *On the Trinity*, II, 8, 29.
[66] *Lehrbuch*, II, 162 ff.

by Emperor Constantius, and the substitution of a Semi-Arian formula for the Nicene Creed. The conflict which ensued was waged first between the Arians and Semi-Arians, then by the Semi-Arians among themselves. The result was an alliance of the Semi-Arians and Athanasianists which effected the restoration of the Nicene faith. This was a remarkable event.

The second moment occurred during the migration of peoples from the East to the West. This was the period when the old Roman empire was crumbling. The Ostrogoths, Burgundians, Suevi, and the Lombards, tribes to which the future of Europe belonged, had accepted Arianism. Would this mean the victory of Arianism? The tide turned with the conversion of the Franks to Catholicism and Athanasianism (496). In this great moment in the life of the Church, historical event united with the voice of Scripture and the experience of the Church to testify to the fundamental significance of the doctrine of the Holy Trinity.

BIBLIOGRAPHY

1. The Elimination of Monarchianism

BARDY, G. *Paul de Samosata.* 1923.

EVANS, E. *Tertullian's Treatise Against Praxeas.* London: SPCK, 1948.

KRETSCHMAR, G. *Studien zur Frühschristlichen Trinitätslehre.* 1956.

LOOFS, F. *Paulus von Samosata.* 1924.

PRESTIGE, G. L. *God In Patristic Thought.* 2nd ed.; London: SPCK, 1952.

RAWLINSON, A. E. J. *Essays on the Trinity and the Incarnation.* New York: Longmans, Green and Co., 1928.

2. Arianism

ARIUS. Fragments of letters to Eusebius of Nicomedia, Alexander of Alexandria, and Emperor Constantine are in *MSG*, Vol. 18, 547-84.

GWATKIN, H. M. *Studies in Arianism.* 2nd ed.; London: Bell, 1900.

————. *The Arian Controversy.* London: Longmans, Green and Co., 1889.

HEFELE, C. F. VON, *Konziliengeschichte.* 9 vols., 1855 —. 2nd ed., vols. 1-3, 1873-90.

KOELLING, W. *Geschichte der Arianischen Häresie.* 2 vols. 1874-1883.

MANSI, J. DOM. *Collectio Sacrorum Conciliorum.* Florence and Venice, 1759-98; new print, 1903. See especially Vol. II, pp. 635-1082 for the reports by Eusebius, Socrates, Sozomen, Theodoret and Philostrobius on the Council of Nicea.

NEWMAN, J. H. *The Arians of the Fourth Century.* 3rd ed.; London: Longmans, Green and Co., 1871.

NPNF, Second Series, Vols. I-II, containing the church histories of Socrates and Sozomen in English.

————. Second Series, Vol. XIV, containing the transactions of the Ecumenical Councils in English.

SNELLMANN, P. *Die Anfänge des Arianischen Streites.* 1904.

3. Athanasianism

ATHANASIUS, *MSG,* Vols. 25-28. Selected writings are found in *NPNF,* Second Series, Vol. IV, and in *LCC,* Vol. III.

BETHUNE-BAKER, J. F. *The Meaning of Homoousios.* Vol. VII in Cambridge Texts and Studies, 1901.

CROSS, F. L. *The Study of St. Athanasius.* Oxford University Press, 1945.

HOUGH, L. H. *Athanasius, the Hero.* New York: Methodist Book Concern, 1906.

LAUCHERT, F. *Die Lehre des heiligen Athanasius.* 1895.

PAINE, L. L. *Critical History of the Evolution of Trinitarianism.* 1900.

SCOTT, H. M. *Origin and Development of the Nicene Creed.* 1896.

SWETE, H. B. *The Holy Spirit in the Ancient Church.* London: Macmillan Co., 1912.

WEIGL, E. *Untersuchungen zur Christologie des heiligen Athanasius.* 1914.

4. The Creeds

BURN, A. E. "The Athanasian Creed and Its Early Commentaries," *Texts and Studies,* Vol. 4, No. 1. Cambridge: Cambridge University Press, 1896.

FOULKES, E. F. *The Athanasian Creed.* London: Hayes and Co., 1872.

OMMANNEY, G. W. D. *The Athanasian Creed.* London: Rivington, 1875.

————. *Early History of the Athanasian Creed.* London: Rivington, 1880.

SWAINSON, C. A. *The Nicene and the Apostles' Creeds: together with the Creed of Athanasius.* London: Murray, 1875.

CHAPTER X

THE DOCTRINE OF TWO NATURES AND ONE PERSON IN CHRIST

Introductory Observations

The first stage of real christological development began with the attempt to solve the trinitarian problem. The starting point of the development was the consideration: If Christ is really our Redeemer, then he must be God. In order to avoid the appearance of polytheism the question had to be answered: How is the Christ or Logos related to the one God? As the result of much debate and controversy, the doctrine of the Trinity finally emerged: There is one divine being in three distinct persons—Father, Son, and Holy Spirit—all participating in the same divine essence and differing only in function. The first stage of development decided the real deity of Christ.

The second stage of the christological development was reached when men turned their attention to the humanity of Christ. It was necessary and inevitable that they should do so. It was all the more necessary since, as Harnack says, "no single outstanding church-teacher really accepted the humanity in an unqualified way." [1] It is true that in dealing with Docetism the Church had learned to insist upon the real humanity of Christ. But much was still to be learned on this subject. In emphasizing the humanity of Christ against the docetic conception, the Church had used expressions which referred chiefly to the genuineness of his corporeality. Tertullian and Origen had spent their genius upon this problem. It was Apollinaris who was to precipitate the issue by propounding the christological problem seriously and suggestively.

[1] *History of Dogma,* IV, 139.

The third stage of the development came when men, satisfied as to the divinity and humanity of Christ, were compelled to ask the next question: What is the relation between the divine and the human in Christ? Tertullian, with fine prophetic intuition, had anticipated the final christological result when he said: "We see His double state, not intermixed but conjoined in one person, Jesus, God and man." [2] It is necessary to trace the development as it proceeded gradually and painfully, sometimes even violently, toward the truth.

The present study will deal with the second and third stages of the development. Whereas the preceding chapter dealt with Christ's prehistoric existence and divine nature, this chapter deals with his historical existence as the incarnate Son of God, the connection of the divine nature with the human nature of the Son of Mary, and the mutual relations of the two. We agree with Thomasius that this is Christology in the stricter sense of the word.

I. The Problem as Posed by Apollinaris

As we have mentioned, the first one to propose and deal with the christological problem in a serious and suggestive way was Apollinaris, Bishop of Laodicea (d. *ca.* 390). He was a man of fine intellectual gifts, a voluminous writer, a capable and enthusiastic defender of Nicene Christology, and at one time a bulwark of orthodoxy. For a while he was the friend of Athanasius.

To Apollinaris the christological problem was fundamentally a religious one. Like Athanasius, he viewed Christ's soteriological work as changing man's sinful mortality into sinless immortality. With the thought of redemption constantly before him, Apollinaris said that Christ is both God and man. If Christ is only man, he did not save the world, and if only God, he did not save it through suffering. If Christ was only man, or if only God, he was not a mediator between man and God. Apollinaris was convinced that Christ, in order to be our Redeemer, must be God and man. This conviction raised the important and puzzling question: How can perfect humanity and perfect divinity be maintained in one person? "If a perfect God were united with a perfect man," reflected Apollinaris, "then there would be two (sons), one by nature the Son of God, and the other by

---

[2] *Against Praxeas,* 27.

171

adoption." [3] The personal unity of Christ must be maintained. If we hold to the perfect humanity of Christ, his sinlessness is not guaranteed, neither is there any way of establishing harmony between the two wills. Christ would be a peccable and mutable being, unfit for carrying out the work of redemption. How was the problem to be solved? In the mature form of his teaching he followed the trichotomic view of man expressed in I Thess. 5:23 and said that in Christ the divine Logos had replaced the human mind. For this certain scriptural passages, such as John 1:14 and Rom. 8:3, were quoted. This meant that Christ was human according to the animated body only, and that the Son of God had assumed the flesh of Mary's son and absorbed it into his divinity. Although this exalted the divinity of Christ, it did so by denying his real humanity. Apollinaris was paving the way for Monophysitism.

The mistakes of Apollinaris' Christology were clearly seen by the orthodox Fathers of that day, especially by the Cappadocians. First, in objecting to the mutilated humanity of Christ, the Cappadocians pointed out that in such a being the facts of the gospel history could not be harmonized, for example, the absence of omniscience, and the struggle of the human will with the divine will in Christ (Luke 22:42). Apollinaris would necessarily be driven to Docetism. Their second main objection was that the Apollinarian Christ was incapable of effecting redemption. Sin affects not only our bodies and animal souls but likewise our minds. A complete and perfect redemption demands a human as well as divine Redeemer whose body redeems our bodies, whose soul redeems our souls, and whose mind redeems our minds. Only by becoming what we are in all the parts of our being could Christ have brought humanity into communion with God. To conceive of a man without a mind is impossible. A mutilated human being is unworthy to be saved, for that which cannot be added to cannot be cured; but that which is united to God is already saved. If half of Adam fell, it was the half also which was added to and saved; but if the whole Adam fell, the addition was made to the whole that was born, and he was wholly saved. [4]

The historical significance of Apollinaris lies in the fact that he

---

[3] Athanasius, *Against Apollinaris*, I, 2.

[4] Gregory of Nyssa, "Against Eunomius, Book II," *NPNF*, V, 101 ff. Cf. also Ayer, *op. cit.*, pp. 494 ff., and *LCC* III, 215 ff.

proposed the christological problem of the two natures in Christ for the Church's consideration. Loofs says: "Apollinaris set forth the questions with such acumen and with such completeness that the discussion, which lasted for more than three hundred years up to the ecumenical synod at Constantinople in 680, could add only a few points that were really new. Even the technical terms of the later controversies are found, for the most part, with him." [5]

Apollinaris, his teachings, and his followers, were condemned at Rome in 377, at Antioch in 378, by the so-called Second Ecumenical Council at Constantinople in 381,[6] and again by Rome in 382. The Apollinarians were excluded from the Church and later joined the ranks of the Monophysites. The Decree of Chalcedon (451) was very explicit in its rejection of Apollinarianism. It declared that Christ is "true God and true man of a reasonable soul and body (*ek psyches logikes kai somatos*)," and that he is "of the same substance with us according to his manhood." Even in 691, the Quinisextum Synod remembered to condemn "Apollinaris, leader of wickedness, who impiously declared that the Lord did not assume a body endowed with both soul and mind." [7] C. E. Raven, a thoroughgoing scholar on this subject, says: "Apollinaris can only be condemned by those who are prepared to allow that the whole Greek school from Justin to Leontius and John of Damascus is similarly at fault, since the divergences between them and the heresiarch are merely verbal and superficial." [8] The fact is that none of the Greek theologians succeeded in seriously establishing the perfect humanity of Christ, Cyril of Alexandria included.

As to aims, the Church has completed two stages in its christological growth. In the Arian controversy, the Church had established the true divinity of Christ; and in the Apollinarian conflict, his true humanity. The Church was now ready for the third stage, and its problem was to discover correct terms with which to express the relation of the divine and the human in the God-Man. The solution of the problem was attempted from two directions. Two schools, the

---

[5] *Leitfaden*, p. 266.

[6] *NPNF*, XIV, 172 ff.

[7] Mansi, *Collectio*, XI, 936.

[8] C. E. Raven, *Apollinarianism* (New York: The Macmillan Company, 1924), p. 18.

Antiochean and the Alexandrian, devoted their energies toward answering the question: How are the divinity and the humanity related in Christ?

II. THE PROBLEM AS DEBATED BY THE SCHOOLS OF ANTIOCH AND ALEXANDRIA

Kurtz describes the situation fittingly when he says: "Each of these two schools represented one side of the truth of the Church's doctrine; in the union of the two sides the Church proclaimed the full truth. On the other hand, each of the two schools proceeded more and more one-sidedly to emphasize its own side of the truth, and so tended toward positive error. Thus arose two opposite errors, the separating of the natures and the confusing of the natures, which the Church rejected one after the other, and proclaimed the truth that lay at the root of both." [9]

The Antiochean School

The Antiochean school during this period was represented first by Diodorus of Tarsus (d. 378),[10] but chiefly by Theodore of Mopsuestia (d. 428),[11] Nestorius (d. ca. 451),[12] and subsequently by Theodoret (d. 457). This school was marked by an aversion to metaphysical speculation and to the deeper mystical element in Christianity. It rejected allegorical exegesis and established a grammatico-historical method of scriptural interpretation. The men whom we have named were diligent exegetes who studied the life of the historical Christ, especially his human and moral development. They were naturally opposed to Docetism and Apollinarianism. Their chief emphasis was upon the humanity of Christ without intending in the least to deny his divinity.

They held that Christ is possessed of a perfect humanity which consists of a body and a reasonable soul. He is also endowed with a free will or "power of self-determination." The humanity which Christ assumed was subject to mutability, physical weakness, and sinful

[9] *Church History,* Par. 52, 2.
[10] Only a few fragments of his work are extant. See bibliography.
[11] Only fragments of his commentaries and dogmatic writings are extant.
[12] On Nestorius, see below.

174

affections. By the use of his human will Christ overcame the tempter, sin, and all fleshly lusts, and arrived at perfection. The process of divinization which took place in the humanity of Christ had a saving and sanctifying effect on the human race which is connected with him. Kurtz describes this process of divinization thus: "The historical development of the God-Man is with him, that is, Theodore of Mopsuestia, the type and pattern of the historical redemption of mankind. Christ assumed a complete human nature with all its sinful affections and tendencies; but he fought these down and raised his human nature by constant conflict and victory to that absolute perfection to which by the same way He leads us through the communication of His Spirit." [13]

But what is the relation between the divine and the human in Christ according to the Antiocheans? These writers were very careful to exclude any confusion of the two natures. Since Christ is both divine and human, it follows that the divinity has its residence (enoikesis) in the humanity. The Logos resides in the man Jesus as in a shrine; this indwelling is also compared to Christ's indwelling in the hearts of believers. The relation is therefore a connection or conjunction (synapheia). This does not constitute a union according to essence, nor according to energy, but rather a union according to grace. The Logos entered into an intimate relation with the humanity of Jesus because he was pleased with it. It is therefore a moral union. Knowing in advance what would become of the man Jesus, the Logos entered into fellowship with his person in the womb of the Virgin Mary. As the man Jesus succeeded more and more in the struggle with sin and became sanctified by the Spirit of God, the fellowship grew closer and closer. It finally reached its highest degree of intimacy in the resurrection and ascension of Jesus.

How are these two natures to be brought into the unity of one person? Here is the difficulty, and it is here that the Antiochean theology has been condemned. One is given the impression that there are two persons. Theodore of Mopsuestia, realizing this, labored to avoid such an accusation. He said: "The Son is rightly confessed to be one, since the distinction ought of necessity to remain, and the unity of person ought to be guarded without interruption." [14] Never-

[13] Kurtz, loc. cit.
[14] On the Incarnation, XV, 1.

theless, this unity meant no more than the harmonious adjustment of the will of Jesus to the will of the Logos, so that Jesus became the perfect organ of the willing and acting Logos. Theodore seemingly secured the unity of the two natures. "When we distinguish the natures," he observed, "we maintain that the nature of God the Word is perfect; perfect, too, the person—for it is not possible to speak of a distinct existence which is impersonal; perfect, too, the nature of the man, and the person likewise. When we look to the conjunction of the two, then we say that there is one person." [15] He illustrated the thought by the words of Christ concerning a nuptial pair: "They are no longer twain, but one flesh" (Matt. 19:6). To summarize, the reasoning of the Antiocheans was simply this: if we fasten our attention exclusively upon the two natures, both of which are personal, we observe two persons; but if we keep in mind the perfect and harmonious union of will into which they have entered, then we have only one person.

The Antiocheans, however, did not really succeed in meeting the objection of their opponents, the Cappadocians, and later, Cyril of Alexandria. The Antiocheans expressed the relation between the two natures in Christ by the word *synapheia*. The union was not a genuine personal union. While Theodore of Mopsuestia used the phrase "two natures and one person," the term "person" still meant no more than the appearance of one being—a *prosōpon*—under which the Logos and the man Jesus pursued their common existence. In this view there is no room for a real incarnation of the Logos in the sense of John 1:14, "The word was made flesh." Theodore said that this verse must not be taken literally; the Logos simply adopted the flesh of Jesus and made it his habitation. The judgment of the Church has been that the separation between the two natures insisted upon by the Antiocheans is too radical. The human nature developed independently of the divinity; therefore a real participation of the divinity in the experience of the human life is not admissible. Contrary to the intention of the Antiocheans, the real union of the two natures in the person of Christ was destroyed. Mary is therefore only *anthropotokos* in the literal sense; only by metaphor may she be called "*Theotokos*," or Mother of God, as the worshipers of the Virgin had begun to style her.

[15] *Ibid.*, VIII.

The Alexandrian School

The Alexandrians moved in a different direction from the Antiocheans. The starting point of this school was the divine side of Christ's person and the incarnation of the Logos as taught by the orthodox teachers of the Church and given doctrinal expression by Athanasius in his controversy with Arianism.

The Teachings of Athanasius

Athanasius had insisted upon a complete humanity—one that remains essentially different from the divinity of the Logos. The states of humiliation and exaltation affected only the humanity of Christ. The Logos really became "flesh" (John 1:14) by taking upon himself flesh and soul from the Virgin Mary and making them his own. As a result, the two natures became one person in an abiding union of divinity and humanity. By reason of the incarnation the real subject of this union is the Logos who has the flesh as his organ of revelation and work. With this union in mind, Athanasius went on to teach that the divinity and humanity enjoyed equal participation in the works of Christ during his earthly pilgrimage, since they were the works of one subject. The divinity had a part even in the sufferings of Christ, though with the restriction that the divinity did not suffer in itself but in the flesh. The suffering of the body was transferred by the Logos to himself. He suffered the weakness of the flesh because the flesh was his own body. Mary is also spoken of as "*Theotokos.*" [16]

Harnack makes the criticism that Athanasius did not succeed entirely in escaping Docetism. His conception of the divinity of Christ forced him into a special interpretation of the historic Christ and his history. Athanasius' Redeemer is the God who, it is true, became man, but who in reality only accommodated himself to human nature, its limitations, and sufferings. Whenever Athanasius dealt seriously with Christ's humanity, the history of the Redeemer was divided into what God

[16] Our special reference is to the letter of Athanasius addressed to Bishop Epictetus of Corinth (*NPNF,* IV, 570 ff.) In the interests of chronological precision it should be remembered that Athanasius wrote before the time of the Antiocheans. We have dealt with his position at this point because the Alexandrian theologians started with his Christology. It should also be kept in mind that Athanasius did not deal intentionally with the person and natures of Christ. In the West, Tertullian had spoken of "two substances and one person," and this formula was destined to aid Eastern speculation in solving the problem.

and what man had done.[17] The charge of <u>Docetism</u> has always been brought against the theologians who followed a course different from that of the Antiochean School.

The Later Alexandrians

After the time of Athanasius, the system of the Alexandrian School received its first contributions from <u>the Cappadocians</u>, especially from the two Gregories. Completed and rounded out by <u>Cyril of Alexandria (d. 444)</u>, this school betrayed its heretical tendency in <u>Eutyches</u> and <u>Monophysitism</u>. The emphasis of this school was upon the union of the two natures, and upon the person as the means of safeguarding the validity of Christ's redemption.

<u>Gregory Nazianzus (d. 390)</u> took the position that in the incarnation the <u>humanity of Christ had</u>, by the process of mixing or commingling (*synkrasis, anakrasis, mixis*), <u>entirely disappeared in the divinity</u>. He compared the divinity and humanity of Christ to the sun and the stars; the sun shines with such brilliancy as practically to extinguish the stars. <u>Gregory of Nyssa (d. *ca.* 400)</u>[18] also said that Christ's passive body had mixed with his active divinity, and that the human had been transformed into the divine. He likened the human nature of Christ to a drop of vinegar which is completely enveloped and absorbed in the vastness of the ocean. These theologians founded their doctrine of incarnation on the principle: *Natura humana capax divinae* ("human nature is capable of becoming divine"). When the objection was made that the perfect God cannot unite with imperfect humanity, they responded that the mutable and peccable body was in itself perfectly dignified since birth, growth, and nourishment of the body are only processes of life established by the Creator Himself; sin and death did not touch him. <u>So strongly did these theologians emphasize the union of both natures that the two natures actually seemed to disappear.</u> The natures seemed to continue only *in abstracto.* Gregory Nazianzus spoke of the body of Christ as continuing its life in heaven. Gregory of Nyssa spoke of the *idiomata* of both natures, and of a free will in Christ's humanity which was guided and deter-

---

[17] See Harnack's final judgment of Athanasius; *Grundriss,* pp. 177 ff.

[18] For a detailed discussion with reference to sources, see J. N. D. Kelly, *Early Christian Doctrine* (New York: Harper & Bros., 1958), pp. 263 ff.

mined by the will of his divinity. It is evident that the great Cappadocians had not yet arrived at a consolidated theory or system with regard to the two natures and one person in Christ. This was to come later with Cyril of Alexandria.

III. THE PROBLEM AS DEBATED BY NESTORIUS AND CYRIL

Nestorius

Nestorius, who became the Patriarch of Constantinople in 428, was of the School of Antioch. It is interesting to see how different scholars have judged him. Kurtz describes him as "an eloquent and pious man, but hasty and imprudent, with little knowledge of the world and human nature, and immoderately severe with heretics." [19] Harnack calls him "naively self-conceited, storming and short-sighted, but sincere and not without noble traits." [20] Seeberg characterizes him as a man of pedantry, equipped with the dogmatic fanaticism that is usually peculiar to the later generations of schools.[21]

In his zeal for orthodoxy Nestorius not only persecuted the Arians, Apollinarians, Novatians, and Macedonians, but he also started a crusade against those who spoke of Mary as "mother of God." "To speak correctly," said Nestorius, "Mary is only the mother of Christ." [22] His position, which was perfectly correct, was that a human mother could not give the divine nature to the Logos, and hence the divinity of Christ had not originated from Mary. It does not follow from this, however, as Luther pointed out, that it is wrong to say that God was born of Mary.[23] Luther argues that it would be the same as if we said: This woman has given birth to a child; the child's soul, however, is not of her nature but of God, and therefore she cannot be the mother of the child. But, says Luther, a woman is the mother of the entire child including the soul, although the soul, in a special sense, has its origin from God. For this reason, Luther continues, we are justified in saying that Mary is the Mother of God. Because of the position from which Nestorius argued, Luther scolds him as "an

---

[19] *Op. cit.,* Par. 52, 3.

[20] *Grundriss,* p. 250.

[21] *Lehrbuch,* II, 214.

[22] "According to a more exact expression the Holy Virgin is named the mother of Christ (*Christotokos*)." Ayer, *op. cit.,* p. 501.

[23] See Luther's treatise "On the Council and the Churches," *PE,* Vol. V.

unlearned, rude, proud man . . . eloquent with a loud voice who wanted to be a self-made Doctor or Master." [24]

There was a deeper reason why Nestorius was opposed to the word "*Theotokos.*" As a pupil of the Antiochean School he objected to the transference of the *idiomata* of Christ's human nature to the Logos. Luther saw this clearly and continued his own discussion along that line.

Nestorius was condemned at the Third Ecumenical Council in Ephesus (431) for dividing the one Christ into two persons or two hypostases.[25] Luther defends the accused against this charge. On the basis of the historical material that was accessible to him, he insists that Nestorius meant to teach and did teach a Christ of two natures in one person only. This cannot be denied. But what was the foundation for the unjust charge? As a pupil of the Antiochean School which emphasized the reality of the two natures in Christ, Nestorius defined the relation of the one to the other as a *"synapheia,"* a mere connection or conjunction. His teaching was like that of Theodore of Mopsuestia. Beginning with the conception in the womb of Mary, the Logos entered into a relation with a complete man. This relation became so intimate that it resulted in one person. Yet the Logos only resided in the man Jesus as in a shrine. It is not a physical or an essential union. Each nature has its own properties, and we must distinguish between the created and the uncreated. Only the human nature can be born, suffer, die, and be raised from the dead; only the divine nature is eternal, omnipotent, omniscient, omnipresent. In thinking of Christ there must be a constant distinction between the two natures. This made Christ appear to be not a real God-Man, but a God-bearing man.

True to the divisive character of Antiochean Christology, Nestorius rejected the *communicatio idiomatum* ("communication of attributes"). His real reason in rejecting the "*Theotokos*" was this: It is impossible for the Logos to be born. Nothing human must be predicated of the divinity. Concerning the heresy of Nestorius we can say nothing more than that he taught the theology of the Antiochean School. It was a Christology that could hardly avoid an emphasis upon the

[24] *Ibid.,* pp. 217-18.
[25] See Ayer, *op. cit.,* pp. 507 ff. and *NPNF,* XIV, 191 ff.

humanity of Christ, and that endangered the unity of his person.

We shall now try to show that the Alexandrian Christology, as systematized by Cyril, was in line with the development of orthodoxy in the Church, and that it did indeed help to establish important elements of truth in the christological dogma as it was finally crystallized in the Creed of Chalcedon and in Part Two of the *Symbolum Quicunque*.

Cyril of Alexandria

Cyril of Alexandria (d. 444) was unrelentingly opposed to Nestorius, whose heresy consisted in teaching the Christology of the Antiocheans, especially that of Theodore of Mopsuestia. Up to the appearance of Cyril, this Christology had had a legitimate place in the Church's endeavors to solve the christological problem.

It is true that there were certain personal elements which were involved in the conflict between Cyril and Nestorius. The charge is that Bishop Cyril was a man who used questionable means to establish and to further the cause for which he stood. Even Luther expresses his disgust with the Third Ecumenical Council at Ephesus (431), at which Cyril succeeded in bringing about the condemnation of Nestorius.[26] Loofs remarks that the modern historian, with his wider knowledge of older sources to which Luther had no access, is compelled to render an even more severe verdict.[27] Ecclesiastical rivalry between the two sees of Alexandria and Constantinople played an important part in the whole controversy. The emperor, who was favorably disposed to Nestorius, had intended to investigate charges against Cyril at a council. But Cyril turned the tables by preferring charges against the Patriarch of Constantinople and by using violence. He had the good fortune, in connection with his church politics, to fight in the interests of piety, like Athanasius in his day. "Cyril offered," says Loofs, "a further development of the traditional line, represented by the Apologists, by Clement and Origen, by Methodius, Athanasius, and Gregory Nazianzus, which was running parallel with the trend of popular piety."[28] Thomasius remarks that Nestorius

---

[26] Luther, *loc. cit.*

[27] *PRE*, XIII, 736, 60; cf. 741 ff.

[28] *Leitfaden*, p. 292.

rejected the *"Theotokos"* so emphatically that the general feeling was that the attack was directed against the christological conception which was connected with that term.[29] Harnack remarks that while Cyril was offensive in the methods he used, he was honest in the principles for which he stood. It must not be overlooked that he wrote his work *De incarnatione unigeniti* before the outbreak of the Nestorian controversy.[30]

Cyril's teaching did not start with the historic Christ but, like Athanasius and Gregory Nazianzus, with God the Logos who became man. This Logos-God, who is unchangeable, assumed impersonal human nature including the mind, without sacrificing anything to this human nature. In this union the Logos became the subject. The religious interest in these assertions of Cyril was that the activity of the Redeemer had to be the work of the unalterable God himself; otherwise the death of Christ could not have effected our redemption. By employing the conception of the two natures, the human which is impersonal and the divine as the subject of both, Cyril avoided using the word "mixture" which the Cappadocians had used.

With Cyril the emphasis was upon the personal union of the two natures of the God-Man. Before the incarnation, abstractly, there were two natures, but after the incarnation there was only one, a divine-human nature. Cyril was wont to say that Christ was one from two natures (*ek dyo physeōn heis*). The position of Cyril is described in the following statement: Only before the union and *in abstracto* can we speak of two natures; after the incarnation and *in concreto* we can speak only of one divine-human nature. In this respect the Monophysites have claimed Cyril.

On this basis a *communicatio idiomatum* is taught. While the Logos himself is incapable of suffering, he suffered in the human nature which became his own in the incarnation. Because of this doctrine Nestorius accused Cyril of dragging the divinity into the sphere of the finite.

Such was the christological system of Cyril. There are two natures and yet a unity. The one is not changed into the other, nor are

[29] Thomasius, *op. cit.,* I, 322.
[30] See *MSG*, 75, 1189 ff.

the two confused with each other. Neither is there an adjoining of one nature to the other (*synapheia*), nor an indwelling of the divinity in the humanity (*enoikesis*). Each nature preserves its attributes. Cyril's system really offered no reasonable solution of the problem. But did Cyril intend a real solution of the problem? The fact is, he simply stated the mystery of godliness (I Tim. 3:6) in harmony with the orthodox traditions of the Church as expressed by Athanasius and the Cappadocians, avoiding the mistakes of his predecessors, and completing their system.

IV. Eutycheanism, Monophysitism, and the Creed of Chalcedon

In the Nestorian controversy both Cyril and Nestorius had been deposed from office through the decision of Emperor Theodosius II (431). In 433, a truce between the Antiochean and Alexandrian Schools was proclaimed by means of a confession which was not antagonistic to the opinions of the Antiocheans.[31] This confession was prepared by the Antiocheans and signed by Cyril. Cyril was able to retain his office and influential position in the Church. The confession represented concessions on both sides. The union of the two schools was not based on any doctrinal settlement of the christological problem. Such a situation was keenly felt, even among the adherents of Cyril. Cyril died in 444 and was succeeded by Dioscurus, who, like his predecessor, attempted to make the Alexandrian See the dominating institution in the Church of the East. He persecuted the Antiocheans, labored to do away with the doctrine of the two natures, and favored creeds which had an Apollinarian bias.

At this juncture Eutyches, the abbot of a monastery near Constantinople and an adherent of the new Alexandrian School, came forward with an extreme opinion in which a heretical element may easily emerge when the Alexandrian Christology is pressed too far. He taught that after the incarnation Christ had only one nature. Eutyches also said that the body of Christ, which is the body of God, is not consubstantial with our own.

Eutyches was condemned and deposed by a synod at Constantinople over which the Patriarch Flavian presided (448). Leo I of Rome sided with Flavian and, in a famous letter (usually called Leo's

---

[31] See the English version of the creed in Ayer, *op. cit.,* pp. 510-11.

Tome),[32] addressed to Flavian in the summer of 449, Leo asserted the doctrine of one person and two natures in Christ. In August of the same year, the emperor convoked an ecumenical council at Ephesus at which Dioscurus presided. The council undertook to purify the Church of the leaven of Antiochean Christology in a high-handed manner. The clarifying utterance from Leo was not permitted to be read. On the contrary, the doctrine of the two natures was condemned, Eutyches was restored, and Flavian, Eusebius, and Theodoret were deposed.

Leo branded the convention with the name "Robber Synod," condemned its resolutions, and demanded a new council under the influence of the Roman See. In the meantime he secured the influence of Pulcheria, the emperor's sister for his cause. The emperor died in 450 and was succeeded by Pulcheria and her husband Marcianus. Both were hostile to Dioscurus of Alexandria and in sympathy with Leo. A new ecumenical council was called in 451 to meet in Nicea. In order to suit imperial pleasure the place of meeting was changed to Chalcedon. At this council Dioscurus was deposed, the doctrine of the two persons and its defenders were anathematized, and Theodoret was reinstated. Cyril was declared to have been orthodox, and on the basis of Leo's Tome, christological definitions were formulated which have always been regarded by the Latin, Greek, and conservative Protestant churches as the final solution of the christological problem. It will be of interest to read the verdict as pronounced by the Creed of Chalcedon:

> We, then, following the holy Fathers, all with one consent, teach men to confess one and the same Son, our Lord Jesus Christ, the same perfect in Godhead and also perfect in manhood; truly God and truly man, of a reasonable soul and body; consubstantial with us according to the manhood; in all things like unto us, without sin; begotten before all ages of the Father according to the Godhead, and in these latter days, for us and for our salvation, born of the Virgin Mary, the Mother of God, according to the manhood; one and the same Christ, Son, Lord, Only-begotten, in two natures, inconfusedly, unchangeably, indivisibly, inseparably,[33] the distinction of natures being by no means taken away by the union, but rather the property of each nature being preserved, and concurring in one person and one subsistence, not parted

[32] See the English text in *NPNF,* XIV, 254 ff., and *LCC,* III, 359 ff.

[33] *Asynchytōs, atrepōs, adiairetōs, achōristōs.* Cf. *NPNF,* XIV, 264; Ayer, *op. cit.,* p. 520; and *LCC,* III, 371 ff.

or divided into two persons but one and the same Son and Only-begotten, God the Word, the Lord Jesus Christ; as the prophets from the beginning have declared concerning Him, and the Lord Jesus Christ Himself has taught us, and the creed of the Holy Fathers has handed down to us.[34]

The leading ideas of this Chalcedonian Christology were embodied in the second part of the Athanasian Creed.

V. The Settlement Unsuccessfully Challenged by Monophysitism and Monotheletism

Monophysitism

The so-called Monophysite struggles began immediately after the Council of Chalcedon. Those who opposed the Creed of Chalcedon, with its recognition of the two natures, were now called Monophysites. A great hubbub took place, chiefly in Egypt and Palestine. The whole Church was in a feverish excitement. Monophysite sects were formed in Egypt, Syria, and Armenia. Strongly opposed to the teaching of the two natures in Christ, they sought to defend their position by appealing to the teaching of Cyril. As to positive teaching they soon split among themselves. One class (Severians), although opposed to a human nature in Christ as contrasted with a divine nature, held that the body of Christ was corruptible before the resurrection. Another class (Julianists) declared the opposite to be true. Still another faction was willing to accept the Chalcedonian Creed with a Cyrillian interpretation. In 527 Justinian ascended the imperial throne. He regarded it as his life's task to win back the dissenting Monophysites in the interest of the state. He was assisted in his attempt by the monk Leontius of Byzantium.[35] The Monophysites contended that the teaching of two natures in the Creed of Chalcedon implies the doctrine of two hypostases. To meet this criticism, Leontius introduced the term "*enhypostasia*." The human nature, he maintained, possesses no hypostasis of its own. Instead, it exists in the divine physis of Christ. On the basis of this interpretation of Chalcedon, Justinian favored the introduction of the phrase into the Trisagion of the Liturgy (cf.

---

[34] *LCC*, III, 373.

[35] Cf. "Leontius," *Catholic Encyclopedia* (New York: Universal Knowledge Foundation, Inc., n.d.), IX, 180 ff. For extracts from Leontius' writings, see *LCC*, III, 375 ff.

Isaiah 6:3), stating that God was crucified for us, so that the Trisagion read as follows: "Holy God, Holy Mighty, Holy Immortal, who was crucified for us, have mercy on us." Justinian was persuaded by the empress Theodora that the Monophysites would be satisfied if the writings of Theodore of Mopsuestia, the controversial writings of Theodoret against Cyril, and the letter of Bishop Ibas to Maris, the Persian were condemned. The alleged errors of these men were collected in the so-called *Three Chapters*. Of these men Theodoret and Ibas had been recognized as orthodox at Chalcedon, and even Theodoret, although excommunicated in 451, had been received back into the Catholic Church. While the Oriental bishops took a favorable attitude, the West was reluctant to obey the emperor. Pope Vigilius pursued a course of indecision. Justinian finally convened the Fifth Ecumenical Council at Constantinople in 553, which confirmed the decrees of the emperor. In addition to the former heresies, the Council also anathematized fifteen doctrinal tenets of Origen. However, Justinian did not reach the end he had in view. The Monophysites continued their separation and exist today as the Coptic, Jacobite, Ethiopean, and Armenian churches.[36] The Council included Pope Honorius among its anathemas.[37]

Monotheletism

A second attempt to change the decision of Chalcedon was made in the Monothelite controversy (633-680). Emperor Heraclius, persuaded by certain Monophysite bishops of Armenia and Syria, endeavored to reconcile the contending parties by saying that "Christ accomplished His work of redemption by the exercise of one divine human will."[38] The one Christ works the human and the divine things through a divine human energy. Some of the Catholic bishops saw nothing unorthodox in this view, and the movement received the support of Patriarch Sergius of Constantinople and even of Pope Honorius of Rome. Opposition arose on the orthodox side. The

[36] For the proceedings of the council, see *NPNF*, XIV, 289 ff.; *LCC*, III, 378 ff.; Ayer, *op. cit.*, pp. 541 ff.

[37] On the problem of reconciling this condemnation with the doctrine of papal infallibility, see *NPNF*, XIV, 351-52; see also *Catholic Encyclopedia*, VII, 452 ff.

[38] Mansi, *op. cit.*, XI, 564 ff.

monk Sophronius, who was soon to become Patriarch of Jerusalem, raised his voice in protest and a new controversy arose. Theodore I and his successors rejected the Monothelite doctrine which Emperor Heraclius had espoused and promulgated, and the West severed church fellowship with the East. Finally, at the Sixth Ecumenical Council at Constantinople (680), it was decided on the basis of a letter by Bishop Agatho of Rome that Christ has "two natural wills or willings . . . not contrary one to the other . . . but His human will follows, not as resisting or reluctant but rather as subject to His divine and omnipotent will." [39]

We have followed, in a cursory manner, the course of the christological development. In conclusion, let us repeat the conciliar decisions by which the christological problem was finally solved and crystallized into dogma: Christ is divine—Nicea (325); Christ is human—Constantinople (381); Christ is one in person—Ephesus (431); Christ is two in nature—Chalcedon (451); although not possessing "two faces"—Constantinople (553); yet possessing two wills—Constantinople (680). *Summary*

In the eyes of Harnack (and many others) this development is a glaring proof of the Hellenization of the gospel. The dogmas of the Trinity and of the two natures, Harnack said, are foreign to the simple gospel as Jesus preached it. Aulén, on the other hand, writes: "When we note the fundamental ideas behind the formulations of the dogmas of the ancient Church, they do not appear as Hellenization, but rather imply the most determined opposition against both forms[40] of that process of Hellenization which endeavored to get a foothold in the Church." [41] Whenever a church loses sight of the second person of the Trinity incarnate in the historical Jesus, it proclaims a gospel other than that of the New Testament.

---

[39] The letter of Agatho is found in *NPNF,* XIV, 329 ff. See also Ayer, *op. cit.,* pp. 660 ff., and *LCC,* III, 382 ff.

[40] Dynamistic Monarchianism and the Antiochean theology led to the conception of Christ as an intermediary being, while Modalism and the later Alexandrian theology tended to remove the concrete human features from the person of Jesus.

[41] *The Faith of the Christian Church,* trans. Eric H. Wahlstrom and G. Arden (Philadelphia: Muhlenberg Press, 1948), pp. 217-18.

BIBLIOGRAPHY

1. Elimination of Monarchianism

BARDY, G. *Paul de Samosata.* 1923.
EVANS, E. *Tertullian's Treatise against Praxeas.* London: SPCK, 1948.
KRETSCHMAR, G. *Studien zur frühchristlichen Trinitätstheologie.* 1956.
LOOFS, F. *Paul von Samosata.* 1924.
PRESTIGE, G. L. *God in Patristic Thought.* 2nd ed.; London: SPCK, 1952.
RAWLINSON, A. E. J. *Essays on the Trinity and the Incarnation.* London and New York: Longmans, Green and Co., 1928.

2. Arius

ALEXANDER, Bishop of Alexandria. Circular to Bishop Alexander in Constantinople.
————. Document of deposition of Arius addressed to all Catholic bishops. In Greek, *MSG*, Vol. 18.
ARIUS. Letter to Alexander of Alexandria.
————. Letter to Emperor Constantine.
————. Letter to Eusebius of Nicomedia.
ATHANASIUS. Writings. See below.

GWATKIN, H. M. *Studies in Arianism.* 2nd ed.; London: Bell Press, 1900.
————. *The Arian Controversy.* London: Longmans, Green and Co., 1889.
HEFELE, K. J. VON *Konziliengeschichte.* Vol. I. 2nd ed.; 1873 —.
KOELLING, W. *Geschichte der arianischen Häresie.* 2 vols. 1874-1883.
MANSI, J. DOM. *Collectio Sacrorum Conciliorium.* Reports on the Council at Nicea by *Eusibius, Socrates, Sozomen, Theodoret* and *Philostrobius.* Florence and Venice: 1759-1798. Newprint, 1903.
NEWMAN, J. H. *The Arians of the Fourth Century.* London and New York: Longmans, Green and Co., 1908.
RELTAN, H. M. *A Study in Christology.* London: SPCK, 1917.
SNELLMANN, P. *Die Anfänge des arianischen Streites.* 1904.
SOCRATES. *Church Histories,* Book I. English translation in *NPNF*, Second Series, Vols. I-II. Also *LCC*, Vol. III.
SOZOMEN. *Church Histories,* Book I. English translation in *NPNF*, Second Series, Vols. I-II. Also *LCC*, Vol. III.
Transactions of the Ecumenical Councils. NPNF, Second Series, Vol. XIV.

3. Athanasius

ATHANASIUS. *Works. MSG*, Vols. 25-28. New edition by H. G. OPITZ, 1934 —.
————. Selected Writings. *NPNF*, Second Series, Vol. IV. Also *LCC*, Vol. III.
BETHUNE-BAKER, J. F. "The Meaning of Homoousios," *Cambridge Texts and Studies*, Vol. VII. Cambridge: Cambridge University Press, 1901.

CROSS, F. L.   *A Study of St. Athanasius.* Oxford: Clarendon Press, 1945.

HOUGH, L. H. *Athanasius, the Hero.* New York: Eaton and Mains, 1906.

LAUCHERT, F. *Die Lehre des heiligen Athanasius.* 1895.

PAINE, L. L. *Critical History of the Evolution of Trinitarianism.* Boston and New York. 1900.

SCOTT, H. M. *Origin and Development of the Nicene Creed.* Chicago: Chicago University Press, 1896.

SWETE, H. B. *The Holy Spirit in the Ancient Church.* London: Macmillan Co., 1912.

WEIGL, E. *Untersuchungen zur Christologie des heiligen. Athanasius.* 1914.

4. Apollinaris

AYER, J. C. *Source Book for Ancient Church History.* New York: Charles Scribner's Sons, 1948.

BETHUNE-BAKER, J. F. *Introduction to the Early History of Christian Doctrine.* London: Methuen and Co., 1938.

CASPARI, C. P. *Alte und Neue Quellen.* 1897.

DRAESEKE, J. *Appollinaris von Laodicea, sein Leben und seine Schriften.* in *Texte und Untersuchungen.* 1892.

LIETZMANN, H. *Apollinaris von Laodicea und seine Schule.* 1904.

RAVEN, C. E. *Apollinarianism.* New York: Macmillan Co., 1924.

VOISIN, G. *L'Apollinarisme.* 1901.

5. The Antiochean School

DIODORUS. Fragments. *MSG*, Vol. 33. 1959—.

THEODORE OF MOPSUESTIA. Fragments. *MSG*, Vol. 66; also ed. by H. B. Swede, 2 vols., 1880 ff.

THEODORET. *Works. MSG*, Vols. 80-84.

AYER, J. C. *Source Book for Ancient Church History.* New York: Charles Scribner's Sons, 1948.

KUEHN, H. *Theodor von Mopsuestia und Julius Africanus als Exegeten.* 1880.

NORRIS, R. A. *Manhood and Christ: a Study in the Christology of Theodore of Mopsuestia.* New York: Oxford University Press, 1963.

SPECHT, F. A. *Der exegetische Standpunkt des Theodor von Mopsuestia und Theodoret.* 1871.

SULLIVAN, F. H. *The Christology of Theodore of Mopsuestia.* 1956.

6. Nestorius

AYER, J. C. *Source Book for Ancient Church History.* New York: Charles Scribner's Sons, 1948.

BETHUNE-BAKER, J. F. *Nestorius and his Teaching.* Cambridge: Cambridge University Press, 1908.

FENDT, L. *Die Christologie des Nestorius.* 1910.

LOOFS, F. *Nestoriana.* 1905.

————. *Nestorius and His Place in the History of Christian Doctrine.* Cambridge: The University Press, 1914.

Transactions of the Ecumenical Councils. NPNF, Second Series, Vol. XIV.

VINE, A. R. *An Approach to Christology*. London: Independent Press, 1948.

WEIGL, E. *Die Christologie vom Tode des Athanasius bis zum Ausbruch des nestorianischen Streites*. 1925.

7. *Cyril of Alexandria*

CYRIL. *Works. MSG*, Vols. 68-77. See especially: (1) the second of his three letters addressed to Nestorius (*MSG*, Vol. 77); (2) the five books against Nestorius addressed to Bishop Celestine I in Rome (Vol. 76); (3) three doctrinal letters *De recta fide* addressed to Theodorius II and the ladies of his court (Vol. 76); and (4) the third of his three letters to Nestorius, to which there are attached the twelve anathemas against Nestorius and the defense of these (Vol. 77).

AYER, J. C. *Source Book for Ancient Church History*. New York: Charles Scribner's Sons, 1948.

BEHRMANN, A. *Die Christologie des heiligen Cyrillus von Alexandria*. 1902.

8. *Eutycheanism, Monophysitism, and the Final Settlement in the Creed of Chalcedon*

AYER, J. C. *Source Book for Ancient Church History*. New York: Charles Scribner's Sons, 1948.

HAASE, F. *Dioskur nach monophysitischen Quellen*. 1908.

JUNGLAS, J. P. *Leontius von Byzanz*. 1908.

KELLY, J. N. D. *Early Christian Doctrines*. New York: Harper and Bros., 1958.

KUHN, P. *Die Christologie Leos I*. 1894.

OSWEPIAN, G. *Die Entstehungsgeschichte des Monotheletismus*. 1897.

OTTLEY, R. L. *The Doctrine of the Incarnation*. London: Methuen and Co., 1896.

PRESTIGE, G. L. *Fathers and Heretics*. London: SPCK, 1954.

SELLERS, R. V. *Two Ancient Christologies*. London: SPCK, 1940.

Transactions of the Ecumenical Councils. NPNF, Second Series, Vol. XIV.

CHAPTER XI

THE PROBLEMS OF ANTHROPOLOGY AND SOTERIOLOGY

I. The Eastern View of Man's Original State

The East did not take the lead in discussing the problems of sin and grace. The practical mind of the West had the chief interest in this sphere of Christian thought. The dominating interest of the East, so much inclined to speculation, was in the doctrine of the Trinity and in Christology.

The condition of man's will, in its relation to saving grace (anthropology), did become a matter of interest in the East because of a threefold opposition: (1) Stoicism, which reduced free will to a minimum by teaching that man is in the hands of fate; (2) Gnosticism, which taught that men are by nature either spiritual, physical, or carnally minded, being inexorably doomed to a life of sin and excluded from the capability of regeneration, and that regeneration is not an ethical but a natural process; (3) Manichaeism with its doctrine that man had come into being as the creature of the devil, and therefore, was evil from the beginning.

Against these influences the Greek Fathers strongly emphasized man's freedom and his accountability. Stimulated by this interest, a number of matters belonging to the field of anthropology came under discussion, among them: (1) the original state of man and (2) the fall and its consequences. The former subject, the original state of man, included (a) the problem of the image of God in the first man (reason and free will, moral perfection, immortality of the soul). Closely connected was (b) the exact conception of the East concerning man's original righteousness. The second of the above-mentioned subjects, the fall and its consequences, had reference to the effect of the fall on the will. Man's knowledge (reason) was darkened, his judgment concerning right and wrong became increasingly uncertain. Man came under the dominion of sensuality and his will became weakened, a condition which became general in the human race. The thought of the Greek Fathers on original sin is well described by two older historians in the field of Christian doctrine:

Hagenbach remarks:

> Opinions were not as yet fully developed concerning the moral depravity of each individual, and the sin of the race in general was considered as the effect of the first sin. They were so much disposed to look upon sin as the free act of man's will that they could hardly conceive of it as simply an hereditary tendency transmitted from one to another. The sin of every individual, as found in experience, had its type in the sin of Adam, and consequently appeared to be a repetition rather than a necessary consequence of the first sin. In order to explain the mysterious power which drives man to evil they had recourse to the influence of the demons, strong but not absolutely compulsory, rather than to a total bondage of the will as the result of original sin.[1]

While the Greek Fathers admitted the universality of sin and even emphasized the first sin as an act in which the whole race had participated, they would not admit that the sinful condition was necessarily universal among men, for fear that such an admission might detract from the guiltiness of sin.

Kurtz says:

> Opposition to Gnosticism and Manichaeism led the older Fathers to emphasize as strongly as possible the moral freedom of men, and induced them to deny inborn sinfulness as well as the doctrine that sin was imprinted in men in creation, and to account for man's present condition by bad training, evil example, the agency of evil spirits, etc.[2]

But Irenaeus, as we have seen, expressed his belief in original sin, and Gregory of Nyssa also made strong statements in this direction. However, the consequences of a consistent doctrine of original sin were not drawn. On the contrary, some expressions from men like Athanasius, Gregory of Nyssa, Clement of Alexandria, and Cyril of Alexandria plainly imply a rejection of original sin. Chrysostom is

[1] K. R. Hagenbach, *History of Doctrine* (2nd ed., Edinburgh: T. T. Clark, 1850—), I, 231.

[2] Kurtz, *op. cit.*, Par. 53, 1.

credited with the statement, "We baptize infants also though they are not defiled with sin." [3]

II. WHAT KEPT THE EAST FROM LEADING IN THE PROBLEMS OF SOTERIOLOGY?

The East was not especially interested in the discussion of divine grace as related to man's freedom. Grace, that is, redemption through Christ, liberation from the old sinful life, and regeneration by baptism, was such a powerful factor in the consciousness of the early Christians that a dogmatic reflection was not especially invited. On this point all were in general accord. As Christians they felt the power of the Spirit, so pulsating within them and so furnishing them with the strength for their ethical tasks that there seemed to be no need for dogma-making along that line.

A further explanation of why it was the West and not the East which cultivated the field of soteriology for future doctrinal decisions must be seen in a characteristic difference between the Greek and Latin parts of the Church, a difference which can be traced back as far as the Greek Apologists. The Greek Fathers, unlike the practical Latins, were attracted by speculative subjects. From the time of the Apologists the Greeks regarded Christianity chiefly as a revelation of truth. Christianity was looked upon as a higher philosophy or as absolute truth when compared with the relative truth found in Judaism and heathenism.

With the idea of the Logos a certain accommodation to the Hellenic conception of reason and freedom as possessed by the natural man entered in. This was not without influence upon the soteriological views of Greek Christianity, according to which man was regarded as possessing the power to act in conformity with the light of reason. The Greeks, particularly the Anti-Gnostic fathers, were not thoroughgoing Pelagians. Such men as Irenaeus, Clement and Cyril of Alexandria, Origen, Athanasius, Basil, the Gregories, and Cyril of Jerusalem admitted that man's will had been weakened by the fall and that the assistance of grace was needed.[4] According to them, freedom

---

[3] See the whole passage in James Hastings, *Encyclopedia of Religion and Ethics* (New York: Charles Scribner's Sons, 1908-1920), II, 393.

[4] For references, see J. N. D. Kelly, *Early Christian Doctrines* (New York: Harper & Bros., 1958), pp. 174 ff.; 346 ff. and Thomasius, *op. cit.,* I, 445 ff.

and grace stand side by side in producing the acts of goodness; or, more correctly, man's free will begins and grace follows in a supplementary manner (Semi-Pelagianism). Faith is man's own work. A real regeneration as a creative act of divine grace, including a renewal of man's will, was not and could not be taught in consistency with these views. There were individual voices which spoke in other tones. Because of his theory of a pre-cosmic fall, Origen, for example, said that children come into the world already stained with sin.[5] Chrysostom employed Semi-Pelagian terms: "It depends upon us and upon God," he said: "We must first choose the good, then God will do His part. God does not anticipate our will that our freedom may not suffer; but after we have chosen, He grants much help." [6]

III. The Teaching of the West

As has been remarked, the Latin Fathers were considerably more interested in practical questions than were those of the East. While the Latin Church also discussed and advocated human freedom, its emphasis was upon the facts of sin and grace. The difference in tendencies was of a latent nature; in the main the two parts of the Church were in agreement with each other. The provocation to conflict required only the overemphasis of one of the two tendencies. In the course of time the conflict came. But before we discuss this situation, we must consider man's natural depravity as it was developed by the Latin Church Fathers.

It must be admitted that the Church Fathers of the East approached the doctrine of man's natural depravity as inherited from his ancestors. They spoke of a guilt that is common to the whole race. But Tertullian, in his *On the Soul*, was really the first to teach original sin. Loofs, who points to Tertullian's dependence on Stoic views, calls it "a kind of original sin." [7] As an advocate of traducianism, Tertullian believed that the individual soul consists of a human substance, and that it comes into existence with the body in and through generation as a transmission from the seed of Adam. Thus the way was prepared for the recognition of inherited sin. The soul has its sinful

[5] *Against Celsus,* VII, 50.
[6] *Homily on Hebrews,* 1-3.
[7] *Leitfaden,* p. 163.

condition as a result of its relation to Adam. Our race is infected not only with Adam's death, but also with sin, which has become, so to speak, a natural element in mankind, a second nature, a *malum animae* ("evil of the soul"), a *vitium originis* ("blemish of origin").

But Tertullian did not succeed in drawing the evangelical conclusions from his doctrine of natural depravity. His conception of grace does not fit into a system of soteriology such as was later constructed by Augustine. Tertullian's opposition to Gnosticism led him to lay strong emphasis upon man's free will even before conversion. But it was especially his legalistic conceptions regarding the relation between God and man that kept Tertullian from an evangelical view of grace. God is the offended judge and man is the offender and debtor who must settle with the divine majesty through such works of satisfaction as self-humiliation, asceticism and, if possible, martyrdom. Then man will experience grace as a creative principle infused into his heart. In this way Tertullian was a forerunner of Occidental Catholicism.

Yet to Tertullian and other teachers of the West, there was a larger emphasis upon man's real sinfulness and a corresponding emphasis upon grace. Cyprian defended infant baptism on the ground that the child also is sinful and therefore needs regeneration.[8] Hilary was strong in his expressions on the universality of man's natural depravity.[9] Ambrose was even more outspoken on both sin and grace.[10] He spoke of man's sin as a contagion which he traced back to conception and which he described as a guilt that needs to be forgiven. In his teaching of grace Ambrose was deeper than any of his predecessors, and he was the first to express a belief in prevenient grace. He pointed to the first turning of man's will as an effect of divine grace.[11]

It is to be noted, however, that the difference between the East and the West on this whole subject had not yet become disruptive. On the one hand, the East had no thought of denying the universality of man's sinfulness and the need of grace for his salvation. On the

[8] Though an infant has not committed actual sins, it is in need of forgiveness because it "has contracted the contagion of the ancient death at its earliest birth," "Letter to Fidus," *ANF,* V, 353-54.

[9] *Homily on Psalm 119:* "In the error of the one, i.e. Adam, the whole human race went astray." Quoted by Seeberg, *Textbook,* II, 339.

[10] *Exposition of Luke,* 7:132, 234, *passim.*

[11] "I dare say that by himself man cannot enter the way of life, unless God go before" (*nisi Deum habeat praevenientem*); *ibid.,* 11:84.

other hand, the Latin Fathers were far from denying the personal responsibility of man and his free will in accepting or rejecting the gracious influences of God. As was stated above, there was a difference in tendency in the two sections of the Church, but this was as yet latent in character. Up to this time there had been no occasion for a conflict, since neither of the two tendencies had been asserted strongly enough to exclude the other.

IV. AUGUSTINE AND THE PELAGIANS

A Preliminary Study of Pelagianism

Pelagius (d. after 418) was a British or Irish monk of much ability and learning. He left behind him a considerable number of writings of which, besides a few fragments in Augustine's works, only a commentary on the thirteen Epistles of Paul, a letter to Demetrius, and an address (*Libellus fidei ad Innocentium*) have been preserved.[12] Two of Pelagius' most enthusiastic supporters were Caelestius and Julianus of Eclanum (d. 450). The latter was an effective advocate of Pelagian views, which he developed into a system by adding rationalistic and naturalistic elements. The most pertinent of his writings are his *Libra IV ad Turbantium* and *Libra VIII ad Florum*, of which we have many fragments in Augustine's *Contra Julianum*[13] and especially in the *Opus Imperfectum*.[14]

The teachings of the Pelagians can be covered by briefly describing their conception of human freedom, of sin, of the universality of sin, and of grace.

Does man come into harmony with God by making the right use of his natural ability to choose between good and evil from case to case? Or does this harmony come about through an influence of divine grace upon the life of man so that the will of the regenerated functions freely in the direction of the good? This was the problem in the controversy. The Pelagians affirmed the first of these two

[12] The extant writings of Pelagius are included in the works of Jerome (*MSL*, 30). The various confessions of faith are collected by A. Hahn, *Bibliothek der Symbole* (3rd ed.), XVIII, pp. 288 ff.; cf. Alexander Souter, *Pelagius' Exposition of Thirteen Letters of St. Paul*, 3 vols. (Cambridge: The University Press, 1922-1927); also H. Zimmer, *Pelagius in Irland* (1901). Cf. Ayer, *op. cit.*, pp. 457 ff.

[13] *MSL*, Vol. 45.

[14] *Ibid.*

questions. Pelagius stressed the power of contrary choice (*possibilitas utriusque partis*) or what we call formal freedom.[15] He never tired of praising the inalienable power of man's nature to do what is right (*bonum naturae*). Pelagius argued that since God has enjoined His law upon man, therefore man must have the power to fulfill it.[16] There is nothing in man that compels him to sin. That *bonum naturae* ("goodness of nature") has enabled many pagans to develop the highest virtues. It is even possible for man to lead a sinless life.[17]

Man's freedom as the natural power to choose from case to case and in act after act indicates the Pelagian conception of sin. Sin is not seen in a condition of man's nature, in an inclination, or in tendencies of the will. This led the Pelagians to reject the doctrine of original sin or of a sinful inclination transmitted from parents to children. The position was taken that not the soul (*anima*), but only the flesh (*caro*) is traceable to Adam.[18] The fall of Adam was looked upon as an insignificant act with no meaning for his posterity.[19] Man's sensual nature, his concupiscence, was regarded as entirely indifferent. On this issue Julian had a severe conflict with Augustine. Physical death was not the consequence of sin, but merely a necessity of the human organism. It was admitted, however, that spiritual death (*mors animae*) had passed from Adam to his children. This would not justify our speaking of an imputation of guilt from an inherited sinful condition. Such an imputation of guilt would constitute an injustice of which God would be incapable.[20] Children, therefore, do not need to be baptized for the forgiveness of sins.[21]

The apparent universality of sin was explained by pointing to man's sensual nature which, although entirely innocent in itself, becomes the occasion for temptation and sinning.[22] In addition to this, Pelagius mentions the attraction of evil examples as the occasion for individuals

---

[15] *Letter to Demetrius*, 3; cf. Augustine, *On the Nature of Christ*, I, 19 and XVIII.

[16] Pelagius on Romans 11:8.

[17] Pelagius on Romans 8:3; cf. Augustine, *On Nature and Grace*, 8.

[18] Pelagius on Romans 7:8; Augustine, *Opus Imperfectum*, I, 61; IV, 14, 19-20.

[19] Julian, *op. cit.*, VI, 11-12.

[20] Pelagius on Romans 5:15 ff.

[21] Caelestius, quoted by Augustine in *On the Grace of Christ*, Book II; in *On Original Sin*, VI, 6.

[22] Pelagius, quoted by Augustine in *On the Grace of Christ*, I, 11 (X)

to sin. These evil examples have their power in the continued practice of sinning, the *longus usus peccandi, longa consuetudo vitiorum* ("the long usage of sinning, the long custom of vice")[23] and Pelagius is compelled to admit a necessity of sinning.[24] This is a very significant admission! The universality of sin is explained by a sinful condition in the human race which defeats the original assertions of the goodness of nature. Pelagius does not really want to make this admission. His interest does not go beyond isolated individuals and isolated human acts. He fails to see the ethical unity of the race and the ethical unity in the individual.

The Pelagian teaching on grace corresponds with these views of human nature and free will. The Pelagians did not believe in a real grace, that is, in a grace conceived of as the divine influence in man, much less in a creative divine influence upon man's spiritual powers. To them grace was first of all an enlightenment of man's reason, enabling him to see the will of God so that man of his own powers can choose and act accordingly.[25] Grace consists in the revelations of the divine will through the law, especially as given in Christ's precept and example, and also in promises, discipline, warnings, trials, etc.[26] All this is merely for the purpose of assisting man who chooses and acts in perfect independence. Since grace is nothing but an assistance, and since man can do the right without such aid, Caelestius argued that grace is not absolutely, but only relatively necessary. In his work of grace God merely facilitates the right action of man's will.[27] The requirement on man's part is that he should make himself worthy of such aid.

It was Loofs who called attention to the fact that Pelagianism was not a new doctrine with which the Church, under the theological leadership of Augustine, was unexpectedly confronted. Pelagius, with Caelestius and Julian, simply gave blunt and systematized expression to certain tenets of the popular Catholicism of that day. The elements of this theology are found in the Greek Apologists of the second century and in the whole moralistic-intellectualistic and rationalistic

---

[23] Pelagius, *Letter to Demetrius*, 8.
[24] Pelagius on Romans 7:20.
[25] *Letter to Demetrius* 2, 4 ff., 8.
[26] *Ibid.*, 8; cf. Augustine, *On Original Sin*, 26, 30.
[27] Pelagius, quoted by Augustine in *On the Grace of Christ*, I, 26 (XXV).

popular philosophy of the centuries before Augustine. The moralizing influence of Stoicism is especially observable.[28]

On the basis of the text of Pelagius' *Commentary on Paul to the Romans*, rediscovered by Souter, and the investigations of Zimmer, Loofs has also called attention to the energy with which Pelagius has stressed justification by faith alone. Walker, in his history, seconds Loofs by remarking, "No man between Paul and Luther so emphasized justification by faith alone."[29] On this question the student will be interested to hear Seeberg. He admits that Loofs has correctly quoted the teaching of Pelagius on justification. But Seeberg insists that, in the case of Pelagius, the formula "justification by faith" does not have the meaning that it appears to have because in the Pelagian conception of Christianity it is impossible to find a logical place for that teaching of Paul. Seeberg adds, "Pelagius was a rationalist and a moralist, and he had no understanding of the inner relation between sin and grace."[30] Loofs agrees with this when, in connection with a criticism of both Augustine and Pelagius, he says that Pelagius "was prevented by his moralism from appreciating the religious significance of faith."[31] This whole investigation has shown that Pelagius was a man of personal piety, that for his salvation he wanted to rely upon the forgiveness of sins through Christ, and that he had a deeper conception of the guilt of the sinner than the history of the past warrants us to believe.[32]

This investigation does not change the fundamental structure of Pelagian theology as pictured above. In this theology the divine law appears as a collection of moral demands and sin is thought of as a heap of separate stones with no organic unity in a depraved nature. Christian perfection is viewed as a cluster of individual virtues and works with no demand for a regenerated heart as the necessary source of the truly Christian life. Fisher remarks correctly that Pelagius'

---

[28] See Loofs' article "Pelagius and the Pelagian Controversy" in *PRE*, XV, 747 ff. Cf. also *Leitfaden*, 417 ff.

[29] Williston Walker, *A History of the Christian Church* (New York: Charles Scribner's Sons, 1959), p. 186.

[30] *Lehrbuch*, II, 495.

[31] *Leitfaden*, p. 420.

[32] See *Letter to Demetrius*, 8; Augustine, *Opus Imperfectum*, I, 171.

"conception of character is atomistic." [33] In the conflict between Augustine and the Pelagians two fundamentally different conceptions of Christianity clashed with each other. It is a conflict that will never be entirely settled.[34]

Augustine and His Teaching

Before he was converted, Augustine defended human freedom in opposition to the Manichaeans. On reflecting how his own conversion had come to pass, he came to the conviction that man in his natural condition is incapable of any positive co-operation with divine grace in conversion, and that the enkindling of faith depends solely upon the grace of God. He found himself unable to change his will; and now that change had come as a gift. It is a mistake to believe that the change in Augustine's conviction was caused by the Pelagian controversy. We know that already in 396, before he knew of Pelagius, he had been moved for exegetical reasons (Rom. 9:16; I Cor. 4:7; Phil. 2:13) to believe that faith is the gift of God. Even before that time, in 386, he prayed for faith as a gift: *Da fidem!* [35] Consideration should also be given to the fact that, on sin, grace, and faith, Ambrose was in many ways a precursor of Augustine, with passages which "do not fall a whit behind the famous statements of Augustine." [36]

The following works of Augustine are of chief importance for the study of this fundamental experience in his life: *Liber de 83 quaestionibus* (388-396); *De libero arbitrio* (388-395); *Quaestiones ad Simplicianum* (397); *Confessiones* (400). In connection with the Pelagian controversy: *De peccatorum meritis et remissione* (412); *De spiritu et littera* (412); *De natura et gratia* (415); *De perfectione justitiae hominis* (415); *De gestis Pelagii* (417); *De gratia Christi et de peccato originali* (418); *De nuptiis et concupiscentia* (419); *Contra duas epistulas Pelagianorum* (420); *Contra Julianum* (421); *De gratia et libero arbitrio* (427); *De correptione et gratia* (427); *De praedestinatione sanctorum* (428); *De dono perseverantiae* (429). *Opus imperfectum contra Julianum* (until his death).

---

[33] Fisher, *op. cit.,* p. 190.
[34] Cf. the interesting characterization by Harnack, *History of Dogma*, V, 172.
[35] *Soliloquies,* I, 1, 5.
[36] Harnack, *History of Dogma,* V, 49.

The following is an endeavor to present Augustine's views on sin and grace in the form of a brief outline.[37]

In his conflict with Manichaeism, Augustine had learned not to look for man's sinfulness in natural qualities received at creation. The original man was just, and his will was in harmony with God as well as with himself. The will was master over the carnal impulses. There was no suffering. To this God had added the help (*adjutorium*) to remain in this blessed state.[38] In this state man was able not to sin and die, but not incapable of sinning and dying (*posse non peccare et non mori*, not *non posse peccare et non posse mori*). Man's will was free and under no compulsion. Should man apply his freedom in the wrong direction, his state would become one in which it was impossible not to sin and not to die (*non posse non peccare et non mori*).[39]

The fall of Adam was a great sin. Pride was the motive.[40] He wanted to be his own master and refused to obey God. This fall was not just a single act, for his will became evil. Turning from God he turned to himself. Thus Adam became a sinner with a sinning will.[41] The soul lost its *adjutorium* and with it the control over the body. The mind became carnal and was turned to things low, changeable, mutable and uncertain.[42]

The sin of Adam was the sin of the whole human race. For this Augustine quoted Rom. 5:12 (where the Vulgate uses *in quo* for *eph ō*). We all were in Adam, and all were he.[43] Augustine taught that human nature in its totality was seminally present in the first man. As a personal act the first sin was not our act but the act of another; yet it was truly the common act of mankind in its collective or undistributed form of existence. "We sin willingly." (*Non inviti tales sumus*).[44] Therefore, guilt is imputed to the whole race. It is the guilt of the entire race by right, because the will of his posterity

---

[37] Quotations are from the English version of his works as found in *NPNF*, especially Vol. V.
[38] *On Rebuke and Grace*, 33-34 (XII).
[39] *Ibid.*, 10 (VI); II (VII); 32 (XI); 33 (XII).
[40] *On Marriage and Concupiscence*, II, 58; *On Nature and Grace*, 33 (XXIX).
[41] *Opus Imperfectum*, I, 71; *City of God*, XIV, 11.
[42] *On Free Will*, I, 16; 35.
[43] *On Merits and Remission of Sins*, I, 11 (X); III, 14 (VII); *passim*.
[44] "We are such not against our will." Quoted by Seeberg, *Textbook*, I, 344.

was operative in Adam's sin. Children are included in this condition of sin though actual sins have not been committed; their salvation in case of death can be admitted only if they were baptized.[45]

Such was Augustine's conception of original sin. The means for the transmission of sin from parents to child was seen in the impure character of the sexual desire which, in his view, is not separable from sin. He wrote: "When it shall come to the act of generation, it is not possible that allowable and honorable intercourse should occur without the burning of lust, so that what springs from reason might be transmitted and not what springs from lust." [46] We see that Augustine differed from Luther. While to Luther inherited sin was essentially unbelief, to Augustine it was the dominion of sensuality over the spirit. "The corruption of the body which oppresses the soul is not the cause, but the penalty of the first sin; neither does the corruptible flesh make the soul a sinner, but the sinful soul makes the flesh corrupt." [47] It has often caused surprise that Augustine could not decide whether to accept traducianism or creationism.[48] One would expect him to have been a traducianist.

Man's restoration comes through grace alone. This grace is in no sense just relatively, but absolutely necessary. It attaches itself to the remnant of the divine image in man, in his need of redemption and in the capacity for salvation.[49] Grace begins with baptism, which is the first act through which God establishes a relation between himself and man who needs grace. Even children cannot be saved without baptism. Through baptism, the guilt of original sin is removed.[50] Grace received by faith does what the law with its demands was unable to do, namely, to overcome concupiscence. Now the motto is "Grant what Thou commandest," no longer "Do what I command." [51] Grace operates as a divine creative act.[52] In this process of renewal the Holy Spirit works

---

[45] *City of God*, XIII, 14; *On Merits and Remission of Sins*, I, 10 (IX); 11 (X); *passim.*

[46] *On Merits and Remission of Sins*, II, 22 (XV); 36 (XXII); *On Marriage and Concupiscence*, I, 24 (XXII); 27 (XXIV).

[47] *City of God*, XIV, 3; *passim.*

[48] *On The Soul and Its Origin*, II, 20 (XIV); 21 (XV); *passim.*

[49] *City of God*, XXII, 24; *On the Spirit and the Letter*, 47 (XXVII).

[50] See the argument in *On Merits and Remission of Sins*, and on *The Baptism of Infants.*

[51] *On the Spirit and the Letter*, 22 (XIII).

[52] *On the Grace of Christ*, 25 (XXIV).

faith in man, dispelling the spiritual ignorance which had come over man through the fall. Man assents to divine truth and arrives more and more at a higher knowledge of spiritual things.[53] Faith as mere assent does not save; it must become a faith in Christ, in which "both hope and love are added." [54] Through this "infusion of love" the will of man is liberated more and more so that concupiscence loses its power over him. In this way nature is repaired and man is transformed. It is of the greatest importance to observe that the transformation of the natural man into a spiritually minded man is not the result of a natural psychological development as the Pelagians believed, but that it is the result of a supernatural divine influence upon his will. It is this process for which Augustine uses the term "justification" (he also uses the terms *renovatio, vivificatio, regeneratio, sanctificatio*). By this term he means that, after the beginning of the new life has been made with the forgiveness of his sin,[55] man actually becomes righteous.[56] Augustine needed this emphasis upon forgiveness as the first gift of grace in order to secure peace for the sinner who has not yet had an opportunity to exercise his faith in works of love. So closely did he connect the anticipated renovation with this act of forgiveness that he failed in interpreting Paul as the Reformation succeeded in doing.[57] There was a deplorable absence of an emphatic distinction between justification and sanctification as Paul and Luther taught it. Grace to Augustine was essentially an inspiration of a good will[58] in the form of a gradual process.[59]

[53] *Commentary on St. John*, XXVII, 6; XXII, 5; XXIX, 6.
[54] *Ibid.*, XXIX, 6.
[55] *On the Spirit and the Letter*, 51-52 (XXIX).
[56] *Ibid.*, 45 (XXVI).
[57] *Ibid.*, 51 (XXIX); *Sermons*, 158, 4-5.
[58] *On Rebuke and Grace*, 3 (II).
[59] Both Rome and Wittenberg have appealed to Augustine. The followers of Luther (likewise the followers of Calvin) can claim him on the doctrine of natural depravity and of free grace in the forgiveness of sin without antecedent works of merit. Rome can claim Augustine because he conceived of justification as a gradual process which made man actually righteous. Nonetheless, we must not forget (1) that Augustine, like Luther, saw in the forgiveness of sins through baptism a divine act of justification which was preceded by no meritorious work (compare with this the Roman Catholic *meritum de condigno*), and (2) that the principle of justifying love, which Augustine always regarded as a work of the Holy Spirit, brings him closer to the position of the Reformers.
In this connection Nygren's conception of Augustine is of special interest. Augustine, he maintains, came to Christianity with a Hellenistic prepossession,

Grace, in Augustine's view, is irresistible and predestinating. This doctrine, in its completed form, was added after he had developed his doctrine of sin and grace. This was finished before the Pelagian controversy began in 412. Not until 416, in his letter to Pauline of Nola, did Augustine offer his teaching of predestination.

In grace, says Augustine, we have the will of God with regard to man's salvation. If grace lays hold on man, there can be no resistance, for God carries out his will in the human heart no less than in nature. His grace is irresistible. It is *given freely* and is "prevenient" to human action.[60] God accomplishes this through, not against man's will, to which God gives freedom from the old servitude to the end that man choose the good.[61] Thus man is liberated from the power of concupiscence. In these statements Augustine would not deny the freedom of the will. He would simply say that the will always makes its choice with freedom. The choice of the will depends, however, upon the inclination of the heart. If the heart is inclined toward the natural, the will cannot and will not choose the spiritual. When grace changes the inclination of the heart, the will then freely chooses the spiritual things.[62] In the operation of changing the heart grace acts in such a way that man's will cannot resist.[63] For this reason we can say: Man is converted not because he wills the spiritual; rather he wills the spiritual because he is converted.

the Eros motif; man's ascending desire for the *summum bonum* was the dominant feature in his thought. In his study of Paul, Augustine was confronted with the Agape motif of Christianity, with God's descending love for men. This meeting of the Eros and Agape motifs produced "a characteristic third which is neither *Eros* nor *Agape,* but *Caritas.*" *Caritas,* to Augustine, is primarily love to God, not God's own love. It is love directed upwards, the means to possess in the Creator the *summum bonum.* But has any man the power to raise himself to God? To this question Augustine answers: By grace only. Thus *gratia* became the key word of Augustine's interpretation of Christianity. According to him, "everything in our life," as Nygren observes, "depends ultimately on God's grace." "It is at this point," Nygren adds, "that Augustine is furthest from the Hellenistic theory which served as a starting point for his doctrine of *Caritas. . . .* Without grace there is no access to God. Without grace *Caritas* has no air beneath its wings for its flight to god" [*Agape and Eros,* pp. 526 ff.]. But "the end is and remains the ascent of *Caritas* to God" [*Ibid.,* pp. 449 ff.].

[60] *On Rebuke and Grace,* 45 (XIV); *Commentary on St. John,* LXXXVI, 2.
[61] *On the Spirit and the Letter,* 52 (XXX); *Epistles,* 159, 2; *Enchiridion,* 25, 100.
[62] *On Grace and Free Will,* 31 (XV), 4 (II).
[63] *On Rebuke and Grace,* 45 (XIV).

To this Augustine added that God gives the gift of perseverance, the *donum perseverantiae*, to the elect.[64] Man needs this gift if he is to be saved, and God grants it. According to Augustine the gift of perseverance is not granted in individual instances, from case to case; rather it is given in a way that keeps man in a state of grace from which individual good acts naturally issue.[65]

Why do not all who are called yield to grace? Augustine answers this question with the doctrine of predestination. Some men have been predestined to salvation from eternity. Their number is fixed and unchangeable. They are to "fill up the gap which the rebellion and fall of the devil had left in the company of the angels." [66] To the predestined (*electi*) God gives the grace of perseverance. This grace belongs to their predestination. They may stumble and fall but they cannot do so permanently.[67] Since justification, in the eyes of Augustine, is a gradual process, the elect will always remain uncertain whether they have received the gift of perseverance. Hence they ought to rejoice in their salvation with fear and trembling, for the non-elect too may appear to be true Christians who have been called, justified, and regenerated through baptism. Yet they will not be saved, for they are not elected.[68]

Normally the elect are among the called who are gathered into the Church. Augustine considers it possible that some of the elect may never have heard the gospel in this life.[69]

To the question why God chooses some and leaves others to their fate, the only answer is "I so will." To this answer the creature must humbly bow before his Creator. Augustine avers that God cannot be blamed for the rejection of the non-elect; the fact is, they fall by their own will, and God simply passes them by. Man is in no position to call God to account. God would be righteous even if he were to punish all. "He who is delivered has good reason for thankfulness, he who is condemned has no ground for finding fault." [70]

[64] *Ibid.*, 34, (XII); *On the Gift of Perseverance*, 1 (I).
[65] Cf. Seeberg, *Textbook*, II, 536-37.
[66] *Enchiridion*, 29; *City of God*, XXII, 1.
[67] Cf. *On the Gift of Perseverance*.
[68] *On Rebuke and Grace*, 24 (IX).
[69] *On the Predestination of the Saints*, 17 (IX); *Epistles*, 102, 2, 12, 14-15; *On Baptism*, V, 27-38.
[70] *On the Gift of Perseverance*, 17 (VIII).

Does Augustine teach a predestination to damnation? Usually he speaks of the non-elect as people whom God passes by, whom the Almighty "permits" to be deceived and hardened. Occasionally he speaks of some men predestined by God to everlasting death and damnation.[71]

In a brief outline, this is Augustine's teaching of predestination. Is the great African a representative of an absolute determinism? Harnack is inclined to answer this question in the affirmative,[72] while Loofs states flatly, "Augustine was no determinist."[73] Seeberg, on the other hand, thinks that it is difficult to arrive at a definite conclusion. As to his concept of God, Augustine seems to hold deterministic views. When speaking about man, he never denies man's responsibility because man did not lose the power of willing through the fall. However, the deterministic view is evidently the overtone in this great composition on sin and grace. Seeberg prefers to call Augustine's position a "modified determinism."[74]

The religious significance in Augustine's teaching of predestination is fittingly expressed by Nygren in this statement: "The Augustinian doctrine of predestination . . . is the most emphatic confession of the unmotivated and spontaneous nature of Divine love. Augustine has taken seriously the idea: 'You have not chosen me, but I have chosen you.'"[75]

V. SEMI-PELAGIANISM AND THE TEMPORARY SETTLEMENT OF THE CONTROVERSY

The crudities of Pelagianism were rejected by the Church when it excommunicated Caelestius, the friend of Pelagius, at a synod in Carthage in 412. The Church condemned Pelagianism at a general synod in Carthage in 418 and again at the Third Ecumenical Council at Ephesus in 431.[76] But the rejection of Pelagianism did not mean the acceptance of everything in the Augustinian system. It was Augustine's doctrine of predestination which gave offense, even to those

---

[71] *Commentary on St. John*, XLIII, 13; XLVIII, 6; C, 2; *Enchiridion*, 26, 100; *City of God*, XV, 1.
[72] *History of Dogma*, V, 218.
[73] *Leitfaden*, p. 411.
[74] *Lehrbuch*, II, 539-40.
[75] Nygren, *op. cit.*, p. 468.
[76] Cf. Seeberg, *Textbook*, I, 368 ff. and Ayer, *op. cit.*, pp. 400 ff.

who otherwise favored him in his controversy with Pelagius. We now come to a series of conflicts known as the Semi-Pelagian Controversies.

Due to Augustine's doctrine of predestination, there was a considerable agitation among the monks in Egypt. By pushing the doctrine of predestination to its two logical conclusions, some relaxed into a state of optimistic but rash confidence, some became the victims of distressed consciences and were plunged into the abyss of hopeless despair, and others fell into the error which ascribes merit to the human factor in salvation. In 427 Augustine wrote his treatises *On Grace and Free Will* and *On Rebuke and Grace*,[77] in which he endeavored to counteract the disastrous consequences of his doctrine.

More violent was the opposition which arose in southern Gaul. At Massilia there was a monastery which was presided over by John Cassianus, a disciple and a friend of Chrysostom. The monks of this monastery and the theologians belonging to the same school protested against Augustine's doctrine of predestination. Among them was the famous Vincent of Lérins, who set forth the criteria of Catholic doctrine in his *Commonitorium pro Catholicae Fidei Antiquitate et Universitate* (434),[78] insisting that only that is genuinely Catholic and orthodox which has been "believed always, everywhere, and by all." An application of this principle to Augustine's theory of predestination made it very evident that on this point Augustine was far from being Catholic.

These opponents of Augustine's doctrine of predestination were called Semi-Pelagians. Most of them could, with more precision, be styled Semi-Augustinians. They admired Augustine in everything except predestination. They strongly emphasized man's sinfulness, particularly its sensual aspects. The sin of Adam was regarded as a hereditary disease. Since the fall a weakness prevails in the human will. They found this to be their starting point in Augustine's teaching of the natural depravity of man.

They abhorred Augustine's doctrine of predestination and characterized it as new, therefore in conflict with tradition; and as dangerous because it defeats the end of preaching, and weakens the moral energy

---

[77] *NPNF*, V, 436 ff.

[78] *MSL*, 50, 637 ff. See the English text in *LCC*, IX, 36 ff.

or leads into despair. Augustine's doctrine of predestination, they held, supposes that God, the Creator, is of diverse natures. In opposition to all this these opponents declared that grace is absolutely general, that Christ died for all, and that predestination must be based upon foreknowledge.

The Semi-Pelagian features of these Semi-Augustinians were not absent. They taught that, while man had suffered a great weakening of his spiritual powers in the fall and was therefore unable to free himself by his own will, he was able to wish to have the Physician and to believe in Him. God comes to the assistance of the weakened human will. Grace is concomitant with and not prevenient to human merits. Grace co-operates with man's free will. Cassianus[79] approached Pelagius when he said that grace is an enlightenment and instruction through the law by which a spiritual understanding is given. But who takes the initiative in the working out of our salvation? Cassianus said that sometimes God takes the first step, and sometimes man does. But in all cases it is co-operation. Thus *sola gratia*—Augustine's finest contribution—was sacrificed. Augustine wrote *On the Predestination of the Saints* and *On the Gift of Perseverance*[80] against the Massilians.

Defenders of Augustinianism

After the death of Augustine in 430, Prosper of Aquitania (d. 460) raised the standard on behalf of the Augustinian doctrine and waged a stern warfare with all its opponents. His chief work, *Liber Collationum*, and his polemical, *Carmen de Ingratis*, were written against those who did not attribute all good to divine grace.[81] He characterized Semi-Pelagianism as an impossible *tertium quid* arising from Augustinianism and Pelagianism. Whereas Pelagius had taught that man takes the initiative and the Church taught that grace makes a beginning, the Semi-Pelagians ambiguously straddled the fence. Prosper also criticized the Semi-Pelagian attitude on original sin. On the one hand, he said, they admitted that man's sinful condition was inherited. On the other hand, however, they spoke of seeds of virtue in man, which showed that the sin from Adam was not regarded as total depravity.

---

[79] The works of Cassianus are in *MSL*, Vols. 49-50.
[80] *NPNF*, V, 493 ff.
[81] See his writings in *MSL*, Vol. 51.

In another writing which came from the Augustinian circle and which appeared anonymously under the title *De vocatione gentium*,[82] an attempt was made to construct a doctrine of sin and grace on the basis of Augustinian conceptions. Care was taken, however, to avoid the most objectionable features. It is not the human will, by its merits, that makes the beginning toward salvation, but the elective will of God, which does not exclude the free exercise of man's will.

In order to save the universality of grace (I Tim. 2:4) along with the Augustinian conception of a special election of a limited number, the author of this work introduced the distinction—peculiar to himself —between general and special grace. By general grace the writer meant God's dealings with individuals and peoples independent of His special revelation, as through the voice of nature, endowments, providence, traditions, and influence of the Spirit (Acts 17:28; 14:14). This general revelation is sufficient to induce men to turn to God and seek him. For those who are really saved, there is the special grace through the revelation in Christ. The general grace has a pedagogical significance in that it leads men to the special grace in revelation. This special grace is enjoyed by only a part of humanity. The best co-operation of such general and special grace is seen in people under the influence of Christianity. Grace in its manifold forms of influence (invitation through examples, dangers, miracles, intuitions, suggestions) takes the initiative everywhere and influences the will in its relation to salvation in Christ. Behind this grace stands God's irrevocable decree of election with regard to certain individuals. Why are not all men saved? Here the writer takes refuge in theological mystery. It is certain that the lost perish only by their own fault.

Among the defenders of Augustinianism belongs also the unknown author of the *Hypomnesticon*, quoted in Article XVIII of the Augsburg Confession.[83] The aim of the writer was to reinstate the doc-

---

[82] *MSL,* 51, 647 ff. The idea of a twofold covenant of God with men has held a prominent place in Calvinistic theology. The distinction is made between a covenant of works and one of grace, or between a covenant of general grace and one of "special" grace. The covenant of works, or general grace, is universal; the covenant of special grace includes only the elect. Cf., for example, the Westminster Confession, Chapter VII, and Charles Hodge, *Systematic Theology* (New York: Scribner, Armstrong, & Co., 1874), II, 117 ff., 354 ff.

[83] *Hypomnesticon* ("Memorandum") *contra Pelagianos et Caelestianos* by an unknown author. The text is found in some older editions of the works of Augustine.

trines of Augustine, but at the same time to remove the offensive features of the system without endangering anything that was essential to the *sola gratia*. Through the fall, man's free will was lost in things spiritual and in things pertaining to salvation. Freedom of will was retained only with regard to what concerns this present life, that is, with regard to purely external matters (*res externae*) such as building a house, and with regard to external things in the moral sphere—civil righteousness and its opposite—such as murder, theft, etc. Freedom in spiritual things is restored through prevenient grace which flows from the wounds of Christ and works faith and the power for good works in man. It is, however, within man's power to resist God's gracious influences. Predestination is distinguished from prescience or foreknowledge. God foresaw who would accept Christ, and these he predestinated to salvation before the foundation of the world. He also foresaw who would continue in godlessness, but he did not predestinate them to their doom.

Voices against Augustine

The *Praedestinatus* is another anonymous writing, dated about 450. Its title was given to the work by its first editor. It seems to have been composed by a Semi-Pelagian whose aim was to satirize and thus bring into disrepute the Augustinian doctrine of predestination.[84]

A very outspoken Semi-Pelagianism was taught by Bishop Faustus of Reji, who was born in Britain and died about 495. He went beyond Cassianus and was the most promising spokesman of the Semi-Pelagians. His principal writing is *De gratia Dei et humanae mentis libero arbitrio*, which was written soon after the Synod of Arles in 475. It may be called the program of the Semi-Pelagians.[85]

Faustus spoke against Pelagius in strong terms, calling him *doctor pestifer*. He criticized Pelagius for regarding the natural powers of man as sufficient to attain salvation and for denying original sin. Holding the monastic idea, Faustus taught that original sin had its source in the sexual desire. Death came as a consequence of the fall. The free will, while not extinct, is *infirmatum et attenuatum* ("weak and

---

[84] *MSL*, 53, 587 ff. Cf. Hans von Schubert, *Der sogenannte Praedestinatus* (1903).

[85] See his writings in *MSL*, Vol. 58; also in *Corpus Scriptorum Ecclesiasticorum Latinorum* (Vienna, 1866——), hereinafter referred to as *CSEL*, Vol. XXI.

enfeebled"). Man cannot exercise it for his salvation without the aid of grace. But Faustus rejected the predestinarian conception of a divine monergism and taught that the will of man, by virtue of the freedom left in him, makes the beginning. Salvation is accomplished by the co-operation of the human and the divine factors, the latter taking the initiative. It is emphasized that the Lord invites only the willing and seeking ones. What did Faustus understand by grace (*adjutorium divinum*)? It is the illumination of man's will, preaching with its promises and warnings, and God's guiding hand in a man's life. It is not, as it was with Augustine, the regenerative power of grace in the heart.

The Temporary Settlement

Both sides had received a thorough hearing. The voice of Faustus was decidedly Pelagian, and his book was approved by many because of its rationality. A strong reaction against Augustinianism appeared among the Scythian monks of Constantinople as much as fifty years later (*ca.* 520). Fulgentius of Ruspe, in the name of a council, replied with an able apology (*De veritate praedestationis et gratia Dei*) for the doctrine of Augustine.[86] He was followed by two able Gallic bishops, Avitus of Vienna and Caesarius of Arles, who won a decided victory over Semi-Pelagianism at the Synod of Orange (529).[87]

What doctrine was accepted at Orange? A predestination of man to perdition was rejected. Beyond this statement no utterance was delivered on the doctrine of predestination. Neither did the Synod accept Augustine's doctrine of irresistible grace. Regarding sin and grace, the utter inability of the natural man in things spiritual and the necessity of attributing every good movement to grace were clearly confessed. Grace was declared to be prevenient. Not only sanctification but even the first impulses of our willing belong to the work of grace.[88]

The following paragraphs are given as a summary of the consensus upon which the followers of Augustine (for example, Prosper, Fulgen-

[86] See *MSL,* Vol. 65.

[87] Cf. F. Arnold, *Caesarius von Arelate und die gallische Kirche seiner Zeit* (1894).

[88] Cf. Ayer, *op. cit.,* pp. 472 ff.

tius, Caesarius, and Maxentius,[89] in harmony with the Roman See) stood united:

God foreknows all things, both good and evil. His prescience as such is not causative. He wills and foreordains only what is good. Predestination, therefore, has reference exclusively to the children of God.

While God foreknows all evil persons and influences, he does not foreordain them. Evil is not present in God; hence it cannot be the object of divine predestination.

When the regenerated fall it is not because they were not earnestly called, but they fall by reason of their own perverted will. Grace is universal and election is through Christ. When man perseveres in grace unto the end it is to be attributed to the grace of God alone. It is therefore impossible that a child of God should become a child of the devil through predestination. God, however, does not predestinate unto salvation those who resist him and fall.

The grace of God and the merits of Christ are for all. God earnestly desires and wills the salvation of all men (I Tim. 2:4).

To use the language of the Scythian monks: "We believe that the natural free will is able to do nothing but to distinguish and to covet the fleshly things or the things of this world; but as to the things of the eternal life it can neither think the same nor will them nor covet them nor do them; it is then that the Holy Spirit is poured out in our hearts and works inwardly in it." [90] This doctrine was approved by Bishop Boniface II of Rome.

The Church received a great heritage in the statements of the Synod at Orange: the teaching of man's complete depravity, of the loss of his spiritual freedom, of the absence of any merit in his salvation, which is by grace alone. Faith and the new life are produced by grace. This grace is attached to the sacrament of baptism, but with the admission that grace may also work independently of the sacraments, through the Word. The double predestination of Augustine was bypassed. The Middle Ages will show the return of Semi-Pelagianism and the establishment of principles that made the Reforma-

[89] John Maxentius was the leader of the Scythian monks who leaned toward Monophysitism. Pelagianism, in the eyes of many, was a heresy akin to Nestorianism.

[90] Cf. Arnold, op. cit., pp. 331 ff.

tion necessary. In all these developments, the history of Augustinianism continues.

BIBLIOGRAPHY

1. Primary Sources (dates in parenthesis)

Augustine and Grace

LIBER DE 83 QUAESTIONIBUS (388-396)
DE LIBERO ARBITRIO (388-395)
QUAESTIONES AD SIMPLICIANUM (397)
CONFESSIONES (400)

Augustine and the Pelagian Controversy

DE PECCATORUM MERITIS ET REMISSIONE (412)
DE SPIRITU ET LITTERA (412)
DE NATURA ET GRATIA (415)
DE PERFECTIONE JUSTITIAE HOMINIS (415)
DE GESTIS PELAGII (417)
DE GRATIA CHRISTI ET DE PECCATO ORIGINALI (418)
DE NUPTIIS ET CONCUPISCENTIA (419)
CONTRA DUAS EPISTULAS PELAGIANORUM (420)
CONTRA JULIANUM (421)
DE GRATIA ET LIBERO ARBITRIO (427)
DE CORREPTIONE ET GRATIA (427)
DE PRAEDESTINATIONE SANCTORUM (428)
DE DONO PERSEVERANTIAE (429)
OPUS IMPERFECTUM CONTRA JULIANUM (until his death)

2. Secondary Sources on Augustine and the Pelagians

BOHLIN, T. *Die Theologie des Pelagius in ihrer Genesis.* Upsala, 1957.
COPINGER, W. A. *A Treatise on Predestination, Election and Grace.* London: James Nisbet and Co., 1889.
FERGUSON, F. *Pelagius.* Cambridge: Cambridge University Press, 1956.
JAUNCY, E. *The Doctrine of Grace up to the End of the Pelagian Controversy.* London: SPCK, 1925.
KLASEN, F. *Die innere Entwickelung des Pelagianismus.* 1882.
LUTHARDT, CH. E. *Die Lehre vom freien Willen und sein Verhältnis zur Gnade.* 1863.
MOZLEY, J. B. *Treatise on the Augustinian Doctrine of Predestination.* 3rd ed.; London: Murray and Co., 1883.
NYGREN, ANDERS. *Agape and Eros.* Philadelphia: Westminster Press, 1953.
NYGREN, G. *Das Prädestinationsproblem in der Theologie Augustins.* 1956.
ROTTMANNER, O. *Der Augustinismus.* 1892.

SOUTER, ALEXANDER. *Pelagius' Exposition of Thirteen Letters of St. Paul.* 3 vols. Cambridge: Cambridge University Press, 1922—.

TENNANT, R. *The Sources of the Doctrines of the Fall and Original Sin.* Cambridge: Cambridge University Press, 1903.

————. *The Origin and Propagation of Sin.* Cambridge: Cambridge University Press, 1902.

WARFIELD, B. B. *On Augustine and the Pelagian Controversy.* An introductory essay to *NPNF*, Vol. V.

WIGGERS, G. *An Historical Presentation of Augustinianism and Pelagianism.* Translated by RALPH WALDO EMERSON. 2 vols. Andover: Gould, Newman, and Saxton, 1840.

WILLIAMS, N. P. *The Doctrines of the Fall and Original Sin.* London and New York: Longmans, Green and Co., 1927.

CHAPTER XII

THE SACRAMENTS

We shall confine our review of the sacraments to the development of baptism and the Lord's Supper in the ancient Church. Tertullian was the first to speak of the *sacramentum baptismatis et eucharistiae*.[1] The task of giving authoritative definitions of baptism and of the Eucharist were considered only periodically by different synods.

I. BAPTISM

Baptism in the name of the triune God was looked upon as the door of admission into full membership in the Christian family. It was regarded as the means of forgiveness of all past sins, and as the sacrament by which, according to later views, the Holy Spirit is received for illumination and for regeneration.[2] The first demand for the administration of the sacraments by clerics came from Ignatius, who spoke of the sacraments as belonging to the special work of the bishops.[3]

Baptism, of course, was not meant to work magically. Without repentance and faith it would avail nothing. The gifts of baptism and the rite of its administration were not regarded as of necessity simultaneous. Yet an inner logical connection was seen between the two.[4] Later, in the Catholic Age, the use of water was supplemented by an anointing with oil. The water symbolized the removal of sin; the anointing with oil, the positive gift of the Spirit. This double act was preceded by a renunciation of the devil and by the rite of exorcism.

---

[1] *Against Marcion,* IV, 34.

[2] Justin, *Apology,* I, 7, 61; Tertullian, *On Baptism,* 1; Irenaeus, *Against Heresies,* III, 17, *passim.*

[3] *Letter to Smyrna,* VIII, 1-2.

[4] Cf. Tertullian, *On Repentance,* 6.

Somewhat later there followed the ceremony of breathing the Holy Spirit (cf. John 20:22). Baptism itself was by thrice-repeated immersion. (In Spain the immersion was only once.) During the centuries after Tertullian, other symbolical features were added. The sign of the cross was made on the forehead and breast. Later a grain of salt was put into the mouth (Mark 9:50). Eye, nose, ear, and tongue were touched with spittle and the words spoken: *Ephphatha,* "Be opened" (Mark 7:34). In Italy, a piece of money was laid into the hand as a symbol of the entrusted talent (Luke 19:12).[5]

According to Clement, baptism imparts regeneration, illumination, remission of sins, purification, divine sonship, and immortality. It confers a bright impress of righteousness by the communication of the Holy Spirit.[6]

Origen speaks of baptism as a unique means of obtaining forgiveness of sin. Of course, the candidate must turn his back upon sin.[7] In baptism the believer is united with Christ. As in the case of Jesus, the Holy Spirit descends upon the Christian in his baptism. Even infants, defiled with sin, must be baptized.[8]

The strongly realistic tendencies of Tertullian, which we have described in Chapter VIII, led him to conceive of the Spirit as an attenuated material substance influencing the water of baptism. The Spirit is spoken of as *substantia baptismatis.* As the Spirit hovered over the waters at the beginning, so he continues to linger over the water of the baptized.[9] Later, however, Tertullian modified the statement: "Not that in the waters we received the Holy Spirit, but in the water . . . we are cleansed and prepared for the Holy Spirit."[10] Unless a man receives baptism he cannot be saved. The only exception is for martyrs, whose blood is a "second font."[11] The effects of baptism include remission of sin, deliverance from death, regeneration, and the Holy Spirit.[12] However, without repentance baptism would be

---

[5] See Tertullian, *On the Crown,* 3.
[6] *The Instructor,* I, 6. *Stromateis,* IV, 18.
[7] *Homily on Luke,* 21.
[8] *De Principiis,* II, 10, 7. For further references, see Kelly, *op. cit.,* p. 208.
[9] *On Modesty,* 9; *On Baptism,* 3-14.
[10] *Ibid.,* 5.
[11] *Ibid.,* 16.
[12] *Against Marcion,* I, 28.

without value.[13] Baptism is administered to little children, although the delay of baptism, he says, is preferable because both the children and their sponsors may fail to fulfill their promises. Besides, "Why does the innocent period of life hasten to the 'remission of sins'?"[14] However the reservations expressed in this pre-Montanistic tract are not repeated by Tertullian in his later treatise, *On the Soul*. In this later writing he considers the souls of all men to be "in Adam," i.e., burdened with original sin, until by baptism they are "enrolled anew in Christ."[15]

Cyprian, the pupil of Tertullian, also sees in baptism the saving work of God in man. Because of the Novatian schism he became involved in a controversy with Bishop Stephen of Rome over the validity of schismatic baptism. While Stephen denied the validity of such baptism, Cyprian was willing to recognize baptism by the Novatians. As a result, the Roman position led to a weakening of the importance of baptism proper. Its administration was delegated to the presbyter. The imposition of hands and the sealing with chrism, however, was reserved for the bishop.[16] Here we have the beginning of "confirmation" as a separate sacrament.[17]

After Nicea, the teachings of Cyril of Jerusalem are fairly representative of the views about baptism during this period. According to him, baptism confers two basic benefits: the forgiveness of past sins

[13] *On Repentance*, 6.

[14] *On Baptism*, 18.

[15] *On the Soul*, 40. Joachim Jeremias explains the absence of these reservations as due to the fact that the former treatise is addressed to catechumens and neophytes, the latter to Christian parents. It is difficult to see why Tertullian should have regarded the children of converts to Christianity as less sinful than the children of Christians. More probably the difference reflects a deepening conception of original sin in the writer himself. In addition, the frequent denial of a "second repentance" endangered the salvation of all the baptized. In the decades following Constantine, the custom of the Greek mystery religions to postpone the rite until the children "can take in something of the mystery" seems to have produced a real crisis. Thus Basil the Great, Gregory of Nazianzus, Ambrose, and Augustine, for example, were not baptized until the ages of 27, 29-30, 33-34, and 32, respectively.

[16] Cf. Kelly, *op. cit.*, pp. 210-11.

[17] Penance developed as a separate sacrament in a similar way. When the original sequel of repentance and baptism became inverted by the practice of infant baptism, penance became a "second plank after shipwreck" and acquired the status of a sacrament. Cf. *ibid.*, pp. 436 ff.

and sanctification for the years ahead. "You go down dead indeed in sin, and you come up alive unto righteousness." [18] The operation of the Spirit, in his thought, is closely linked with the baptismal waters. As a matter of fact, he, and others after him, for example, his namesake Cyril of Alexandria, were inclined to a view of consubstantiation of the water and Spirit.[19]

In the West, Augustine put a lasting stamp on the doctrine of baptism. Augustine's teaching appears especially in his writings against the Pelagians. He taught that it is the guilt of man's natural depravity, first of all, that is removed by baptism. Concupiscence, which before baptism constitutes man's special and real guilt, is no longer imputed to him. It is admitted that together with the forgiveness of the guilt attached to the general sinful condition, the sins committed by heart, mouth, and hand, are also forgiven (*per accidens*). But it is especially the inherited guilt which baptism removes. This was the new thought that was introduced by Augustine. Up to this time it was the sinful acts committed before baptism that were spoken of as the special objects of removal through the forgiving grace of baptism. This Augustinian thought soon took hold of the Church. There was a lasting truth which has served not only to complement, but also to counteract the insufficient conceptions of the Eastern Church on this subject.

To sum up, baptism, according to Augustine is: (1) the sacrament for removing the guilt of the sinful condition with which man is born. (2) The inherited sinful desire remains after baptism as a morbid leaning to sin. But (3) with baptism the Holy Spirit is received as the beginning of a renovation in a continued forgiveness of the daily sins in which that languor is more and more reduced. (4) The objective character of baptism was safeguarded by insisting that, while baptism does not bring salvation to the unconverted, it does stamp them with a *character dominicus* in which the Lord claims them as his property. For this reason they are not to be rebaptized when they become converted or return to the Church. Their original baptism is simply to be recognized. (5) Nor are children, who later become conscious of the meaning of baptism, to be rebaptized. They simply

---

[18] *Catechetical Lectures,* III, 12.
[19] *Ibid.,* III, 4-5. Cf. Kelly, *op. cit.,* pp. 428-29.

step into conscious possession of the forgiveness of sin and of the Spirit.[20]

II. THE LORD'S SUPPER

A. The Lord's Supper in the Early Church

The Biblical Material

The Lord's Supper has been much in the limelight in recent New Testament scholarship. Yet in a work like ours, we cannot enter upon a critical analysis of these findings. We must content ourselves with stating a few basic principles.

In the New Testament we have four accounts of the Institution: Matt. 26:26-29, Mark 14:23-25, Luke 22:15-20, and I Cor. 11:23-25.

In these accounts three theological motives are to be discerned: (1) At the Last Supper Jesus acted not as priest, but as the head of a family. He gave his body not to God, but to his disciples. Hence the Supper is sacramental in character though it proclaims his sacrificial death on Golgotha. (2) It affirms the covenant of God with his people. (3) It is an anticipation of the messianic banquet. To these three points, Paul added a fourth element: participation in the Supper is a constituent factor of the Church of the New Testament (I Cor. 10:17). In addition, the sixth chapter of the Gospel of John must not be overlooked. The discourse in which Jesus presents himself as the bread of life is a *scandalon* or stumbling block to the Jews. The disciples, however, by partaking of the Supper, bear witness to the world that they believe in the historical Jesus as the Incarnate Son of God. As the Logos, according to John, has become "flesh," not "man," so in the Supper he gives not his "body" but his "flesh," which promises resurrection and eternal life.

The meaning of *estin* in the words of the distribution cannot be directly determined on the basis of the New Testament texts. To arrive at an understanding we must approach the problem in the light of the Hebrew mode of speech. Unlike the Greek mind which is analytic, describing that which is, the Hebrew mind thinks in terms of action. A word in Hebrew is action, event; it can be seen (Jer.

---

[20] The main sources for Augustine's position are: *On Baptism, Against the Donatists,* and "Answer to Letters of the Donatist Bishop Petilian," *NPNF,* IV, 411 ff., and the anti-Pelagian writings, especially *On the Merits and Remission of Sins* and *On the Baptism of Infants* (*NPNF,* V, 15 ff).

2:31). The event in this case is that by means of bread Christ continues his presence in the Church. The bread is truly the body of Christ in the celebration of the Supper. He is present in substance, not statically but dynamically.[21]

The Practice of the Holy Communion in the Early Church

The early Christians celebrated the Eucharist (in the *Didache*, IX, 5, the name *eucharistia* occurs for the first time) in the evening, as had been the case at the original institution. The use of candles in some churches still reminds us of this. At first, when Christians were few, the service had the form of a Christian fellowship meeting with a meal which was called the *agape*. But the growth of the Church soon necessitated the separation of the two. The first step was to let the Eucharist precede the *agape*. The next step was to celebrate the Eucharist in the morning and the *agape* in the evening. About the end of the fourth century, the *agape* was taken out of the churches and held in private homes, which soon led to its entire discontinuance.

At first, when the Christians had no houses of worship, the liturgical form was very simple. The bishop or leader began with a prayer of praise and thanksgiving spoken over the bread and wine (*eucharistian poieitai*).[22] The congregation answered with "Amen." Next followed the brotherly kiss (*philema hagion*) to indicate the reconciliation of hearts. Then the broken bread and the cup were passed. After the third century, the liturgy was further developed and used in the *Missa fidelium*, which gathered the baptized members of the Church and separated them from those still under catechetical instruction (*Missa catechumenorum*). We have this more fully developed liturgy for the Lord's Supper in the *Apostolic Constitutions*.[23] According to the

---

[21] Cf. Oscar Cullmann and J. Leenhardt, *Essays on the Lord's Supper* (London: Lutterworth Press, 1958), pp. 44 ff.

[22] Justin Martyr, *Apology*, I, 66.

[23] Book VII, 25; VIII, 12-15. In *ANF*, Vol. VII. The various liturgies of the ancient Church are discussed at great length by Hans Lietzmann in *Messe und Herrenmahl* (1926). Lietzmann set forth the theory that the original celebration was not a memorial of Christ's death (cf. Acts 2:6, the eucharistic prayer of the *Didache*). The sacrificial aspect was first introduced by Paul, who claimed to have received it by special revelation (I Cor. 11:23). This Pauline version was later adopted by the synoptic writers. Lietzmann's interpretation of the verb in question, *paralambano*, is highly improbable, for elsewhere in the same Letter (15:1, 3) it clearly refers to the tradition Paul has received in the Church. (Cf. R. Kittel, *Wörterbuch zum Neuen Testament*, IV, 14).

liturgy of James, used in Jerusalem about the third and fourth centuries, the service began with the reading of several prayers. Then followed the *offertorium*, that is, the gifts of bread and wine, which were gathered by the deacon. The loaf chosen for the celebration was called *hostia*. The liturgy continued with a benediction, the brotherly kiss, the washing of hands by the administering clergyman, and the warning of the communicants against receiving the sacramental gift unworthily. There followed the preparation of the elements, which were guarded against insects by fans used by two sub-deacons. Then the bishop, or the presbyter as his substitute, in an impressive garment, continued:

"Lift up your hearts." The congregation answered: "We lift them up to the Lord." Bishop: "Let us give thanks to the Lord, our God." Congregation: "This is worthy and right." Next followed a prayer for the sanctification of the gifts. After another prayer, the bishop said: "The holy to the holy." The congregation answered: "One is holy; One is God; One is Jesus Christ, to the honor of God the Father, blessed in all eternity. Amen. Glory be . . ." During the Communion, Psalm 34 was sung. The distribution took place with the simple words: "The Body of Christ, the Blood of Christ, the Cup for eternal life," the communicant answering, "Amen." Certain localities developed their own liturgies which, however, show their dependency upon the orginal one. At Alexandria we have the Liturgy of Mark; at Constantinople the Liturgy of Basil, which, in more abbreviated form, issued into the widely used Liturgy of Chrysostom and is in use even today in the Eastern Orthodox church. Among the Western liturgies, the one by Gregory the Great was increasingly recognized.

B. Gradually Developing Doctrinal Concepts

The history of the Eucharist in the ancient Church does not represent a logical development doctrinally. A dogma of the Lord's Supper was unknown. Neither synods nor councils concerned themselves with eucharistic doctrine. The phrase in the Apostles' Creed, *communio sanctorum*, is ambiguous. It may refer to fellowship with the saints or to participation in "holy things," that is, the sacraments.

The Post-Apostolic Fathers and, as a matter of fact, almost all the Fathers of the ancient Church except the earlier Alexandrians, impress one with their natural and unconcerned realism. To them the Eucharist was in some sense the body and blood of Christ. The *Didache* speaks of it as the spiritual food for eternal life.[24] Ignatius, by pointing to John 6:54, calls it "the medicine of immortality" and "the antidote to prevent us from dying." [25] Justin Martyr says, "We receive it not as common bread or common drink . . . it is the flesh and blood of that Jesus who was made flesh." [26]

In Irenaeus we observe a strange emphasis upon the Eucharist as an offering of bread and wine. To this we shall have occasion to return later. Here we are interested in whether Irenaeus can be taken as a representative of a realistic conception of the Eucharist. It is a historical fact that the old distinction in Protestant theology between an earthly and heavenly matter (*materia terrestris* and *materia coelestis*) in the Lord's Supper goes back through Luther to Irenaeus, who spoke of a matter *epigeiou te kai ouraniou*.[27] In the passage quoted above, he argues against the Gnostics: "Because our flesh is nourished in the Eucharist by the body and blood of our Lord, therefore it is not possible for our bodies to fall victims to death and decay." The meaning of Irenaeus is that through the prayer of the Church (*epiklēsis*) the Holy Spirit unites the Logos with the elements, bread and wine, and makes them something that they were not before, namely, body and blood of Christ.[28] This was not meant to be transubstantiation, but it is the union of the Logos with the elements that makes these the body and blood of the Lord.

In the West, Tertullian spoke regularly of the bread as the "body of the Lord." His argument was based on the intimate relation of body and soul: "The flesh feeds on the body and blood of Christ, that the soul may likewise fatten on its God." [29] At other times, he sees in the bread only a *figura corporis*, which "represents" (*repraesentat*) the body of Christ.[30] But as Kelly correctly observes, "the verb *repraesentare*, in Tertullian's vocabulary retained its original signifi-

---

[24] *Op cit.,* X, 3.
[25] *Letter to Ephesians,* XX, 2; *To Smyrneans,* VII.
[26] *Apology,* I, 66.
[27] *Against Heresies,* IV, 18, 5.
[28] *Ibid.,* IV, 17, 5; V, 2, 3.
[29] *On the Resurrection of the Flesh,* VIII; *On Prayer,* XIX; *On Idolatry,* VII.
[30] *Against Marcion,* III, 19; IV, 40; I, 14.

cance of 'to make present.' " [31] While accepting the equation of bread and body, "he remains conscious of the sacramental distinction between them." [32] This interpretation is vindicated by what Tertullian says in his explanation of the Fourth Petition, "Give us this day our daily bread, *spiritually*. For Christ is our Bread; because Christ is Life, and bread is life. . . . Then we find too that His body is reckoned in the bread (*in pane*)." [33] The living Christ, then, is the gift of the Eucharist, but he is offered *in pane*. As was later the case in Luther, an instrumental relationship exists between the elements and Christ.

In the same passage Tertullian expresses still another idea. In petitioning for daily bread, he continues, "we ask for perpetuity in Christ, and indivisibility from His body." [34]

The bread, then, represents not only the body of the historical Jesus, but also the Church of Jesus Christ, for the one bread makes one body of the many members (I Cor. 10:17).

A different situation confronts us when we turn to the Alexandrian fathers. True, they too use the conventional realistic language. But their bias to allegory and their Platonizing method—to seek the spiritual reality behind the physical phenomena—alters the perspective.

To drink the blood of Jesus, Clement says, "is to become partaker of the Lord's immortality." [35] The eucharistic wine is a mixture of the Logos with material substance. Yet what appears to be a reference to the Eucharist turns out to be an allegory communicating a Gnostic mystery: "For so He imparts of Himself to those who partake of such food in a more spiritual manner, when now the soul nourishes itself, according to the truth-loving Plato [!]." [36]

Origen concurs fully with this sentiment of Clement. Although he writes that the "bread becomes (*gignesthai*) by prayer a sacred body" [37] and recommends showing reverence for the consecrated elements, the Logos and his words are much more important to him. The bread which the Lord held in his hand, Origen says, is not his body. Instead, it is the word in whose image (*in cuius mysterio*) the

---

[31] Kelly, *op. cit.*, p. 212.
[32] *Ibid.*
[33] *On Prayer*, VI.
[34] *Ibid.*
[35] *The Instructor*, II, 2; cf. *Who Is the Rich Man?* XXIII, 4.
[36] *Stromateis*, V, 10.
[37] *Against Celsus*, VIII, 33.

bread was to be broken.[38] Hence the words of Christ, of whom the elements are a symbol, are the efficacious gift of the Supper. The outward rite is for the simpler Christians, that they may have a thorough instruction in the faith.[39]

The Eucharist was also the center of worship, the sacrifice of the Christian people. Originally it had the significance of an offering of praise (*sacrificium laudis*), an offering of the lips (Acts 5:8, 8:3-4; Heb. 13:15; cf. Hos. 14:3; Ps. 50:25, 116:17) on the part of the participating congregation for the gifts of God in bread and wine which are now brought as offerings for distribution among the poor. But soon the saying of these eucharistic prayers over the oblations were made the special duty of the officers of the Church,[40] namely the bishops (or presbyters) and the deacons, who were compared with the priests and the Levites of the Old Testament and their offerings. Soon the real act of offering was seen, not in the offering of the congregation, but in the dedication of those gifts for use in the Eucharist. Gradually the *touto poieite* ("this do"), the words of Christ in the institution of the Supper, acquired the meaning that was later given this phrase in the Decrees of Trent. The next step in the development is seen in the words of Cyprian: "The bishop now imitates that which Christ did, and he offers the true and full sacrifice in the Church to God the Father." [41] This seemed natural, because bread and wine were held to be the body and blood of Christ. Cyprian simply stated what was already the belief of his age.

Origen's view of the Supper left a permanent mark upon Eastern Christianity. The Antiocheans, owing to their peculiar Christology which denied the organic unity of the two natures in Christ, leaned toward the symbolic conception. Theodore of Mopsuetia, in interpreting I Cor. 11:34, spoke of the elements as symbols of the death of Christ.[42] Theodoret maintained that the Lord does not change the elements; instead, he adds his grace to objects of nature. The elements remain what they are, "but they are thought and believed to be what

---

[38] *Homilies on Exodus*, XIII, 3.

[39] *Commentary on Matthew*, Sermon 85.

[40] *Commentary on John*, XXXII, 24. For further references, see Kelly, *op. cit.*, pp. 213-14.

[41] *Epistles*, 63. Cf. Ayer, *op. cit.*, pp. 234 ff.

[42] Cf. G. E. Steitz, *Die Abendmahlslehre der griechischen Kirche* (1864), referred to in the article "Abendmahl" by Loofs in *PRE, I*, 55.

they have become, and are worshiped as what they are believed to be." [43]

The future, however, belonged to the realistic conception of the eucharistic elements, though men like Eusebius, Athanasius, Gregory of Nazianzus, and Basil the Great were still aware of a substantial difference between the elements and the body and blood of Christ. The elements are to them *symbola* and *antitypa*. When they say that bread and wine are "changed" (*metaballein*) through the "*epiklesis*" of the Holy Spirit, they want to emphasize that the elements are no longer common bread and wine, but objects set aside for a holy purpose. What they actually teach is a "transformation" or "transvaluation" of the elements.

This may also be said of Cyril of Jerusalem. He, too, uses the term *metaballein* with respect to the eucharistic elements. As Christ changed water into wine at Cana, so "it is not less trustworthy to believe that He did the same when He said, This is my body." However, Cyril calls attention to the fact that we receive the body of Christ under the sign (*en typo*) of the bread. At the same time he says the Eucharist is a "holy and most awful sacrifice," an "unbloody service," in which "we offer Christ as slain for our sins." [44]

The idea of transformation was further developed and expounded in a striking manner by Gregory of Nyssa. He teaches a twofold conversion; first, a transformation of the eucharistic elements into the very body and blood of Christ, and secondly, a "transelementing" (*metastoichiōsis*) of our body and blood into the body and blood of the Lord. The first is effected through consecration; the second, through eating and drinking. The first is analogous to the incarnation. That which happened there happens anew in every Eucharist, and by eating the eucharistic bread man is liberated from the poison that makes him a victim of death. "For in no other way can anything enter the body but by being transfused through the vitals by eating and drinking." [45]

Chrysostom indulges in a description of a very coarse and sensual kind of presence, speaking of the identity of the eucharistic body with

[43] Quoted from Thomasius, *op. cit.*, I, 420.

[44] *Mystical Catechisms*, IV-V. For detailed references, see Kelly, *op. cit.*, pp. 442-43, 451, and *PRE*, I, 53.

[45] *Great Catechism*, XXXVII; *NPNF*, V, 504 ff.

the body born of the Virgin and crucified under Pontius Pilate. This body, he says, we hold in our hands and bury our teeth in it, for the elements have been refashioned (*metarrythmizein*) or transformed (*metaskeuazein*). However, Loofs[46] and other scholars maintain that this realistic language notwithstanding, Chrysostom did not hold the later Roman doctrine of transubstantiation. Basically he was an Antiochean theologian. The expressions are nothing more than the emotional outburst of a great pulpit orator.

Cyril of Alexandria contributed nothing new to the eucharistic doctrine. He simply stated that which was commonly believed, namely that the consecrated elements are the body and blood of Christ, and that the eucharistic body is identical with the body born of the Virgin.

Finally, John of Damascus (d. 750) summarized the doctrine in the following manner: "The bread and wine are not merely figures (*typa*) of the body and blood of Christ . . . but the deified body of the Lord itself." This does not mean that the body which was taken up into heaven descends, "but that the bread itself and the wine are changed (*metaballontai*) into the God's body and blood," by the energy of the Holy Spirit who performs those things that are supernatural. In every eucharistic celebration, then, "the Holy Spirit repeats the miracle of the Incarnation." [47] Of course, the Eucharist, according to John of Damascus, is also an unbloody sacrifice offered by the priest for the living and the dead.[48] On the whole, however, the sacrificial element in the teachings of the Greek fathers was held in check by the fact that they considered immortality rather than the forgiveness of sins the primary gift of the Eucharist.

This gift of immortality is the older Eastern doctrine of *metapoiōsis* ("transformation") as compared with the Western doctrine of *metaousiōsis* ("transubstantiation") to which the Eastern Church later consented at a synod at Constantinople in 1277. The difference between the doctrine of transformation and transubstantiation may be stated as follows: according to the Eastern view, the substance of the elements remains, while their "form," i.e., the source of their activity, is changed. According to the Western view, the substance of the

[46] *PRE,* I, 55.
[47] *Exposition of the Orthodox Faith,* IV, 13. *NPNF,* IX, 81 ff.
[48] *On Images,* Second Oration, 17.

bread and wine have been replaced by those of the body and blood of Christ.

The Western Church

Both Hilary and Ambrose express themselves in terms which at times have a realistic, and on other occasions a symbolic ring. Thus, Hilary, for example, may write, "Indeed we receive in a mystery the flesh of His body." [49] Ambrose remarks that through the mystery of sacred prayer the elements are transfigured into the flesh and blood of Christ.[50] On the other hand, the eucharistic sacrifice is to him only an image of divine reality.[51] More definite are the statements in two spurious writings that have at times been ascribed to him, *De sacramentis* and *De mysteriis*. In the former it is stated that through prayer the very nature of the elements is changed (*mutatur*). According to Loofs, even these writings lack the realism of the later Roman dogma. At most we may say that these writings prepared the way for the dogma to come.[52]

Augustine is of special interest regarding the concepts of the Lord's Supper in the West. His teaching, however, presents a peculiar dualism. Again we must remind ourselves of his definition of a sacrament as a visible sign of an invisible grace.

To Augustine the bread is only a sign of the body of Christ. The real body is the mystical body, the Church. Thus it is the Church that is symbolized in the Lord's Supper. Therefore, only real Christians receive a benefit. The benefit of the Supper consists in that it symbolizes our union with Christ, the spirit of love proceeding from him and operative in the Church.[53] This is Augustine's symbolical conception of the Eucharist. The sacrament is to remind us of Christ's suffering and to stimulate us for the union of love as members of his body which is the Church.

There is also another strain in the language of Augustine on the Lord's Supper. He speaks of a manducation ("chewing") of the flesh of Christ, and of a drinking of his blood. The elements are

[49] *On the Trinity,* VIII, 13.
[50] *An Exposition of the Faith,* IV, 124.
[51] *On Psalm 38,* Chap. 25.
[52] For references and criticism, see *PRE,* I, 60 ff.
[53] *City of God,* XXI, 25, 2; *Letters,* 185, 11, 50; *passim.*

called the body and blood of Christ (*corpus et sanguis Christi*). The bread is the body through the benediction of Christ. Converted Jews drink the blood which once they poured out. Loofs[54] and Seeberg[55] insist that such expressions are not irreconcilable with Augustine's symbolical conception, and they refer to the fact that Augustine repeatedly denies the ubiquity of the body of the glorified Christ. The body, he says, is confined in one place in heaven.[56]

Augustine also made use of the idea of his age that the Eucharist is a sacrifice. It is to remind Christians of the original offering.[57] The Eucharist has the significance of asserting the redeeming power of Christ's offering before God. Occasionally Augustine would say that the congregation of believers, in the union with Christ in the Supper, presents itself as an offering to God. The aim is first to express the consciousness that Christ's offering was for our redemption, and second to remind us of the duty to offer our own lives to Christ.[58]

Note that both the Eastern and the Western churches proceed from the premise that the body of Christ is locally retained in heaven. Hence the eucharistic body is in every case a new creation; according to the Eastern Church, by the energy of the Holy Spirit who, at the petition of the priest, descends upon the elements; according to the Western dogma, by virtue of the words of the institution faithfully repeated by a duly ordained priest. In other words, in the West it is held that Christ himself performs the miracle, while the view of the Eastern church is trinitarian at this point. In this respect a similarity exists between the Eastern tradition and Calvin. Note also the designation of the elements as "figures" and "symbols" in the theology of both the Eastern and the Reformed tradition. Luther belongs in a class to himself. In his eyes the "real presence" is the inevitable result of the *communicatio idiomatum*. Consequently, the ministrant of the Supper does not "make" the presence; he simply proclaims it. The uniqueness of Christ's presence in the Supper is this, that here he is present for the recipient as his gracious Savior.

---

[54] *PRE*, I, 61 ff. and *Leitfaden*, pp. 373-74.

[55] Seeberg, *Lehrbuch*, II, 545-46.

[56] *City of God*, XXII, 29 4; *Letters*, 187, 12, 41; *passim*.

[57] *Against Faustus*, XX, 18; *passim*.

[58] *On the Creed*, 11 (*NPNF*, III, 373); *Commentary on John*, Tract L, 13 (*NPNF*, VII, 282); *passim*.

One more factor must be noted. The symbolical view of the Greek Fathers, of Augustine, and of Zwingli and others is conditioned by a Platonic ontology. The things of this world are only an image of reality. The ascendancy of sacramental realism coincided with the rise of Aristotelianism in the West. The "idea" is understood as an energy operative *in* matter. From this point of view, Thomas Aquinas and Luther have much in common.

BIBLIOGRAPHY

1. Baptism
BARTH, KARL. *The Teaching of the Church regarding Baptism.* London: SCM Press, 1948.
Christian Baptism. Edited by A. GILMORE. London: Lutterworth Press, 1959.
CULLMAN, OSCAR. *Baptism in the New Testament.* London: SCM Press, 1961.
FLEMINGTON, W. F. *The New Testament Doctrine of Baptism.* London: SPCK, 1948.
JEREMIAS, JOACHIM. *Infant Baptism in the First Four Centuries.* Translated by DAVID CAIRNS. London: SCM Press, 1960.
LAMPE, G. W. H. *The Seal of the Spirit.* London: Longmans, Green and Co., 1951.

2. The Lord's Supper
"Abendmahl," *PRE*, Vol. I. Also in *Religion in Geschichte und Gegenwart,* Vol. I.
ADAMSON, ROBERT M. *The Christian Doctrine of the Lord's Supper* Edinburgh: T. & T. Clark, 1905.
ANDERSEN, A. *Das Abendmahl in den ersten zwei Jahrhunderten.* 1906.
ANGUS, S. *The Mystery Religions and Christianity.* London: Murray, 1925.
BRILIOTH, YNGVE. *Eucharistic Faith and Practice.* London: SPCK, 1930.
CLARK, N. *An Approach to the Theology of the Sacraments.* London: SCM Press, 1956.
CULLMANN, OSCAR. *Early Christian Worship.* Translated by A. STEWART TODD and JAMES B. TORRANCE, London, SCM Press, 1953.
————— and LEENHARDT, J. *Essays on the Lord's Supper.* London: Lutterworth Press, 1958.
DIX, GREGORY. *The Shape of the Liturgy.* Westminster: Dacre Press, 1949.
EICHORN, A. *Das Abendmahl im Neuen Testament.* 1898.
ELERT, W. *Abendmahl und Kirchengemeinschaft in der alten Kirche.* 1954.
FRITSCHKOPF, B. *Die neuesten Erörterungen über die Abendmahlsfrage* 1921.

GARDNER, P. *The Origin of the Lord's Supper.* London and New York: Macmillan Co., 1893.

GORE, C. *The Body of Christ.* London: Murray, 1904.

HEITMUELLER, W. *Taufe und Abendmahl bei Paulus.* 1903.

HIGGINS, A. J. B. *The Lord's Supper in the New Testament.* London: SCM Press, 1960.

HOFFMAN, J. *Das Abendmahl im Urchristentum.* 1903.

JEREMIAS, JOACHIM. *The Eucharistic Words of Jesus.* Translated by ARNOLD EHRHARDT. New York: Macmillan Co., 1955.

"Klaō," Wörterbuch zum Neuen Testament, Vol. III. Edited by R. KITTEL.

LAMBERT, JOHN G. *The Sacraments of the New Testament.* T. & T. Clark, 1903.

LIETZMANN, H. *Mass and the Lord's Supper.* Translated by DOROTHEA H. G. REEVE. Leiden: E. J. Brill, 1953—.

LILLEY, J. P. *The Lord's Supper, Its Origin, Nature and Use.* Edinburgh: Hamilton, 1891.

McDONALD, A. B. *Christian Worship in the Primitive Church.* Edinburgh: T. & T. Clark, 1934.

Meaning and Practice of the Lord's Supper. Edited by H. T. LEHMANN. Philadelphia: Muhlenberg Press, 1961.

OULTON, J. E. L. *Holy Communion and Holy Spirit.* London: SPCK, 1951.

SCHWEITZER, A. *Das Abendmahl auf Grund der wissentschaftlichen Erforschung des neunzehnten Jahrhunderts und der historischen Berichte.* 1901.

SEEBERG, R. *Das Abendmahl im Neuen Testament.* 1905.

SIMPSON, J. G. *The Sacraments of the Gospel.* London: Longmans, Green and Co., 1914.

STONE, D. *A History of the Doctrine of the Holy Eucharist.* London and New York: Longmans, Green and Co., Vol. I. 1909.

STRANGE, C. *Die Bedeutung der Sakramente.* 1927.

WETTER, G. P. *Das Christliche Mysterium, Studien zur Geschichte des Abendmahls.* 1921.

CHAPTER XIII

CONCLUDING OBSERVATIONS: THE CHRISTIANITY OF THE EAST AND OF THE WEST

In the preceding chapters, the dogma of the ancient Church has been traced in its development from the first elementary statements in the Rule of Faith into the more matured expressions of the so-called ecumenical creeds of Christendom. These creeds cover (1) Christ in his trinitarian relation or his pre-existence and (2) Christ in his historical post-existence as God-Man. In addition, the decisions of the Synod at Orange (529) on the relation of the saving will of God to the spiritual power of man in the acts of his salvation are also important. Though the twenty-five canons of this synod have not been counted among the ecumenical creeds of Christendom, they present to us a remarkable anticipation of Evangelical teaching on the roles of God and man in the appropriation of redemption.

With this faith as a common possession, East and West still differed widely in many of their views of theology and piety.

I. EASTERN CHRISTIANITY

The direction for Greek theology was received from Origen. While much of his teaching was refused, there was, nevertheless, something in his theology that continued to be characteristic of Christian thought among the Greeks. The significance of Origen lay in his combination of a threefold interest. He was interested in the Church's tradition, in the authority of the Scriptures, and in Hellenic philosophy. His high regard for the Scriptures and his own example as the first real exegete brought impulses for an extensive interpretation of the

New Testament and stimulated the growing interest in a recognized canon. (Chief in urging a canon of Holy Scriptures was Athanasius.)[1] The permanent trait which Greek theology received from the school of Alexandria was the endeavor of Origen to unite the gospel in the form of apostolic tradition with Neo-Platonic philosophy. The Alexandrian theologians were convinced that Christianity and Neo-Platonism were in essential agreement. This relation to Neo-Platonism also characterized the teaching of so prominent a theologian as Methodius of Olympus (d. 311). In contrast, he rejected the many spiritualistic heresies of Origen and his allegorical method of interpreting Scripture, and corrected him by referring to the theology of Irenaeus.[2]

The meaning of salvation in Greek theology must be given brief consideration. It was not fully the same as in Latin theology. This explains certain characteristics which must not be overlooked. Among the Greeks, the guilt of sin was not felt with the same intensity as was its effect, which was seen in the corrupting influences of sin, particularly in the blinding of man's spiritual vision to the knowledge of God. Jesus, as Savior, was taken to be more the restorer of sin's injury than the remover of its guilt. His work was to bestow incorruption (*aphtharsia*). This must not be taken to mean that the idea of Christ's death as a ransom (*lytron*) was absent; indeed, this idea was professed by John of Damascus.[3] The stress, however, was upon Christ as the giver of divine life, the remover of the corruption wrought by sin, the restorer of the real God-likeness in a deification (*theopoiesis*) and in the communication of God's glory (*doxa*). The idea of Christ's death bringing the forgiveness of sin had no stress among the Greeks. They failed to appropriate the Pauline idea of justification. They overlooked the causal connection between the regeneration of the heart and the good works that were to follow. Faith lost its scriptural meaning of a personal attitude, that is, of *fiducia* ("trust") in the forgiving grace of God, and became an orthodoxy with regard to the formal statements of dogma.[4]

[1] Cf. his famous *Easter Letter* of A.D. 367 (English text in *NPNF*, IV, 551-52.)
[2] Cf. Nygren, *op. cit.*, p. 414.
[3] *Exposition of the Orthodox Faith*, III, 27.
[4] On some of the aspects discussed here, see E. Scholz, *Die Lehre des heiligen Basilius von der Gnade* (1881); F. K. Huehmer, *Des heiligen Gregor von*

There was another trait in Eastern theology, the "mystagogical" one. The Greek mind had a deep interest in truth. To Socrates, virtue was practically identical with knowledge. Paul wrote, "The Greeks seek after wisdom" (I Cor. 1:22). In the eyes of the Gnostics, religion was a type of higher knowledge. To Clement and Origen, faith was a lower state in religion, to be developed into knowledge.

Closely related to this interest was a seemingly opposite concern. It was found that philosophical truth expressed in dogmatic statements was in danger of losing its influence on the life of its followers. This observation produced the cultivation of the Greek mysteries. These mysteries were intended to reveal and to communicate the truth more fully and to keep the faculties of the worshiper in a state of continual activity. The intellectual, discursive activity of the soul was to be submerged into a state of immediate perception of the divine mystery by means of allegory, symbol, and presentation. The Gnostics made much of this. It also affected the Church, especially in the East. We refer to the *Mystagogical Cathechisms* of Cyril of Jerusalem.[5] Christian theologians were advised to use the mysteries as symbols of heavenly things. The Trinity and the doctrine of the incarnation, especially, were represented in forms of the mysteries. While the pagan mysteries did grow out of an interest to safeguard the continued life of the philosophical principles, the embodiment of Christian truth in mystery forms issued in a ritualism through which Christian life became petrified and lost its creative power.

A factor which contributed toward making Eastern Christianity a mystical religion was the influence exercised by the writings which appeared in the last quarter of the fifth century under the name of Dionysius the Areopagite.[6] The writer of this literature is believed to have been a pupil of Paul (Acts 17:34), but the writings are of pseudonymous origin, dating from the fifth century (about 482), and

---

Nazianz Lehre von der Gnade (1890); K. Holl, *Enthusiasmus und Bussgewalt beim griechischen Mönchtum* (1898); E. Weigel, *Die Heilslehre des heiligen Cyril von Alexandrien* (1905); J. Aufhauser, *Die Heilslehre des heiligen Gregor von Nyssa* (1910). Cf. Aulén's treatment of the atonement in the Greek fathers, *Christus Victor.*

[5] *LCC*, IV, 64 ff.

[6] The Greek text is found in *MSG*, Vols. 3 and 4. Compare with J. Parker, *The Works of Dionysius the Areopagite* (London: Skiffington, 1887). See also Nygren, *op. cit.*, pp. 576 ff., and Ayer, *op. cit.*, pp. 560 ff.

probably written by a Syrian. They are composed of four tracts: *The Names of God, The Mystical Theology, The Heavenly Hierarchy*, and *The Church's Hierarchy*. Their contents reveal the ideas of Proclus (d. 485), one of the last representatives of the Neo-Platonic School at Athens. It seems to have been the aim of these writings to incorporate Neo-Platonism into the teachings of the Church and thus to remove it as an opponent.

On the basis of a Neo-Platonic abstract conception of the Godhead, in which the trinitarian relation and the incarnate Christ in union with the Father is recognized, a doctrine was proposed as follows. The Divine Being, which cannot be expressed in predicates and attributes, is to be thought of as the center of hierarchies of created beings. Closest to God, in a first periphery, is the heavenly hierarchy, represented by three orders of angels ranging from the highest to the lowest. Then follows the ecclesiastical hierarchy which also has three orders: bishops, priests, and deacons. The lay hierarchy which extends from the monks down to the other laity comes last. At the head of these orders stands Christ as the highest hierarch. The Word, sacraments, and gifts of the Spirit are the means through which the process of a gradual deification takes place. These theories of the Areopagite served as the frame for expressing characteristic elements in the piety of Greek Christianity which were continued in the Christianity of the West. The aim was to arrive at a union with God in a mystical fashion without employing intellect and understanding. The influence proceeded from the highest hierarchy, the angels, and through the priesthood down to the laity, by employing a whole system of initiations. By a worship that stimulated spiritual devotions the soul is to be lifted up into a participation of the divine (*theopoiesis*). It is the hierarchy that effects the union of man with God. Christ himself is the source and power of the hierarchy. Here is the authority in religion. This principle converted Christianity into a cultic institution directed by the priesthood. It must be admitted that this whole mystagogical theology was expressive of a deep-seated trait in the religious practice of devotion among the Eastern races.

Parallel with the adoption of the ecumenical creeds, a lower type of religion was in the process of development in the field of practical piety. This type manifested itself in the worship of saints, angels, the Virgin Mary, the cross, images, and relics. From about the fourth century, this *Christentum zweiter Ordnung* ("Christianity of the second order"), as Harnack called it,[7] became so strong that in the Greek church, with the Seventh Ecumenical Council at Nicea (787),[8] it resulted in a dogma that sanctioned the veneration of images. The report of the circumstances in that conflict, in which the theologians, and especially the monks, advocated the veneration of images, while the emperor, along with the army, violently opposed the practice, may be left to Church history. It seems that the state looked upon the worship of images as the indulgence of a private mystical piety that tended to have a weakening influence upon the virility of a nation which found itself in a life and death struggle with the forces of Mohammedanism. On the other hand, the following may be enumerated in explanation of the advocacy of image worship: Neo-Platonism, with its persistent influence upon the theologians of that day, stood for the principle that the heavenly forces work through earthly symbols and images. Monophysitism, as taught by the later Alexandrian School, particularly by Cyril, had a strong undercurrent of Greek piety. A picture of Jesus as man was looked upon as the symbol of his deity. John of Damascus contributed much to the final decision by his *Three Orations on the Images*.[9]

II. WESTERN CHRISTIANITY

As Origen was in a special way the father of Eastern theology, so Tertullian and Augustine have been the special makers of Western theology and Christianity. Our interest must be first in the pre-Augustinian and in the pre-Gregorian expressions of Western Christianity.

A review of the situation must recall the teachings of Tertullian in which he laid foundations for the theology of the West. With Tertullian we must mention Cyprian and the bishops of Rome. There were other theologians who also contributed. Some of them had been under the influence of Greek scholars: Hilary, Faustinus, Victorinus

---

[7] Harnack, *Grundriss*, p. 272.
[8] See the documents in *NPNF*, XIV, 521 ff.
[9] *MSG*, 94. Cf. *Exposition of the Orthodox Faith*, IV, 16.

Rhetor, Rufinus, Jerome, Ambrose. These men were channels for the transmission of Origen's exegesis and the theology of the Cappadocians into the West. Others were more Latin in character: Optatus, Pacian, Prudentius, and Zeno. Among all Western theologians before Augustine, Ambrose was the most influential.

In the following we shall enumerate a number of factors that constituted the characteristics of Western Christianity and theology. Western Christianity was governed by the interest in the authority of a recognized creed, namely the so-called Roman Symbol. The note was sounded by Tertullian when he demanded *crede quod traditum est* ("Believe because it is tradition").[10] He calls the Roman Symbol "a law of faith." [11] In the mind of Tertullian, furthermore, there goes with this demand to submit to the Rule of Faith the conception that the biblical foundations for the Symbol are rational, comparable to the natural knowledge of God. Reason and faith, therefore, are not antithetical. Tertullian was a believer in what was later expressed as *Credo ut intelligam* ("I believe in order that I may know"). Like the Apologists, he believed that Christianity is the truly rational religion.

With this view was associated that peculiar legalism which soon appeared as a characteristic of Western Roman Christianity. As the East inclined to speculation, so the West was interested in that moral righteousness which had its first orientation in a peculiar combination of Stoic moralism (Seneca, Cicero) with Judaistic legalism. Grace, to Tertullian, comes through the law, which teaches man to do the good and to earn eternal life as a reward. In his description of the process of the soul's salvation Tertullian moves in legal terms. There is man's deficiency in consequence of an inherited sinful condition. In baptism man is judged as one who has been forgiven. Now there is the demand upon the Christian to fulfill the law and even to accumulate merits before God. Man's shortcomings call for a repentance which must express itself in satisfactions. A question that troubled the Church for a long time was whether repentance after baptism was admissible for all sins, and whether the way was open for more than one repentance. In the principles advocated by the Roman

[10] *On the Flesh of Christ,* 2.
[11] *On the Veiling of Virgins,* 1.

bishop Callixtus foundations were laid for repentance as an institution on the basis of a further development of the teaching of Tertullian and Cyprian. The gradual result was an elaborate system of legalism.

At the same time a characteristic of Western Christianity was its interest in the institutional features of the Church. This was natural. The Romans expressed their highest ideals in the state with its organization, its rights, its authorities, its offices, and laws. Legalism dominated in the field of soteriology. This was followed in the Church by an interest in the institutional conceptions of Christianity with their aim of providing for tangible assurances of salvation in absolution and multiplied sacramental acts. The development into the institutional introduced the problem of the relation of the spiritual forces within the Church to the hierarchically organized Church. This was a problem for the East as well as the West, but in Western Christianity the movement was characterized by the interests of nascent Roman Catholicism.

Tertullian's contribution to Western theology and Christianity has been discussed. Augustine was also a powerful factor: (1) On the doctrine of the Trinity, he stressed the Unity, thus recognizing a legitimate element in Monarchianism, to which Rome had been holding. It found expression in Part One of the so-called Athanasian Creed which originated and came into use in the West. The devotion with which Augustine dealt with this problem in his *De Trinitate* ("On the Trinity") impressed upon the Church the lesson that this dogma must be a fundamental in the Christian Church forever. (2) In the conflict of Augustine with Pelagianism and Semi-Pelagianism, the soteriological interest of Western theology was thoroughly discussed. The special problem of the West was: What shall I do to be saved? The chief message of the theologians about the time of Augustine, and even before him (Ambrose and Hilary), was the way of salvation. (3) Through the Donatistic controversy the objective character of the means of grace and of the Church had been safeguarded.

Both the Eastern and the Western forms of Christianity represent the beginning of denominational types with further characteristics to be developed during the Middle Ages.

Book Two

THE MIDDLE AGES

CHAPTER I

THE MIDDLE AGES

INTRODUCTORY NOTES

In the closing chapter of Book One an estimate was given of the theological work in the ancient Church. A christological dogma had been worked out which constituted the central and integral part of a trinitarian conception of God and his relation to man. In addition, the conflicts concerning the doctrine of sin and grace had yielded certain evangelical conceptions. At this point, the classical countries of Christianity experienced the Mohammedan invasion. Both the Christian life and the spirit of theological work were quenched by the invasion. New objects for Christianization appeared in the settling of the Germanic peoples that had emigrated from the East. They soon turned from Arianism, which they had adopted in passing the gates of Constantinople, to Athanasian Christianity. By and by they began to produce theological scholars. We read of them at the court of Charlemagne, in Spain, and in England. In the main, they were yet like children, wondering at the dogmatic creation of the past. Gradually they began to think for themselves. The philosophy of the East, that potent factor for the stimulation of dogmatic work, had been suppressed under the Islamic invasion. In theology, Rome had nothing to contribute. Its contribution to the age beginning with Gregory the Great was the education of the new races in the elementary matters of religion.

The rise and the degeneration of the papacy and of Scholasticism furnish objects for interesting studies. The conception of the Church, the interest of the hierarchy, legalism, asceticism, repentance, sin and grace, mysticism, the interactions between philosophy and theology—all these will claim much attention in this very brief review of the Middle Ages. Neo-Platonism and Aristotelianism again became objects of interest and constituted new temptations for the adulteration of Christian doctrine, as the Reformation would later claim.

THE THEOLOGY OF GREGORY THE GREAT

Gregory the Great may be compared to the two-headed Janus of the Romans. He looked back upon six centuries of Christianity and forward to a new age which derived its character from the tasks growing out of the collapse of antiquity and the migration of new races into Europe.

Born about 540, Gregory was destined to rule dogmatic thought in the Church undisputed for five hundred years, and to remain dominant in the Roman church. The son of a Christian senator at Rome, he began public life as a Roman prefect. He took monastic vows, founded cloisters, became an abbot, and was elected pope in 590. As pope he sought political independence and security for the papacy, by his political sagacity safeguarding the secular interest of the curia. In England he is remembered for the missionary expedition he sent to the Anglo-Saxons in 596. He made his influence dominant, especially along practical lines, through untiring correspondence, through his other writings, and through liturgical reforms. His chief writings are *Exposition on Job* in thirty-five books called *Moralia* and *Dialogue on the Life and Miracles of Pious Fathers in Italy*, with appended thoughts on the immortality of the soul. He died in 604.

Gregory was a wise and energetic churchman, a shrewd politician, a lovable and imperative shepherd of souls. His theology issued into regulations for Church life. Under forms familiar to Augustinianism, he brought into the dogmatic storehouse of the Church the popular type of religious thought, adding many superstitious elements derived from paganism.[1] His theology, though described as a *mixtum compositum*, remained within the bounds of the orthodoxy laid down in the first four ecumenical councils.

Gregory's teaching included the following.

The Scriptures, including the Four Gospels, and "Tradition," covering the four ecumenical councils from Nicea to Chalcedon, constitute a full and equal dogmatic authority.[2]

[1] Cf. *PRE*, VII, 88-89.
[2] *Epistles*, I, 25.

God exists as three persons in one divine substance.[3] Christ is the God-Man, truly God, of one essence with the Father, also truly Man, joined to us.

Christ, being sinless, became our Mediator and Redeemer through his incarnation and death in order to remove God's wrath against sin. The redemption is also considered a price paid to Satan, who was deceived in the bargain and could not control the sinless God in Christ. Christ is also Teacher, Revealer of God, of his will, of our sinfulness, and an example for us.[4]

In his teaching on sin, Gregory was theoretically Augustinian. He stressed the consequences of the fall and spoke of original sin, of an inherited guilt, and of death as the punishment for sin. He held to Augustine's teaching concerning the condemnation of children who died without baptism. His doctrine of grace also had an Augustinian stamp. Through baptism, sin is forgiven and faith is implanted.[5] Faith through the preached and inwardly digested Word produces the love and will for the good. Here Gregory furnished a point of contact for the Reformers.

At heart, Gregory was a Semi-Pelagian. He believed that God justified man by imparting His commandments, which man had to fulfill and might even surpass.[6] This teaching submerged the monergism of grace which Augustine's doctrine of predestination had championed.[7] Similar inconsistency was the differentiation between the prevenient and the subsequent grace of God. In Gregory's concept of penance the emphasis was also Semi-Pelagian. He defined penance as contrition, confession, absolution, and satisfaction. The unsearchable God, he said, leaves no sin unpunished. In baptism the inherited original sin is forgiven; but for all actual sins there must be "satisfactions." The satisfactions of the ancient Church were a testimony of true sorrow for sin. Gregory made them self-inflicted, temporal punishments by which to escape eternal punishment. The merit of Christ and the power of the Church then centered in the ability to convert eternal punishments into temporal ones, and to

[3] *Moralia*, XXXIII, 10, 20; XXII, 17, 42; III, 14, 26.
[4] *Ibid.*, IX, 38, 61.
[5] *Ibid.*, IX, 34, 54.
[6] *Ibid.*, IX, 34, 54.
[7] *Ezekiel*, I, 9, 2.

decrease or do away with temporal punishments through the intercession of Christ and the saints, through masses (for the living and the dead), and through the use of relics and amulets. The stimulus for the employment of these powers was the fear of losing salvation. The invention of an elaborate casuistry introduced the theology of fear and of ethical conceptions that had no root in Scripture. With Gregory, the sacrament of penance appears in an already-finished form.

Upon this Semi-Pelagian background, the Eucharist was changed by Gregory from God's action to man's deed—from a sacrament into a sacrifice for our redemption. The benefit received from the mass (Ambrose was the first to employ this term) was no longer merely the forgiveness of sins, but bodily blessings, magically communicated.[8] Even the dead could be partakers of such blessings if the mass were offered for them.

Gregory's doctrine of purgatory expanded time and space to make more room for the working of his system. His scriptural proof for the existence of purgatory was Matt. 12:32.[9]

Theoretically, Gregory thought of the Church as belonging to the saints of all ages. Practically, the Church was to him a *civitas Dei*, a temporal state with the pope at its head, and therefore a *corpus mixtum* comprising the good and the bad. In this sphere the priesthood rules above all, including the state. It rules over body and soul, through the sacraments and magic rites and through the power to dispense the spiritual treasures which the Church possesses.[10]

To summarize the estimate of Gregory the Great: (1) He was the guardian of traditional orthodoxy on the Trinity and on Christology. He offered nothing new except through his accentuation of popular beliefs. (2) He put tradition on an equal basis with the Scriptures. (3) On anthropology and soteriology he was Semi-Pelagian, and gave to repenetance and the Eucharist an interpretation

---

[8] See Gregory's *Canon of the Mass.*

[9] In the Patristic Age, Augustine considered purgatory to be "a matter either ascertained or left doubtful whether believers shall pass through a purgatorial fire and in proportion as they have loved with more or less devotion the goods that perish, be more or less quickly delivered from it." (*Enchiridion*, 69).

[10] For further references, see Seeberg, *Textbook*, II, pp. 17 ff.

in harmony with this view. (4) On church and priesthood he was hierarchical.

Gregory transformed virtues into rites, ordinances, and religious acts. He made the miracle a characteristic trait in religion. He classified angels, devils, saints, and sacraments, and emphasized fear and hope rather than a sure trust in God through Christ. He opened wide the door for what Harnack has called "the Christianity of a second order" by approving officially the invocation of saints and martyrs. He crystallized many of the elements of the religious superstition which in that day of passing paganism had made its way into the Church. He externalized internal graces into acts and ceremonies after the fashion of the mystery religions, and extended the power of the Church beyond space and time to the very gates of heaven through the teaching of purgatory.

CHAPTER II

THEOLOGICAL MOVEMENTS DURING THE CAROLINGIAN RENAISSANCE

From the time of Gregory the Great to that of Charlemagne, the Western Church was not theologically enriched. Islam had conquered territories rich in theological lore and the East had shaken off the powerful influence of Greek philosophy. In the seventh and eighth centuries Arianism was crushed through the conversion of England (especially through Gregory's mission to the Anglo-Saxons) and through the conversion of Germany to Rome and to Athanasianism (especially through the influence of Chlodwig). Theology now centered in the northern lands, which had no doctrinal background. These countries sought only to absorb and learn from the past to which they were heirs. In the East, the monergistic and monotheletistic controversies ran their course with no visible participation by the West, which was engaged chiefly in making compendiums and excerpts and in fashioning institutions. Under Charlemagne, however, a revival took place.

Charlemagne dominated the history of his period, not only in the state but also in the Church. He felt called to exercise judgment and power in Church affairs, even in such details as Church discipline, liturgical arrangements, education of the clergy, Church art, missions, the placing of bishops, and the settling of papal affairs. This ultimately involved matters of doctrine. His judgments, which were practical or pragmatical rather than visionary, were brought to bear on four major issues: Adoptionism in Spain, veneration of images in the East, the *filioque* of the Nicene Creed, and the miraculous virgin birth.

Later, under the reign of his successors, two other issues attracted the interest of the Frankish theologians: the teaching of a double predestination by Gottschalk, and the teaching of transubstantiation by Radbertus.

I. THE ADOPTIONISTIC CONTROVERSY

The adoptionistic controversy was merely a repetition, on a Spanish background, of the old christological controversy concerning the divine and human in Christ.[1] The Spanish theologians Elipandus of Toledo and Felix of Urgel, on the basis of theological developments up to Augustine, defended the christological conception which emphasized the human in Christ and declared that his divinity was the result of an act of adoption by God.[2] They were opposed by the Asturians, Beatus and Heterius of Libana (785), whose interest centered in the divine Christ made man for us. In order to safeguard the mystic-realistic conception of the Lord's Supper, they accused the Spaniards of Nestorianism. The teaching of the two Spanish scholars was condemned by three synods under Charlemagne, who probably desired to assert himself as ruler and preserver of the Church's orthodoxy. Pope Hadrian I agreed. The teaching of John of Damascus was declared orthodox. A sound refutation of Adoptionism was never made. It crept out again among scholars of the later Middle Ages as, for example, in Alcuin's *Seven Books against Felix*.

II. THE ICONOCLASTIC CONTROVERSY

After a long and fierce controversy, the Seventh Ecumenical Synod at Nicea (787)[3] assigned salutation and respectful reverence to the images of Christ and the saints. The Synod had been convened by the Empress Irene of Constantinople, and delegates of Pope Hadrian I had participated in it. Charlemagne had not been consulted, nor was anyone present to represent him. Resenting this slight, the emperor directed a critical examination of the decrees of the Synod. He found cause for censure and disapproval on the ground that the Latin trans-

---

[1] Nestorian diophysitism against Eutychian monophysitism.
[2] Cf. the Mozarabic Liturgy containing Augustine's formula: *Passio filii adoptivi.*
[3] *NPNF*, XIV, 533 ff.

lation of the decree ascribed adoration and divine homage, *adoratio* and *servitium*, to the images. With sharp criticism the *Libri Carolini* (790) rejected both the adoration and veneration as well as the destruction of images. The *Libri* declared that adoration belongs only to God; veneration belongs to the saints and their relics. The significance of images lies in the fact that they beautify the churches, awaken the memories of the past, and take the place of the Scriptures for the illiterate. His view was reasserted in 794 at Frankfort[4] against the diplomatic vacillation of the pope. With the breaking up of the imperial power of the Carolingians it was inevitable that this viewpoint should give way to the image worship approved by Nicea and Rome. However, the West was never willing to admit the veneration of images as the perfection of the christological dogma and the climax of the religious life of the believer. Thus began a cleavage between East and West.

III. THE FILIOQUE CONTROVERSY

In discussion of the doctrine concerning the procession of the Holy Spirit, the cleavage between East and West was widened. On the basis of an Augustinian modalism, as expressed in Part One of the Athanasian Creed, the West thought of the Holy Spirit as proceeding from the Son as well as the Father. Gradually this teaching, without official act, caused the insertion of the *filioque* into the Nicene Creed. Its presence was defended by Bishop Theodulf of Orleans in his book, *On the Procession of the Holy Spirit*. The Synod of Aachen (809) accepted the insertion with the half-hearted approval of Pope Leo III, who discredited Charlemagne's right to alter an ancient symbol of the Church. The *filioque*, though never popularized, became the accepted formula of the West, while it was flatly condemned in the East.

IV. CONTROVERSY ABOUT THE MIRACULOUS BIRTH OF JESUS

The controversy concerning the miraculous birth of Jesus centered in the perpetual virginity of Mary. The question was treated along conservative lines by the monk Ratramnus. He conceded the virginity of Mary even after the birth of Jesus, but warned against a Docetism

[4] *Ibid.*, pp. 583 ff.

which, by denying all natural processes in connection with his birth, would make Christ a phenomenon instead of a true man. His teaching was opposed by Radbertus, a fellow monk, who followed the miracle-seeking, mystical trend of his day in the way prepared by Augustine[5] and by Ildefonsus of Toledo.[6] Radbertus insisted upon a supernatural birth as well as a supernatural conception of Jesus in every respect. The interest of the age in safeguarding the holiness and sinlessness of Mary supported Radbertus and directed the way for future development in such matters.

V. THE PREDESTINATION CONTROVERSY

The conflict between the received practice of the Church and genuine Augustinianism had led the Church to a position not far removed from Semi-Pelagianism. The Carolingian theology had taken over this attitude. How blindly this theology proceeded is shown by the *Libri Carolini* which endeavored to prove its orthodoxy by translating Pelagius' *Libellus fidei ad Innocentium*. This confession retained great influence throughout the entire Middle Ages. It went by the name *Sermo Augustini*. (Even history itself plays jokes!) Consequently, when genuine Augustinianism was revived in the ninth century by Gottschalk, it was either falsely interpreted or resolutely cast aside. The spirit of Gregory and the needs of ecclesiastical practice—that is, Semi-Pelagian tendencies — triumphed anew and with finality.

The monk Gottschalk of Orbais had not only studied Augustine but *experienced* him in the miseries of his life. For this reason, he recognized that the Church carried a Semi-Pelagian heart beneath its deceiving cloak of Augustinian formula. Gottschalk's attacks upon the prevalent doctrine and practice of the Church were passionate and vehement, and they aimed at nothing less than a reformation. Briefly stated, he taught: The unchangeable God has settled definitely the course and destiny of the world from all eternity. Election and rejection are due to an inscrutable decree of God. He has not determined

[5] *On Nature and Grace,* 42 (XXXVI).
[6] *On the Perpetual Virginity of St. Mary against Three Infidels.* The *Catholic Encyclopedia,* VII, 649, calls the book "a bombastic work which displays however a spirit of ardent piety and assures Ildephonsus a place of honor among the devoted servants of the Blessed Virgin."

some for salvation and others for death, but he foreknows the attitude each man will take toward his grace. Foreknowledge and predestination are simultaneous in God. The significance of foreknowledge is that it explains the justness of divine rejection. Evil is of man's will. God does not determine a man's willing evil, only his punishment. Salvation is not through merit but only through grace. The work of Christ is efficacious only for the elect, but no one knows who they are. Yet, Augustine's emphasis on the psychological and formal freedom of man has no place in Gottschalk's system.

The antagonists of Gottschalk saw no place in this doctrine for good works, priest or sacrament, nor for the whole ecclesiastical system. Affairs reached a crisis because of the preaching of Gottschalk, now a priest, on a journey into upper Italy. Complaints against him were made to Hrabanus, his abbot, by the Bishop of Verona. In 848, the Synod of Mayence, dissatisfied with the confession laid down by Gottschalk and with his accusation of Semi-Pelagianism against Hrabanus, condemned him. The Synod of Chiersy (849) did likewise, and Hinkmar, the Archbishop of Rheims, imprisoned him. He died (869) without recanting.

The Augustinian doctrine of predestination had been brought favorably to the attention of scholars, even of Gottschalk's antagonists. It was treated in a manner halfway between Gregory and Gottschalk by four theologians of Alcuin's school: Prudentius of Troyes, Remigius of Lyon, Lupus of Ferrieres, and Ratramnus of Corbie. The mutual antagonism of the Alcuin and Hinkmar circles played a large part in the controversy. A compromise was reached at the Synod of Valence (885), which simultaneously accepted the double predestination of Augustine and the validity of the sacraments. In 859, at Savonieres and Langres, and in 860, at Toucy, further compromises were made and an academic peace restored on the following basis: God has assuredly predestined to life; in accordance with this purpose Christ died for all; the free will of man was weakened through the fall but not destroyed. Pure Augustinianism was rejected in favor of practical piety.

VI. The Eucharistic Controversy

Until this period the theology of the West had been concerned only occasionally with the Lord's Supper. Ambrose and Gregory had expressed themselves realistically, while Augustine had rejected a corporeal presence of Christ in the sacrament. Popular piety inclined increasingly to the view that in the mass the actual body of Christ is received. This tenet was rooted first of all in the general craving for the miraculous and in the crude conception of religion at that time. In addition to this, men, with their exceedingly vivid consciousness of sin, believed that they could be certain of forgiveness only if the mass were an actual repetition of the sacrifice on Calvary.

The treatise of Radbertus *On the Body and Blood of the Lord* was the first monograph on the subject.[7] The author, who was abbot of the monastery at Corbie (842-853), attempted a compromise between the theory of Augustine and the religious conceptions of the Church of his day, and propagated for the first time a real, though internal and mysterious, transubstantiation.

At the words of the priest, God (who can do everything he wills), causes a miracle to take place: the consecrated elements are really changed into the historical body of Christ. The empirical observation that the accidents of color, form, and taste do not change is explained by the assertion that the change takes place not as an outward, but as an inward mystery. The lack of visible proof is intended to confirm the faith of the Christian. Whereas all truly receive the sacramental elements, Radbertus contends that only those who spiritually comprehend Christ receive his body and blood. This is truly Augustinian. Radbertus sought to co-ordinate the miracle with faith, and he was not yet ready to separate the communion from the sacrifice of the mass.

The first opposition to this doctrine was raised by Hrabanus, the aged Archbishop of Mayence. He remained closer to Augustine than Radbertus. The effect of the Supper consists of a spiritual union of the individual with the mystical body of Christ. Bread and wine are not the body of Christ himself, but only a symbol of it. Hrabanus' symbolical view, however, was no longer so pure as Augustine's, for even he recognized a certain change in the elements after the consecration.

Ratramnus, also a monk of Corbie, was drawn into the controversy by Emperor Charles the Bald, who asked him for an "opinion" on the

---

[7] For selections in English, see *LCC*, IX, 94 ff.

matter of a real or mysterious reception of the Lord's body by believers. Ratramnus answered, in a treatise bearing the same title as that of Radbertus,[8] that bread and wine are not changed into the historical body and blood of Christ.[9] The sacramental elements are only a symbol. The presence of Christ, though real and true, is purely spiritual, and the effect of participation consists in a spiritual communion with the Lord. The Augustinian spiritualism of Ratramnus could not maintain itself against the practice of the Church, which supported the conception of Radbertus.

BIBLIOGRAPHY

The Middle Ages

LCC, Vols. IX-XIV.

MANSI, J. DOM. *Collectio Sacrorum Conciliorum.* Florence and Venice: 1759-1798. New print 1903.

MIGNE, J. P. *Patrologiae cursus completus* — — — *qui ab Aevo Apostolico ad Tempora Innocentii III (anno 1216) pro Latinis et ad Concilii Florentini Tempora (anno 1439). Series Scriptoresque Ecclesiae Graecae,* 161 vols, 1857-1904; Paris: pro Graecia Floruerunt, 1867. *Series Latina,* 221 vols.; Paris, 1844-1904.

MIRBT, C. *Quellen zur Geschichte des Papstums.* 4th ed., 1924.

Cambridge Medieval History. Edited by H. M. GWATKIN and J. P. WHITNEY. 12 vols. New York: Macmillan Co., 1911-36.

HAUCK, A. *Kirchengeschichte Deutschlands.* 5 vols. 1887–.

HEFELE, VON K. J. *Konziliengeschichte.* 9 vols. 1855–. 2nd ed., 3 vols., 1873–. 8 vols.; Paris, 1907–.

Life in the Middle Ages. Edited by C. G. COULTON. Cambridge: Cambridge University Press, 1955.

McGIFFERT, A. C. *History of Christian Thought.* New York and London: Charles Scribner's Sons, 1933.

OBERMANN, H. *The Harvest of Medieval Theology.* Cambridge: Harvard University Press, 1963.

SEEBERG, R. *Dogmengeschichte.* Vol. III. 4th ed., 1930.

STAEHELIN, E. *Die Verkündigung des Reiches Gottes in der Kirche Jesu Christi.* 1953, 1955. Vols. II-III.

TAYLOR, H. O. *The Classical Heritage of the Middle Ages.* 3rd ed.; New York: Macmillan Co., 1901.

[8] Translated under the caption "Christ's Body and Blood" in *LCC*, IX, 118 ff.
[9] The statement that "the substance of the bread and wine are substantially converted into another substance, that is, the body and blood of Christ" probably did not originate at this period. Its author seems to have been not Haimo of Halberstadt (d. 853) as sometimes held, but Haimo, the abbot of Hirschau at the close of the eleventh century. Cf. Seeberg, *Lehrbuch* (1913), III, 76; also *PRE*, VII, 348.

_____. *The Medieval Mind*. 2 vols. London: Macmillan Co., 1911.
TROELTSCH, E. *The Social Teachings of the Christian Churches*. Translated by OLIVE WYON. Glencoe, Ill.: Free Press, 1949. Vol. I.

Gregory the Great

GREGORY. *Letters*. Edited by P. EWALD and L. M. HARTMANN. 1891–.
_____. Selected writings in *NPNF*, Vols. XII, XIII.
_____. *Commentary on Job*. *LCC*, Vol. IX. *MSL*. Vols. 75-79.

DUDDEN, F. H. *Gregory the Great, His Place in History and Thought*. London and New York: Longmans, Green and Co., 1905.
HOWORTH, H. H. *Gregory the Great*. London: Murray and Co., 1912.
MANN, H. K. *Lives of the Popes in the Early Middle Ages*. London: Kegan Paul, Trench, Trübner and Co., 1905. Vol. I.
McCLAIN, J. M. *The Doctrine of Heaven in the Writings of S. Gregory the Great*. Washington: Catholic University of America Press, 1956.
SHARKEY, N. S. *Gregory the Great's Concept of Papal Power*. Washington: Catholic University of America Press, 1950.
SNOW, A. *St. Gregory the Great*. London: Burns, Oates and Washbourne, Ltd., 1924.

The Adoptionistic Controversy

HEFELE, VON K. J. *Konziliengeschichte*. III, 642 ff.
MANSI, J. DOM. *Collectio Sacrorum Conciliorum*. Vols. 12, 13.
MSL. Vols. 96, 99, 100, 101, 104.

The Iconoclastic Controversy

BURY, J. B. *A History of the Later Roman Empire*. London and New York: Macmillan Co., 1889.
HEFELE, VON K. J. *Konziliengeschichte*. III, 604 ff.
MANSI, J. DOM. *Collectio Sacrorum Conciliorum*. Vols. 12, 13.
MARTIN, E. J. *A History of the Iconoclastic Controversy*. London: SPCK, 1930. New York: Macmillan Co., 1930. *MSL*, Vol. 98.

The Filioque Controversy

HEFELE, VON K. J. *Konziliengeschichte*. III, 749.
MANSI, J. DOM. *Collectio Sacrorum Conciliorum*. Vol. 14.
MSL, Vols. 101, 105.
SWETE, H. B. *The Holy Spirit in the Ancient Church*. London: Macmillan Co., 1912.
WILLIAMS, C. *Descent of the Dove*. New York: Meridian Press, 1956.

Controversy about the Miraculous Birth of Jesus

MSL. Vols. 120, 121.

The Predestination Controversy

HEFELE, VON K. J. *Konziliengeschichte*. IV, 130 ff.
MANSI, J. DOM. *Collectio Sacrorum Conciliorum*. Vols. 14, 15.
MSL. Vols. 112, 115, 119, 121, 122, 125, 345 ff.

The Eucharistic Controversy

MSL. Vols. 112, 120, 121, 125.

STONE, D. *A History of the Doctrine of the Holy Eucharist.* New York and London: Longmans, Green and Co., 1909. Vol. I.

CHAPTER III

THE DEVELOPMENT OF PAPAL SUPREMACY

During the Middle Ages, Christian religion was a matter of national concern. The Western church fell heir to the Roman Empire. Both the Germanic and the Slavic peoples accepted Christianity, and national churches were the result. Gregory the Great was not able to bind all the new churches to Rome. The close relationship of the Carolingians with the papacy from the eighth century on resulted at first in imperial theocracy rather than in papal hierarchy. After the imperial power had disintegrated, when the Church remained the only bond of union among Christian peoples, the old ways of Gregory were chosen once more. The sovereignty of the pope was soon established. Though it was not yet dogma, Church law demanded that the pope be regarded as superior to the emperor. This was the trend of development during the Middle Ages.

The *Pseudo-Isidorean Decretals* (*ca.* 845) present as ancient papal rights all the claims ever advanced by the papacy. They stress the independence of the hierarchy from the laity and the supremacy of the pope over the bishops and the national churches. The authority of the papacy in future conflicts with the emperor, papal claims to supremacy over Church and state, and the right to appoint bishops and other Church dignitaries, though bolstered by decree after decree, found their final authority in these decretals. Efforts to construct a new system of Church jurisprudence centered in the authority of the pope placed the *Decretals* on a par with the decrees of the ancient councils. But mistrust lingered about them for a long time.

To carry through the ideals of Pseudo-Isidore required a papacy regenerated from the immorality and inefficiency of the tenth century, and a comprehensive Church-wide movement. The aim was achieved through the emperors, with the support of the monastery at Cluny.

The Cluniac movement began as a reformation of the monasteries. Gradually it developed into a general Church movement. As this was first of all a purely religious movement, it received the ready support of the emperors. The zeal of Cluny was directed against immorality in the monasteries, marriage of priests, simony, etc. This zeal soon found a check had been placed upon it; the state wished to rule the Church according to its own laws and will. Recognition of this goal of the state awakened the curialistic tendency of Pseudo-Isidore. The Church's secularization, it was held, was due to the control of the state! Therefore, the Church and the bishops must be independent of the emperor and placed under the authority of the pope. (On account of his experience with the rebellious dukes of the empire, Otto I (936-73) had created the institution of ecclesiastical principalities. The unmarried bishops were expected to be more loyal to the emperor than the dukes, who often strove only for political aggrandizement of their own dynasties.) The canon law of the Roman church must take the place of the laws of the national churches. The right of investiture was to be given to the pope; fees paid to the emperor in return for bishoprics were to be branded "simony" (Acts 8:18-24). Detachment from the world was understood to mean detachment from the state; thus, an ecclesiastico-political program resulted from what had started as a religious one. A tragic fate willed that the emperors themselves should create the necessary premises of the conflict. Henry II (1002-1024) and Henry III (1039-1056) reformed the morally degenerate papacy (Synod of Sutri, 1046). Immediately the regenerated papacy began to strike at the very foundation of the state.

That which was only germinal in Pseudo-Isidore was proclaimed with perfect candor by Gregory VII (1073-1085). The Church is of divine origin, while the state is rooted in the sinful order of the world (according to Augustine's *City of God*). The pope is the universal head of the Church. The bishops are his representatives and responsible to him alone. Their nomination and ordination are his exclusive privilege. The pope, who has the power of the keys in heaven, has that power all the more on earth. The princes are his liegemen. They must kiss his feet, not the feet of the emperor. The emperor receives his glory from the pope as the moon from the sun. While the pope may depose the princes and the emperor, no human authority can depose the pope.

These demands should not be traced back to a sacerdotal craving for power in Gregory. Gregory felt that he was called to establish God's kingdom on earth. Within himself he felt God thinking and working, and for that reason he was convinced that he could shake the world to its foundations. There was a peculiar religious heroism lying behind his delusion, but this heroism and his dramatic conflict with Emperor Henry IV (1056-1106) belong to Church history.

After the death of Gregory, the representatives of reform movements lacked spiritual fervor. The terms of the Concordat of Worms (1122) show that the curialists were forced to content themselves with a compromise. It is true that the pope invested the bishops, but they were chosen under imperial influence. The bestowal of secular sovereignty remained the exclusive right of the emperor. The later struggle between Frederick I and Alexander III, and between the last emperors of the house of Hohenstaufen with Innocent III, was a mere struggle for secular supremacy in Italy. As a lasting *status quo*, neither the supremacy of the state nor that of the Church was ever completely or factually established.

In this conflict for supremacy in Italy, the papacy rested its claim to sovereignty upon a legal basis. To attain its purpose, it fostered collections of synodical canons and papal decrees which might serve as binding sources of law. Ivo of Chartres (d. 1116) was one of the greatest jurists to take this matter in hand. At Bologna the study of canon law was made a separate course of study. At this university Gratian (d. 1140) wrote his *Decretal*, the most complete collection of canon law up to that time. Its importance lies in the fact that it assigned a place in the lawbooks to the dogma and sacraments of the Church, and established the Scriptures, tradition, and the decrees of the councils and the pope as the binding doctrinal authorities. Anselm's emphasis upon the juridical point of view in his theory of atonement and upon the significance of the priest in the sacrament of penance contributed to the strengthening of papal supremacy. The Church became a courthouse; then, along the same line of development, a house of merchandise; and then a "den of thieves." Luther's burning of the papal bull was only a side issue to the main event of burning the books of canon law.

Only the rise of a new piety prevented the religious zeal of the earlier Cluniac movement from being submerged in this rising tide of legalism.

BIBLIOGRAPHY

Corpus Juris Canonici.

MIRBT, C. *Quellen zur Geschichte des Papstums.* 1924.

MSL. Vols. 161, 162.

BOEHMER, H. *Kirche und Staat in England und in der Normandie im 11 und 12 Jahrhundert.* 1899.

BOWDEN, J. W. *Life and Pontificate of Gregory VII.* London: Rivington, 1849.

CARLISLE, R. W. and A. J. *A History of Medieval Political Theory.* Edinburgh: W. Blackwood, 1936-50.

GREENWOOD, T. *Cathedra Petri.* 6 vols. 1856—.

HALLER, J. *Das Papsttum, Idee und Wirklichkeit.* 5 vols. Stuttgart and Basel: 1951-53.

JALLAND, T. G. *The Church and the Papacy.* London: SPCK, 1944.

KIDD, B. J. *The Roman Primacy to A.D. 461.* London: SPCK, 1936.

KRUEGER, G. *The Papacy: The Idea and its Exponents.* Translated by F. M. S. BATCHELOR and C. A. MILES. New York: G. P. Putnam's Sons, 1909.

RULE, M. *The Life and Times of St. Anselm.* 2 vols. London: Kegan Paul, Trench, Trübner, and Co., 1883.

SCHULTE, J. F. *Geschichte der Quellen des Kirchenrechts.* 1875. Vols. 1, 2.

TOUT, T. F. *The Empire and the Papacy.* New York: Macmillan Co., 1921.

ULLMANN, W. *The Growth of Papal Government in the Middle Ages.* London: Methuen and Co., 1955.

————. *Medieval Papalism: The Political Theories of the Medieval Canonists.* London: Methuen and Co., 1955.

VINCENT, M. R. *The Age of Hildebrand.* New York: The Christian Literature Co., 1896.

CHAPTER IV

THE AWAKENING OF
THE NEW PIETY

Carolingian learning and the new piety were related as are mechanical learning and the inner understanding of that learning. In the early Middle Ages, men had been content to accept the Church's doctrines as they were and to conserve them with slavish dependence. The mass of the people had seen in Christianity not a new divine, spiritual life of the individual, but rather an external institution. During the eleventh and twelfth centuries, the maturing spirit of the young nations experienced a new understanding of Christianity. It is true that the doctrines themselves remained undoubted. A genuinely religious need was striving to liberate forces and treasures which lay bound in the Church's teaching, striving to establish through them a life of inward, personal piety. Men desired to strike water from the rock. They wanted to experience what until then they had only subscribed to. An impetuous, outspoken, religious subjectivism came forth which asked with Augustinian seriousness about sin and grace, about God and the certainty of salvation. Certainty, experience, and conversion were the three characteristics of this new piety

The impulse of the new piety arose in the monasteries of Lorraine and Cluny. It was supported by the laity rather than the clergy, for it threatened heavy demands upon the priests. The new piety is most clearly visible in the enthusiasm for the Crusades and the fostering of innumerable monastic foundations. This piety aimed at a strict discipline for the monasteries, monastic regime for the secular clergy, supremacy of the Church over nations, rulers, and subjects, and the subordination of the present to the future life. By a peculiar twist of logic, freedom from and victory over the world were held to be attainable solely through the dominion of the Church over the world. Such antagonistic qualities as ambition and humility, sensuality and self-denial, brutality and sentimentality characterize this period. Basic to the development of the new piety was the growth of mysticism. It was mysticism, indeed, added to the ascetic ideals of monasticism, which produced the new piety.

Mysticism had been a constituent part of philosophical Christianity from the beginning. It had an especially strong hold on the theology and piety of the Eastern church. Its first exponent of importance in this period was John Scotus Erigena.[1]

The background of this scholar, who was not a cleric but a sort of court philosopher and independent thinker, was not only in Augustine and Gregory, but also in Philo and Neo-Platonism. He was well versed in classical Greek, using the Septuagint by choice, and had a deep sympathy for the speculation of the East. He translated the writings of Dionysius the Areopagite into Latin.

John's chief work, De divisione naturae, bridged the way from Neo-Platonism to the speculative mysticism of the Middle Ages. According to his system, God created an ideal world, from which the real world emanated with man as its center. Man contains in himself all the properties of all creatures of the world. In this man sin is found without cause; it separates him into two sexes and a multitude of individuals. In Christ the original man is restored to unity and resolved into the original world of ideas and absorbed into God.

The influence of John Scotus was not discernible in his own day. His teaching met little opposition, since he refrained from attacking the doctrine of the Church. Moreover, he was not understood by his fellow theologians, nor did he understand the needs and problems of his time. His theological efforts were thoroughly disappointing to those who appreciated his learning. In his treatise On Divine Predestination (849), he identified predestination with foreknowledge and denied the reality of sin. In the controversy concerning the Eucharist, he emphasized the symbolic value of the elements and lent no support to the realists. His works reveal the beginnings of Scholastic investigation. After his death, they were repeatedly condemned. He was

[1] A. Gardner, Studies in John the Scot (London: Clarendon Press, 1900). Cf. also Nygren, op. cit., pp. 594 ff.

not a true mystic, lacking as he did the exalted religious experience and the yearning which characterize the mystic. His chief contribution to the age was the foundation he laid and the stimulation which he gave to mystical thinking in the future.

Other representatives of the new piety appeared prior to Bernard. A mysticism that led to piety was fostered by Ratherius (d. 974), a speculative thinker with a large following. Classical expression was given to the aims of the movement by Othloh of Emmeram (d. 1083). He gave subjective treatment to all of the materials of doctrine and faith and popularized the mystic attitude. From his time on, the laity welcomed contemplation, if not speculation. New monastic orders arose with a rigorous discipline. Even the papacy was won over and sanctioned the movement. One of the immediate results was the enthusiasm engendered for the Crusades.

The new piety and the Crusades interacted upon one another. From the intimate connection of many thousands through the Crusades with the land of the Gospels, new attitudes were developed. Chief among these attitudes was the desire to follow Christ in all the stages of his sufferings. The true humanity of Jesus was re-emphasized and the religious objective of Adoptionism was maintained in this way. Negative asceticism, self-denial and emphasis upon self-abnegation, received a positive purpose, namely, to follow Jesus and to become like him. Mysticism, embracing Christ, as indicated by Augustine and enlarged by John Scotus, became a mighty current. The Church now possessed a threefold Christ: the transcendental, the sacramental, and the historical. Christian piety embraced the humble, holy, patient, sacrificing Lord and called forth ultimate resources of human invention to serve him.

In the teachings of Hugo (d. 1141),[2] preceptor of the abbey school of St. Victor near Paris, we find the first outstanding representative of new piety. A survey of his system of contemplation, based primarily on Augustine, is found in his work, *Commentary on the Heavenly Hierarchy of St. Dionysius the Areopagite according to the Interpretation of John the Scot*. He emphasized the three stages through which the soul attains knowledge of divine things. The first stage is sensual perception, the power for which has not been greatly di-

---

[2] See a brief selection of his writings in *LCC,* X, 300 ff.; XIII, 86 ff.

minished in man through the fall. The second stage consists in a search after the secret spiritual meaning of that which is perceived. In this the faculties of man are much more beclouded. The third stage consists in an untrammeled vision of the essence of things, which is possible only through the Spirit of God. The motive behind Hugo's scheme was the personal experience of salvation and of union with Christ. "We are truly made partakers of this redemption if we through faith are united to the Redeemer himself, who through the flesh entered into fellowship with us." [3]

Bernard of Clairvaux (d. 1153),[4] the most powerful personality and the greatest religious genius of his time, gave classic expression to the general mood of the new piety. He created a coherent system of the order of salvation which was Christ-centered, built on religious experience, and culminated in mystic ecstasy.

It was the man Jesus, whom the Crusades had rediscovered for the Western world, in whom Bernard was interested. The metaphysical Logos-Christ or the sacramental Christ was of little concern to him. Augustine had recognized the significance of the man Jesus and of his humility for faith. Bernard devoted himself to Jesus in a far more determined and glowing manner. Jesus, the joy of his heart, is the great king, not in spite of his humility, lowliness, and obedience, but because of them. In them, as well as in the patience, love, and purity of Jesus, the divine reality is revealed to pious experience. Everyone can become sure of God in an immediate vision. (For this, Luther praised the monk of Clairvaux as one of the truest saints of the Middle Ages.) Bernard linked this fundamental idea with Augustine's Neo-Platonic stages of contemplation in a unique manner reminiscent of Origen, Methodius, and Ambrose. Nevertheless, the whole system is an independent and new creation which rests upon one man's experience.

The chief sources of Bernard's mystic piety are his eighty-six sermons on the Song of Songs. The first presupposition of the spiritual life is the believing recognition of the Church's doctrines. If we meditate profoundly (*sedula meditatio*) on the holiness and purity of Jesus, we are overwhelmed by the mighty consciousness of our sin-

---

[3] *LCC*, X, 307.

[4] Cf. the discussion on Bernard and a selection of his writings in *LCC*, XIII, 47 ff. See also Nygren, *op. cit.*, pp. 635 ff.

fulness and we feel the wrath of God in all its severity. When we gaze at the sweetness of Jesus and his mercy, we become certain of forgiveness at the hands of a God who does not impute sin. That is the first stage of the mystical way to God, which is to say the way to conversion. According to an illustration used by Bernard, contrition is a kissing of Jesus' feet. Then follows repentance, which is a kissing of his hands. Reflecting on the love of God in Jesus awakens the impulse to imitate Jesus' love, patience, humility, and above all, his obedience. The perfect surrender of the will of the individual to the will of God is the most distinctive mark of the imitation of Christ.

Last follows the kissing of Jesus' lips, the climax of ecstasy. The third and highest stage, it is an absolutely spiritual experience of God which is not transmitted by sensuous means but which is enacted spontaneously in the soul. Nor is it always a mere psychological impression or agitation of the soul; it is an ascent of the soul to the Godhead.

In following the mysticism of the ancient Church, especially that of Augustine, Bernard ran the risk on the one hand of degrading the historical in religion to a transitory stage and on the other of losing himself in pantheism, as was the case before him with Methodius of Olympus, and after him with Amalrich of Bena and the sects of the Free Spirit. Bernard met these dangers by placing less emphasis upon the Augustinian differentiation between common faith, which reaches only to the man Jesus, and the mystical vision of the Godhead. The way to pantheism is blocked, according to Bernard's advice, in that one is to devote oneself more to God's will than to loving contemplations of him. The different stages of mystical experience, according to Bernard, are of equal value insofar as the same thing is experienced in the previous stages as in the ecstasy, except that in the third stage the experience is immediate and stronger. The certainty of forgiveness is dependent on the complete devotion of the will. Bernard's mysticism has a specifically Christian character. The ecstasy is not an end in itself. Like Sadhu Sundar Singh, Bernard received in the ecstasy a mighty impulse to manifest by works of love to his brethren, the powers of grace he had been given. The active life (*vita activa*) follows the contemplative life (*vita contemplativa*).

Not only was Bernard's Christianity adapted to the Church; it frequently reached evangelical heights. Everything—the breaking forth of the primal feelings of guilt, fear, and love, as well as the desire for holiness—is traced back to the working of grace. Bernard is genuinely Pauline in denying the possibility of merits and asserting that the forgiveness of sins and the granting of eternal life is by grace only. The only merit a man may have is to hope in his Savior and to have a humble readiness to receive God's grace. "The righteousness of man consists in the pardon of God." [5]

Bernard's subjectivism was indeed strong, but his ecclesiastical and hierarchial consciousness was just as strong. Bernard was convinced that the individual comes in touch with the gracious influences of Christ only through the medium of the Church (the sacraments). He was a firm believer in the Gregorian principle that it is the duty of the ecclesiastical hierarchy to compel the world to serve the interest of the heavenly and divine. Bernard was the most influential Church diplomat as well as the greatest mystic of his age.

BIBLIOGRAPHY

BERNARD. *MSL*, Vols. 182-185.
HUGO. *MSL*, Vols. 175-177.
OTHLOH. *MSL*, Vol. 146.
RATHERIUS. *MSL*, Vol. 136.
SCOTUS ERIGENA. *MSL*, Vol. 122. *LCC*, Vol. XII.

GARDNER, A. *Studies in John the Scot.* London: Clarendon Press, 1900.
GILSON, E.. *The Mystical Theology of St. Bernard.* Translated by A. H. C. Downes. New York: Sheed and Ward, 1940.
MORRISON, J. C. *Life and Times of St. Bernard.* London: Macmillan Co, 1877.

[5] Cf. Loofs, *Leitfaden*, p. 524.

CHAPTER V

THE RISE OF SCHOLASTICISM

The Church's more rapid decline in its quest for earthly might was hindered by the revival of a new interest in philosophy and theology known as Scholasticism. Its beginnings date from about 1100; the period ends with the Reformation.

Scholasticism grew out of the same roots as the new mystic piety. Man wanted to know in order to become inwardly certain of salvation. By knowledge, Scholasticism understood the rational understanding, while the new piety understood it to be a spiritual experience. With the new piety the interest was personal and subjective whereas with Scholasticism the interest was more scientific and objective. The instrument of rational understanding and proof was dialectics, as men had learned from Aristotle. Dialectics was the art of proving a thing through logical considerations. At this point the peculiar character of medieval thought becomes evident. Men thought from the inside out and not empirically. The presuppositions from which men proceeded were settled by authority and not by critical and observant research. The authority of the Scriptures, the Fathers, the councils, and the papal decrees were inviolable; they were considered divine law. Men were not concerned about seeking the truth but only about proving it and systematizing the divinely revealed metaphysics through methodical reflection.

Scholasticism was not merely an unfruitful formalism. It was a truly creative movement. It fused the theology of revelation and ancient philosophy into a natural theology, and produced a worldview of remarkable breadth and completeness. Scholasticism was remarkable in spite of its compromising character (revelation and reason), for it derived everything from God and then summarized everything in him. Theology became the only possible world-view, and philosophy was made the handmaiden of theology.

The rise of Scholasticism definitely curbed the growth and power of the monastic orders. It raised new units of influence in the schools, attracted prominent teachers, and directly caused the development of modern universities.

In their attempt to prove the reasonableness of the Church's doctrines, the Schoolmen were confronted with the philosophical problem of the relationship between the idea of a thing and its reality, between thinking and being. Nominalism and realism became the names of opposing schools of thought on this philosophical problem.

The terms are based on the different conceptions of the reality of generic ideas (universals) by Plato, Aristotle, and the Stoics. The problem is: Do the universals exist only as subjective conceptions, or do they exist as objective realities? If the latter, do they exist separately from the individual things or in them? Furthermore, are they corporeal or incorporeal? For instance, is the concept "man" a reality or is it only the intellectual abstraction derived from the common properties of individual beings called men? According to Plato, man carries within himself a conception of the idea of an absolute good and beautiful. He cannot have attained this impression by experience, since the absolute good does not exist in this sensible world. Rather, the soul has viewed this idea in its pre-existence and has retained a memory of it. Reason is the immortal part of the soul and constitutes its very essence. The rational perceptions of the soul, the ideas (universals), therefore, possess reality, since they are recollections of eternal and unchangeable, corporeal though spiritual objects: *universalia ante rem*. Whatever is truly reasonable is also truly real. Plato's teaching of the ideas underwent a certain modification by Aristotle. He reduced the ideas to spiritual forces (energies) which are active in matter: *universalia in re*.

Either type of realism was welcomed by the Church for its apologetic value. The reality of the Church's doctrines seemed to be guaranteed if their reasonableness could be effectively demonstrated. The moderate realism of the Aristotelian type was found to conform best to the interest of the Church and the needs of the time.

The ancient conception of the universals had suffered a further modification through the teachings of the Stoics, who maintained that the ideas were mere intellectual abstractions (*nomina*) derived from the common attributes of things: *universalia post rem*. This nominalistic theory was branded dangerous and destructive. It could find little favor with the Church, for it endangered the objective reality of fundamental beliefs of the Church; e.g. the doctrine of the Trinity.

The chief champion of nominalism during this period was Roscellinus of Compiegne (d. *ca.* 1125). His theory was orientated along the line of logic, but he did not fully realize its metaphysical significance. Roscellinus found a stern opponent in Anselm of Canterbury, who demonstrated to his contemporaries the pagan consequences of the nominalist position. The extreme realism of William of Champeaux met with as little success. The main current of thought was supplied by the moderate realism of the Roman philosopher, Boethius. His translations of the *Categories of Aristotle* and the *Isagoge of Porphyry* provided the scientific tools with which to solve the problems of Scholasticism.

The four outstanding scholars of this period were: Anselm, Abelard, Hugo, and Peter Lombard.

Anselm was abbot in the monastery of Bec in Normandy, and from 1093, Archbishop of Canterbury. He died in 1109 after a bitter conflict with King Henry I.

Anselm's theological and religious conflict made it necessary for him to oppose the nominalism of Roscellinus, whose denial of the reality of the generic ideas, Anselm maintained, would lead to the dissolution of the Church's doctrine of the Trinity. Instead of the one triune God, we would have three gods. In his *Monologium*, therefore, Anselm taught a moderate realism. The philosophical problem was a side issue with him. His real interest was centered in theological speculation. He leaned heavily upon Augustine. The teaching of the Church laid down in the Bible and by the three ecumenical symbols possessed inviolable authority for him. Unlike the older school, Anselm wanted to become inwardly certain of truth by religious experience. This tendency he had in common with the new piety. By rational thinking he tried to demonstrate the truth of the Church's dogma to Christians, Jews, and Gentiles (*Cur Deus homo?*). "I believe in order to understand." This progress from simple faith to religious knowledge is very momentous. By combining faith and knowledge, practical piety and theological speculation, Anselm became the foremost pathfinder of Scholasticism.

Abelard, a pupil of Roscellinus, surpassed the influence and importance of Anselm. He was born in 1079 at Palais, Bretagne, the son of a French knight. In Paris he became the youthful rival of William of Champeaux and created a real sensation in his lectures on Ezekiel. His brilliant personality and his pre-eminent intellectual gifts won the hearts of many. After his love affair with Heloise, he entered the abbey of St. Denis, and again caused difficulties with his treatise *Concerning the Divine Unity and Trinity*, which was condemned at Soissons as Sabellian. He could boast of enthusiastic followers, but he also had uncompromising persecutors, the most prominent of whom were Norbert and Bernard of Clairvaux. Bernard, the mystic, saw in Abelard, the rationalist, the principle of evil itself. At the Synod of Sens (1141), Bernard procured the condemnation of some of Abelard's statements. Even an appeal to Rome did not save Abelard. Peter of Cluny offered him a place of refuge at that monastery, where he died in 1142. Prominent works by Abelard are *Christian Theology*, *Introduction to Theology*, *Sic et Non*, and *Commentary on Romans*.

His rationalistic tendences notwithstanding, Abelard was not a rationalist after the fashion of the eighteenth century. He never questioned the authority of the Bible. His position is best defined as a type of mediating theology. His mediating view in the conflict between realism and nominalism has become known as "conceptualism."

In his defense of the Christian dogma against the radical scholars of the time, the followers of Avicenna and Averroes at Paris, Abelard employed dialectic as the scientific instrument of theology. In this he was guided by his Scholastic optimism which believed that reason could not contradict revelation. The duty of the scholarly theologian, according to him, was to come through doubt to inquiry, and through inquiry to truth. By contrast with Anselm, Abelard wanted to understand in order to believe. He never invaded the province of authority; rather, he saw it as the task of reason to support doctrine.

In *Sic et Non*, Abelard was the first to apply the dialectic method to the treatment of theology. The work poses a long list of isolated questions of doctrine, then groups concordant or contradictory opinions on each from the Bible, the Fathers, the decrees, and the canons. The thesis itself does not come up for discussion; instead the value of the different authorities is weighed by the application of rational investigation. While statements from the Fathers, the decrees, or the canons may be false or historically spurious, a quotation from the Bible is absolutely inviolable.

How does Abelard compare with Anselm? While Anselm demanded willing surrender to the doctrinal system as a whole, Abelard thought of a gradual trial by reason, by which the theologian arrives at complete comprehension of doctrines. Anselm says, *Credo ut intelligam* ("I believe, that I may know"), because he considers doctrine supernatural and feels that it can be comprehended only through a science of experience (*experientis scientia*). Abelard says, *Intelligo ut credam* ("I know, that I may believe"), because in his opinion a reasonable perception of the object of faith is both possible and necessary. Anselm works comprehensively. He experiences the doctrine in its entirety. Abelard is clever, but Anselm is gifted with genius. With Anselm, human reason creates or produces a new reason from doctrine. Abelard is content to show that the individual doctrine is reasonable. In Abelard the old conviction of the Apologists that Christianity is the climax of all philosophy lived on.

One cannot value Abelard's significance for Scholasticism highly enough. The characteristic feature of Scholasticism appears clearly in Abelard's theological work. Ecclesiastical positiveness is brought into close union with a sober dialectic and scientific method. This combination foreshadowed the great change which the thirteenth century was to bring, the displacement of Plato (the pure Neo-Platonic idealism in Augustine's theology) by Aristotle (the critical and empirical tendencies in later Scholasticism). Though Abelard was mercilessly condemned by the Neo-Platonic authorities of his times, the immediate future thought differently of him. His pupil, Alexander III, ascended the papal throne (1159–81).

Hugo was the son of a North German noble. While traveling in France he was moved to enter the monastery of St. Victor at Paris. He died in 1141, at the age of forty-four, as rector of the monastery's famous school.

Under the influence of his German training, Hugo followed a historical biblical outline in his discussion of theology.[1] His book *De sacramentis Christianae fidei* is the first important textbook on dogmatics in the Western Church, and reveals the brilliant systematic ability of its writer.[2]

The significance of Hugo's thought consists in the fact that he knew how to unite the lines of thought which came from Anselm, Abelard, and Bernard. Hugo summarized the speculative, rational, and mystical elements into the establishment of a strictly ecclesiastical theology. The sting was pulled out of dialectics when the rationality of a dogma was subjected to the super-rational background of faith. In this limited sphere theology could mix with philosophy without danger.

Peter the Lombard was born at Navarra in Italy. He studied at Bologna, Rheims, and Paris. In France he came into personal contact with Bernard, Abelard, and Hugo. He later taught at the cathedral school of Notre Dame, and was finally made Bishop of Paris. He died there about 1160.

Peter combined the dialectical method of Abelard with the orthodoxy of Hugo, from whom he also inherited his systematic talent. As he collated the various pronouncements on the dogmas of the Church he compared and weighed them and finally set forth the Scriptures as the highest authority. In keeping with the mind of Abelard, Peter held that reason had only a formal significance. It was used only as a means of salvation against the contradictions of the authorities.

His *Four Books of Sentences* was written in Paris before 1150. In its four divisions he treats of God, creation, original sin, Christ, the Holy Spirit, the sacraments, and eschatology. The present division into 182 distinctions is of a later date. The *Sentences* became the medieval textbook on dogmatics. The objective treatment of the material made this work a suitable guide for divergent theological schools. The *Sentences* are marked by the absence of a true conception of the gospel. Augustine is interpreted in the spirit of the day. The teaching of the Church concerning the sacraments is preserved and fixed according to the contemporary conception. This conception

[1] Rupert of Deutz and Honorius Augustodunensis were his forerunners in Germany. For a selection of Rupert's works, see *LCC*, IX, 249 ff.

[2] This title is best translated "Concerning the Mysteries of Christian Faith," for it is not a discussion of sacraments in our sense of the word. By *sacramentum* Hugo understands everything that God has done for men.

attained dogmatic value and Peter Lombard is held in high esteem by the Roman church for his important contribution in this field.

BIBLIOGRAPHY

ABELARD, PETER. *MSL*, Vol. 178.
ANSELM. *MSL*, Vols. 158, 159.
BOETHIUS. *MSL*, Vols. 63-64.
HONORIUS AUGUSTODUNENSIS. *MSL*, Vol. 172.
HUGO. *MSL*, Vol. 176.
LCC, Vol. X.
PETER LOMBARD. *MSL*, Vol. 192.
RUPERT OF DEUTZ. *MSL*, Vol. 167.
WILLIAM OF CHAMPEAUX. *MSL*, Vol. 163.

ADAM, K. *The Spirit of Catholicism.* New York: Macmillan Co., 1937.
BARTH, KARL. *Anselm: Fides Quaerens Intellectum.* Translated by IAN W. ROBERTSON. Richmond: John Knox Press, 1960.
CARRE, M. H. *Realists and Nominalists.* London and New York: Oxford University Press, 1946.
COPLESTONE, F. C. *History of Philosophy.* Westminster, Md.: Newman Press, 1957-59.
GILSON, ETIENNE. *The Spirit of Medieval Philosophy.* Translated by A. H. C. DOWNES. New York: Charles Scribner's Sons, 1936.
GRABMANN, M. *Die Geschichte der Scholastischen Methode.* 2 vols. 1909, 1911.
HASKINS, C. H. *The Renaissance of the Twelfth Century.* Oxford: Oxford University Press, 1927.
MACDONALD, A. J. *Authority and Reason in the Early Middle Ages.* London: Oxford University Press, 1927.
POOLE, R. L. *Illustrations of the History of Medieval Thought.* London: Williams and Norgate, 1920.
RASHDALL, H. *The Universities of Europe in the Middle Ages.* 3 vols. Oxford: Clarendon Press, 1895.
REINERS, J. *Der Aristotelische Realismus in der Frühscholastik.* 1907.
———. *Der Nominalismus in der Frühscholastik.* 1910.
RIGG, J. M. *St. Anselm of Canterbury.* London: Methuen and Co., 1896.
SIKES, J. G. *Peter Abelard.* Cambridge: Cambridge University Press, 1932.
WELCH, A. C. *Anselm and His Work.* New York: Charles Scribner's Sons, 1901.
WULF, M. DE. *Histoire de la Philosophie Medievale.* Translated by E. C. MESSENGER. 2 vols. 1924-25. New York: Longmans, Green and Co., 1936-38.

CHAPTER VI

DOCTRINAL ISSUES OF THE ELEVENTH AND TWELFTH CENTURIES

Early Scholasticism was concerned mainly with the discussion of the doctrine of God, original sin, the christological problem, and the teaching concerning Mary; it was especially instrumental in clarifying the conception of the sacraments and of the Church. Conflicting tendencies, while creating some disturbances of minor importance, directly caused two very bitter and pointed controversies: the Berengar-Lanfranc controversy over the Lord's Supper, and the conflict over the doctrine of the atonement which involved Anselm, Abelard, and Bernard.

I. The Berengar-Lanfranc Controversy

Since the first medieval conflict over the Lord's Supper, Radbertus' realistic conception of the sacrament had gained ground. The Augustinian tradition was unable to check this gain. With the beginning of the new learning a fresh scientific interest in this problem became manifest. A last, though futile attempt was made to curb the trend toward sacramental realism in its crassest form.

Berengar (d. 1088), a pupil of Fulbert of Chartres, was the man who renewed the attack upon the theory of Radbertus. Confident of his dialectics and reason, he uncovered the logical contradictions of the doctrine of transubstantiation. Appealing to the Scriptures, his religious interest compelled him to reject the idea that the communicants receive "pieces of Christ's flesh." He demanded the entire Christ and revived the Augustinian-Ratramnian spiritual concept of the sacrament. The corporeal presence is denied, for Christ's body exists undivided in heaven. The substance of the elements remains unchanged. Bread and wine are merely emblematic of the body and blood of the Savior, but they receive a new relation to the invisible body of Christ. His body, passion, and death cannot be comprehended by the senses. Union with Christ takes place inwardly and spiritually. With this spiritualization the presence and reception of the entire Christ, as demanded in the interest of true piety, is conceivable. Only believers receive the body of Christ. Only they experience the matter of the sacrament.

At a synod held in Rome, 1059, Berengar was forced to confess that "after the consecration the true body and blood of Christ are present, not only sacramentally but also perceptibly and that they are handled by the hands of the priests and broken, not only mysteriously (*in sacramento*) but in truth (*in veritate*) and ground by the teeth of the faithful." [1]

Tired of submission and placing his confidence in the archdeacon Hildebrand, who later became Pope Gregory VII, Berengar revived his view shortly after 1065. A passionate literary feud was the result. The chief writings were Lanfranc's *On the Body and Blood of the Lord* (against Berengar) and Berengar's reply *On the Holy Supper,* against Lanfranc. Other opponents of Berengar were Hugo of Langres, and especially Guitmund of Aversa, who wrote the treatise *Three Books on the Truth of the Body and Blood of Christ in the Eucharist.* For a few years Hildebrand was able to protect Berengar. When he became pope, he could no longer do so. In 1079 Berengar again had to surrender to Rome.

The new doctrine of the sacrament was scientifically elaborated by the opponents of Berengar. There was not much new in the result, for the theologians were bound to the Roman confession of 1059. Transubstantiation, that is, the teaching that the substance of bread and wine is actually changed into the body and blood of Christ, was

---

[1] Karl Mirbt, *Quellen zur Geschichte des Papstums* (4th ed., 1924), p. 144. As the observant reader will notice, this confession anticipates a rejection of Calvin's peculiar view of the Real Presence.—The Confession contains the doctrine of transubstantiation without the technical term. Expressions such as *convertere, commutare, conficere,* etc., were being used by the men of either party. Modern scholars are still at variance as to the first instance of the term transubstantiation. Cf. Loofs, *Leitfaden,* pp. 504-505; Charles Gore, *The Body of Christ* (London: Murray and Co., 1904), pp. 116 ff.

now the official teaching of the Church. Only the accidental properties (color, taste, and form) of the elements remain. In every host
the entire body of the historical Christ is present and received by
believers and unbelievers alike.

A number of problems remained to be solved. Starting with
Christology, the first attempts were made to solve the problem of
ubiquity. According to nature, it was said, Christ is present in one
place, that is, in heaven; through grace and by virtue of his divine
omnipotence, which extends even to the flesh of Christ, the body of
the Savior is present both in heaven and upon earth at the same time.
The flesh does not descend from heaven; it remains where it is, yet it
exists *tota et integra et substantialiter* wherever it pleases Him. Hence,
in a thousand masses all the hosts contain the entire Christ in all
their parts.[2]

A further consequence of transubstantiation was the sentence of
Lanfranc: "Even sinners and those who partake unworthily receive
the real body of Christ." [3] Lanfranc added, however, that the unworthy communicant receives it only according to its essence, not
as a saving power. In this sense Alger of Liege and Lanfranc made a
distinction between the communion of the believing and that of the
unbelieving. Though the unbelieving receive the true body of Christ,
only the believing enter into a spiritual communion with him.

Some followers of Berengar tried to take a mediating viewpoint by
advancing the theory of impanation. They admitted that Christ is
really, even bodily, present in the sacrament, but without any change
in the elements. Just as the human nature remained unchanged in the
incarnation, so in the impanation the bread and wine are substantially
unchanged. Just as in the man Jesus the true Godhead was present in
the closest union with him, so it is present in the bread and wine.
This theory, while being condemned at this time, developed during
the later Middle Ages into the theory of consubstantiation.

The Church gave its definite approval to the doctrine of transubstantiation at the Fourth Lateran Council at Rome in 1215. This
doctrine, with the other sacraments, was placed beside the dogmas of
the ancient Church. It was considered a dogma of the same impor-

[2] For references, see Seeberg, *Lehrbuch,* III, 200 ff.
[3] Mirbt, *op. cit.,* p. 145.

tance as the doctrine of the Trinity or Christology. In the first chapter of the confession called *Innocentium*, it is said: "The Body and Blood are truly (*veraciter*) contained in the Sacrament of the Altar under the appearance of bread and wine, after the bread has been changed into the Body, and the wine into the Blood, through the power of God. Only the rightly ordained priest can perform this sacrament." [4]

II. The Doctrine of the Atonement

Anselm of Canterbury was the first to present a harmonious and consistent doctrine of the atonement, in his epoch-making book *Cur Deus Homo?* He rejected the conception of Christ's work as a lawsuit with the devil and substituted a new theory on the subject.

The key to Anselm's range of ideas is the fundamental idea of the kingdom of God. God is the lord and king of the world. In the beginning he created the angels to inhabit his kingdom. After their fall, God created man as a substitute for the loss which he had suffered. Through willful disobedience Adam also sinned and refused God's purpose. Sin, therefore, is embedded in the will, and consists of the lack of the righteousness which man owes God. God's honor is offended. His honor consists in this, that his will and plan should come to completion and every creature should subject itself to him. All men have sinned in Adam and with him.

It was impossible for God to remit this sin simply out of mercy, for such an action would have brought disorder into his kingdom. There must be either punishment or satisfaction. Punishment or eternal condemnation would have defeated God's own eternal plan for man's salvation in his kingdom. There had to be satisfaction. Was man able to render an adequate satisfaction? He could not. Anything man might have been able to do by way of contrition would have been inadequate. Neither would any new obedience atone for the transgressions of the past. Nonetheless, man had to render satisfaction.

Thus the incarnation of the Son of God was necessary. Only as God-Man (*Deus-Homo*) could Christ take our place and render that satisfaction. The satisfaction did not consist in Christ's earthly life of obedience, for as one living in this world he owed such obedience

---

[4] *Ibid.*, p. 179.

to God. The significance of a real satisfaction lay exclusively in giving up his life. He was not obligated to do this, because he was sinless and did not need to die. The value of Christ's death was heightened by his voluntary submission. God had to reward the voluntary self-sacrificing death of a sinless one. The God-Man was not in need of a reward for himself, for everything that the Father has is already his, and in his sinlessness he owes no debt that might be remitted. Therefore, he gives his reward, the fruit of his work, to those for whose salvation he became man, namely, to his brethren who are burdened with debt.

Anselm's system is presented in much too judicial a fashion. The relation between God and man appears as that of a ruler to his subjects. There is a stress upon the term satisfaction that makes the New Testament conception of God's love recede into the background. Another defect of Anselm's system lies in his failure to include Christ's active obedience in his work of redemption. Furthermore, the application of Christ's merit to the individual lacks justifying faith as the appropriating factor. This was the special contribution of the Reformation. Anselm, in this endeavor to systematize the doctrine of the atonement, recognized the fundamental truths of Scripture and of Christian experience involved in man's sin, namely, God's justice and the means of redemption. Despite his imperfect expression, Anselm drew lines that have served as a foundation for arriving at more evangelical forms of teaching. Anselm shares with Latin theology the danger of making redemption partly a movement upward from man to God and only partly a downward movement from God to man.

Abelard's teaching on sin is subjectivistic and relativistic. It charms the modern mind. Sensual appetites, sexual desires, and man's deeds are morally irrelevant in themselves. They become sinful only through a willing consent to evil. The essence of sin consists in a conscientious, disobedient contempt of God. It is evident that such a conception of sin does away with the Church's doctrine of original sin. Abelard reduced the significance of original sin to a mere hereditary punishment inflicted by God upon all descendants of Adam.

Abelard's view of the atonement is perfectly in line with this superficial conception of sin. The only thing which he has in common with Anselm is the rejection of the claim of the devil upon mankind. As for the rest, he severely criticized Anselm's position. In order to forgive Adam's sin, shall God be pleased with a crime which would far surpass Adam's sin, that is, the slaying of his Son? The case of Mary, whom God exempted from the curse of original sin, demonstrates that God can forgive without Christ. Christ's birth, passion, and death reveal God's infinite love for mankind and awaken in us a reciprocal love and gratitude. This disposition of love is the basis both of justification and the forgiveness of sin (*caritas justificat*).

Strange to say, with this subjective or moral conception of the atonement, Abelard held another view which was the nearest approach that he made to the objective view of the atonement. "Through His merits He has obtained for us everything good that we have." [5] Christ's merits, however, are not his death, but his perfect love. Inasmuch as our love is insufficient, our merits are also insufficient. Our merits are supplemented by Jesus' instruction, his complete fulfillment of the law, and his effective intercession for us. Abelard related the sacramental idea to his teaching of the atonement. The love which is efficacious for the forgiveness of sin is infused into us through the sacraments. Thus besides the rational-psychological way to forgiveness he saw a sacramental-supernatural way independent of it. One recognizes the mediating theologian who, convinced of the rightness of reason, will not give up the genuine faith of the Church.

The larger stress of God's love in the teaching of Abelard is correct, but it is just as one-sided as Anselm's system. While Anselm failed to make clear the subjective application of Christ's merits through faith, Abelard practically reduced the work of Christ to an incitement of trust and love in man's heart toward God. Christ is not the originator of man's redemption; he is only the teacher and herald of the redemption completed through God's love.

The greatest antagonist of Abelard was Bernard of Clairvaux. Like Abelard, Bernard stressed the need for meditating upon the love of Christ so that our hearts may be aroused to responding love, but it was unbearable to him that in the teaching of Abelard there was no place for the blood of Jesus and his cross. Abelard's view that Christ was only a teacher was shocking to Bernard. As it was not the example of Adam that made us sinners, so it is not the example of

[5] *MSL,* Vol. 178, p. 869.

Christ that suffices for our redemption. The mystical element in Bernard's theology expressed the view that Christ was the Second Adam who suffered vicariously and wrought our redemption as the head of a new spiritual race.

According to Hugo, sin is disobedience to God, for which man suffers the punishment of spiritual ignorance and carnal concupiscence. Christ came to placate the offended God, and through the sacraments Christ communicates to us his renewing and sanctifying grace.

It is of the greatest significance that Peter Lombard followed Hugo in his teaching on original sin. The voluntaristic conception of Anselm and Abelard is pushed to the background, and carnal concupiscence is made the essence of sin. The corruption of human nature is transmitted to the child through sexual pleasure and infects the soul, which is created separately by God in each individual.

In his teaching on the atonement, Peter unites—in an unsatisfactory way—nearly all the theories on the work of Christ which tradition offered him, even the theory of the deception of the devil. However, like Anselm, Abelard, and Hugo, Peter denies any claim of the devil upon the sinner. As a perfect sacrifice Christ was able to procure salvation for us.

In a more concise statement of how that happens,[6] Peter takes the subjective view first: God's love is revealed in Christ's death. Through the cross, responding love for God is kindled in us and we are thereby justified. Next to that stands the objective view: God himself was made flesh, since a mere man or angel might easily have sinned. The God-Man conquers the devil, redeems us from eternal punishment and infuses his grace into us through the sacraments.

Peter Lombard's doctrine of the atonement indicates a mere summary of various theories, but no settlement of the problem.

BIBLIOGRAPHY

1. *Berengar-Lanfranc Controversy*
   ALGER. *MSL*, Vol. 180.
   BERENGAR. *Liber de sacra coena adversus Lanfrancum.* Edited by A. F. and E. T. VISCHER. 1834.
   GUITMUND. *MSL*, Vol. 149.

[6] *Sententiae,* Book III, Dist. 18-20.

HEFELE, VON K. J. *Konziliengeschichte.* 9 vols., 1855–. 2nd ed., 3 vols., 1873–. 8 vols.; Paris, 1907–.

LANFRANC. *MSL,* Vol. 150.

MANSI, J. DOM. *Collectio Sacrorum Conciliorum.* Florence and Venice: 1759-1798. New print, 1903.

PETER LOMBARD. *MSL,* Vol. 192.

2. *The Doctrine of the Atonement*

ABELARD, PETER. *MSL,* Vol. 178.

ANSELM. *MSL,* Vol. 159.

————. *Prologium, Monologium, . . . Cur Deus Homo.* Translated by S. N. DEANE. Chicago: Open Court Publishing Co., 1926.

BERNARD. *Epistola,* 190. *MSL,* Vol. 182.

AULEN, G. *Christus Victor.* Translated by A. G. HEBERT. London: SPCK, 1953.

MCINTYRE, JOHN. *St. Anselm and His Critics.* Edinburgh: Oliver and Boyd, 1954.

WELCH, A. C. *Anselm and His Work.*

WILLIAMS, W. *The Mysticism of St. Bernard of Clairvaux.* London: Burns, Oates, and Washbourne, 1931.

CHAPTER VII

THE CHURCH AND THEOLOGY OF THE THIRTEENTH CENTURY

The thirteenth century was the golden age of Roman Catholicism. The church party of Gregory VII had attained its purpose. The pious expectation of biblical eschatology had become materialized on earth. The Church militant was also the Church triumphant. "The kingdoms of this world are become the kingdom of our Lord and his Christ" (Rev. 11:15), for the vicar of Christ was the undisputed sovereign of kings and bishops, Church and state, the lord over the temporal and eternal welfare of men. No pope has ever been more powerful than Innocent III (1198-1216), and except for the Vatican decree of 1870, no pope has ever uttered such great boasts as he. "The pope holds a position between God and man. Though less than God, he is greater than man. He judges everybody, but is himself judged by none." [1] Innocent read references to himself into passages like Isa. 42:8, John 1:16, and Romans 8:29.

These unparalleled claims of the papacy were seconded and defended in the name of piety and theology by the new mendicant orders and the great teachers of the high Scholastic period. At the time when some groups began to call attention to the contradiction between the simple earthly life of Jesus and the might and splendor of his vicar in Rome, these new orders made their appearance to demonstrate to the world that a genuine imitation of the poverty of the Savior still had a place within the Church.

The idea of this new type of monastic life originated with Francis of Assisi (1182–1226). The son of a wealthy Italian merchant, he left

---

[1] *MSL,* Vol. 217, p. 568. The passage occurs in a sermon preached on the occasion of Gregory's consecration as Bishop of Rome, February 22, 1198.

all he had and followed Jesus in his lowliness with the greatest sincerity. In Francis, Bernardian mysticism found its noblest representative in this period. As Bernard had been instrumental in fostering the new piety among the nobility, so the new piety was promulgated among the populace of the then efflorescent cities through Francis. A monastic order that wants to live from alms cannot establish itself in romantic solitude. The headquarters of the mendicant friars had to be among the hurly-burly of city life. Thus the mendicant friars had a splendid opportunity to take advantage of the teaching positions at the new centers of learning, the universities.

Theological thought in the thirteenth century received a strong impetus from a new and intensified study of Aristotle by the scholars of the West. Hitherto only part of Aristotle's logical writings had been known in the West, through the translation of Boethius. From 1150 to 1210, Aristotle's *Natural Philosophy*, *Politics*, *Metaphysics* and *Ethics* were gradually introduced. The translations were made, not from the original Greek, but from Arabic. Special credit for this translation goes to the Spanish and Sicilian Jews who performed their work by order of the Archbishop of Toledo and Emperor Frederick II. Not until later, when the Latin Empire was established in Byzantium, was it possible to obtain Latin translations from the original Greek.

It was significant that the West became acquainted with the works of Aristotle in their entirety not only through translations from Arabic but also through Arabian commentaries. For this reason the Church at first blamed Aristotle himself for the Neo-Platonic, pantheistic speculation of the Jewish-Arabian scholars.[2] His philosophical writings were prohibited under pain of excommunicaton as late as 1210 and 1215. The change came when the genuine Aristotle was distinguished from the Arabic Aristotle. By 1231, the study of Aristotle was generally permitted insofar as he was purified "from every suspicion of error." After that the ban was broken. In 1255, the study of Aristotle was made obligatory by the University of Paris. He was often spoken of as the *praecursor Christi in naturalibus* and compared

---

[2] Among the most influential of these writers were Avicenna (d. 1037), Avicebron (d. 1070), and especially Averroes (d. 1198). See Averroes, *Tahafut al Tahafut* ("The Incoherence of Incoherence"), trans. Simon van der Bergh in 2 vols. (London: Luzac and Co., 1954).

to John the Baptist, as the *praecursor Christi in gratuitis*. Albertus Magnus declared Aristotle's philosophy the rule of truth, the highest perfection of human reason.

The new material and problems raised by this study of Aristotle called for a new method of study. Hitherto systematic work in the schools had been devoted to writing a commentary on the *Sentences* of Peter Lombard. This method was now replaced by writing a *summa*, a very elaborate but carefully balanced treatment of all the objects of theology, resembling the superb Gothic architecture of the age. With incomparable strength and an acumen never again attained, the best talents of the Middle Ages devoted themselves to the work of fusing the Augustinianism of the Church and of ecclesiastical law with the Aristotelian philosophy. At the same time, the scholars held to the presupposition that both existed by equal right and that neither natural nor revealed theology might be discarded.

The older Franciscan school had precursors in theologians like Praepositinus of Cremona, William of Auxerre, and William of Auvergne. Members of this school started with the theology of the twelfth century and their chief authority was Augustine. At the same time, modern tendencies asserted themselves in the new style of problematics and the more intensive use of dialectic.

The real founder of high Scholasticism and the foremost exponent of the older Franciscan school was Alexander of Hales (d. 1245). His colossal *Summa universae theologiae* signifies the deepest cleavage between the theology of the twelfth and that of the thirteenth century.

Alexander attempted to produce a homogeneous system upon the threefold foundation of the strictest orthodoxy, the new piety, and Aristotelian philosophy. His system was not a superficial arrangement of contrasted theses, like Abelard's *Sic et Non*, but a search for the truth from the cognition of the principle. In this, Alexander adhered to Augustinianism, permitting Aristotle to determine only his method of thought. Many of his new transpositions and solutions became historically significant and are partially valid today, for example: his distinction between the *fides informis* of the natural man, which relies on authority, miracle, and rational arguments, and the *fides formata* or *infusa*, which so illumines man by the divine light that he comes to the immediate certainty of God and divine beings without further proof; his doctrine of the primitive state; his combining of the Aristotelian conception of form with the doctrine of grace; his distinction between the *meritum de condigno* and the *meritum de congruo*;[3] his introduction of "attrition" (imperfect sorrow for sin, such as arises from fear of punishment); and his comment on the preference given to the study of the *Sentences* at the expense of Bible study.

Another representative of this school was Bonaventure (*doctor seraphicus*), born in the Papal States in 1221. He died as a cardinal and general of the Franciscan Order in 1274. Augustine was his chief authority, and he put Plato above Aristotle. His theological position is characterized by three catchwords: illumination, voluntarism, and positivism; that is, the mystic contemplation of God, the enjoyment of God (*frui Deo*) by a voluntary submission of the intellect in obedience to Christ, and the blind surrender of the conscience to the laws and commandments of the Church. Thus arose the strange alliance between the boldest, most absolute mysticism and the most scrupulous, ingenious traditionalism as it can be observed in Bernard and later in Duns Scotus and Occam.[4]

It was the Dominicans who brought Scholasticism to its height. Albertus Magnus (*doctor universalis*), the son of a German nobleman, was the leader in this movement. He died in 1280 as a professor at Cologne. Albertus was a great teacher and a prolific writer. His writings include works on theology, philosophy, biology, zoology, botany, astronomy, and alchemy.[5] The conflict between Platonism and Aristotelianism remained unsolved in his system.

The greatest perfection of the movement was reached in Thomas Aquinas, son of an Italian aristocrat. In 1243 he entered the Dominican order and studied under Albertus Magnus at Cologne. He later taught at Paris, Naples, and Rome. He died in 1274 on his way to the council at Lyons. This accomplished scholar was a literary genius with an all-embracing interest. He wrote commentaries on Aristotle and on books of the Old and New Testaments, and provided a dogmatic and ethical *summa*, the *Summa Theologica*. He and his school found an implacable opponent in the Franciscan order. In this conflict Aquinas

---

[3] For an explanation of these terms, see p. 289.

[4] For a selection of Bonaventure's writings, see *LCC*, X, 379 ff.

[5] H. Balls, *Albertus Magnus als Zoologe* (1928) and *Albertus Magnus als Biologe* (1947).

was the victor. After he had been made the official theologian of the Dominicans, the Church also decided in his favor. In 1323 he was canonized; he was proclaimed *doctor ecclesiae* in 1567, and in 1880, "patron of all Catholic schools."

As Augustine is the Christian Platonist *par excellence*, Aquinas is the Christian Aristotelian in a supreme degree. He tried hard to expurgate the pantheism of the Arabian commentators from Aristotle's writings and to harmonize the teaching of the great philosopher with Christian theism. He also wanted to harmonize two other opposing schools of thought, namely, the rationalists and the mystics. The rationalists (Abelard and his followers) obliterated all distinctions between natural and supernatural truth and treated the mysteries of faith as conclusions of reason. The mystics (John Scotus Erigena, for example) removed every distinction by teaching that even truth of the natural world is known to man only by special illumination. Against these tendencies, Aquinas maintained that natural knowledge belongs to the realm of reason while supernatural truth is a matter of revelation. However, there are not two sets of truth; rather, the two supplement each other. Reason and revelation, philosophy and theology, are parts of one system.

The purpose of revelation, Aquinas says, is to give man knowledge about God. This knowledge is mediated to man in a twofold way: first, by natural reason, which can prove the existence of God; second, by special revelation, by which man may know God as he is in himself (doctrine of the Trinity).[6] Aquinas' conception of God combines Platonic and Aristotelian ideas, since God is both perfect being and pure actuality, primary cause and primary agent. Likewise, his doctrine of grace reflects his Aristotelian bent of mind. Because nothing in the corporeal world can act unless it is moved by God, God is the First Mover in all things spiritual.[7] Salvation is "from predestination, which never fails, and from grace: for whoever has grace, by this fact is worthy of eternal life." Predestination to life is absolute, whereas damnation is the fault of man who "fails to obtain it [grace]

---

[6] A. C. Pegis, *The Basic Writings of Saint Thomas*, 2 vols. (New York: Random House, 1945), I, 18 ff.

[7] *Ibid.*, II, 980. Cf. Thomas Bonhoeffer, *Die Gotteslehre des Thomas von Aquin als Sprachproblem* (1961).

through mortal sin." [8] Predestination therefore is irresistible, but not grace. As may be seen, Aquinas follows Augustine quite closely but is anxious to warn the faithful against the spirit of complacency.

Unlike Anselm, Thomas Aquinas denied the absolute necessity of Christ's passion. Christ suffered out of love and obedience. He obtained a merit. His death is not only sufficient but "superabundant."

The disruption of the Thomistic synthesis was effected in two different ways. On the one hand, the humanists detached themselves from the Augustinian heritage of the Church and developed an independent view of the world in Hellenic fashion. On the other hand, Luther struck violently at this artificial edifice. Rediscovering the personal God of the Bible, he shattered the structure of the Scholastics into fragments. This is the real and abiding significance of the Reformation. [9]

In spite of the great advance in ecclesiastical power and theology, opposition to the Church became very noticeable during the thirteenth century. The West had come into contact with the flourishing scientific and impressive social life of the Arabian countries through the Crusades. This contact created a skeptical sentiment as to the absolute truth of the Church. Men were beginning to arrive at the proposition of a twofold truth according to which a doctrine might be possible in theology but impossible in philosophy. In Palermo, probably at the brilliant imperial court of Frederick II, the notorious saying originated that the three impostors of mankind were Moses, Jesus, and Mohammed. The pitiless conflict of the popes with Frederick II and the last rulers of the Hohenstaufen dynasty was void of any spiritual objectives. It was a mere struggle for political hegemony in Italy. No wonder that the papal ban could neither impair nor change the plans of the emperors. In its desire to rule the world, the Church forfeited its spiritual power and became a part of the world.

Likewise the rising tide of nationalism in the Western world began to oppose the international and super-national claims of the Church. The Latin of the Church was beginning to lose its exclusive position. A new national literature in the vernaculars of the various countries was coming into existence. Poets like Walther von der Vogelweide

[8] Pegis, *op. cit.,* I, 257.
[9] Cf. G. S. Hendry, *God the Creator* (1937), pp. 60 ff.

(d. *ca.* 1230) and Dante (1265-1321) sided strongly with the emperors in their conflict with the popes and unhesitatingly assailed the unscrupulous and immoral strategy of the papacy.

Furthermore, the growth of the universities (Bologna, founded in the eleventh century; Paris and Oxford, twelfth century; Heidelberg, 1396), added to the disintegration of the solidarity of the Scholastic world-view. The study of Aristotle fostered a new interest in the natural sciences, as evidenced in the work of Roger Bacon (d. 1292). To be sure, these tendencies could fully succeed and mature only much later.

The Church was also attacked and opposed in the name of genuine piety. Old heresies were revived, as in the case of the dualistic-Manichaeistic Cathari.[10] New heretical groups sprang up, for example, the Waldensians, who taught a biblicism pure and simple. The Church tried to win them back or to exterminate them. In so doing, the Church revived the dreadful pagan persecutions of the first centuries. The Church itself gave reason to believe that the papacy was the seven-headed beast of Revelation, and ever since this belief has not been without its advocates. The golden age of Roman Catholicism ended with the pope a prisoner at the mercy of the French king and the grand intellectual structure of Thomas undermined by Duns Scotus.

BIBLIOGRAPHY

ALBERTUS MAGNUS
ALEXANDER OF HALES
AQUINAS, THOMAS
————. *Thomas's Treatise on Man.* Edited by J. F. ANDERSON. Englewood Cliffs, N. J.: Prentice Hall, 1962.
————. *Thomas's Summa theologica.* Edited by Fathers of the English Dominican Province. London: Burns & Oates, 1947-48.
————. *Thomas's Commentary on the Metaphysics of Aristotle.* Edited by JOHN R. ROWAN. Chicago: H. Regnery Co., 1961.
BONAVENTURA
INNOCENT III. *MSL,* Vols. 2-14-217.
LCC, Vol. X.
PEGIS, A. C. *The Basic Writings of St. Thomas.* 2 vols. New York: Random House, 1945.

[10] Cf. H. J. Warner, *The Albigensian Heresy* (London: SPCK, 1922—).

Secondary Sources

CUTHBERT, T. *Life of St. Francis of Assisi.* 1913.

D'ARCY, M. C. *Thomas Aquinas.* London: Benn, 1930.

GILSON, E. *Philosophy of St. Thomas.* Translated by E. BULLOUGH. St. Louis: Herder Book Co., 1937.

GOHEEN, T. *The Problem of Matter in the De Ente Essentia of Thomas Aquinas.* Cambridge: Harvard University Press, 1940.

GRABMANN, M. *Der Einfluss Alberts des Grossen auf das Mittelalterliche Geistesleben.* 2nd ed. 1955.

————. *Introduction to the Theological Summa of St. Thomas.* Translated by JOHN S. ZYBURA. London: Herder Book Co., 1930.

————. *Thomas Aquinas: His Personality and Thought.* Translated by V. MICHEL. New York: Longmans, Green and Co., 1928.

JOERGENSEN, J. *St. Francis of Assisi.* Translated by T. O'CONOR SLOANE. New York: Longmans, Green and Co., 1912.

ROBINSON, PASCHAL. *The Writings of St. Francis of Assisi.* Philadelphia: Dolphin Press, 1906.

CHAPTER VIII

THE TEACHING ON SIN AND GRACE—THE SACRAMENTS

The Doctrine of Sin and Grace

As typical scholars of the West, the Scholastics made the greatest contribution to theology along the practical lines of anthropology and soteriology.

In describing the original state of man they distinguished between the natural endowment of man and the additional endowment of grace. The natural endowment consists in the harmony of man's natural powers and the absence of concupiscence. The endowment of grace is a *donum superadditum*, an additional gift to control the inferior sensitiveness in man. Through this additional endowment man was also able to make himself acceptable in the sight of God.

As to the conception of sin, the Franciscans favored the traditional Semi-Pelagian tenets of the age, whereas Thomas kept closer to the Augustinian heritage of the Church.

Original sin was defined as something negative, the lack of original righteousness or the loss of the additional endowment. The fall caused no important alteration in man's nature. According to Thomas, natural depravity is something positive: it is concupiscence and involves both guilt and punishment. Since all of these teachers held to the doctrine of creationism, concupiscence was said to have its origin in the flesh and to be propagated by generation.

The conditioned original sin is materialized through actual sin. The chief sources of actual sin are seven: pride, covetousness, lust, anger, gluttony, envy, and sloth. These are the capital sins (*peccata capitalia*). They are subdivided into *peccata mortalia* and *venialia*. A sin is mortal if it is a willful transgression of the law of God and separates from God. Venial sins are only a *version*, a deviation from God, without punishments. The natural possibility of sinning comes from God, who is the cause of everything; the depravity of the action, however, comes from the free will of man. Though the universality of sin was generally conceded, the Scholastics made an exemption in the case of the Virgin Mary. Whereas all agreed that Mary was exempted from actual sin, the Dominicans objected to denying original sin in Mary. No formal decision was reached until 1854, when Pope Pius IX sanctioned belief in the immaculate conception of Mary.

On grace, Thomas, following Augustine, taught that God is the moving power in effecting man's conversion. Still Thomas insists that man is free in the use of his will to prepare for grace. Grace is viewed from the standpoint of Aristotelian form, which is first a disposition in God that becomes active in its object. By the infusion of grace into man, he is restored and his nature is repaired. Justification is not a judicial act of God; it is a gradual process of human recovery. Through the infusion of grace man also receives love, which changes his attrition to contrition and his *fides informis* to *fides formata*. Man's good works are so perfected in him that he can justly claim eternal life from God (*meritum de condigno*), while before this infusion took place it seemed only appropriate that God should recompense the honest moral endeavor of man. The merits of man's works had been *de congruo*.

A man may earn more merits than are necessary for his own salvation if he is willing to follow the evangelical counsels in addition to all the commandments of the gospel. The supererogatory works of Christ and the saints have created a treasury of superabundant merits (*thesaurus supererogationis meritorum*). The treasury is at the disposal of the pope and is administered by the priests for the benefit of the souls in purgatory.

This brief outline of the order of salvation clearly indicates that the religious life of Roman Catholicism does not center in faith but in love and good works. Consequently, no certainty of salvation is attainable. The pious man is always kept in suspense as to his final destiny. No wonder that the grandest hymn of the Middle Ages is not a hymn in praise of victorious faith but an expression of fear and apprehension: *Dies irae, dies illa* ("Day of wrath, that mournful day").

THE DOCTRINE OF THE SACRAMENTS

All the lines of interest in medieval theology converge in the teaching concerning the sacraments. This teaching was conditioned by a twofold interest: (1) the practical concern of the individual for some tangible form of salvation, and (2) the hierarchical tendencies of the age to bind the salvation of the individual to the Church. The sacraments became both a means of grace and a means to rule.

Since the term *sacramentum* had been used in the preceding centuries for any significant religious act, the exact number of the sacraments had remained undetermined. To baptism and the Eucharist, Abelard had added confession and extreme unction. His pupils added matrimony. These five sacraments were also recognized by Hugo. Robert Pullus (d. 1150) attained the same number by omitting extreme unction and matrimony but including penance and ordination. Through a combination of these the number seven was finally reached. This has been the established number, since Peter Lombard, finally receiving official sanction at the council of Florence in 1439.[1]

The Franciscans upheld Augustine's definition of a sacrament as a visible sign of an invisible grace. Thomas, however, made the sacramental matter the vehicle of grace except in the case of ordination. In this sacrament, according to Aquinas, the spiritual power proceeded from the officiating bishop.

In each sacrament the matter, the visible element, is distinguished from the form, the words used in the rite. The two terms have retained a connotation from Aristotelian philosophy: *materia* signifies the unformed substance of a thing, *forma* its shaping energy. In the Eucharist, bread and wine are the unformed matter until the words of institution change them into the sacramental body and blood of Christ.

The primary effect of the sacraments is to restore his original righteousness to man through the impartation of the redemptive merits of the Savior. The three sacraments which cannot be repeated (baptism, confirmation, and ordination) also communicate a *character spiritualis,* that is, an indelible, indestructible mark imprinted on the

[1] Mirbt, *op. cit.,* p. 44.

soul for all time. This conception has served as a convenient means to uphold the belief in the unity and sanctity of the Church in spite of prevailing dissensions and unbelief among the baptized and the undeniable unworthiness of many priests.

The validity of the sacraments depends exclusively on a virtue inherent in themselves. They are effective *ex opere operato*. The only requirement is that the officiating priest have the intention of doing what the Church does, and that likewise the recipient, in order to participate in the blessing of the sacrament, have the disposition of faith and not be in the state of mortal sin.

The definitions of each sacrament contained in the papal bull *Exultate Deo* of 1439[2] were based chiefly on Thomas Aquinas. They are still authoritative in the Church of Rome.

The matter of baptism is a triple immersion in or sprinkling with water; its form is the words: "I baptize thee in the name of the Father, and of the Son, and of the Holy Ghost." Inasmuch as it confers justifying grace upon the recipient, his sins, original as well as actual, are forgiven, and their guilt and punishment are removed. The baptized is made a saint in the kingdom of God in spite of the fact that a spark, a *fomes peccati*, remains which might at any moment be kindled into a flame.

Confirmation is the anointing of the baptized with consecrated chrism, signifying the communication of the Holy Ghost to make him a strong and perfect Christian. In the ancient Church, as in the East to the present time, this anointing was connected with the rite of baptism and administered by the priest. In the Church of Rome the ordinary minister now is the bishop. The matter of this sacrament is holy chrism; its form, "I sign thee with the sign of the cross, and confirm thee with the chrism of salvation, in the name of the Father, and of the Son, and of the Holy Ghost."

Theological speculation as well as practical piety culminates in the doctrine of the Eucharist, which is both a sacrament and a sacrifice. In the mass, the heavenly Christ unites Himself with the elements of bread and wine, and at the same time, the priest offers Christ up to God. In the eyes of the realists, the mass was a continual "representation" of the sacrifice of Christ on Calvary, whereas the nominalists

---

[2] Mirbt, *loc. cit.*

were inclined to regard it as a daily "repetition." Its matter is bread and wine; its form, the words of institution. According to Thomas, the substance of the elements is changed into that of the celestial body of Christ. The accidental properties, however, remain unchanged. The elements become essentially the body of Christ, though not with respect to the dimensions of his body and blood. This change is effected by virtue of the sacramental words when properly recited by a consecrated priest.

Since the whole Christ was held to be present in each of the elements, the tendency to withhold the cup from the laity gradually, though slowly, became the established custom of the Church. The conception of the Eucharist as a sacrament became secondary to that of a daily sacrifice. Holy Communion was believed to have been instituted not for eating and drinking but for adoration and worship, and this contributed to an ever increasing aggrandizement of the sacerdotal hierarchy. The exhibition of the sacramental Christ in the mass and in eucharistic processions (*Corpus Christi* festivals since 1264)[3] turned out to be the greatest display of sacerdotal power.

The effect of this sacrament consists in the strengthening of sanctifying grace and the remission of venial sins. As a sacrifice, the Eucharist is a propitiatory, effectual oblation for the benefits of those present or absent, living or dead.

The Scholastics distinguished the sacrament of penance from the Christian virtue of repentance. Whereas this virtue is a permanent requirement, the necessity of receiving the sacrament is limited to certain occasions, specifically, to remove mortal sin and to assure the communicant of the absence of such sin before Holy Communion.

The history of penance is long and intricate.[4] The severe discipline of the ancient Church had gradually been mitigated. Public penance proved distasteful to the northern people. It was gradually supplanted by private confession to the priest. The earliest trace of this is found

---

[3] Mirbt, *op. cit.*, pp. 203-204.

[4] O. W. Watkins, *A History of Penance* (London and New York: Longmans, Green and Co., 1920). B. Poschmann, *Die abendländische Kirchenbusse im Ausgang des christlichen Altertums* (1928); *Die abendländische Kirchenbusse im frühern Mittelalter* (1930); and *Poenitentia Secunda; Die kirchliche Busse im ältesten Christentum* (1940). R. C. Mortimer, *The Origins of Private Penance in the Western Church* (Oxford: Clarendon Press, 1939). C. Vogel, *La discipline penitentielle en Gaulle* (1952).

in the monasteries of Cassianus (fifth century) in southern Gaul. From the monastic discipline the practice was transferred to the secular clergy, and then to the laity. It was welcomed by the laity to quiet the fear of punishment, purgatory, and hell. On the one hand, confession deepened the consciousness of sin, but on the other it weakened the moral life, for it became habitual. The conception became universal that through intercessions and satisfactions punishment for sin could be absolved. The old order of contrition, confession, satisfaction, and absolution was changed to let absolution precede satisfaction. The confession itself was looked upon as forgiving the sins; satisfaction as the means of escaping temporal punishments for sins and acquiring merits. Whoever neglects penitential works must suffer in purgatory, but whoever neglects repentance and confession is irrevocably lost. These satisfactions came to be looked upon as good works which removed the punishment for sin, and when performed without being required, to their classification as good works, procuring merit where there was no sin which required compensation.

As soon as a real value became attached to satisfactions, exchanges, transfers, reductions, substitutions, attenuations, redemptions or commutations, and a traffic in spiritual indulgences logically followed. Payments of money were accepted instead of the performance of penances. The hiring of others to do works of penance for a sinner was permitted. The first indulgences appeared in southern France in the eleventh century.[5] The first plenary indulgence was granted in 1040 by Benedict IX. Indulgences, according to the official interpretation, only remit the canonical punishments connected with sin. The erroneous conception that they forgive sin proved too popular and worked disastrously for the continuation of the practice.

The acts of the penitent are the matter of this sacrament: the contrition or the attrition (Thomas)[6] of the heart, the confession before the priest, and the satisfaction through penitential works. The words of the priest, "I absolve thee," constitute its form. The forgiveness of sin is not obtained through the contrite disposition of the

[5] A. M. Lepicier, *Indulgences, their Origin, Nature, and Development* (Kegan Paul, Trench, Trübner and Co., 1895).

[6] C. Meyer, *The Thomistic Concept of Justifying Contrition* (Mundelein, Ill.: St. Mary of the Lake Seminary, 1949).

sinner, but is dependent on the keys of the Church. In 1215 Innocent III, made yearly confession at Easter obligatory.

About 888, the Western Church began to emphasize the ancient custom of anointing the sick. Soon this practice received a sacramental character (extreme unction) inasmuch as it was connected with the remission of sins and was considered a substitute for penance. The matter of extreme unction is consecrated olive oil with which the priest anoints the eyes, ears, nostrils, lips, hands, feet, and loins of the sick in immediate danger of death. Its form is the accompanying prayer: "Through this holy unction and His most precious mercy may the Lord forgive thee all thy sins of sight . . ." The effect of extreme unction is the healing of the soul by the remission of venial sin, the cleansing from the remains of sin, and, if God sees fit, the restoration of health to the body.

The last two sacraments exclude each other: the recipient of ordination is prohibited from marriage and *vice versa*. Ordination is instituted to rule the Church; matrimony, to multiply its membership. The power and grace to rule and to perform the sacred duties of the Church are bestowed upon the recipient of ordination through seven successive acts of blessing. This sacrament is administered by the bishop and imparts an indelible character. The matter is found in the rites of the laying on of the hands, the anointing, and the handing over of the paten and chalice. The words of the consecrating bishop constitute the form: "Receive authority to offer sacrifice in the Church for the living and the dead . . . Receive the Holy Ghost; whosesoever sins you remit, they are remitted unto them . . ."

No teaching is more inconsistent and vacillating than that concerning matrimony. Unlike all the other sacraments, the recipients are the agents, for matrimony itself, not the benediction of the priest, constitutes the sacrament. Consequently, the form is found in the mutual consent of the contracting parties. Its matter is left undefined. Its effect is the impartation of sanctifying mutual love which enables husband and wife to bear with each other's weakness and to procreate and educate their children in fear and love of God. As a sacrament, matrimony is indissoluble. It may be repeated in case of the death of one of the contractors. In spite of the contradictory teachings regarding matrimony, its sacramental conception helped to preserve a holy place for it in the world of ascetic and monastic ideals. The requirement of a voluntary, mutual consent and the restriction placed upon intermarriage of relatives proved to be of great importance for the civilization of the West.

BIBLIOGRAPHY

BACH, J. *Die Siebenzahl der Sakramente.* 1864.

GIHR, N. *Die heiligen Sakramente der katholischen Kirche.* 2 vols. 1902-1903.

HAHN, G. L. *Die Lehre von den Sakramenten.* 1864.

KENNEDY, D. J. "Sacraments," *Catholic Encyclopedia,* Vol. 13. New York: Robert Appleton Co., 1907-1912.

LEA, H. C. *A History of Auricular Confession and Indulgences in the Latin Church.* 3 vols. Philadelphia: Lea Bros. and Co., 1896.

MACDONALD, A. J. *Berengar and the Reform of the Sacramental Doctrine.* London: Longmans, Green and Co., 1930.

MSL, Vol. 31.

SCHANZ, P. *Die Lehre von den heiligen Sakramenten.* 1893.

STONE, D. *A History of the Doctrine of the Holy Eucharist.* London and New York: Longmans, Green and Co., 1909.

CHAPTER IX

CHURCH AND STATE IN THE FOURTEENTH AND FIFTEENTH CENTURIES

Thomas set forth the infallibility and unrestricted sovereignty of the pope over Church and state.[1] At the Second Council of Lyons in 1274, official sanction was given to this doctrine. In the papal bull *Unam Sanctam* (1302), Boniface VIII formulated what had been taught and approved, but in a way that proved offensive to his time. He held that the pope possesses both swords, the spiritual and the secular, and that unconditional submission to the pope is necessary for eternal salvation.[2] Boniface's claims were supported by two jurists —the Italian monk, Augustines Triumphus,[3] and the Spaniard, Alvarus Pelagius.[4]

Western Europe was by no means ready to surrender to these claims. Boniface met with the most disgraceful disaster. He was taken prisoner by the French king, an event which ushered in two of the most ignominious periods in the history of the papacy: the Babylonian Captivity of the Church, 1307–77, and the Great Schism, 1378–1415.

During the later Middle Ages, Europe was in the transition from barter economy to money and credit economy. The Holy See became the foremost international money institute. The Church's system of taxation, which exploited individuals and peoples, together with the traffic in indulgences proved destructive to the morals of the Church and the national wealth of the European peoples. Opposition arose

[1] Mirbt, *op. cit.*, pp. 199 ff.
[2] *Ibid.*, pp. 210-11.
[3] *Summa de potestate ecclesiae* (1473). Cf. Mirbt, *op. cit.*, p. 216.
[4] *De planctu ecclesiae* (1474).

in Western Europe, which at this time was experiencing a rising tide of national consciousness. At the same time the awakening nationalism fostered a revival of the Carolingian idea of a national church. This movement early became noticeable in England, which had never been under the charm and pressure of the romantic idea of the Holy Roman Empire.

Occam was the first who argued against the claims of the papacy in the name of reason and the Scriptures.[5] The very idea of the papacy was for him against both reason and the Bible, which themselves are fully harmonious. This criticism of the hierarchical system was something new, and it paved the way for the triumph of the Reformation in English history.

Far more radical than Occam was John Wyclif (d. 1384).[6] According to him, the power which the pope claims for himself properly belongs to the poor and pious, who could be united in a national church to be ruled by the law of Christ contained in the infallible Bible.

On the Continent these revolutionary ideas were proclaimed by John Huss, who died for them in 1415.[7] After his death, his followers tried to enforce these ideas with the sword and the torch.

The same tendencies toward a national church were felt in Spain, and notably in France, as the Pragmatic Sanction of Bourges, 1438, demonstrated. Through French influence the national conception of the Church prevailed at the three great councils of reform.

The collapse of the imperial power (the interregnum, 1254–73) greatly strengthened the self-consciousness of the federated princes and cities in Germany and Italy. After the restoration of imperial power, Emperor Ludwig of Bavaria (1314–1347) engaged in a lifelong, ardent struggle against the unbridled claims of the Church. His allies in this conflict were the German cities, the Italian Ghibelins (including Dante), a minority party of the Franciscans which was at odds with the hierarchy over the mendicant principle of their order, and

---

[5] *Dialogus* and other political writings, edited by Goldast, 1614, and R. Scholz, 1914.

[6] His works have been edited by the Wyclif Society, 19 vols. (1884—). Cf. *LCC*, XIV, 21 ff.

[7] His works have been edited by W. Flajshan (Chicago: University of Chicago Press, 1903—). Cf. *LCC*, XIV, 187 ff.

the famous writer Marsilius of Padua, professor at Paris. In his diatribe *Defensor pacis*,[8] Marsilius set forth the principle of popular sovereignty in both Church and state. The pope is the first and supreme officer of the Church, but as a fallible human being, he is responsible to the whole Church: to clerics and laity, men and women. The pope is to be judged according to the only infallible authority, the Bible, by a general council, to which the Church has delegated her power.

French scholars of the Sorbonne, for example, Conrad von Gelnhausen, Henry von Langenstein, Peter d'Ailli, and John Gerson, persistently defended these conciliar ideas over against the curial conception of the Church. Their efforts resulted in three great attempts at practical reform: the councils at Pisa (1409), Constance (1414–18), and Basel (1431–49). At the fifth session of the Council of Constance, the conciliar conception of the Church was solemnly approved. Nevertheless, the revived papacy soon defied the conciliarists openly and boldly.[9]

The intrusion of the ego-centered Roman law, together with the trend toward a money-based economy, contributed to the deterioration of the social standards of the lower classes. Pessimism prevailed, kindling revolutionary communistic ideas as well as ardent apocalytic expectations.

The Church tried to regain over the people the influence which it had lost over the state. New churches were built; the number of the clerics and monks increased enormously; the traffic in relics flourished; the importance of the sermon received new emphasis; the Bible was translated and printed in the popular idiom.[10]

A sad counterpart was the spread of superstition. Through Thomas Aquinas the belief in witches found its way into Christian dogmatics, and Pope Gregory IX put the Dominicans in charge of the cruel judicial process of the Inquisition.

As to the upper classes, the Renaissance in Italy constitutes the most conspicuous movement. It was initiated by the poets Petrarca (d. 1374) and Boccaccio (d. 1375). As the name indicates, the Renaissance was a rebirth of the philosophical and cultural ideas of Graeco-Roman

---

[8] *Defensor pacis* (1324). Cf. Mirbt, *op. cit.*, pp. 217 ff.

[9] See *LCC*, XIV, 91 ff.

[10] Cf. M. Reu, *Luther's German Bible* (Columbus, Ohio: Lutheran Book Concern, 1934).

civilization. The driving force of the movement is found in the desire to proclaim and to enjoy the innate rights and values of human nature. The Renaissance produced such great artists as Michelangelo and such notorious criminals as Rodrigo, who later became Pope Alexander VI, and his son, Cesare Borgia. The anti-Christian tendencies of the movement were repressed for a time by the intense religious awakening of the Reformation, but they survived as an undercurrent and would come to the surface again toward the end of the seventeenth century. As a cultural and aesthetic movement, the Renaissance celebrated its greatest achievements in the field of literature and art. It invaded the very ranks of the upper hierarchy, even the Vatican.

Less radical than the Renaissance in Italy was the humanist movement at Paris, Oxford, and the German universities. This movement helped to discredit the subtle method of Scholasticism and to arouse a new interest in the ancient languages. Reuchlin, a great scholar of Hebrew, published his first Hebrew grammar in 1506, and in 1516 Erasmus' first edition of the Greek New Testament came off the press. Men of similar disposition were Laurentius Valla, who criticized the so-called *Constantinian Donation*, Marsilio Ficino, and Giovanni Pici della Mirandola in Italy, Cardinal Ximenes in Spain, John Colet and Thomas Morus in England, and Ulric von Hutten in Germany. Either their insight into the corruption of the church or their interest in a thorough reform, however, was too superficial. In the end, the common tenets of Greek philosophy bound them all to the church of Thomas Aquinas. The Church could bear them all!

BIBLIOGRAPHY

HYMA, A. *From the Renaissance to the Reformation.* Grand Rapids, Mich.: W. B. Eerdmans Co., 1951.

OWST, G. R. *Preaching in Medieval England 1350–1450.* Cambridge: Cambridge University Press, 1926.

REU, M. *Luther's German Bible.* Columbus, Ohio: Lutheran Book Concern, 1934.

ROBSON, J. A. *Wyclyf and the Oxford School.* Cambridge: Cambridge University Press, 1961.

SPINKA, M. *John Huss and the Czech Reform.* Chicago: Chicago University Press, 1941.

CHAPTER X

THEOLOGY AND PIETY IN THE LATER MIDDLE AGES

DUNS SCOTUS AND HIS FOLLOWERS

The Englishman John Duns Scotus (d. 1308) marked the turning point in medieval Scholasticism. Against the Aristotelian tenets in the system of Thomas, Duns Scotus stands out as the representative of the older Platonian-Augustinian school of thought. Concerning the problem of the universals, he taught that the genus is inherent in the individuals (*universalia in re*). His realism was modified by his emphasis on the individuality of a thing and by the stress which he laid on experience as a source of human knowledge. Endowed with a remarkable keenness of mind, the scholarly Duns Scotus discovered and laid bare the weakness and defects in the theology of Thomas. The peaceful alliance of theology with philosophy which Thomas had achieved in his *Summa* was short lived. Duns Scotus distinguished, at least in principle, between philosophical knowledge and the religious approach to an assurance of metaphysical reality. He rejected the intellectual, speculative method of his Dominican rival. For Duns Scotus theology was a practical science. He conceded very little to logical demonstration. The fruition of the Godhead is effected not through the intellect but through the will. Thus he discredited a forceful tenet of the Scholastic age and reintroduced a principle which proved very effective in shaping the theology which was to come. In spite of this genuinely Augustinian trend of thought, Duns Scotus remained within the approved limits of the traditional Semi-Pelagian interpretation of the great African theologian.

Duns Scotus' emphasis upon the authority of Scripture and of the Church compensates for his absence of emphasis on the speculative foundations of theology. Since it is the Church which has approved and authorized the extent and content of the Scriptures, however, the authority of the Church remains of foremost importance to him.

The interpreter of Duns is handicapped by the subtlety of his terminology and his apparent endeavor to protect heterodox teachings behind the shield of orthodoxy. For good reasons Duns Scotus could be called an Abelard *redivivus*. But he was far too shrewd to commit himself openly, as did that great savant of the twelfth century.[1]

Although Duns Scotus, like Thomas, may occasionally define God as the infinite being, it is the voluntaristic conception of Augustine which prevails in his theology. His conception of God bears all the characteristics of what we call the "otherness" of God. In this respect Duns Scotus marks a milestone toward the rediscovery of the personal God of the Bible. God is pure will dominating the world. While Thomas said that God wills the good, Duns Scotus contended that whatever God wills is good. This absolute will of God is limited only by his own goodness or by the nature of a thing. If he wills, God may save Judas, but he cannot save a stone. A certain arbitrary element was here imparted to the nature of God which prepared the way for the subtle and futile discussions of later theologians on the possibilities and probabilities in the plans of God. On the other hand, by his stress on the will of God, Duns Scotus disentangled the concept of God from the many logical necessities under which Anselm had put God's dealings with the world.

Duns Scotus denied that Christ has rendered a superabundant satisfaction to God. The merit of Christ consists in the willingness of God to accept and to put a value upon whatever is done or suffered.

Duns Scotus, unlike Augustine, applied the same voluntaristic principle to his teaching on anthropology. Original sin is defined as the loss of original righteousness. The natural powers of men are unimpaired. Man can produce within himself the attrition by which he will receive and merit the justifying grace by a merit of congruity. In this respect Duns Scotus is a true exponent of the Semi-Pelagian tradition in the Franciscan order.

The same holds true as regards his views on the sacraments. The

---

[1] Cf. the divergent opinion among modern scholars on the teaching of Duns Scotus concerning universals. While some have called him a nominalist, others have defined his position as excessive realism. Cf. Seeberg, *Lehrbuch*, III, 569-70.

Augustinian tradition of his order is well maintained in spite of his orthodox terminology. In the doctrine of the Eucharist his real sympathies are with the theory of consubstantiation. However, in order to avoid a seeming heterodoxy, Duns Scotus introduces into the discussion the theory of the *transsubstantiatio adductiva;* that is, the earthly elements are not changed into the body and blood of Christ, but rather, some particles of them are annihilated by the sacramental union, so that the sacramental Christ is coexistent with the bread and wine in the Eucharist.

The respective followers of Thomas and Duns Scotus formed opposing schools of thought: the Thomists and the Scotists. Both schools produced men of great scholarship. The dominating figure of the fourteenth century was William of Occam (d. 1349 at Munich), who, like Duns Scotus, was an Englishman and a member of the Franciscan order. He started with the Scotist theology of his order, but his theology developed into a system of its own, marked by a revival of nominalism. Occam was considered the modernist of his day.

The revival of nominalism started with the Thomist, Durandus de Porciano, and the Scotist, Peter Aureoli. It was Occam who made it the dominating philosophy at the Sorbonne and at most of the universities in Germany. According to Occam, all knowledge is derived from intuitive observation of the individual thing. It is only by way of logical abstraction that the intellect creates a generic conception (conceptualism), a common name, to designate it. This conception may be called a universal, but it has no reality outside the concrete thing. The human intellect, however, substitutes a name (*terminus*) for this conception (terminism).

Even more than his countryman, Duns Scotus, Occam combined in his nature a critical radicalism and a practical conservatism which is typical of the Anglo-Saxon race. He shared the disposition of the skeptics with regard to the demonstrability of the Church's doctrines. He did not shrink from openly attacking the hierarchy. Nevertheless, he wanted to remain a loyal son of Rome. Since the papacy was not sacrosanct to him, the authority of the Bible was a far more practical matter to him than to Duns Scotus. Mainly through Occam the Bible became, at least in theory, the doctrinal authority of the fourteenth century. Whatever is not contained in the Scriptures, the Christian is not bound to believe. <u>The Scriptures are truth because they are inspired.</u> Inspiration is conceived of as a dictation by the Holy Spirit. In practice, his biblicism remained ineffective since he continued to work under the illusion of the age that the doctrines of his Church were identical with the teachings of the Bible.

In the doctrine of the Eucharist, Occam tried to overcome the quantitative relationship between the body of Christ and the earthly elements. In his treatise *De sacramento altaris* he devoted much time and effort to proving that a thing may lose its attribute of quantity without losing its essential identity. As the rational soul is locally inseparable from man, but as a whole is present in the whole of man as well as in every part of him, so "the entire body of Christ is really contained under the whole host and under each part of the host." [2] <u>As to the biblical basis of the theory of transubstantiation, Occam expressed his doubts openly.</u> Nevertheless, he defended it, simply in obedience to the Church.

> Although it is expressly set forth in the canonical Scriptures that the body of Christ is to be offered to the faithful under the species of bread, yet that the substance of the bread is really converted or transubstantiated into the body of Christ is not found expressed in the canon of the Bible; but this doctrine is believed to have been divinely revealed to the Holy Fathers, or to have been proved from passages of the Bible by a diligent and skillful examination.[3]

<u>Occamistic modernism</u> held the field in theology, almost unrivaled, for nearly a hundred years. Its stronghold on the continent was the <u>Sorbonne at Paris.</u> Peter d'Ailli and Gerson, the most prominent and influential leaders of the great movement to reform the church in both head and members, were its professed followers. In Germany it was Gabriel Biel (d. 1495), professor at Tübingen, who made Occamism live longer there than in any other country of Western Europe. Biel's pupil, John Nathin, taught Martin Luther the Occamistic theory of his master at the University of Erfurt.

According to Biel, fallen man still possesses the rectitude of his natural will. His freedom is not corrupted by sin. He may turn to God of his own free will. Such a turning is meritorious and will be rewarded by God with the infusion of grace.

[2] T. Bruce Birch, *The De sacramento altaris of William of Ockham* (Burlington, Ia.: Lutheran Literary Board, 1930), p. 189.
[3] *Ibid.,* p. 173.

Despite these Pelagian tendencies, the modernists frequently expressed themselves in predestinarian terms. Predestination, they said, is absolute and is the sole cause of man's salvation. It becomes effective, Occam added, only "on account of some meritorious work of man." Seeberg maintains[4] that this apparent contradiction is best explained by the fact that the predestinarian views of these men are little more than a theoretical deduction from their voluntaristic conception of God. The Pelagian understanding of man actually dominated the practice.

As time passed, the hair-splitting subtleties of nominalism, its empty criticism, and its futile attempts at reform could no longer command the interest of the younger generation. After 1450 a return to the teachings of the "ancients" (Thomas and Duns Scotus) became apparent. More and more Thomas was looked upon as the normative exponent of Catholic doctrine. The theologian of this group who is best known among Protestants is the Thomist friar, Thomas Vio (Cajetanus), the papal envoy sent to confer with Luther at Augsburg in 1518. Spanish theologians of the next century, from whom the hierarchy recruited its brain trust during the threatening crisis of the sixteenth century, put the finishing touch to the work of these ancients.

THE MYSTICS

Neither the rationalization of the Church's doctrine in the system of Thomas, nor the unintelligible positivism advocated by Duns Scotus and the nominalists could satisfy the religious need of the times. A stream of outspoken religious subjectivism was breaking forth as in the eleventh and twelfth centuries. Historically, the rise of the new mysticism is to be traced back to the nunneries which had been placed under the spiritual supervision of the Dominican Order. The new mysticism was Thomistic in principle although the Aristotelian outlook was broadened by Platonic and Neo-Platonic principles which reached the West through the writings of the Areopagite and John Scotus Erigena. For this reason the Dominican mysticism in Germany and the Netherlands was to some extent more philosophical (in danger

[4] *Lehrbuch* (1913), III, 647-48. For the effect which these teachings had on Luther and his spiritual struggle in the monastery see U. Saarnivaara, *Luther Discovers the Gospel* (St. Louis: Concordia Publishing House, 1951), pp. 25 ff.

of pantheism) and less biblical than the Bernardian type of mysticism. It showed little interest in the historical foundations of Christianity. Its interest was centered in the emancipation of the soul, its illumination, and blissful communion with God. The German mystics were genuine Occidentals with a deep appreciation of an active life of duty. Some of them rank foremost in the history of Christian preaching. As a church movement the mystics did not depart in any marked degree from the teaching and practice of the Church. In stressing the religious experience of the individual, the movement stands out as a forceful champion of the empirical tendencies of the age.

In the fifteenth century, the movement became general and began to influence lay piety. Although the hierarchy had succeeded in wiping out mystic-sectarian lay organizations like the Cathari, Albigenses, and the Sect of the Free Spirit, it could not kill the spirit of these movements. Even the Waldensians survived the Inquisition and papal excommunication. In the century preceding the Reformation such lay organizations as the Brothers of the Common Life became the foster soil for mystic speculation and practical piety.

Among the most eminent of the Dominican mystics were the following:

(1) Meister Eckhart (d. 1327).[5] The Inquisition brought charges of pantheism against him and the bull of the pope issued two years after his death declared "twenty-eight of his propositions to be pantheistic in nature, seventeen heretical, and eleven dangerous."

(2) Henry Seuse (Suso), the poet among the mystics.

(3) John Tauler. His mysticism is more truly evangelical and Jesus-centered.[6]

(4) John Ruysbroeck.

(5) Thomas à Kempis (d. 1471), the alleged author of *The Imitation of Christ*, which has had the widest circulation of any devotional literature.[7]

Finally, (6) the anonymous author of *German Theology* which was edited by Luther in 1516 and re-edited in 1518. Luther's praise of

[5] For the works of the mystics and recent studies on them, see *LCC*, XIII, 170-71, 208-209, 246-47, 264-65, 285-86, 321, 352 ff., and 393.

[6] Cf. E. Filthaus, *Johannes Tauler* (1961).

[7] J. E. G. de Montmorency, *Thomas à Kempis* (London: Methuen & Co., 1906).

the book will hardly stand the test of facts. He seems to have been misled by its serious devotional fervor.[8] As regards its contents, the book is thoroughly Neo-Platonic.

Mystic piety also experienced a revival in England and other European countries. In England this type of piety was greatly fostered by such saints as Richard Rolle (d. 1349), Walter Hilton (d. 1396), who wrote *The Scale of Perfection,* and Juliana of Norwich (d. about 1414), author of *Revelations of Divine Love.* Through the anonymous book, *The Cloud of Unknowing,* English mysticism became thoroughly tinged with Neo-Platonism.

REVIVAL OF AUGUSTINIANISM

The emphasis on the will of God in nominalistic theology, as well as the serious searching after personal religious experience, fostered a revival of Augustinian thought. The Pelagian tenets in contemporary theology were defied; the absolute necessity of divine grace was again set forth. The doctrine of predestination received a new emphasis and Augustine's definition of the Church as *congregatio praedestinatorum* received new emphasis. Most eminent among this group were the distinguished English scholar, Thomas Bradwardine (d. 1349) and the Augustinian friar, Gregory of Rimini (d. 1358).[9]

To this school of thought belong also the so-called forerunners of the Reformation: Wyclif, Huss, Goch, Wesel, and Wessel. The name "forerunner" is hardly justifiable. True enough, all of them felt disturbed over the corruption of the Church; all hurled bitter charges against the numerous abuses of the Church or openly attacked some of its doctrines. Wyclif, for example, denounced transubstantiation as something worse than paganism, saying the words of institution were to be taken figuratively.[10] He denied the necessity of the sacrament of penance and assailed the sale of indulgences as blasphemy. However, none of them was able to strike at the root of the evil, for every one, without exception, remained under the influence of the

[8] *Luther's Works,* 55 vols. (St. Louis: Concordia Publishing House and Philadelphia: Muhlenberg Press, 1957—), hereinafter referred to as *LW,* I, 73.

[9] Cf. Carl Stange on Luther's high estimate of Gregory of Rimini in *Studien zur Theologie Luthers* (1928), I, 13 ff.

[10] See the tract "On the Eucharist," *LCC,* XIV, 61 ff.

Scholastic definition of grace as *gratia infusa,* and under the legalistic conception of the gospel as a new law.

ERASMUS

Since the general tendencies and importance of the Renaissance have been discussed in the previous chapter, a few remarks on the theology of Erasmus may suffice in concluding the discussion on the Middle Ages.

With regard to the problem of the freedom of the human will, Erasmus was an outright Pelagian. In his teaching on grace, he formally accepted the Scholastic terminology. Objectively, however, a wide gap is apparent between him and the Scholastics. The infusion of grace through the sacraments has no place in his system. The conception of grace was reduced to a divine ethical stimulus derived from the example of Jesus. As for the rest, there are a number of very interesting points in his world of thought. Erasmus took a critical position toward the *homoousios* of the ancient Church and toward the sacrament of penance. He favored the symbolical interpretation of the Lord's Supper. He accepted the inspiration of the Scriptures as it had been set forth by the later Scholastics, but attributed only a diversified authority to the books of the New Testament. He taught that the Church is under divine obligation to keep the Sabbath. Erasmus, who remained in the Roman church, may be looked upon as a forerunner of the Catholic modernists. Luther was thoroughly unsympathetic toward him.[11]

CONCLUDING REMARKS

We have come to a close of our brief discussion of medieval theology. In summarizing its tendencies we may say that medieval theology is a theology of merit, speculation, and mysticism. To the pious of that age these were the three "heavenly ladders" for the soul's ascent to God. When we say that medieval theology is a theology of merit we ought to say that it is also a theology of grace. Nygren remarks, "it is characteristic of it that it regards as one these two things which, in the evangelical view, are simply exclusive of each

[11] Cf. the discussion of Erasmus in *LCC,* XIV, 281 ff., especially p. 286, and the English text of the *Enchiridion,* pp. 295 ff.

other." [12] This shows us the lasting impression which Augustine made upon the Middle Ages. The Catholic doctors were neither Pelagians promulgating an outright Eros type of religion, nor were they followers of the New Testament with its emphasis on God's Agape. They were rather disciples of Augustine, in whose thought Eros and Agape were merged into the synthesis of *caritas*. At the close of the Middle Ages, this synthetic character of Christianity was seriously challenged, first by the revival of classical learning, in which Eros gained new momentum, and secondly, in the Reformation, with its stress on Agape. For Luther, God was Agape, who established fellowship with us on our own level in Christ Jesus. This revolutionary change in Christian thought leads us to a new era in the history of Christian thought: the Reformation.

BIBLIOGRAPHY

BIEL. *Oposcula et Textus*. Edited by CHARLES FECKES. 1929–.
————. *Treatise on the Power and Utility of Money*. Translated by R. B. BURKE. Philadelphia: University of Pennsylvania Press, 1930.
BRADWARDINE, Thomas. *Anglia Sacra*, Vol. I. 1691.
DUNS SCOTUS. *Works*. Edited by WADDING, 13 vols., 1639. Re-edited by VIVES, 26 vols., 1891 –.
ECKHART, *Works*. Edited in part by FRANZ PFEIFFER in *Deutsche Mystiker des 14 und 15 Jahrhunderts*, Vol. 2, 1857, and in *Die Klassiker der Religion*, Vols. 14-15, 1919. New edition, Stuttgart, Kohlhammer Verlag.
ERASMUS, *Works*. Edited by BEATUS RHENANUS, 3 vols. 1540. Edited by JOHN CLERICUS, 10 vols., 1703-1706. *LCC*, Vol. XIV.
GOCH. *Works*. *Bibliotheca Reformatoria Nederlandia*, Vol. 6. 1909.
GREGORY OF RIMINI. *Lectura in I et II Librum Sententiarum*. 1482.
HILTON, WALTER. *The Scale of Perfection*. Edited by EVELYN UNDERHILL. Naperville, Ill.: Allenson, 1948.
JULIANA OF NORWICH. *Revelations of Divine Love*. Edited by JAMES WALSH. New York: Harper & Bros. 1948.
RUYSBROECK, *Werke*. Edited by J. B. DAVID. 6 vols. 1858-69.
SUSO, HEINRICH. *Werke*. Edited by KARL BIHLMEYER, 1907. Edited by W. LEHMANN, 2 vols., 1911.
————. *Exemplar: Life and Works of Henry Suso*. Translated by SISTER ANN EDWARD. 2 vols. Dubuque, Iowa: Priory Press, 1962.
TAULER. *Works*. *Deutsche Texte des Mittelalters*, Vol. II. 1910.
WESEL. *Works*. *Monumenta Medii Aevi*, Vol. I. 1757.
WESSEL. *Works*. Groningen, 1614.
WILLIAM OF OCCAM. *Works*.

[12] Nygren, *op. cit.*, p. 621.

WILLIAM OF OCCAM. *The Cloud of Unknowing.* Edited by EVELYN UNDER-HILL. Naperville, Ill.: Allenson, 1912.

ALLEN, P. S. *The Age of Erasmus.* New York: Oxford University Press, 1914.

BIRCH, T. BRUCE. *The de Sacramento Altaris of William of Occam.* Burlington, Iowa: Lutheran Literary Board, 1930.

CHAPIRO, JOSE, *et al. Erasmus and Our Struggle for Peace.* Boston: Beacon Press, 1950.

FILTHAUS, E. *John Tauler.* 1961.

HARRIS, C. H. *The Place of Duns Scotus in Medieval Thought.* 2 vols. New York: Humanities Press, 1959.

HARRIS, C. R. H. *Duns Scotus.* 2 vols. Oxford: Clarendon Press, 1927.

HOOK, W. F. *Lives of the Archbishops of Canterbury.* London: Bentley, 1865. Vol. 4.

HORSTMANN, C. *Yorkshire Writers: Richard Rolle . . . And His Followers.* London: Swan, Sonnenschein and Co., 1895.

LEFF, A. *Bradwardine and the Pelagians.* Cambridge: Cambridge University Press, 1957.

MANGAN, J. J. *Life, Character, and Influence of Desiderius Erasmus of Rotterdam.* 2 vols. New York: Macmillan Co., 1927.

OBERMANN, H. A. *Archbishop Thomas Bradwardine.* 1958.

PHILLIPS, M. M. *Erasmus and the Northern Renaissance.* New York: Macmillan Co., 1959.

SMITH, PRESERVED. *Erasmus.* Dover Publications: New York, 1962.

ULLMANN, KARL. *Reformatoren vor der Reformation.* 1841-42. 2nd ed., 1866.

Book Three

THE REFORMATION

CHAPTER I

LUTHER AS A REFORMER

I. General Observations

With the exception of some lonely voices of the spiritualistic type and the messages of Wyclif and Huss, the Middle Ages had produced no concerted criticism of the doctrine of the Church. The reformatory movements during the late Middle Ages had been directed against evils and abuses pertaining to pretensions and morals of the clergy and to Church government. The Reform Councils of the fifteenth century had called for a reformation "in head and members." With Luther and Zwingli, criticism turned decisively to the doctrinal foundations.

In the Evangelical "remedy" there was such religious and theological depth that a doctrinal reformation of the Church could no longer be resisted. Luther arose and became a reformer without any intention on his part; the occasion offered itself when his conscience urged him to protest against an abuse of the indulgences. Providentially this protest, in the form of Ninety-five Theses nailed on the door of a church in Wittenberg, started the movement on its way. Looking back upon his life, Luther himself declared: "God led me on like a horse whose eyes have been blindfolded that he may not see those who are rushing toward him." He added: "A good work is seldom undertaken or accomplished through wisdom or foresight . . . everything must be accomplished in the midst of error or ignorance." [1]

The Middle Ages were marked by a constant confusion of spiritual and secular interests. Neither the state nor the Church was free to act upon the foundations peculiar to and characteristic of itself. Each had to consider the interests and the demands of the other. It was

[1] *Luther's Works,* Erlangen edition (hereinafter referred to as *EA*), 57:31-32.

difficult for the Reformation to extricate itself from this situation. Luther, although very insistent upon the separation of Church and state, found it necessary to put the government of the young Church into the hands of the princes who functioned through consistories. He looked upon these princes as chief members of the Church (*praecipua membra ecclesiae*). This was a temporary expedient which was to cease when the members of the Church were sufficiently mature to take over the government themselves. Articles XVI and XXVIII of the Augsburg Confession later expressed the principle of separation of Church and state.

Neither the Renaissance nor humanism nor spiritualism had the inner strength to overcome the old and to usher in the new age. Either their will and thought were not serious and deep enough to shatter the Catholic system of the Middle Ages or else they denied every connection with the past. The new development depended upon the Reformation initiated by Luther—that broad movement which in its first prophetic stage worked itself out with an unprecedented force. The Lutheran Reformation brushed aside humanism, which wanted to overcome the ills of the age and to regenerate the world through an aesthetic rationalism, the spirit of classicism, and a blending of religion with paganism. Humanism sought a reform of Christianity by removing its dogmas or stripping them of their supernatural features and reducing religion to moralism. The Lutheran Reformation, likewise, discredited Socinianism, which was an endeavor to use the Bible to construct a body of rationalistic doctrines: the rejection of Christ's divinity, the denial of an objective conception of the atonement, and making justification a moral process. Spiritualism in the form of Anabaptism also was brushed aside by the powerful development of the conservative Reformation.

The Reformation was in keeping with the deeply religious interest that inspired the Middle Ages. As was stated, that interest now became doctrinal. Soteriological orientation was the dominating note. What especially attracts our attention is the intensity of religious thought in that age. For a comparison we refer to the ecclesiastical legislation on repentance in the Middle Ages and to the various forms of repentance which were observed in the monastic period of Luther's life. Luther turned against the traditional view of repentance connected with the institution of indulgences. He assailed the pardoning power of the pope; the validity of indulgences for the dead; and the Roman theory that the abundant merits of Mary and the saints, which were available for money, supplemented the merit of Christ, as the basis for the forgiveness of sins. Luther said in the first of his Ninety-five Theses that believers must learn that their whole life must be a repentance. In the place of repentance as a sacrament with meritorious works, he rediscovered the biblical concepts of faith and justification. Good works in the form of a "new obedience" follow faith as confidence (*fiducia*) in forgiveness through Christ; but these works must never have the significance of satisfaction. Repentance as mere attrition has no value; evangelical contrition is coupled with faith. Full oral confession must not be forced by laws, because "who can understand his errors?" (Ps. 19:12). Luther early recognized the impossibility of confessing all mortal sins.[2] It occurred to him that man is under obligation to confess his sins only to God,[3] and that the confession required by the Church is but a human ordinance. We can confess to whomsoever we will; we are free to omit confession to man altogether, if we confess to God.[4] From this position Luther never wavered, although he always warmly commended voluntary private confession.[5]

Lutheran writers have characterized the Lutheran Reformation as simply a return to apostolic conditions. It is true that Luther, like the other Reformers, aimed at a return to scriptural principles. But it is a mistake to think that the Lutheran Reformation aimed merely at a re-establishment of former conditions. The Reformation received much of its content from men and conditions which existed long after apostolic times. The Reformers were heirs of the ancient Church; and of the influence of Irenaeus, Origen, Athanasius, the Cappadocians, Tertullian, and Augustine. Among the medieval leaders whose thought influenced the Reformers were Anselm, Bernard, and some of the Scholastics. The heritage of the religious experience of the Church was also important. The Reformation was not a return to

[2] *WA*, 1:322; 2:60; 6:162, 545.
[3] *WA*, 6:158 f.
[4] *WA*, 8:161, 175, 181-182; *EA*, 28:248, 302; 29:353; 10:401; 23:86-87.
[5] *WA*, 8:168, 173, 176, 178; *EA*, 23, 26-27; 28:249 f., 308.

the pattern of Church life in apostolic times. It was characterized by Luther's rediscovery of the gospel and his consistent attempt to make the gospel relevant to the needs and conditions of his contemporaries. It is this which makes the Church resulting from the Reformation deeply human, universal, and ecumenical in character.

Luther was a prophet, a real religious genius, with a wonderful faculty for realizing in the clear depth of his own experience all the emotions and needs of his age. His message was a response to the questions people asked in their hearts.

Luther was much attracted by the writings of the mystics, whose thoughts he followed from the age of Augustine through Bernard down to the Schoolmen. He liked the practical emphasis of the German mystics on the way to God and their translation of the ideas of the dogmaticians into practical religious truths expressed in the mother tongue. He was also attracted by the religious and evangelical depth which was found in such writings as *The Imitation of Christ* by Thomas à Kempis, the sermons of John Tauler, and the *Theologia Germanica*, an edition of which Luther published in 1516. But his aversion to quietism, his vivid sense of personality in God and man, and his strong ethical interest kept him from embracing mysticism as such.[6]

The Augustinian and Pauline character of the Lutheran Reformation is conspicuous. Luther departed from Thomas Aquinas and Duns Scotus, and expressed his agreement with Augustine's monergism of grace by stressing man's inability to bring about the new spiritual life through his own natural powers. This led Luther to a determinism such as he asserted in his *On the Bondage of the Will* against Erasmus (1524). The agreement with Augustine led him back to a study of Paul. Thus he came to write his *Lectures on Romans* (1515-16). In 1521, Melanchthon published his *Loci*, which was essentially a treatment of the same epistle. This gave the Lutheran Reformation that decidedly Pauline and Augustinian character in opposition to Pelagianism and to Semi-Pelagianism in all its forms. The Johannine element ought not to be overlooked, for Luther was no less interested in the Johannine doctrine of the incarnation than in the Pauline teaching of justification by faith. In his own words, "St. John's Gospel is the

[6] Cf. the discussion on this subject in Loofs, *op. cit.*, pp. 636, 691, 693.

one, tender, true, chief Gospel, far, far to be preferred to the other three and placed high above them." [7]

Luther witnessed the bankruptcy of Scholasticism. He found himself unable to keep company with the humanists but he delighted in their attacks upon Scholasticism, although differing from them in the type of polemics. Luther occasionally utilized Scholastic thought forms, speaking, for example, in Occamistic terms of the matter of ubiquity. But he turned decidedly against what the Scholastics taught on freedom of the will, grace, faith, righteousness, works, and merits. He accused Thomas Aquinas of being responsible for the dominance of Aristotle, whom Luther called the destroyer of godly doctrine.[8] He used to say that nobody will become a theologian unless he undertakes to study theology without Aristotle. For Luther, the Scholastics were unsafe leaders in matters of the gospel and the essentials of salvation.

Historians are attracted to Luther the reformer, but the Reformation grew out of the experiences of Luther the man. We need only think of how much he wrote on repentance and assurance of salvation. Soteriology was the central interest of his reform. His leading question was: How shall I find a gracious God? We see this interest in his sermons, catechisms—indeed in all his writings. The purely speculative features of theology had no interest for him. He dealt with fundamentals: God's holiness, his love, man's sinfulness, law and gospel, Christ, faith, justification. He was led to this by his own experience and by his conception of repentance. In Luther's system we observe the purity of the religion of redemption to which we referred as one of the leading interests in the construction of the history of doctrine.

It is interesting to trace the development of Luther as a reformer. The time was ripe for the birth of the principles of the Reformation, but these principles had to be experienced in the soul of some forceful personality before they could become dynamic for subsequent ages. In its main features the Reformation was the experience not of an

---

[7] *PE*, 6:443-44. See Walter von Loewenich, *Luther und das johannaeische Christentum* (1935); Carl Stange, *Der johannaeische Typus der Heilslehre Luthers im Verhältnis zur paulinischen Rechtfertigungslehre* (1949); James Atkinson, *Luthers Einschätzung des Johannesevangeliums* in Vilmos Vajta, *Lutherforschung heute*, pp. 49 ff.

[8] *WA*, 8:127.

individual, but of the Church. Luther was the forceful personality chosen to precipitate the movement and to give it substance. Luther's development as a reformer was a gradual one. That fact should never be forgotten. In recent years Reformation research has given a great deal of attention to the early stages of that development.

The doctrines of the earlier Luther may be seen in the time between 1513 and 1517, the period which marked the transition from the teaching of the Middle Ages. According to Seeberg, these were the years during which Luther arrived at new thoughts on sin, law, the gospel, Christ, faith, justification, sacrifice in the mass, the seven sacraments, and the authority of the Church. With respect to other teachings, however, Luther was still Roman Catholic. The positions Luther arrived at after the nailing of the Ninety-five Theses were a result of his public conflict with the official Church over the matter of repentance. These additional new thoughts pertained particularly to faith, works, law and gospel, sin and grace, justification, and atonement. From 1517 on, Luther's development continued in many ways. He began to question the biblical warrant for such doctrines as the divine right of the papacy, the invocation of saints, purgatory, and the sacrifice of the mass. In 1519, and later, his opposition to Rome moved him to expressions in which he avoided clear testimony to the real presence in the Lord's Supper. Opposition to the "Enthusiasts" made it necessary for him to affirm the realistic features in the doctrine of the Eucharist. Luther, under the influence of historical motives, found himself in a continuous state of doctrinal development; that is, errors to the right and to the left taught him the truth of Scripture.

The Lutheran Reformation was conservative. History of doctrine, particularly symbolics, has always taken note of Luther's conservatism with regard to the Church's tradition in matters of practice, in liturgy, and in like matters. Luther's position was: Preserve what is good, because in all matters of Church practice nothing that is good can be against Scripture. Luther always refused to lose the net gains of ancient times. This position has brought on the Lutheran church an oft-repeated charge of being a halfway reformation. Against this criticism note the care that has always been taken, even in matters of practice, to profess the gospel and to eliminate all work-righteousness and all humanistic negation of grace. The Reformed churches have been inclined to an opposite principle (Puritanism) which reads: Keep only what is expressly commanded in Scripture. Here the fear prevails that the human elements, the created things, in their service of symbolizing or communicating the divine and the spiritual, may take the place of what is to be taught or to be communicated and may develop into an idolatry or a magical mediation of the spiritual.

In doctrinal respects the conservatism of Luther can also be seen. Luther accepted the ecumenical creeds of Christendom. The Augsburg Confession refers to the Nicene Creed and the Apostles' Creed as documents of authority. So highly did Luther regard the Athanasian Creed, with its Chalcedonian Christology concerning the two natures of Christ and their relation, that he wrote: "It has been composed in such a way that I do not know whether anything more important and glorious has been written since the time of the Apostles." [9] On the basis of his views of the personal union, Luther further elaborated the relationship between the two natures. He accepted from Augustine the doctrine of man's natural depravity and its result with regard to man's will. His soteriology started with the Augustinian heritage, but avoided Augustine's confusion of justification with sanctification. Luther's reinterpretation of Paul made a proper distinction between these two topics of soteriological interest. By rooting forgiveness in justification by faith, Luther secured for the sinner the certainty of his salvation. At the same time the holiness of life as fruit from the root was safeguarded.

Luther's theology was established upon the principle of an organic union between the divine and the human: God is present for our salvation in and through Christ. Luther saw this organic union between God and Christ in the incarnation of the Logos as expressed by the trinitarian relation. He saw it also in the personal union of the two natures of Christ, whereby Christ's humanity participated in the attributes of his divinity (*genus majestaticum*). Luther was convinced of the organic relation between the divine and the human. On this matter he felt himself in harmony with the Christology of Cyril of Alexandria as against that of Theodore of Mopsuestia and Nestorius.

Luther maintained a similar organic union in the means of grace.

[9] *EA*, 23:251 ff.

319

To him, the Bible was the Word of God—it did not just contain the Word. The same idea prevailed in his conception of the sacrament. He saw the same organic relation of the divine and the human in the relation between the invisible and the visible Church. To him, there were not two churches, one invisible and one visible. Both were together in organic relation.

The failure to see Luther's emphasis on the organic union in all these respects can prevent a proper estimate of his theology. Here was the ultimate source of his difference from the Zwinglian Reformation.

Luther's rediscovery of the gospel was of utmost importance for civilization and culture. By recalling the Church to its peculiar task of proclaiming the good news, the Reformation emancipated science, literature, and the state from the tutelage of the hierarchy, and endowed those areas of life with a consciousness of their God-given destiny.

Luther significantly influenced literature and philosophy. To German literature he gave not only its common language but also an inexhaustible richness of graphic idiomatic expression. Profound, too, was the influence of Luther's thought upon philosophy in its rational as well as in its speculative tendencies. Luther anticipated some of the basic ideas of Kant. He conceived of space and time as thought forms of the empirical world and stressed that the concepts of God and immortality are affirmations of faith but not of speculation and reason. German Idealism as a whole cannot be thought of apart from the Reformation, for it was the Reformation which emphasized the significance of the personal life and, far more forcibly than the Renaissance, established the unique value of personality. It was the Reformation which called for a joyous and positive, not a calm and stoical, relation to life as directed by God. It was the Reformation which pointed emphatically to the pre-eminence of the will in human action. It was Luther who stirred such a thinker as Kierkegaard to action in his struggle against the secularization of the Christian faith in the system of Hegel.[10]

In conclusion we briefly refer to Nygren's penetrating analysis of the Reformation. Luther, according to Nygren, accomplished a

[10] Cf. Regis Jolivet, *Introduction to Kierkegaard* (New York: E. P. Dutton and Co., Inc., 1946).

"Copernican revolution" in the history of Christian thought in that he insisted on "opposition to all egocentric forms of religion, upon a purely theocentric relation to God." [11] Against the egocentric attitude which had come to mark the Catholic conception of love, Luther set a thoroughly theocentric idea of love.[12] Love, in Luther's thought, was concerned not with man's love for God but strictly with the love with which God loves us. This means that Luther rediscovered the great paradox of the New Testament which declares that God is willing to establish fellowship with men on our own level, the level of sin rather than of self-made holiness. Our fellowship with God, then, rests for us on the basis not of holiness but of sin; and for God, upon his entirely unmotivated, groundless love, which justifies not the man who is already righteous and holy, but the sinner. There is no other justification than the justification of the sinner, no other fellowship with God than that on the basis of one's own sin and the groundless divine love. In this sense, the justified Christian man is *simul justus et peccator*—in himself a sinner but justified and taken into fellowship with God by the divine love. The sinner is treated as only a man who is in himself righteous ought, by human standards, to be treated. On the basis of this understanding of God's love, Luther renewed the primitive Christian Agape tradition, which had been interrupted at an earlier stage in the Church. He restored Jesus' message of fellowship with God—"I have not come to call the righteous, but to call sinners" (Mark 2:17)—and Paul's gospel of the justification of the sinner.[13]

II. High Points in Luther's Thought

The Tower Experience

On July 17, 1505, Luther entered the Augustinian monastery at Erfurt. Here he was taught the doctrines of Occam and Biel: that man, of his own pure, natural strength, is able to do meritorious works before the infusion of grace, and to love God and Christ above all things. It was precisely this teaching which failed him. Moreover he could not find peace for his troubled soul in the sacrament of penance.

[11] Nygren, *op. cit.*, p. 681.
[12] *Ibid.*, p. 683.
[13] *Ibid.*, p. 687.

In addition, the doctrine of predestination caused Luther much anguish. In both of these problems Luther received fatherly assistance from John Staupitz, his superior. Staupitz taught Luther that repentance begins with the love of God, which is revealed in the cross and kindles a reciprocal love in the heart of man. Predestination, according to Staupitz, is grounded solely in the undeserved divine mercy and love.[14]

Another problem, however, remained unsolved. In the preface to the Wittenberg edition of his works (1545), Luther relates the following incident:

> Meanwhile, that same year (1519), I had again turned to the exposition of the Psalter, confident that after the academic treatment of the Epistles of St. Paul to the Romans and Galatians and the Epistle of the Hebrews I was better trained. Certainly I had been possessed by an unusually ardent desire to understand Paul in his Epistle to the Romans. Nevertheless, in spite of the ardor of my heart I was hindered by the unique word in the first chapter: "The righteousness of God is revealed in it." I hated that word "righteousness of God," because in accordance with the usage and custom of the doctors I had been taught to understand it philosophically as meaning, as they put it, the formal or active righteousness according to which God is righteous and punishes sinners and the unjust.
>
> As a monk I led an irreproachable life. Nevertheless, I felt that I was a sinner before God. My conscience was restless, and I could not depend on God being propitiated by my satisfactions. Not only did I not love, but I actually hated the righteous God who punishes sinners. . . . Thus a furious battle raged within my perplexed conscience, but meanwhile I was knocking at the door of this particular Pauline passage, earnestly seeking to know the mind of the great Apostle.
>
> Day and night I tried to meditate upon the significance of these words: "The righteousness of God is revealed in it, as it is written: The righteous shall live by faith." Then, finally, God had mercy on me, and I began to understand that the righteousness of God is that gift of God by which a righteous man lives, namely, faith, and that this sentence: The righteousness of God is revealed in the Gospel, is passive, indicating that the merciful God justifies us by faith, as it is written: "The righteous shall live by faith." Now I felt as though I had been reborn altogether and had entered Paradise. In the same moment the face of the whole of Scripture became apparent to me. My mind ran through the Scriptures, as far as I was able to recollect them, seeking analogies in other phrases, such as the work of God, by which He makes us strong, the wisdom of God, by which He makes us wise, the strength of God, the salvation of God, the glory of God.

[14] Cf. U. Saarnivaara, *Luther Discovers the Gospel* (St. Louis: Concordia Publishing House, 1951), pp. 25 ff.

Just as intensely as I had before hated the expression "the righteousness of God," I now lovingly praised this most pleasant word. This passage from Paul became to me the very gate to Paradise. Afterwards I read Augustine's treatise *On the Spirit and the Letter*, and, contrary to my expectation, I discovered a similar interpretation of the righteousness of God: that with which we are endued when God justifies us. Although up until now this had been imperfectly explained, and he does not clearly expound everything concerning imputation, he nevertheless seemed to teach the righteousness of God by which we are justified.

Better equipped after these considerations, I began to interpret the Psalms the second time. The result would have been an extensive commentary, but I was again interrupted the following year by the summons of Emperor Charles V to the Diet at Worms.[15]

The *Table Talks* also contain several accounts of this discovery. In one passage from 1532, Luther says that this experience took place in the tower and *hypocaustum* (heated day room) of the monastery.[16] In another passage he adds that at this time he learned the proper distinction between the law and the gospel.[17]

The Luther research of the last half century has made a valiant effort to solve the problem concerning both the date and meaning of Luther's tower experience. It has been dated variously as early as 1508 or 1509 by Seeberg, and as late as 1518 by Grisar and Saarnivaara, while other scholars have pointed to any of the years between 1512 and 1516. As a matter of fact, the dating of the tower experience is contingent upon the understanding of the experience. All scholars agree that in the passages under consideration Luther refers to the decisive event of the discovery of the gospel of the Reformation. But they do not agree on what this gospel is. Evidently the passage we have quoted is a *locus classicus* for the Reformation doctrine of justification. We must ask: What was Luther's original doctrine of justification?

Basing his argument chiefly on Luther's first lectures on the Psalms (1513–15) and especially his lectures on Romans (1515–16), Holl,[18] like Seeberg[19] before him, maintains that, according to Luther,

---

[15] *Ibid.*, pp. 25 ff. For another translation see Hanns Lilje, *Luther Now*, trans. Carl J. Schindler (Philadelphia: Muhlenberg Press, 1952), pp. 66-67.

[16] *Tischreden*, 3:3232.

[17] *Ibid.*, 5:5518. Cf. Saarnivaara, *op. cit.*, pp. 37-38.

[18] "Die Rechtfertigungslehre in Luthers Vorlesung über den Römerbrief, 1910," *Gesammelte Aufsätze*, I (1948), 111 ff.

[19] Seeberg, *Lehrbuch* (1917), IV, I.

man is justified in view of the fact that the believing sinner will become righteous in fellowship with God. Justification is an "analytical judgment." It is an act of grace and also an estimate of the moral condition of the believer. In this way, Holl and his followers think that they can enlist Luther against the purely forensic view of justification held by Melanchthon and the orthodox teachers of the seventeenth century, whose teaching seems to endanger the inseparable connection between justification and sanctification.

In the preface quoted above, Luther maintained that he had been taught to understand the word righteousness philosophically as meaning the formal or active retributive righteousness of God. In 1905, the Roman Catholic scholar Denifle showed that sixty teachers of the Roman church interpreted the word as meaning "God's undeserved justifying grace." [20] "What conclusions are we to draw from this fact?" Saarnivaara asks, "Are we to conclude, as some scholars do, that Luther made a mistake?" Saarnivaara wants none of this. He says that the tower experience as interpreted by Holl would be no discovery at all because it entailed nothing but the traditional Augustinian-Catholic view of justification. According to Augustine, the sinner was justified by fulfilling the law through the power he received from God. To be justified meant to be made righteous, albeit by the grace of God. This was not a new discovery. Luther had known for a long time that the grace of God is indispensable for man. Yet one thing he did not know prior to the tower experience: "that man is righteous in the sight of God, not because he has become, or started to become righteous, but because Christ has fulfilled the Law for him and because God imputes the 'good works' of Christ to him." [21]

In all his writings prior to the end of 1518, Saarnivaara maintains, Luther's view of justification remained essentially Augustinian. He understood justification primarily from the ethical point of view as the actual renewal of man.[22] Toward the end of 1518, Luther published his "Sermon on the Threefold Righteousness" [23] and early in 1519 another "Sermon on the Twofold Righteousness." [24] In the

---

[20] Cf. Saarnivaara, *op. cit.*, p. 40.

[21] *Ibid.*, p. 41.

[22] *Ibid.*, pp. 82 ff.

[23] *WA*, 2:41 ff.

[24] *WA*, 2:143 ff. Cf. Saarnivaara, *op. cit.*, pp. 92 ff.

former, Luther distinguished three kinds of sin and, corresponding to them, three types of righteousness. The first sin and righteousness are according to the civil law. The second sin is essential, inborn, original, although alien to the individual because it is the sin of Adam imputed to him. The righteousness that corresponds to this kind of sin is likewise inborn, essential, original in Christ but imputed to the sinner as "alien righteousness." "This is . . . our lot, capital, foundation, rock, and our whole substance wherein we glory forever," and becomes our own through faith. The third sin is actual, which is the fruit of original sin. "The righteousness that corresponds to this is the actual righteousness, flowing out of faith . . ."

In his sermon on twofold righteousness, Luther reaffirms this position. As the sin of Adam is alien to man, so the righteousness of Christ is alien to the sinner. Just as man's alien sin issues into actual sin, so his alien righteousness produces good works in him. "This is the Gospel and the example of Christ." "Relying wholly on the righteousness of Christ," notes Saarnivaara, "Luther has now an altogether new tone in his whole life. . . . He is able to believe confidently that grace is actually his and that he is already righteous before God through the merit of Christ." [25]

In a number of articles, Wilhelm Walther (d. 1924) protested most vigorously against Holl's ethicizing interpretation of the Reformation doctrine of justification. Even if, at an earlier time, Luther had suggested or intended to suggest what Holl says (which Walther refused to accept), there is nothing to confirm this view in Luther's later writings. Justification, according to Luther, is valid and complete simply because of Christ's active and passive obedience. [26]

More recently, Karl Barth and his school have strongly opposed Holl's interpretation of Luther. For them, the question is a side issue of their intense aversion to the ethicizing tenets in the theology of Ritschl. Althaus has also expressed his disapproval of Holl and of his disciple, Hirsch. [27] Although Althaus grants that the term *justificare* in Luther's writings may have the double meaning of declaring just and of making just (in this respect there is no difference between Luther and Melanchthon till 1532), justification *propter Christum*

[25] Saarnivaara, *op. cit.,* p. 95.
[26] *Neue Kirchliche Zeitschrift,* No. 11 (1923).
[27] *Zeitschrift für systematische Theologie* (1923), pp. 107 ff.

always means the sinner's justification solely by virtue of Christ's perfect obedience to God. Holl's attempt to make this stumbling block acceptable to the modern mind showed a deplorable lack of insight into the true nature of the sinfulness of mankind. On the other hand, Althaus does not wish to belittle Karl Holl's effort to emphasize Luther's fervent desire for true holiness.[28]

Of late, Regin Prenter has expressed his disapproval of Holl's and Seeberg's interpretation of Luther. The source of these two scholars' presentations, he says, is the theology of yesterday, inherited partly from Schleiermacher and partly from the revivalistic pietism of the nineteenth century which regarded empirical piety as possessing in itself a definite value before God. In the eyes of Luther, the progress of sanctification, which Holl equated with growth in the plan of real justification, is "not an object of psychological observation, but an object of faith and hope." To Luther our "alien righteousness" is not an imputed, abstract contribution of Christ (as in seventeenth-century orthodoxy) but the living Christ himself, who justifies us not somewhere in *foro coeli* but dwelling in us by faith.[29]

In the act of justification the believer experiences the grace of divine predestination. As the sinner is justified by faith, so by faith he is assured of the eternal decree of God as a decree unto salvation. The *Deus absconditus* is no other God save the *Deus revelatus*. Since the divine revelation, however, can be apprehended only by faith, there will always remain some mysteries in God which are unfathomable to man.[30]

Luther's Concept of Religion

The medieval Schoolmen tried to arrive at a concept of God in two different ways. First, portraying God as blissfully resting in himself, they sought to prove to the inquiring mind the essence and attributes of the "Highest Being." Second, they shaped the idea of

[28] Cf., for example, Luther's *Treatise on Baptism, PE,* I, 51 ff.

[29] Regin Prenter, *Spiritus Creator* (1953), pp. 41 ff., 69 ff. Independently of Saarnivaara, the German scholar, E. Bizer, in *Fides ex Audito* (1958), p. 112, has arrived at the same conclusion: Luther discovered the gospel after the posting of the Ninety-five Theses. The two sermons on the righteousness of God contain, for the first time, a new understanding of the gospel.

[30] Cf. Luther's treatise *On the Bondage of the Will, WA,* 18:600 ff. in the English translation by J. I. Packer and R. O. Johnston (Westwood, N. J.: Fleming H. Revell Co., 1957).

God and religion into a system of legalistic moralism and placed God and man on the same level as two parties contracting to an agreement. As the Rewarder of good and evil, they taught, God could be decisively influenced by the deeds of man.

Luther found it impossible to bring these two modes of thought into a lasting wedlock. God is almighty or he is not God. Almighty God stands as the Lord of the world and of history, challenging the will of every man, whom he claims entirely for himself. The Catholic differentiation between the "commands" which unconditionally obligate every man, and the "evangelical counsels" which need to be followed only by those who wish to attain to a special perfection, collapses. Holy God wishes the entire heart of man, and, because God is perfect, he wants to lead man to perfection. Thus the unqualified command to love God and our neighbor (Matt. 22:37 ff.) is once more set forth in its original rigor.

Luther rejected a doctrine of God conceived in abstract, metaphysical terms and established a genuinely religious understanding of God. The greatness of God is known in his moral superiority which desires moral perfection in man also. Every moral defect, no matter how insignificant, and every negligence in love, no matter how petty, provokes the wrath of the holy God and separates us from him. Luther digs still deeper. It is not to be thought that man prepares his approach to God through manifold laborious and pious deeds, and that morality forms the presupposition of man's fellowship with God. The opposite is true. We are invited to listen to the foolish preaching of the Gospel, so obnoxious to the feeling of man. Holy God anticipates sinful man, and his goodness overcomes all human sin. In his inmost heart God is "pure love," "merciful will," "pure beneficence." [31] His grace is free, not conditioned upon merits.[32] All work-righteousness is thereby excluded. The fact is that God saves none but the sinner, instructs none but the simple and ignorant, enriches none but the poor, and vitalizes none but the dead.

Luther makes a clear-cut distinction between the philosophical approach to a knowledge of God and the religious-theological way to assurance. Philosophy, being occupied with a rational investigation of

[31] *EA*, 14:49; 7:68, 159.
[32] *WA*, 43:607.

God's essence and nature, fails to attain its objective, for human reason after the fall is unable to understand God. Nor does philosophical speculation afford any comfort to man. If God, according to the human intellect, is considered the sole cause of the universe, the idea of God and the devil are blended into one conception of a horrifying, monstrous being.[33] Luther never loses sight of the fact that it is sinful man who is searching for God. Theology, therefore, is a practical science in the eyes of the Reformer, to help man in his distress of sin and guilt. God who is hidden from the eyes of the sinner (*Deus absconditus*) revealed himself to man in Christ Jesus, who is *Deus incarnatus*.[34] In Christ crucified there is a true knowledge of God; in him we behold what God is: "a furnace of love." [35] To designate these two ways Luther uses the terms *theologia gloriae* and *theologia crucis*.[36] The "theologians of glory," he says, are vain sophists. Having set their minds on high things such as God's infinite power, wisdom, and justice, they despise God in his suffering, weakness, and foolishness.[37] But "professing to be wise, they became fools" (Rom. 1:22). For the cross is the power of God unto salvation.[38]

Faith, as the only appropriate response to God's revelation in Jesus, has a double significance in Luther's theology. First, it is the means by which man appropriates the merits of Christ. Second, it has a profound epistemological significance. God becomes known not through the intellect nor through mystical or moral experience. Instead, God is known by faith which transcends the intellectual, emotional, and volitional endowment of man. Consequently faith, in the eyes of Luther, must not be equated with knowledge about God or with religious experience. Faith is not experience, although it is experienced, for it has its seat in the living soul of man. Faith's objects are *occulta*, things not seen but hoped for (Heb. 11:1). As compared with knowledge, the proper realm of faith is the future, not the present

[33] *WA*, 37:455, 461; 40: I, 77, 99, 174, 607-08; 43:179, 459.

[34] *WA*, 18:644-45, 689.

[35] *WA*, 36:424-25.

[36] "The Heidelberg Disputation," *LW*, 31:37 ff.; cf. W. von Loewenich, *Luther's Theologica Cruci* (2nd ed., 1933).

[37] *LW, loc. cit.*

[38] Thesis XX: *Ergo in Christo crucifixo est vera theologia et cognitio Dei.*

or the past. In Luther the door is closed to religious intellectualism and moralism as well as to mystic pietism.[39]

Seen from this point of view, Luther's theology is eminently existential. Like Paul before him and Kierkegaard after him, Luther's name looms large as a protagonist in the religious war against Aristotle, Thomas, and Hegel. To him,

> The proper subject of theology is man, guilty of sin and condemned, and God the Justifier and Savior of man, the sinner. Whatever is asked or discussed in theology outside this subject, is error and poison. All Scripture points to this, that God commends His kindness to us and in His Son restores to righteousness and life the nature that has fallen into sin and condemnation. The issue here is not this physical life—what we should eat, what work we should undertake, how we should rule our family, how we should till the soil. All these things were created before man in Paradise and were put into man's hands when God said (Gen. 1:28), "Have dominion over the fish of the sea and over the birds of the air." The issue here is the future and eternal life; the God who justifies, repairs, and makes alive; and man, who fell from righteousness and life into sin and eternal death. Whoever follows this aim in reading the Holy Scriptures will read holy things fruitfully.
>
> Therefore this theological knowledge is necessary: A man should know himself, should know, feel, and experience that he is guilty of sin and subject to death; but he should also know the opposite, that God is the Justifier and Redeemer of a man who knows himself this way. The care of other men, who do not know their sins, let us leave to lawyers, physicians, and parents, who discuss man differently from the way a theologian does.[40]

Despite the emphasis on God's revelation in Christ, Luther does not deny the validity of divine revelation apart from the person of Jesus Christ. For Luther the knowledge of God is twofold. "Men naturally know," he says, "that there is a God, but what His will is, or what is not His will, they do not know." [41] All men have the "general" but not the "particular" knowledge of God. This "general" knowledge is the source of the religious consciousness of man. As such it has some positive value. It mediates to men not only the bare fact of God's existence, but also that he has created heaven and earth and that he is

---

[39] Loewenich, *op. cit.*, pp. 54 ff.

[40] *LW*, 12:311-12. Cf. L. Pinomaa, *Der existentielle Charakter der Theologie Luthers* (1940).

[41] *Commentary on St. Paul's Epistle to the Galatians*, trans. Philip S. Watson (Westwood, N. J.: Revell, 1953), hereinafter referred to as *Commentary on Galatians*, p. 277.

just and that he punishes the wicked.[42] However, man has perverted this general knowledge of God which has led to idolatries in the world including the false piety of the monks.[43]

Luther, then, does not deny the validity of a so-called "natural revelation" but is opposed to the "natural theology" of the Scholastics. His conception of a general or natural knowledge of God has virtually nothing in common with the "natural" and "revealed" knowledge of traditional theological thought.[44] The natural theology of the Scholastics is gained by the exercise of reason. Their knowledge of God is derived from "the things that are made." On this basis they endeavor to prove the existence of God and his attributes. They desire to ascend to God by means of reason and speculation. In Luther, on the other hand, the natural knowledge of God is granted to man through nature as a medium of divine revelation. All creatures and all created ordinances, in the eyes of Luther, are *larvae Dei*, masks of God. They "contain Christ" inasmuch as the God whose "mask" they are is the very one who reveals himself, albeit in a special way, in Jesus Christ.[45] For "there is no other God."[46] Natural theology and natural knowledge of God are no less a matter of faith than revealed theology and the knowledge of Jesus Christ.

The doctrine of the wrath of God reaches a wonderful spiritual depth in Luther's theology. Luther learned to understand God's wrath as His "strange work" (*opus alienum*)[47] by means of which God pursues his "proper work" (*opus proprium*) of love.[48] The proper works of God, so Luther says, are the works of his mercy: to forgive sin, to justify and save those who believe in Christ. His strange works are to judge, condemn, and inflict punishment upon the unbelieving. Although they are alien to his very nature, God is compelled to undertake them lest his gracious will suffer frustration

[42] *Ibid.*

[43] *Ibid.*, p. 278.

[44] Watson, *Let God be God* (London: Epworth Press, 1947).

[45] *Ibid.*, p. 79.

[46] On the problem of our knowledge of God, cf. *ibid.*, pp. 73 ff.; John Dillenberger, *God Hidden and Revealed* (Philadelphia: Muhlenberg Press, 1953); Wilhelm Link, *Das Ringen Luthers um die Freiheit der Theologie von der Philosophie* (1955); and Bernhard Lohse, *Ratio und Fides* (1958).

[47] Cf. Isa. 28:21.

[48] *WA*, 3:426; 42:356; *LW*, 13:135, *passim*

by them that hate him. As to strange works, God does not exercise them directly but rather indirectly through the "tyrants," namely, Satan, sin, death, hell, and the law.

Luther did not regard God's wrath as a mere reflection in man's consciousness.[49] Rather it is really there in all its fearfulness, shattering the sinner, for God's wrath is the necessary affirmation of his righteousness over against the awfulness of human sin. God's wrath, therefore, is an eminently ethical reaction. Aside from Christ the divine wrath is a severe reality for the world, but in Christ God's wrath is conquered.[50]

Luther's concept of hell is explained in like manner. Under the influence of the divine law, man experiences the wrath of God in his conscience. The pangs of a bad conscience are the very nature of hell. If the devil had no guilty conscience, even he would be in heaven.[51] This inward idea of hell, however, is merely pre-eschatological. After the final manifestation of God's glory on the day of judgment, godless man as a whole, in his soul and body, will bear the eternal wrath of God.[52]

God is experienced as steadfastly active and operative in the whole creation. If man has recognized God in his works of grace, he recognizes Him also in the world. It is in this uninterrupted activity of grace that Luther sees the action that is worthy of God in the proper sense.

> Almighty is He, so that nothing but His might alone operates in all things and through all things and over all things. . . . The little word "mighty" must not mean here a quietly resting Might, such as we mean when we say that a temporal king is mighty, although he sits still and does nothing; but it is an operative might and constant activity which moves and works without pause. For God rests not, He works without cessation.[53]

> All creatures are God's masks and He disguises whom He desires to let co-operate with Him and help Him do all kinds of things which He can do and even does without their assistance.[54]

> He is everywhere present, in death, in hell, among the fiends, yea, even

[49] Seeberg, *Lehrbuch,* IV, 176.

[50] L. Pinomaa, *Der Zorn Gottes in der Theologie Luthers* (1938); Theodosius Harnack, *Luthers Theologie* (1862) I, 253 ff.

[51] *EA, Op. Lat.,* 10:375.

[52] *EA,* 41:319.

[53] *WA,* 7:574.

[54] *EA,* 11:115.

in their hearts. For He has made everything and He rules everything, so that it must do what He wills.[55]

A miracle, in the eyes of Luther, is not primarily an unexpected supernatural intervention in the customary drift of things. The daily course of the world itself, with its abundance of living movements and operative powers, is the greatest miracle of all. This does not mean that, in the eyes of Luther, man's activity is eliminated. Although God could create fruit out of the ground without plowing and sowing, and perpetuate the human race without the sexual life of man, it is his will and design to perpetuate his works through the toil of human beings. But the relationship between God's operative power and our work is not a matter of necessity. God is free to work however he wants. It is we who are bound to comply with his plan in order to obtain the necessities of life. Just as little children will not receive a gift from St. Nicholas unless they pray and hang up their stockings at night, so we shall not be provided with necessities unless we work. But our work, like the hanging of stockings by children, is not the means of bringing forth food out of the earth, it is the *conditio sine qua non.*[56]

The Meaning of Christ for Luther

Luther wholeheartedly embraced the christological dogma of the ancient Church. This is not to be looked upon as a deplorable survival of Scholastic tenets in his thinking, as Ritschl and his followers thought. Rather, Luther's conception of Christ is the necessary correlation to his idea of justification. In the interest of redemption, Luther's Christ is separate from sinners and higher than the heavens. The genuine redemptive theology of Athanasius is revived in Luther's teaching of Christ. Though weighed down by sin and guilt, we may be assured that we have "a brother in heaven who is at the same time the Son of God." [57] "God desires to be known only through Christ; He is the mirror, the means, and the way by which we know God." [58] "Whoever does not find or receive God in Christ, shall at no time and in no place have or find God outside of Christ." To be more exact:

[55] *WA*, 19:219.
[56] *WA*, 12:442; 17:2; 20:272; *passim.*
[57] *WA*, 49:282.
[58] *WA*, 40: I, 602.

God shows himself to us through the medium of Christ's humanity.[59] Luther's strong interest in the unity of Christ's natures as well as his position in the eucharistic controversy issue from this point of view. True God and true man are one person, and from this teaching issues that of the *communicatio idiomatum*.

It was not metaphysical speculation that prompted Luther to uphold the decision of the Fourth Ecumenical Council; it was simply his genuinely religious desire to read the heart of God in the earthly life of Jesus. Man as a sinner cannot commune with the *Deus absolutus* and *nudus*, the absolute and naked God (that is, the God not revealed). The only God we know is the God who is revealed, dressed, and clothed, *Deus revelatus, vestitus, indutus* in his promises and Word "so that from the name God we cannot exclude Christ, whom God promised to Adam and the other patriarchs." [60]

The man Jesus reveals two different things to us: First, he shows us the spiritual sense of the law and clarifies the magnitude of God's demands. Second, he shows us in his human deeds and sufferings the loving will of God made visible. His proper office is to declare grace and the forgiveness of sins. But Christ's significance is not exhausted in a mere announcement of grace and forgiveness. He brings us peace, not by preaching, as did the Apostles, but by granting it. He gives us grace and forgiveness of sins; he makes us living and righteous. He frees us from death and from sins. These are divine works which the creature cannot do; even the angels are unable to perform them. These works belong to the highest creative majesty and permit us to experience that Christ is true God.[61]

Luther's teaching of the suffering of Christ is a grand prelude on the love of God. First, the death Christ suffered was vicarious—a punishment for man's sin. On the cross he experienced the wrath of God. "For God cannot be well-disposed, not gracious to sin, nor can He take away His wrath and punishment until payment and satisfaction have been made for it." [62] Luther was far from conceiving of the satisfaction rendered by Christ in a pecuniary manner, as an exact *quid pro quo*. Instead, the satisfaction which Jesus rendered was

---

[59] *Ibid.,* p. 77; *EA,* 7:68; 10:181.
[60] *LW,* 12:312.
[61] *WA,* 40: I, 81.
[62] *EA,* 7:175-76; 11:290, *passim.*

forensic, that is, it was adequate in proportion to the sin of man. It was also ethical, for Jesus took the cross upon himself in willing obedience to the Father and out of love for men. Jesus was unique even in his Godforsaken-ness because he was the Son of God. While the condemned endure the divine wrath with resentment and hatred for God, Jesus was and remained the Righteous One. "He contradicted Himself, as it were, when He cried out that God had forsaken Him, and yet called Him 'My God,' proving thereby that He was not entirely forsaken." [63]

In Luther's eyes reconciliation implies redemption. The dying Jesus is the conqueror of sin, death, hell, and Satan. In this respect Luther's doctrine of the atonement, in the words of Aulén, belongs to the "classic type." [64] The Suffering Servant is at the same time the *Christus Victor*. Good Friday and Easter are closely united in Luther's thinking. The *Christus miserabilis* of Anselm is blended into one picture with the *Christus gloriosus* of Byzantine theology. Luther did not write a single passion hymn; but his Easter hymns are meditation on both the suffering and the exalted Lord.[65] Christ's resurrection announces not only that guilt and punishment have been removed, but also that the night of sin is ended. It is here that Christ displays his creative power in the real sense, by also giving us the Holy Spirit that we may imitate him and begin to stifle and to slay sin.[66] Christ himself operates in us as the exalted Lord and fights in us against sin.[67]

Law and Gospel

Luther was very outspoken on the distinction between law and

---

[63] Remark on Ps. 22:1; *WA*, 5:602.

[64] G. Aulén, *Christus Victor* (London: SPCK, 1931), pp. 117 ff. Excellent though this study is, it presents, in our opinion, a one-sided view of Luther. The author seems to underrate the importance of those passages in Luther which have a bearing on the cross in its effect upon God. Satisfaction, according to Luther, is by God and to God. Cf. our article "The Cross in Lutheran Theology," *The Lutheran Church Quarterly* (1944), pp. 61 ff.

[65] Cf. the Easter hymn "Christ Jesus Lay in Death's Strong Bands," *Service Book and Hymnal* (Minneapolis: Augsburg, 1958), No. 98.

[66] *EA*, 14:161-62.

[67] *WA*, 1:364-65; 3:433. In this connection, see Luther's explanation of the second article of the Apostles' Creed in the Small Catechism: "I believe that Jesus Christ . . . is my Lord, who has redeemed me, a lost and condemned creature, delivered me and freed me from all sin, from death, and from the power of the devil . . ." See also the more detailed explanation of the same article in the Large Catechism.

gospel. The law commands; the gospel gives. There is much law in the words of Christ and Paul, for example, in the Sermon on the Mount and the Epistles, and in the Old Testament there is much gospel, in the many promises of grace. This means that we have both law and gospel in both the New Testament and the Old.

The law reveals our sinfulness, frightens us, distresses us, and prepares us for the gospel of grace. From this standpoint, Luther eliminates from the law proper the Jewish legal code, the Mosaic law in its national features and ceremonial elements. Even the moral law as a demand, when it first comes to man, never evokes in man a free and glad response to do the will of God. Instead, man feels rebellion and resistance. The law discloses the depth of his depraved condition. For this reason we need the law. This is why Luther turned so energetically against the Antinomians. We need the law even after the new life has begun, for the justified man still remains a sinner. He is always *simul justus et peccator*[68] and is in need of the law to deepen his repentance.[69]

The gospel as free gift must go together with the law as demand and as guide. It is the remedy for the sickness. The gospel gives man the spirit to keep God's commands from the heart. It begets in him an infinitely rich love so that he cannot do otherwise than live and act according to God's will. This is an experience that runs through the whole life of the Christian. The judgment of God and the terror of the conscience (*Anfechtung*) is to be taken with the comfort of the gospel and a joyful response to the divine imperative as inseparable aspects of the Christian life.

Luther's Concept of Sin

As to the origin of sin, Luther's thought is strictly infralapsarian. God is not the author of evil. The evil in our lives is our own guilt, not the fault of God. But why did God permit Adam to fall? Why has God created us to be infected with Adam's transgression, when he could have prevented Adam's fall and could have created us for something else or from a previously purified sperm? Because he is God, Luther says, "His will has neither cause nor reason." Although revealed in Jesus Christ, God at the same time remains a God "con-

[68] See p. 321.
[69] Cf. Gerhard Heintze, *Luthers Predigt von Gesetz und Evangelium* (1958).

cealed in majesty" (*absconditus in majestate*). Mortal man must not try to penetrate into the hidden will of God.[70] Luther held to the traducianistic view of propagation. In body and soul, the child is wholly the offspring (*tradux*) of his parents.[71]

Opposing the psychological understanding of "flesh" in the Middle Ages, Luther turned back to the language of Paul, in whose thought "flesh" expresses a religious judgment over the whole man—body, soul, and spirit.[72] *Totum hominem esse carnem* ("the whole man is flesh").[73] Luther says that Paul, like Christ in John 3, includes not only unchastity but also idolatry, envy, strife, hatred, and the like, among the sins of the flesh (Gal. 5:19 ff.).[74] Even man's religion and worship of God belongs to the realm of the flesh. It is for his own sake that natural man loves God. He regards religion as an effective tool for his own self-aggrandizement. He is *curvus* or *curvatus in se:* crooked, ultimately bent back upon himself.[75] The difference between Augustine and Luther is significant in spite of the fact that they use the same terminology. When Augustine says that man is *curvatus* he means that man is bent to the things of the flesh, to the inferior things of the cosmos.[76] Luther, on the other hand, means that man is by nature always seeking his own selfish ends. He is possessed by a self-seeking will. "Man can do nothing but seek only his own and love himself above all things. . . . Thus in what is good and virtuous man seeks himself, that is, that he may please himself."[77] This is the very essence of concupiscence: pollution by egocentricity, not by sexual desire.

Can this hereditary condition be charged to the individual if it is given to him with his personal existence? The personal existence cannot be called to account, but the soul, which forms itself anew with every decision of the will in its fundamental impulses, is responsible for the direction which it gives to the will. It is certainly true that we do not sin against our own will; instead, our will is

---

[70] *On the Bondage of the Will, WA,* 18:634 ff.
[71] Cf. *EA,* 10:304; 11:246; 19:15.
[72] *WA,* 40: II, 83-84, 111.
[73] *WA,* 18:742.
[74] *Preface to Romans, PE,* 6:453.
[75] *WA,* 18:504, *passim.*
[76] See the references in Nygren, *op. cit.,* p. 485.
[77] *WA,* 56:237 and *LCC,* XV, 89.

always at hand to assist us when we do something evil. For this reason Luther uses the significant term "personal sin"[78] for original sin. In Luther's thought the distinction between venial and mortal sins is false and dangerous. Every sin separates us from God and places the sinner under the wrath and judgment of God. Sin is essentially unbelief, since only faith gives man a right attitude toward God.[79]

The Christian Life

Luther turned against the Aristotelian and Scholastic ethics of the Middle Ages. Good works do not make a person good. The opposite is true: a person must be good before he can do good works.[80] Hence, where justification is concerned, works are altogether out of place. There faith alone reigns. Against the Scholastic emphasis on human abilities, Luther stressed the all-importance of faith for the Christian life: "The first and highest, the most precious of all good works is faith in Christ . . . for in this work [i.e. faith] all good works must be done and receive from it the inflow of their goodness, that men may understand it." [81] Through faith alone is man saved, albeit through a faith which "comes to take pleasure in God's commandments." [82]

According to Luther, Christian ethics has two basic marks. First, it finds its norm in the will of God expressed in the structures of life and in Scripture. Monastic works are "unbelieving good works," for they do not have a Word of God in which the monk may put his trust. Second, no compulsive action can please the unconditional demand of the divine will. Instead, the right love must spring freely and joyfully from the heart. Luther's ethics is an ethics of love. For a God, Luther says, "who has so prodigally lavished upon me His blessings, I will in turn freely, joyously and for nothing do what is well-pleasing to Him, and also be a Christian toward my neighbor, as Christ has been to me." [83] By faith and love, man is placed between God and his neighbor. He can be likened to a vessel or tube "through

[78] *WA*, 10: I, 508.
[79] *WA*, 3:582; *EA*, 12:110-11.
[80] *WA*, 2:492.
[81] *PE*, 1:187.
[82] *PE*, 6:452.
[83] *WA*, 7:35.

which the stream of divine blessings must flow without intermission to other people." [84]

Luther's ethics of love is also an ethics of freedom. Uniformity of conduct becomes impossible: "Love rises above all law." To love "is no commandment and all commandments." [85] The theory of later Lutheran orthodoxy about "the third use of the law," according to which the Christian life must conform to a fixed pattern, has no place in Luther's thought. Christ is not to be imitated by the believer but "rather to be accepted in faith, because Christ had His special office for the salvation of man, an office which no one else has." [86] Compared with Christ, the Sinless One, no human life is ever sinless. On this side of eternity the Christian is *simul justus et peccator*, both righteous and a sinner, holy and profane, an enemy of God and yet a child of God.[87] Perfection is not an ethical disposition in the soul, quantitatively increasing or decreasing. A Christian is righteous and holy by virtue of an alien righteousness and holiness, the righteousness and holiness of Christ.[88] Thus Luther could say, "The one doctrine which reigns in my heart [*in corde . . . regnat*], is that of faith in Christ, from whom, through whom, and unto whom all my theological thinking flows back and forth day and night." [89] Hence, in the eyes of Luther, if the Church loses the article of justification, it loses everything.[90] This doctrine is indeed *articulus stantis et cadentis ecclesiae*, "the article on which the Church stands or falls." Having become one person with Christ by faith, this "faith is not an idle quality but the excellency thereof is such that it produces works that are pleasing to God." [91] This faith confounds, as Luther says, the foolish dreams of the monastic way of life and re-establishes a sure trust in a way of life in which I, as husband or wife, father or mother, ruler or citizen, may serve my neighbor. The earthly station in which a Christian

---

[84] *WA*, 10: I, 100.

[85] *WA*, 17: II, 95. Cf. Gustaf Wingren, *Luther on Vocation,* trans. Carl C. Rasmussen (Philadelphia: Muhlenberg Press, 1957), pp. 146-47.

[86] Wingren, *op. cit.,* p. 172.

[87] *Commentary on Galatians,* p. 226.

[88] *Ibid.,* p. 39, *passim.*

[89] *Ibid.,* p. 16.

[90] *Ibid.,* p. 40.

[91] *Ibid.,* p. 170.

has received the call to eternal life is a vocation (*Beruf*) God has appointed for him.[92]

The Two Kingdoms

Luther expresses his concept of the two kingdoms in many of his writings. In Luther the term has a twofold meaning, a sociological and an instrumental one. The kingdom of God or of Christ is the sum total of all who believe in and profess the name of Christ, whereas the kingdom of the world means the organized society of men. The kingdom of God is realized in the Church and the kingdom of the world in the state. At the same time, the terms mean the two different ways in which God governs the world. Seen from this perspective, both kingdoms have soteriological and eschatological significance. God preserves his creation from satanic destruction through the state. This is accomplished through the exercise of law and order. The state, therefore, is a servant of God. [93] Since the works of restraining evil and punishing the wicked are God's *opera aliena*, the state is only "the kingdom of the left hand of God," [94] for it is "the kingdom of sin." [95] On the other hand, God accomplishes his *opera propria* through the gospel as proclaimed in the Church. The Church, therefore, is "the kingdom of His right hand." [96]

Luther's view of the state can be fully appreciated only within the framework of his concept of the "natural orders." Man as a social being is a part of certain orders or stations of life such as the family, his vocation, the state, and the empirical Church. These orders, Luther maintains, are a part of God's design to continue his creation (family and the economic order) or to preserve it from disorder caused by sin and the devil, "the prince of this world."

> Once again he [the psalmist] refers to all God's work in general, . . . to all His ordinances and institutions which He established by His word and command . . . such as the station of father and mother, . . . of

[92] *Ibid.*, p. 170; *PE*, 1:183, and many other passages. Cf. Wingren, *op. cit.*, and the literature referred to. See also W. H. Lazareth, *Luther and the Christian Home* (Philadelphia: Muhlenberg Press, 1960).
[93] *PE*, 4:290, *passim*. Cf. Philip S. Watson, *The State as a Servant of God* (London: SPCK, 1946); Eivind Berggrav, *Man and State* (Philadelphia: Muhlenberg Press, 1951); and Lilje, *op. cit.*, pp. 160 ff.
[94] *WA*, 52:26.
[95] *WA*, 42:79.
[96] *WA*, 52:26.

servant and maid, marriage, the station of lords and subjects. . . . Where such stations operate as they should, there things go well in the world. . . . Now God declares concerning these stations that they must remain if the world is to stand. . . .[97]

What the jurist calls "natural law"[98] is to Luther the will of God expressed in the structures of the world and is a part of his belief that God reveals himself to all men as Lord of nature and history. To this extent Luther was a conservative, but he was not a reactionary defending the *status quo* at all cost. Nor was he an exponent of the principle of "legitimacy." It matters not to God, he said, "where an empire comes from; it is His will that it shall be ruled."[99] He regards the historical form of government as subject to change, for all government must serve the one purpose, to safeguard and protect the life of its people.[100]

The two kingdoms, Church and state, must not be confused. If the secular government is interpreted spiritually, if one would venture to rule a country or the world with the gospel, he would not maintain the world but lead his country into chaos. If, contrariwise, a person tried to propagate the gospel with the sword, he would destroy the spiritual character of the Church. In either way, the saving will of God would be frustrated.[101] Both kingdoms must remain until the Last Day, the state and its officials, as well as the Church, being subject to God. Though different in their purpose and function, Church and state have their objective unity in God, and the Christian is a citizen of both realms. He is united to God by faith, and called to serve his neighbor in love, for every believer occupies a certain station in life as father, teacher, judge, and the like. Believers are all one in Christ, yet they differ from each other as to their station in life.[102]

[97] *LW*, 13:358. For further references, cf. George Forell, *Faith Active in Love* (New York: American Press, 1954), pp. 112 ff.; Franz Lau, *Äusserlich Ordnung und weltlich Ding in Luthers Theologie* (1933); and Heinz H. Zahrnt, *Luther deutet Geschichte* (1952).

[98] Cf. Franz X. Arnold, *Zur Frage des Naturrechts bei Luther* (1937).

[99] *PE*, 2:156.

[100] *PE*, 3:224.

[101] *PE*, 3:237. Cf. Luther's exposition of the Sermon on the Mount, *AE*, 21:1 ff., especially pp. 99 ff.

[102] On the whole problem under discussion, compare Harald Diem, *Luthers Lehre von den zwei Reichen* (1938); Ernst Kinder, *Geistliches und weltliches Regiment nach Luther* (1940); Gustaf Tornvall, *Geistliches und weltliches Regiment bei Luther* (1947); Franz Lau, *Luthers Lehre von den beiden*

Church and Ministry

Luther was not the religious individualist Protestant liberalism pictured him to be. In his lectures on Genesis, Luther said that the first "theological" word in Scripture refers to the Church.[103] When planting the tree of life, God, as it were, built a temple that Adam might worship him. The Church is the first institution which God established, before the home and the state.[104] As the Church is the first institution, so it will be the final one. All worldly institutions and kingdoms will come to an end (I Cor. 15:24); however, Christ will never abolish his spiritual kingdom, but will deliver it up to God.[105] Christ and the Church belong together; neither will come to an end. The Church is the kingdom of God in its earthly form.[106] As God is both revealed and hidden in his creatures, who are the *larvae Dei*, and in Christ, who as man was subject to the law and the wrath of God, so God is both revealed and hidden in the Church. The Church is the people of God, in whose midst he dwells. Like Christ, it "is outwardly known by the holy possession of the Cross." The more the Church is despised, the more it is true to its very nature. This also applies to the individual believer. A mystical or moral experience is no test of God's election. A sinner may be closer to God than someone men would call a saint. *Abscondita est ecclesia, latent sancti* ("the Church is hidden, the saints are hidden"). No religious society, such as the radicals of the Reformation (for example, Schwärmer) attempted to establish, is the true Church; nor is he potentially a saint who holds membership in an external organization, as the Church of Rome claims.

Luther never sets the "invisible" Church against the "visible" one as if the visible were not a true church. The Church is constituted by the preaching of the Word and the administration of the sacraments. Where the Word is, there, in Luther's eyes, is the Church; and where the Word is proclaimed some will always believe. "God's Word

Reichen (1953); Johannes Heckel, *Im Irrgarten der Zwei-Reiche-Lehre* (1957); Gottfried Forck, *Die Königsherrschaft Jesu Christi bei Luther* (1959); and Watson, *The State as a Servant of God.*

[103] *LW*, 1:94.
[104] *LW*, 1:103 ff.
[105] *WA*, 52:522.
[106] *PE*, 5:286.

cannot be present without God's people, and God's people cannot be without God's Word." [107]

According to Luther, the Church is both the workmanship and the workshop of the Holy Spirit. It is the Holy Spirit who through his gifts (the Word and the sacraments) calls, gathers, enlightens, and sanctifies the whole Christian Church on earth, as Luther says in the explanation of the third article in his Small Catechism. Consequently *extra ecclesiam nulla salus*, "outside the Christian Church" (that is, where the gospel is not), there is no forgiveness, and hence no holiness. [108]

The preceding implies that for Luther the Word and sacraments are the chief marks of the Church. Occasionally he may add other marks such as the keys, ministry, prayer, suffering, and, to a lesser degree, the effect of the Word in the lives of the people. [109]

The Church, Luther says, is holy because it possesses the Word through which the Holy Spirit offers forgiveness of sins. For this reason the Roman church, too, is holy, for there "remain in it baptism, the sacrament, the voice and text of the Gospel, the Holy Scripture, the ministries, the name of Christ and the name of God." [110] Hence the Church is indeed one. Its continuity is contingent upon the Word which, as previously stated, cannot but elicit some response of faith. Luther's interest was centered in the succession of believers (*successio fidelium*), not in the so-called "apostolic succession of the ministry."

In keeping with his emphasis on faith and the Word, Luther rejects the Roman distinction between the priesthood and the laity. In speaking of the ministry the term "priest," he maintains, is altogether out of place. The ministerial office is not a priestly office. Instead, "all Christians are priests in equal degree." [111] "We are all priests, and there is no difference between us." [112] Every baptized believer, women included, "can baptize and administer the Word of life." [113] The keys, too, "belong to the whole Church and to each of its mem-

[107] *PE*, 5:271.
[108] Explanation of the third article in the Large Catechism.
[109] *PE*, 5:269 ff.
[110] *Commentary on Galatians*, p. 39.
[111] *LW*, 40:39.
[112] *PE*, 2:283.
[113] *LW*, 40:25.

bers." [114] "However, no one may make use of this power except by the consent of the community or by the call of a superior. For what is the common property of all, no individual may appropriate himself, unless he be called." [115] It is therefore the call that makes the ministry, the nature of which is functional. Ordination is simply the public, solemn confirmation of the call. It confers no "indelible character." Indeed, a minister may become a layman again.

As indicated, the call need not be extended by a local congregation. Neither the episcopal nor the congregational system, in Luther's eyes, is required by the New Testament. In Lutheranism there is room for both forms of church government. "Polity has no religious significance in the Lutheran church." [116] Likewise, Luther regarded the liturgy as an *adiaphoron*, that is, as neither right nor wrong. He composed no "prayer book." He treated the liturgical life as a matter of freedom.[117] Melanchthon later said in Article VII of the Augsburg Confession that Church order and liturgy are not necessary for the true unity of the Christian Church.

Word and Sacrament

The Church is constituted by the proclamation of the gospel. In emphasizing the importance of the Word, Luther opposed the Roman view that the Church is built through the infusion of grace in a quasi-physical manner. On the other hand, he opposed the idea of the spiritualists that the Holy Spirit operates immediately on the mind of man.

The Word makes the sacrament. From the Word the sacrament derives its nature, as Augustine taught: "When the Word is added to the element, it becomes a sacrament." [118] The sacraments are means and instruments of grace, ordained by God. Like the Word, they have their origin in Christ who, as the Logos of God, is also the

[114] *LW*, 40:27. Cf. the whole treatise *Concerning the Ministry, ibid.,* 40:3 ff. and the criticism of the sacrament of ordination in *Babylonian Captivity of the Church, PE,* 2:273 ff.
[115] *PE,* 2:281.
[116] Lilje, *op. cit.,* p. 131.
[117] See Luther's *Preface to the German Mass* (1526), *PE,* 6:170. For further discussion of Luther's views on polity and liturgy, cf. Lilje, *op. cit.,* pp. 122 ff.; Nygren (ed.), *This Is the Church* (Philadelphia: Muhlenberg Press, 1952), pp. 175 ff.; and Wilhelm Brunotte, *Das geistliche Amt bei Luther* (1959).
[118] Large Catechism, Part IV, 18.

original *sacramentum Dei*[119] ("sign of God") and *opus Dei* ("living and active organ of God's redemptive love"). The sacraments are instituted for the purpose of nourishing faith.[120]

Baptism is the work of God, not of the officiant, for the man who baptizes officiates not by his own authority, but in the stead of God.[121] In baptism man is incorporated into the Church of Christ. Baptism signifies two things: "Death and resurrection; that is, full and complete justification." [122] However, without faith it avails nothing, for "faith justifies and fulfills that which baptism signifies." [123] Baptism embraces the whole Christian life which "is nothing else than a daily baptism, once begun and ever continued." [124] Thus understood, baptism effects regeneration, that is, it makes a man a member of the Church militant. Luther says in the Small Catechism (Part IV): "It signifies that the old Adam in us, together with all sins and evil lusts, should be drowned by daily sorrow and repentance, and be put to death, and that the new man should come forth daily, and rise up, cleansed and righteous, to life forever in God's presence."

In discussing baptism, Luther puts the emphasis on faith, without which no one can be saved. How, then, does this view of baptism agree with the practice of infant baptism? Do infants believe? Luther answered the question in the affirmative. In opposition to the Roman view that a sacrament is effective *ex opere operato* and in opposition to the rejection of infant baptism on the part of the Anabaptists, Luther developed the idea of "infant faith." Faith, he argued, is a *donum Dei*, a gift of God. It comes from hearing the Word. In his baptism, the infant child hears the Word, though he is not subjectively conscious of it. Luther, of course, realizes that infant faith cannot be described as trust, obedience, or the like. What he means to say is simply this: The child addressed by the Word is put into a new relationship with God, who grants the child forgiveness of sins, life, and salvation. This does not mean, according to Luther, that infant baptism is a substitute for conversion. As the child grows in

[119] *WA,* 10: I, 2, 15, 21. Cf. Erich Roth, *Sakrament nach Luther* (1952), pp. 10 ff.
[120] *PE,* 2:224.
[121] *Ibid.*
[122] *Ibid.,* p. 230.
[123] *Ibid.,* p. 228.
[124] Large Catechism, Part IV, 65.

years he must learn to respond subjectively to the promise of God
with repentance, trust, and obedience. In all the passages pertaining
to this problem, Luther is actually saying that men, including infants,
are holy only by virtue of the imputation of the grace of God that
appeared in Jesus Christ. As always, Luther is very anxious to avoid
the error which makes faith a work of man.[125]

For Luther the Lord's Supper is a real means of grace. In this sacrament Christ offers the fruit of his death to all who eat and drink. It
is the sacrament of fellowship with the Lord. The Supper is also an
"image of love," signifying the communion of saints.[126] The communion is thus twofold. First, we partake of Christ. Second, we partake of all the saints, and they partake of us, so that through this
sacrament of love we become one bread, one cup, one body, one
congregation.

In the Supper men do not act, but God acts. Just as Luther found
the divine activity of Christ in his human deeds, so the *communicatio
idiomatum*, according to Luther, leads inevitably to the doctrine of
the real presence, the personal presence of the incarnate Son of God.
"In, with, and under" the bread and wine are present the body and
blood of Christ, not just the effects of Christ's atoning sacrifice.

In no uncertain terms, Luther rejected the Roman view of the mass
as a sacrifice. On the cross, Christ obtained our forgiveness; in the
Supper, he "distributes and imparts it [forgiveness] through the Word
as also in the Gospel whenever it is preached." [127] To Luther the
mass is a sacrament and testament and cannot be a sacrifice any more
than the other sacraments.[128] It is a sacrifice only in the sense that it
is an act of praise and thanksgiving in which we offer ourselves and
all that we have to God,[129] yea, that Christ offers us, and we offer
ourselves to him.[130]

[125] Cf. Large Catechism, Part IV, 65, and Luther's treatise *Concerning Baptism,
LW*, 40:225 ff. For a complete review of the whole problem, see Karl Brinkel,
Die Lehre Luthers von der Fides Infantium bei der Kindertaufe (1958).
   [126] *EA*, 27, 29, 44-45.
   [127] *EA*, 29:285 f.
   [128] *PE*, 1:312.
   [129] *Ibid.*, p. 313.
   [130] *Ibid.*, pp. 314-15. Cf. Ruben Josefson on "The Church and Baptism" and
"The Lutheran View of the Lord's Supper" in Nygren, *This Is the Church*, pp.
243 ff.; V. Vajta, *Luther on Worship*, trans. U. S. Leupold (Philadelphia: Muhlenberg Press, 1958), pp. 149 ff.; and H. Sasse, *This is My Body* (Minneapolis:
Augsburg Publishing House, 1959), pp. 78 ff.

The Word and the Bible

Luther's theology is a theology of the cross. It may also be described as a theology of the Word. "The Word, I say, and the Word only, is the vehicle of the grace of God." [131] In order to understand the Reformer's view of the Word it is necessary to relate his theology of the Word to his theology of the cross. God has effected our redemption in the cross of Jesus. Yet a crucified Messiah is an offense to human sense. We must leave our own wisdom and listen to that Word which, contrary to reason, proclaims the Crucified One to be "God with us." [132]

Luther uses the term "Word of God" in several senses:

First of all, Christ is the very Word of God. In God there was a "Speech or Word" that preceded the existence of all creatures.[133]

Second, creation, which reveals God, is a Word of God. "Thus you must be ashamed of yourself when you look at the sun which preaches this to you every day." [134] Flowers and trees, leaves and grass, birds and berries, in Luther's words, proclaim the goodness of God.

In the third place, God's redemptive deeds in history are a Word of God to be seen and heard. Luther observed that the Hebrew word *dabar* not only means "to speak," but also denotes the thing spoken of. A concrete action of God is to Luther a Word of God.[135] The exodus and the cross are the two central Words of God in history. Yet any historical event may become a Word of God proclaiming his judgment or election.[136]

Fourth, the Word of God addresses us either as law or gospel. The Scholastics of the Middle Ages had also distinguished between law and gospel. They called the Old Testament the "old law" and the New Testament the "new law." Following Augustine, they talked of the old law as "letter," containing only "shadows" and "figures" of the things to come; and of the new law as "spirit," announcing the reality of man's redemption. For Luther, distinctions between the two

[Handwritten margin note: Note the many different meanings Luther gives to the term "Word of God."]

---

[131] *WA*, 2:509.
[132] See Regin Prenter, "The Living Word" in *More About Luther* ("Martin Luther Lectures," Vol. 2; Decorah, Iowa: Luther College Press, 1958).
[133] *LW*, 22:12 (Sermon on John 1:1).
[134] *LW*, 21:126.
[135] *LW*, 1:16. Cf. Peter Meinhold, *Luthers Sprachphilosophie* (1958).
[136] See H. Zahrnt, *Luther deutet Geschichte* (1952).

Testaments were of little concern. He was primarily concerned with law and gospel as two fundamentally different aspects of the divine Word, the law as command and the gospel as promise, which may be found everywhere in the Bible.[137]

Fifth, the Word is, to Luther, the oral Word, the Word of preaching. "Christ did not command the Apostles to write, but only to preach."[138] Again, "The church is a mouth-house, not a pen-house."[139] The gospel is not what you find in books but rather a "spoken and living Word," a voice which resounds and which is heard everywhere.[140]

Finally, Luther speaks of the Bible as the Word of God. Scripture is the Word of God because it is the original witness to the redemptive work of God and because it participates in the nature of that which it records. When Luther speaks about Scripture as the Word of God he sets it in opposition to the traditions of men in the Catholic church and the private revelations and "inner word" of the radical Reformers. The written Word, according to Luther, has a twofold function. First, it is to sustain the oral proclamation in the Church. To continue to be the Word of God, the oral Word needs the written Word.[141] The second function of the written Word in relation to the oral Word is to preserve the proclamation in the Church from error and false doctrine. Even the Fathers—and Luther adds, "I speak of the holy and good ones"—when they built without the Scriptures, built wood, straw, and hay.[142]

Formally Luther followed the terminology of the later Middle Ages in speaking of the Holy Spirit as the author and writer of the Bible. Luther did not draw the same conclusions from these statements as did the orthodox Lutheran teachers of the seventeenth century.[143] In his eyes, the Scriptures were not "errorless." For instance, commenting on Gal. 1:11, he said. "Now the histories in the Scriptures are

---

[137] Cf. Prenter, *op. cit.*, p. 67.

[138] *WA*, 10: I, 626.

[139] *Ibid.*, pp. 2, 48.

[140] *WA*, 12:259 f.

[141] Cf. Jaroslav Pelikan, *Luther the Expositor* (St. Louis: Concordia Publishing House, 1959), pp. 68 ff.

[142] *PE*, 5:171.

[143] For this reason M. Reu, *Luther and the Scriptures* (Columbus, Ohio: Wartburg Press, 1944) is unreliable. It gives a distorted view of Luther.

oftentimes chopped up and out of order (*concisae et confusae*), so that they cannot be easily harmonized as, for example, the denials of Peter and the history of the passion of Christ. Paul does not recite the entire history. Therefore I labour not, neither am much troubled about harmonizing it." [144] Luther rejected the Solomonian authorship of Ecclesiastes. [145] He wished to see Esther eliminated from the canon of the Old Testament. [146] In discussing the New Testament, he revived the ancient differentiation between *homologoumena* and *antilegomena*. [147] He expressed dislike for Hebrews [148] and for Revelation. [149] He was especially offended by the Letter of James. [150] His criticism was theologically motivated:

> All the genuine sacred books agree in this, that all of them preach Christ and deal with Him. That is the true test by which to judge all books, when we see whether they deal with Christ (*Christum trieben*) or not. . . . What does not teach Christ is not Apostolic, even though St. Peter and St. Paul taught it; again, what preaches Christ would be Apostolic, even though Judas, Annas, Pilate and Herod said it. [151]

It is not surprising that the concept of the Word of God as a living Word had far-reaching consequences for the hermeneutical principle operative in Luther's exegesis. Karl Holl has summarized Luther's contribution to the interpretation of Scripture in the following seven points: (1) Scripture has only one meaning. (2) The literal, grammatical interpretation is prior to any other understanding of the text. (3) Every single passage must be seen in the light of the whole Bible. (4) In interpreting the Bible, we are concerned not with its letter, but with its subject matter. (5) The subject matter of the Bible is always clear and intelligible. (6) Because the Scriptures are clear, they are their own interpreters. (7) If the fundamental clarity of Scripture is recognized, its undeniable obscurities and difficulties in details may be freely admitted. [152]

These principles have been put in the right perspective of Luther's

[144] *Commentary on Galatians*, p. 74.
[145] *PE*, 6:394.
[146] *EA*, 62:131.
[147] *PE*, 6:476.
[148] *Ibid.*, pp. 476-77.
[149] *Ibid.*, pp. 479 ff.
[150] *Ibid.*, pp. 477 ff.
[151] *Ibid.*, p. 478.
[152] Karl Holl, *Gesammelte Aufsätze zur Kirchengeschichte* (1948), pp. 544 ff.

theology of the cross, says Regin Prenter, by another German scholar, Heinrich Bornkamm.[153] The Bible bears witness to the redemptive acts of God among the people of Israel and in the incarnation and cross of Jesus. These acts are events in history. The pre-existent Christ of the Old Testament and the Incarnate Person perform the same work of God. As historical events, these acts must be interpreted literally. As redemptive acts, they must be interpreted from the center of the Bible, which is Christ.

BIBLIOGRAPHY

Works

> D. *Martin Luthers sämmtliche Schriften.* 24 quarto vols. Edited by J. C. WALCH. Jena, 1740–53. St. Louis: Concordia Publishing House, 1880–1910.
>
> Erlangen Edition. 67 quarto vols. 1826–1857. Selections from this edition, translated into English by J. N. LENKER, 14 vols., 1903–.
>
> *Weimar Edition.* 1883–.

Selected Works

> *Braunschweig-Berlin Edition.* Edited by BUCHWALD, KAWERAU, KOESTLIN, *et al.* 8 vols. English translation based on this edition, *Works of Martin Luther.* 6 vols. Philadelphia: Holman Company and Muhlenberg Press, 1915–.
>
> *Luther's Correspondence.* A selection edited by PRESERVED SMITH and C. M. JACOBS. London: Murray and Co., 1913 and 1918.
>
> *Luther's Works.* Edited by JAROSLAV PELIKAN and HELMUT T. LEHMANN. 55 vols. St. Louis: Concordia Publishing House and Philadelphia: Muhlenberg Press, 1953–.
>
> *LCC,* Vols. XV-XVIII.
>
> *A Compend of Luther's Theology.* Edited by H. T. KERR. Philadelphia: Westminster Press, 1943.
>
> *What Luther Says.* Edited by EWALD M. PLASS. 3 vols. St. Louis: Concordia Publishing House, 1959.

Recent Luther Research

> ALTHAUS, PAUL. *Die Theologie Martin Luthers.* 1962.
>
> BAINTON, ROLAND H. *Here I Stand.* Nashville: Abingdon Press, 1950. New York: Mentor Books.
>
> BLAYNEY, I. W. *The Age of Luther.* New York: Vantage Press, 1957.
>
> BOEHMER, HEINRICH. *Luther in the Light of Recent Research.* Translated by CARL F. HUTH, JR. New York: The Christian Herald, 1916.
>
> BORNKAMM, HEINRICH. *Luther's World of Thought.* Translated by MARTIN H. BERTRAM. St. Louis: Concordia Publishing House, 1958.

---

[153] *Luther und das Alte Testament* (1948). Cf. Prenter, *op. cit.,* pp. 75-76.

CARLSON, E. M. *The Reinterpretation of Luther.* Philadelphia: Westminster Press, 1948.

GERRISH, B. A. *Grace and Reason.* Oxford: Clarendon Press, 1962.

GRISAR, HARTMANN. *Martin Luther, His Life and Work.* St. Louis: Herder Book Co., 1935.

HERMANN, R. *Gesammelte Studien zur Theologie Luthers und der Reformation.* 1959.

HIRSCH, E. *Lutherstudien.* 1954.

HORST, S. *Luther in den Wandlungen seiner Kirche.* 2nd ed., 1951.

JOERGENSEN, A. T. *Martin Luther, Reformer of the Church.* Translated by RONALD M. JENSEN. Minneapolis: Augsburg Publishing House, 1953.

KOESTLIN, J. *The Theology of Luther.* Translated by CHARLES E. HAY. 2 vols. Philadelphia: Lutheran Publication Society, 1897.

KOOIMAN, W. J. *By Faith Alone.* Translated by BERTRAM LEE. London: Lutterworth Press, 1954.

LILJE, HANNS. *Luther Now.* Translated by CARL J. SCHINDLER. Philadelphia: Muhlenberg Press, 1952.

MACKINNON, J. *Luther and the Reformation.* 4 vols. London and New York: Longmans, Green and Co. 1925–.

PAUCK, W. *The Heritage of the Reformation.* Boston: Beacon Press, 1950.

REU, M. *Thirty-five Years of Luther Research.* Chicago: Wartburg Publishing House, 1917.

RUPP, GORDON. *The Righteousness of God.* London: Hodder and Stoughton, 1953.

SCHEEL, O. *Martin Luther, vom Katholizismus zur Reformation.* 2 vols. 1897.

SCHWIEBERT, E. G. *Luther and His Times.* St. Louis: Concordia Publishing House, 1950.

THIEL, R. *Luther.* Translated by GUSTAV K. WIENCKE. Philadelphia: Muhlenberg Press, 1955.

THULIN, O. *Martin Luther, sein Leben in Bildern und Zeitdokumenten.* 1958.

VAJTA, VILMOS: (ed.) *Luther on Worship.* Translated by U. S. LEUPOLD. Philadelphia: Muhlenberg Press, 1958.

WOLFF, O. *Die Haupttypen der neueren Lutherforschung.* 1938.

The Young Luther

BOEHMER, HEINRICH. *Road to Reformation.* Translated by JOHN W. DOBERSTEIN and THEODORE G. TAPPERT. Philadelphia: Muhlenberg Press, 1946.

ERIKSON, E. H. *Young Man Luther.* New York: Norton Press, 1958.

FIFE, R. H. *The Young Luther.* New York: Macmillan Co., 1928.

————. *The Revolt of Martin Luther.* New York: Columbia Press, 1957.

HIRSCH, E. *Initium theologiae Lutheri.* 1920.

KUIPER, B. K. *Martin Luther: The Formative Years.* Grand Rapids, Mich.: Eerdmans, 1943.

MEISINGER, K. A. *Der katholische Luther.* 1952.

RUPP, GORDON. *The Righteousness of God.* London: Hodder and Stoughton, 1953.

STANGE, CARL. *Die Anfänge der Theologie Luthers.* 1957.

SCHEEL, O. *Dokumente zu Luthers Entwickelung.* 1911-12.

SCHUBERT, HANS VON. *Luthers Frühentwickelung.* 1916.

Luther and Scripture

DAVIES, R. E. *The Problem of Authority in the Continental Reformers.* London: Epworth Press, 1946.

OSTERGAARD-NEILSEN, H. *Scriptura Sacra et Viva Vox; eine Lutherstudie.* 1957.

PELIKAN, JAROSLAV. *Luther the Expositor.* St. Louis: Concordia Publishing House, 1959.

PRENTER, REGIN. "The Living Word," in *More about Luther.* "Martin Luther Lectures," Vol. II. Decorah, Iowa: Luther College Press, 1958.

QUANBECK, W. A. "Luthers' Early Exegesis," in *Luther Today.* "Martin Luther Lectures," Vol. I. Decorah, Iowa: Luther College Press, 1957.

SITTLER, JOSEPH A. *The Doctrine of the Word in the Structure of Lutheran Theology.* Philadelphia: Muhlenberg Press, 1948.

TORRANCE, T. F. *Kingdom and Church: A Study in the Theology of the Reformation.* Edinburgh: Oliver and Boyd, 1956.

CHAPTER II

ZWINGLI AND HIS THEOLOGY

I. Zwingli and Luther Contrasted

In 1540 Calvin wrote the following significant words to Farel concerning Zwingli and Luther: "If they are compared with each other, you yourself know how greatly Luther excels." [1] He was correct in noting the pre-eminence of Luther. But the two men ought not to be compared. They may be contrasted, for they are antipodal: men "quite unlike in temperament, cast of mind, and culture." Individualities are incommensurable; this is especially the case with personalities of far-reaching influence. If a comparison is in order, Zwingli was far closer to Savonarola in his religio-political activities, while in some fundamental philosophico-theological principles he was closer to Calvin.

Zwingli took the humanistic approach. It was a time when the atmosphere was heavy with humanism. Just as humanism had turned for help to the treasures of antiquity, its ideals, philosophy, art, literature, original texts, so Zwingli was led to revert to the Bible and the early patristic writers. To him the Bible was a divine law by which the conduct of the individual, the ethics of the state, and the practice of the Church were to be regulated. He did not become a Reformer as the result of having passed through soul-renewing experiences proceeding from a consciousness of sin, repentance, and grace, as was the case with Luther. It was his classical and biblical studies which made Zwingli what he was. He always remained a moderate biblical humanist. Zwingli's humanistic-philosophical cast of mind stands out clearly all through his doctrinal system. We see

---

[1] *Si inter se comparantur, scis ipse quanto intervallo Lutherus excellat.* See A. L. Herminjard, *Correspondence des Reformateurs francais*, Vol. VI, 191. Cf. A. Lang, *Johannes Calvin* (1909), p. 64.

it in his use of the Bible, in his world-view, in his desire for the strict independence of the spiritual and earthly spheres, in his doctrine of sin, in his Christology, in his attitude toward the sacraments, and in his view of Church and state. "The root of all these differences between Zwingli and Luther is to be found in the fact that Luther's understanding of the Holy Scriptures was conditioned chiefly by his religious experience, while that of Zwingli was conditioned in great measure by his humanistic training." [2] This explains the intellectual-moralistic tone in Zwingli's conception of Christianity.

Zwingli's scope of reformatory activity was from the first much larger than that of Luther. Zwingli had learned to know men and life before he became a student of the Scriptures. It was natural for him to include commonwealth and government in his reformatory endeavors. He followed theocratic ideals. In this his views were akin to those later developed by Calvin. Luther suggested that state and Church might be brought together in a case of necessity, but Zwingli believed that they belonged together as naturally as body and soul in man. In other words, Zwingli advocated a union of Church and state. According to him, the secular power should supervise the discipline of the Church; at the same time, the Bible of the Church was to be the governmental code of law. The validity of civil law depends upon its conformity to the Scriptures. Should the government fall short of being a Christian government, revolution would become the program of the day. [3]

Zwingli's political activity was not limited to the direction of his native city, nor to the affairs of Switzerland. In correspondence with Landgrave Philip of Hesse he was engaged in political schemes of the widest and most daring character. Charles V was to be dethroned, Philip of Hesse to be made emperor of Germany, the Roman Catholic king of France to be used as an ally, and the fleet of Venice to be included in the coalition. If Luther had known of these plans he would never have met Zwingli at the Colloquy of Marburg (1529). It was difficult even for the Elector of Saxony to convince Luther

[2] Loofs, *Leitfaden*, p. 799.
[3] Zwingli, "Schlussreden," *Werke*, Vol. I. Translated as "Sixty-seven Articles or Conclusions," *Corpus Reformatorum* (hereinafter referred to as *CR*), Vol. 89, and Schaff, *Creeds of Christendom* (New York: Harper & Bros., 1919), III, 196 ff.

that it was the duty of the Protestant princes to meet Emperor Charles V with armed resistance, should he move against the Smalcald Federation to crush the power of Protestantism. Luther took the position that the gospel needs no carnal weapons. Zwingli fell in the battle of Kappel (1531), clothed in the armor of a soldier. In a monument at Worms, he is shown with the Bible in one hand and the sword in the other. Thus striking was the contrast between Zwingli and Luther.

There has been a great deal of argument whether Zwingli was dependent upon Luther. Zwingli himself refused to be called a pupil of Luther, insisting that he had begun to preach the gospel in 1516, but he was acquainted with everything Luther wrote after 1518. He followed with interest what Luther wrote subsequent to the Leipzig Disputation of 1519,[4] the time from which the humanist Zwingli became more consciously a Reformer and was religiously deepened. Many of his expressions on sin, repentance and recourse to the grace of God in Christ sound to the reader like the thoughts of Luther. In his *Articles of Belief* there are many echoes of Lutheran ideas, for instance, the independence of the gospel from the official church (Art. 1); Christ as the only way of salvation (Arts. 2-5); and the insufficiency of our own works—only insofar as they are the works of Christ are ours good works (Arts. 7, 8, 14).

Zwingli, however, emphasized his independence of Luther: "I am not ready to bear the name of Luther, for I have received little from him. What I have read of his writings is generally founded in God's Word."[5] Zwingli could not avoid being influenced by such a writing as Luther's *Commentary on Galatians.* Seeberg remarks: "Zwingli started with the Erasmian ideas of reformation. This led him to the Scriptures. But it was Luther's range of ideas that continually guided him in his interpretation. At the central point of his apprehension of religious truth, Zwingli is dependent upon Luther."[6]

It was certainly true that Zwingli did not take over all the fundamental thoughts of Luther. He was too critical to do so. The hu-

---

[4] See Walther Koehler, *Ulrich Zwingli und die Reformation in der Schweiz;* pp. 60-61; cf. also Arthur Rich, *Die Anfänge der Theologie Huldrych Zwinglis* (1949).

[5] *Werke,* I, 254; *CR,* Vol. 89 (Zwingli, 2), pp. 145-46.

[6] Seeberg, *Lehrbuch,* IV, 356-57.

manistic-philosophical basis of his whole conception of Christianity asserted itself more and more, especially in his systematic writings. It has been advanced that Zwingli's reformation lacked the truly religious motives which meant so much to Luther. There are grains of truth in this statement. The difference between the two men is seen at such points as the following. Luther would not part with infant baptism, because baptism was the only means of bringing children to their Lord and Savior; Zwingli stressed that baptism was a means of supplying members for his folk church. Luther emphasized the doctrine of justification by faith because it brought peace to his soul; Zwingli stressed it because it was a weapon for destroying the Romish works of merit. Luther made much of the sacraments because to him they were veritable channels of grace; Zwingli retained them as outward marks of the Christian because Christ had instituted and commanded them. While all this and more must be admitted, it should not be overlooked that in the last analysis it was Zwingli's religious thoughts, as expressed in his conceptions of God, predestination, the Church, and the conditions of salvation that provided the driving power of his reformatory work. He was different from Luther in the building of his theological system.

What then was Zwingli's significance for the cause of the Reformation?

Zwingli never held the commanding position occupied by Luther. To the day of his death Luther remained the decisive authority for those who were associated with him. Even the hand of death did not chill his marvelous potency. His theological and religious influence was augmented with the passage of the years. With Zwingli it was different. He had many sympathizers, men like Oecolampadius, Leo Jud, Haller, Bullinger, and others; but they never considered him their leader. In his presence they felt themselves independent theologians and thinkers.

Neither can the literary production of Zwingli be compared with the fundamental significance of the writings of both Luther and Calvin. True, Zwingli wrote much and he wrote beautifully. "In Zwingli's writings there runs a muse whose loins are girt-up. Learned ballast is lacking. An unrestrained rhetorical diction holds the reader to the subject in a living manner from beginning to end. Rooted firmly in the present, the practical man wrote not for libraries but for living men whom he wished to influence." [7] The same writer states, "His writings procured for him no real spiritual leadership. They are all hastily manufactured products of the moment. One may marvel at the literary fruitfulness of Zwingli in the years from 1522 to 1531; but not one of his writings possesses monumental features." [8]

In more recent times, historians of the liberalistic trends have praised Zwingli as being the pioneer of modernistic ideas among the Reformers.[9] Measured by present-day tenets of modernism, Zwingli believed in the fundamentals of conservative Protestantism, including the divinity of Christ and his atonement as a vicarious sacrifice. The traits in his system that were different from the positions of Luther, Melanchthon, Calvin, Bullinger, Bucer, and others were bound to attract the attention of later, more liberal Protestantism. His stress upon reasonableness as a criterion of truth and his special interest in the things pertaining to this side of eternity were a symptom of his humanism. Luther's interest in humanism was limited to the formal matters in which this movement was fit to aid the gospel (such as language). Zwingli kept an interest in humanism as such. At a time when the other Reformers looked upon the Scriptures as the only source of truth, Zwingli co-ordinated the ideas of classical antiquity with the Bible on many occasions, insisting that Christianity has no exclusive claim upon what is true and good. While Christianity was to him the perfect religion, he insisted that the pagans had real religion and the opportunity to make themselves pleasing to God. To Luther, the fundamental dividing line between Christianity and paganism was a chasm that could not be bridged. Zwingli bridged the chasm with a wider conception of religion, which he put as a *tertium quid* and as a solution to a problem of the relation of Christianity and paganism.[10] To Zwingli it was not the sinfulness and guilt

[7] Paul Tschackert, *Die Entstehung der lutherischen und reformierten Kirchenlehre* (1911), I, 257.

[8] *Ibid.,* p. 229.

[9] This observation was made by Richard Rothe with his interest in a *Kulturprotestantismus,* Wilhelm Dilthey, and Ernst Troeltsch, professors of philosophy at Berlin University. Special mention should be made of the writings cited in our bibliography on Hulderich Zwingli by Professor W. Koehler, himself Reformed and a great admirer of Zwingli.

[10] See Rudolf Pfister, *Die Seligkeit erwählter Heiden bei Zwingli,* 1952.

of man's natural condition that invited divine grace, but rather the fact that man was the crown of creation and occupied an important place in God's cosmos.[11] Many historians examine Zwingli's teachings in order to point to him as the herald of modern tendencies. Zwingli's doctrine of man will be discussed further.

II. SOME CHARACTERISTICS OF ZWINGLI'S THEOLOGY

The Holy Scriptures

Zwingli wholeheartedly accepted the Reformation doctrine of *sola scriptura*. The principle that all doctrinal and ecclesiastical questions must be settled in accordance with the teaching or example of the Bible underlies his whole reforming program. Yet the student of Zwingli cannot fail to notice a fundamental difference between him and Luther. To Luther, Scripture, containing law and gospel, points out two different ways in which God deals with man. To Zwingli, this distinction means very little. The Word of God in both Testaments "is so alive and strong and powerful that all things have necessarily to obey it." [12] Revelation is intellectualized. "The word Gospel is equivalent of good news or tidings which God gives to men in matters in which they are either ignorant or doubtful." [13] The gospel gives man a sure knowledge of God.[14]

As the Word of God, Scripture is clear. It needs neither interpreters nor commentators.[15] Tradition is useless, if not downright harmful. Man must be taught by God. Strictly speaking, the spoken or material Word is no means of grace at all, let alone the sacraments.[16] This means that Zwingli did not regard Scripture merely as an external authority after the fashion of the late Scholastics, but instead his obedience to the Bible was grounded in an inward conviction of the divine

---

[11] See Koehler, *loc. cit.*
[12] "Of the Clarity and Certainty of the Word of God," *LCC,* XXIV, 71.
[13] *Ibid.,* p. 83.
[14] *Ibid.,* p. 86.
[15] *Ibid.,* p. 79.
[16] The position that the outward Word has the power "to bring with it its own inward enlightenment and assurance" (*ibid.,* p. 53), seems untenable to us. Compare, for example, the remark of Zwingli, "a channel or vehicle is not necessary to the Spirit"; *Ratio Fidei,* translated as "Reckoning of the Faith," *Book of Concord,* ed. H. E. Jacobs (Philadelphia: General Council, 1916), II, 168. Cf. R. E. Davies, *The Problem of Authority in the Continental Reformers* (1946), pp. 62 ff.

truth. Faith is not given through the Word, though the proclamation of the gospel usually precedes faith.

The Doctrine of God

Here we touch upon the centrality of Zwingli's system. The point of orientation—the point of departure—for Zwingli's entire structure of thought is this very doctrine. The word which succinctly characterizes his system is "theocentric." Zwingli would brook no meddling with the absolute sovereignty of God. His monotheism was very strict and unbending, with a tendency toward Unitarianism.[17] Zwingli had been driven to this position by his disgust at the pagan worship of the relics and images at the shrine of Einsiedeln. His diametrical reaction was to make the doctrine of God the center and core of all his thinking.

What then is God? He is the First Moving Cause, the Absolute Causality who occasions and cares for all things by his providence. Nothing ever happens by accident or by free will. As a consequence of this determinism, Zwingli declares that all evil, as well as all good, is due to the causality of God. This includes the fall of Adam. God cannot be accused of sin, since he does not stand under the law. "If in man there is absolutely no free counsel, then we are compelled to confess that thefts, murders, and all sorts of crimes are done by divine providence. For thus, I say, we acknowledge providence as caring for and accomplishing all things." [18] Nevertheless, "one and the same deed, say adultery or murder, is no crime insofar as it is the work of God its author, mover, and instigator; but insofar as it is the work of man, it is a crime and sin. For the former is not bound by the law, but the latter is indeed condemned by the law. For what God does, He does without hindrance; the other does it by an entire evil inclination." [19] Hence it is that "although God in the beginning knowingly and providently formed man who was to fall, nevertheless at the same time He decided to reveal His Son in human nature that He might repair the fall." [20]

[17] His acceptance of the trinitarian dogma was rather conventional, his biographers say. Cf. *PRE,* 21:814.

[18] *CR,* IV, 113.

[19] *Ibid.,* p. 112.

[20] Cf. his "Treatise on Providence," *ibid.,* p. 5.

The Doctrine of Man

Zwingli's view of man is dualistic or Platonic. While the body is by generation, the soul is directly from God. It is a vital substance. The soul not only has life in itself but gives life to the body the moment it enters its dwelling place. *Expressis verbis*, Zwingli accepts the Greek view of the soul as the form-giving energy ("entelechy") of the body.

Death does not affect the soul; it liberates the soul from its earthly prison. In death the body enters upon a state of sleep until the Last Day when it will be reunited with the soul. When Jesus said, "God is a God not of the dead but of the living" (Matt. 22:31-32), Zwingli maintains, Jesus was speaking not of the resurrection of the body but of the immortality of the soul.[21]

Zwingli's concept of sin is likewise colored by his humanism. Adam was created in a state of innocence, but he sinned and, in him, all mankind. Sin is disobedience. No longer is the sinner able to fulfill the will of God. Original sin is not damnatory; it is only "sickness" (*morbus est et conditio*), not guilt. "It is the infirmity and defect of shattered nature—a defect which one derives from birth without his own fault." [22] From the beginning God willed the fall in order to manifest his goodness in the elect.[23]

Predestination

The Augustinian heritage asserts itself most strongly in Zwingli's view of predestination. "I know," he says, "that the Supreme Divinity which is my God freely regulates all things; what He does is not dependent on any creature." [24]

For Zwingli the doctrine of predestination serves a double purpose. By emphasizing divine election as the only ground of salvation, Zwingli declines the Catholic view of merit as well as the Anabaptist estimate of believers' baptism as a sure sign of salvation.

Man's work is not meritorious, nor is man saved on account of his faith. Instead, God elects a man to eternal life regardless of that man's

---

[21] "Exposition of the Faith," *LCC,* XXIV, 273 ff. Cf. also the reference in Pfister, *op. cit.,* pp. 49 ff.

[22] Werke II, 287; *CR,* 91 (Zwingli, 4), 307.

[23] Jacobs, *op. cit.,* II, 162.

[24] *Ibid.*

ethical or religious qualities. Because God is free, he may choose children or even heathen. In his *Exposition of the Faith*, Zwingli included such heroes and worthies as Hercules, Theseus, Socrates, Aristides, Antigonus, Numa, Camillus, the Catos, and Scipios among the elect.[25] Zwingli was not ready to admit that such a view would nullify the work of Christ, as Luther and his friends maintained.[26] Zwingli was quite emphatic in stressing that Christ is the only way to the Father. Man is elected in Christ. This does not mean, according to Zwingli, that every elect person need have heard of Christ in his life. The elect who hear the gospel will respond in faith, and those who do not have this privilege will respond with a virtuous life, for the law is written upon the hearts of all men and the knowledge of God may precede the knowledge of Christ.[27] In Zwingli, the law is a part of the gospel, and the gospel, in his eyes, is a "new law." Christ is a believer's law.[28] It is evident that Augustinian and Erasmian ideas form the basis of Zwingli's view of election.[29]

Faith has only a peripheral significance in Zwingli's system. It is only a confirmatory sign of election. The elect are informed of election by means of God-instilled faith. True, Zwingli spoke of justification by faith; but he never had Luther's deep religious interest in that doctrine.[30]

Christology

In speaking of the person of Christ, Zwingli adhered strictly to his world-view, which distinguished rigidly between the divine and the human. It is true that in separating the two natures he maintained the unity of the person of Christ. He argued that the distinct properties and works of the two natures do not disrupt the unity of the person any more than body and soul constitute two persons in man. Nevertheless, he distinguished so strictly between the two natures that in the mind of the Lutherans he laid himself open to the charge of Nestorianism. Christ, after his ascent, is omnipresent according to

[25] *LCC*, XXIV, 275.
[26] Jacobs, *op. cit.*, II, 160 ff.; *LCC*, XXIV, 212 ff., 251 ff., 254 ff., *passim*.
[27] *Werke*, III, 180.
[28] *Ibid.*, I, 213.
[29] Cf. the many references in Pfister, *op. cit.*, especially pp. 65 ff.
[30] Cf. *LCC*, XXIV, 34.

his divinity; but according to his humanity, he is limited to a definite locality in heaven. In this language we miss the appreciation of the organic relation of the two natures in the living historic person of Christ. This divisive Christology was to appear with great force in a disruptive controversy over the Eucharist.[31]

In order to explain why Scripture often speaks of one nature of Christ in terms of the other nature, or ascribes the properties of one nature to the entire person, Zwingli, in his conflict with Luther, introduced his theory of the "interchange" or *alloiosis*—a figure of speech (*phrasis loquendi*) by which the Scriptures say one thing, but mean another. Luther criticized this method of interpretation sharply in his polemical writings against Zwingli.

The Church

The true Church is the company of the elect who have been predestined by God to eternal life. This Church is known to God alone. Those who are members of this Church know by faith that they are elect, but they remain ignorant of who the other members may be. The elect are secure and safe, for those who truly believe are ordained to eternal life. This Church includes many elect who do not have faith and who in this life may never hear the gospel.

The Church is also understood by Zwingli as the number of all who profess the name of Christ and participate in the sacraments. This Church is perceptible to the senses and is called the Church only in man's judgment. There are, according to Zwingli, two churches: the invisible Church, which comprehends only the elect, and the visible Church, which is composed of all who are enlisted under Christ and use the sacraments of the Church.[32]

Like Luther, Zwingli turned against the Anabaptists, who gathered only those people into their religious societies who could be shown to be saints. On the other hand, the difference between Zwingli and Luther is significant.[33] Zwingli failed to establish any intimate connection between the two churches. Some of these ideas found their way in modified form into Lutheranism through eighteenth-century pietism, the view that religious experience is a sure proof of salvation.

[31] Cf. the references cited in note 26, above.
[32] Jacobs, *op. cit.,* II, 166 ff., *passim.*
[33] Cf. pp. 355 ff.

Like Zwingli, the pietists tended to direct a troubled conscience to reflect on its own faith, "to have faith in faith," as if man were justified "on account of faith." [34]

The Sacraments

Christ, the head of the Church, has instituted certain rites which are to be administered by his Church: baptism and the Eucharist. The question is whether they are really means of grace. According to Zwingli, the sacraments can communicate nothing to the elect, for the elect are already assured of their election and salvation by their faith, and this certainty is strengthened for them by Christ, the infallible pledge. Why then were the sacraments instituted? They are "a sign of a sacred thing—i.e., of grace that has been given" previously to every individual.[35] By partaking of the sacraments the individual church member professes his membership. The sacraments are signs of union and allegiance by public profession. They are *Eidespflichte*, sacrificial and not sacramental in significance. The sacrament has no supernatural content; it is merely an external symbol of something which has already been accomplished inwardly.

Baptism, in particular, is the rite in which "the body is washed with the purest element; but by this it is signified that we have been gathered by the grace of divine goodness into the assembly of the Church and of the people of God, in which we must live uprightly and purely." Baptism is only a sign and symbol of an inner regeneration.[36] It is a pledge and covenant seal. "It is given and received for the sake of fellow-believers, not for a supposed effect upon those who receive it." [37] Nor is baptism "the confirmation of an existing faith in that which we have already learned and to which we are pledged." [38] This view of baptism caused a serious rift between Zwingli and some of his early supporters. Such men as Conrad Grebel and Felix Manz fully shared Zwingli's view of the immediacy of the Holy Spirit's work in

[34] According to Paul, man is justified "through faith" *dia pisteōs* or *ek pisteōs* or *pistei* (Rom. 3:21 ff.), but not "on account of faith." Christ is the sole causal ground of salvation, while faith is the organ or instrument by which man lays hold of Christ.

[35] Jacobs, *op. cit.*, II, 169.

[36] *Ibid.*

[37] *LCC*, XXIV, 136.

[38] *Ibid.*, p. 138.

the soul of man. They too regarded the sacraments as mere external rites. Luther was justified when he numbered Zwingli among these Enthusiasts. Differing from Zwingli, these "Swiss Brethren" nonetheless considered baptism the sign of existing faith. They rejected infant baptism as a meaningless ceremony, having no basis in Scripture. In their eyes, the Church was to be gathered anew in every generation from those who had been truly converted by the operation of the Holy Spirit. In such a Church there was no room for children, not even for those of believing parents. The first case of "believer's baptism" occurred on January 21, 1525. Lest the practice gain momentum, the council of Zurich took harsh measures against Grebel and his friends. In November, 1526, the city established death by drowning as the penalty for participation in the Anabaptist movement. The story of this movement belongs to Church history.

This conflict of Zwingli with Grebel and his friends over infant baptism was no less significant than Zwingli's conflict with Luther over the Lord's Supper. The rejection of infant baptism constitutes even today a more serious obstacle to Christian unity than the divergent opinion of Zwingli and Luther on the Lord's Supper. In addition, the conflict was a more tragic one from the personal point of view, for Grebel and Zwingli stood united on the basic presupposition of the Christian faith, namely, on the concept of the immediacy of the Holy Spirit's operation.[39]

The Eucharist is also a sign and symbol, in Zwingli's thought. At first Zwingli stood under the influence of Erasmus, the aristocratic humanist who was very anxious to maintain at least a semblance of identity with the approved doctrine of the Church. Both held to a certain Real Presence of the body of Christ. At the same time, the position was taken that only the common people, the "simple minded," had need of the sacrament. No change from this position is noticeable in Zwingli's early correspondence or in Thesis 18 of his *Schlussreden,* 1523.[40] Koehler points out four factors which contributed to bring about a change in the view of Zwingli: (1) the famous letter of the Dutch humanist, Honius, laid before Luther, suggesting that the

---

[39] Cf. the article on Conrad Grebel in *The Mennonite Encyclopedia* (Scottdale, Pa.: n.d.), II, 566 ff.

[40] See Schaff, *op. cit.,* III, 197 ff.

words "this is my body" be taken to mean "this signifies"; (2) the teaching of Karlstadt, and, as a result of it; (3) Luther's increasing emphasis on the real presence; and (4) Zwingli's break with Erasmus which removed him more decisively from the views of Romanism.[41] It was especially the letter from Honius that made a deep impression on Zwingli. He felt it as "flesh of his own flesh." Under the impact of this letter and the other factors referred to, Zwingli began to develop what is known as the symbolical interpretation of the Supper. He had already begun to look upon the Eucharist as a *Gemeinschafts-mahl* ("meal of fellowship") with Christ and fellow believers. More and more he stressed faith as the special constituent factor of the Supper. Christ in his humanity is present "not in essence and reality" but only "by the contemplation of faith." [42] That is to say: Christ is present only by means of the imaginative or pictorial power of faith. The external eating and drinking are only addenda to the inward eating and drinking. The outward transaction is a pictorial representation of the inward reality. The Eucharist is an act of profession and allegiance whereby we confess that we are adherents of Christ and members of his body. It is chiefly a memorial, which we celebrate in remembrance of Christ's death and by which we show forth that death. Finally it is a thanksgiving (*eucharistia*) to God for the gift of his Son and his redeeming work.

Zwingli, being guided by several considerations, kept away from any doctrine of a real-presence: (1) Scripture declares that "the flesh profiteth nothing" (John 6:63-64). As a matter of fact, his whole argument revolved about this particular passage of the New Testament. (2) His world-view would not permit any close conjunction of the heavenly and the earthly. (3) His Christology maintained that the humanity of Christ is limited to a definite place in heaven. In his divinity, of course, Christ is omnipresent in heaven and upon earth; but in his humanity he is limited to the same conditions as other creatures. He cannot be present in the Supper according to his human nature because in this he is tied to "the right hand of God" in heaven. Calvin later found himself in agreement with Zwingli. The

---

[41] Walter Koehler, *Zwingli und Luther, ihr Streit über das Abendmahl* (1924), Vol. I.

[42] Jacobs, *op. cit.,* II, 170.

cases in Scripture where divine attributes such as omnipresence, omnipotence, and omniscience are predicated of Christ's humanity must be interpreted by the *alloiosis*. Zwingli's caricatures of those who believed in the real presence were very coarse. He called such people "flesh-eaters" and "blood-drinkers," and he referred to the Lutherans in words which compared them to the Israelites who lusted after the fleshpots of Egypt.

At the Marburg Colloquy (1529) there were differences between Luther and Zwingli besides the one on the Lord's Supper. Zwingli, at that time, accommodated himself to the well-known positions of Luther to such an extent that he subscribed to the Marburg Articles,[43] which codified many points of agreement. Luther was not able to accept Zwingli's hand of fellowship because, under the circumstances, this would have been a declaration on his part that he looked upon the disagreement concerning the Lord's Supper as a matter of indifference. It is a mistake to believe that Luther expressed ill feeling toward the Zwinglians. In a thorough investigation, Hans von Schubert has pointed out the peaceful, cordial, and hopeful mood in which Luther found himself at the close of this colloquy. The much-quoted remark, "Ye have another spirit than we," was a purely objective statement and not spoken in a spirit of invective. In letters written at that time —for instance, to his wife—Luther expressed hope for a growing union to extend also to the difference on the Lord's Supper.[44]

We may briefly summarize the difference between Zwingli and Luther as follows:

(1) *The relation of the two natures in the person of Christ.* Zwingli inclined to the Nestorianizing, a side-by-side relation between the divine and the human in the historic Christ, after the fashion of the Antiochean School (Theodore of Mopsuestia). Luther, on the other hand, stood for the organic, personal union, following the Alexandrian School (Cyril).

(2) *The Word of God.* Zwingli emphasized the "inner" Word

---

[43] See text of the Marburg Articles in Jacobs, *op. cit.,* II, 69 ff.; also in H. Sasse, *This Is My Body* (Minneapolis: Augsburg Publishing House, 1959), pp. 269 ff.

[44] See pp. 381-82. Cf. also Hans von Schubert, *Bekenntnisbildung und Religionspolitik, 1529-1530* (1910).

with a concession to tenets of the Anabaptists, which made Luther stress the written and spoken Word.

(3) *Man's natural depravity*. Zwingli would only admit a weakness in man which does not become real sin until it results in sinful acts. Luther insisted that this natural, sinful condition is the real, special sin of mankind. This difference affected the conception of infant baptism.

(4) *The conception of infant baptism*. To Zwingli, baptism was a badge of recognition as a Christian, a kind of initiation into the Church. To Luther, baptism was a sacrament of regeneration, of forgiveness of sin, and of an imputation of Christ's righteousness.

Although there was a great deal of agreement between the two men with respect to justification by faith and good works, Zwingli's humanistic approach to the inner problems of religion differed from Luther's doctrine of sin and grace.[45]

Reformed Confessions Influenced by Zwingli

At this point we shall list the oldest confessions of the Swiss Reformation. They do not have the importance for the Reformed churches that the Augsburg Confession has for the Lutheran church. The interest of the Reformed is in their later confessions that emerged under the influence of Calvin. The four confessions issuing from the Swiss Reformation influenced by Zwingli are:

(1) *The Sixty-seven Articles* (Schlussreden), 1523. These Articles resemble the Ninety-five Theses of Luther, 1517, "but they mark a considerable advance in Protestant conviction."[46] They firmly maintain the primacy of Scripture over against the Church and proclaim faith in Christ as the only way to salvation. In addition, they attack the primacy of the pope, the sacrifice of the mass, fasts, pilgrimages, etc.[47]

(2) *The Ten Theses of Berne*, 1528. This brief document was written by two theologians of Berne and revised at their request. It was

---

[45] Cf. J. L. Neve, *Story and Significance of the Augsburg Confession* (Burlington, Iowa: Lutheran Literature Board, Inc., 1930), p. 46.

[46] Schaff, *op. cit.*, I, 364.

[47] For the full text of the first two confessions, see *ibid.*, III, 197 ff. Cf. the introductory remarks in *ibid.*, I, 363 ff. A comprehensive edition of all Reformed confessions was made by Karl Mueller, *Die Bekenntnisschriften der Reformierten Kirche* (1903).

published by Zwingli. Broadly speaking, the Theses reaffirm the anti-Roman theology of the Sixty-seven Articles of Zwingli, but also reject the real presence of Luther and his defense of pictures in churches as set forth in his writing, *Against the Heavenly Prophets in the Matter of Images and Sacraments*, 1525.[48]

(3) *The Reckoning of the Faith* (Ratio fidei) presented to Emperor Charles V at Augsburg, 1530. In twelve articles Zwingli declared his faith in the orthodox doctrines of the Trinity and the person of Christ as laid down in the Nicene and Athanasian Creeds. He also committed himself on the doctrine of election, the meritorious work of Christ, and the nature of the Church and of the sacraments. He rejected images and the doctrine of purgatory. In such matters as original sin and the sacraments, he departed much further from traditional theology than the Lutherans. On the other hand, he protested against being identified with the Anabaptists, affirming his belief in a Christian society and in government as a holy office ordained by God.[49]

(4) *The Exposition of the Christian Faith*, dedicated to King Francis I, 1531. Writing three months before his death and in bold language, Zwingli set forth his understanding of the Christian faith on basically the same topics and in the same spirit as in the previous document.[50]

Following the premature death of Zwingli in 1531, but preceding the age of Calvin, a number of confessions were composed which were a little nearer to Lutheranism, due largely to the union efforts of the Strassburg Reformers, Bucer and Capito.

(1) *The First Confession of Basel*, 1534, was written by Oecolampadius and revised in its present form by Oswald Myconius. It re-emphasized in twelve articles Zwingli's theology in its anti-Roman and anti-Anabaptist form. As for the Lord's Supper, a slight concession was made to Lutheranism, inasmuch as Bucer's interpretation of the Supper (Christ as food of the soul) was recognized.[51]

---

[48] *LW*, 40:73 ff.

[49] See the English text in Jacobs, *op. cit.*, II, 160 ff. Cf. also the introductory discussion in Schaff, *op. cit.*, I, 366 ff.

[50] The English text is given in *LCC*, XXIV, 245 ff. Cf. Schaff, *op. cit.*, I, 368-69.

[51] The text is omitted in Schaff, *op. cit.*, but compare his discussion of this confession in *ibid.*, I, 386 ff.

(2) *The Second Confession of Basel,* better known as the *First Helvetic Confession,* was drawn up by Bullinger, Myconius, and others in 1536. It is the first confession to express the faith of all the Reformed cantons of Switzerland. It is the Swiss counterpart of the Wittenberg Concord, which the Swiss refused to sign. It consists of twenty-seven articles. Its doctrine of the sacraments is essentially Zwinglian, but like the first Confession of Basel, it employs the sacramental language of Bucer.[52]

(3) Anticipating later development, we must also include here the *Second Helvetic Confession,* the final confession of the Zwinglian family. It was composed by Bullinger in the later years of his life (1562) for his own use, and published in a revised form at the request of Frederick III, Elector of the Palatinate, in 1566. Of all the Continental Reformed symbols, this is the most widely adopted and the most authoritative with the exception of the *Heidelberg Catechism.* It is a lengthy document of thirty articles. It opens with a statement on the Holy Scriptures. The Apocrypha are excluded from the canon (Art. I, Sec. 9).[53] Concerning man in his fallen state, this confession evades the doctrine of total depravity. Man is said not to have been turned "into a stone or stock," an expression found in Article II of the Lutheran Formula of Concord. Man sins willingly (Art. IX). Predestination is single. God has from eternity elected the saints whom he will save in Christ (Art. X). In the doctrine of the sacraments the influence of Bucer and Calvin is very evident: the sacraments are defined as signs and seals of God's promises for us as well as pledges on man's part to consecrate himself to God. They consist of three things: the Word, the thing, and the thing signified (Art. XIX).[54]

[52] See the Latin and German text in *ibid.,* III, 211 ff., with introduction, I, 388 ff.

[53] Schaff is not quite correct when he says that this is the first exclusion of the Apocrypha from the canon (*op. cit.,* I, 396). *The French Confession,* 1559 (Art. III) and the *Belgic Confession,* 1561 (Art. IV and V) both enumerate the traditional sixty-six writings of the Bible as the sure and sole rule of faith. *The Belgic Confession* (Art. VI) includes an enumeration of the apocryphal writings, stating that these do not possess the dignity of canonicity. Unlike these and other Calvinist symbols, the Lutheran confessions do not contain a single article on the inspiration and the canon of Scripture.

[54] Schaff, *op. cit.,* I, 390 ff., in addition to an excellent introduction gives an English translation of the *Second Helvetic Confession* in an abbreviated form. The Latin text is given in full in III, 233 ff.

BIBLIOGRAPHY

Works

Published by Melchior Schuler and Johannes Schulthess, 8 vols. Zurich, 1828–.

Critical edition in the *Corpus Reformatorum*. 1905–.

Selected Works

Edited by S. M. JACKSON *et al.* 3 vols. 1912–.

LCC, Vol. XXIV.

Research on Zwingli

BURCKHARDT, P. *Huldreich Zwingli: eine Darstellung seiner Persönlichkeit und seines Lebenswerkes.* 1918.

COURVOISIER, JACQUES. *Zwingli.* Geneva, 1947.

FARNER, OSKAR. *H. Zwingli.* 3 vols. 1943–.

———. *Zwingli the Reformer: His Life and Work.* Translated by D. G. SEAR. New York: Philosophical Library, 1952.

FINSLER, G. *Ulrich Zwingli.* 1873.

———. *Zwingli Bibliographie.* 1897.

HUNDESHAGEN, K. B. *Beiträge zur Kirchenverfassungesgeschichte.* 1864.

JACKSON, S. M. *H. Zwingli, the Reformer of German Switzerland.* New York: G. P. Putnam's Sons, 1901.

KOEHLER, W. *Ulrich Zwingli und die Reformation in der Schweiz.* 1919.

———. *Huldrych Zwingli.* 1943. 2nd ed., 1952.

LOCHER, G. W. *Die Theologie H. Zwinglis im Lichte seiner Christologie.* 1952.

MOERIKOFER, J. K. *Huldreich Zwingli nach den urkundlichen Quellen.* 2 vols. 1867–.

RICH, ARTHUR. *Die Anfänge der Theologie H. Zwinglis.* 1941.

SIMPSON, SAMUEL. *U. Zwingli, the Swiss Patriot and Reformer.* London: Hodder and Stoughton, 1902.

STAEHELIN, R. *Huldreich Zwingli: Sein Leben und Wirken.* 2 vols. 1895 and 1897.

ZELLER, E. *Das theologische System Zwinglis.* 1853.

CHAPTER III

THE EUCHARISTIC CONTROVERSY

The controversy over the Lord's Supper between Luther and Zwingli was to some extent a revival of the difference between the realistic and spiritualistic conception of the sacrament in the previous history of the Church.[1] Throughout his life Luther was a believer in the realistic conception, although there was a time in his development when, in his antipathy to the pope, he might have been open to some kind of a symbolical interpretation. In a letter addressed to the people of Strassburg, in 1524, he admits that if Karlstadt or someone else had told him five years before that in the sacrament there is nothing more than bread and wine, he would have rendered him a great service. "For I was well aware," he continues, "that by these means I could strike the hardest blow against the papacy. . . . But I am captured by the Word of God and cannot find a way out. The words are there and are too strong for me." [2] The source of Luther's teaching on the sacrament is the Word of God, not the heritage received from the Middle Ages.

The first signs of criticism of the Roman dogma appear in connection with the dispute on the indulgences. According to the teaching of Rome, a sacrament is effective *ex opere operato*, as an ordinance ordained by God, provided the recipient does not obviate the effect by an actual sin or by the intention to commit a sin. Luther rejected this doctrine as early as 1518. "Not the sacrament but the faith of the sacrament justifies." [3] Unbelief is the real *obex* ("bar, impediment") which renders a sacrament ineffective. Neither the elements nor the

---

[1] See pp. 219 ff., 250 ff.

[2] *WA*, 15:394. Cf. the whole passage in Hermann Sasse, *This Is My Body* (Minneapolis: Augsburg Publishing House, 1959), p. 81.

[3] *WA*, 1:324, 544. Cf. Sasse, *op. cit.*, p. 83.

rite avail anything unless the bread and wine are received in faith. This does not mean that Luther denied the objective character of the sacrament. It is valid as an ordinance of Christ, yet efficacious for salvation only if received in faith.

About two years later Luther began to object to the Roman doctrine of the mass as a sacrifice. As time progressed the sacrificial aspect of the mass became the main target of his criticism. The first evidence is found in the *Treatise on the New Testament*, published in August, 1520. "We must let the mass be a sacrament and testament, it is not and cannot be sacrifice." [4] We should give our spiritual sacrifices, ourselves and all that we have in the mass. Although such sacrifices do occur even apart from the mass, "yet it is more mighty and more acceptable" when it takes place in the assembly of believers.[5] To be sure, we are not to present such a sacrifice before God "in our own person"—Luther is very anxious to eliminate the idea of human merits —"but we are to lay it on Christ and let him present it." [6] In short, "we do not offer Christ as a sacrifice, but Christ offers us." [7]

In his famous writing *On the Babylonian Captivity of the Church* (1520), Luther sees the "captivity" of the "sacrament of the bread" first in withholding the cup from the laity, next in the doctrine of transubstantiation, and finally in the interpretation of the mass as a sacrifice. This, he adds, "is the most wicked abuse of all . . . and . . . has brought an endless host of others in its train." [8]

The Reformer continued his criticism of this third captivity of the Supper especially in *The Misuse of the Mass* (1521)[9] and in *The Abomination of the Secret Mass* (1525).[10] Finally, in the *Smalcald Articles* (1537), which the Lutheran church received into the *Book of Concord*, Luther calls the mass, among other things, "the most precious papal idolatry," "the dragon's tail" that has brought forth "a brood of vermin and the poison of manifold idolatries" (the doctrines of purgatory, of indulgences, etc.).[11]

---

[4] *PE*, 1:312.
[5] *PE*, 1:313.
[6] *PE*, 1:314.
[7] *Ibid.*
[8] *PE*, 2:186 ff.
[9] *LW*, 36:127 ff.
[10] *LW*, 36:307 ff.
[11] "Smalcald Articles," Part II, Art. II, *Book of Concord,* ed. Theodore G. Tappert (Philadelphia, Muhlenberg Press, 1959), pp. 293 ff.

Closely connected with the rejection of the mass as a sacrifice is Luther's objection to the doctrine of transubstantiation. In the *Babylonian Captivity* he repudiates this doctrine as a Thomistic opinion conditioned by Aristotelian metaphysics. It has no foundation in Scripture, he says. As the human nature is not transubstantiated in the incarnation, so in the Supper the elements remain unchanged. The real presence remains. The intellect may not grasp this presence, but faith will. As to his own view, Luther says that Pierre d'Ailli has given him much food for thought. D'Ailli taught, like his master Occam, that the substance of bread and wine remain as well as their accidents. "At the same time," Luther concludes, "I permit other men to follow the other opinion." [12] Such a matter should not be made an article of faith.

In the meantime a new movement began to make its influence felt in Luther's homeland. While the Reformer was detained at Wartburg, representatives of "the theology of the inner light" made their appearance in Wittenberg in December, 1521. Luther called them *Schwärmer*. They advocated radical social measures to usher in the kingdom of Christ (Thomas Muenzer and others).[13] In Wittenberg they were joined by Karlstadt, a colleague of Luther at the university, who soon became outspoken in his rejection of the sacramental character of the Supper. Having been expelled from Saxony, Karlstadt found refuge in southern Germany and eventually in Basel where his anti-Lutheran tracts were secretly printed.[14] In these tracts Karlstadt mainly set forth two things. First, the Supper is not a sacrament. It neither offers forgiveness of sins nor is a pledge of the forgiveness of sins. Its meaning is purely memorial. Second, in the institution of the Supper Jesus intended to say "Take and eat this bread, this do in remembrance of me." By the word "this," Jesus pointed to his own body as if he were saying "here sits the body that will be given for you." Concern over this controversy was felt in Strassburg, and when approached by seven Strassburg preachers,[15] Luther replied with

---

[12] *PE*, 2:187 ff.

[13] See Karl Holl, *Gesammelte Aufsätze zur Kirchengeschichte*, pp. 420 ff.

[14] The text is printed in *D. Martin Luthers sämmtliche Schriften,* ed. Johann Georg Walch in modern German (St. Louis, 1880-1910), hereinafter referred to as *ST. L.,* XX (1890), 92 ff., 2306 ff., 2312 ff.

[15] *WA, Briefwechsel,* 3:381 ff.

his *Letter to the Christians at Strassburg in Opposition to the Fanatic Spirit* (1524).[16] Feeling the necessity of a more comprehensive refutation Luther wrote *Against the Heavenly Prophets in the Matter of Images and Sacraments*[17] late in December, 1524, and in January, 1525. He sensed that Karlstadt's subjectivism would end in a denial of the Christian faith as founded on Scripture. The Bible, he emphasized, is the ground of faith and "we are not to deviate from the words as they stand, nor from the order in which they stand."[18] In addition, God deals with us in the gospel in a twofold manner: outwardly through the oral word and through material signs; inwardly through the Holy Spirit, faith, and other gifts. The outward factors must precede, for the inward experience is effected by the outward.[19] As to the Supper, Christ has placed "the strength and power of his suffering in the sacrament, so that there we lay hold on it and find it according to the word, 'This is My body given for you for the forgiveness of sins.' "[20]

Karlstadt's criticism of Luther made a deep impression on Zwingli and the men who inaugurated the Anabaptist movement. This started the first great conflict over the Lord's Supper. In the eyes of the Swiss, Luther's Reformation was a half-way Reformation because he retained the "Catholic" doctrine of the real presence and the concept of the sacraments as real means of grace. From the Wittenberg point of view, Zwingli was a *Schwärmer*, like the Anabaptists, since for them the sacraments were mere signs of that divine grace which is bestowed by God independently of the outward words as well as of the sacramental elements.

Johannes Bugenhagen, in the fall of 1525, was the first of the Wittenberg theologians to attack Zwingli openly.[21] Meanwhile, Oecolampadius of Basel tried to win over the cities in southwestern Germany to Zwingli's cause.[22] His own interpretation, however, differed slightly from that of Zwingli. He argued that, since Jesus spoke in Aramaic, a language which does not have the copula *est*, the trope

[16] *LW*, 40:61 ff.
[17] *LW*, 40:73 ff.
[18] *LW*, 40:157.
[19] *LW*, 40:146.
[20] *LW*, 40:210.
[21] *St. L.*, 20:500-501.
[22] Cf. Sasse, *op. cit.*, pp. 140-41.

is to be found not in the *est*, as Zwingli had said, but rather in the word *corpus*. The words of Jesus do not mean "this signifies my body" but rather they are to be understood as "this is the figure of my body." The Lutheran sentiment in this part of the country found its expression in the so-called *Syngramma Suevicum* written in 1525 by Johannes Brenz and signed by fourteen pastors of Swabia.[23] The *Syngramma* clearly teaches not only the real presence but also the *manducatio indignorum*, that the worthy and the unworthy alike receive the body of Christ.

So far there had been no direct conflict between Luther and Zwingli, although each had referred to the other in occasional remarks. At the request of Oecolampadius and his friends in southern Germany, Zwingli began the fight with his *Amica exegesis, id est expositio eucharistiae negotii ad Martinum Lutherum*[24] and a German article[25] against Luther's *Sermon on the Sacrament of the Body and Blood of Christ against the Enthusiasts*, written in March, 1526.[26] Zwingli saw the Anti-Christ at work in Luther's interpretation of the Supper and was convinced that he would prevail if Luther "continued to offer stubborn resistance." Luther's reply was his treatise, *Dass diese Worte Christi: Das ist mein Leib, noch feststehen, wider die Schwarmgeister*[27] ("That These Words of Christ, 'This is my body,' Still Stand Firm Against the Fanatics"). This book drew a reply from Zwingli in June 1527, entitled *Dass diese Worte, Das ist mein Leib, ewiglich den alten Sinn haben werden*[28] ("That These Words, 'This is my body,' Shall Forever Retain Their Old Meaning"). In March, 1528, Luther published his famous *Grosses Bekenntnis vom Abendmahl*[29] ("Larger Confession of the Lord's Supper"). Zwingli and Oecolampadius closed the controversy with a common reply in August, 1528.[30]

In the following discussion the contents of these separate writings are not given in detail; rather, an attempt is made to understand the

[23] See the text in *St. L.,* 20:520 ff.
[24] *Werke, CR,* 3:459 ff.
[25] *Ibid.*
[26] *WA,* 19:482 ff. (*LW,* 36:331 ff.).
[27] *WA,* 23:38 ff. (*LW,* 37:3 ff.).
[28] *Werke, CR,* 2 b:16 ff.; *St. L.,* 20, 1122 ff.
[29] *WA,* 26:241 ff.
[30] *Werke, CR.* 2 b:94 ff.; *St. L.,* 20:1228 ff.

arguments put forward by either party.[31] To begin with, Luther and Zwingli had much in common. Both were men of the Bible and both regarded the Bible as powerful, certain, and clear.[32] Luther was well aware of the fact that Scripture frequently uses symbolical language, and Zwingli recognized the fact that the words of Scripture are frequently to be understood in their literal sense. Why then did they differ with respect to the solemn words of Christ, "This is my body"? In the last analysis, the difference between the two Reformers is not an exegetical one. Instead, the divergent views reveal a fundamentally different approach to the truth of the gospel.

Zwingli's objections to Luther can be summarized under two main propositions: (1) the real presence is unnecessary; (2) it is impossible. A figurative understanding of the words of institution is necessary, Zwingli maintains, or else an absurdity, or even several absurdities, would arise. For Zwingli the greatest of these absurdities is the idea that bodily eating and drinking can have a spiritual effect. Neither the outward words nor the sacramental elements can convey the Spirit. *Finitum non est capax infiniti!* A channel or vehicle is not necessary for the Spirit.[33] The Spirit contacts the soul directly. The sacraments neither convey nor distribute the grace of God. Bodily eating profits nothing (John 6:63), let alone gives such spiritual blessings as forgiveness of sins. To eat his body means to believe in him who gave his flesh on the cross.[34] Zwingli does not explain the words of institution by themselves, as Luther did, but rather on the basis of other passages, for instance, I Cor. 10:1 ff. and especially John 6 in which, as he himself admits, there is no reference to the sacrament.[35]

Luther, on the other hand, maintains that the sacrament is *des Herren Abendmahl, nicht der Christen Abendmahl* ("the Lord's Supper, not the Church's supper").[36] In obedience to Christ, we are bound to honor God and believe his words and not to question the necessity or possibility of eating the body of Christ. God always

---

[31] Cf. Sasse, *op. cit.,* pp. 144 ff.
[32] See, for example, Zwingli's "Of the Clarity and Certainty of the Word of God," *LCC,* XXIV, 29 ff.
[33] Jacobs, *Book of Concord,* II, 168.
[34] *LCC,* XXIV, 198.
[35] *Ibid.,* pp. 211 ff.
[36] *WA,* 23:278 (*LW,* 37:142).

works and manifests himself through an outward sign. The flesh of Christ, indeed, avails much. It is an incorruptible, immortal, and imperishable flesh. The words of institution are clear. Their literal meaning must stand unless a clear article of the Christian faith would necessitate a symbolical interpretation of them. Christ's words, "This is my body," are the whole gospel.[37]

There is a close affinity between the incarnation and the Supper in Luther's thought. To him both are an expression of Christ's descent to the very level of sinful man. The glory of our God, Luther says, is precisely this, that "for our sake, He lowers Himself to the deepest depth, into the flesh, into the bread, into our mouth, heart and bosom."[38] Like baptism,[39] the Eucharist bears witness to the totality of our redemption. "If one eats Him spiritually through the Word, He remains spiritually in us, in our soul. If one eats Him bodily, He remains bodily in us and we in Him. For He is neither digested nor transformed by us; rather He transforms us unceasingly, the soul into righteousness, the body into immortality."[40] In the light of Luther's total view of the sacrament this remark must not be interpreted in the manner of the Greek Fathers. Luther does not teach that the earthly elements are a *pharmakon tēs athanasias* ("medicine of immortality"). What he wants to stress is that both soul and body are delivered by Christ from the power of sin, of death, and the devil. Since the incarnate Christ is both the giver and the gift of the sacrament, we, as spiritual-bodily beings, receive him as the spiritual-bodily Christ.[41]

Next to the absurdity that bodily eating and drinking can help the soul, in the eyes of Zwingli, is the absurdity that the body of Christ can be present in this world. Scripture, as well as the creeds, plainly declares that "He ascended into heaven, and sitteth on the right hand of God the Father Almighty." If he were present in the bread "then the Last Day has already come. . . . He is already seated on the judgment throne."[42] "The flesh may fume but the words of Christ

[37] *LW*, 36:288.
[38] *WA*, 23:157.
[39] Cf. Large Catechism, Part IV, 44-45.
[40] *EA*, 30:133. Cf. Ernst Sommerlath, *Der Sinn des Abendmahls* (1930), pp. 82 ff.
[41] Cf. Prenter, *Spiritus Creator*, p. 277.
[42] *LCC*, XXIV, 216.

stand firm; He sits at the right hand of the Father, He has left the world, He is no longer present with us.[43]

Zwingli believes in a qualitative difference between the divine and the human nature of Christ and, unlike Luther, is not willing to admit an exchange of properties (*communicatio idiomatum*). According to his divine nature, Christ never left the right hand of God, and with his human nature, he ascended into heaven, which in the eyes of Zwingli and the medieval Schoolmen, is a place.[44] Sasse puts the problem very aptly:

> The obvious weakness of his Christology is the inability to see the real unity of the God-man. Zwingli was not a Nestorian, just as Luther was not a Monophysite. But within the framework of the Chalcedonian Creed Zwingli came close to the Nestorian doctrine which, while emphasizing the two natures, was unable to say how these two natures could be in one person.[45]

In answering the objections of Zwingli, Luther developed what became known as the doctrine of the "ubiquity" of the body of Christ. In his treatise on *The Adoration of the Sacrament* (1523), he said that "the body which you receive, the Word which you hear, are the Word and body of Him who holds the whole world in His hand and who inhabits it from the beginning to end (*an allen Enden*, i.e. everywhere)".[46] If the divine and human natures in the person of Christ are inseparably united, it would follow that his human nature must share the omnipresence of his divine nature. The right hand of God to which Jesus ascended is not a local right hand. Like John of Damascus,[47] Luther understands the right hand of God to mean the glory and power of the Godhead in which the Son participates as God and *homoousios* with the Father.[48]

Luther speaks of the presence of God in a twofold sense. God is present everywhere. As Creator and Lord, he is above the universe

---

[43] *Ibid.*, 214.
[44] *Ibid.*, 212-13.
[45] Sasse, *op. cit.*, p. 150.
[46] *WA*, 11:450; *LW*, 36:298.
[47] *On the Orthodox Faith*, IV, 2. Sasse remarks, "It is interesting to observe that Luther here, as in other points of the Eucharistic doctrine (e.g., about the fruit of the sacrament) comes nearer to the Eastern fathers, while Zwingli and Calvin remain dependent on the early Augustine" (*op. cit.*, p. 159).
[48] "The right hand of God is the almighty power of God which at one and the same time can be nowhere and yet must be everywhere." *LW*, 37:57. Cf. *WA*, 23:133.

and its limitations. God's omnipresence is shared by the eternal Logos. In the incarnation, the Logos lost none of his divine attributes but imparted them to his human nature. Although God is everywhere, he cannot be found everywhere, at least not as the God of love and grace. There is a significant difference between his omnipresence and his "presence for us." As the God of mercy, he is found only where he wants himself to be found: in the manger, on the cross, in his Word, and in the sacramental elements.

There are two characteristics of this presence of God. First, it is realized in the visible, earthly means of creation, that is, in the humanity of Christ, in the water of baptism, and in the bread and wine of the Supper. Second, under these means the revelation of God remains hidden because these means are an offense to reason. God's revelation can be received and given only in faith and to faith. As the cross would avail us nothing without the Word of God, so the sacramental signs are all in vain if the Word is absent.[49] Hence apart from the celebration there is no sacrament (*extra usum nullum sacramentum*).

If his opponents assert that the ubiquity of the body of Christ is impossible, Luther calls attention to the fact that even philosophy recognizes more modes than that which is called the "local" or "circumscriptive." This mode of presence belongs to a physical body. The circumference of the body coincides with the boundary of the space that it fills. But the presence of Christ in the Supper is not of that kind. In addition to the local presence, even the theologians of the Middle Ages, like Thomas,[50] recognized another presence, the *praesentia definitiva*. This doctrine found its final form in the teaching of Occam, whose theory Luther explains in the Large Confession as follows: (1) The body of Christ may be present in a corporeal, circumscriptive way as was the case when Jesus walked bodily on earth. "He can still employ this mode of presence when He wills to do so, as He did after His resurrection and as He will do on the Last Day."[51] (2) Christ also possesses the incomprehensible, spiritual mode of presence (*praesentia definitiva or diffinitiva*) according to which "He neither occupies nor vacates space, but penetrates every creature,

[49] *LW*, 40:212-13.
[50] See Sasse, *op. cit.*, pp. 48-49, 156.
[51] *WA*, 26:335; *LW*, 37:222.

whenever He wills." [52] Jesus employed this mode of presence when he left the sealed tomb and came through locked doors. According to this mode, he was also present in the bread and wine on the night when he instituted the sacrament; for the glorification of Jesus began, according to Luther, not with his resurrection and exaltation, but with the incarnation. (3) Since Christ is one person with God, he also possesses the divine, heavenly mode of presence (*praesentia repletiva*). According to this mode, Christ transcends all creatures and at the same time is in all creatures.

Luther concludes his argument by saying that he does not wish to deny that God has more than these three modes whereby Christ's body can be present wherever he wants to be present. Luther does not regard his own answer as exhaustive or dogmatic in nature. Against the background of the commonly held conception of heaven as a space within the universe, Luther wanted to show that it is not impossible, as Zwingli had said, for the body of Christ to be present in the Supper.[53] Because of the incarnation, Jesus is true God and true man in one person, and the right hand of God is not a place, but a position of eminence. These are the truths which Luther tries to uphold.

Christ is "substantially" present in the Supper. However, Luther used the term "substance" not in the static sense as if "something" accedes to the sacramental elements. He did not teach a temporary union of two substances. To Luther substance is a dynamic term, signifying *ens in actu* ("being in action"). To say that Christ is "substantially" present means for Luther that he is personally present. Neither consubstantiation nor impanation adequately expresses Luther's view.[54] The Lutheran formula "in, with, and under" has a limiting significance. It expresses positively an instrumental relationship between the elements of the sacrament and the actual self-

---

[52] *WA, loc. cit.; LW, loc. cit.*

[53] *WA*, 26:336-37; *LW*, 37:223. Cf. the Formula of Concord, Art. VII ("Solid Declaration"), ll. 94 ff., in Tappert, *op. cit.*, pp. 386-87.

[54] Cf. Genrich, *Die Christologie Luthers im Abendmahlstreit* (1929), pp. 69 ff. The term "consubstantiation" is nowhere found in Luther, nor does the Formula of Concord (Art. VII) so interpret the Reformer's doctrine. A discussion as found in Occam on how a "substance can be a quantum without a quantity" does not occur in Luther (T. Bruce Birch, *op. cit.*, pp. 339 ff.).

communication of Christ. The union is an *unio sacramentalis*.[55] The real presence is not localized in the host (against Rome); nor is it actualized by a contemplation of faith (against Zwingli).

How can the bread be called the body of Christ if it remains natural bread? Luther answered this question by referring to the figure of speech called synecdoche. Just as a mother, pointing to the cradle in which her baby lies, says, "This is my child" so, Luther maintains, we say of the bread, "This is the body of Christ." Zwingli and others objected that Luther did not understand the sacramental words literally. They argued that to say the body of Christ is in, with, and under the bread, is not the same as to say that this *is* the body of Christ. Luther maintained that the synecdoche takes the reality of the body as well as the reality of the bread seriously, just as Paul was serious when he addressed the Corinthians and Galatians as the Church of God, though not all members of those churches were true children of God.[56]

In Luther's thought, the Word and the sacramental action are inseparable. There is no sacrament without the Word nor without the eating and drinking. In the rite the words of institution are not merely informatory, as the Zwinglians held, nor does the recitation of these words "make" the real presence. They proclaim and reveal the omnipresent body and blood of Christ as the God-appointed means of man's salvation.[57]

At the invitation of Landgrave Philip of Hesse, both parties met at Marburg, in October, 1529, to discuss their differences.[58] Before parting, they signed articles that had been drafted by Luther, dealing with such fundamentals as the Trinity, the two natures of Christ, original sin, faith, justification, baptism, absolution, civil government, ecclesiastical traditions, and the Lord's Supper.[59] With respect to the

[55] Formula of Concord, Art. VII, 35. Cf. Luther's statement: *in usu, non in objecto, spiritus est;* i.e., a material and outward thing becomes spiritual when it is done in the Word (*WA*, 23, 189).

[56] *WA*, 18:187 (*LW*, 40:197); *WA*, 26, 444.

[57] On the proper meaning of consecration, Luther remained inconsistent. Cf. in Vajta, *op. cit.*, pp. 100-101, n. 62 and Sasse, *op. cit.*, pp. 164 ff., 371.

[58] The most recent attempt to reconstruct the colloquy was made by Walter Koehler, *Das Marburger Religionsgespräch 1529, Versuch einer Rekonstruktion,* 1929. Sasse has put into English what was actually said at Marburg (*op. cit.*, pp. 223 ff.). Cf. *WA*, 30:III, 110 ff.

[59] *WA*, 30:III, 160 ff. See the English text in Sasse, *op. cit.*, pp. 269 ff.

Supper there was agreement in the demand for both kinds, in the rejection of the sacrifice of the mass, in the assertion that the spiritual partaking of Christ's body and blood "is especially necessary for every true Christian," [60] and that the sacrament is ordained by God as a comfort and strengthening of faith. As to the presence of the body and blood of Christ in the bread and wine, no agreement was reached; each party, however, promised to deal with the other in Christian love, fervently praying that God would confirm them in the right understanding.

Actually little was accomplished, for each side could read its own interpretation into the *Marburg Articles*. A "difference of spirit" separated Luther and Zwingli. The Lord's Supper was the chief occasion for the difference to become conspicuous at that time. Nevertheless, Luther was hopeful. He wrote a letter full of optimism to his wife.[61] In a later letter addressed to Johannes Agricola (October 12) he used stronger expressions, saying that his opponents had humbled themselves beyond measure.[62] At the same time Zwingli wrote of his opponent, "Truth has prevailed so manifestly that, if ever a person has been defeated, it is the impudent (*impudens*) and stubborn (*contumax*) Luther." [63]

In 1530, an imperial diet was held at Augsburg. Disunited as they were, the Protestants presented three different confessions. The Lutheran party presented to the emperor what became known as the *Augsburg Confession*, drafted by Melanchthon. Article X on the Supper reads: "It is taught among us that the true body and blood of Christ are really present in the Supper of our Lord under the form of bread and wine and are there distributed and received. The contrary doctrine is therefore rejected." [64] Philip of Hesse suggested a change in this article so that the Zwinglians also could subscribe,[65] but

---

[60] Sasse, *op. cit.,* p. 272.

[61] *Ibid.,* pp. 269 ff.; see also Jacobs, *op. cit.,* II, 69 ff.

[62] *WA, Briefwechsel,* 5: No. 1479.

[63] Quoted from Sasse, *op. cit.,* p. 274.

[64] The translation follows the German (official) text. The Latin version is still shorter: "Our churches teach that the body and blood of Christ are truly present and distributed to those who eat in the Supper of the Lord. They disapprove (*disprobant*) of those who teach otherwise."

[65] Theodor Kolde, *Die älteste Redaktion der Augsburger Konfession* (1906), pp. 40 ff.

the Lutherans could not be moved. The language was left in its original formulation, but the rejecting phrase was purposely put into the mildest form. Zwingli submitted his *Ratio Fidei* to the emperor. This was a document in which he reproduced practically all those points which had been offensive to the Lutherans at Marburg and which he seemed to have recalled by signing the *Marburg Articles*. As to the Supper, he says that the body of Christ is present only by the contemplation of faith.[66]

Little importance was attached to Zwingli's confession even by the South Germans who, on July 11, presented their own confession, the *Confessio Tetrapolitana*.[67] The document was composed by the Strassburg theologians Bucer, Hedio, and Capito. Besides the city of Strassburg, the cities of Constance, Memmingen, and Lindau added their consent. The sacraments are defined as "sacred symbols" and "visible signs of invisible grace" (Chap. XVI). The language in the discussion of the Eucharist (Chap. XVIII) is ambiguous. Sasse says of Bucer, "We may look to Bucer for the origin of the custom of theologians to speak of a Real Presence when a Real Presence is not actually meant." [68] The *Tetrapolitana* anticipates the teaching of Calvin and of the Reformed confessions in general. While we receive the earthly elements outwardly, the souls of believers receive the body of Christ inwardly by faith. Luther's *manducatio oralis* and *manducatio indignorum* are implicitly rejected in the *Tetrapolitana*.[69]

The following summer Zwingli wrote his *Exposition of the Christian Faith* and sent it to the King of France. Considering the views on the Word and on the sacraments expressed in both the *Ratio* and the *Exposition*, one is tempted to question the sincerity of Zwingli at Marburg. How could he reconcile the statement of Article VIII of the *Marburg Articles* to the effect that normally the Spirit gives faith through the oral word and that through baptism children are received into God's grace (Art. XIV) with the view expressed in the *Ratio Fidei* that no channel or vehicle is necessary to the Spirit, and that "the

---

[66] Jacobs, *op. cit.*, II, 170 ff.
[67] See the English version in *ibid.*, 179 ff.
[68] Sasse, *op. cit.*, p. 306.
[69] Referring to the attempts of Bucer to win the Swiss over to the *Tetrapolitana*, the Reformed theologian Karl Mueller remarks, "Their friendly attitude notwithstanding, the Swiss declined to exchange their own clear teaching of the sacrament for the obscure language [of this document]." *PRE*, 19:564.

sacraments are far from conferring grace, that they do not even convey or distribute it"? He adds "In this matter, most powerful Caesar, I may seem to thee too bold but my opinion is fixed" (Art. VII). The unity created at Marburg was certainly an illusion.[70]

Zwingli died in the battle of Kappel, October 11, 1531. In Zurich, the mantle of the prophet fell on Heinrich Bullinger. At Strassburg, Bucer continued his efforts to bring about a better understanding between Zurich and Wittenberg. In the *First Helvetic Confession* (1536), composed by Bullinger and others, the Swiss divines renounced the purely symbolical interpretation of the sacraments and expressed themselves in terms that are close to Bucer's view.[71]

Bucer continued to negotiate with Wittenberg and was invited by Luther to meet him at his home in May, 1536. As a result the two parties signed the so-called *Wittenberg Concord*.[72] The first article says that with the bread and wine the body and blood of Christ are truly and substantially present, offered, and received. The second article rejects transubstantiation, a local inclusion of the body of Christ and his presence apart from the rite of the sacrament. The relation between Christ's body and the bread is described as "sacramental union." The third article teaches the validity of the sacrament independent of the worthiness of the minister and of the recipient.

Luther was satisfied with the mild expression that the body of Christ is present and offered "with" (*cum*) the bread. He did not insist on the prepositions "in" and "under." He likewise permitted the expression *manducatio impiorum* to be changed to *manducatio indignorum*, for Bucer understood the term *impii* as referring to people who have never heard of the gospel. The objectivity of the Supper, in Luther's eyes, was not such that the rite performed by or for Jews or Turks would still be a valid Eucharist.[73]

The *Wittenberg Concord* was a success in that it brought the Protestants of southern Germany into the Lutheran church. It was a failure in that Bucer's aspirations for a broader union were not ful-

[70] See Sasse, *op. cit.*, pp. 276 ff.

[71] (Arts. XX [XXI] – XXII [XXIII]). See the text in Schaff, *Creeds of Christendom*, III, 223 ff.

[72] See the English version in Jacobs, *op. cit.*, II, 253 ff.

[73] Cf. "Bucer's Exhortation to His Colleagues" in Jacobs, *op. cit.*, II, 287 ff.

filled. He tried in vain to persuade the Swiss leaders to accept the *Concord*.[74]

By this time <u>Melanchthon showed some signs of defecting from Luther's view of the Lord's Supper</u>. From the beginning, he had laid special emphasis on the celebration of the Church. He was averse to equating the bread with the body of Christ and located the real presence in the action itself.[75] Luther's view of the ubiquity of the body, as well as Zwingli's purely symbolical interpretation were, in Melanchthon's opinion, contrary to the teaching of the ancient Church. At Marburg, Melanchthon defended the real presence on the basis of Scripture and on "the almost unanimous consent of the Fathers." [76] Gradually his belief in the unanimity of the Fathers was shaken[77] and he became more receptive to Bucer's practical view that divergent opinions on the Supper could be tolerated within the Church. Unlike Luther, he based the real presence on the will of Christ. *Praesentia est voluntaria* ("When he wills, Christ can be present") *ubique* ("everywhere"). He replaced Luther's concept of the ubiquity of Christ's body with the idea of the so-called "multivolenspresence." [78] Against Zwingli, Oecolampadius, Bucer, and Calvin, Melanchthon denied that the body of Christ can be in only one place (i.e., heaven). Christ can be in several places at the same time *arcano modo* ("in mysterious manner"); "in which several places are like one point to the body of Christ." [79]

In 1540 Melanchthon prepared a new edition of the *Augsburg Confession* for a colloquy to be held between Protestant and Catholic theologians at Worms. To facilitate negotiations and to make it easier for the Protestants to present a united front, Melanchthon made several alterations in the Latin text of the *Augsburg Confession*.[80] No changes were made in the German text, the authority of which remained unquestioned. Article X in the new (*Variata*) edition reads as follows:

---

[74] On this topic see Koehler, *Das Marburger* . . . , II, 432 ff.; Ernst Bizer, *op. cit.,* pp. 65 ff.; Sasse, *op. cit.,* pp. 301 ff.

[75] Cf. Vilmos Vatja (ed.), *Luther und Melanchthon,* pp. 102-103, n. 69.

[76] See Sasse, *op. cit.,* pp. 227-28.

[77] This was in part due to a collection of patristic sayings composed by Oecolampadius, the so-called *Dialogues.*

[78] For references, cf. Seeberg, *Lehrbuch,* IV, 447 ff.

[79] Quoted from Sasse, *op. cit.,* p. 316.

[80] An English version is found in Jacobs, *op. cit.,* II, 103 ff.

"Of the Lord's Supper they (i.e. our churches) teach that with (*cum*) the bread and wine the body and blood of Christ are truly offered (*exhibeantur*) to those who eat in the Lord's Supper." The word *exhibeantur* replaces the *distribuantur* of the *Invariata* of 1530. In addition, the words "truly and substantially present" are omitted. Likewise, the rejection of "those who teach otherwise" has been deleted. The preposition *cum* had also been used in the *Wittenberg Concord*. It can mean the same as *in* and *sub;* but it can also be understood as "simultaneously with." It was evidently understood in that sense by Calvin, who was present at Worms and signed the *Altered Augsburg Confession* (1540).

The differences between Luther and Melanchthon became increasingly apparent in the next few years.[81] In 1543 Melanchthon and Bucer drew up some articles for the introduction of the Reformation into the city of Cologne. They said about the Lord's Supper that "whoever firmly trusts in the words of Christ and in the visible signs eats truly and to salvation the flesh of Christ." Luther's view that even without faith the body of Christ is eaten, although not to salvation, was neither asserted nor denied. When Luther read the document he said "the shoe pinched him hard." [82] He found a great deal stated about the benefits of the sacrament, but "only a mumbling about its substance" [83] and he declared, "After so many confessions which I have published, I must send out one more: and I shall do it soon and it will be my last." [84] The document appeared in September, 1544, under the title *Kurzes Bekenntnis vom heiligen Sakrament* ("Shorter Confession of the Holy Sacrament").[85] Concerning the Supper, the pope, Luther maintained, was closer to the truth than Zwingli and his followers. Luther regarded himself as at one with Rome in teaching the real presence of the body of Christ, though not locally included in the bread. Hence those who eat of the bread do not receive pieces of Christ's flesh; rather each communicant receives the whole Christ. He who denies the real presence is in danger of losing

[81] Cf. Julius Koestlin, *The Theology of Luther,* II, trans. Charles E. Hay (Philadelphia: Lutheran Publication Society, 1897), pp. 184 ff.

[82] *WA, Briefwechsel,* 10:617-18 (No. 4014).

[83] *Ibid.*

[84] *WA,* 54:120 (Enders, *op. cit.,* 16:6).

[85] *WA,* 54:141 ff.

also the two natures united in the one person of Christ. This publication meant the entire failure of the union efforts of Bucer.

BIBLIOGRAPHY

BIZER, ERNST. *Studien zur Geschichte des Abendmahlstreites im 16. Jahrhundert.* 1940.

BRILIOTH, YNGVE. *Eucharistic Faith and Practice.* London: SPCK, 1930. See especially pp. 94 ff.

GENRICH, P. W. *Die Christologie Luthers im Abendmahlstreit.* 1929.

GOLLWITZER, HELMUT. *Coena Domini.* 1937.

KOEHLER, WALTER. *Zwingli und Luther, ihr Streit um das Abendmahl.* Vol. I, 1924; Vol. II, 1953.

SASSE, HERMANN. *This is My Body.* Minneapolis: Augsburg Publishing House, 1959.

SCHWEIZER, J. *Reformierte Abendmahlsgestaltung in der Schau Zwinglis.*

SOMMERLATH, ERNST. *Der Sinn des Abendmahls.* 1930.

CHAPTER IV

MELANCHTHON, THE CO-LABORER OF LUTHER

Luther, for all the depth of his religious genius, was not at his best when it came to guarded theological definition. We see this in the Smalcald Articles. Luther said of Melanchthon his co-worker:

> I was born for warring with factious spirits (*Rotten*) and devils. For this reason my books are stormy and warlike. To me it has fallen to uproot trees, to clear away thorn and brush, and to fill up mudholes. I am a rough pioneer who has to blaze the trail and even up the path. But Magister Philip proceeds quietly and with a clean hand, building, planting, sowing and watering with pleasure according to the rich gifts with which God has endowed him.[1]

Melanchthon had the didactical gift for method, form, and system. Up to the end of his life he was asked to formulate the results of the many conferences and colloquies into tangible and suitable statements.

On the other hand, Melanchthon was a man of irenic disposition. He was ready to serve the cause of union and tranquility. This was a trait which often worried not only Luther but also many of his co-laborers, and which occasionally hindered the right development of things. Reaction against this conciliatory trait in Melanchthon started the development of anti-Melanchthonian factions. This was especially observable in the controversies after Luther's death. The changes in the *Augsburg Confession* in the *Variata* editions, 1540 ff.,[2] are striking instances of the vacillating attitude of Melanchthon for the purpose of effecting a reconciliation with Rome and of establishing a united Protestant movement.

[1] See *PRE,* 12:528.
[2] For an English translation see Jacobs (ed.), *Book of Concord,* II, 103 ff. Cf. also Franz Hildebrandt, *Melanchthon: Alien or Ally?* (Cambridge: Cambridge University Press, 1946).

Melanchthon, a grandnephew of the famous John Reuchlin, was born in 1497 in southwestern Germany. At the age of thirteen he entered the University of Heidelberg and later continued his studies in the humanities and Scholastic theology at Tübingen. He arrived in Wittenberg in August, 1518. Throughout his long career he held a chair in the arts faculty but lectured also in theology. A humanist by persuasion, Melanchthon, under the magnetic spell of Luther, opened his heart to the gospel and became, next to Luther, the most influential leader of the German Reformation. He died in 1560.[3]

MELANCHTHON'S DISCOVERY OF THE GOSPEL

Like Luther, Melanchthon went through a spiritual crisis early in his life. Both Scholasticism and humanism assigned priority to reason in the religious quest of truth. The good can be taught. Properly taught, man will do what God requires of him. Thus Melanchthon regarded the promotion of morality (*formare mores*) as his supreme task. August 29, he delivered his inaugural address before the assembled university, "On the Improvement of Studies." [4] Disgusted with the frigid glosses and jangling comments of the Scholastics, he pleaded for a renaissance of true learning and of "a reasonable and sincere piety" through a study of original sources: the ancient classics and the Scriptures in Greek, Latin, and Hebrew. Through his friendship with Luther he soon learned to detect the fallacy inherent in the humanist belief in the power of reason.[5] *Vincitur affectu ratio* ("reason is held in bondage by passion"), he says.[6] The affections are not obedient to reason. Man is not free. "Love of self is the root of all evil." [7] This sinful disposition cannot be overcome by the law, for the law does not give what it commands.[8] It is by the grace and Spirit of God that man is cleansed and impelled to do the good.[9] As in his humanistic period, Melanchthon's interest was centered in the

[3] See Werner Elert's essay "Humanitat und Kirche: zum 450. Geburtstage Melanchthons," *Zwischen Gnade und Ungnade* (1948).

[4] *De corrigendis adulescentiae studiis* (*CR*, 11:15 ff.).

[5] For references see Adolf Sperl, *Melanchthon zwischen Humanismus und Reformation* (1959), pp. 101-102.

[6] Robert Stupperich (ed.), *Melanchthons Werke in Auswahl* (1951—), I, 36.

[7] *CR*, 21:55.

[8] *CR*, 21:53.

[9] *Ibid.*

good life. But he knew that the virtuous life could be realized only through the power of the Holy Spirit. It is the Holy Spirit who also offers the believer forgiveness of past sins. Thus, a man may have confidence that his sins will no longer be imputed to him (*propter Christi meritum*).[10] The benefit of Christ is, therefore, a renewal which includes the forgiveness of sin.[11] This is the form in which Melanchthon discovered the gospel. The forgiveness of sins remains subordinate to the ethical renewal of man. As he himself later admitted, he had not as yet given sufficient attention to the doctrine of justification.[12]

THE LOCI COMMUNES OF 1521

Although Melanchthon had been called to the chair of Greek in the University of Wittenberg, he spent the major part of his first years teaching sacred literature, especially the Gospel of Matthew, and the Epistles of Paul to the Romans and to Titus. His notes on Romans fell into the hands of his students, who published them. To these notes Melanchthon had given the name *Lucubratiuncula* ("Night Works"). In addition to these Melanchthon prepared another set of lectures, the *Institutio Theologica*.

The *Lucubratiuncula* were published without the consent of the author. After some unsuccessful attempts to suppress the circulation of the book, Melanchthon decided to revise it. This he did, no doubt making use of the *Theological Institute on Romans*. The composite and revised work was published in Wittenberg in 1521 under the caption *Loci Communes Rerum Theologicarum* ("Leading Conceptions in Theology"). It was the first dogmatics of the Protestant Church. It is said that during the life-time of its author it went through eighty editions. The editions of 1535 and 1543 express certain changes with respect to the doctrine of the will in the process of conversion.

In writing the *Loci*, Melanchthon was guided by Paul's Letter to the Romans. God wills to be known, he says, by a new method, "the foolishness of preaching." [13] Hence there is no reason to put much

[10] *CR*, 21:56.
[11] Stupperich, *op. cit.,* I, 16-17, 38.
[12] *CR*, 1:158.
[13] Charles Leander Hill, *The Loci Communes of Philip Melanchthon* (Boston: Meador Publishing Co., 1944), p. 67.

labor on the greatest topics such as, the Unity and Trinity of God, on the great mystery of creation, and on the mode of the incarnation. The Scholastic theologians busied themselves with these topics in vain, "trifling a whole lifetime about universals, formalities, connotations, and I know not what other meaningless words." [14] Instead, this is Christian knowledge: to know Christ's benefits, to know about the law, sin, and grace. [15]

The problem of the forgiveness of sins occupied the center of Melanchthon's thought. The Scholastics, he maintained, obscured the topic of sin in their distinctions between actual and original sin. [16] "Scripture does not call the one 'original' and the other 'actual' for original sin is clearly some actual depraved desire." [17] "All sin is a 'vice,' a depraved affection and a depraved motion of the heart against the Law of God." [18] Sin's essence is self-love. [19] "Flesh not only designates the body, rather all affections and emotions of the natural man." [20] Flesh refers to the whole nature of man, including "the most illustrious powers of nature." [21] As may be seen, this understanding of sin and flesh is in full accord with that of Luther.

Next, "the proper function of the Law is the revelation of sin." [22] "In justifying sinners, God's first work is to reveal our sin, to confound our conscience, to shatter it, to terrify it." [23]

In contrast to the law, the gospel is "the promise of grace and righteousness." [24] Rejecting the Scholastic notion of *"gratia infusa,"* Melanchthon states that the word *gratia*, on the basis of its Hebrew and Greek equivalents, plainly signifies "favor," as the mercy and gratuitous benevolence of God. "In a word, grace is nothing but the forgiveness of sins." [25] Melanchthon, then, maintains very carefully the proper distinction between law and gospel.

[14] *Ibid.*, p. 68.
[15] *Ibid.*
[16] *Ibid.*, p. 81.
[17] *Ibid.*, p. 82.
[18] *Ibid.*
[19] *Ibid.*, p. 83.
[20] *Ibid.*, p. 234.
[21] *Ibid.*, p. 237.
[22] *Ibid.*, p. 162.
[23] *Ibid.*
[24] *Ibid.*, p. 169.
[25] *Ibid.*, p. 171.

Melanchthon dismisses entirely the notion of work-righteousness. "Our works however good they may be do not constitute our righteousness." [26] We are justified when we believe in the gospel: "when we cling to Christ," believing "that the righteousness of Christ is our righteousness, that His satisfaction is our expiation, that His resurrection is ours . . . for righteousness is faith alone in the mercy and grace of God in Jesus Christ." [27] At one point in the *Loci*, Melanchthon equates the term "justification" with "sanctification." "Justification has just begun and is not fully completed." [28] Just as "sanctification is not yet perfected in us." [29] As in Luther's eyes, the Christian, according to Melanchthon, is *simul justus et peccator*.[30]

In no uncertain terms Melanchthon rejects the Scholastic distinction between *fides informis* and *fides formata*. "Scholastic faith is nothing but a dead opinion." [31] But an opinion held concerning "things to be believed" and the accuracy and dependability of the biblical narrative is not faith at all.[32] Faith is "reliance upon the divine mercy promised in Christ." [33] In a word, faith is *fiducia*, trust in God and a ready response to the will of God "in every vicissitude of life and death." [34] Like Luther, Melanchthon conceived of faith not as a dormant conviction but rather as an active principle incessantly driving man to do the will of God. For he who possesses faith "possesses all things and can do all things." [35]

---

[26] *Ibid.*, p. 172.

[27] *Ibid.* In his introduction, Hill remarks that the forensic notion of justification is not voiced in the *Loci*: "In fact this theory of justification did not come into definite form until very late in the doctrinal writings of the Lutheran Church. It was not formulated until 1549 or the date of the appearance of the third edition of the *Loci*" (p. 61). This statement, in our eyes, is contrary to historical evidence. In the *Institute*, Melanchthon speaks of the non-imputation of sin (cf. *CR*, 21:56). In the *Theses* for the Baccalaureate of Theology (November 9, 1519) he wrote, *Omnis iustitia nostra est gratuita Dei imputatio* ("All our righteousness is by the gracious imputation of God"). On the genuineness of the *Thesis* see Sperl, *op. cit.*, pp. 110-11. The idea of the non-imputation of sin and of the imputation of faith *propter meritum Christi* is at the very core of Article IV in the *Apology* of the *Augsburg Confession*, 1531.

[28] Hill, *op. cit.*, p. 197.

[29] *Ibid.*, p. 234.

[30] *Ibid.*, p. 235.

[31] *Ibid.*, p. 178.

[32] *Ibid.*, p. 176.

[33] *Ibid.*, p. 177.

[34] *Ibid.*, p. 193.

[35] *Ibid.*, p. 194.

DIVINE PREDESTINATION

At first glance, Melanchthon seems to be as predestinarian as Luther in his *On the Bondage of the Will*. In introducing the subject, Melanchthon says, "All things that happen, happen of necessity according to divine predestination." [36] Upon closer scrutiny, it is evident that Melanchthon does not discuss the problem of predestination at all. In the whole section, "On the Powers of Man, Especially Free Will," the author makes no reference to the eternal destiny of man. Instead, he deals with the problem of psychological determinism. The alleged discussion of predestination is a part of the larger exposition of the "powers of man, especially of free will." [37] As in the *Lucubratiuncula*, Melanchthon retains a dualistic psychology which says that man is divided into two parts: the faculty of cognition and the faculty of the will, affections or appetites [38] by which faculty man is subject to "love, hate, hope, fear, and the like." [39] As stated above, reason is unable to subdue man's affections. Hence, there is no such thing as freedom of the will. [40] Rather, all things happen according to divine predestination. It is only by the Spirit of God that man's moral nature may be restored and preserved. All genuine morality is contingent upon the redemptive grace of God. In the final analysis, therefore, the doctrine of divine predestination is meant to serve the humanist ideal of the noble life.

In saying that all things happen according to divine predestination, Melanchthon does not want to deny "that there is a certain kind of liberty in external things." [41] You may, for example, greet or not greet a certain man, etc. [42] The natural man may even conquer one affection by another, like Alexander the Great, who conquered the love of pleasure by a still greater love of glory. [43]

Little wonder that Melanchthon should hesitate to imbue the minds of young people with the doctrine of predestination. [44] A discussion

[36] *Ibid.,* p. 72.
[37] *Ibid.,* pp. 69 ff.
[38] *Ibid.,* p. 71.
[39] *Ibid.,* p. 72.
[40] *Ibid.*
[41] *Ibid.,* p. 75.
[42] *Ibid.,* p. 76.
[43] *Ibid.,* p. 77.
[44] *Ibid.,* p. 74.

of predestination geared to the attainment of the good life may indeed prove disastrous to the pursuit of morality.[45]

THE PROBLEM OF RELIGIOUS AUTHORITY

As to the formal principle of the Reformation, the principle *sola Scriptura*, Melanchthon's position in the *Loci* is biblicistic through and through. Concerning the composition of the *Loci*, he says he had nothing in view but to assist "the studies of those who wish to be conversant with the Scriptures.[46] The Scriptures—to be more exact, the canonical Scriptures—are the only source of the Christian faith.[47] In the commentaries of both the ancient Greek and Latin writers there are many things diametrically opposed to truth.[48] But "nothing ought to be considered an article of faith which the Scriptures do not openly teach." [49] "Neither Pontiffs nor councils nor the universal church have any right to change or decide any matter of faith." [50] Melanchthon believes in the Nicene Council, as he states, only "because I believe the Scriptures." [51] Unfortunately, in the early Church, "Christian doctrine was weakened through its fusion with Platonic philosophy." [52] In later times the Church has embraced the subtle pratings of Aristotle,[53] the wrangler.[54]

Also pointing to his exclusive biblicism is his statement that the state should be administered according to the gospel.[55] Although in keeping with what Melanchthon had said previously, this position is not consistently maintained in the *Loci*, as is evident from the discussion "On Human Laws" [56] and "On Magistrates." [57]

The difficulty of maintaining consistently that the state should be governed by the precepts of Scripture is accentuated by the views

[45] Cf. Sperl, *op. cit.*, pp. 123 ff.
[46] Hill, *op. cit.*, p. 65.
[47] *Ibid.*, pp. 64-65, 137.
[48] *Ibid.*, p. 65.
[49] *Ibid.*, p. 137.
[50] *Ibid.*, p. 131.
[51] *Ibid.*, p. 137.
[52] *Ibid.*, pp. 70, 112.
[53] *Ibid.*, p. 64.
[54] *Ibid.*, p. 113.
[55] *Ibid.*, p. 125. Cf. Sperl, *op. cit.*, pp. 95 ff.
[56] Hill, *op. cit.*, pp. 130 ff.
[57] *Ibid.*, pp. 262 ff.

expressed on natural law. On one occasion, Melanchthon argues that the precepts of Scripture should be sufficient. At the same time he maintains that some natural laws are imprinted by God on human minds "to serve as a rule for the judgment of character." [58] Among these, he says, are the following: (1) God ought to be revered; (2) because man is born into a definite society, no one ought to be injured; (3) human society demands that we use all things in common.[59] But having said that the worship of God is a principle written upon the natural mind of man, Melanchthon nevertheless deduces this principle from the Bible. <u>Melanchthon's teaching of natural law evidently is a foreign element in the *Loci Communes* of 1521</u>, as C. Bauer has rightly observed.[60] With respect to this second principle, Melanchthon does not deny the duty of magistrates to punish the criminal "so that the many may not be injured." [61] Nor is he an advocate of a socialist economic order. Property is to be shared, he says, "through contracts, buying, selling, leasing, farming out, and in other ways." [62]

MELANCHTHON'S EARLIEST CONTRIBUTION TO RELIGIOUS EDUCATION

Between 1525 and 1529, the Elector of Saxony ordered official visitations of the churches to investigate the religious and moral condition of the people. Melanchthon was among the men commissioned to conduct this investigation. An alarming state of affairs was discovered. The religious ignorance and moral condition, not only of the common people but also of many of the clergy, were appalling. In order to meet the situation and to make these visitations as fruitful as possible, Melanchthon was instructed by the Elector to draw up articles to guide the Church officers and ministers in the needed reform. This document was published in 1528.[63] It was the first official form for teaching the fundamentals of the Christian religion according to the

---

[58] *Ibid.*, pp. 112.
[59] *Ibid.*, pp. 113.
[60] "Die Naturrechtsvorstellungen des jüngeren Melanchthon" in *Festschrift für G. Ritter* (1950) p. 255.
[61] Hill, *op. cit.*, p. 114.
[62] *Ibid.*, p. 115.
[63] *Unterricht der Visitatoren als die Pfarrherren im Kurfürstentum zu Sachsen.* See its text in *CR,* 26:41 ff. A separate edition was published by Hans Lietzmann in 1912.

doctrines of the Reformation. As such it was a forerunner of Luther's catechisms and the *Augsburg Confession*. As a Church manual (*Kirchenordnung*) it also dealt with principles of Church discipline and public education. The publication of this document marks a Reformation milestone.

By the time of drafting of the *Augsburg Confession* Melanchthon was eminently prepared for the task. During thirteen years of struggle for the fundamentals of the Reformation, he enjoyed the daily fellowship of Luther and with him witnessed the growth of Wittenberg from a small provincial university into an international institute of higher learning. Students of that day were flocking to Wittenberg from all countries in order to hear Luther and Melanchthon. Coming from the Scandinavian countries, from Finland, the Baltic states, from Poland, Hungary, from France and England, we find all these future preachers and teachers of their respective countries at the feet of Luther and Melanchthon, the *praeceptor Germaniae*. The writing of the *Loci*, the *Articles of Visitation*, the joint preparation with Luther of the so-called *Schwabach Articles*, Luther's separation from humanism and from the Pelagianism of his day, the elimination of spiritualism with its theology of the "inner light" and the problems posed by Zwingli—all these schooled and enabled Melanchthon to write the *Augsburg Confession*, the Magna Charta of Protestantism in general and of Lutheranism in particular.

Melanchthon's View of Justification, 1530 and 1531

While we shall give a resume of the theology of both the *Augsburg Confession* and its *Apology* in the next chapter, it may be profitable to acquaint the student more fully with Melanchthon's teaching of the "material principle of the Reformation," the doctrine of justification by faith alone, as found in the lengthy fourth article of the *Apology* of the *Confession*.[64]

In the *Augsburg Confession* (Art. IV) Melanchthon stated briefly that our righteousness before God is not conditioned "by our own merits, works, or satisfactions but that we receive forgiveness of sin and become righteous before God by grace, for Christ's sake, through faith" (*gratis, propter Christum, per fidem*). The Roman theologians

[64] Tappert, *op. cit.*, pp. 107-168.

replied that "it is entirely contrary to Holy Scripture to deny that our works are meritorious." [65] The chief purpose of the *Apology* was to battle against the disparaging attitude of the Roman party as regards faith over against good works in justification. While the Catholic doctors were willing to concede that faith plays a necessary part in justification, they regarded faith merely as a preparation for or the beginning of justification, and put much emphasis on love (good works) as implementing faith (*fides charitate formata*). Over against this Roman view Melanchthon, in the *Apology*, stressed faith as the one and only means of justification. This, however, does not mean that he re-introduced a human element into the concept of justification. In the *Apology* he was not interested in the psychological, immanental aspect of faith. Faith, as he says, is not a human power. For him to be justified *sola fide* is the same as to be saved *sola gratia*. Faith justifies not because it is a superethical quality of the soul, but because it is the means of apprehending the merits of the Savior.[66]

The transcendental aspect of Melanchthon's view of God's dealing with men is clear from the following linguistic peculiarities of the *Apology:* (1) the author's preference for the passive voice of the verbs in question, *iustificari* (to be justified), *pronuntiari* (to be pronounced), *reputari* (to be accounted), indicates that he conceives of justification as an act done not by men, but rather in men by God; (2) the wonderful array of nouns used by Melanchthon in describing the content of justification, such as a "promise of a gracious forgiveness of sins," a "true and firm reconciliation," an "acceptance and adoption into the number of God's children," an "enrollment in the book of life," a "beginning of life eternal," an "imputation of the righteousness of Christ or of the Gospel"; (3) the equally impressive group of adjectives, describing the righteousness of the Christian as "passive, of another person or lying outside of ourselves and imputed." Attention should also be given to the way in which Melanchthon stresses the unconditional nature of justification. Proceeding from the mercy and good will of God, justification takes place *gratis*, without works either preceding or following faith.

"To be justified," Melanchthon says, "means to make (*effici*) un-

---

[65] "Confutation of the Augsburg Confession," in Jacobs, *op. cit.,* II, 211.
[66] *Apology*. IV, 86.

righteous men righteous or to regenerate them." [67] This definition shows that Melanchthon did not hestitate to follow the terminology of his Roman adversaries: to be justified is to be made righteous. However, Melanchthon would not accept the moralistic implications inherent in Roman theology. To be justified is the same as to attain the remission of sins, he writes in the same context.[68] Evidently Melanchthon uses the term *"justum efficere,"* which in Roman theology signifies the "effective" view of justification, to express in his own thought the "forensic" view. To be made just, according to him, is the same as to be pronounced or accounted just.[69]

As stated, Melanchthon equates justification with the remission of sins. Forgiveness, however, in his eyes, is contingent on the work of the Savior. It is this basic fact in the redemptive work of Christ which Melanchthon has in mind when he says that God imputes the righteousness of Christ to man. Man is just in the eyes of God "on account of the righteousness of another one, viz. of Christ." We are righteous by the imputation of an *aliena iustitia*.[70] Since it is by faith that man apprehends the righteousness of Christ, Melanchthon also says that we are justified by faith and that "faith itself is imputed for righteousness . . . faith is the righteousness of the heart." [71]

THE THEOLOGY OF THE OLDER MELANCHTHON

In 1532 Melanchthon published a new *Commentary on Romans*, and in 1535 he brought out a new and revised edition of the *Loci Communes*. These publications reflected a new and final stage in his theological development. The humanistic bent of his mind became progressively more apparent. This fact expressed itself in a number of concessions which he made, first, to reason, and, second, to tradition.

Luther had pronounced a solemn anathema against Aristotle, that "condemned, conceited, rascally heathen" from whom nothing can be learned "either of the things of nature or the things of the Spirit."

[67] *Ibid.*, 72, 117.
[68] *Ibid.*, 76.
[69] With respect to the terminology in the article under discussion, see Carl Stange, "Zur Rechtfertigungslehre in der Apologie," *Studien zur Theologie Luthers*, I (1928), 453 ff.
[70] *Apology*, IV, 76.
[71] *Ibid.*, 92.

Yet for the formal training of the mind Luther was ready to retain the Logic, Rhetoric and Poetics of the Stagarite.[72] Melanchthon seized upon this concession of Luther and based the training in the schools of higher learning on the axiom *carere igitur Aristotelis monumentis non possumus* ("therefore we cannot dispense with the literary legacy of Aristotle"). This predilection for Aristotle and the ancients in general made it difficult for Melanchthon to accept the Copernician theory of the universe. Apart from Scripture, which he maintained taught that God established the earth forever,[73] the teaching of Copernicus would upset the study of the liberal arts (*conturbare artes*).[74] However, neither Melanchthon nor Luther interfered with the promulgation of the Copernican theory at the University of Wittenberg.[75]

Under the impact of humanism, Melanchthon came dangerously close to the Scholastic idea of a natural theology, according to which the being and attributes of God are evident to reason. Although the human will has been corrupted through the fall, Melanchthon said, reason has retained its integrity at least in the process of thinking, for the image of God was in the mind (*imago Dei erat in mente*).[76] Following this line of argument, Melanchthon moved away from the determinism of his earlier period. In his *Commentary on Romans* and in the *Loci* of 1535 he says that God's election is determined by something in man (*aliqua causa electionis in nobis*), insofar as man has the ability to reject or not to reject the grace of God. Three causes are concurrent in the conversion of man, he maintains: the Word of God, the Holy Spirit, and the will of man assenting to and not opposing the Word of God, for man has "the faculty to lay hold of grace." [77]

This high estimate of the powers of man inevitably changed Melanchthon's attitude toward the law. As stated above, he had given some consideration to the concept of natural law in the *Loci* of 1521. At that time, the idea had only marginal significance for him. In the

---

[72] *PE,* II, 146-47.
[73] Cf. Pss. 68, 79; Eccles. 1:4; and elsewhere.
[74] *CR,* 13:217.
[75] See Werner Elert's discussion of this issue in *Morphologie des Luthertums,* I (1931), 363 ff.
[76] *CR,* 21:801.
[77] See the chapter on the "Freedom of the Will" in the 1535 and subsequent editions of the *Loci.*

later editions the idea of natural law held a prominent place. The law of nature, he said "is the knowledge of the divine law imbedded in the nature of man." On the basis of this law, man knows that God is one, mind, eternal, wise, just, and good, the creator of all things, a benefactor to the just while punishing the unjust.[78] Furthermore, by virtue of the divine light within him, man knows how to distinguish between good and evil, how to lead an ordered social life. This natural law was reaffirmed by God in the Decalog. Hence the Decalog has an abiding significance for the Christian Church. While some traces of these ideas may be found in the *Loci* of 1521, Melanchthon now presented a well-rounded doctrine of "the threefold use of the Law." First, the law is meant by God to be a coercive factor in human society (the pedagogical or political use); second, the law reveals sin in that it accuses and terrifies the conscience (the theological, and in the eyes of Melanchthon, the principal use of the law); third, it is a rule of life for the reborn, teaching them the works that are pleasing in the sight of God (the didactic use).[79] Melanchthon used this concept against the Antinomians who taught that the law should be eliminated from the teaching of the Church.[80]

In the world of sin, the law needs a protector. This protector is the state. The government is a minister of God and custodian of both tables of the Decalog. While the ministry exercises a spiritual power through the gospel, the government should preserve external peace and order. The primary duty of the state is to serve the glory of God for, on the basis of natural law, all men know of God and of their duty to worship him. The state should also promote the cause of true religion and piety, suppress all false doctrines and idolatrous practices since the bishops are unwilling to reform the church. As an additional duty, the state, through the establishment of schools, should foster the study of the liberal arts and of theology, for in conformity with Isa. 49:23, the state shall be a nursing mother and the prince a nursing father to foster teachers and students of "the doctrine of God and of those arts that are necessary in the church." Hence, to obey the government, in the eyes of Melanchthon, is a religious duty. These views explain, at least in part, the absolutism of the Protestant princes

---

[78] "De lege naturae" in 1543 edition.
[79] "De usu legis" in 1543 edition.
[80] See pages 748 ff.

in Germany, the pronounced class consciousness of the different estates, and the decline of personal liberty in the Age of Orthodoxy.[81]

In this discussion, the similarity, no less than the dissimilarity, between Melanchthon and Luther is striking. When the bishops failed Luther, he too called upon the temporal powers to recognize their responsibility and to reform the Church. For Luther this was clearly a concession to a dire exigency. He appealed to the princes in their capacity as the most prominent lay members of the Church. Luther's appeal to the princes was necessitated by a concrete emergency. In the eyes of Melanchthon, on the other hand, the government has a spiritual function by nature. The views expressed reflect the normal relation between church and state. Melanchthon became the father of the territorial church (*Landeskirche*) with the prince as the *summus episcopus* of the Church. This made the prince an arbiter of the religion of his subjects. Thus, the principle *cuius regio eius religio* was decreed in Augsburg, 1555.

Another concession to reason is seen in Melanchthon's definition of faith. In 1521 he rejected the Scholastic understanding of faith as assent to things set forth in Scripture. He took the historical reliability of Scripture for granted but refused to designate man's reliance upon it as faith. Faith, he said, "is nothing other than reliance on the divine mercy promised in Christ." [82] In the *Loci* of 1543, he wrote "And this is a true definition of faith: faith is assent to the whole Word of God set before us and therefore also to the promise of reconciliation freely given on account of Christ, the Mediator. . . ." In distinction from an "uncertain opinion," he adds that, it is most common to regard faith as a "firm assent" (*firma assensio*). This was the origin of the definition of faith which became normative in later Lutheran orthodoxy: faith includes the three elements: *knowledge, assent, and trust*. The notional element is now a significant aspect of faith. The gospel was in danger of becoming equated with the doctrine of the gospel, *die reine Lehre* ("pure doctrine"), which the Church is to maintain and promote.

---

[81] Cf. the chapter "De magistratibus civilibus" in the *Loci* of 1543. It should be remembered, however, that the same tendencies were at work in Catholic France, and that in many cases the German princes were simply imitating the absolute-monarch of France.

[82] Hill, *op. cit.,* p. 177.

As a teaching body the Church is visible. It is the *coetus vocatorum* ("assembly of the called"). This Church is a mixed society, for in her midst are many who are not really regenerated but who give only intellectual assent to the doctrine of the gospel. The Church's mark is the proclamation of the gospel through which God is efficacious among its members. This concept of the Church presupposes the ministry as a teaching profession and loyalty to the doctrine of the gospel as a true mark of the ministry. Melanchthon expressly rejects the idea of episcopal succession as necessary for the continuity of the Church. The visible Church consists of two classes of people: *docentes* and *audientes*, those who teach and those who listen to the Word. This trend in Melanchthon produced in later Lutheranism the unfortunate institution of a *Pastorenkirche*, a church consisting of a well educated ministry and a laity resigned to inertia with no other religious obligation except to hear the sermon. Melanchthon made the amazing statement: "I believe in the Creed, I make use of the sacraments, I am baptized, and obey the ministry, hence I am a Christian." [83] This and similar statements must not be interpreted as if Melanchthon were preaching salvation granted to all who hold the pure doctrine of Church. Trust (*fiducia*) remained the first and controlling element of faith with him. Nor did he lose sight of the concept of the Church as an object of faith, since it is only by faith that we know of the elect as members of the visible Church. The fact remains, as Seeberg remarks,[84] that as the teaching of the Church became progressively more articulated and consequently more difficult for the laity to apprehend, the spiritual and moral requirements for Church membership became progressively more lax. This tendency was further abetted by the purely forensic conception of justification as a mere theoretical imputation of Christ's substitutionary satisfaction somewhere *in foro coeli*. To Luther, on the other hand, our alien righteousness is the personal Christ who dwells in us by faith.

The humanistic veneration of antiquity finally led Melanchthon to put an increasing emphasis on tradition. While Luther, too, had a high regard for the fathers and councils of the ancient Church, but always subjected them to the authority of Scripture, the older Mel-

[83] *CR,* 24:402; see also the chapter "De ecclesia" in the *Loci* of 1543.
[84] Seeberg, *Lehrbuch,* IV, 454.

anchthon practically equated Scripture and tradition. Scripture, the Ecumenical Creeds, the *Augsburg Confession,* the doctrine of Luther, the teaching of the University of Wittenberg—all these are the source of truth which the Church must confess. Melanchthon wanted to have nothing to do with any "new dogma." As shown in the previous chapter, he defected from Luther's doctrine of the Lord's Supper because the teaching of the ubiquity of the body of Christ could not be proved from the writings of the ancients. For the same reason he took an adamant stand against the "new" teachings of the Anabaptists and Anti-trinitarians, and approved of the execution of Servetus at Geneva. The most notorious example of Melanchthon's traditionalism is to be seen in his endorsement of the Leipzig Interim with its Semi-Pelagian teachings, approval of the mass, and the like.[85]

CONCLUDING REMARKS

In his book *Melanchthon: Alien or Ally?*, Franz Hildebrandt says, "The confessor is greater than the professor, the role of Luther more gratifying than that of Melanchthon."[86] Schiller's famous dictum, *Von der Parteien Hass und Gunst verzert, schwankt sein Charakterbild in der Geschichte*[87] may well be applied to Melanchthon. While the so-called Gnesio-Lutherans lost all confidence in him, the mediating trait of his theology was bound to reassert itself later in the age of syncretism and union endeavors in Germany and America. Heinrich Heppe, for example, regarded Melanchthon as the Protestant theologian *par excellence* because he preserved a commendable *via media* between Luther and Calvin, declining to accept the doctrine of ubiquity as held by Luther or the teaching of a double predestination as professed by Calvin. For this reason, Heppe maintained, not the Lutheran church but rather the German Reformed is the true heir of the Protestant Reformation.[88] As has been shown, Melanchthon defected from Luther in some of the fundamentals of Luther's theology. On the other hand, a kind of Lutheran overtone cannot be denied with respect to the religious and theological outlook of

---

[85] See pp. 451 ff.
[86] p. xi.
[87] "His portrait fluctuates in history depending on the prejudice of the parties."
[88] Heinrich Heppe, *Die konfessionelle Entickelung der altprotestantischen Kirche Deutschlands* (1854).

Magister Philip. Above all, he must be credited with having led German Humanism into the channels of Protestantism. He did this by bringing faith and science into the closest contact. Thus the history of German Humanism came to be distinct from that of the Latin countries.

BIBLIOGRAPHY

Works.

In the *Corpus Reformatorum*, Vols. 1-28. 1844—.
Loci Communes of 1521. Translated by CHARLES LEANDER HILL. Boston: Meador Publishing Co., 1944.
Melanchthon's Werke in Auswahl. Edited by ROBERT STUPPERICH. 5 vols. 1951—.
Melanchthon: Selected Writings. Edited by E. E. FLACK and LOWELL SATRE. Minneapolis: Augsburg Publishing House. 1962.

Research on Melanchthon

HILDEBRANDT, FRANZ. *Melanchthon: Alien or Ally?* Cambridge: Cambridge University Press, 1946.
LENTZ, H. H. *Reformation Crossroads.* Minneapolis: Augsburg, 1958.
MANSCHRECK, C. L. *Melanchthon, the Quiet Reformer.* New York: Abingdon Press, 1958.
RICHARD, J. WM. *Philip Melanchthon, Preceptor of Germany.* New York and London: G. P. Putnam's Sons, 1898.
SPERL, ADOLF. *Melanchthon zwischen Humanismus und Reformation.* 1959.
STUPPERICH, ROBERT. *Der unbekannte Melanchthon.* 1961.
VAJTA, VILMOS (ed.). *Luther und Melanchthon.* 1961.

CHAPTER V

EARLIEST LUTHERAN CONFESSIONAL WRITINGS

In order to do justice to the historical situation of the particular symbols of Lutheranism, a distinction must be made between two periods. The earlier confessions (the *Catechisms*, the *Schwabach Articles*, the *Augsburg Confession*, the *Apology* and the *Smalcald Articles*), are confessional expressions of the prophetical period of the Reformation. The *Formula of Concord* represents the doctrinal results of a long period of theological controversy within the Lutheran Church itself, which may be called the didactical period of the Reformation.

THE SCHWABACH ARTICLES

The *Schwabach Articles* are a document of closest relation to the *Augsburg Confession*. They were drafted in June, 1529, on the instruction of the Elector of Saxony by the Wittenberg theologians, most probably by Melanchthon, with the assistance of Luther. These articles were written before the *Marburg Articles* had been composed by Luther, as has been shown by H. von Schubert.[1] The intention was to use them as a basis for negotiations with the upper German cities, which were under the influence of Martin Bucer at Strassburg. Bucer was mediating between Luther and Zwingli on the issue of the Lord's Supper. The Articles did not accomplish doctrinal union at the meeting held in the Schwabach on October 16. Philip of Hesse

[1] *Zeitscrhift für Kirchengeschichte* (1908). Cf. J. L. Neve, *Introduction to the Symbolical Books* (Columbus, Ohio: Wartburg Press, 1956), pp. 88-89, and *Story and Significance of the Augsburg Confession* (Burlington, Iowa: Lutheran Literary Board, Inc., 1930), pp. 41-42.

was urging a political union of German Protestantism. Luther was opposed to such a union, because he saw it as an act of disloyalty to the rightful government, and the Elector of Saxony inclined more and more to a policy of non-activity toward the emperor. Nevertheless, the Protestants of Northern Germany wanted to let their friends, who leaned toward Bucer, know what their position was, particularly on the Lord's Supper. Though agreement was not reached, these *Schwabach Articles* still had their value. At the Augsburg Diet (1530), the Articles served Melanchthon in the construction of the doctrinal elements of the *Augsburg Confession*. The *Schwabach Articles* indicated to Melanchthon, those points on which the Lutheran party in Augsburg were of one mind. This document was shrouded in secrecy because of its political implications, and did not become known until its publication by Luther during the session of the Diet of Augsburg. The *Augsburg Confession* rendered the *Schwabach Articles* superfluous. We mention them here because they were of far greater importance than the *Marburg Articles*, and because they constituted the first relatively complete confessional documents of Lutheranism.

The tone of the *Schwabach Articles* is decidedly polemical against Rome, as for instance in Article XV, where the prohibition of marriage and ordinary food and drink to priests, together with the urging of the monastic life and vows of every kind, are declared to be nothing but damnable doctrines of the devil. The mass is spoken of as the greatest of all abominations. In Article X there is strong emphasis upon the real presence of Christ's Body and Blood in the Eucharist, in opposition to "the other side."

The contents of the Schwabach Articles can be indicated here only by the topics under discussion, which are as follows: (1) The Trinity; (2) The Incarnation of the Son of God; (3) The Work of Christ; (4) Original Sin; (5) Justification by Faith; (6) Faith, the Gift of God; (7) The Preached Word; (8) The Two Sacraments; (9) Baptism; (10) The Eucharist; (11) Private Confession; (12) The Christian Church; (13) Christ's Return to Judgment; (14) The Government; (15) Monastic Vows and Other Prohibitions; (16) The Mass; (17) Ceremonies of the Church. Space will not be taken to point out the matters in which the *Augsburg Confession* shows the influence of the

Schwabach Articles. Calinich and Knaake have gone into details on this subject.[2]

THE AUGSBURG CONFESSION

The *Augsburg Confession* of 1530 and 1531 was destined to become the official confession of the Lutheran Church. There had been no plan, however, to establish a new dogma. In an epilogue to Part I (Article XXI) Melanchthon insisted there had been no departure from the teachings of the "Catholic" Church as represented by the Fathers, that is from Athanasius to Leo the Great and perhaps to Gregory the Great. The confessors wanted to take the position that errors in doctrine which had crept in and which never had been codified in a real creed, should not claim to be Christian Catholic doctrine. An example is the Semi-Pelagianism of the Middle Ages, which was sanctioned first by the condemnation of Gottschalk (853) and later by the teaching of men like Thomas Aquinas and Duns Scotus. The decrees of the Fourth Lateran Council (1215) were a list of teachings that were Roman Catholic, but could not claim to be Christian Catholic in character. There was much self-deception in the presumption that the early Church was in entire harmony with the doctrinal positions of the Reformers. This must not surprise us when we remember that church history at that time was yet in its swaddling clothes. The plan of the Lutherans was to proceed on the ground that they were in entire harmony with the teachings of the early Catholic Church, and their *Apology*, as they first called their document, needed to refer only to some abuses which they had removed. In other words, the plan was to present to the emperor only what the Confession deals with in its second part (Articles XXII-XXVIII). So it came about that Melanchthon at first concentrated on the Articles of Abuses, the so-called *Torgau Articles.*[3]

In a pamphlet, *The Four Hundred Four Theses*,[4] addressed to the emperor, the Lutherans were portrayed as radicals whose views were

[2] Robert Calinich, *Luther und die Augsburgische Konfession* (1861); J. K. F. Knaake, *Luther's Anteil an der Augsburgischen Konfession* (1863); cf. J. W. Richard, *Luther and the Augsburg Confession* (1909).

[3] The text is found in *CR*, 26:161 ff.; English translated by Jacobs, *Symbolic Books of the Lutheran Church*, II, 75 ff.

[4] Critical edition and investigation by W. Gussmann, *Quellen* II (1930), and J. Ficker, *Zwingliana* V (1933), pp. 152 ff.

[Margin annotations:] Against unrecognized heresies which had uncritically been accepted into the life of the Roman Church.

The Lutherans planned to prove that they were merely adhering to what had been taught in the early church.

identical with those of recognized heretics. This convinced Melanchthon and his assistants that the chief part of the Confession to be presented to the emperor ought also to deal with the teachings of the Wittenberg reformers. Thus it came about that Melanchthon, largely on the basis of the Schwabach-Marburg articles, composed Articles I-XXI which now constitute the chief part of the *Augsburg Confession*.

A certain systematic arrangement is observable in the twenty-one doctrinal articles of the Confession. Article I begins with God, and Article XVII closes the body of doctrines with "the Return of Christ to Judgment." Articles XVIII-XXI were added to supplement some of the doctrines discussed in the previous articles.

The articles discuss major topics. (1) God and Christ, Articles I and III; (2) the doctrine of man, Articles II, XVIII, and XIX; (3) faith and good works, Articles IV, VI and XX; (4) The church and ministry, Articles V, VII, VIII, XIV, XV; (5) The Sacraments, Articles IX-XIII; (6) the Christian in society, Article XVI: (7) the doctrine of the Last Things, Article XVII.[5]

One

Article I on the Trinitarian relation in the Godhead and Article III on the Incarnation and Christ's work of reconciliation reaffirm the Nicene and Chalcedonian theology and approve the condemnation of the ancient heresies.

Two

The anthropological, including the hamartological interest of the Confession is dealt with in Article II on man's natural depravity. This depravity is defined as a condition in which man is born "without fear of God and without trust in God and with concupiscence." Man's depravity is further characterized as "truly sin," bringing "eternal death," if there is not a regeneration "through baptism and the Holy Ghost." This "organic basis" for Lutheran theology is asserted against

---

[5] The final article of this section, Art. XXI, "The Cult of Saints," was added by Melanchthon in the middle of June for reasons that can only be surmised. Like the articles of the second part, it is based on the *Torgau Articles* dealing with abuses that had crept into the Church.

the Pelagians and Roman Catholic Semi-Pelagians who denied that
original sin is truly sin "and who to obscure the glory of Christ's merit
and benefits argue that man can be justified before God by his own
strength and reason."

In Article XVIII, the question of the influence of natural depravity
on man's will is discussed. Although man retains a certain outward
freedom in matters of civil righteousness (*in rebus civilibus*), through
the Fall he lost the "power without the Holy Ghost, to work the
righteousness of God, that is spiritual righteousness" (*justitia spiritualis*). "This righteousness, if experienced by the regenerated, is
wrought in the heart when the Holy Ghost is received through the
Word."

Article XIX on the Cause of Sin is a postscript to the Confession
before its delivery. This article supplements Article II by insisting
that while God created and preserves man, the cause of sin must not
be sought in God, but "in the devil and ungodly men."

Three

Articles IV, VI and XX offer the central doctrine of Man's Salvation. Article IV of Justification, which can be traced through the
whole Confession as the fundamental interest, is addressed against
Pelagianism and Semi-Pelagianism (1) "that men cannot be justified
before God by their own strength, merits or works, but (2) are freely
justified for Christ's sake through faith (*propter Christum, per fidem*)
when they believe that they are received into favor and that their
sins are forgiven for Christ's sake, who, by His death, hath made
satisfaction for our sins." As a postscript, just before delivery, the
statement was added: "This faith God imputes for righteousness in
His sight. Romans 3 and 4."

Closely associated with the article on justification is Article VI of
the New Obedience: "This faith" (*fides illa*), spoken of in Article IV,
is bound (*debeat*) "to bring forth good fruits." "It is necessary
(*oporteat*) to do good works." These good works are not optional.
However, they must be of the sort which are "commanded by God"
(*mandata a Deo*); not the works of a self-chosen sanctity (*consilia
evangelica*). The warning is attached: "But not that we should rely
on those works to merit justification before God, for remission of sins

and justification are apprehended by faith. . . . We are freely receiving remission of sins, without works, by faith alone. . . ."

Article XX on Faith and Good Works, a lengthy article constituting one-third of all the doctrinal articles (again a postscript to the first draft), eloquently confirms this fundamental doctrine of the Reformation.

Four

The brief Article VII defines the Church as the "assembly of saints," or according to the German text, the "assembly of believers" [6] among whom the Gospel is preached in its purity and the sacraments are administered according to the Gospel." This one holy Church is to continue forever. This Church is not at all invisible, as has sometimes been stated. Melanchthon states in the Apology (VII-VIII, 20) that it is not a "Platonic republic" nor an imaginary Church which is to be found nowhere, for believers as well as the Word and sacraments are entities existing in space and time. However the Church is an object of faith, because the genuineness of a man's faith is known to God alone. In fact, in this life, as Article VIII adds, "many false Christians, hypocrites and even open sinners remain among the godly." This definition of the Church unites the concept of the Church as a fellowship and as an institution, for the fellowship of believers is constituted by the Word and sacraments.

The marks of the Church are seen in the Gospel and the sacraments. The emphasis on the preaching of the Word in purity and the right administration of the sacraments points to the ideal in the doctrinal presentation of the saving Gospel. The continuity of the Church is to be found in a "succession of believers." Church government, including the episcopate, is not a mark of the Church.[7] Neither episcopate nor presbyterial succession belongs to the essence of the Church.

Concerning the unity of the Church, Article VII declares "it is enough to agree concerning the teaching of the Gospel and the administration of the sacraments." It is not necessary that human traditions or rights and ceremonies be alike everywhere. The Lutheran Church has never issued a "Common Prayer Book."

[6] The interchange of these two terms reflects a genuine biblical understanding of sainthood. Sainthood is not a moral attribute.
[7] Cf. also Art. XXVIII, "Ecclesiastical Power."

The nature of the ministry is functional. Ministers are "heralds of the Gospel."[8] However nobody should publicly teach, preach, or administer the sacraments "without a regular call" (*nisi rite vocatus*, Article XV). A Christian is made a minister by the call.

In the *Augsburg Confession* Melanchthon did not express himself on the nature of ordination. In Article XIII of the *Apology* he stated that the laying on of hands may be called a sacrament if it is interpreted in relation to the proclamation of the Word, but ordination does not impart a sacerdotal character "as though the new covenant needed a priesthood like the Levitical." Ordination belongs not to the *esse*, only to the *bene esse* of the church. The lack of ordination does not invalidate the Word or the sacraments. Nor does the moral character of the minister contribute anything essential to the Word and sacraments. The sacraments are valid *ex opere operato*, but will not justify "without a good attitude in the one using them." (*Apology*, VII-VIII, 21). This discussion shows that the *Augsburg Confession* is opposed to all those who regard ecclesiastical order as divinely instituted, on the one hand, and to spiritualistic individualism, on the other.

Article XV, supplemented by sections in Article XXVIII, offers guiding thoughts concerning rites and usages not commanded by Scripture but which have grown out of the history of the Church. The approach to these discussions may be seen in the closing statement of Article VII: "Nor is it necessary that human traditions, rites or ceremonies, instituted by men, should everywhere be alike." Here the problem of the *adiaphora* is involved. The guiding principles in matters of rites and usages in the Church are the following: (1) Divinely commanded ceremonies such as the sacraments must be maintained. (2) With respect to ceremonies not divinely commanded there must be liberty. (3) Ceremonies should not be multiplied (Article XXIII), because (a) they tend to obscure the doctrine of grace, (b) they may lead men to think lightly of the real commandments, (c) they may burden men's consciences. (4) There are rites and usages which ought to be observed, namely, (a) such as are profitable for good order and helpful to a Christian way of life, *e.g.* the Lord's day, Easter, Pentecost, and similar holy days; (b) where an observ-

---

[8] Cf. Helmut T. Lehmann, *Heralds of the Gospel* (Philadelphia: Muhlenberg Press, 1953).

ance is dictated by love; i.e. not to give offence, and (c) as added by the *Formula of Concord* (Article X), where it is the Christian's duty to profess the truth.

Five

The nature and meaning of the sacraments is discussed in Articles IX-XIII. Directed against Zwingli, Article XIII declares that the sacraments are "not merely marks of professon among men"; they are real means of grace, "signs and testimonies of the will of God toward us." Since Confession and Repentance are included in this article, it appears that the *Augsburg Confession* fixes the number of sacraments at three. This impression is confirmed by the statement in the *Apology* which says that "the genuine sacraments . . . are baptism, the Lord's Supper and absolution."

Article IX does not aim at a complete doctrine of baptism. Here there is much in common with Rome. Though valid *ex opere operato,* baptism is effective if the grace offered is accepted by man. Baptism is a divine appointment and as such is necessary for salvation. It is through baptism that man is received into the Church the realm of the redeeming work of God, apart from which there is no salvation. Children, too, are to be baptized.[9]

Article X on the Lord's Supper is very brief. Melanchthon was satisfied with affirming the Real Presence and, by implication, the *manducatio oralis et indignorum.* The rejection of "those who teach otherwise" is put in the mildest possible form (*improbant secus docentes*). Evidently the article was meant to be an invitation to those under the influence of Bucer to join the Lutheran confession.[10]

The sacrament of Penance is comprised of two elements: the sacramental action before the priest and the inward disposition of the sinner, i.e. repentance. With respect to the former, Article XI declares

---

[9] The most extended discussion of baptism in the Confessional writings is found in Luther's *Large Catechism,* Part IV. Baptism, he maintains here, is the work of God, but without faith it is of no use. It is something which the Christian has to study and practice all his life. Concerning infants, Luther says, "we bring the child with the purpose and hope that he may believe, and we pray to God to grant him faith." A person baptized in infancy should not be rebaptized later, for his baptism would be valid though he did not believe when he was baptized—"which, however, cannot be proved."

[10] This hope of Melanchthon's did not materialize.

that private confession and absolution should be retained, but that the enumeration of all trespasses and sins is neither necessary nor possible. Concerning the second aspect, repentance is said to consist of two parts: genuine contrition and faith in Christ. The good works that must follow are not in any ways "works of satisfaction," but rather the inevitable fruit of true repentance.[11] The Article also rejects the teaching of those who hold that a person who has become godly cannot fall again[12] and also the rigorism of the ancient Novatians, who denied restoration, even after repentance, to those who were guilty of grave sins.

In the Large Catechism (Part IV) Luther recognized only two sacraments: Baptism and the Lord's Supper. Baptism, he says, "comprehends also the third sacrament, formerly called Penance, which is nothing else than baptism." For "if you live in repentance, you are walking in Baptism." While the Roman practice dealt with offences and sins against regulations, this article focuses attention upon the promises of the Gospel accepted by faith.

Six

The *Augsburg Confession* has one article on civil affairs (Article XVI). In substance the Article declares that civil government is a divine institution; that it is right for a Christian to hold private property, and that marriage is pleasing to God. The Article is aimed at the Anabaptists of that day who confused Church and state and equated the Kingdom of Christ with a definite political and social order. In the more elaborate treatment in the *Apology*, Melanchthon stressed three points; (1) a Christian is bound by conscience to obey the government; (2) he may avail himself of public redress; and (3) he may sit as judge and determine matters by imperial and other existing laws[13] and may also participate in a "just," i.e. defensive, war.

---

[11] This understanding of confession is further developed in Art. XXV.

[12] Such was the teaching of some of the Anabaptists. Cf. *Die Bekenntnisschriften der evangelisch-lutherischen Kirche* (1952), pp. 67-68, n. 2.

[13] Against Karlstadt, Luther maintains that the Decalog stands only insofar as it agrees with natural law, that the Decalog was the *Sachsenspiegel*, i.e., the civil code, of the Jews. Hence, every nation has a right to promulgate a civil code of its own, including those commandments which are in agreement with natural law (*LW*, 40:97-98).

Seven

Article XVII, on Christ's return to judgment, professes the ecumenical faith in the second Coming of Christ, the resurrection of the dead, and life everlasting. On the negative side it rejects the "restoration of all" and the doctrine of a millenium as held by some of the Anabaptists.[14] Its rejection is expressed in the following words: "Rejected, too, are certain Jewish opinions . . . which teach that, before the resurrection of the dead, saints and godly men will possess a worldly kingdom and annihilate all the godless."

The conciliatory tendency of the Lutherans at Augsburg most likely led them to pass over the Roman teaching of purgatory. Later, in the *Smalcald Articles*, Luther minced no words in condemning the doctrine of purgatory and the traffic in purgatorial masses, referring to the pope as the "very Antichrist." [15]

In Part II of the *Augsburg Confession* "an account is given of the abuses which have been corrected." They are, briefly speaking, as follows: in the Lord's Supper, both kinds are given to laymen (XXII), priests are permitted to marry (XXIII), the celebration of the mass without communicants has been abolished (XXIV), in Confession enumeration of sins has been discontinued (XXV), church regulations and traditions, especially the distinction of foods, are no longer observed as necessary for salvation (XXVI), marriage has been restored to its proper place, with monastic vows being held in disrepute (XXVII), and finally, the episcopal office has been restricted to its spiritual functions (XXVIII).

The Apology of the Augsburg Confession

This document was published by Melanchthon immediately after his return from Augsburg. It was necessitated by the official reply to the *Augsburg Confession* by the Roman theologians in their so-called *Confutation.*[16] The chief and permanent value of the *Apology* lies in the fact that it is the oldest and most authentic interpretation of the *Augsburg Confession* by the author himself. The aim of the *Apology* was (1) to reject the claim of the Romanists that through the *Confu-*

[14] Cf. *Bekenntsschriften*, pp. 72-73, n. 2, n. 3.
[15] *Smalcald Articles*, Part II, Art. I, IV.
[16] See the English text in Jacobs, *op. cit.*, II, 209 ff.

tation the *Confession* had been refuted, (2) to articulate the differences between Wittenberg and Rome by tracing them back to the fundamental difference of Law and Gospel, sin and grace. The doctrine of justification by grace through faith (*propter Christum, per fidem*) is the pivot of the whole *Apology*.[17]

THE SMALCALD ARTICLES

These Articles were written by Luther in case the Wittenberg theologians should decide to attend the general council which the pope had promised to convene at Mantua. They met at Smalcald in 1537. The Articles, in three main divisions, are highly polemical. The vehemence of Luther's conviction is evident everywhere. Part I, in four brief articles, treats the doctrine of the Trinity and of the Incarnation. Concerning these matters, Luther states, there is no dispute or contention. "Therefore it is not necessary to treat them at greater length." Luther added them in order to stress the non-sectarian, ecumenical character of the Reformation. In addition he was certain that the trinitarian faith, including the Incarnation, lies at the heart of Christian theology. Part II is likewise a group of four articles which make it clear that, despite the common endorsement of the creeds of the Ancient Church, "the two parties disagreed in their interpretation and application of these creeds." [18] Against the background of the Incarnation and the death of Christ, the doctrine of justification by faith, in the eyes of Luther, is the *articulus stantis et cadentis ecclesiae* (the article with which the Church stands and falls). Consequently, "nothing in this article can be given up or compromised, even if heaven and earth and things temporal should be destroyed. . . . On this article rests all that we teach and practice against the pope, the devil, and the world." [19] This fact explains Luther's bitter criticism of the Mass,[20] the monastic way of life,[21] and the papacy.[22] Part III

---

[17] For more extensive discussion of the *Apology*, consult the literature cited in the Bibliography under *Augsburg Confession*.

[18] Tappert, *op. cit.*, p. 292, n. 5.

[19] Part II, Art. I.

[20] *Ibid.*, Art. II.

[21] *Ibid.*, Art. III.

[22] *Ibid.*, Art. IV.

consists of fifteen articles which, as Luther says, "we may discuss with learned and sensible men, or even among ourselves." They treat of the nature and forgiveness of sin, Law and Gospel, the sacraments, the ministry, the Church, good works, and human traditions.

The *Tractatus* (Treatise) of Melanchthon, which is printed as an appendix to the *Smalcald Articles*, unlike the Articles, was officially adopted at Smalcald. It consists of two parts, one concerning the pope, the other concerning bishops in general. In the first part Melanchthon tries to show that the Roman claim that the pope is the supreme head of the Church by divine right cannot be substantiated either from the Scriptures or from the tradition of the ancient Church. In addition, Melanchthon regards the pope's claim to be supreme over the secular power by divine right as intolerable, and looks with deep resentment upon the assertion that man's salvation depends on obedience to the pope. Because of these extravagant claims, Melanchthon maintains, it is evident "that the marks of the Antichrist coincide with those of the pope's kingdom and his followers." [23]

In the second part of the *Treatise* Melanchthon rejects the hierarchal structure of the Church. Contrary to the claim of the Romanists, he says, the Church retains the right of electing and ordaining pastors, and of exercising jurisdiction, since the power of the keys was given to the whole Church, "and not merely to certain individuals." [24] In the *Augsburg Confession* and its *Apology* Melanchthon looked forward to a Church reformed and cleansed of the abuses of the bishops. In the *Treatise* he no longer held this hope. The Gospel alone is necessary, not bishops. For administrative reasons the ministry may be graded one; yet spiritually, all ministers are alike, "whether they are called pastors, presbyters, or bishops." [25]

[23] "Treatise on the Power and Primacy of the Pope," 39.

[24] *Ibid.,* p. 67.

[25] *Ibid.,* p. 61. High-church-minded Lutherans have usually maintained that, according to the *Treatise,* the concept of a presbyterial succession belongs to the essence of the Church. This view is hardly germane to the tenor of the Treatise, for the argument teaches its climax in a solemn affirmation of the priesthood of all believers in whom the power of the keys is vested (p. 69). For a more detailed analysis of the *Smalcald Articles* see W. D. Allbeck, *Studies in the Lutheran Confessions* (Philadelphia: Muhlenberg Press, 1952), pp. 194 ff.

Luther's Catechisms

Both *Catechisms* came off the press in 1529. They are divided into five parts: the Decalogue, Apostles' Creed, the Lord's Prayer, Baptism, and the Lord's Supper.[26] Although prepared simultaneously, "the *Small Catechism* is not merely a condensation of the *Large Catechism*, nor is the *Large Catechism* simply an expansion of the *Small Catechism*. They differ in tone and purpose. Written for use in the households of plain people, the *Small Catechism* bears no trace of polemics so evident in the *Large Catechism*, which was written particularly for ministers." [27]

Apart from being manuals for instruction, the *Catechisms* have a definite confessional significance. The *Augsburg Confession* and the *Small Catechism* are the two documents regarded as the "particular confessions of the Lutheran Church" which are officially recognized by all the Lutheran churches of the world. In their struggle with Calvinism, the Lutherans turned increasingly to the *Small Catechism* as the banner of their faith.

Closely related to the confessional significance of the two *Catechisms* is their theological significance. Their theology is both ecumenical and evangelical. Luther again wanted to drive home the central truth of the Scriptures. Man is both creature and sinner who is redeemed by Christ, whose atoning death is appropiated by faith. This is the Gospel as proclaimed in the one, holy, catholic Church through both Word and sacrament. Justified by faith, the Christian will of necessity bring forth good works.[28]

BIBLIOGRAPHY

The Schwabach Articles
  Die Bekenntnisschriften der evangelisch-lutherischen Kirche. Edited by the *Deutsche Evangelische Kirchenausschuss.* 2nd ed., 1952. See especially pp. 52 ff. English translation appears in *H. E. Jacobs; The Book of Concord; Or, The Symbolical Books of The Evangelical Lutheran Church with Historical Introduction, Notes, Appendixes*

[26] For the latest critical edition see *Die Bekenntnisschriften*, pp. 499 ff.; English translation by Tappert, *op. cit.*, pp. 337 ff.

[27] Tappert, *op. cit.*, p. 337.

[28] See the fine analysis of the Catechisms in Allbeck, *op. cit.*, pp. 213 ff. (especially the remarks on p. 219), and the literature cited there. See also our discussion of the Formula of Concord in Chapter VII.

and Indexes. Philadelphia: General Council Publication, 1916. II, 69 ff.

REU, MICHAEL. *The Augsburg Confession.* Chicago: Wartburg Publishing House, 1930.

EA, 24:322 ff.; *WA,* 30:III, 172 ff.; *CR,* 26:141 ff.

The Augsburg Confession

CR, 26:97 ff.

Critical edition in *Bekenntnisschriften der lutherischen Kirche.* 2nd. ed., 1952.

Book of Concord. Edited by THEODORE G. TAPPERT. Philadelphia: Muhlenberg Press, 1959.

ALLBECK, W. D. *Studies in the Lutheran Confessions.* Philadelphia: Muhlenberg Press, 1952.

ASMUSSEN, HANS. *Warum noch lutherische Kirche?* 1949.

NEVE, J. L. *A Guide to the Augsburg Confession.* Columbus, Ohio: Lutheran Book Concern, 1927.

REU, MICHAEL. *The Augsburg Confession.* Chicago: Wartburg Publishing House, 1930.

SCHLINCK, EDMUND. *The Theology of the Lutheran Confessions.* Translated by PAUL F. KOEHNEKE and HERBERT J. A. BOUMAN. Philadelphia: Muhlenberg Press, 1961.

CHAPTER VI

BUCER, CALVIN, AND THE CONFESSIONAL STANDARDS OF CALVINISM

I. Martin Bucer

Martin Bucer (Butzer) was born in the Alsace, 1491. In 1506 he entered the Dominican order. He became a follower of the Reformation in 1518; yet the humanistic and spiritualistic tendencies current in Switzerland and along the Rhine remained potent factors in his thought. Later he became the reformer of Strassburg. His residence on the Rhine, so near Switzerland, brought him into contact first with theological influences of Zwingli and his group and later with Calvin. His location was a factor in making him the type of mediating theologian for which he is known in history. In 1549, on account of the Counter-Reformation, he was forced to leave Strassburg and accepted the invitation of Cranmer to come to England as professor at Cambridge. He soon became an influential factor in Protestant circles there. He died at Cambridge in 1551.

Several things attracted the English reformers to Bucer: (1) His mediating position on the Lord's Supper was bound to appeal to them. In this matter he had enjoyed the confidence of Philip of Hesse, and had been untiringly active in efforts at mediating between the cities of the South and the Lutherans of northern Germany. While the Augsburg diet was in session he played a leading role in formulating the *Tetrapolitana* with its mediatory position regarding the Eucharist. (2) Like Bugenhagen in the north, Bucer was endowed with a gift when it came to the practical affairs of the Church, and he employed this gift in organizing Protestant churches in numerous cities in South Germany and in Hesse. (3) In connection with this practical inclination he followed the ideals of the Christian life which became characteristic of Calvin's reformation. Especially in his book, *De regno Christi*, dedicated to King Edward VI of England, he developed a conception of the relation between Church and state which is strongly suggestive of the ideas of Calvin.

Bucer's theology was influenced to a large extent by Luther. This influence is particularly discernible in Bucer's teachings on sin, grace, and justification. Occasionally the Strassburg theologian defined justification as including election, the remission of sins, and newness of life. At other times Bucer says that justification consists first of forgiveness, and then of the restoration of the divine image in man.[1]

Even his doctrine of predestination bears a resemblance to that of Luther. Strictly speaking, predestination means the election of the saints to everlasting life. In the wider sense of the term, it signifies God's providential rule over all things. From this point of view, Bucer also teaches a predestination of the godless, for they too have a place in the whole economy of God.[2]

Unlike Luther, Bucer postulates a more intimate connection between law and gospel. The "substance" of the divine ordinances is said to be the same in both Testaments. This explains Bucer's attempt to regulate the Christian life in a way that later became normative in Calvinism[3] The Church, in his eyes, is the kingdom of Christ. Its purpose is the administration and care of the eternal salvation of the elect. In the Church Christ Himself, our Lord and King, gathers and rules his elect through his ministers by means of the Word and discipline.[4]

In summary it should be noted (1) that it was largely Bucer, in connection with Melanchthon, who transmitted Luther's conception of Christianity to Calvin; and (2) that it was Bucerism, together with Melanchthonism, that prepared the way for the German Reformed church as it exists today (especially along the Rhine) and which put

---

[1] Cf. quotation of relevant passages of Bucer's commentary on Romans in Otto Ritschl, *Dogmengeschichte des Protestantismus*, III, 147. Cf. also Seeberg, *Lehrbuch*, IV, Part II (1920), 553.

[2] *Commentary on the Gospels*, II, 25b, 201b.

[3] The "closed Sunday" has its origin in Bucer's theology. Cf. Otto Ritschl, *op. cit.*, III, 128-29.

[4] Especially developed in *De Regno Christi;* cf. the *Tetrapolitana*, Art. XV.

upon this church the peculiar stamp of a mild Calvinism in the doctrine of the eucharist, evading, however, the Calvinistic emphasis upon predestination.

II. JOHN CALVIN

Calvin, as churchman and theologian, established a continuity with the heritage of Zwingli, whose followers were now led by Bullinger. This was done in the *Zurich Consensus* of 1549. The biographer of Calvin, E. Staehelin, pronounces this confessional document "the solemn act by which the Zwinglian and Calvinistic reformations were joined in everlasting wedlock as the one great Reformed Church." [5] Still, Calvin was not a follower of Zwingli. While there is a noticeable approach to Zwingli in the *Consensus*, the teaching of Calvin follows the manner of Bucer's mediation. Calvin's historical significance lies in his ability to put the stamp of his theology on all the various Protestant teachings in Western Europe which had hesitated at Luther's realism, his distinction between law and gospel, and his conception of a separation of Church and state. Calvin gradually united the diverging tendencies within the Reformed churches, and by further development of these tendencies made them into a new type of Protestant Christianity.

Calvin was the greatest among the theologians of the Reformed group. He was not a prophet such as Luther, who left so much unpolished gold to the Church that generation after generation continues to study his writings, seemingly without exhausting them. Calvin, like Melanchthon, succeeded in actually coining his own theological thought. Calvin can be studied, exhausted, and mastered. He was not creative in the sense that he produced a new world of religious thought. In the main he worked with the ideas of Luther, Augustine, and others. Seeberg remarks: "He possessed the wonderful talent of comprehending any given body of religious ideas in its most delicate refinements and giving appropriate expression to the results of his investigations." [6] He was the greatest exegete of the Reformation period, excelling Luther in keen logical thought, and surpassing both Luther and Melanchthon in systematizing the new conception of Christianity which had been brought to light through

[5] E. Staehelin, *Johannes Calvin*, II, 121.
[6] Seeberg, *Textbook*, II, 394.

the Reformation. As a man of the second generation of Reformers, he had a distinct advantage over Luther, Zwingli, and Melanchthon— the advantage of perspective. But with him that large view over the whole situation was a native gift. He had a remarkable ability for organization and with it, the Frenchman's gift for ruling.

Calvin was a Christian statesman. As such he modified and applied in his own way the principles of Protestant religion to the needs of locality and time. Since he lived and labored in a republic, he became an aristocratic republican. Under favorable conditions, such as existed in the Anglo-Saxon world, this aristocratic republicanism could easily be broadened into a genuine democratic concept of government. Luther turned at an early age from the study of jurisprudence to that of theology, but Calvin was a perfectly trained lawyer. To some extent this may account for his legalistic conception of Christianity which reminds us of Tertullian, the father of Roman Catholicism.

Calvin never met Luther but he was thoroughly familiar with his writings and he accepted his teachings in most of the so-called fundamentals. His estimate of Luther was high. In a letter addressed to Farel, 1551, he said: "If they (Luther and Zwingli) are compared, you yourself know how far Luther excels." [7] Shortly before Luther's death Calvin addressed him as his most honored father. Luther, in 1539, wished Calvin well and sent him greetings through Bucer. Especially during the years of his banishment from Geneva and his stay at Strassburg (1538-1541), Calvin inclined strongly toward Lutheranism. This attitude was cultivated to a considerable degree by his personal acquaintance and friendship with Melanchthon, whom he met at the colloquies at Worms and Regenburg, 1540 and 1541. Calvin was spoken of as a South German Lutheran.

This cordial relationship between Calvin and the Lutherans was later terminated by a new conflict over the Lord's Supper. The mediating position in the Articles drawn up by Melanchthon and Bucer for introducing the Reformation to the city of Cologne revealed the situation. Reports were circulated that Luther, because of his silence, had yielded in his teaching of the real presence. This prompted Luther, two years before his death, to publish his *Shorter Confession of the Holy Sacrament.*[8] Luther's *Confession* was very

---

[7] *CR,* 39:24.   [8] See p. 385.

embarrassing to Calvin. Though different from Zwingli, Calvin could not accept Luther's doctrine of the ubiquity of the body of Christ. The dilemma in which he found himself is revealed in a letter he wrote to Melanchthon, dated November 28, 1552: "You can imagine how painful it would be for me to find myself estranged from the man [Luther] whom I love and honor more than any other and whom God not only adorned with incomparable gifts but whom He, as His most prominent servant, entrusted the administration of the highest things." [9] But with all these pleasant words, Calvin was very determined in the rejection of Luther's teaching on this point.

The Lutherans began their polemical activity against Calvin with a publication by Joachim Westphal in 1552.[10] Calvin at first ignored this and other attacks, but later replied in two successive writings.[11] A heated controversy was in progress with many theologians of both sides participating. Calvin replied in a third and final writing.[12] The whole controversy brought further embarrassment to Melanchthon. In his *Last Admonition*, Calvin made the statement that he had received the Augsburg Confession in the sense in which it had been interpreted by its own author, Melanchthon. His reference was, of course, to the altered edition of 1540, to which he and others had subscribed at the colloquy in Worms, 1540.[13]

Scripture and the Knowledge of God

Luther had affirmed the truth of Scripture and its sole authority for Christian doctrine. He developed no theory of inspiration and moved with great freedom in judging the canon inherited from Judaism and the early Church. He recognized a form of doctrine in the Bible which served as a basis for criticism of whole books and passages in

---

[9] *CR*, 42:416.

[10] *Farrago confusanearum et inter se dissidententium opinionum de coena Domini* ("A Hodge-Podge of Miscellaneous and Amongst Themselves Dissenting Opinions on the Lord's Supper").

[11] *CR*, 37:1 ff., 41 ff. For an English translation of the "Second Defence" see *Tracts and Treatises*, (Grand Rapids, Mich.: Eerdmans, 1958), II, 245 ff.

[12] *CR*, 37:137 ff.; *Tracts and Treatises*, II, 346 ff.

[13] ". . . in regard to the Confession of Augsburg . . . [as it was published at Ratisbon] it does not contain a word contrary to our doctrine. If there is any ambiguity in its meaning, there cannot be a more competent interpreter than its author, to whom, as his due, all pious and learned men will readily pay this honour." *Ibid.* p. 355.

the canon. Luther found this criterion in the doctrines of the incarnation and of justification by faith, particularly as it was set forth in the Fourth Gospel and in the Pauline Epistles to the Romans and Galatians. In other words, according to Luther all Scripture teaches Christ.

Calvin was thoroughly sympathetic to this view. He, too, saw Christ everywhere in the Bible. However, Calvin's approach to the subject is much more in keeping with human logic and reason.

In the *Institutes* Calvin sets forth the doctrine of Scripture within the wider context of the knowledge of God. "There is within the human mind, and indeed by natural instinct, an awareness of God." [14] This awareness can never be fully erased from the mind of man. Hence actual atheism, Calvin holds, is impossible.[15] The whole universe reflects the workmanship of God.[16] To this knowledge of God in nature, God added the light of his Word.[17] The Word clarifies the otherwise confused knowledge of God in our minds.[18] In addition to the knowledge of God as Creator, the Word reveals God as Mediator and Redeemer.[19] Lest the oracles of God granted to the patriarchs be forgotten, God inspired the patriarchs to pass them down to posterity.[20] This is the origin of the Bible. The revelation in Scripture excels the revelation in creation for the former can communicate to us what the latter cannot.[21] The Bible has its authority from God, not from the Church which is grounded upon the Bible.[22] Although the canon is the bequest of the Church, Scripture "indeed is self-authenticated." [23] God is the author of the Bible.[24] The Scriptures have sprung from heaven.[25] God willed that the law be put down and sealed in writing. In addition, the prophets composed "under the dictation of the Holy Spirit." [26] Later came the Apostles as "sure

[14] *The Institutes of The Christian Religion*, I, 3, 1.
[15] *Ibid.*, I, 3, 3.
[16] *Ibid.*, I, 3, 11.
[17] *Ibid.*, I, 6, 1.
[18] *Loc. cit.*
[19] *Loc. cit.*
[20] *Ibid.*, I, 6, 2.
[21] *Ibid.*, I, 6, 4.
[22] *Ibid.*, I, 7, 1 f.
[23] *Ibid.*, I, 8, 5.
[24] *Ibid.*, I, 7, 4.
[25] *Ibid.*, I, 7, 1.
[26] *Ibid.*, IV, 8, 6.

and genuine scribes [amanuenses] of the Holy Spirit." [27] Law and gospel, then, plus the history related in the Bible, are oracles of God.

If the Scriptures are the very oracles of God, rational proofs to establish the authority of the Bible seem to be unnecessary. Nevertheless Calvin offers, throughout Chapter VIII of Book I of the *Institutes*, a whole list of such proofs, repeating in part what had been said by the theologians of the ancient Church and the Schoolmen of the Middle Ages as well as anticipating the orthodox theologians of the seventeenth century, both Reformed and Lutheran.[28]

In criticism of Calvin's view of the Bible, Hunter correctly remarks:

> To complete his doctrine, Calvin would need to show reason for believers that its compilers were in such wise under the guidance of the Holy Spirit that they included nothing which was not divinely inspired and excluded nothing which was. The witness of the Holy Spirit in each believer's heart would then be the testimony to the trustworthiness of His own editorship.[29]

Calvin did not offer such a reason, nor could he or any other defendant of the authenticity and completeness of the Bible offer it, for the simple reason that Scripture itself nowhere defines the extent of its canon. For example, were the lost letters of Paul to the Corinthians and Laodiceans not inspired? The Apostle evidently put these letters on the same level with his extant epistles to the churches in Corinth and Colossae. Contrariwise, in the eyes of Luther, whom Calvin respected as a true man of God, not every statement, not even every writing of the Bible, is a trustworthy witness to Christ.[30] The doctrine of the canon is indeed one of the most perplexing for orthodox fundamentalistic theology.

---

[27] *Ibid.*, IV, 8, 9. In a footnote to this passage the editors of the *Institutes* (*LCC*, II, 1157) remark that this statement does not "support the view that Calvin's doctrine of the inspiration of the Scriptures was one of verbal inerrancy." In our view, the weight of evidence is against their opinion. Calvin's exegetical works seem to support those who have long held that the great Reformer was the father of the theory of verbal inspiration as taught by the orthodox men of the seventeenth century, both Reformed and Lutheran. Cf. A. M. Hunter, *The Teaching of Calvin* (London: J. Clarke and Co., 1950), pp. 72 ff.

[28] Cf. pp. 468 ff.

[29] A. M. Hunter, *op. cit.*, pp. 69 f.

[30] See pp. 347 ff. Cf. also R. E. Davies, *The Problem of Authority in the Continental Reformers* (London: Epworth Press, 1946), pp. 93 ff., and T. H. L. Parker, *The Doctrine of the Knowledge of God: a Study of Calvin's Theology* (Grand Rapids, Mich.: Eerdmans, 1959).

The Doctrine of God: Predestination

The concept of God and the doctrine of predestination are inseparably interwoven in Calvin's thought. As in the case of Luther, the thought of God is continually in the mind of Calvin; still, his attention is not focused primarily on the love of God. Instead, the concept of the divine majesty and honor is his primary concern. However, the formal treatment of the topic belongs not to the doctrine of God but to the doctrine of salvation. A soteriological interest is by no means lacking. Calvin's definition of predestination, the *decretum horrible*,[31] reads as follows:

> We call predestination God's eternal decree, by which He determined with Himself what He willed to become of each man. For all are not created in equal condition; rather eternal life is foreordained for some, eternal damnation for others. Therefore as any man has been created to one or the other of these ends, we speak of him as predestined to life or to death.[32]

Election does not depend on faith "as if Scripture taught that we are merely given the ability to believe, and not, rather, faith itself." [33] Nor is it doubtful or ineffectual until confirmed by faith. Man may be elected even in the state of unbelief.

God elects or rejects nations and individuals according to his good pleasure. He may give grace to the one, "because He is merciful, and not give to all because He is a just judge." [34]

Calvin expressly denies that the destruction of the non-elect is merely a matter of God's foreknowledge. In God there is neither future nor past, but all things are present. In his omniscience, he not only conceives all things through ideas, "as we have those things which our minds remember," but He truly looks upon them as things and discerns them as things placed before him.[35] Nor is Calvin ready to accept the distinction between will and permission as if God permits the destruction of the impious but does not will it. God is sovereign in every respect and nothing comes to pass unless he wills it.[36] His omnipotence suffers no limitation.[37] Adam fell by the divine

[31] *Institutes,* III, 23, 7.
[32] *Ibid.,* III, 21, 5.
[33] *Ibid.,* III, 24, 3.
[34] *Ibid.,* III, 23, 11.
[35] *Ibid.,* III, 21, 5; 22, 1.
[36] *Ibid.,* III, 23, 8.
[37] *Ibid.,* III, 23, 7.

will "because the Lord had judged it to be expedient." [38] God created Adam that he should perish by his defection.[39] Election precedes the Fall, yea, even creation, for it is unthinkable, Calvin says, that God should have created man, the noblest of his creatures, without a determined end.[40] Predestination is supralapsarian.[41]

The eternal election of the individual is made effective through the call. Being engrafted in Christ, the elect may rest assured that he will never be cut off from salvation.[42] Justification is a sign of election.[43] To the elect God also gives the gift of perseverance.[44] He who truly believes in Christ cannot fall away.

Like Luther in his conflict with Erasmus, Calvin had to answer those who held that the doctrine of predestination makes God the author of sin and that it leads to ethical indifference. The main opposition came from Albert Pighius, a staunch defender of the papacy, and from Sebastian Castellio, a one-time friend of Calvin. Against Pighius, Calvin wrote his *Defensio sanae et orthodoxae doctrinae de servitute et liberatione humani arbitrii*.[45] He addressed himself to Castellio in the highly acrimonious *Brief Reply in Refutation of the Calumnies of a Certain Worthless Person*.[46] With a Pelagian bent of mind, Pighius accused Calvin of ethical indolence, a strange accusation indeed, for no one emphasized man's duty to serve God in daily life and outward conduct more than Calvin. Besides, Calvin does not deny that fallen man possesses the ability to will. In the Fall, he says, man "was not deprived of will, but of soundness of will." [47] Man would not be man if he had no power to will. This belongs to him by

---

[38] *Ibid.*, III, 23, 3, 8.

[39] *Ibid.*, III, 23, 7.

[40] *Ibid.*, III, 23, 7.

[41] *Loc. cit.* Cf. "Articles concerning Predestination," *LCC*, XXII, 179. Charles Hodge remarks that the position of Calvin on this point has been disputed. He quotes from the *Consensus of Geneva*: God elects from the damned race of Adam whom He pleases, and rejects whom He wills. (*Systematic Theology*, II (1874), 316.) But in writing the *Consensus* Calvin was moved by harmonizing and apologetic motives. Besides, the final draft of the *Institutes* was made seven years later, in 1559.

[42] *Institutes*, III, 21, 7.

[43] *Loc. cit.*

[44] *Ibid.*, III, 24, 6-7; II, 3, 11; *passim.*

[45] *CR*, 34:225 ff. W. A. Hauck, *Die Erwählten: Prädestination und Heilsgewissheit nach Calvin* (1950).

[46] See English text with introduction in *LCC*, XXII, 331 ff.

[47] *Institutes*, II, 3, 5.

nature. But to will ill, is of a corrupt nature; to will well, of grace.[48]
Like Luther, Calvin distinguishes between necessity and compulsion.[49]
Man sins not by outward compulsion, but spontaneously by the necessity of innate evil.

Motivated by humanistic tendencies, Castellio attacked Calvin's doctrine of predestination. Calvin's reply is shot through with venomous acrimony. The doctrine under attack is scriptural, says Calvin. God is not the author of sin, for man sins voluntarily. As history shows, God is using evil deeds well. "It is not right to exact from God a reason for His actions." [50] Rather is it becoming to man to wait quietly for the revelation of the mystery. In the meantime, no precise reason for the hidden judgment of God can be rendered. As may be seen, Calvin, like Luther, ultimately appeals to the hidden counsels of God (the *Deus absconditus*).

The Concept of Sin

Like Augustine, Calvin conceived of mankind as a mass of perditions. All men stand condemned and convicted before God because, through Adam's transgression, all have become entangled in the curse. A contagion imparted by Adam resides in all. Infants, too, "are guilty not of another's fault but of their own." [51] Calvin defines original sin as "a hereditary depravity and corruption of our nature, diffused into all parts of the soul, which makes us liable to God's wrath, then also brings forth in us those works which Scripture calls 'works of the flesh' (Gal. 5:19)." [52]

The nature of sin is unfaithfulness, the root of the fall. From it arose ambition, pride, ungratefulness, and disobedience.[53] The whole man lies under the power of sin, yet the chief seat of sin is the will of man.[54] The fall stripped man of all such supernatural gifts as faith, love of God, charity toward neighbor, and zeal for holiness

---

[48] *Loc. cit.*

[49] *Loc. cit.;* cf. Luther, "On the Bondage of the Will," *WA,* 18:634; English translation by J. I. Packer and O. R. Johnston (London: James Clark & Co., 1957), pp. 102-103.

[50] *LCC,* XXII, 342. Cf. Hunter, *op. cit.,* pp. 93 ff.; P. Jacobs, *Praedestination und Verantwortlichkeit bei Calvin* (1937); W. A. Hauck, *op. cit.*

[51] *Institutes,* II, 1, 8.

[52] *Ibid.*

[53] *Ibid.,* II, 1, 4.

[54] *Ibid.,* II, 2, 27.

and righteousness. At the same time, the natural gifts, such as soundness of mind and uprightness of heart, were corrupted. Yet reason, by which man distinguishes between good and evil, was not completely wiped out. Man, in contradistinction to the animal, is capable of pursuing the study of the arts and sciences, and of leading an ordered social life.[55] Likewise, fallen man has retained the faculty of willing. To will is an indestructible endowment of human nature. As to content, however, the will is corrupt. "Simply to will is of man; to will ill, of a corrupt nature; to will well, of grace." [56]

Justification and Sanctification

Calvin held to a strictly forensic view of justification. Man is justified solely by the intercession of Christ's righteousness. In the words of Calvin, "This is equivalent to saying that man is not righteous in himself but because the righteousness of Christ is communicated to him by imputation," and he adds, "something worth carefully noting." [57] To the accusations of his Roman adversaries that such a view of justification would destroy the necessity of good works, Calvin replies, as Luther did before him, that a living faith is never devoid of good works and that the justification of man inevitably involves man's renewal and sanctification. Like the Lutherans in their conflict with Osiander, Calvin was very careful to balance the religious and the moral aspects of redemption. As Christ contains both righteousness and sanctification within himself, so the sinner must first possess Christ, but cannot possess him without being made a partaker in his sanctification, for Christ cannot be divided into pieces.[58]

The Incarnation and the Cross of Christ

Calvin accepted the Chalcedonian doctrine of the two natures of Christ. Christ is God incarnate. The Son of God became the Son of Man "not by confusion of substance but by the unity of person." [59] It is not permissible to commingle the two natures, as Eutyches did, nor to pull them apart. Calvin however declined to follow Luther's

[55] *Ibid.,* II, 2, 12 ff.
[56] *Ibid.,* II, 3, 5.
[57] *Ibid.,* III, 11, 23.
[58] *Ibid.,* III, 16, 1-2.
[59] *Ibid.,* II, 14, 1.

understanding of the doctrine of the *communicatio idiomatum.* The divine nature does not communicate ubiquity to the human nature, nor was the divine nature confined "within the narrow prison of an earthly body." [60] From these premises Calvin concludes that in the Eucharist "the whole Christ is present, but not in his wholeness." [61]

According to Calvin the sinlessness of Jesus was not the result of the virgin birth. Jesus was sinless, he maintains, because the sanctifying power of the Spirit kept Jesus' generation as pure as would have been true before the fall.[62]

God and man are estranged by sin. It takes a mediator to bridge the gulf between God and ourselves. In order to accomplish this, the mediator must be both God and man. Only as God could Christ conquer sin and swallow up death; while only as man could he, in our stead, be obedient to the Father, pay the penalty which we deserved and present our flesh as a satisfaction to God. The work of Christ implies two things: the reconciliation of God and the redemption of man.[63]

The office of Christ is threefold. He was appointed to be prophet, king, and priest. As prophet, he teaches perfect wisdom; as king, he exercises his spiritual rule in the Church through his word and the Spirit; as priest, he reconciles us to God and pleads for us as the everlasting intercessor.[64]

The incarnation, in the eyes of Calvin, was not absolutely necessary. It stemmed from a heavenly decree[65] upon which man's salvation depended. Why then was God made man, and why did he die at all? In the light of the cross, Calvin replies, man learns to know his own misery as well as the greatness of God's love. To be consistent with the holiness of God, a way had to be found to counter man's disobedience with obedience, to satisfy God's judgment and to pay the penalty of sin.[66] According to Calvin then, the absolute decree of God is the sole cause of man's salvation. The decree becomes effec-

---

[60] *Ibid.,* II, 13, 4; 14, 1.
[61] *Ibid.,* IV, 17, 30.
[62] *Ibid.,* II, 13, 4.
[63] *Ibid.,* II, 12, 1 ff.
[64] *Ibid.,* II, 15, 1 ff.
[65] *Ibid.,* II, 12, 1.
[66] *Ibid.,* II, 17, 3.

tive in the elect, not in view of faith but rather in view of the merits of Christ.

The Sacraments

The sacraments, to Calvin, are "a sort of appendix" joined to the Word.[67] Their whole power rests in the Word, and apart from it they are nothing. Calvin approves of the saying of Augustine, "Let the Word be added to the elements and it will become a sacrament." [68] The important function of the sacraments is to confirm and seal the promises of the Word.[69] "The testimony of the Gospel is engraven upon the sacraments." [70] They are "the Word made visible (*verbum visibile*), or a sculpture and image of that grace of God which the Word more fully illustrates." [71] "From the physical things set forth in the sacrament we are led by a sort of analogy to spiritual things." [72] They are "tokens of the covenant" and "pillars of our faith." [73] The sacraments are signs of the condescending grace of God to lead us, his creatures "who always creep on the ground, cleave to the flesh, and do not think about or even conceive of anything spiritual." [74] Thus there is in God's action a correspondence between the visible sign and the thing signified, that is, the spiritual reality proffered in the sacraments. When the Spirit was given to the Apostles on Pentecost, the people saw cloven tongues of fire, "because the preaching of the Gospel was to spread through all tongues and was to possess the power of fire." [75]

R. S. Wallace aptly states:

> The aspect of the Gospel which the sacraments chiefly bring before our eyes in clarifying for us the promises given in the Word is that of our mystical union with the body of Christ. For Calvin, this union with Christ is one of the most important doctrines for anyone to grasp who would understand the Christian faith and the Christian life and the Christian ordinances.[76]

[67] *Ibid.*, IV, 17, 3.
[68] *Ibid.*, IV, 17, 4.
[69] *Ibid.*, IV, 17, 5.
[70] Commentary on II Cor. 5:19.
[71] Commentary on Gen. 17:9.
[72] *Institutes*, IV, 17, 3.
[73] *Ibid.*, IV, 14, 5.
[74] *Ibid.*, IV, 14, 3.
[75] Commentary on Acts 2, 3; on John 1:32.
[76] R. S. Wallace, *Calvin's Doctrine of the Christian Life* (Edinburgh: Oliver and Boyd, 1959), p. 143. We owe much to this excellent study of Calvin.

As Christ in his human nature performed all that is necessary for the salvation of man, so we must be brought into some kind of communion with the "flesh" or body of Christ in which he accomplished his redemptive work. "His flesh as a channel conveys to us that life which dwells intrinsically, as we say, in His divinity." [77] We are incorporated into "a holy brotherhood," [78] the Church. Not only our souls but also our bodies are involved in this union. We are incorporated with him in one life and one substance. [79] Thus engrafted, we "may grow more and more together with Him, until He perfectly joins us with Him in heaven." [80] The sacraments are eschatological signs.

In revealing himself, God takes up into his activity an earthly action, and unites a human element with himself, for the time being. This is what Calvin has in mind when he describes the relationship between the elements and the thing signified as "sacramental union." The affinity which the things signified have with their symbols "is so close that the name of the thing signified is frequently given to the symbol." [81] Thus the bread is figuratively the body of Christ, as an expression of a metonymy. This figure of speech is commonly used in the Scriptures, Calvin says, "when mysteries are under discussion." His definition of a sacrament is wider than Luther's. Without reservation he includes under the term "sacrament" all those signs in the Old Testament "which God ever enjoined upon men to render them more certain and confident of the truth of His promises," as for instance, the tree of life in the Garden of Eden, the rainbow of Noah and his descendants, the smoking fire pot (Gen. 15:17), circumcision, the miracles accompanying the exodus, the fleece watered with dew and conversely, the earth bedewed, leaving the fleece untouched (Judg. 6:37-38), the brazen serpent, etc. "Since these things were done to support and confirm their feeble faith, they were also sacraments." [82] The only difference between the sacraments of the Old Testament and those of the New is this, that whereas "the former foreshadowed

[77] Commentary on John 6:51.
[78] *Institutes,* II, 12, 2.
[79] Commentary on I Cor. 11:24.
[80] *Institutes,* IV, 17, 3.
[81] *Ibid.,* IV, 17, 21.
[82] *Ibid.,* IV, 14, 18; also 15, 9; 17, 21.

Christ promised while He was yet awaited; the latter attested Him as already given and received." [83]

In keeping with the original meaning of the Latin word *sacramentum*, Zwingli limited the significance of the sacraments to an expression of man's loyalty to God and to a badge of the Christian faith. Calvin, on the other hand, does not approve of making the first and only thing that which is secondary in the sacraments. "Now, the first point is that the sacraments should serve our faith before God; after this, that they should attest our confession before men." [84]

With this definition of the meaning of the sacraments in mind, Calvin applies himself to a thorough investigation of the two genuine sacraments of the New Testament: baptism and the Lord's Supper.

Baptism is to him "the sign of the initiation by which we are received into the society of the Church, in order that, engrafted in Christ, we may be reckoned among God's children." [85] It is a token and seal of the remission of sins, and as such, effective for the whole of life, never spending its force, so that no other sacrament, such as the Roman sacrament of repentance, is necessary. It is likewise a token of the mortification of the Old Adam, and a lasting testimony of the believers' union with Christ. Baptism is unrepeatable. Infant baptism[86] is to be continued in the Church just as in the old dispensation infants were included in the covenant which God had made with his people. The necessity of baptism is conditional, not absolute, for in the final analysis, salvation is contingent upon divine election. "God," he says, "adopts our babies before they are born." [87] Hence, "emergency baptism," as continued in the Lutheran church, is meaningless to Calvin and regarded as an infringement upon the ecclesiastical ministry if administered by laymen, especially by women.[88]

Both Luther and Calvin seem to agree that baptism is a real means of grace. Yet there is a marked difference between the two. This becomes apparent when the question is asked how the benefits of baptism are communicated and received. Is it by the Holy Spirit in

[83] *Ibid.*, IV, 14, 20.
[84] *Ibid.*, IV, 14, 13.
[85] *Ibid.*, IV, 15, 1 ff.
[86] *Ibid.*, IV, 16, 1 ff.
[87] *Ibid.*, IV, 15, 20.
[88] *Ibid.*, IV, 15, 20 ff.

the rite itself, or is it by the Holy Spirit in connection with the rite?

In answer to the question "What benefits does baptism confer?", Luther had written: "It worketh forgiveness of sins, delivers from death and the devil, and gives everlasting salvation to all who believe, as the words and promises of God declare." [89] Speaking on what to him was the heart of baptism, he says:

> It is not the water, indeed, that produces these effects, but the Word of God which accompanies and is connected with the water, and our faith which relies on the Word of God connected with the water. For the water, without the Word of God is simply water and no baptism. But when connected with the Word of God, it is a baptism; that is, a gracious water of life and a 'washing of regeneration' in the Holy Ghost as St. Paul says to Titus in the third chapter, verses 5-8.[90]

Calvin's interpretation of the problem under discussion is as follows:

> These things, I say, He performs for our soul within as truly and surely as we see our body outwardly cleansed, submerged, and surrounded with water. For this analogy or similitude is the surest rule of the sacraments, that we should see spiritual things in physical, as if set before our eyes. For the Lord was pleased to represent them by such figures, not because such graces are bound and enclosed in the sacrament so as to be conferred upon us by its power, but only because the Lord, by this token, attests His will toward us, namely, that He is pleased to lavish these things upon us. And He does not feed our eyes with a mere appearance only, but leads us to the present reality and effectively performs what it symbolizes.[91]

The chief interest of Calvin, pertaining to baptism as to the Supper, is in the pedagogy of the rite, in the promise of grace, and in the assurance that God will do to the elect what he promises through symbols and analogies. The benefits are not communicated through the work of the Word as being in any necessary connection with baptism. The rite has only representational, symbolical, and confirmatory significance.[92]

As to the Lord's Supper, Calvin maintains that the words of Institution must not be understood literally, but sacramentally, i.e. according to the usage of Scripture whereby the sign is given the name of the thing signified. For evidence he refers to such statements in Scripture

---

[89] *Small Catechism,* Art. IV.

[90] *Ibid.*

[91] *Institutes,* IV, 15, 14.

[92] Cf. G. W. Richard, *The Heidelberg Catechism* (Philadelphia: Reformed Church Publishing Board, 1913), p. 89.

as: "the lamb is the Passover" (Exod. 12:11), "the rock from which water flowed in the desert (17:6) was Christ" (I Cor. 10:4). There is a mystery of a "sacramental union" by which "those things ordained by God borrow the name of those things of which they always bear a definite and not misleading signification, and have the reality joined with them." [93] "Brevity is obscure," says Calvin. The statements, "Christ is the Son of God," and "This [the bread] is the body of Christ" are two different propositions. Contrary to Luther, Calvin maintains that the words of institution "are not subject to the common rule and are not to be tested by grammar." Instead, the bread is called the body in a sacramental sense.[94] Calvin resents being called a "Tropist." [95] The bread is not a bare figure, as Zwingli taught, "rather with good reason the bread is called body, since not only does it represent the body but also presents it to us." [96]

The gift communicated is the flesh of Christ. The controversy with the Lutherans, especially with Westphal,[97] Calvin maintains, does not concern reception, only the mode of reception.[98] Calvin can say that the *materia* or *substantia* of the Supper is the flesh or the body of Christ, or that it is "Christ with His death and resurrection" [99] In this respect, there seems to be no difference between Calvin and Luther, at least not in the eyes of Calvin himself. However, when he enters upon a discussion of the mode of communication and reception of the body of Christ, Calvin finds himself in decided opposition both to the Lutherans and the Romanists.

To Calvin Luther's teaching of ubiquity is a "monstrous notion." [100] As Christ's body was circumscribed on earth after the manner of a human body, so it is now ciurcumscribed in heaven, "a place higher than all the spheres." [101] There it will be contained until the Last Day.[102] According to his divinity, he is present with us always, but not according to his humanity. Consequently there can be no descent

---

[93] *Institutes,* IV, 17, 21.
[94] *Ibid.,* IV, 17, 21.
[95] *Ibid.*
[96] "Short Treatise on the Lord's Supper," *LCC,* XXII, 147.
[97] Cf. pp. 458 ff.
[98] *CR,* 9:74.
[99] *Institutes,* IV, 17, 33; *passim.* Cf. Wallace, *op. cit.,* pp. 199 ff.
[100] *Institutes,* IV, 17, 30.
[101] *Commentary on Ephesians,* 4:10.
[102] *Institutes.* IV. 17, 26; *passim.*

of the body of Christ into the bread of the Supper, nor can the body become invisibly present on earth, for visibility is a proper and inseparable quality of a body.[103] Calvin deems it utterly unlawful to draw the body of Christ back under the corruptible elements of the Supper and imagine it to be present everywhere. In order to enjoy a participation of the body, the Lord bestows this benefit upon us through the operation of the Holy Spirit. Christ descends in the Spirit, or Calvin may say that the believers are lifted up to Christ by the Holy Spirit.[104]

In the Supper Christ is received by faith; but eating is not the same as believing (as Zwingli had said), for faith as a habit of the soul does not of necessity imply an objective event taking place in the sacrament. Genuine faith is like an empty vessel receiving something other than itself.[105] Calvin, likewise, disapproves of the Lutheran teaching of the oral manducation. According to Luther, Christ communicates himself to the recipient by means of the bread. In Calvin's view, Christ always remains distant from the bread. The Supper affords the believer an opportunity to commune with Christ simultaneously with the reception of the elements.[106] Against the background of this view it stands to reason that Calvin must scorn the Lutheran teaching of the reception of Christ's body by the unworthy.[107]

In conclusion, the question may be in order: Is Calvin closer to Luther or to Zwingli? The Union theologians of Germany have long approved the former alternative. Personally, we are inclined to question this theory. If Zwingli had met with Calvin in 1529, we believe, the Zurich Reformer would gladly and sincerely have signed all the *Marburg Articles*. For proof we may refer to the "everlasting wedlock" between Zurich and Geneva established by Bullinger in the *First Helvetic Confession*, 1536. Like that of Zwingli and Bucer Calvin's Christology reflects a Nestorian tendency. The following statement bears this out: "Although the whole Christ is everywhere, still the whole of that which is in Him is not everywhere." [108] This

---

[103] *CR*, 9:230.
[104] *Institutes*, IV, 17, 12, *passim*.
[105] *Ibid.*, III, 11, 5. Cf. Wallace, *op. cit.*, pp. 211-12.
[106] Cf. *Small Catechism*, Art. IV, and many other passages.
[107] *Institutes*, IV, 17, 33. Cf. Calvin's reply to Tilemann Heshusius (*LCC*, XXII, 282 ff.), and other passages.
[108] *Institutes*, IV, 17, 30.

view is remembered in the history of theology as *"the extra illud Calvinisticum"* In addition, Zwingli, Bucer, and Calvin conceived of heaven and the "right hand of God" as a place far removed from our world, to which Christ was removed at his ascension and where he will remain until the Last Day. Calvin also had a coarse physical concept of the resurrection body of Christ. When it says in Scripture (John 20:19) that Christ went in to his disciples through closed doors, Calvin remarks that either "the hardness of the stone yielded at His approach" or, as is more probable "the stone was removed at His command and immediately after He passed through, returned to its place." [109] Such notions, of course, made it impossible for Calvin to understand, let alone to appreciate, Luther's teaching of the ubiquity of the body of Christ.[110]

Church and Ministry

Calvin had a high conception of the Church. He did not regard the Reformation as a separatist movement.[111] He believed in the one, holy, catholic Church from which the Roman communion had separated itself. The Church, he said, is "the pillar and ground of the truth" and separation from it "is the denial of God and Christ." [112]

Strictly speaking, the Church is the company of all the elect from the beginning of the world, "not only the saints presently living on earth." [113] This Church is invisible to men. From this invisible Church Calvin distinguishes the visible Church, which is the whole multitude of men spread over the earth "who profess to worship God and Christ." [114] The marks of the visible Church are the proclamation of the Word in purity and truth, and the administration of the sacraments according to the institution of our Lord.[115] Important as discipline is for Calvin, he does not include it in the *Institutes* as a third

---

[109] *Ibid.,* IV, 17, 29.

[110] It stands to reason that Calvin, like Luther, rejected in no uncertain terms the Roman doctrine of transubstantiation and of the sacrificial aspect of the Mass (*Institutes,* IV, 17, 12 ff.; the whole of chapter 18; and elsewhere).

[111] *Institutes,* IV, Chap. 2.

[112] *Ibid.,* IV, 1, 10 ff.

[113] *Ibid.,* IV, 1, 7.

[114] *Ibid.,* IV, 1, 7.

[115] *Ibid.,* IV, 1, 9. This definition of the Church agrees almost verbatim with that of Art. VII of the *Augsburg Confession,* the altered version of which Calvin had signed in 1540.

mark of the Church. Yet in his *Reply to Sadolet* he writes that "there are three things on which the safety of the Church is founded and supported: doctrine, discipline, and the sacraments; and to these a fourth is added: ceremonies by which to exercise the people in offices of piety." [116]

Calvin introduced the doctrine of the ministry in the *Institutes* by saying, "Now we must speak of the order by which the Lord willed His Church to be governed." [117] A comparison with the *Augsburg Confession* on this point is interesting. In Article V Melanchthon said that the ministry was instituted that man might obtain saving faith. Calvin's wording shows that he put a higher estimate on the ministry as an order distinct from the congregation. As referred to above,[118] Calvin was opposed to emergency baptism by laymen and was likewise opposed to the laity presiding at the Supper, for both the administration of baptism as well as the serving of the Supper are "a function of the ecclesiastical ministry." In the same manner Calvin maintained that the power of the keys is given to the ministry of the Church.[119] Luther, on the other hand, held that the power of the keys was entrusted to all believers so that each one might act as a Christ to his neighbor. Ministers, Calvin says, are the mouth of God; they perform a work delegated to them by the Lord Himself.[120]

Calvin maintained that some of the offices in the New Testament are temporary while others, among which are the offices of pastors, teachers, elders, and deacons, are permanent. Those who rule in the Church and carry out the ministry of the Word, Calvin says, Scripture calls indiscriminately "bishops," "presbyters," "pastors," and "ministers." [121] The degree nearest to this office is that of the doctors of the Church. In the *Ecclesiastical Ordinances of Geneva* (1541), provision is made for two lectures in theology, one each in the Old and New Testament, and also for a preparatory school for instruction in the languages and humanities.[122]

Next is the office of the elder. Elders are charged with the censure

[116] *LCC,* XXII, 232. Cf. *LCC, XXI,* 1023, n. 18.
[117] *Institutes,* IV, 3, 1.
[118] See p. 430.
[119] *Institutes,* IV, 1, 22.
[120] *Ibid.,* IV, 3, 1.
[121] *Ibid.,* IV, 3, 8.
[122] *LCC,* XXII, 62-63; *Institutes,* IV, 3, 4.

of morals along with the pastors. They form a kind of senate, chosen from godly, grave and holy men, having jurisdiction over the correction of faults.[123] Finally, the Church also should have deacons to serve the church in administering to the poor.[124] According to the *Ecclesiastical Ordinances* these four orders are instituted by our Lord for the government of the Church, and a Church well ordered ought to observe this form of government.[125]

With respect to the making of a minister, Calvin, like Luther, put the primary emphasis on the call. While the call is absolutely essential, Calvin says in the *Institutes* that the rite of ordination by the laying on of hands is merely an apostolic custom whose "careful observance, however, is useful for the dignity of the ministry." [126] In the *Ecclesiastical Ordinances* on the other hand, it is recommended to abstain from the practice of the laying on of hands altogether because of the superstition connected with the Roman sacrament of Ordination.[127]

If a man is made a minister by the external call, who then should choose the ministers? Calvin felt that Scripture provides no sure rule in this matter. Should a pastor be chosen by a single person or by his colleagues and the elders, or should he be chosen by the whole Church? In answering the question, Calvin expresses a preference for a plural authority rather than of an individual.[128] The laying on of hands, he says, ought to be reserved for pastors alone.[129] There was

[123] *Institutes*, IV, 3, 8, "Ecclesiastical Ordinances," *LCC*, XXII, 63-64. According to the *Ordinances for the Supervision of Churches in the Country* (1547), absenteeism from Sunday service without proper excuse and arriving late after the sermon has begun is to be punished by a payment of three sous. A person cursing or renouncing God or his baptism for the first time is to be put on bread and water for ten days. If he repeats his sin, more rigorous corporal punishment is suggested. If unmarried persons cohabit as man and wife, they are to be imprisoned for six days on bread and water and to pay sixty sous. Within five years, from 1542-1546, seventy-eight persons were exiled and fifty-eight were sentenced to death. This was at a time when the city of Geneva had about 20,000 people. (*LCC*, XXII, 77 ff.).

[124] *Institutes*, IV, 3, 9; *LCC*, XXII, 64 ff.

[125] *LCC*, XXII, 58.

[126] *Institutes*, IV, 3, 13.

[127] *LCC*, XXII, 59. Calvin never received ordination by the laying on of hands. He was called to Geneva by the consistory and magistracy, the people expressing their consent. Cf. Hunter, *op. cit.*, p. 202. It must be remembered that Calvin, unlike Luther and Zwingli, had not been previously consecrated as a priest.

[128] *Institutes*, IV, 3, 15.

[129] *Ibid.*, IV, 3, 16. Cf. Hunter, *op. cit.*, pp. 200 ff.

a very fundamental difference between Luther and Calvin on this matter. Not only the work of the pastors as ministers of the Gospel, but a certain organization for the administration of doctrine, *cultus*, and discipline in the Church was made a matter of divine right and was regarded as a command of Scripture. For Luther the scriptural examples of Church government indicated that the gifts bestowed by the Spirit upon the congregation of believers must work themselves out in an orderly fashion for the edification of souls; for Calvin they were so many paragraphs of a divine command.

The Functions of the State

For Calvin the Church is an institution by divine right and as such serves for the salvation of souls. For Luther the Church is essentially the congregation of saints gathered around the means of grace, and as such, becomes an institution only by human right. Calvin stresses the independence of the Church from the state.[130] It was on Calvinistic territory in England and America that this idea of Calvin was first developed and realized. However, Calvin held that the state, in addition to its duty of safeguarding peace and order, must see to it that the right kind of doctrine and worship are maintained, and also that the sins against the first table of the commandments be punished. He demanded that the state conform its laws to the divine law.[131] The officers of the Church were to be the judges in state affairs involving religion and morals. This was the situation: in spite of the admission that the state is sovereign and must be obeyed as long as this can be done without sin,[132] the Church dictated to the state in matters of religion and morals, and demanded that the state help Christianize the world and permeate the social order and civilization with the ethical principles of Christianity—with force where this becomes necessary. Zwingli had stressed the same principle. Thus the Roman Catholic practice of using the state for realizing the ideals of the Church came into Protestantism by the back door.

Calvin's reference to the Church as a divine institution and his conception of the state as a handmaid of piety was the source of

[130] *Institutes,* IV, 11, 4 ff.
[131] *Ibid.,* IV, 20, 2. Cf. "Belgic Confession," Art. XXXVI in Schaff, *Creeds of Christendom,* III, 432-33.
[132] *Institutes,* IV, 20, 22 ff.

the intolerance which Calvin displayed on certain occasions. The most dramatic such occasion was the execution of Michael Servetus on October 27, 1553. To judge the affair dispassionately, one must keep in mind the following: (1) Servetus himself was the product of religious freethinking grafted upon the basic principle of Protestantism, the supreme and final authority of the Bible. Servetus, along with Calvin and the other Reformers, accepted the Scriptures as the only norm of faith, but Servetus failed to recognize the genuine religious and evangelical interest underlying the ancient dogmas of the Trinity and of the two natures of Christ. (2) The tone and temper which Servetus displayed in promoting his views were, in the eyes of many, not only in the eyes of Calvin, insolent and arrogant. He was also suspected of leading a dissolute life. He is alleged to have said that he did not marry because there are enough women in the world without marrying. At the Geneva trial, however, he replied that he did not remember having said it, but he admitted that he might have said it in jest and to conceal his impotence, caused by a rupture and operation at the age of about five.[133] Views of this nature gave impetus to the libertinism that prevailed in Geneva, whose adherents departed from the very fundamentals of Christian doctrine and morals. Calvin's consent to the execution of Servetus cannot, of course, be excused; it can only be explained on the ground that, had the libertine movement gone unchecked, the effect upon religion and morality would have been disastrous.[134]

Calvin also sought a field for the activity of his followers in the sphere of social economy. Trade and industry were to be used for God's glory. Here Calvin and his followers can claim successes which Lutheranism never had. The explanation for this lies in the fact that the sea-faring countries—Holland, France, and England, were far more developed commercially than were Germany and the states of central Europe. Wealth is easily followed by a higher articulation of the cultural interests. Seeberg calls attention to the fact that, under central

---

[133] Cf. Roland H. Bainton, *Hunted Heretic: the Life and Death of Michael Servetus* (Boston: Beacon Press, 1960), p. 191.

[134] Servetus' *Christianismi Restitutio* (Vienna, 1553) was reprinted at Nuremberg in 1790. It was translated into German by B. Speiss, *Wiederherstellung des Christentums* (2nd ed., 1895-96). See Bainton, *op. cit.,* pp. 221-22, and Hunter, *op. cit.,* pp. 230 ff.

European conditions as in Poland, Hungary, and Germany, Calvinism did not have this same success.[135]

From Calvin's view of the relation between Church and state, we may separate his philosophy of the state and particularly his views of the relation of the citizens to the sovereign. To the individual citizen Calvin preached loyalty, even in cases where sovereigns are tyrants and neglect their duty. His reason is that "they have their government only from Him [God]" and that it is the "Most High" who "removeth Kings and setteth up Kings and giveth [the kingdom] to whomsoever He will." He says, "We shall not hesitate to regard the most iniquitous tyrant with the honor due to the station in which the Lord has deigned to place him."[136] Calvin cited Scripture to be observed so that "seditious thoughts may never enter our minds."[137] With regard to the government of cruel tyrants he says: "Nothing remains for us than to serve and to live."[138] Again: "For us it is to obey and suffer."[139] It is in the same paragraph that Calvin says: "This observation I always apply to private persons." One exception he will admit and even stress: "If they command anything against Him it ought not to have the least attention; nor, in any case, ought we to pay any regard to all that dignity attached to magistrates."[140] After these instructions for private persons have been given, he added the following very significant paragraph which, in certain situations, especially in countries under Calvinistic influence, has determined political history. Calvin writes:

> If there be, in the present day, any magistrates appointed for the pro-
> tection of the people and the moderation of the power of kings such as
> were, in ancient times, the Ephori, who were a check upon the kings

[135] Outstanding Luther scholars, such as Heinrich Boehmer and Reinhold Seeberg, emphatically protest against the picture of Luther's ethics which Troeltsch has drawn as the basis of Luther's social ideas. Seeberg calls this picture "badly misdrawn." *Lehrbuch,* IV, Part II (1920), 276 ff. Cf. also the study by W. A. Mueller, *Church and State in Luther and Calvin* (Nashville, Tenn.: Broadman Press, 1954). This volume reflects the bias of the Nonconformist. Of special interest for Lutheran thought and work on the subject is Werner Elert; *Morphologie des Luthertums,* Vol. II (1932). Cf. also G. W. Forell, *Faith Active in Love* (New York: American Press, 1954).

[136] *Institutes,* IV, 20, 25-26.

[137] *Ibid.,* IV, 20, 27.

[138] *Ibid.,* IV, 20, 28.

[139] *Ibid.,* IV, 20, 31.

[140] *Ibid.,* IV, 20, 32.

among the Lacedaemonians, or the popular Tribunes upon the Consuls among the Romans, or the Demarchi upon the Senate among the Athenians; or with power such as perhaps is now possessed by the Three Estates in every kingdom when they are assembled; I am so far from prohibiting them, in the discharge of their duty, to oppose the violence and cruelty of kings, that I affirm that, if they connive at kings in their oppression of the people, such forbearance involves the most nefarious perfidity, because they fraudulently betray the liberty of their people, of which they know that they have been appointed protectors by the ordination of God.[141]

In the Netherlands, in Scotland, in England, and in America, situations arose in which the citizenship of a "lower government" functioned in judgment of the higher government. Zwingli, who had also preached obedience to the government, made provisions for revolutions in case of unfaithfulness to the "rule of Christ." [142] Zwingli recognized authority as residing in the sovereignty of the people. The majority has the right to dethrone godless kings.[143]

Calvin's Humanism

There must be a few remarks on a certain humanism which colored the theology of Calvin. His commentary on Seneca's *De clementia* indicates his interest and inclination. The form of his writings shows the balance and moderation of the humanists. He also betrays influences from the biblicistic features of the humanism of Erasmus and others. Calvin combined scholarship with religion, culture with morality. This, in a way, had been Melanchthon's aim, although he had made practical use of it only in his organization of the university studies. Zwingli, on the other hand, was a decided follower of humanism. Calvin's strong inclination to Luther and Melanchthon kept him from sacrificing any of the evangelical essentials. Humanism to him was not just a means of interpreting the Bible as it was Luther, but a new world of moral culture to which he felt himself attracted. His Lutheran opponents in the succeeding centuries of conflict have always

[141] *Ibid.,* IV, 20, 31.
[142] Zwingli, *Werke,* ed. Schuler and Schulthess, I:156, 449.
[143] *Ibid.,* I, 370; cf. IV:42, 59. See also G. Beyerhaus, *Studien zur Staatsanschauung Calvins* (1910); H. Huscher, *Der Staat in Calvins Gedankenwelt* (1923); H. Baron, *Calvins Staatsanschauung und das konfessionelle Zeitalter* (1924); K. Froehlich, *Gottesreich, Welt und Kirche bei Calvin* (1930); J. T. McNeill, *John Calvin on God and Political Duty* (New York: Liberal Arts Press, 1956).

dwelt upon this trait in Calvin and Calvinism.[144] In studying the differing traits in Luther and Calvin it has been observed that, in the aim of making the thoughts of Luther more tangible, Calvin, like Melanchthon, rationalized the more deeply religious tenets of Luther.[145]

THE CONFESSIONS OF CALVINISM

To this class of documents belongs the *Tetrapolitana*, the Confession of the four cities of Strassburg, Constance, Memmingen, and Lindau, 1530. The authorship belongs to Bucer and Capito of Strassburg.[146] It consists of twenty-three articles.

Calvin wrote the *Catechism of Geneva*, the first draft of which was made in 1536. The final form dates back to 1541. Using the question and answer method, Calvin treats successively the Creed, the Law, Prayer, and the Sacraments. In the French edition the Catechism is divided into fifty-five lessons for the fifty-two Sundays of the year and the three great festivals. This Catechism served as a model for a number of similar catechisms which have gradually superseded it (the *Heidelberg* and *Westminster Catechisms, et al.*).[147]

Next we mention the *Consensus of Zurich*, 1549. Through this document of twenty-six articles, Calvin succeeded in winning over the theologians of Zurich and Berne to his peculiar interpretation of the Lord's Supper. In the words of Staehelin, "It was the solemn act by which the Zwinglian and Calvinist Reformation joined in everlasting wedlock." [148]

Among the other symbols written by Calvin are (1) the *Consensus of Geneva, 1552*, and the *French Confession, 1559*. The latter was composed jointly with his pupil, De Chandieu. The former is an elaborate argument for the doctrine of absolute predestination. It was signed by the pastors of Geneva but beyond the city it acquired no confessional significance.[149] *The French Confession of Faith* was dedi-

[144] Cf. Heinrich Schmid, *Geschichte der synkretistischen Streitigkeiten* (1846), pp. 14 ff.

[145] Cf. Seeberg, *Lehrbuch*, IV, 627 ff.

[146] Frequent reference was made to this document in the chapter on the conflict between Luther and Zwingli over the Lord's Supper.

[147] Cf. the text in *LCC*, XXII, 83 ff.; *Tracts and Treatises*, II, 33 ff.; and Schaff, *op. cit.*, I, 467 ff.

[148] English translation in *Tracts and Treatises*, II, 199 ff.

[149] Cf. Schaff, *op. cit.*, I, 474 ff.

cated to the French king to prove that his Protestant subjects were to do nothing else than to live in purity according to the Gospel. It teaches election to salvation only, saying in Article XII that, as to the rest of humanity, God leaves them in corruption and condemnation "to show in them His justice." [150]

Among the symbols produced by the followers of Calvin, there are (1) the *Scotch Confession of Faith*, 1560; (2) the *Heidelberg Catechism* of Germany, 1563; (3) the *Canons of the Synod at Dort*, 1618 f.; (4) the *Westminster Confession* 1647; and (5) the *Helvetic Consensus Formula*, 1675. The *Heidelberg Catechism* is actually the confessional shibboleth of German Calvinism. In a manner that became typical of German Calvinism and which prepared the way for the Prussian Union of 1817, this Catechism ignored Calvin's doctrine of predestination but affirmed his concept of the Lord's Supper.[151]

As may be gathered from this review, no single confession in Calvinism is comparable to the *Augsburg Confession* in Lutheranism. All of these confessions have only regional significance. The unifying factor is not a single confession but rather the theology of Calvin as expressed above all in the *Institutes*.[152] The Lutheran churches in the Lutheran World Federation are rallied around the *Unaltered Augsburg Confession;* the Reformed churches, because of Calvin's emphasis upon the organizational aspect, are gathered in the "Alliance of Reformed Churches Holding the Presbyterian System."

BIBLIOGRAPHY

Works by Martin Bucer
> *Commentary on John.* 1528.
> *Commentary on Matthew, Mark and Luke.* 2 vols. 1527.
> *Commentary on Romans.* 1536.
> Summary of *A sermon preached in the city of Weissenburg.* 1523.

[150] *Ibid.*, I, 490 ff.; III, 356 ff.

[151] Naturally, there are many editions of the *Catechism* in both German and English. For the text see Schaff, *op. cit.*, III, 307 ff. In addition to these symbols we might add the *Thirty-nine Articles of the Church of England,* for their doctrine of the Supper is unmistakably expressed in the language of Calvin (Art. XXVIII). For the Reformed Confessions in Eastern Europe that have the hallmarks of Calvin's theology, see Schaff, *op. cit.*, I, 565 ff.

[152] The first edition was prepared in 1536; the third and final one in 1559. See the excellent introduction in *LCC*, XX, xxix ff.

The Kingdom of Christ, included in *Scripta Anglicana,* 1577 and in *LCC,* Vol. XIX.
Werke. Edited by ROBERT STUPPERICH. 1952—.

Research on Bucer

ANRICH, G. *Martin Butzer.* 1914.
ELLIS, H. "Martin Bucer and the Conversion of John Calvin." Reprinted from the *Princeton Theological Review,* Vol. XXII, No. 3.
————. "The Genesis of Martin Bucer's Doctrine of the Lord's Supper." Reprinted from the *Princeton Theological Review,* Vol. XXIV, No. 2 (1926).
HOPF, CONSTANTIN. *Martin Bucer and the English Reformation.* Oxford: Basil Blackwell, 1946.
KLINGENBURG, G. *Das Verhältnis Calvins zu Butzer auf Grund der Wirtschaftlichen Bedeutung der beiden Reformatoren.* 1912.
LANG, AUGUST. *Der Evangelienkommentar Martin Butzers und die Grundzüge seiner Theologie.* 1900.
PAUCK, WILHELM. *Das Reich Gottes auf Erden, eine Untersuchung zur englischen Staatskirche des 16. Jahrhunderts.* 1930.

Works by John Calvin

In the *Corpus Reformatorum,* Vols. 29-87.
English edition by Calvin Translation Society. 51 vols., 1843 ff. Reprinted Grand Rapids, Mich.: Eerdmans, 1948.
Opera Selecta. Edited by W. NIESEL and D. SCHLEUMER. 5 vols. 1926 ff.
Commentaries. 45 vols. 1948—.
Tracts and Treatises. 3 vols. Grand Rapids, Mich.: Eerdmans, 1958.
LCC, Vols. XX-XXIII.

Research on Calvin

BECKMAN, J. *Vom Sakrament bei Calvin.* 1926.
BEYERHAUS, G. *Studien zur Staatsanschauung Calvins.* 1910.
DOMERGUE, E. *Jean Calvin.* 7 vols. 1899 ff.
DOWEY, EDWARD A., JR. *The Knowledge of God in Calvin's Theology.* New York: Columbia University Press, 1952.
FROEHLICH, K. *Gottesreich, Welt und Kirche bei Calvin.* 1930.
GRASS, H. *Die Abendmahlslehre bei Luther und Calvin.* 1954.
GRIMM, H. J. *The Reformation Era.* New York: The Macmillan Company, 1954.
HARKNESS, G. *John Calvin: The Man and His Ethics.* New York: Abingdon Press, 1958.
HENDERSON, R. W. *The Teaching Office in the Reformed Tradition: A History of the Doctrinal Ministry.* Philadelphia: Westminster Press, 1962.
HOOGSTRA, J. T. (ed.). *John Calvin: Contemporary Prophet.* Grand Rapids, Mich.: Baker Book House, 1959.
HUNT, R. N. C. *Calvin.* London: Centenary Press, 1933.
HUNTER, A. M. *The Teaching of Calvin.* London: J. Clarke and Co., 1950.

HUSCHER, H. *Der Staat in Calvins Gedankenwelt.* 1923.

JANSEN, J. F. *Calvin's Doctrine of the Work of Christ.* London: J. Clarke and Co., 1956.

MACGREGOR, G. *Corpus Christi: The Nature of the Church According to Reformed Tradition.* Philadelphia: Westminster Press, 1958.

MCNEILL, J. T. *John Calvin on God and Political Duty.* New York: Liberal Arts Press, 1956.

NIESEL, W. *The Theology of Calvin.* Translated by HAROLD KNIGHT. Philadelphia: Westminster Press, 1956.

SCHUBERT, H. VON. *Calvin.* 1909.

STAEHELIN, E. *Johannes Calvin.* 2 vols. 1863.

TORRANCE, T. F. *Calvin's Doctrine of Man.* Grand Rapids, Mich.: Eerdman's, 1957.

WALLACE, R. S. *Calvin's Doctrine of the Christian Life.* Edinburgh: Oliver and Boyd, 1959.

CHAPTER VII

CONTROVERSIES AMONG LUTHERANS AND THE FORMULA OF CONCORD

It will be remembered that in the ancient Church the simple rules of faith, as expressed in the so-called Apostles' Creed, were soon developed into the definitions stated in the later creeds. In like manner the great prophetic age of Protestantism was followed by a didactic age.[1] Controversies were bound to arise. They came in the form of deep conflicts which caused divisions among the Lutherans and made settlements necessary. Many of the controversies, which lasted for almost thirty years (1548–1577), were not edifying in character. But they were necessary for the final establishment of Lutheranism. "Pathological" reviews, such as those given by Jacob Planck in his *Entstehung des protestantischen Lehrbegriffs* (1781–1800), are out of place in the present discussion. What must be remembered is that the Lutheran church will always aim to find her bond of unity in the pure doctrine of the Word. The controversies reviewed in this chapter represent the endeavor of the Lutheran church to achieve this kind of unity.

The controversies involved not only individuals but theological faculties and territories. The Gnesio-Lutherans, as they called themselves, had their centers in the city of Magdeburg and the University of Jena in ducal Saxony. Their leader was Matthias Flacius. Other theologians among them were Nicholas von Amsdorf, Wigand, Heshusius, and others. They were bitterly opposed to the Philippists, the followers of Melanchthon who, in their eyes, yielded too much to Calvinism and Romanism. The Melanchthonian party included George

---

[1] Cf. Seeberg, *Lehrbuch*, IV, Part II (1920), 481 ff.

Major, Victorine Strigel, Caspar Cruciger, *et al.* It had its stronghold in the Universities of Wittenberg and Leipzig. Between these two parties stood a large group of theologians which sought to preserve a position free of both extremes. These men were predominant in the University of Rostock in the north and at Tuebingen in the south.

The work of unification was eventually accomplished in the *For-mula of Concord* (1577), its chief authors being Jacob Andrea of southern Germany and Martin Chemnitz, a respected theologian in the North. The *Formula* was subscribed to by approximately two-thirds of the Lutherans in Germany, which meant it had the status of a symbolical writing. As such it was incorporated into the *Book of Concord,* published in 1580, in commemoration of the delivery of the *Augsburg Confession,* 1530.

As to standards for the doctrinal deliverances, the *Formula of Concord* recognized: (1) the Scriptures as the only source of Chris-tian life and doctrine; (2) the Ecumenical Symbols as confessions of the ancient Church; (3) the *Augsburg Confession* "as symbol of our time," interpreted by the *Apology* and the *Smalcald Articles,* with the *Catechisms* of Luther as popular presentations of the same doctrine.

The *Formula of Concord* is divided into two parts: (1) the Epi-tome and (2) an extensive discussion, the "Solid Declaration." It consists of twelve articles, dealing exclusively with differences among the Lutherans in the post-Reformation age.

The irenic tendency is noticeable. Where errors were to be pointed out (in cases such as controversies with Flacius, Osiander, Agricola, Major, Amsdorf, Strigel, Melanchthon), the names of the teachers were not mentioned. It was to be a "formula of concord" on the basis of Luther's theology. Luther's name alone is mentioned.

We can best find our way through the apparent chaos of contro-versial issues by organizing our material as Thomasius and Tschackert have done and by dealing with (1) the controversies affecting the heart of Lutheranism, namely, the Antinomian and the Osiandrian con-flicts; (2) the controversies bearing upon the conflict between Luther-anism and Melanchthonianism or Philippism, namely, the adiaphoristic, the majoristic, and the synergistic conflicts; (3) the controversies which cleared up the relation between Lutheranism and Calvinism, namely, the Crypto-Calvinistic conflict over the Lord's Supper and the person of Christ; to which we shall add the discussion of predestination.

THE ANTINOMIAN CONTROVERSIES

In his *Instructions for the Visitation of the Saxon Churches* (1527), Melanchthon had written "that the ministers should also preach the Law in order to bring people to repentance." As a result, he was attacked by John Agricola, who contended that repentance is produced not by the law but by the gospel. Luther sided with Melanchthon. Ten years later Agricola staged the real controversy by attacking Luther himself. He maintained that there is no need whatever for the preaching of the law: "The Decalogue belongs to the hall of justice, not to the pulpit." "Man is overpowered by the kindness of God, and thereupon renounces his former life and shrinks from incurring the displeasure of his heavenly Father.[2] Six public disputations were held by Luther. Although Agricola recanted, he never really gave up his views. He felt that he was called to establish the doctrine for free grace against Luther.

A second Antinomistic controversy arose through such men as Andrew Poach and Anthony Otto, of whom the latter stood on the side of Amsdorf. They gave utterance to statements like these: "The best art of the Christian is to know nothing of the law," "Evangelical preachers must preach the Gospel and not the Law," "Law, good works, and new obedience do not belong to the kingdom of God, but to the world, to Moses and the dominion of the pope."[3] This type of radicalism received its answer in the following historical statements which are reminiscent of Luther in his second disputation with Agricola: "The Law of God has a threefold duty—(1) to produce outward righteousness among the ungodly through threats and promises (*usus legis politicus*); (2) to produce contrition in the heart of the sinner so that in the terrors of conscience he will accept the grace of God offered to him in Christ (*usus legis paedagogicus*); (3) to serve the converted Christian as a guide and a canon in the doing of works 'commanded by God' (*usus legis didacticus*)."

[2] Cf. Seeberg, *Textbook*, II, p. 251.

[3] For references to the primary sources, cf. Seeberg, *Lehrbuch,* IV, pp. 488 ff.; *Textbook,* II, pp. 365-66.

In Article V, the *Formula of Concord* undertook to solve the difficulty by defining the terms repentance and gospel. The law, in its strictest sense, is the divine revelation of God's will, his wrath, and his punishment of sin and unbelief. Even the proclamation of the suffering and death of Christ as a revelation of divine wrath directs people toward the law. The gospel, in its strictest sense, is the divine revelation of God's grace in atonement, forgiveness, and salvation. Everything that threatens and condemns is law, and everything that comforts and offers grace is gospel. Repentance and faith are co-ordinate, for the law by itself begets either pride or despair. Hence both must be preached to the end.

Article VI of the *Formula* introduced a special discussion of "the third use of the Law." It shows the need of the law after conversion. If Christians were perfectly renewed they would not need the law; but since renewal has only begun and they still have the old Adam, they also need the law and its instructions, warnings, and punishment. Actually, then, the third use of the law is the same as the second, albeit in the life of believers. The difference from Calvinism is striking. In the *Heidelberg Catechism* and elsewhere, the third use (the didactic one) is the proper function of the law.

A distinction is made between the works of the law and the fruits of the Spirit: (1) The law demands newness of life, but gives no power to produce it; the gospel brings the Holy Spirit and renews men's hearts, instructs them through the law, admonishes, and, if they sin, punishes them; (2) the unregenerate can produce only the works of servants, while the regenerate, as children of grace, produce works as the fruits of the Spirit.[4]

THE OSIANDRIAN CONTROVERSY

Osiander's special teaching on justification is part of a comprehensive system. On the doctrine of justification he regarded himself as being, in the main, on the Lutheran side against Romanism. But he

---

[4] C. F. W. Walther, founder of the Lutheran Church—Missouri Synod, has written a classic commentary on this problem entitled *The Proper Distinction between Law and Gospel* (St. Louis: Concordia Publishing House, 1929). Cf. also Ragnar Bring, *Gesetz und Evangelium und der dritte Gebrauch des Gesetzes in der lutherischen Theologie* (1943) and Lauri Haikola, *Gesetz und Evangelium bei Matthias Flacius Illyricus* (1954) and *Usus Legis* (1958).

objected to a mere imputation of Christ's righteousness as the basis of the sinner's adoption. This does not mean that he did not hold Luther's doctrine of atonement. In fact, he taught that Christ, by his innocent sufferings, had endured "the wrath of God and obtained for us the forgiveness of sins";[5] also that he had "fulfilled the Law purely and perfectly for us and for our benefit, in order that it might not be imputed to us, nor we be accursed because we do not in this life perfectly fulfill the Law."[6] Approaching the views of mysticism, Osiander taught that justification through faith is a process of becoming righteous by the indwelling of the divine nature of Christ in the believer. Osiander emphasized "the Christ in us" while Luther emphasized "the Christ for us" as the source of man's renewal.[7] Francis Stancaro, an Italian monk opposed to Osiander, introduced the view that Christ is our righteousness according to his human nature only.

In Article III the *Formula of Concord* was obliged to make a pronouncement upon these matters because of the controversy which arose. The emphasis was placed on the following items: (1) "Our righteousness rests not upon one or the other nature of Christ, but upon His whole Person, who alone, as both God and man, is in His entire and most perfect obedience, our righteousness." (2) The most perfect obedience of Christ, which was manifested in doing and suffering, constitutes the merits of Christ which God imputes to us for righteousness; to justify means to absolve for the sake of Christ. (3) This justification is apprehended by faith as the organ which appropriates the merit of Christ.

THE CONFLICTS WITH MELANCHTHONIANISM

The Adiaphoristic (Interimistic) Controversy

After having defeated the Smalcald Federation of the Protestant princes (1547), Charles V was ready to restore the unity of the Church. The Augsburg Interim,[8] which had been drafted by a Roman theologian of the old school and finished by Bishop John Pflug in company with John Agricola (then court-preacher at Brandenburg),

[5] Cf. Seeberg, *Lehrbuch,* IV, pp. 496 ff.; *Textbook,* II, pp. 369 ff.
[6] *Ibid.*
[7] Cf. Emanuel Hirsch, *Die Theologie des Andreas Osiander* (1919); H. W. Heidland, *Die Anrechnung des Glaubens zur Gerechtigkeit* (1936).
[8] Text in J. E. Bieck, *Das dreifache Interim* (1721), pp. 266 ff.

was published on May 15, 1548. It contained twenty-five articles which all the churches of Germany, Romanist as well as Protestant, were to accept as an interim measure until a General Council could be held to accomplish the final settlement. For Saxony, the Augsburg Interim was worked over into the Leipzig Interim.[9]

The content of this Leipzig Interim reveals its character. The doctrine of justification was impregnated with the teaching of an infused righteousness. Faith was removed from its central position in the order of salvation and counted among the virtues which merit reward. The teaching on the power and authority of the Church amounted to this, that the Lutheran pastors must place themselves under the sovereignty of the Roman bishops. In matters of worship, the Mass was restored with practically all the abandoned ceremonies (the seven sacraments, the worshiping of images, fasting, even the *Corpus Christi* procession). The *Catholic Encyclopedia* characterizes the Interim in the following words:

> The points of doctrine were all explained in the sense of the Catholic dogma, but couched in the mildest and vaguest terms; and wherever it was feasible, the form of the concept approached the Protestant view of those subjects. In matters of ecclesiastical discipline two important concessions were made to the Protestants, *viz.*, the marriage of the clergy and the communion under both kinds.[10]

A remark of Lindsay is interesting at this point:

> Nothing that Charles ever undertook proved such a dismal failure as this patchwork creed made from snippets of two Confessions. However lifeless creeds may become, they all—real ones—have grown out of the living, Christian experience of their framers, and have contained the very life-blood of their hearts as well as their brains. It is a hopeless task to construct creeds as a tailor shapes and stitches coats.[11]

Melanchthon, Bugenhagen, and the rest of the Wittenberg theologians were now under the jurisdiction of Elector Maurice who had joined the emperor and had contributed to the defeat of the Smalcald Federation. By permitting the Interim to pass without protest they became guilty of a grave offense against the Church. It was a time when in other parts of Germany some four hundred clergymen were

[9] *Ibid.*, pp. 361 ff.; English text in Jacobs, *op. cit.*, II, 260 ff.
[10] VII, 77.
[11] Thomas M. Lindsay, *A History of the Reformation* (New York: Charles Scribner's Sons, 1907), I, 390-91.

driven from their homes or imprisoned because of their resistance to the Interim. Melanchthon's inner attitude was expressed when he was first approached by Maurice. He wrote: "I will not encumber my conscience with this book." [12] But as soon as it became too dangerous to protest, his action conformed to the following principle: Do the best you can under these present circumstances and save as much as you can. The result of this attitude toward the Interim was that the Lutherans lost confidence in Melanchthon and became distrustful of his school, the Philippists.

Although it means trespassing upon the specific field of Church history, we cannot resist quoting here from a few letters which were addressed to the conscience of Melanchthon. Corvinus, who had been imprisoned for three years because of his writings against the Interim, pleaded with Melanchthon (in Latin):

> Oh, my Philip, oh, I say, our Philip, return through the immortal Christ to the former candor, to the former sincerity, to the former constancy! Do not make the minds of our people languish by your fright and half-heartedness! . . . You must not be the cause of such immense offenses within the Church! Do not permit your so excellent writings, words, acts, by which you have done so wonderfully much for the Church and schools, to be turned in such a way through that fault of disregard, innovation, moderation! Think of how much courage your plans give on the one hand to the opposition, and on the other hand, how it robs our side! We pray that, mindful of your profession, you and your Wittenberg men would conduct yourselves as you did in the beginning of this matter, that is, that you would think, speak, write and do what becomes Philip, the Christian teacher, not the court-philosopher.

On July 22, 1548, Caspar Aquila had written to Melanchthon: "Thou holy man, reply and breathe, defend the Word and Name of Christ and His glory, which is the highest possession on earth, from that virulent sycophant." (This concluding allusion was to Agricola who was the Protestant party in the framing of the Interim.)

Calvin also expressed his censure in a letter which lacerated Melanchthon's heart. He wrote: "Your condition is another one than that of many; for it is more disgraceful for the leaders or standard-bearers to tremble than for the mass of soldiers to flee." [13]

---

[12] *CR,* VI, 839.

[13] Quotations from Fritschel, *The Formula of Concord* (Philadelphia: Lutheran Publication Society, 1916), pp. 46 ff. Cf. also Calvin, "The Adultero-German Interim," *Tracts and Treatises,* III, 189 ff.

Matthias Flacius, professor of Hebrew at Wittenberg and a former pupil of Melanchthon, was the chief leader of the opposition against the Interim. Such men as Amsdorf, Wigand, Westphal and others were associated with him at Magdeburg, the city of refuge. The Lutheran congregations everywhere suffered especially from the introduction of the old Roman ceremonies to which they offered a passive resistance. The Interimists had made the declaration that such ceremonies are *adiaphora*, i.e. neither commanded nor prohibited; therefore, they fall into the category of freedom regarding ceremonial practices. It was at this point that Flacius began his attack upon the Wittenbergers in his publication, *De veris et falsis Adiaphoris* (1549). He proceeded upon the same principles which Melanchthon had established in the *Augsburg Confession* (Articles XV and XXVIII) and in the corresponding Articles of the *Apology*. He emphasized the fact that circumstances may arise, under which *adiaphora* may cease to be such. The existing situation made Flacius see that the whole heritage of Luther, together with the fundamental positions of the Reformation on justification, good works, repentance, the Church, and the ministry were at stake. In view of this danger, Flacius sounded a warning against making any concessions whatever, even in the matter of ceremonies. He established himself squarely upon the principle which Lutheranism has adopted, that in the case of conflict regarding the truth, and where offense might be given, nothing is an *adiaphoron*.

The position of Flacius with regard to *adiaphoron* occasioned the writing of Article X of the *Formula of Concord*. The discussion was limited to *adiaphora* of a churchly nature (which was different from the time of Pietism when the discussion was about matters of pleasure and recreation). In other words, it centered around the use or non-use of ceremonies in the Church. Things that are "contrary to God's Word, are not to be regarded *adiaphora*." Likewise, "when there are useless, foolish spectacles that are profitable neither for good order, nor Christian discipline, nor evangelical propriety in the church, these also are not genuine *adiaphora* or matters of indifference." But there are genuine *adiaphora* or matters of indifference. Is the Church, then, free to do as it pleases? The *Formula's* answer is: "At a time of confession, at a time when the enemies of God's Word desire to suppress the pure doctrine of the holy Gospel, the entire church, yea, every Christian, but especially the ministers of the Word as the presidents of the congregations of God, are bound according to God's Word, to confess the doctrine and what belongs to the whole of religion, freely and openly, not only in words, but also in works and with deeds; and that then, in this case, even in such *adiaphora*, they must not yield to the adversaries. . . ."

The Majoristic Controversy

The Leipzig Interim had omitted Luther's *sola fide*, emphasized the necessity of Christian virtues for salvation, and had even stressed the reward merited by good works. In a controversy with Nikolaus von Amsdorf, George Major, a pupil of Melanchthon, maintained that "good works are necessary to salvation, since no one is saved by wicked works and no one without good works." [14] While such a statement grew out of a desire to defend the attitude of the Wittenberg theologians toward the Interim, it was also calculated to establish the profound connection between faith and the new life. Amsdorf declared that the statement could be defended only by a "Pelagian, a Mameluke, and a denier of Christ." [14] Flacius also became a participant in the controversy. Amsdorf even went so far as to say that "good works are injurious to salvation" and that God does not care for works,[14] meaning by this, of course, if there is any reliance on them for salvation. Amsdorf's party, which was strictly Lutheran, disowned Amsdorf's statement and insisted that the new obedience must proceed from the inward impulses of the new heart.

In Article IV, the *Formula of Concord* starts on the basis of Article VI of the *Augsburg Confession*, of "the New Obedience," and records the following points of agreement between the Lutheran theologians: (1) It is the will of God that believers shall walk in good works which, however, must not include the works of self-chosen sanctity, but only such as are commanded by God. (2) Works pleasing to God can be done only by persons who through faith are reconciled to God and renewed by the Holy Ghost. The works of such persons are good notwithstanding the imperfection of

---

[14] Cf. Seeberg, *Lehrbuch*, IV, pp. 485 ff.; *Textbook*, II, pp. 364-65.

the works. (3) Faith, therefore, must be the mother and source of truly good works.

Concerning the controversial points, the Article states in the Solid Declaration that Scripture, as well as the *Augsburg Confession* and its *Apology*, frequently employs such words as "necessity," "necessary," "needful," "should," and "must" to indicate that we are bound to do good works. It is wrong, therefore, to criticize propositions and formulas expressing the necessity of good works. However, the word "necessity" should not be interpreted to mean that good works are to be done under outward compulsion instead of evangelical freedom.

Furthermore, it should be understood that good works do not contribute to man's justification. They are not necessary from the viewpoint of justification which is *sola fide*.

Although good works do not sustain salvation, as the Council of Trent declared—for faith is the beginning middle and end of everything—salvation may be lost by a life in willful sin. Finally, the statement of Amsdorf that good works are detrimental to salvation ought to be rejected. A living faith will of necessity do good works. However, a Christian ought not to trust in their being meritorious to eternal life.

The controversy shows that both parties were moving in Melanchthonian categories. The inner connection between justification and sanctification was no longer understood. Justification was considered a purely juridical act "in heaven." The ineffable grace of God was in danger of becoming "cheap grace."

The Synergistic Controversy

In the Interim it was said that "the merciful God does not work with man as with a block but draws him so that his will also cooperates if he be of understanding years." [15] This statement appealed to some theologians who did not intend to surrender anything of the *sola gratia* of Luther. Among them were John Pfeffinger of Leipzig and Victorine Strigel of Jena. Adopting Melanchthon's saying of the three efficient causes in conversion,[16] Pfeffinger said of the third, the

[15] Jacobs, *op. cit.*, II, 262.
[16] See pp. 396 ff.

will of man, that it does not resist, but adapts itself to the working of the Holy Spirit.[17] In public disputation with Flacius, Strigel maintained that sin has not destroyed but only weakened the free will of man. His attitude towards grace is not merely passive but only "more passive than active." Strigel's interest was centered in the formal freedom of the will.

After some initial criticism voiced by Amsdorf and others, it was Flacius who, in his disputation with Strigel, again became the champion of the strict Lutherans. He acknowledged a co-operation of the will which, however, did not begin until after the actual moment of conversion. Conversion is wrought exclusively by the Holy Spirit in such a way that man is entirely passive. Man is converted as an object of conversion, even when his will raves and howls. "God alone converts man—He does not exclude the will, but every efficacy or operation of it." [18]

It was natural that the discussion should run over into the doctrine of original sin. In that disputation Strigel used the illustration of the magnet: "When the magnet is touched with the juice of garlic it loses its quality of attraction, and, after it is touched again with the blood of an animal, the attraction is restored." [18] "But all the time," Strigel said, "the magnet does not cease to be a magnet." [18] Thus original sin is merely "accidental" to man and his will. At this point Flacius stepped forward with the assertion that original sin is not accidental but is the "essential substance" of man. The essential nature of man has been transformed by sin. He used the most extreme expressions: "The image of God has been replaced by the true and living image of the devil, the nature of man has been distorted into a diabolic nature, and every point of attachment to divine influences has been lost." [19]

It must be observed that Flacius, like the Scholastics of the Middle Ages, distinguished between the stuff of which a thing is made and the form which it takes. He meant the latter when he said that sin

---

[17] For references, consult Seeberg, *Lehrbuch,* IV, 490 ff.

[18] Seeberg, *Lehrbuch,* IV, 490 ff.; *Textbook,* II, 367 ff.

[19] These views are expressed in a tract published as an appendix to a large work entitled *Clavis Scripturae* (1567).

is the substance of man.[20] But even in the eyes of his friends the statement smacked of the Manichaean heresy and they turned against him when he refused to retract it.

Article I of the *Formula of Concord* rejects both Pelagianism and Synergism. Man's inherited, dreadful, and abominable disease is truly sin. On account of this corruption "and because of the fall of the first man, our nature or person is under the accusation and condemnation of the Law of God" (Solid Declaration). In addition, the Epitome emphasizes that a distinction must be made between nature and sin. The difference is as great as the difference between the work of God and the work of the devil. Besides, the Son of God assumed our nature in the unity of his person, though without sin.

CONTROVERSIES ABOUT THE RELATION BETWEEN CALVINISM AND LUTHERANISM

The Westphal Controversy

In 1540 Melanchthon prepared an altered edition of the Augsburg Confession, the so-called *Variata*,[21] to which Calvin was quite ready to subscribe. Because of this fact, Calvin was frequently regarded as an Upper German Lutheran. But in 1549 he succeeded in bringing about a union between himself and Bullinger at Zurich (the *Consensus Tigurinus*).[22] They repeated their view that the real presence is impossible because the body of Christ is locally contained in heaven (Art. XXI). Hence, in the Supper we receive the body of Christ only spiritually by faith (Art. IX). This, along with the spread of Calvinism to Western Europe and Germany, especially to the Palatinate and even Saxony, moved Joachim Westphal, a prominent pastor of Hamburg, to sound the alarm. He issued a publication[23] in which he revealed the difference between Calvin and Luther on the Eucharist and warned

---

[20] Seeberg remarks: "Flacius was not a heretic; but in the heat of the controversies of those days he was so labeled and this dictum has often been repeated." (*Lehrbuch*, IV, 495). Flacius did not conceive of sin as a physical change in man. He expressly rejected the idea that, in the act of regeneration God creates, as it were, a new physical heart. He referred to both the fall into sin and the restoration to holiness as a moral transformation (*loc. cit.*). Cf. U. S. Leupold, "The Flacian Controversy and Its Significance Today," *The Lutheran Church Quarterly* XVI (1943), 197 ff.

[21] English text in Jacobs, *op. cit.*, II, 103 ff.

[22] Cf. Schaff, *op. cit.*, I, 471 ff. Cf. p. 420.

[23] *Farrago Confuseanarum, etc.* See p. 422, n. 10.

the Lutheran Church of the undermining influences which were at work. In view of this development Calvin replied three times.[24]

The case of Frederick III in the Palatinate reveals the situation. When the Lutheran estates at the Diet of Augsburg, in 1564, accused him of having broken the Augsburg Religious Peace Treaty of 1555 by introducing Calvinism, he replied that he had never read Calvin, that he did not know what Calvinism was, and that he still adhered to the *Augsburg Confession*, i.e., the *Variata*. A year before, though, he had publicly introduced the *Heidelberg Catechism!*

In like manner the city of Bremen was lost to Lutheranism through Albert Hardenberg, while his associate, John Timmann, sided with Westphal. In the palatinate, on the other hand, Tilemann Heshusius[25] defended Luther's view against Wilhelm Klebitz. This shows that the Lutheran church was in a struggle for its very existence, especially because Melanchthon refused to make a public statement. When, for example, the elector of the Palatinate asked Melanchthon for his opinion on the matter, he replied, "It is not difficult, but dangerous, to answer." [26]

The "Crypto-Calvinistic" agitations were also extended to Electoral Saxony where the Philippists had been working into the hands of Calvin. Melanchthon had passed away and his son-in-law, Caspar Peucer, a physician, was now the recognized leader of the party. When the plot of the party was finally revealed, he was arrested but later released.

The Lutheran party restated its doctrine under the leadership of John Brenz at a Synod held at Stuttgart, 1559. This synod maintained Luther's understanding of the Real Presence, but denied any sort of transubstantiation of the elements. Christ is not locally included in

---

[24] *First Defense* (1554), *Second Defense* (1556), and *Last Admonition* (1557). In the *Last Admonition* Calvin said that the *Augsburg Confession* "does not contain a word contrary to our doctrine. If there is any ambiguity in its meaning there cannot be a more competent interpreter than its author, to whom, as his due, all pious and learned men will readily pay this honour." (*Tracts and Treatises*, II, 355). Calvin's reference, of course, is to the 1540 edition. Yet he certainly deceived himself as to the vitality of the old Lutheran position when he fancied Westphal's publications to be of no account and accordingly replied quite superciliously.

[25] See Calvin's reply in *LCC*, XXII, 257 ff.

[26] Quoted by Seeberg, *Lehrbuch*, IV, 509.

the elements, but is present by virtue of the union of the divine and human natures in the one person.[27]

The Melanchthonian party presented its views in an anonymous publication, *Exegesis perspicua*.[28] Against the background of Zwingli's and Calvin's concept of the two natures in Christ, it taught that the communion in the sacrament is a spiritual communion of Christ's divinity with the believer. The Supper is a seal of his promise. It said that Luther was drawn into the controversy with Zwingli because Zwingli regarded the sacrament merely as a token of man's profession. The Reformed[29] recognized this error but the Lutheran party, in attacking the former and abandoned error, continued to oppose those who now teach better. Luther retained some ideas that originated in the Roman teaching of transubstantiation and his followers refuse to abandon them. We must not adhere too tenaciously to the original founder of Protestantism (Luther), but must allow room for the better insights that came later with Melanchthon and Calvin. The doctrine of ubiquity and of the *manducatio indignorum*, etc. should be dropped.[30] This publication was a real eye-opener to the Lutherans, even to Elector Augustus, who personally disliked the Gnesio-Lutherans, especially Flacius, and it hastened the downfall of the Melanchthonians.

The Solid Declaration of the *Formula of Concord* deals with the Eucharist (Art. VII) and the Person of Christ (Art. VIII). It also treats the Descent into Hell from the standpoint of the personal union of Christ's two natures (Art. IX).

In Article VII the *Formula* uses painstaking care to guard the interpretation of Article X of the *Augsburg Confession* on the Lord's Supper by describing the kind of "real presence" which Luther meant in his controversy with his opponents and in his agreement with the South Germans in the Wittenberg Concord. The bodily presence is taught on the basis of the words of institution. Thus it is taught that, on account of the sacramental union between the earthly elements

---

[27] *Confessio et doctrina theologorum, etc.*, 1561.

[28] Its author was Joachim Cureus, a physician (d. 1573). It was first published in 1574 and edited by W. Scheffer, 1853.

[29] Calvin's followers in Germany called their church "the church reformed according to the Word of God," thereby implying that Luther's Reformation was incomplete.

[30] See Fritschel, *op. cit.*, pp. 189 ff.

and the heavenly gifts, Christ's body and blood are truly and essentially present and are received with the bread and wine. It is not, however, a "physical or earthly presence." From such a view of the real presence it follows that communicants receive the Body of Christ with the mouth, which, however, does not mean a Capernaitic eating, for it takes place in a supernatural, incomprehensible, heavenly way. Along with this sacramental mode of receiving Christ's essential body by worthy and unworthy communicants, there also goes a spiritual reception by faith alone, which can also take place outside of the use of the sacrament. The pious, indeed, receive the body and blood of Christ as an infallible pledge and assurance that their sins are forgiven and that Christ dwells in them and wishes to be efficacious in them. The discussions in this Article are so thorough and exhaustive that all loop-holes for the vagueness of Melanchthon, the mediating suggestions of Bucer and the definitions of Calvin, are completely stopped. There can be no mistake, henceforth, as to the distinction between Lutheranism and Calvinism. To have made this clear in every respect is the significance of this Article.

The *Formula of Concord* carried its decisions back to the doctrine of the Person of Christ, where the difference between Luther and Zwingli had already appeared. The Zurich Reformer had taken the position that, according to his body, Christ cannot be present in the Supper because omnipresence belongs to the divine nature only. Calvin agreed with Zwingli. Here the *Formula*, in its system of the personal union and the *communicatio idiomatum*, teaches also the *genus majestaticum*, according to which certain attributes of the divine nature (omnipotence, omnipresence, omniscience) are communicated to Christ's human nature so that the whole Christ, in one undivided Person, can be and is present where in the Word He promises to be present.

In the brief Article IX on the "Descent into Hell," we can see again the Lutheran emphasis upon the personal union of God and man in Christ. "The entire person, God and man, after the burial, descended into hell, conquered the devil, destroyed the power of hell, and took from the devil all his might." This brief article on Christ's descent into hell was occasioned by the teaching of John Aepinus of Hamburg. In the later version of his teaching he made a distinction between the

Inferno, the punishment for all descendants of Adam, and *Gehenna*, the irrevocable condemnation of all who die in unbelief. Christ, he said, by vicariously suffering the former, had thereby redeemed believers from the pains of *Gehenna*.

The descent into hell then, according to Aepinus, belongs to Christ's state of humiliation. It took place in his soul while his body remained in the grave. Aepinus was opposed esepecially by George Karg (Parsimonius) of Bavaria, who rejected a local view of hell and maintained that man cannot know how and when the descent took place. It is sufficient for us to know that Christ has destroyed the power of hell. Article IX agrees with Karg's view. It refers to Luther's famous sermon preached on Easter Eve at Torgau, 1533, when Luther, aware that he was using figurative language, spoke of the descent as a display of Christ's victory over hell and the devil.[31] On other occasions, however, Luther identified the descent into hell with the suffering of Christ on the cross.[32] This means that Luther had no dogma of the *descensus*. The two different aspects held together in Luther's theology were put asunder by later theologians. While the orthodox Lutherans followed the first line of thought, Calvin and his followers put their weight behind the second alternative. Consequently, the doctrine of the descent into hell was one of the problems that kept the Lutherans and Calvinists apart in the seventeenth century. For the Lutherans it belonged to the state of Christ's exaltation; in the eyes of the Calvinists it was the final step of the humiliation of the Redeemer.[33]

The Doctrine of Predestination

Calvin expressed his view on predestination in the *Institutes* and, above all, in the *Consensus of Geneva*, 1552.[34] He had developed the doctrine of double predestination as an aspect of the sovereignty of God. Luther stated a similar view in his reply to Erasmus, *On The Bondage of the Will*, and he never retracted it. But he was moved by a somewhat different motivation. As the caption of his writing indicates, Luther approached the problem "existentially," from the stand-

---

[31] See the English version of this sermon in Jacobs, *op. cit.*, II, 249 ff.
[32] *WA*, 5:604; 44:423-24; *passim*.
[33] Cf. F. H. R. Frank, *Die Theologie der Konkordienformel*, III, 435 ff.
[34] Cf. p. 443.

point of man held in the bondage of evil. His main concern was to stress the universal reign of sin and the monergism of divine grace.

The literature published in the period under discussion was not occasioned by a conflict among the Lutherans. Instead, it reflected the disagreement between the Lutherans and the Reformed. In Heidelberg, Heshusius attacked not only Calvin's doctrine of the Lord's Supper, but likewise his teaching of predestination. The same situation prevailed in Strassburg where John Marbach, a Lutheran, attacked Jerome Zanchi on both points. A temporary settlement was affected by the *Formula of Union* which acknowledged both the universality of the atonement and of the call as well as a special election to eternal life. As to the reprobate, the *Formula* said that God "permits" them to persevere in sin.

The *Formula of Concord* expressed itself on the doctrine of predestination in Article XI. No article in any of the other older confessional writings could be quoted. The two main authors of this Article ventured out on their own theological positions. The one, Martin Chemnitz, had expressed himself in his *Catechism*, which was composed for the churches in the duchy of Brunswick, 1574;[35] the other, Jacob Andrea, in the *Swabian Formula* of the same year. Luther is quoted only once (from his preface to Romans). His most important writing concerning predestination, *On The Bondage of the Will*, is bypassed in silence.

A brief summary of the argument on predestination is as follows: A distinction must be made between God's foreknowledge, which extends to everything in the universe, and his election, which is concerned only with the pious children of God. Election, however, is not to be posited only in the secret, inscrutable counsel of God. Such a doctrine leads either to despair or to false security on the part of the godless. Instead, it is to be understood in the light of Christ. The atonement is universal and is seriously offered to all in general through the promises of the gospel and individually through the sacraments. Election is to be known not from God's secret counsel but from revelation alone. In our search for election we must adhere exclusively to God's revealed Word. The elect are those who heed the call. Election rests solely on the grace of God, for He "owes us

[35] See the text in Frank, *op. cit.*, III, 329 ff.

neither His Word, nor His Spirit, nor His Grace." [36] God draws men through the means of grace. At least, this is the common ordinance of God.[37] The reason why not all who hear the Word come to faith is not to be seen in God. He wants all men to be saved. The cause of damnation is the devil and man himself, who resists the divine call. It is not God but the devil who makes some vessels of divine wrath.[38] But God punishes sin with sin, the impenitence of man with obduracy and blindness.[39]

The argument in this Article is not in keeping with Luther's *On The Bondage of the Will*. In this writing Luther holds to the doctrine of double predestination. According to his inscrutable will, Luther maintains, God saves some while hardening others. God willed the fall of Adam. Why? He is *Deus absconditus*, even in his revelation. Is God then unjust? The answer must be: No![40] For he is under obligation to no one.

Lutheranism in general has not followed Luther's line of argument. The *Formula of Concord* has been, broadly speaking, much more acceptable. In a way better than Luther, the *Formula* leaves the mystery where it belongs, i.e. with God. Salvation is free; divine grace is inclusive. God wills that all men should come to the knowledge of truth. God is not the author of sin, nor does he will the damnation of anyone. The biblical teaching of predestination is not a theory that solves the riddles of the universe. "It is an expression of faith that puts life and its insoluble mysteries into the hand of God." [41]

The closing Article of the *Formula of Concord* (XII) consists of

[36] Solid Declaration, 60.

[37] *Ibid.*, 76.

[38] *Ibid.*, 79.

[39] *Ibid.*, 83.

[40] Cf. an article by Otto W. Heick, "Let Man Be Man," *The Lutheran Quarterly*, IV (1954), 143 ff.

[41] Anders Nygren, *Commentary on Romans*, trans. C. C. Rasmussen (Philadelphia: Muhlenberg Press, 1949), p. 370. Nygren's criticism of a rational doctrine of predestination as improper in the light of Romans 9 applies also to Philip Schaff's remark that Articles II and XI of the *Formula of Concord* contain illogical and contradictory assertions. The doctrine of human depravity, as set forth in Article II, says Schaff, leads logically to the double predestination of Calvin which is rejected in Article XI. In his eyes the Lutheran system is inconsistent (*op. cit.* I, 314 f., 330). Actually it is no more inconsistent than Paul himself when he says: "Work out your own salvation with fear and trembling, for it is God who worketh in you both to will and to do of his good pleasure" (Phil. 2:12 f.).

a list of sectarian doctrines which the authors wished to disavow: the teachings of the Anabaptists, such as Menno's view of the incarnation that Christ did not assume his body from Mary, but only through Mary,[42] the negative attitude toward infant baptism, and the state, etc., errors of the Schwenkfeldians, of the "New Arians," and of Antitrinitarians of the day.

AN ESTIMATE OF THE FORMULA OF CONCORD

The *Formula of Concord* represents the development of Lutheran doctrine in the later part of the Reformation Age. It consolidated German Lutheranism and put a stop to the further conquest of Lutheran territory by Calvinism, which remained limited, in the main, to its original influence in the South and to the West along the Rhine. Through the *Augsburg Confession,* as interpreted by the *Formula of Concord* on the one side, and by the *Heidelberg Catechism* with all the Reformed Confessions as its background on the other side, the consciousness of Lutheranism and Calvinism as two distinct churches of Protestantism was decisively expressed. From now on, not earlier, we have the names "Lutheran" and "Reformed" as adopted by the churches themselves. The name "Lutheran" had been used by Rome since 1520 to designate those who adhered to the cause of the Reformation. With the introduction of Calvinism into the Palatinate, the distinction was made between Lutherans and Calvinists. After 1585, the followers of Luther began to call themselves "Lutherans." The followers of Calvin refused the name "Calvinists" and used the title "Reformed" to indicate that they, as a church, were aiming to reform German Lutheranism from the Romish leaven within it.[43]

The *Formula of Concord* gave expression to a consensus already inaugurated. It accomplished the purpose which it had in view. This included the rejection of Calvinism. While this had become a necessity, it must not be overlooked that, in very many points of evangelical Christianity, Calvin with his great gifts of theological interpretation, was fundamentally a follower of Luther. In certain articles the *For-*

[42] Cf. "The Incarnation of Our Lord" in J. C. Wenger (ed.), *Complete Writings of Menno Simons,* trans. L. Verduin (Scottdale, Pa.: Herald Press, 1955), pp. 783 ff. Cf. also our Volume II, Chapter I.

[43] Cf. Heinrich Heppe, *Ursprung und Geschichte der Bezeichnung reformierter und lutherischer Konfession* (1859).

mula of Concord also took a position against Melanchthon but, outside of this, it was in perfect harmony with the leading thoughts of Melanchthon's theology, which permeated all Lutheran teaching. While Melanchthonianism was merely an influence within Lutheranism, Calvinism was in the process of becoming a new and independent church with the program of eliminating historic Lutheranism.

Among the replies to the *Formula of Concord* by the Reformed, the *Newstad Admonition* (*Neostadiensium Admonitio*, 1581) was especially significant for two reasons: (1) This book was written with great thoroughness by Zacharias Ursinus, one of the authors of the *Heidelberg Catechism*. (2) It was written at the instruction of Count Casimir, of Neustadt in the Palatinate, and published in the name of the Newsted theologians. These theologians at first labored for a Melanchthonian, middle type of Protestantism, but in fact they found themselves entirely on the side of Calvin, agreeing with him even in the doctrine of predestination, although not pressing this point to the extent it was done in other countries.

An impression of the *Newstad Admonition* may be had from the captions of its twelve chapters: (1) The person of Christ, a review of the true doctrine. (2) The Lord's Supper, a review of the true doctrine. (3) Refutation of the false accusation of our churches with regard to false dogmas. (4) The authority of the *Augsburg Confession*. (5) The true meaning of the *Augsburg Confession*. (6) Regarding the authority of Dr. Luther. (7) Concerning the unjust condemnation of our doctrine in the *Book of Concord*. (8) Proof of false assertions in the *Book of Concord*. (9) Proof of contradictions in the *Book of Concord*. (10) The procedure of the theologians in bringing about concord and the part of a Christian magistrate in church controversies. (11) The inconvenience in the carrying out of this concord. (12) An epilogue on the true method for establishing Christian concord in the churches.[44]

BIBLIOGRAPHY

ALLBECK, W. D. *Studies in the Lutheran Confessions.* Philadelphia: Muhlenberg Press, 1952.

Formula of Concord. German and Latin text in *Bekenntsschriften der*

[44] On the replies of the Lutheran camp and counter replies of the Reformed, see *PRE*, XIII, 710, and Schaff, *op. cit.,* I, 332 ff.

lutherischen Kirche. English text in *Book of Concord.* Edited by THEODORE G. TAPPERT. Philadelphia: Muhlenberg Press, 1959.

FRANCK, F. H. R. *Die Theologie der Konkordienformel.* 4 vols. 1858 ff.

FRITSCHEL, GEORGE J. *The Formula of Concord.* Philadelphia: Lutheran Publishing Society, 1916.

KRAUTH, C. P. *The Conservative Reformation and its Theology.* Philadelphia: J. B. Lippincott and Co., 1875.

NEVE, J. L. *Introduction to the Symbolical Books of the Lutheran Church.* Columbus, Ohio: Wartburg Press, 1956.

RICHARD, J. W. *The Confessional History of the Lutheran Church.* Philadelphia: Lutheran Publishing Society, 1909.

SCHLINCK, EDMUND. *Theology of the Lutheran Confessions.* Translated by PAUL F. KOEHNEKE and HERBERT J. A. BOUMAN. Philadelphia: Muhlenberg Press, 1961.

TSCHAKERT, PAUL. *Die Entstehung der lutherischen und reformierten Kirchenlehre.* 1910.

CHAPTER VIII

THE AGE OF PROTESTANT
ORTHODOXY

LUTHERAN ORTHODOXY

In the *Book of Concord* the Lutheran churches arrived at a common
expression of faith and theology. The book, first published in 1580,
included, besides other material, the nine confessions which the Lutheran church, as a whole or in part, acknowledges as testimonies of
the faith: the *Apostles' Creed*, the *Nicene Creed*, and the *Athanasian
Creed*, all inherited from the ancient church; and six original creeds:
the *Augsburg Confession* (1530), its *Apology* (1531), the *Smalcald
Articles* (1537) and two *Catechisms* of Luther (1529), and the *Formula
of Concord* (1577). As discussed in the previous chapter, the *Formula of Concord* was a milestone in the doctrinal development of
the Lutheran church. Its promulgation ushered in the age of strict
orthodoxy which prevailed up to the Pietistic movement at the close
of the seventeenth century.

In the decade following the publication of the Book of Concord,
Electoral Saxony went through a second stage of the Crypto-Calvinistic controversy. When Elector Augustus died in 1586 he was succeeded by Christian I, who in 1589 made Nicholas Crell (or Krell)
chancellor. Supported by some former students of Melanchthon, Crell
issued a number of regulations openly favoring Calvinism. Resisting
pastors were either jailed or banished. But the reign of the powerful
chancellor came to an abrupt end by the premature death of the
elector in 1591. Even before the funeral of the elector, Crell was
arrested. His trial dragged on for ten years. Ignoring the religious
charges, an imperial court at Prague sentenced him to death for political crimes, since, it was said, he had alienated the elector from the

emperor by giving military support to France. He was beheaded in Dresden, October 9, 1601. As deplorable as the tragic end of this man may seem, Crell was no innocent martyr who died for his religious convictions. Actually he had grossly abused his position to undermine, in a stealthy manner, the confessional status of the land.

The Lutheran reaction to Crell's Crypto-Calvinism is expressed in the so-called *Saxon Visitation Articles, 1592*, which discuss the difference between Lutheranism and Calvinism concerning the doctrines of the Lord's Supper, the Person of Christ, baptism, and predestination under four headings. These *Articles* never acquired general authority and have long ceased to be binding even in the Church of Saxony.[1]

Of the leading theologians mentioned previously, Nicholas von Amsdorf died in 1565, Joachim Westphal in 1574, and Matthias Flacius in 1575. Of the co-authors of the *Formula of Concord*, Martin Chemnitz died in 1580, Jakob Andreae in 1590, and Nicholas Selnecker in 1592. In 1582, Chemnitz, Selnecker, and a less known theologian published an *Apology of the Book of Concord*. Building on Melanchthon's *Loci*, Chemnitz also wrote the *Loci* theologici which was published posthumously in 1591. These *Loci* continued to be used as a textbook for Lutheran dogmatics until they were supplanted by Leonhard Hutter's *Compendium locorum theologicorum* (1610). Chemnitz is best remembered for his monumental *Examen Concilii Tridentini*, a refutation of the Council of Trent in four volumes, 1565-1573. The *Magdeburg Centuries* belong to the same period. They are a church history by centuries in thirteen volumes published under the editorship of Flacius. The first three volumes represent a work on biblical dogmatics written by Johannes Wigand and Matthaeus Judex. These volumes were intended to be a counter-production to Melanchthon's *Loci*. The whole venture was intended to prove that Lutheranism stands on apostolic ground. It was opposed by the Roman theologian, Caesar Baronius, with his *Annals*, 1588–1607.

The seventeenth century was the period of Lutheran high orthodoxy. Represented by a galaxy of men, this period produced the great

---

[1] These *Articles* are omitted in recent editions of the *Book of Concord*, but were found in the older, much-used edition of the Lutheran Symbols by J. T. Mueller. A German, Latin, and English text is given by Schaff, *op. cit.*, III, 181 ff. Cf. also the English version in Jacobs, *op. cit.*, II, 299 ff., and the critical remarks and Latin text in Schaff, *op. cit.*, I, 345 ff.

dogmatic systems of Lutheranism. In the earlier part of this century we have John Gerhard (d. 1637) at Jena. He was considered to be the standard dogmatician. A younger contemporary of Gerhard was J. F. Koenig at Rostock (d. 1664). His *Theologia positiva acroamatica* formed the basis of most of the dogmatic lectures in the second half of the seventeenth century. The climax of orthodoxy is seen in the works and writings of Abraham Calovius (d. 1686) and J. A. Quenstedt (d. 1688), both of Wittenberg. The latter has been called "the bookkeeper of Lutheran orthodoxy." Both men wielded an enormous influence in the Lutheran Church. David Hollaz (d. 1695) and J. W. Baier (d. 1713) belong to the declining period of Lutheran orthodoxy. Baier's *Compendium theologiae positivae* passed through many editions, the latest by C. F. Walther, the founder of the Missouri Synod, 1879. Among conservative Lutherans it was often customary to refer to these men and others of the same period as the "fathers" of the Church.[2]

Orthodoxy, however, was more than just a system of pure doctrine. The Treaty of Augsburg, 1555, had granted religious liberty to the "relatives of the Augsburg Confession" in the empire. The right was reserved for the civil authorities to decide which of the two versions of the Christian faith, the Roman Catholic or the Lutheran, was to be practiced in their given territories. This arrangement was expressed by the formula "*cuius regio eius religio.*" In addition to its religious significance, the *Augsburg Confession* became a political document of great importance. The Treaty of Augsburg had established a most intimate connection between Church and state. The latter had become a confessional state. All officers and civil servants were obligated by oath to defend the *Augsburg Confession.* The princes, and in the case of the free cities, the magistrates, supported the Church in its claim to bring the whole life of its members, their culture, education, and even the criminal code, under the rule of the Church. Relying on the government, the orthodox clergy kept the Lutheran territories "pure" of Catholics, Calvinists, Anabaptists, religious individualists, and the like. Hence, the orthodox system was bound to decline at the very

---

[2] Cf. the biographical sketch in H. Schmid, *The Doctrinal Theology of the Evangelical Lutheran Church,* trans. Charles A. Hay and Henry E. Jacobs (Minneapolis: Augsburg Publishing House, 1961), pp. 665-71.

moment when this unity of Church, state, and culture began to disintegrate. Lutheran orthodoxy, and Calvinistic orthodoxy as well, is, in every respect, a Protestant counterpart to the period of high scholasticism in the Middle Ages.

As had been the case then, so now there was only room for one independent, religious movement, i.e. mysticism. The mystics, when they remained orthodox in doctrine, were widely appreciated. Foremost of the mystics of this period was John Arndt (d. 1621), whose *Vier Bücher vom Wahren Christentum* ("Four Books of True Christianity") are the most widely read devotional books of Lutheranism. They have been translated into most European languages. Some of his ideas are drawn from the Medieval mystics, especially from Tauler, and are not always in keeping with Lutheran doctrine. Strict orthodoxy and mystic piety are more happily united in Heinrich Mueller (d. 1675), author of *Der himmlische Liebeskuss* and *Geistliche Erquickungsstunden* ("The Kiss of Heavenly Love and Hours of Spiritual Refreshment"). Christian Scriver (d. 1693), author of *Der Seelenschatz* ("The Treasure of the Soul") should also be remembered.

The seventeenth century was also the classical period of the Lutheran chorale (Philip Nicolai, John Meyfart, Paul Gerhardt and many others). Last, but not least, the music of Heinrich Schuetz (d. 1672) and of Johann Sebastian Bach (1685-1750) was thoroughly rooted in the orthodox piety of this age. Having spent the active years of his life in the first half of the eighteenth century, which saw the decline of orthodoxy, Bach's talent was little appreciated toward the close of his life and he was soon forgotten after his death. It was not until 1829 that his *Matthaeuspassion* experienced a veritable resurrection in Berlin. The chorale, as well as the music of Schuetz and Bach, have a mystic undertone. As a matter of fact, the language of Nicolai's hymn, "O Morning Star, so Pure and so Bright," is so saturated with the erotic language of Bernardian mysticism that, in an unaltered form, it is totally unacceptable today. But at the same time Nicolai ranks among the foremost defenders of Lutheranism over against Calvinism.[3] Likewise, Bach did not feel at home in the

---

[3] Nicolai is also the author of *Der Freudenspiegel des ewigen Lebens* ("The Joyous Mirror of Eternal Life"), a devotional book written in the same erotic language.

atmosphere of the Reformed court of Anhalt-Coethen (1717-1723). It was Lutheran orthodoxy from which he received inspiration and stimulus for his great compositions.[4]

Reformed Orthodoxy

The Reformed church also went through an age of orthodoxy, which was counteracted at an early stage by the inroads of Arminian thought.

The cohesive force of Calvinism was not a confession comparable to the *Augsburg Confession,* but rather the theology of Calvin himself. His *Institutes* were the textbook *par excellence* of Reformed theology. Calvinism was not included in the Treaty of 1555. Yet the Calvinists in the German empire came forth with the claim that they too were "relatives of the Augsburg Confession." It must be remembered that Calvin himself had signed the Confession, albeit the altered version of 1540.

Western Calvinism had four main centers: Geneva, including the French speaking churches; German speaking Switzerland and the Rhineland; the Netherlands; and the British Isles.[5]

In Zurich, Heinrich Bullinger (d. 1575) succeeded Zwingli as leader of the Reformation among the German speaking Swiss. Bullinger was the co-author of the *First Helvetic Confession* and the sole author of the *Second Helvetic Confession.* He also effected the union of the Zurich Reformation with the Reformation movement in Geneva through the *Consensus of Zurich.*[6] Depending on Zwingli for his conception of the sacraments, Bullinger nevertheless had been influenced earlier by Luther and Melanchthon. In his concept of justification as effective without works, he was closer to the Gnesio-Lutherans than to the Philippists. Bullinger hesitated to apply the principle of rigid logic to the doctrine of predestination, as was the case with Calvin. Wolfgang Musculus (d. 1563) and Benedictus Aretius (d. 1574) followed a similar line of thought. Although influenced by Luther, they were closer to Bucer and Capito of Strassburg.

[4] Cf. Hans Besch, *Johann Sebastian Bach, Frömmigkeit und Glaube* (1949), I, 176.
[5] Cf. Otto Ritschl, *Dogmengeschichte des Protestantismus,* III, 243 ff.
[6] Cf. p. 443.

In Germany, Victorine Strigel, a Lutheran, joined the Reformed Church in 1566. Of the two authors of the *Heidelberg Catechism*, the one, Zacharias Ursinus (d. 1583), was a student of Melanchthon, while the other, Caspar Olevianus (d. 1582), received his training in Geneva. Together with Johannes Piscator, Johann Heinrich Alting, and others, these men represented the Heidelberg school, which was the most influential theological faculty of German Calvinism up to the outbreak of the Thirty Years War (1618-1648).

The most renowned theologian of German Reformed Protestantism was Bartholomew Keckermann. He was born in Danzig, 1571. He attended the universities in Wittenberg, Leipzig, and Heidelberg. In the latter he was appointed professor of Hebrew. In 1601 he returned to his native city as professor of philosophy. He died in 1609. Keckermann was the chief representative among the Reformed theologians who took a renewed interest in Aristotle. Following Aristotle,[7] he distinguished between two kinds of scholastic disciplines: contemplative and operative. The former has to do with established facts (physics, mathematics), the latter deals with principles for a harmonious ordering of life (ethics, economics, and political science). For Keckermann theology is an operative discipline. It is a system of special aptitude making us wise unto eternal salvation. The method is analytical. Starting with the goal of life, which is the fruition of God, the sources and means of salvation are to be investigated and man is to be shown how they are to be applied. This understanding of theology reflects the influence of both Calvin and Ursinus, co-author of the *Heidelberg Catechism*.[8]

The men discussed thus far arrived at their position relatively independent of Calvin. As time progressed, his influence gained momentum and the doctrine of predestination was generally accepted. Theodore Beza (d. 1605) succeeded him in Geneva. His views on predestination were unquestionably supralapsarian or even "supra-creationistic"[9] (i.e., preceding the creation of the world) as Otto

---

[7] Cf. Aristotle, *Nicomachean Ethics,* VI, 2-4.

[8] Calvin, *Institutes,* I, 1, 2; *Heidelberg Catechism,* Question 1. Cf. Althaus, *Die Prinzipien der deutschen reformierten Dogmatik der aristotelischen Scholastik* (1914), pp. 26 ff.; H. E. Weber, *Der Einfluss der protestantischen Schulphilosophie auf die lutherische Dogmatik* (1908), pp. 14 ff.

[9] Ritschl, *op. cit.,* III, 295.

Ritschl maintains. He defined predestination as "the eternal and immutable decree which, in order of time, is antecedent to all causes of salvation and damnation.[10] According to this view, God elected a certain number of his creatures to be vessels of grace, and a certain number to be vessels of wrath. Creation serves as an order of both redemption and reprobation. Among those theologians who followed Beza's view were Jerome Zanchi at Strassburg (d. 1590), Lambert Danaeus (d. 1595) at Geneva, Leyden, *etc.*, Francis Gomarus (d. 1641) at Leyden, and the British theologians, William Perkins (d. 1602) and William Twisse (d. 1645), prolocutor of the Westminster Assembly. On the other hand, the *Canons of Dort (1619)* and the *Formula Consensus Helvetica*, drawn up in 1675, whose principal authors were J. H. Heidegger (d. 1698) and Francis Turrentini (d. 1687), gave symbolical authority to the infralapsarian view. However, both the supralapsarians as well as the infralapsarians, were agreed on the "five points of High Calvinism": (1) double predestination by God, (2) the total depravity of man, (3) atonement limited to the elect, (4) the irresistibility of grace, and (5) the gift of perseverance. For Beza and others all of this does not imply that God is the author of sin. God created Adam as a moral being with freedom of the will. Though God willed the fall, he did not effect the fall.[11]

Lutherans and Calvinists in Conflict

The irritation of the Lutherans during this period was chiefly against the Reformed. They felt that their territory had been invaded. The Palatinate was lost to Calvinism. Hesse and Anhalt in Thuringia became centers of Calvinistic propaganda. The city of Bremen was lost and the small principality of Lippe was also lost to Calvinism. Because of influences from the Palatinate and from Hesse, Elector Sigismund of Brandenburg, a Hohenzollern, turned to the Reformed. Although the Hohenzollern dynasty did not force Calvinism upon its subjects, these rulers were untiring in their effort to bring about a union between the two great churches of the Reforma-

[10] *Ibid.,* 294.
[11] *Ibid.,* 295-96.

tion.[12] While Germany was ravaged by the Thirty Years War, the Calvinist countries—Switzerland and above all Holland—enjoyed a period of peace and prosperity. The "spiritual" views of Calvinism and the pliability and humanism of the school of Melanchthon were favored at the courts and by the princes. Historic Lutheranism was to be "reformed." This was the reason why the Lutherans looked upon the Calvinists as their most dangerous opponents.[13] Beginning in 1570, no less than six colloquies were held between representatives of the two churches, and two calls were issued from the quarters of the Reformed in the Palatinate appealing for confessional peace. In addition, the British divine, John Durry (Duraeus) spent fifty years of untiring activity in bringing about the union of Continental Protestantism. He was encouraged in his endeavors by the British statesman, Sir Thomas Roe, and the Swedish chancellor, Oxentierna.

The most important of the colloquies was the one held at Leipzig, March 3 to 23, 1631. The conference was called by the princes of Brandenburg, Saxony, and Hesse, but the protocol was signed by the six participating theologians. The *Augsburg Confession* was made the basis of the discussion. The discussion was honest, without rancor, yet the historic differences stemming from the interpretation of the Lord's Supper were not removed. It may truthfully be said that the Leipzig Colloquy is in the same class as the Marburg Colloquy between Luther and Zwingli. As in the case of Marburg, nothing practical or tangible resulted.[14]

The friction between the two churches continued unabated. The doctrine of the Person of Christ and of the Lord's Supper remained a reason for separation. Soon the controversy concerning the distinction between Fundamentals and Non-Fundamentals caused addi-

---

[12] The student of church history will remember that these endeavors were not successful until 1817. The problem is still acute. History shows that the Union did not terminate the friction between the two churches. There has been less irritation between Lutherans and the Reformed in Hanover, for example, where no union was attempted, than in Prussia, where the union movement was effected by an autocratic king.

[13] Schaff remained utterly unaware of the difficulties created for the Lutherans by Reformed propaganda; *op. cit.,* I, 345-46.

[14] For fuller information, compare J. L. Neve, *The Lutherans in the Movements for Church Union* (Philadelphia: Lutheran Publishing House, 1921), pp. 49 ff. On the Leipzig Colloquy, compare also Schaff, *op. cit.,* I, 558 ff.

tional difficulties[15] and the doctrine of predestination made the gulf ever more apparent.

Apart from the doctrine of the Lord's Supper and the related problem of the two natures of Christ, the controversy between Lutheran and Reformed revolved around the doctrine of predestination. Prior to the *Formula of Concord* there had been a local conflict about this issue in Strassburg between Marbach and Zanchi (1563).[16] Nine years after the *Formula's* publication predestination became a hotly debated issue at the Colloquy held in Montbelliard. The chief debaters were Andreae and Beza.[17] The Colloquy had some repercussions in the city of Berne, where Samuel Huber (d. 1624) accused his colleague, Abraham Musculus, of endorsing the theses of Beza at Montbelliard. A disputation was held at Berne in April, 1588, and Huber was excommunicated. He signed the *Formula of Concord* and was made professor at Wittenberg in 1592. He virtually eliminated the idea of election. As Adam is the universal corruptor of the human race, so Christ is the universal reparator and Savior. Man is lost by his own persistent unbelief. In Wittenberg Huber was soon opposed by Aegidius Hunnius, who took offense at the rejection of election as taught in the *Formula of Concord*. Huber lost his professorship in 1594, but found refuge in the duchy of Brunswick where he died in 1624.

To some extent Hunnius implemented Article XI of the *Formula of Concord*. Election, he held, is not absolute, but *ordinata*. God elects him who by faith accepts the merits of Christ. Election is in view of faith. Hunnius distinguished between the antecedent will of God and his subsequent will. The former will is universal; God wills that all men be saved. The latter is selective. Dependent on his foreknowledge, God has elected those who he foreknows will repent and believe. This version of the doctrine under discussion became

---

[15] In a way the so-called "Syncretistic Controversy" was also a conflict within Lutheranism. George Calixtus, a theologian of the Melanchthonian school, sided with the Reformed delegates at the convention at Thorn. For details see our Vol. II.

[16] See p. 463.

[17] Cf. Neve, *op. cit.*, pp. 54-55. Montbelliard is a district in eastern France. Through marriage it had become a part of Wurttenberg in 1397. It was permanently ceded to France in 1801. Today it is one of the three centers of French Lutheranism.

normative for the Lutherans in the seventeenth century. Hollaz defined predestination as "the eternal decree of God to bestow eternal salvation upon all whom God foresaw that they would finally believe in Him.[18]

In the opening years of the seventeenth century, a Dutch Calvinist, Jacob Arminius, raised objections to Beza's doctrine of predestination. This lead to an important controversy in the Reformed Church and undermined the whole Calvinistic scheme of salvation, splitting the church into two factions, the Calvinist and Arminian wing.[19]

The Lutherans, likewise, were disturbed by two domestic controversies: the crypto-kenotic and the Rathmann controversies.

The Swabian theologian, Johannes Brenz, one of the authors of the *Formula of Concord*, asserted that Christ, even in the state of humiliation, possessed and exercised divine glory, although not openly. "He lay dead in the tomb, in humiliation; living He governed heaven and earth in majesty; this indeed during the time of His humiliation, before His resurrection." Chemnitz, on the other hand, though he ascribed the possession of divine glory to Christ, taught a partial renunciation of the use of it during His earthly life. The *Formula of Concord* expressed no definite judgment on this question. Later (1619) a controversy arose between the followers of Brenz, who were the theologians of Tuebingen, and the followers of Chemnitz, at the University of Giessen. The former maintained an "absolute presence" of the humanity of Christ from the first moment of his conception in the womb of Mary. They taught that there was a difference only in the manner in which Christ exercised his dominion, hidden in the state of humiliation, under the form of a servant, but gloriously in the state of exaltation. The Giessen theologians rejected the "absolute presence." On the basis of the *communicatio idiomatum* they did not deny that Christ possessed divine attributes in the state of his humiliation, but they taught that the use of these attributes was not so much a natural outcome of the possession as it was an expression of his divine will. They taught that Christ renounced the use of the

[18] Cf. Ritschl, *op. cit.*, III, 134 ff., and Heinrich Schmid, *op. cit.*, pp. 270 ff. In the nineteenth century C. F. Walther declined to follow the Fathers of the seventeenth century with respect to this particular teaching. Election, he taught, is not in view of faith, but rather to faith. Cf. our Vol. II.

[19] For details, see our Vol. II.

divine attributes until the completion of his work of redemption. In the *Decisio Saxonica* (1624), the Saxon theologians by and large supported the position of the Giessen school. The later dogmaticians expressed the problem in the formula: *krypsis kteseōs kenōsis chreseōs,* i.e. though the man Jesus was in full possession of all divine attributes, he did not normally make use of them prior to his exaltation.[20]

The second controversy concerned the meaning of Scripture. The dogmaticians, were of one mind in teaching that the Bible can convert and regenerate the mind of man. Hermann Rathmann, a pastor at Danzig (d. 1628), denied that the Scriptures posses this power *extra usum.* To Rathmann, the divine efficacy is separable from the Scriptures and is merely auxiliary. The Holy Spirit joins himself to the Word only in the mind of men when the Scriptures are used savingly. This view was rejected by the dogmaticians because of its affinity to the mystical view of the Bible held by adherents to the theology of the "inner light." [21]

THE IMPACT OF ARISTOTELIANISM

All these divisions notwithstanding, the Lutherans and the Reformed theologians actually proceeded from the same premises in their method, i.e. from Aristotelean logic and from the doctrine of the infallibility of Scripture. They co-ordinated reason and revelation as the sources of religious knowledge and expressed the Christian faith in categories of Aristotelean philosophy.

Quenstedt defined theology as "the science about God and divine things." Theology is twofold: natural and revealed (or supernatural). The natural knowledge of God may be inadequate since it is not a saving knowledge; however it is not useless for it makes man inexcusable before God. It is innate because the concept of God is engraved upon every man by nature; it is acquired by the human mind from the book of nature. God is the "First Cause," the "Prime Mover" or "Thinking Independent Substance." Among others, Gerhard recapitulated the proofs of God developed in antiquity and used

---

[20] For the sources, see Schmid, *op cit,* pp. 389 ff. The Lutherans regarded the *Logos ensarkos* ("the incarnate Logos") as the subject of Phil. 2:7; the Reformed, on the other hand, interpreted the passage as referring to the *Logos asarkos* (to the act of the incarnation itself).

[21] Schmid, *op. cit.,* pp. 506-507.

by the Scholastics of the Middle Ages.[22] The use of reason in theology is perfectly justified, for by it the existence of the true God must be proved and the author of supernatural revelation established. Aulén is correct when he says that when one reads the treatment of the doctrine of God by these theologians, it is difficult to believe that the Reformation stood between them and medieval Scholasticism.[23] For the sake of completeness, however, it cannot be denied that both Melanchthon[24] and Calvin[25] had given special attention to the natural knowledge of God.

Concerning Scripture, Luther's critical remarks about the canon have been discussed previously.[26] Melanchthon, following his conservative trait in matters of tradition, was averse to critical expressions concerning the canon. The position of Johannes Brenz was that of Luther. In a critical estimate of the *Gallic Confession*, he disapproved of the statement in Article III which includes James, Jude and Revelations among the canonical books of the New Testament. These writings, he said, had not been unanimously received in the ancient Church, and Protestantism should not put them on the same level with the other books of the New Testament.[27] Johannes Wigand and Matthaeus Judex, contributors to the *Magdeburg Centuries*, expressed similar criticism of James and Jude. Luther's criticism was chiefly based on the spiritual quality of a book whether or not it bears witness to Christ, i.e. to the Pauline concept of justification by faith. The writers just quoted, on the other hand, though not ignoring Luther's point of view, tended to put more emphasis on the evidence of history. Chemnitz, in his refutation of the Council of Trent,[28] follows much the same line of argument. Later the attitude changed. In the eyes of Gerhard and Quenstedt, for example, all twenty-seven

---

[22] *Ibid.,* pp. 104-105. In his *Loci,* 1542, Melanchthon cited eight facts as proofs of the existence of God; see *ibid.,* p. 106.

[23] Gustaf Aulén, *Das christliche Gottesbild* (1930), p. 252. For source material on the Lutheran dogmaticians, see Schmid, *op. cit.,* pp. 15 ff., 103 ff.; on the Reformed teachers, see Heppe, *Reformed Dogmatics,* trans. G. T. Thomson (London: G. Allen and Unwin, 1950), pp. 1 ff., 47 ff.

[24] Cf. p. 396.

[25] Cf. pp. 423-24.

[26] Cf. p. 469.

[27] Ritschl, *op. cit.,* I, 131.

[28] *Ibid.,* pp. 138-39.

books are canonical though the antilegomena are of second rank.[29]

The situation among the Reformed was different. Calvin had defended the canonicity of all twenty-seven books of the New Testament. Heppe quotes Wolfgang Musculus as having said that Calvin was less bound to the antilegomena than to the rest of Scripture.[30] "After the identification of the concepts 'Word of God' and 'Holy Scripture' had become prevelant," Heppe adds, "Reformed dogmaticians began to declaim against the Old Protestant distinction between canonical and apocryphal writings in the New Testament as against a delusion of the devil." [31]

The concept of inspiration had a parallel development in both churches. It gained momentum steadily while the idea of revelation receded into the background. It became more and more customary to make the authority of Scripture rest not upon God's personal acts of revelation, but upon the manner of their recording, upon inspiration. Scripture was regarded as having been dictated by God. "The 'divineness' of Scripture was derived purely, not from the participation of its authors in the facts of revelation, and in God's saving activity, but from the manner of its recording.[32] Inspiration, it was said, is plenary, including both content and words. Even before the promulgation of the *Formula Consensus Helvetica*, 1675, Polanus, John Buxtorf the Younger, and others maintained that the vowels in the Hebrew text of the Old Testament were "*theopneustos*" (i.e. inspired by God), leaving undecided "whether the very points or, at least, the power of the points" [33] were given by divine inspiration. In order to meet the Catholic claim of the priority of tradition, Zanchi, and others after him, distinguished between the "written and unwritten Word of God." The essence of Scripture is nothing else, they maintained, than "inspired doctrine." The writing of this doctrine on tablets or in books is merely an additional element. Hence, Scripture is older than the tradition of the Church.

Among the Lutheran theologians it was Flacius who first spoke of

[29] Schmid, *op. cit.,* pp. 84 ff.

[30] Heppe, *op. cit.,* p. 14.

[31] Ritschl, *op. cit.,* I, 180-81. The identical distinction was made by Quenstedt at Wittenberg. Cf. Schmid, *op. cit.,* pp. 59-60.

[32] Ritschl, *op. cit.,* p. 18.

[33] *Ibid.,* p. 19.

the verbal inspiration of Scripture. Johann Gerhard developed this idea into a Protestant dogma. For Flacius the relation of the divine and the human in the concept of inspiration was that of an organic union which has always been characteristic of Lutheranism. A dynamic relation exists between the divine and the human, resulting in a mutual "perichoresis" (permeation). In this thought Luther and his followers were in basic agreement with the Alexandrian School of the ancient Church.

It must not be overlooked that Chemnitz and his contemporaries, although not speaking of verbal inspiration, very emphatically taught the inspiration of all the canonical books of both Testaments. The occasion for developing a doctrine of inspiration presented itself in a heated conflict with Rome, particularly with Cardinal Roberto Bellarmin (d. 1621), a Jesuit who had written a three volume work against contemporary heretics. Gerhard treated the subject systematically in his *Locus de Scriptura*, 1610. Like Flacius, he took the position that in Scripture it is God the Holy Spirit who speaks; therefore, Scripture is *theopneustos* (II Tim. 3:16). The writers are "amanuenses." There is no essential difference between Scripture and the Word of God. Gerhard followed the Reformed theologian Polanus in extending divine inspiration to the pointing of the Hebrew vowels. Among the later dogmaticians of the seventeenth century it was primarily Quenstedt who completed the dogma of the inspiration of Scripture for the Lutheran Church of that age. It was he who furnished the outline for discussion of the problem by the three propositions: (1) The holy writers received an outward and an inner impulse from the Holy Spirit for writing. (2) The Holy Spirit also gave them the materials and the words. (3) The Holy Spirit led the writers in such a way that they were guarded against error.[34]

As previously mentioned, these men employed the method of Aristotelean scholasticism. Zabarella of Padua (d. 1589) is usually credited with the revival of this kind of scholasticism which had an effect on Melanchthon. Of the later Lutherans, George Gutke in Wittenberg and Berlin (d. 1634) referred to Aristotle's logic as "God's own logic." Of the Reformed we have already referred to Kecker-

---

[34] Cf. Schmid, *op. cit.,* pp. 42 ff. See also Robert Preuss *The Inspiration of Scripture, a Study of the Theology of Seventeenth Century Lutheran Dogmaticians,* (Edinburgh, Oliver and Boyd), 1955.

mann at Heidelberg and Danzig.[35] A prominent feature of Aristotle's logic is the use of the principle of causality. The orthodox writers of both churches made ample use of this principle. In discussing the Incarnation, Gerhard, for example, speaks of Mary as the material cause; of the Holy Ghost as the efficient cause; of human salvation as the final cause; and of the miraculous conception of Jesus as the instrumental cause.[36] In discussing election, the Reformed speak of the love with which "Father, Son, and Holy Spirit would love one another and glorify one another" as the *causa impulsiva;* of Christ as the *causa electionis*, though "it should not be concluded from this that Christ's redemptive work and merit are the *causa meritoria* simply of God's council and election; for indeed Christ's redemptive work and merits are not the absolute *causa electionis* which is to be sought only in the absolute counsel of love of the Trinity." [37] Actually the merits of Christ are the "sheer *causa salutis*." [38]

The concept of God was depersonalized, God being spoken of as an "It." Aristotle's God is such a spiritual being, that removed from the affairs of man, he spends his time in serene self-contemplation. Corresponding to this depersonalized concept of God, sin was defined as an infraction of the divine law.[39] Though not entirely wrong, this definition lacks depth. Sin is more than breaking the law. Basically sin is unfaithfulness to God who calls man to personal fellowship.[40] In the Bible sin is not primarily a social but a religious concept; likewise, the saint in the New Testament is the man reconciled to God through Christ Jesus. The moral aspect is entirely secondary. Faith also lost its personal character. While Paul wrote: "I know whom I have believed," the dogmaticians were chiefly concerned with "what"

[35] See p. 473. Cf. also Peter Petersen, *Geschichte der aristotelischen Philosophie im protestantischen Deutschland* (1921), especially pp. 315 ff., and H. E. Weber, *Die philosophische Scholastik des deutschen Protestantismus im Zeitalter der Orthodoxie* (1907), especially pp. 74 ff., 105 ff.

[36] Johann Gerhard, *Loci theologici* (1885), I, 495. Cf. Pelikan, *From Luther to Kierkegaard* (St. Louis: Concordia Publishing House, 1950), p. 65.

[37] Heppe, *op. cit.,* pp. 165 ff.

[38] Cf. the causes of election as stated by the Lutheran dogmaticians: the Triune God is the efficient cause, his grace the impulsive or moving internal cause, the merit of Christ the external moving cause, faith the external less principal cause. Schmid, *op. cit.,* p. 287.

[39] Schmid, *op. cit.,* p. 231; Heppe, *op. cit.,* p. 320.

[40] Cf. especialiy Hosea.

is to be believed. They spoke repeatedly of the "things" or "articles" contained in Scripture which must be believed for eternal salvation. Faith is thus "thingified." "As had been the case with Roman Catholicism in the Middle Ages, Protestant scholasticism often multiplied distinction far beyond necessity. The humbler duties of preaching the Gospel and ministering to the spiritual needs of the people were often shunned in favor of the more glamorous field of theological debate." [41] The dogmaticians believed that God's existence could be demonstrated rationally, and that such attributes as omnipotence and goodness are evident in creation. By the proper use of reason even the "rationality of revealed truths must be set forth," [42] for "the maxims of philosophy and the conclusions of theology do not really contradict each other." [43] In the eyes of the orthodox, it was more rational to accept the Bible as trustworthy than to reject it. The transition from the orthodoxy of the seventeenth century to the rationalism of the eighteenth century was at first barely perceptible. It took several decades until orthodox theology saw itself strangulated by the use of reason, which it had enlisted to demonstrate the plausibility of supernatural revelation. [44]

The intimate relationship between philosophy and theology in the orthodox system, however, was not entirely negative. In the controversy with the Reformed over the ubiquity of Christ's body, Lutheranism extricated itself from the Aristotelian concept of substance as a static, quantitative entity, and developed an understanding of the universe that had significant consequences for philosophy. Calvin and his followers were unable to appreciate the Lutheran view of ubiquity because they continued to think of the body of Christ in terms of local extention, and of the ascension as a movement from a lower to a higher place. The Crypto-Calvinistic controversy gave Lutheran theologians an opportunity to realize that, while space and time are aspects of reality as experienced by us, they are not, of necessity, attributes of reality itself. In this way Lutheranism liberated theology from the shackles of Aristotelian physics and made

[41] Pelikan, *op. cit.,* p. 77.
[42] Heppe, *op. cit.,* p. 9.
[43] Schmid, *op. cit.,* p. 32.
[44] Cf. Pelikan, *op. cit.,* pp. 76 ff.

a significant contribution to Kantian and post-Kantian concepts of the universe.[45]

BIBLIOGRAPHY

ALTHAUS, PAUL. *Die Prinzipien der deutschen reformierten Dogmatik im Zeitalter der aristotlelischen Scholastik.* 1914.

ELERT, WERNER. *The Structure of Lutheranism.* Translated by WALTER A. HANSEN. St. Louis: Concordia Publishing House, 1962.

GASS, WILHELM. *Geschichte der protestantischen Dogmatik.* Vol. I. 1854.

HEPPE, HEINRICH. *Reformed Dogmatics.* Translated by G. T. Thomson. London: G. Allen and Unwin, 1950.

KAHNIS, K. F. A. *Der innere Gang des deutschen Protestantismus.* Vol. I. 3rd ed., 1874.

LEUBE, HANS. *Die Reformideen in der deutschen lutherischen Kirche zur Zeit der Orthodoxie.* 1924.

PELIKAN, JAROSLAV. *From Luther to Kierkegaard.* St. Louis: Concordia Publishing House, 1950.

PREUS, H. A. and SMITS, E. (eds.) *The Doctrine of Man in Classical Lutheran Theology.* Minneapolis: Augsburg Publishing House, 1962.

PREUSS, ROBERT. *The Inspiration of Scripture, a Study of the Theology of Seventeenth Century Lutheran Dogmaticians.* Edinburgh: Oliver and Boyd, 1955.

RITSCHL, OTTO. *Dogmengeschichte des Protestantismus.* 4 vols. 1908 ff.

SASSE, HERMANN. *Here We Stand.* Translated by *Theodore G. Tappert.* New York: Harper & Bros., 1938.

SCHMID, HEINRICH. *The Doctrinal Theology of the Evangelical Lutheran Church.* Translated by CHARLES A. HAY and HENRY E. JACOBS, 1875. Minneapolis: Augsburg Publishing House, 1961.

THOLUCK, AUGUST. *Der Geist der lutherischen Theologen Wittenbergs im Verlauf des 17. Jahrhunderts.* 1852.

WEBER, H. E. *Der Einfluss der protestantischen Schulphilosophie auf die lutherische Dogmatik.* 1908.

[45] Defecting from Luther's view of ubiquity, Melanchthon and his school continued to hold fast to the Scholastic view of heaven as a distinct place. For detailed references, see Elert, *Morphologie des Luthertums,* I, 220-21. Elert quotes from the sermon of a Reformed pastor, arguing against the non-local view of heaven: "In [the heaven of the Lutherans] which is everywhere, angels and devils mingle, and the angels carry their own heaven with themselves just as the devils carry their own hell with themselves, a fact which is abominable to hear." Elert also quotes Lavater, a contemporary of Goethe, saying: "Since it takes a cannon ball more than a hundred thousand millions of years to reach the closest planet . . . you can imagine the speed with which Christ ascended into heaven" (*ibid.,* p. 365).

CHAPTER IX

THE RESURGENCE OF CATHOLICISM

INTRODUCTORY REMARKS

Strange as it may seem, during the Middle Ages the Church of Rome, with few exceptions, was without definite, universally binding dogmas. The great works of the Scholastics contain only the private teachings of their respective authors who were themselves divided into different schools with widely divergent tendencies. The sentiment prevailed that the ancient councils and fathers as well as the teachings and practice of the Catholic Church represented the truth of Christianity. The disposition to believe what the Church believes (*fides implicita*) was predominant. Even the mystics took little interest in theology and dogma. Their aim was to bring about a personal revival of the Christian faith and practical reforms within the Church. Then came the Reformation. Putting its own religious experience in a dogmatic garb, the Reformation compelled the Church of Rome to formulate more precisely its own doctrines against Protestantism.

In its struggles to meet the crisis Rome could marshall a number of spiritual forces. A strong form of medieval piety existed—especially in Italy and Spain—and found expression in the rise of a new mysticism and in the founding of new religious orders.[1] A Christian humanism gained momentum and purged Scholasticism of the fruitless formalism of the late medieval period.[2] This was largely the work of Cardinal Cajetan (d. 1534), whose commentary on the *Summa* of Thomas became the standard interpretation of Thomism, and of the Spaniards Melchior Cano (d. 1560) and Francis Suarez (d. 1617).

[1] Prominent among these orders were the Oratories of Divine Love, the first order of which was founded in Italy in 1497, and the Barefooted Carmelites in Spain, which was founded by St. Theresa of Jesus (d. 1582).
[2] Cf. in H. J. Grimm, *The Reformation Era* (New York: Macmillan Co., 1954), the chapter on "The Catholic Reformation," pp. 366 ff.

A number of theologians, engaged in controversies with the Reformation, represented a "Reform Catholicism" which was ready to concede several points to Protestantism. These theologians adhered strictly to the cardinal Roman Catholic viewpoints and sharply rejected the Protestant doctrines. They differed, however, from the older controversialists on account of the appreciation of the problems occasioned by Luther and the other Reformers. Men such as John Driedo (d. 1535), A. Pighius (d. 1542), John Gropper (d. 1559), and Caspar Contarini (d. 1542) discussed the authority of the Scriptures and the Church and their mutual relation, but mainly they treated topics such as freedom, sin, grace, and justification, and the sacraments.

While the men just mentioned kept comparatively close to Augustinianism and Thomism, the more liberal school, which was connected with the Semi-Pelagianism of the Franciscan theology, was greatly abetted by the Jesuit Order, which was then coming into prominence. An original theological significance cannot be attributed to Ignatius Loyola (d. 1556). Only certain formulas and methods of his *Spiritual Exercises* are new. Through these *Exercises* he strengthened the authority of the Church, especially that of the papacy. Because he endeavored to render man's relation to Christianity and the Church as convenient as possible, Ignatius was compelled to lower the moral standards. For this reason the Jesuit Order became the instigator of the Moralist controversies in the succeeding centuries.

THE COUNCIL OF TRENT

After the Religious Treaty of Augsburg in 1555, the Roman Catholic Church realized the necessity of settling its dogma. This occurred at the Council of Trent. Harnack's judgment of the Council is significant: "The Decrees of Trent are the shadows of the Reformation. That it was given to Catholicism to understand itself, to give expression to its distinctive character, and to rescue itself from the uncertainties of the Middle Ages, was a debt it owed to the Reformation."[3] The Decrees of Trent elevated medieval theology to the status of dogma.

The Decrees of this Council are, for the most part, the outcome of a lengthy controversy. Consequently, they are the result of compro-

[3] Harnack, *History of Dogma*, VII, 36.

mises whereby the theology of the Thomists, with its appeal to Augustine, gained a slight superiority over its Nominalistic rival. In questions where no agreement could be reached, it was thought expedient either to condemn opponents by means of negative statements, or to maintain complete silence. The history of doctrine must content itself mainly with presenting the settled doctrinal issues. The most important decrees of the Council of Trent deal with Scripture and tradition, sin, grace, and justification, and the sacraments.

The Decree on the Canon of the Scriptures was settled during the Fourth Session. The discussion centered chiefly around the question concerning the authoritative sources of the Christian truth. The Scriptures and tradition are mentioned as such sources of truth. Until then Roman Catholicism had not stated their mutual relation dogmatically. In spite of the actual superiority of tradition, first place had been assigned theoretically to the Scriptures. As a safeguard against Protestantism the Scriptures and tradition are now co-ordinated. Both are inspired. The extent of the canon is strictly determined by the enumeration of every single writing that belongs to it. The decree recognizes as authoritative the apocryphal books of Tobit, Judith, the Wisdom of Solomon, Jesus Sirach, Baruch, and the two books of the Macabees. The Vulgate is decreed to be the authentic text. The interpretation of Scripture remains a prerogative of the Church. Only that sense of Scripture is to be acknowledged to which the Holy Mother Church has adhered and still adheres. The interpretation of Scripture is contained above all in the consensus of the Church Fathers. This interpretation relates to faith and morals only; in purely grammatical and historical matters a certain freedom was not abolished at Trent.

The exact content and extent of tradition was left undecided, thereby preserving for the Church the freedom to move according to the exigencies of circumstances. This freedom enables the unhampered rejection of Protestant teachings even when it is impossible to furnish arguments from the Scriptures or from the tradition of the past.[4]

The Fifth Session issued a Decree on Original Sin. In view of contrasting opinions existing within Catholicism, a clear decision was

[4] Mirbt, *op. cit.*, pp. 292-93; Schaff, *op. cit.*, II, 79 ff. Cf. A. Maichle, *Das Dekret de editione et usu librorum sacrorum* (1914) and *Der Kanon der biblischen Bücher und das Konzil von Trient* (1925).

not reached. It remained undecided whether man through the fall had lost the righteousness in which he was created, or only the *donum superadditum*. Adam's sin extends to all men by propagation, not merely by imitation. Through baptism not only the guilt is remitted, but also all wherein sin truly consists is wholly rooted up. The concupiscence remaining in the baptized cannot be called sin in the strictest sense of the term. <u>Sin has only weakened but not extinguished man's free will</u>. The controversial question between Franciscans and Dominicans regarding Mary's relation to original sin was not answered.[5]

The doctrine of justification, one of the main issues with Protestantism, was dealt with searchingly in the long-drawn-out Sixth Session. Justification was defined as the "translation from the standing in which man was born as a son of the First Adam into the standing of grace and adoption of the children of God." This translation runs through several stages.

In the first stage prevenient grace is effective in man through the Word. <u>Man perceives that the call of God is intended for him, "to which he may assent and with which he may co-operate</u>." This co-operation, it is claimed, has no meritorious character; hence there is no support of the Nominalist's theology of a real *meritum de congruo*. On the other hand, this also means that the *sola gratia* of the Reformation is likewise rejected.

(b) The second stage is that of justification proper. It includes <u>"not merely the forgiveness of sins, but also sanctification and renewal of the inward man by a voluntary acceptance of grace and of gifts whereby the unrighteous is made righteous</u>." [6] The forensic conception of justification is condemned as a Protestant heresy. The actual moral change of man not only belongs to justification; it is its main element.

(c) The third stage: Subjectively, therefore, "<u>justification cannot be effected by faith alone, hope and love must accompany</u> it. Faith is but the foundation and root of human salvation. For faith does not perfectly join us to Christ nor make us living members of His body,

[5] Mirbt, *op. cit.,* pp. 293 ff.; Schaff, *op. cit.,* II, 83 ff.

[6] Mirbt, *op. cit.,* pp. 294 ff.; Schaff, *op. cit.,* II, pp. 89 ff. Cf. H. Rueckert, *Die Rechtfertigungslehre auf dem tridentinischen Konzil* (1925).

unless hope and love are added to it." [7] This inward psychico-moral disposition is infused into men through the sacraments, particularly through baptism. The Pauline exclusion of works (Rom. 3:28), which was at first taken into consideration, was passed over when the decree was finally drawn up.

(d) The fourth stage: Man's efforts and good works play a co-operative role in his justification. Such good works merit eternal life, even though ultimately they are gifts of God.

(e) In basing justification upon faith and good works, the absolute certainty of present and final pardon can never be attained. The Council evaded a positive attitude to the assurance of salvation, but rejected the Protestant conception of assurance as vain and heretical. The real Catholic frame of mind is a disposition of the soul composed of fear and hope (Gregory I). Accordingly, there is no assurance of election except through special revelation. Justification may be lost, but it can be regained through the sacrament of penance. [8]

The Decree on the Sacraments [9] resulted from the Seventh Session. With regard to the doctrines of the sacraments sharp contrasts among the theological schools in Roman Catholicism were in evidence. According to the teachings of the Thomists, grace is embedded in the sacraments. Certain sacraments confer a spiritual and indelible character upon man. According to the Scotists, an inward spiritual power runs parallel to the external act. In order to conceal this discord, the Council refused to make a positive statement concerning the doctrine of the sacraments, but instead satisfied itself with anathematizing the doctrine of the opponents. The medieval decrees of the Council of Florence on the sacraments were followed as closely as possible. The seven sacraments are, in the words of the Council, instituted by Christ; are necessary for salvation; contain the grace which they confer upon the non-resisting, and are effective *ex opere operato*. Three of them confer a distinctive character upon the soul (baptism, confirmation, and ordination).

The decrees on baptism and confirmation do not furnish anything of importance. In regard to the Eucharist the Council declared decidedly in favor of transubstantiation. "By the consecration of bread and

[7] Mirbt, *Loc. cit.*
[8] *Ibid.*
[9] *Ibid.*, pp. 303-304; Schaff, *op. cit.*, II, 118 ff.

wine a conversion takes place of the entire substance of the bread into the Body of Christ, and of the entire substance of the wine into the substance of His Blood." [10] Consequently, the Body of Christ is present apart from its sacramental use, and the consecrated wafer is an object of veneration. The denial of the cup to the laity is justified on the ground that the whole Christ is present in every particle, and that therefore the eating of the bread alone communicates the full Supper.

Closely related to the Lord's Supper is the Mass, which is of supreme importance to the Roman Catholic church. The theory of the sacrifice of the Mass was not dealt with before the Twenty-second Session (September 17, 1562).[11] An anathema is pronounced upon those who deny that the Mass is a true and proper sacrifice. In the Mass, it is said, the bloody sacrifice once accomplished upon the Cross is "represented" so that "the memory thereof remains even unto the end of the world." [12] Christ is immolated in an unbloody manner. As a sacrifice, the Mass is truly propitiatory. It is an oblation appeasing the Lord. As compared with the sacrifice on Golgatha, "the victim is one and the same now offered by the ministry of priests, who then offered Himself on the cross, the manner alone of offering being different." [13] The Canon of the Mass, which to Luther was an abominable sacrilege,[14] is said to be "pure from every error," and contains nothing "which does not in the highest degree savor of a certain holiness and piety." [15]

The extraordinary importance given to penance at the rise of the Reformation compelled the Council to deal with this sacrament in an especially searching manner. It was decreed that penance is a sacra-

---

[10] Mirbt, *op. cit.,* pp. 305 ff.; Schaff, *op. cit.,* II, 126 ff.

[11] Mirbt, *op. cit.,* pp. 325 f.; Schaff, *op. cit.,* II, 176 ff.

[12] Schaff, *op. cit.,* II, 177.

[13] *Ibid.,* p. 179.

[14] *Vom Greuel der Stillmesse* (*WA,* 18:22 ff).

[15] Schaff, *op. cit.,* II, 180. In addition to being a representation and memorial of the sacrifice of the cross, the *Roman Catechism* of Pius V (II, Ch. IV, Q. 70) speaks of the Mass as a "daily repetition" (*instauratio*) of the sacrifice of Christ. Commenting on this expression, the *Catholic Encyclopedia* (X, 14) remarks that the expression is to be taken "not in the sense of multiplication but simply of an application of the merits of the passion." Yet an obscurity remains. How can a mere "application" be a true immolation? Granted that the Mass is not a "second independent sacrifice," how can it be a sacrifice at all unless it is a multiplication of the sacrifice of the cross?

ment instituted by Christ Himself (John 20:22).[16] All three traditional parts of the sacrament are declared necessary for obtaining salvation. The cardinal conviction of the Reformation is rejected, namely that it is sufficient to have "a terror-stricken conscience, and faith awakened by the Gospel." Attrition is described as a preparation for grace to be received in the sacrament which changes attrition into contrition. The special auricular confession of all mortal sins is required. Absolution is a juridical act in which the priest in God's stead, not only forgives sin, but also imposes the satisfying penalties. The satisfaction, which forms the third part of the sacrament of penance, though not intended to absolve from guilt, proposes to take upon itself the penalties inflicted by the priest, in order that sin become even more odious to man, and that man rid himself of his sinful habit.

Closely related to these penalties of satisfaction are the Indulgences. They were dealt with shortly before the close of the Council during the Twenty-fifth Session. Indulgences are designated as a "usage which is beneficial to the Christian people." [17] The existence of a number of abuses is admitted, especially the opinion that absolution could be obtained for money without the sacrament. This last session of the Council also recognized the effect of the Church upon purgatory through intercessory prayers and the sacrifice of the Mass.[18]

In dealing with the sacrament of extreme unction[19] during the Twenty-fourth Session, the council canonized the viewpoint so far upheld by the Church. During the same session marriage was declared a sacrament, yet the greater merit of the virgin state was maintained.[20]

The sacrament of ordination was discussed in the Twenty-third Session, July 15, 1563.[21] In the previous Session, which dealt with the doctrine of the Mass, it was maintained that the priesthood was instituted by Christ in the night of his betrayal when he constituted the Apostles priests of the New Testament by commanding them and their successors to offer the sacrifice of the Mass with the words, "Do this in commemoration of me." [22]

---

[16] Mirbt, *op. cit.*, pp. 310 ff.; Schaff, *op. cit.*, II, 139 ff.
[17] Mirbt, *op. cit.*, p. 336; Schaff, *op. cit.*, II, 205-206.
[18] Mirbt, *op. cit.*, p. 333; Schaff, *op. cit.*, II, 198-99.
[19] Mirbt, *op. cit.*, pp. 316 ff.; Schaff, *op. cit.*, II, 158 ff.
[20] Mirbt, *op. cit.*, pp. 328 ff.; Schaff, *op. cit.*, II, 193 ff.
[21] Mirbt, *op. cit.*, pp. 326 ff., Schaff, *op. cit.*, II, 186 ff.
[22] Schaff, *op. cit.*, II, 177.

Like baptism and confirmation, ordination confers a character "which can neither be effaced nor taken away." [23] The priesthood, then, constitutes a peculiar order over against the biblical and Protestant concept of the priesthood of all believers. A superiority is granted to the bishops, not on the basis of a different kind of ordination, but rather in view of the fact that the bishops are the successors of the Apostles. The relation of the pope to the bishops was not definitely settled by the Council. The designation of the pope as Vicar of Christ although planned at first, was omitted. Even in the introductory formula of the Decrees of the Council the authority of the Council and the papal authority as represented by the papal legates were co-ordinated without any clear distinction: "This sacred and holy ecumenical, and general Synod of Trent, lawfully assembled in the Holy Ghost, the same three legates of the Apostolic See presiding therein . . . exhorts . . . all and each. . . ." [24]

The Council, however, assigned the publication of the Decrees and the execution of a number of the Canons to the pope, thereby acknowledging his superiority over the Council. It took more than three centuries of development and changes before the papal dogma, which was left unsettled at Trent, was formulated by the Vatican Council.

The decrees of reform passed by the Council affected the life and conduct of the bishops and priests, called for a reform of the monasteries and the establishment of theological seminaries. The eighteenth session abolished the office of the indulgence seller, *etc.*

In its last two sessions the Council expressed the need for a binding formula of faith. Such a formula was prepared on the order of Pius IV by a college of cardinals in 1564. It is known as the *Professio Fidei Tridentinae* ("the Profession of the Tridentine Faith").[25] It consists of twelve articles and was made binding upon all Catholic teachers in seminaries, colleges, and universities. It has also been used as a creed for converts to the Roman faith. It is, in fact, the most concise summary of the doctrinal system of the Church of Rome.

The Council also proposed the preparation of a catechism. The

---

[23] *Ibid.,* p. 189.

[24] *Ibid.,* 77.

[25] See the text in *ibid.,* I, 98 ff.; II, 207 ff.

work was completed in 1566 and published by order of the pope in September. Known as the _Catechismus Romanus_,[26] it is a popular manual of theology and, like Luther's Large Catechism, is intended for teachers of religion. Carlo Borromaeus (d. 1584),[27] Archbishop of Milan, and Peter Canisius (d. 1597),[28] leader of the German Jesuits, led among churchmen and theologians who took a principal part in propagating the Decrees of Trent.

Taken as a whole, the Council of Trent was not a reformation but rather a restoration of Catholic thought and piety.

BIBLIOGRAPHY

CALVIN, JOHN. "Acts of the Council of Trent with the Antidote," 1547, in _Tracts and Treatises_, Vol. III, 17 ff. Grand Rapids, Mich.: Eerdmans, 1958.

CANONES ET DECRETA of the Council of Trent. First published in 1564; many subsequent reprints.

CHEMNITZ, MARTIN. _Examen Concilii Tridentini._ 4 parts. 1565 ff.

Concilium Tridentinum. Goerresgesellschaft. 1901 ff.

Enchiridon symbolorum, etc. Edited by H. DENZINGER and J. B. UMBERG. 1932.

GRASSO, J. B. _Ecclesia et status._ 1939.

GRIMM, HAROLD J. _The Reformation Era._ New York: The Macmillan Company, 1954.

LOYOLA, IGNATIUS. _Spiritual Exercises._ London: Burns and Oates, n. d.

KIDD, B. J. _The Counter Reformation._ London: SPCK, 1933.

MANSI, G. D. _Sacrorum conciliorum._ Vol. 58.

MIRBT, KARL. _Quellen zur Geschichte des Papstums._ 4th ed., 1924.

SCHAFF, PHILIP. _Creeds of Christendom._ 2 vols. New York: Harper & Bros., 1931.

[26] Excerpts from the _Catechism_ are given in Mirbt, _op. cit.,_ pp. 342 ff.

[27] In commemoration of the canonization of Borromaeus in 1610, Pius X published a papal encyclical May 26, 1910, in which he referred to the Reformers of the sixteenth century as "haughty and rebellious men," and "enemies of the cross of Christ whose God is their belly" (Phil. 3:18 f.), and accused the princes and people supporting the Reformation of moral corruption. Upon a protest voiced by the Evangelical Church in Germany and by some political leaders, the Vatican apologized and ordered the German bishops not to publish the encyclical.

[28] See Mirbt, _op. cit.,_ p. 514. Canisius was canonized in 1925. On the occasion of the tercentenary of his death, Leo XIII published the encyclical _Militantis ecclesiae_ in which he labelled the Reformation as a "Lutheran rebellion." See Mirbt, _op. cit.,_ pp. 492.

INDEXES

TOPICAL INDEX

INDEX OF NAMES

Type, 10 on 13, 9 on 11, and 9 on 10 Janson
Display, Garamond
Paper, Spring Grove E. F. with Titanium